PENGUIN MODERN CLASSICS

*The Origins of Totalitarianism*

Hannah Arendt was born into a secular family of German Jews in Hanover in 1906. At university in Marburg, she was taught by the philosopher Martin Heidegger, with whom she developed a romantic relationship, complicated by his later affiliation with the Nazi party. She received her doctorate in philosophy from the University of Heidelberg and began researching antisemitism. In 1933, Arendt was arrested and briefly imprisoned by the Gestapo, after which she fled Germany for Paris, where she worked for the immigration of Jewish refugee children into Palestine. In 1937, she was stripped of her German citizenship. She married the Marxist philosopher Heinrich Blücher in 1940; the same year, she was detained in an internment camp in southwestern France as an 'enemy alien'. After this, she left Europe for the United States, and became an American citizen ten years later.

During her time in the US, Arendt was a research director of the Conference on Jewish Relations, chief editor of Schocken Books, executive director of Jewish Cultural Reconstruction in New York City and a visiting professor at several universities, including Princeton, where she was the first female lecturer.

Hannah Arendt's many books include *The Origins of Totalitarianism* (1951), *The Human Condition* (1958) and *Eichmann in Jerusalem* (1963), in which she coined the famous phrase 'the banality of evil'. She died in December 1975.

HANNAH ARENDT

*The Origins of Totalitarianism*

PENGUIN BOOKS

PENGUIN CLASSICS

UK | USA | Canada | Ireland | Australia
India | New Zealand | South Africa

Penguin Classics is part of the Penguin Random House group of companies
whose addresses can be found at global.penguinrandomhouse.com.

First published in 1951
First published in Penguin Classics 2017

022

Set in 10/12.5 pt Dante MT Std
Typeset by Jouve (UK), Milton Keynes

Printed and bound in Great Britain by Clays Ltd, Elcograf S.p.A.

A CIP catalogue record for this book is available from the British Library

ISBN: 978–0–241–31675–7

www.greenpenguin.co.uk

Penguin Random House is committed to a
sustainable future for our business, our readers
and our planet. This book is made from Forest
Stewardship Council® certified paper.

*To Heinrich Blücher*

# Contents

*Weder dem Vergangenen anheimfallen noch dem*
*Zukünftigen. Es kommt darauf an, ganz*
*gegenwärtig zu sein.*

Karl Jaspers

## Preface to the First Edition

Two world wars in one generation, separated by an uninterrupted
chain of local wars and revolutions, followed by no peace treaty for the
vanquished and no respite for the victor, have ended in the anticipation of a third World War between the two remaining world powers.
This moment of anticipation is like the calm that settles after all hopes
have died. We no longer hope for an eventual restoration of the old
world order with all its traditions, or for the reintegration of the
masses of five continents who have been thrown into a chaos produced by the violence of wars and revolutions and the growing decay
of all that has still been spared. Under the most diverse conditions
and disparate circumstances, we watch the development of the same
phenomena – homelessness on an unprecedented scale, rootlessness to
an unprecedented depth.

Never has our future been more unpredictable, never have we
depended so much on political forces that cannot be trusted to follow
the rules of common sense and self-interest – forces that look like
sheer insanity, if judged by the standards of other centuries. It is as
though mankind had divided itself between those who believe in
human omnipotence (who think that everything is possible if one
knows how to organize masses for it) and those for whom powerlessness has become the major experience of their lives.

On the level of historical insight and political thought there prevails an ill-defined, general agreement that the essential structure of
all civilizations is at the breaking point. Although it may seem better
preserved in some parts of the world than in others, it can nowhere

provide the guidance to the possibilities of the century, or an adequate response to its horrors. Desperate hope and desperate fear often seem closer to the center of such events than balanced judgment and measured insight. The central events of our time are not less effectively forgotten by those committed to a belief in an unavoidable doom, than by those who have given themselves up to reckless optimism.

This book has been written against a background of both reckless optimism and reckless despair. It holds that Progress and Doom are two sides of the same medal; that both are articles of superstition, not of faith. It was written out of the conviction that it should be possible to discover the hidden mechanics by which all traditional elements of our political and spiritual world were dissolved into a conglomeration where everything seems to have lost specific value, and has become unrecognizable for human comprehension, unusable for human purpose. To yield to the mere process of disintegration has become an irresistible temptation, not only because it has assumed the spurious grandeur of 'historical necessity', but also because everything outside it has begun to appear lifeless, bloodless, meaningless, and unreal.

The conviction that everything that happens on earth must be comprehensible to man can lead to interpreting history by commonplaces. Comprehension does not mean denying the outrageous, deducing the unprecedented from precedents, or explaining phenomena by such analogies and generalities that the impact of reality and the shock of experience are no longer felt. It means, rather, examining and bearing consciously the burden which our century has placed on us – neither denying its existence nor submitting meekly to its weight. Comprehension, in short, means the unpremeditated, attentive facing up to, and resisting of, reality – whatever it may be.

In this sense, it must be possible to face and understand the outrageous fact that so small (and, in world politics, so unimportant) a phenomenon as the Jewish question and antisemitism could become the catalytic agent for first, the Nazi movement, then a world war, and finally the establishment of death factories. Or, the grotesque disparity between cause and effect which introduced the era of imperialism, when economic difficulties led, in a few decades, to a profound transformation of political conditions all over the world. Or, the curious contradiction between the totalitarian movements' avowed cynical 'realism' and their conspicuous disdain of the whole texture of reality. Or, the irritating incompatibility between the actual power of modern man (greater than ever before, great to the point where he might challenge the very existence of his own universe) and the impotence of modern men to live in, and understand the sense of, a world which their own strength has established.

The totalitarian attempt at global conquest and total domination has been the destructive way out of all impasses. Its victory may coincide with the destruction of humanity; wherever it has ruled, it has begun to destroy the essence of man. Yet to turn our backs on the destructive forces of the century is of little avail.

The trouble is that our period has so strangely intertwined the good with the bad that without the imperialists' 'expansion for expansion's sake,' the world might never have become one; without the bourgeoisie's political device of 'power for power's sake,' the extent of human strength might never have been discovered; without the fictitious world of totalitarian movements, in which with unparalleled clarity the essential uncertainties of our time have been spelled out, we might have been driven to our doom without ever becoming aware of what has been happening.

And if it is true that in the final stages of totalitarianism an absolute evil appears (absolute because it can no longer be deduced from humanly comprehensible motives), it is also true that without it we might never have known the truly radical nature of Evil.

Antisemitism (not merely the hatred of Jews), imperialism (not merely conquest), totalitarianism (not merely dictatorship) – one after the other, one more brutally than the other, have demonstrated that human dignity needs a new guarantee which can be found only in a new political principle, in a new law on earth, whose validity this time must comprehend the whole of humanity while its power must remain strictly limited, rooted in and controlled by newly defined territorial entities.

We can no longer afford to take that which was good in the past and simply call it our heritage, to discard the bad and simply think of it as a dead load which by itself time will bury in oblivion. The subterranean stream of Western history has finally come to the surface and usurped the dignity of our tradition. This is the reality in which we live. And this is why all efforts to escape from the grimness of the present into nostalgia for a still intact past, or into the anticipated oblivion of a better future, are vain.

Hannah Arendt
Summer 1950

## Preface to Part One: Antisemitism

Antisemitism, a secular nineteenth-century ideology – which in name, though not in argument, was unknown before the 1870's – and religious Jew-hatred, inspired by the mutually hostile antagonism of two conflicting creeds, are obviously not the same; and even the extent to which the former derives its arguments and emotional appeal from the latter is open to question. The notion of an unbroken continuity of persecutions, expulsions, and massacres from the end of the Roman Empire to the Middle Ages, the modern era, and down to our own time, frequently embellished by the idea that modern antisemitism is no more than a secularized version of popular medieval superstitions,[1] is no less fallacious (though of course less mischievous) than the corresponding antisemitic notion of a Jewish secret society that has ruled, or aspired to rule, the world since antiquity. Historically, the hiatus

1 The latest example of this view is Norman Cohn's *Warrant for Genocide. The myth of the Jewish world-conspiracy and the 'Protocols of the Elders of Zion,'* New York, 1966. The author starts from the implied negation that there is such a thing as Jewish history at all. Jews are in his view 'people who . . . lived scattered across Europe from the English Channel to the Volga, with very little in common to them all save their descent from adherents of the Jewish religion' (p. 15). Antisemites, on the contrary, can claim direct and unbroken lineage through space and time from the Middle Ages when 'Jews had been seen as agents of Satan, devil-worshippers, demons in human form' (p. 41), and the only qualification to such sweeping generalizations that the learned author of *Pursuit of the Millennium* sees fit to make is that he deals only with 'the deadliest kind of antisemitism, the kind that results in massacre and attempted genocide' (p. 16). The book also tries rather strenuously to prove that 'the mass of the German population was never truly fanaticized against the Jews' and that their extermination 'was organized and in the main carried out by the professionals of the SD and the SS,' bodies that 'did not by any means represent a typical cross-section of German society' (pp. 212 ff.). How one wishes this statement could be squared with the facts! The result is that the work reads as though it were written about forty years ago by an unduly ingenious member of the *Verein zur Bekämpfung des Antisemitismus* of unhappy memory.

between the late Middle Ages and the modern age with respect to Jewish affairs is even more marked than the rift between Roman antiquity and the Middle Ages, or the gulf – frequently considered to be the most important turning-point of Jewish history in the Diaspora – that separated the catastrophes of the First Crusades from earlier medieval centuries. For this hiatus lasted through nearly two centuries, from the fifteenth to the end of the sixteenth, during which Jewish-Gentile relations were at an all-time low, Jewish 'indifference to conditions and events in the outside world' was at an all-time high, and Judaism became 'more than ever a closed system of thought.' It was at this time that Jews, without any outside interference, began to think 'that the difference between Jewry and the nations was fundamentally not one of creed and faith, but one of inner nature' and that the ancient dichotomy between Jews and Gentiles was 'more likely to be racial in origin rather than a matter of doctrinal dissension.'² This shift in evaluating the alien character of the Jewish people, which became common among non-Jews only much later in the Age of Enlightenment, is clearly the condition *sine qua non* for the birth of antisemitism, and it is of some importance to note that it occurred in Jewish self-interpretation first and at about the time when European Christendom split up into those ethnic groups which then came politically into their own in the system of modern nation-states.

The history of antisemitism, like the history of Jew-hatred, is part and parcel of the long and intricate story of Jewish-Gentile relations under the conditions of Jewish dispersion. Interest in this history was practically non-existent prior to the middle of the nineteenth century, when it coincided with the rise of antisemitism and its furious reaction to emancipated and assimilated Jewry – obviously the

2 The quotations are all drawn from Jacob Katz, *Exclusiveness and Tolerance, Jewish-Gentile Relations in Medieval and Modern Times*, New York, 1962 (Chapter 12), an entirely original study, written on the highest possible level, which indeed should have exploded 'many cherished notions of contemporary Jewry,' as the jacket claims, but did not because it was almost completely ignored by the general press. Katz belongs among the younger generation of Jewish historians, many of whom teach at the Jerusalem University and publish in Hebrew. Why their work is not more speedily translated and published in this country is something of a mystery. With them, the 'lachrymose' presentation of Jewish history, against which Salo W. Baron protested nearly forty years ago, has indeed come to an end.

worst possible constellation for establishing reliable historical records.[3]
Since then, it has been the common fallacy of Jewish and non-Jewish
historiography – though mostly for opposite reasons – to isolate the
hostile elements in Christian and Jewish sources and to stress the
series of catastrophes, expulsions, and massacres that have punctuated
Jewish history just as armed and unarmed conflicts, war, famine, and
pestilence have punctuated the history of Europe. Needless to add, it
was Jewish historiography, with its strong polemical and apologetical
bias, that undertook to trace the record of Jew-hatred in Christian
history, while it was left to the antisemites to trace an intellectually
not too dissimilar record from ancient Jewish authorities. When this
Jewish tradition of an often violent antagonism to Christians and Gentiles came to light, 'the general Jewish public was not only outraged
but genuinely astonished,'[4] so well had its spokesmen succeeded in
convincing themselves and everybody else of the non-fact that Jewish separateness was due exclusively to Gentile hostility and lack of
enlightenment. Judaism, it was now maintained chiefly by Jewish historians, had always been superior to other religions in that it believed
in human equality and tolerance. That this self-deceiving theory,
accompanied by the belief that the Jewish people had always been the
passive, suffering object of Christian persecutions, actually amounted
to a prolongation and modernization of the old myth of chosenness
and was bound to end in new and often very complicated practices of
separation, destined to uphold the ancient dichotomy, is perhaps one
of those ironies which seem to be in store for those who, for whatever
reasons, try to embellish and manipulate political facts and historical
records. For if Jews had anything in common with their non-Jewish
neighbors to support their newly proclaimed equality, it was precisely
a religiously predetermined, mutually hostile past that was as rich in
cultural achievement on the highest level as it was abundant in fanaticism and crude superstitions on the level of the uneducated masses.

However, even the irritating stereotypes of this sort of Jewish
historiography rest on a more solid basis of historical fact than the

3 It is interesting to note that the first modern Jewish historian, J. M. Jost, who wrote
in Germany in the middle of the last century, was much less prone to the common
prejudices of secular Jewish historiography than his more illustrious successors.
4 Katz, *op. cit.*, p. 196.

outdated political and social needs of European Jewry in the nine-teenth and early twentieth centuries. While Jewish cultural history was infinitely more diverse than it was then assumed, and while the causes of disaster varied with historical and geographical circum-stances, it is true that they varied more in the non-Jewish environment than within the Jewish communities. Two very real factors were deci-sive for the fateful misconceptions that are still current in popular presentations of Jewish history. Nowhere and at no time after the destruction of the temple did Jews possess their own territory and their own state; they always depended for their physical existence upon the protection of non-Jewish authorities, although some means of self-protection, the right to bear arms, were granted to 'the Jews in France and Germany well into the thirteenth century.'[5] This does not mean that Jews were always deprived of power, but it is true that in any contest of violence, no matter for what reasons, Jews were not only vulnerable but helpless so that it was only natural, especially in the centuries of complete estrangement that preceded their rise to political equality, that all current outbursts of violence should be ex-perienced by them as mere repetitions. Catastrophes, moreover, were understood in Jewish tradition in terms of martyrology, which in turn had its historical basis in the first centuries of our era, when both Jews and Christians had defied the might of the Roman Empire, as well as in medieval conditions when the alternative of submitting to baptism and thus saving themselves from persecution remained open to Jews even when the cause of violence was not religious but political and economic. This factual constellation gave rise to an optical illusion under which both Jewish and non-Jewish historians have suffered ever since. Historiography 'has until now dealt more with the Christian dissociation from the Jews than with the reverse,'[6] thus obliterating the otherwise more important fact that Jewish dissociation from the Gentile world, and more specifically from the Christian environment, has been of greater relevance for Jewish history than the reverse, for the obvious reason that the very survival of the people as an identifi-able entity depended upon such voluntary separation and not, as was

5 *Ibid.*, p. 6.
6 *Ibid.*, p. 7.

currently assumed, upon the hostility of Christians and non-Jews. Only in the nineteenth and twentieth centuries, after emancipation and with the spread of assimilation, has antisemitism played any role in the conservation of the people, since only then did Jews aspire to being admitted to non-Jewish society.

Whereas anti-Jewish sentiments were widespread among the educated classes of Europe throughout the nineteenth century, antisemitism as an ideology remained, with very few exceptions, the prerogative of crackpots in general and the lunatic fringe in particular. Even the dubious products of Jewish apologetics, which never convinced anybody but the convinced, were towering examples of erudition and scholarship compared with what the enemies of Jews had to offer in matters of historical research.[7] When, after the close of the war, I began to organize the material for this book, which had been collected from documentary sources and sometimes excellent monographs over a period of more than ten years, there did not exist a single over-all presentation of its subject matter that could be said to conform to the most elementary standards of historical scholarship. And the situation has hardly changed since. This is all the more deplorable as the need for an impartial, truthful treatment of Jewish history has recently become greater than it has ever been before. Twentieth-century political developments have driven the Jewish people into the storm center of events; the Jewish question and antisemitism, relatively unimportant phenomena in terms of world politics, became the catalytic agent first for the rise of the Nazi movement and the establishment of the organizational structure of the Third Reich, in which every citizen had to prove that he was *not* a Jew, then for a world war of unparalleled ferocity, and finally for the emergence of the unprecedented crime of genocide in the midst of Occidental civilization. That this called not only for lamentation and denunciation but for comprehension seemed to me obvious. This book is an attempt at understanding what at first and even second glance appeared simply outrageous.

Comprehension, however, does not mean denying the outrageous,

7 The only exception is the antisemitic historian Walter Frank, the head of the Nazi *Reichsinstitut für Geschichte des Neuen Deutschlands* and the editor of nine volumes of *Forschungen zur Judenfrage,* 1937–1944. Especially Frank's own contributions can still be consulted with profit.

deducing the unprecedented from precedents, or explaining phenomena by such analogies and generalities that the impact of reality and the shock of experience are no longer felt. It means, rather, examining and bearing consciously the burden that events have placed upon us – neither denying their existence nor submitting meekly to their weight as though everything that in fact happened could not have happened otherwise. Comprehension, in short, means the unpremeditated, attentive facing up to, and resisting of, reality – whatever it may be or might have been.

For this comprehension a certain familiarity with Jewish history in nineteenth-century Europe and the attendant development of anti-semitism is indispensable though, of course, not sufficient. The following chapters deal with only those elements in nineteenth-century history which indeed belong among the 'origins of totalitarianism.' A comprehensive history of antisemitism remains still to be written and is beyond the scope of this book. So long as this lacuna exists, there is enough justification even in terms of mere scholarship to publish the following chapters as an independent contribution toward a more comprehensive history, although it was originally conceived as a constituent part of the prehistory, as it were, of totalitarianism. Moreover, what is true for the history of antisemitism, that it fell into the hands of non-Jewish crackpots and Jewish apologetics, and was carefully avoided by reputable historians, is true, *mutatis mutandis*, for nearly all elements that later crystallized in the novel totalitarian phenomenon; they had hardly been noticed by either learned or public opinion because they belonged to a subterranean stream of European history where, hidden from the light of the public and the attention of enlightened men, they had been able to gather an entirely unexpected virulence.

Since only the final crystallizing catastrophe brought these subterranean trends into the open and to public notice, there has been a tendency to simply equate totalitarianism with its elements and origins – as though every outburst of antisemitism or racism or imperialism could be identified as 'totalitarianism.' This fallacy is as misleading in the search for historical truth as it is pernicious for political judgment. Totalitarian politics – far from being simply antisemitic or racist or imperialist or communist – use and abuse their own ideological and political elements until the basis of factual reality, from which the ideologies originally derived their strength and their propaganda value – the reality of class struggle, for instance, or the interest conflicts between Jews and their neighbors – have all but disappeared. It certainly would be a serious error to underestimate the role sheer racism has played and is still playing in the government of the Southern states, but it would be an even more serious fallacy to arrive at the retrospective conclusion that large areas of the United States have been under totalitarian rule for more than a century. The only direct, unadulterated consequence of nineteenth-century antisemitic movements was not Nazism but, on the contrary, Zionism, which, at least in its Western ideological form, was a kind of counterideology, the 'answer' to antisemitism. This, incidentally, is not to say that Jewish self-consciousness was ever a mere creation of antisemitism; even a cursory knowledge of Jewish history, whose central concern since the Babylonian exile has always been the survival of the people against the overwhelming odds of dispersion, should be enough to dispel this latest myth in these matters, a myth that has become somewhat fashionable in intellectual circles after Sartre's 'existentialist' interpretation of *the* Jew as someone who is regarded and defined as a Jew by others.

The best illustration of both the distinction and the connection between pre-totalitarian and totalitarian antisemitism is perhaps the ludicrous story of the 'Protocols of the Elders of Zion.' The Nazi use of the forgery as a textbook for global conquest is certainly not part of the history of antisemitism, but only this history can explain why the improbable tale contained enough plausibility to be useful as anti-Jewish propaganda to begin with. What, on the other hand, it can not explain is why the totalitarian claim to global rule, to be exercised by members and methods of a secret society, should become an attractive political goal at all. This latter, politically (though not propagandistically) much more relevant function has its origin in imperialism in general, in its highly explosive Continental version, the so-called pan-movements in particular.

This book then is limited in time and place as well as in subject matter. Its analyses concern Jewish history in Central and Western Europe from the time of the court Jews to the Dreyfus Affair insofar as it was relevant to the birth of antisemitism and influenced by it. It deals with antisemitic movements that were still pretty solidly grounded in factual realities characteristic of Jewish-Gentile relations, that is, in the part Jews played in the development of the nation-state on one side and in their role in non-Jewish society on the other. The emergence of the first antisemitic parties in the 1870's and 1880's marks the moment when the limited, factual basis of interest conflict and demonstrable experience was transcended and that road opened which ended in the 'final solution.' From then on, in the era of imperialism, followed by the period of totalitarian movements and governments, it is no longer possible to isolate the Jewish question or the antisemitic ideology from issues that are actually almost completely unrelated to the realities of modern Jewish history. And this is not merely and not primarily because these matters played such a prominent role in world affairs, but because antisemitism itself was now being used for ulterior purposes that, though their implementation finally claimed Jews as their chief victims, left all particular issues of both Jewish and anti-Jewish interest far behind.

The reader will find the imperialist and totalitarian versions of twentieth-century antisemitism, respectively, in the second and third volumes of this work.

Hannah Arendt<br>July 1967

## Preface to Part Two: Imperialism

Rarely could the beginnings of a historical period be dated with such precision and seldom were the chances for contemporary observers to witness its definite end so good as in the case of the imperialist era. For imperialism, which grew out of colonialism and was caused by the incongruity of the nation-state system with the economic and industrial developments in the last third of the nineteenth century, started its politics of expansion for expansion's sake no sooner than around 1884, and this new version of power politics was as different from national conquests in border-wars as it was from true empire-building Roman style. Its end seemed unavoidable after 'the liquidation of His Majesty's Empire,' over which Churchill had refused 'to preside,' had become an accomplished fact with the declaration of Indian independence. That the British liquidated their colonial rule voluntarily is still one of the most momentous events of twentieth-century history, and after this had happened no European nation could hold on to its overseas possessions. The only exception is Portugal, and her strange ability to continue a fight that all other European colonial powers had to give up may be due to her national backwardness even more than to Salazar's dictatorship; for it was not mere weakness or the exhaustion due to two murderous wars in one generation but also the moral scruples and political apprehensions of the fully developed nation-states that advised against extreme measures, the introduction of 'administrative massacres' (A. Carthill) that might well have broken the nonviolent rebellion in India, and against a continuation of the 'government of subject races' (Lord Cromer) because of the much-feared boomerang effect upon the mother countries. When finally France, thanks to the then still intact authority of De Gaulle, dared to give up Algeria, which she had always considered as much a part of France as the *département de la Seine,* a point of no return seemed to have been reached.

Whatever the merits of this hope might have been if the hot war against Nazi Germany had not been followed by the cold war between Soviet Russia and the United States, in retrospect one is tempted to look upon the last two decades as the time-span during which the two most powerful countries of the earth jockeyed for position in a competitive struggle for predominance in more or less the same regions in which European nations had ruled before. In the same vein one is tempted to look upon the new uneasy détente between Russia and America as the result of the emergence of a third potential world power, China, rather than as the healthy and natural consequence of Russia's detotalitarization after Stalin's death. And if further developments should validate such tentative interpretations, it would mean in historical terms that we are back, on an enormously enlarged scale, where we started from, that is, in the imperialist era and on the collision course that led to World War I.

It has often been said that the British acquired their empire in a fit of absent-mindedness, as consequence of automatic trends, yielding to what seemed possible and what was tempting, rather than as a result of deliberate policy. If this is true, then the road to hell may just as well be paved with no intentions as with the proverbial good ones. And the objective facts that invite a return to imperialist policies are indeed so strong today that one is inclined to believe at least in the half-truth of the statement, the hollow assurances of good intentions on both sides – American 'commitments' to the nonviable status quo of corruption and incompetence on one side, Russian pseudo-revolutionary talk about wars of national liberation on the other – notwithstanding. The processes of nation-building in backward areas where lack of all prerequisites for national independence is in exact proportion to a rampant, sterile chauvinism have resulted in enormous power vacuums, for which the competition between the superpowers is all the fiercer, as with the development of nuclear weapons a direct confrontation of their means of violence as a last resort to 'solve' all conflicts seems to be definitely ruled out. Not only does every conflict between the small, undeveloped countries in these vast areas, be it a civil war in Vietnam or a national conflict in the Middle East, immediately attract the potential or actual intervention of the superpowers, but their very conflicts, or at least the timing of their outbreaks, are suspect of having been manipulated or directly caused by interests and maneuvers that have nothing whatsoever to do with the conflicts and interests at stake in the region itself. Nothing was so characteristic of power politics in the imperialist era than this shift from localized, limited and therefore predictable goals of national interest to the limitless pursuit of power after power that could roam and lay waste the whole globe with no certain nationally and territorially prescribed purpose and hence with no predictable direction. This backsliding has become apparent also on the ideological level, for the famous domino-theory, according to which American foreign policy feels committed to wage war in one country for the sake of the integrity of others that are not even its neighbors, is clearly but a new version of the old 'Great Game' whose rules permitted and even dictated the consideration of whole nations as stepping-stones, or as pawns, in today's terminology, for the riches and the rule over a third country, which in turn became a mere stepping-stone in the unending process of power expansion and accumulation. It was this chain reaction, inherent in imperialist power politics and best represented on the human level by the figure of the secret agent, of which Kipling said (in *Kim*), 'When every one is dead the Great Game is finished. Not before'; and the only reason his prophecy did not come true was the constitutional restraint of the nation-state, while today our only hope that it will not come true in the future is based on the constitutional restraints of the American republic plus the technological restraints of the nuclear age.

This is not to deny that the unexpected revival of imperialist policies and methods takes place under vastly changed conditions and circumstances. The initiative for overseas expansion has shifted westward from England and Western Europe to America, and the initiative for Continental expansion in close geographic continuity no longer comes from Central and Eastern Europe but is exclusively located in Russia. Imperialist policies, more than any other single factor, have brought about the decline of Europe, and the prophecies of statesmen and historians that the two giants flanking the European nations on the east and on the west would ultimately emerge as the heirs of her power seem to have come true. No one justifies expansion any longer by 'the white man's burden' on one side and an 'enlarged tribal consciousness' to unite people of similar ethnic origin on the other; instead we hear of 'commitments' to client states, of the responsibilities of power, and of solidarity with revolutionary national liberation movements. The very word 'expansion' has disappeared from our political vocabulary, which now uses the words 'extension' or, critically, 'overextension' to cover a very similar meaning. Politically more important, private investments in distant lands, originally the prime mover of imperialist developments, are today surpassed by foreign aid, economic and military, provided directly by governments. (In 1966 alone, the American government spent $4.6 billion in economic aid and foreign credits plus $1.3 billion a year in military aid in the decade 1956–1965, while the outflow of private capital in 1965 was $3.69 billion and in 1966 $3.91 billion.)[1] This means that the era of the so-called dollar imperialism, the specifically American version of pre-World War II imperialism that was politically the least dangerous, is definitely over. Private investments – 'the activities of a thousand U.S. companies operating in a hundred foreign countries' and 'concentrated in the most modern, the most strategic, the most rapidly growing sectors of the foreign economy' – create many political problems even if they are not protected by the power of the nation,[2] but foreign aid, even if given for purely humanitarian reasons, is political by nature precisely because it is not motivated by the search for profit. Billions of dollars have been spent in political and economic wastelands where corruption and incompetence have caused them to disappear before anything productive could be started, and this money is no longer the 'superfluous' capital that could not be invested productively and profitably in the home country but the weird out-growth of sheer abundance that the rich countries, the haves as against the have-nots, can afford to lose. In other words, the profit motive, whose importance for imperialist policies was frequently overrated even in the past, has now completely disappeared; only very rich and very

1 The figures are quoted from Leo Model, 'The Politics of Private Foreign Investment' and Kenneth M. Kauffman and Helena Stalson, 'U.S. Assistance to less developed Countries, 1956–65' respectively, both in *Foreign Affairs*, July, 1967.

2 L. Model's article quoted above (p. 641) gives a very valuable and pertinent analysis of these problems.

powerful countries can afford to take the huge losses involved in imperialism.

It probably is too early, and certainly beyond the scope of my considerations, to analyze and ascertain with any degree of confidence these recent trends. What seems uncomfortably clear even now is the strength of certain, seemingly uncontrollable processes that tend to shatter all hopes for constitutional development in the new nations and to undermine the republican institutions in the old. Examples are too many to permit even cursory enumeration, but the rise of an 'invisible government' by secret services, whose reach into domestic affairs, the cultural, educational, and economic sectors of our life, has only recently been revealed, is too ominous a sign to be passed under silence. There is no reason to doubt Mr. Allan W. Dulles' statement that Intelligence in this country has enjoyed since 1947 'a more influential position in our government than Intelligence enjoys in any other government of the world,' [3] nor is there any reason to believe that this influence has decreased since he made this statement in 1958. The deadly danger of 'invisible government' to the institutions of the 'visible government' has often been pointed out; what is perhaps less well known is the intimate traditional connection between imperialist politics and rule by 'invisible government' and secret agents. It is an error to believe that the creation of a net of secret services in this country after World War II was the answer to a direct threat to its national survival by the espionage network of Soviet Russia; the war had propelled the United States to the position of the greatest world power and it was this world power, rather than national existence, that was challenged by the revolutionary power of Moscow-directed communism.[4]

Whatever the causes for American ascendancy to world power, the

3 This is what Mr. Dulles said in a speech at Yale University in 1957, according to David Wise and Thomas B. Ross, *The Invisible Government*, New York, 1964, p. 2.

4 According to Mr. Dulles, the government had to 'fight fire with fire,' and then with a disarming frankness by which the former head of the CIA distinguished himself from his colleagues in other countries, he went on to explain what this meant. The CIA, by implication, had to model itself upon the Soviet State Security Service, which 'is more than a secret police organization, more than an intelligence and counter-intelligence organization. It is an instrument for *subversion, manipulation and violence, for secret intervention in the affairs of other countries.*' (Italics added.) See Allen W. Dulles, *The Craft of Intelligence*, New York, 1963, p. 155.

deliberate pursuit of a foreign policy leading to it or any claim to global rule are not among them. And the same is probably true for the country's recent and still tentative steps in the direction of imperialist power politics for which its form of government is less fitted than that of any other country. The enormous gap between the Western countries and the rest of the world, not only and not primarily in riches but in education, technical know-how, and general competence, has plagued international relations ever since the beginnings of genuine world politics. And this gulf, far from decreasing in recent decades under the pressure of the rapidly developing communication systems and the resulting shrinkage of distance on the earth, has constantly grown and is now assuming truly alarming proportions. 'Population growth rates in less developed countries were double those in the more advanced countries,'[5] and while this factor alone would make it imperative for them to turn to those with surplus food and surplus technological and political knowledge, it is also this same factor which defeats all help. Obviously, the larger the population the less help per capita it will receive, and the truth of the matter is that after two decades of massive help programs all the countries that had not been able to help themselves to begin with – like Japan – are poorer, further away from either economic or political stability than ever. As for the chances of imperialism, this situation improves them frightfully for the simple reason that sheer numbers have never mattered less; white rule in South Africa where the tyrannical minority is outnumbered almost ten to one probably was never more secure than today. It is this objective situation that turns all foreign aid into an instrument of foreign domination and puts all countries that need this help for their decreasing chances of physical survival before the alternative of accepting some form of 'government of subject races' or sinking rapidly into anarchic decay.

This book deals only with the strictly European colonial imperialism whose end came with the liquidation of British rule in India. It tells the story of the disintegration of the nation-state that proved to contain nearly all the elements necessary for the subsequent rise of

5  See the very instructive article by Orville L. Freeman, 'Malthus, Marx and the North American Breadbasket,' in *Foreign Affairs*, July, 1967.

totalitarian movements and governments. Before the imperialist era, there was no such thing as world politics, and without it, the totalitarian claim to global rule would not have made sense. During this period, the nation-state system proved incapable of either devising new rules for the handling of foreign affairs that had become global affairs or enforcing a Pax Romana on the rest of the world. Its political narrowness and shortsightedness ended in the disaster of totalitarianism, whose unprecedented horrors have overshadowed the ominous events and the even more ominous mentality of the preceding period. Scholarly inquiry has almost exclusively concentrated on Hitler's Germany and Stalin's Russia at the expense of their less harmful predecessors. Imperialist rule, except for the purpose of name-calling, seems half-forgotten, and the chief reason why this is deplorable is that its relevance for contemporary events has become rather obvious in recent years. Thus, the controversy about the United States' undeclared war in Vietnam has been conducted from both sides in terms of analogies with Munich or other examples drawn from the thirties when indeed totalitarian rule was the only clear and present, all-too present, danger, but the threats of today's policies in deeds and words bear a much more portentous resemblance to the deeds and verbal justifications that preceded the outbreak of World War I, when a spark in a peripheral region of minor interest to all concerned could start a world-wide conflagration.

To stress the unhappy relevance of this half-forgotten period for contemporary events does not mean, of course, either that the die is cast and we are entering a new period of imperialist policies or that imperialism under all circumstances must end in the disasters of totalitarianism. No matter how much we may be capable of learning from the past, it will not enable us to know the future.

Hannah Arendt
July 1967

## Preface to Part Three: Totalitarianism

### I

The original manuscript of *The Origins of Totalitarianism* was finished in autumn 1949, more than four years after the defeat of Hitler Germany, less than four years before Stalin's death. The first edition of the book appeared in 1951. In retrospect, the years I spent writing it, from 1945 onwards, appear like the first period of relative calm after decades of turmoil, confusion, and plain horror – the revolutions after the First World War, the rise of totalitarian movements and the undermining of parliamentary government, followed by all sorts of new tyrannies, Fascist and semi-Fascist, one-party and military dictatorships, finally the seemingly firm establishment of totalitarian governments resting on mass support:[1] in Russia in 1929, the year of what now is often called the 'second revolution,' and in Germany in 1933.

With the defeat of Nazi Germany, part of the story had come to an

---

1 No doubt, the fact that totalitarian government, its open criminality notwithstanding, rests on mass support is very disquieting. It is therefore hardly surprising that scholars as well as statesmen often refuse to recognize it, the former by believing in the magic of propaganda and brainwashing, the latter by simply denying it, as for instance Adenauer did repeatedly. A recent publication of secret reports on German public opinion during the war (from 1939 to 1944), issued by the Security Service of the SS (*Meldungen aus dem Reich. Auswahl aus den Geheimen Lageberichten des Sicherheitsdienstes der SS 1939–1944*, edited by Heinz Boberach, Neuwied & Berlin, 1965), is very revealing in this respect. It shows, first, that the population was remarkably well informed about all so-called secrets – massacres of Jews in Poland, preparation of the attack on Russia, etc. – and, second, the 'extent to which the victims of propaganda had remained able to form independent opinions' (pp. XVIII–XIX). However, the point of the matter is that this did not in the least weaken the general support of the Hitler regime. It is quite obvious that mass support for totalitarianism comes neither from ignorance nor from brainwashing.

end. This seemed the first appropriate moment to look upon contemporary events with the backward-directed glance of the historian and the analytical zeal of the political scientist, the first chance to try to tell and to understand what had happened, not yet *sine ira et studio*, still in grief and sorrow and, hence, with a tendency to lament, but no longer in speechless outrage and impotent horror. (I left my original Preface in the present edition in order to indicate the mood of those years.) It was, at any rate, the first possible moment to articulate and to elaborate the questions with which my generation had been forced to live for the better part of its adult life: *What happened? Why did it happen? How could it have happened?* For out of the German defeat, which left behind a country in ruins and a nation that felt it had arrived at 'point zero' of its history, mountains of paper had emerged virtually intact, a superabundance of documentary material on every aspect of the twelve years that Hitler's *Tausendjähriges Reich* had managed to last. The first generous selections from this *embarras de richesses*, which even today are by no means adequately published and investigated, began to appear in connection with the Nuremberg Trial of the Major War Criminals in 1946, in the twelve volumes of *Nazi Conspiracy and Aggression*.[2]

Much more documentary and other material, however, bearing on the Nazi regime, had become available in libraries and archives when the second (paperback) edition appeared in 1958. What I then learned was interesting enough, but it hardly required substantial changes in either the analysis or the argument of my original presentation. Numerous additions and replacements of quotations in the footnotes seemed advisable, and the text was considerably enlarged. But these changes were all of a technical nature. In 1949, the Nuremberg documents were known only in part and in English translations, and a great number of books, pamphlets, and magazines published in Germany between 1933 and 1945 had not been available. Also, in a number of additions I took into account some of the more important events

2 From the beginning, investigation and publication of documentary material have been guided by concern for criminal activities, and the selection has usually been made for the purpose of prosecution of war criminals. The result is that a great amount of highly interesting material has been neglected. The book mentioned in note 1 is a very welcome exception from the rule.

after Stalin's death – the successor crisis and Khrushchev's speech at the Twentieth Party Congress – as well as new information on the Stalin regime from recent publications. Thus I revised Part III and the last chapter of Part II, whereas Part I on Antisemitism and the first four chapters on Imperialism have remained unchanged. Moreover, there were certain insights of a strictly theoretical nature, closely connected with my analysis of the elements of total domination, which I did not possess when I finished the original manuscript that ended with rather inconclusive 'Concluding Remarks.' The last chapter of this edition, 'Ideology and Terror,' replaced these 'Remarks,' which, to the extent that they still seemed valid, were shifted to other chapters. To the second edition, I had added an Epilogue where I discussed briefly the introduction of the Russian system into the satellite countries and the Hungarian Revolution. This discussion, written much later, was different in tone since it dealt with contemporary events and has become obsolete in many details. I have now eliminated it, and this is the only substantial change of this edition as compared with the second (paperback) edition.

Obviously, the end of the war did not spell the end of totalitarian government in Russia. On the contrary, it was followed by the Bolshevization of Eastern Europe, that is, the spread of totalitarian government, and peace offered no more than a significant turning point from which to analyze the similarities and differences in methods and institutions of the two totalitarian regimes. Not the end of the war but Stalin's death eight years later was decisive. In retrospect, it seems that this death was not merely followed by a successor crisis and a temporary 'thaw' until a new leader had asserted himself, but by an authentic, though never unequivocal, process of detotalitarization. Hence, from the viewpoint of events, there was no reason to bring this part of my story up to date now; and as far as our knowledge of the period in question is concerned, it has not changed drastically enough to require extensive revisions and additions. In contrast to Germany, where Hitler used his war consciously to develop and, as it were, perfect totalitarian government, the war period in Russia was a time of temporary suspense of total domination. For my purposes, the years from 1929 to 1941 and then again from 1945 down to 1953 are of central interest, and for these periods our sources are as scarce and of the same nature as they were in 1958 or even in 1949. Nothing has happened, or is likely to happen in the future, to present us with the same unequivocal end of the story or the same horribly neat and irrefutable evidence to document it as was the case for Nazi Germany.

The only important addition to our knowledge, the contents of the Smolensk Archive (published in 1958 by Merle Fainsod) have demonstrated to what an extent dearth of the most elementary documentary and statistical material will remain the decisive handicap for all inquiries into this period of Russian history. For although the archives (discovered at party headquarters in Smolensk by German intelligence and then captured by the American occupation force in Germany) contain some 200,000 pages of documents and are virtually intact for the period from 1917 to 1938, the amount of information they fail to give us is truly amazing. Even with 'an almost unmanageable abundance of material on the purges' from 1929 to 1937, they contain no indication of the number of victims or any other vital statistical data. Wherever figures are given, they are hopelessly contradictory, the various organizations all giving different sets, and all we learn beyond doubt is that many of them, if they ever existed, were withheld at the source by order of the government.[3] Also, the Archive contains no information on the relations between the various branches of authority, 'between Party, the military and NKVD,' or between party and government, and it is silent about the channels of communication and command. In short, we learn nothing about the organizational structure of the regime, of which we are so well informed with respect to Nazi Germany.[4] In other words, while it has always been known that official Soviet publications served propaganda purposes and were utterly unreliable, it now appears that reliable source and statistical material probably never existed anywhere.

A much more serious question is whether a study of totalitarianism can afford to ignore what has happened, and is still happening, in China. Here our knowledge is even less secure than it was for Russia in the thirties, partly because the country has succeeded in isolating itself against foreigners after the successful revolution much more

---

3 See Merle Fainsod, *Smolensk under Soviet Rule*, Cambridge, 1958, pp. 210, 306, 365, etc.
4 *Ibid.*, pp. 73, 93.

radically, and partly because defectors from the higher ranks of the Chinese Communist Party have not yet come to our aid – which, of course, in itself is significant enough. For seventeen years, the little we knew beyond doubt pointed to very relevant differences: after an initial period of considerable bloodshed – the number of victims during the first years of dictatorship is plausibly estimated at fifteen million, about three percent of the population in 1949 and, in terms of percentage, considerably less than the population losses due to Stalin's 'second revolution' – and after the disappearance of organized opposition, there was no increase in terror, no massacres of innocent people, no category of 'objective enemies,' no show trials, though a great deal of public confession and 'self-criticism,' and no outright crimes. Mao's famous speech in 1957, 'On the Correct Handling of Contradictions among the People,' usually known under the misleading title 'Let a Hundred Flowers Bloom,' was certainly no plea for freedom, but it did recognize non-antagonistic contradictions between classes and, more importantly, between the people and the government even under a Communist dictatorship. The way to deal with opponents was 'rectification of thought,' an elaborate procedure of constant molding and remolding of the minds, to which more or less the whole population seemed subject. We never knew very well how this worked in everyday life, who was exempt from it – that is, who did the 'remolding' – and we had no inkling of the results of the 'brainwashing,' whether it was lasting and actually produced personality changes. If one were to trust the present announcements of the Chinese leadership, all it produced was hypocrisy on a gigantic scale, the 'breeding grounds for counterrevolution.' If this was terror, as it most certainly was, it was terror of a different kind, and whatever its results, it did not decimate the population. It clearly recognized national interest, it permitted the country to develop peacefully, to use the competence of the descendants of the formerly ruling classes, and to uphold academic and professional standards. In brief, it was obvious that Mao Tse-tung's 'thought' did not run along the lines laid down by Stalin (or Hitler, for that matter), that he was not a killer by instinct, and that nationalist sentiment, so prominent in all revolutionary upheavals in formerly colonial countries, was strong enough to impose limits upon total domination. All this seemed to contradict certain fears expressed in this book (p. 407).

On the other hand, the Chinese Communist Party after its victory had at once aimed at being 'international in organization, all-comprehensive in its ideological scope, and global in its political aspiration' (p. 510), that is, its totalitarian traits have been manifest from the beginning. These traits became more prominent with the development of the Sino-Soviet conflict, although the conflict itself might well have been touched off by national rather than ideological issues. The insistence of the Chinese on rehabilitating Stalin and denouncing the Russian attempts at detotalitarization as 'revisionist' deviation was ominous enough, and, to make matters worse, it was accompanied by an utterly ruthless, though thus far unsuccessful, international policy which aimed at infiltrating all revolutionary movements with Chinese agents and at reviving the Comintern under Peking's leadership. All these developments are difficult to judge at the present moment, partly because we don't know enough and partly because everything is still in a state of flux. To these uncertainties, which are in the nature of the situation, we unhappily have added our own self-created handicaps. For it does not facilitate matters in either theory or practice that we have inherited from the cold-war period an official 'counter-ideology,' anti-Communism, which also tends to become global in aspiration and tempts us into constructing a fiction of our own, so that we refuse on principle to distinguish the various Communist one-party dictatorships, with which we are confronted in reality, from authentic totalitarian government as it may develop, albeit in different forms, in China. The point, of course, is not that Communist China is different from Communist Russia, or that Stalin's Russia was different from Hitler's Germany. Drunkenness and incompetence, which loom so large in any description of Russia in the twenties and thirties and are still widespread today, played no role whatsoever in the story of Nazi Germany, while the unspeakable gratuitous cruelty in the German concentration and extermination camps seems to have been largely absent from the Russian camps, where the prisoners died of neglect rather than of torture. Corruption, the curse of the Russian administration from the beginning, was also present during the last years of the Nazi regime but apparently has been entirely absent from China after the revolution. Differences of this sort could be multiplied; they are of great significance and part and parcel of the national history of the respective countries, but they have no direct bearing on the form of government. Absolute monarchy, no doubt, was a very different affair in Spain, in France, in England, in Prussia; still it was everywhere the same form of government. Decisive in our context is that totalitarian government is different from dictatorships and tyrannies; the ability to distinguish between them is by no means an academic issue which could be safely left to the 'theoreticians,' for total domination is the only form of government with which coexistence is not possible. Hence, we have every reason to use the word 'totalitarian' sparingly and prudently.

In stark contrast to the scarcity and uncertainty of new sources for factual knowledge with respect to totalitarian government, we find an enormous increase in studies of all the varieties of new dictatorships, be they totalitarian or not, during the last fifteen years. This is of course particularly true for Nazi Germany and Soviet Russia. There exist now many works which are indeed indispensable for further inquiry and study of the subject, and I have tried my best to supplement my old bibliography accordingly. (The second [paperback] edition carried no bibliography.) The only kind of literature which, with few exceptions, I left out on purpose are the numerous memoirs published by former Nazi generals and high functionaries after the end of the war. (That this sort of apologetics does not shine with honesty is understandable enough and should not rule it out of our consideration. But the lack of comprehension these reminiscences display of what actually happened and of the roles the authors themselves played in the course of events is truly astonishing and deprives them of all but a certain psychological interest.) I also added the relatively few new items of importance to the reading lists pertaining to Parts I and II. Finally, for reasons of convenience, the bibliography like the book itself is now divided into three separate parts.

II

As far as evidence is concerned, the early date this book was conceived and written has proved to be less of a handicap than might reasonably be assumed, and this is true of the material on both the Nazi and the

Bolshevik variety of totalitarianism. It is one of the oddities of the literature on totalitarianism that very early attempts by contemporaries at writing its 'history,' which according to all academic rules were bound to founder on the lack of impeccable source material and emotional overcommitment, have stood the test of time remarkably well. Konrad Heiden's biography of Hitler and Boris Souvarine's biography of Stalin, both written and published in the thirties, are in some respects more accurate and in almost all respects more relevant than the standard biographies by Alan Bullock and Isaac Deutscher respectively. This may have many reasons, but one of them certainly is the simple fact that documentary material in both cases has tended to confirm and to add to what had been known all along from prominent defectors and other eye-witness accounts.

To put it somewhat drastically: We did not need Khrushchev's Secret Speech to know that Stalin had committed crimes, or that this allegedly 'insanely suspicious' man had decided to put his trust in Hitler. As to the latter, nothing indeed proves better than this trust that Stalin was not insane; he was justifiably suspicious with respect to all people he wished or prepared to eliminate, and these included practically everybody in the higher echelons of party and government; he naturally trusted Hitler because he did not wish him ill. As to the former, Khrushchev's startling admissions, which – for the obvious reason that his audience and he himself were totally involved in the true story – concealed considerably more than they revealed, had the unfortunate result that in the eyes of many (and also, of course, of scholars with their professional love of official sources) they minimized the gigantic criminality of the Stalin regime which, after all, did not consist merely in the slander and murder of a few hundred or thousand prominent political and literary figures, whom one may 'rehabilitate' posthumously, but in the extermination of literally untold millions of people whom no one, not even Stalin, could have suspected of 'counter-revolutionary' activities. It was precisely by conceding some crimes that Khrushchev concealed the criminality of the regime as a whole, and it is precisely against this camouflage and the hypocrisy of the present Russian rulers – all of them trained and promoted under Stalin – that the younger generation of Russian intellectuals is now in an almost open rebellion. For they know everything there is to know about 'mass purges, and the deportation and annihi-lation of entire peoples.'[5] Moreover, Khrushchev's explanation of the crimes he conceded – Stalin's insane suspiciousness – concealed the most characteristic aspect of totalitarian terror, that it is let loose when all organized opposition has died down and the totalitarian ruler knows that he no longer need to be afraid. This is particularly true for the Russian development. Stalin started his gigantic purges not in 1928 when he conceded, 'We have internal enemies,' and actually had still reason to be afraid – he knew that Bukharin compared him to Genghis Khan and was convinced that Stalin's policy 'was leading the country to famine, ruin, and a police regime,'[6] as indeed it did – but in 1934, when all former opponents had 'confessed their errors,' and Stalin himself, at the Seventeenth Party Congress, also called by him the 'Congress of the Victors,' had declared: 'At this Congress . . . there is nothing more to prove and, it seems, no one to fight.'[7] Neither the

5 To an estimated nine to twelve million victims of the First Five Year Plan (1928–1933) must be added the victims of the Great Purge – an estimated three million executed while five to nine million were arrested and deported. (See Robert C. Tucker's impor-tant introduction, 'Stalin, Bukharin, and History as Conspiracy,' to the new edition of the verbatim report of the 1938 Moscow Trial, *The Great Purge Trial*, New York, 1965.) But all these estimates seem to fall short of the actual number. They do not take into account mass executions of which nothing was known until 'German occupation forces discovered a mass grave in the city of Vinnitsa containing thousands of bodies of persons executed in 1937 and 1938.' (See John A. Armstrong, *The Politics of Totalitari-anism. The Communist Party of the Soviet Union from 1934 to the Present*, New York, 1961, pp. 65 f.) Needless to say, this recent discovery makes the Nazi and the Bolshevik systems look even more than before like variations of the same model. – To what extent the mass killings of the Stalin era are in the center of the present opposition can best be seen in the trial of Sinyavsky and Daniel, of which the *New York Times Magazine* pub-lished key sections on April 17, 1966, and from which I quoted.

6 Tucker, *op. cit.*, pp. XVII–XVIII.

7 Quoted from Merle Fainsod, *How Russia Is Ruled*, Cambridge, 1959, p. 516. – Abdur-akhman Avtorkhanov (in *The Reign of Stalin*, published under the pseudonym Uralov in London, 1953) tells of a secret meeting of the Central Committee of the Party in 1936 after the first show trials, in which Bukharin reportedly accused Stalin of changing Lenin's party into a police state and was supported by more than two-thirds of the members. The story, especially the allegedly strong support of Bukharin in the Central Committee, does not sound very plausible; but even if true, in view of the fact that this meeting occurred while the Great Purge was already in full swing, the story does not indicate an organized opposition but rather its opposite. The truth of the matter, as Fainsod rightly points out, seems to be that 'wide-spread mass discontent' was quite

sensational character nor the decisive political importance of the Twentieth Party Congress for Soviet Russia and the Communist movement at large are in doubt. But the importance is political; the light official sources of the post-Stalin period shed on what had happened before should not be mistaken for the light of truth.

As far as our knowledge of the Stalin era is concerned, Fainsod's publication of the Smolensk Archive, which I mentioned before, has remained by far the most important publication, and it is deplorable that this first random selection has not yet been followed up by a more extensive publication of the material. To judge from Fainsod's book, there is much to learn for the period of Stalin's struggle for power in the mid-twenties: We now know how precarious the position of the party was,[8] not only because a mood of outright opposition prevailed in the country but because it was riddled with corruption and drunkenness; that outspoken antisemitism accompanied nearly all demands for liberalization;[9] that the drive for collectivization and dekulakization from 1928 onward actually interrupted the NEP, Lenin's new economic policy, and with it a beginning reconciliation between the people and its government;[10] how fiercely these measures were resisted by the solidarity of the whole peasant class, which decided that 'it's better not to be born than to join the kolkhoz'[11] and refused to be split up into rich, middle, and poor peasants in order to rise against the kulaks[12] – 'there sits somebody who is worse than these kulaks and

---

common, especially among the peasants, and that up to 1928, 'at the beginning of the First Five Year Plan strikes . . . were not uncommon,' but that such 'oppositional moods never come to a focus in any form of organized challenge to the regime,' and that by 1929 or 1930 'every organizational alternative had faded from the scene' if it ever had existed before. (See *Smolensk under Soviet Rule*, pp. 449 ff.)

8 'The wonder,' as Fainsod, *op. cit.*, p. 38, points out, 'is not merely that the Party was victorious, but that it managed to survive at all.'

9 *Ibid.*, pp. 49 ff. – A report from 1929 recounts violent antisemitic outbursts during a meeting; the Komsomol people 'in the audience kept silent . . . The impression was obtained that they were all in agreement with the anti-Jewish statements' (p. 445).

10 All reports from 1926 show a significant 'decline in so-called counter-revolutionary outbreaks, a measure of the temporary truce which the regime had worked out with the peasantry.' Compared with 1926, the reports from 1929–1930 'read like communiqués from a flaming battle front' (p. 177).

11 *Ibid.*, pp. 252 ff.

12 *Ibid.*, especially pp. 240 ff. and 446 ff.

who is only planning how to hunt people down';[13] and that the situation was not much better in the cities, where the workers refused to co-operate with the party-controlled trade unions and addressed the management as 'well-fed devils,' 'hypocritical wall-eyes,' and the like.[14]

Fainsod rightly points out that these documents clearly show not only 'wide-spread mass discontent' but also the lack of any 'sufficiently organized opposition' against the regime as a whole. What he fails to see, and what in my opinion is equally supported by the evidence, is that there existed an obvious alternative to Stalin's seizure of power and transformation of the one-party dictatorship into total domination, and this was the pursuance of the NEP policy as it had been initiated by Lenin.[15] Moreover, the measures taken by Stalin with the introduction of the First Five Year Plan in 1928, when his control of the party was almost complete, prove that transformation of classes into masses and the concomitant elimination of all group solidarity are the condition *sine qua non* of total domination.

With respect to the period of Stalin's undisputed rule from 1929 onward, the Smolensk Archive tends to confirm what we knew before from less irrefutable sources. This is even true for some of its odd lacunae, especially those concerning statistical data. For this lack proves merely that, in this as in other respects, the Stalin regime was ruthlessly consistent: all facts that did not agree, or were likely to disagree, with the official fiction – data on crop-yields, criminality, true incidences of 'counter-revolutionary' activities as distinguished from the later conspiracy fictions – were treated as non-facts. It was indeed quite in line with the totalitarian contempt for facts and reality that all

13 *Ibid.* All such statements are taken from GPU reports; see especially pp. 248 f. But it is quite characteristic that such remarks became much less frequent after 1934; the beginning of the Great Purge.

14 *Ibid.*, p. 310.

15 This alternative is usually overlooked in the literature because of the understandable, but historically untenable, conviction of a more or less smooth development from Lenin to Stalin. It is true that Stalin almost always talked in Leninist terms, so that it sometimes looks as though the only difference between the two men lay in the brutality or 'insanity' of Stalin's character. Whether or not this was a conscious ruse on the side of Stalin, the truth of the matter is – as Tucker, *op. cit.*, p. XVI, rightly observes – that 'Stalin filled these old Leninist concepts with a new, distinctively Stalinist content . . . The chief distinctive feature was the quite un-Leninist emphasis upon *conspiracy* as the hallmark of the present epoch.'

such data, instead of being collected in Moscow from the four corners of the immense territory, were first made known to the respective localities through publication in *Pravda*, *Izvestia*, or some other official organ in Moscow, so that every region and every district of the Soviet Union received its official, fictitious statistical data in much the same way it received the no less fictitious norms allotted to them by the Five Year Plans.[16]

I shall briefly enumerate a few of the more striking points, which could only be guessed at before and which are now supported by documentary evidence. We always suspected, but we now know that the regime was never 'monolithic' but 'consciously constructed around overlapping, duplicating, and parallel functions,' and that this grotesquely amorphous structure was kept together by the same Führer-principle – the so-called 'personality cult' – we find in Nazi Germany;[17] that the executive branch of this particular government was not the party but the police, whose 'operational activities were not regulated through party channels';[18] that the entirely innocent people whom the regime liquidated by the millions, the 'objective enemies' in Bolshevik language, knew that they were 'criminals without a crime';[19] that it was precisely this new category, as distinguished from the earlier true foes of the regime – assassins of government officials, arsonists, or bandits – that reacted with the same 'complete passivity'[20]

16 See Fainsod, *op. cit.*, especially pp. 365 f.

17 *Ibid.*, p. 93 and p. 71: It is quite characteristic that messages on all levels habitually stressed the 'obligations undertaken to Comrade Stalin,' and not to the regime or the party or the country. Nothing perhaps underlines more convincingly the similarities of the two systems than what Ilya Ehrenburg and other Stalinist intellectuals have to say today in their efforts to justify their past or simply to report what they actually thought during the Great Purge. 'Stalin knew nothing about the senseless violence committed against the Communists, against the Soviet intelligentsia,' 'they conceal it from Stalin' and 'if only someone would tell Stalin about it,' or, finally, the culprit was not Stalin at all but the respective chief of police. (Quoted from Tucker, *op. cit.*, p. XIII.) Needless to add, this was precisely what the Nazis had to say after the defeat of Germany.

18 *Ibid.*, pp. 166 ff.

19 The words are lifted from the appeal of a 'class-alien element' in 1936: 'I do not want to be a criminal without a crime' (p. 229).

20 An interesting OGPU report from 1931 stresses this new 'complete passivity,' this horrible apathy which the random terror against innocent people produced. The report mentions the great difference between the former arrests of enemies of the regime when 'an arrested man was led by two militiamen' and the mass arrests when

we know so well from the behavior patterns of the victims of Nazi terror. There was never any doubt that the 'flood of mutual denunciations' during the Great Purge was as disastrous for the economic and social well-being of the country as it was effective in strengthening the totalitarian ruler, but we know only now how deliberately Stalin set this 'ominous chain of denunciations in motion,'[21] when he proclaimed officially on July 29, 1936: *'The inalienable quality of every Bolshevik under present conditions should be the ability to recognize an enemy of the Party no matter how well he may be masked.'*[22] (Italics added.) For just as Hitler's 'Final Solution' actually meant to make the command 'Thou shalt kill' binding for the elite of the Nazi party, Stalin's pronouncement prescribed: 'Thou shalt bear false testimony,' as a guiding rule for the conduct of all members of the Bolshevik party. Finally, all doubts one still might have nourished about the amount of truth in the current theory, according to which the terror of the late twenties and thirties was 'the high price in suffering' exacted by industrialization and economic progress, are laid at rest by this first glimpse into the actual state of affairs and the course of events in one particular region.[23] Terror produced nothing of the sort. The best documented

---

'one militiaman may lead groups of people and the latter calmly walk and no one flees' (p. 248).

21 *Ibid.*, p. 135.

22 *Ibid.*, pp. 57–58. For the mounting mood of plain hysteria in these mass denunciations, see especially pp. 222, 229 ff., and the lovely story on p. 235, where we hear how one of the comrades has come to think 'that Comrade Stalin has taken a conciliatory attitude toward the Trotskyite-Zinovievite group,' a reproach which at the time meant immediate expulsion from the Party at least. But no such luck. The next speaker accused the man who had tried to outdo Stalin of being 'politically disloyal,' whereupon the former promptly 'confessed' his error.

23 Strangely enough, Fainsod himself still draws such conclusions from a mass of evidence that points into the opposite direction. See his last chapter, especially pp. 453 ff. – It is even stranger that this misreading of the factual evidence should be shared by so many authors in the field. To be sure, hardly any of them would go so far in this subtle justification of Stalin as Isaac Deutscher in his biography, but many still insist that 'Stalin's ruthless actions were . . . a way to the creation of a new equilibrium of forces' (Armstrong, *op cit.*, p. 64) and designed to offer 'a brutal but consistent solution of some of the basic contradictions inherent in the Leninist myth' (Richard Lowenthal in his very valuable *World Communism. The Disintegration of a Secular Faith*, New York, 1964, p. 42). There are but few exceptions from this Marxist hangover, such as Richard C. Tucker (*op. cit.*, p. XXVII), who says unequivocally that the Soviet 'system would

result of dekulakization, collectivization, and the Great Purge was neither progress nor rapid industrialization but famine, chaotic conditions in the production of food, and depopulation. The consequences have been a perpetual crisis in agriculture, an interruption of population growth, and the failure to develop and colonize the Siberian hinterland. Moreover, as the Smolensk Archive spells out in detail, Stalin's methods of rule succeeded in destroying whatever measure of competence and technical know-how the country had acquired after the October Revolution. And all this together was indeed an incredibly 'high price,' not just in suffering, exacted for the opening of careers in the party and government bureaucracies to sections of the population which often were not merely *politically* illiterate.' [24] The truth is that the price of totalitarian rule was so high that in neither Germany nor Russia has it yet been paid in full.

---

have been better off and far more equipped to meet the coming test of total war had there been no Great Purge, which was, in effect, a great wrecking operation in Soviet society.' Mr. Tucker believes that this refutes my 'image' of totalitarianism, which, I think, is a misunderstanding. Instability is indeed a functional requisite of total domination, which is based on an ideological fiction and presupposes that a movement, as distinguished from a party, has seized power. The hallmark of this system is that substantial power, the material strength and well-being of the country, is constantly sacrificed to the power of organization, just as all factual truths are sacrificed to the demands of ideological consistency. It is obvious that in a contest between material strength and organizational power, or between fact and fiction, the latter may come to grief, and this happened in Russia as well as Germany during the Second World War. But this is no reason to underestimate the power of totalitarian movements. It was the terror of permanent instability that helped to organize the satellite system, and it is the present stability of Soviet Russia, its detotalitarization, which, on one side, has greatly contributed to her present material strength, but which, on the other, has caused her to lose control of her satellites.

24 See the interesting details (Fainsod, *op. cit.*, pp. 345–355) about the 1929 campaign to eliminate 'reactionary professors' against the protests of party and Komsomol members as well as the student body, who saw 'no reason to replace the excellent non-Party' professors; whereupon of course a new commission promptly reported 'the large number of class-alien elements among the student body.' That it was one of the main purposes of the Great Purge to open the careers to the younger generation has always been known.

## III

I mentioned before the detotalitarization process which followed upon Stalin's death. In 1958, I was not yet sure that the 'thaw' was more than a temporary relaxation, a kind of emergency measure due to the successor crisis and not unlike the considerable loosening of totalitarian controls during the Second World War. Even today we cannot know if this process is final and irreversible, but it surely can no longer be called temporary or provisional. For however one may read the often bewildering zigzag line of Soviet policies since 1953, it is undeniable that the huge police empire was liquidated, that most of the concentration camps were dissolved, that no new purges against 'objective enemies' have been introduced, and that conflicts between members of the new 'collective leadership' are now being resolved by demotion and exile from Moscow rather than by show trials, confessions, and assassinations. No doubt, the methods used by the new rulers in the years after Stalin's death still followed closely the pattern set by Stalin after Lenin's death: there emerged again a triumvirate called 'collective leadership,' a term coined by Stalin in 1925, and after four years of intrigues and contest for power, there was a repetition of Stalin's *coup d'état* in 1929, namely, Khrushchev's seizure of power in 1957. Technically speaking, Khrushchev's coup followed the methods of his dead and denounced master very closely. He too needed an outside force in order to win power in the party hierarchy, and he used the support of Marshal Zhukov and the army exactly the same way Stalin had used his relationships to the secret police in the succession struggle of thirty years ago.[25] Just as in the case of Stalin, in which the supreme power after the coup continued to reside in the party, not in the police, so in Khrushchev's case 'by the end of 1957 the Communist

25 Armstrong, *op. cit.*, p. 319, argues that the importance of Marshal Zhukov's intervention in the inner-party struggle has been 'highly exaggerated' and maintains that Khrushchev 'triumphed without any need for military intervention,' because he was 'supported by the Party apparatus.' This seems not to be true. But it is true that 'many foreign observers,' because of the role of the army in support of Khrushchev against the party apparatus, arrived at the mistaken conclusion of a lasting power increase of the military at the expense of the party, as though the Soviet Union was about to change from a party dictatorship into a military dictatorship.

Party of the Soviet Union had attained a place of undisputed supremacy in all aspects of Soviet life';[26] for just as Stalin had never hesitated to purge his police cadres and liquidate their chief, so Khrushchev had followed up his inner-party maneuvers by removing Zhukov from the Presidium and Central Committee of the party, to which he had been elected after the coup, as well as from his post as highest commander of the army.

To be sure, when Khrushchev appealed to Zhukov for support, the army's ascendancy over the police was an accomplished fact in the Soviet Union. This had been one of the automatic consequences of the breaking up of the police empire whose rule over a huge part of Soviet industries, mines, and real estate had been inherited by the managerial group, who suddenly found themselves rid of their most serious economic competitor. The automatic ascendancy of the army was even more decisive; it now held a clear monopoly of the instruments of violence with which to decide inner-party conflicts. It speaks for Khrushchev's shrewdness that he grasped these consequences of what they presumably had done together more rapidly than his colleagues. But whatever his motives, the consequences of this shift of emphasis from the police to the military in the power game were of great consequence. It is true, ascendancy of the secret police over the military apparatus is the hallmark of many tyrannies, and not only the totalitarian; however, in the case of totalitarian government the preponderance of the police not merely answers the need for suppressing the population at home but fits the ideological claim to global rule. For it is evident that those who regard the whole earth as their future territory will stress the organ of domestic violence and will rule conquered territory with police methods and personnel rather than with the army. Thus, the Nazis used their SS troops, essentially a police force, for the rule and even the conquest of foreign territories, with the ultimate aim of an amalgamation of the army and the police under the leadership of the SS.

Moreover, the significance of this change in the balance of power had been manifest before, at the occasion of the suppression by force of the Hungarian Revolution. The bloody crushing of the revolution,

26 *Ibid.*, p. 320.

terrible and effective as it was, had been accomplished by regular army units and not by police troops, and the consequence was that it did by no means represent a typically Stalinist solution. Although the military operation was followed by the execution of the leaders and the imprisonment of thousands, there was no wholesale deportation of the people; in fact, no attempt at depopulating the country was made. And since this was a military operation and not a police action, the Soviets could afford sending enough aid to the defeated country to prevent mass starvation and to stave off a complete collapse of the economy in the year following the revolution. Nothing, surely, would have been farther from Stalin's mind under similar circumstances.

The clearest sign that the Soviet Union can no longer be called totalitarian in the strict sense of the term is, of course, the amazingly swift and rich recovery of the arts during the last decade. To be sure, efforts to rehabilitate Stalin and to curtail the increasingly vocal demands for freedom of speech and thought among students, writers, and artists recur again and again, but none of them has been very successful or is likely to be successful without a full-fledged re-establishment of terror and police rule. No doubt, the people of the Soviet Union are denied all forms of political freedom, not only freedom of association but also freedom of thought, opinion and public expression. It looks as though nothing has changed, while in fact everything has changed. When Stalin died the drawers of writers and artists were empty; today there exists a whole literature that circulates in manuscript and all kinds of modern painting are tried out in the painters' studios and become known even though they are not exhibited. This is not to minimize the difference between tyrannical censorship and freedom of the arts, it is only to stress the fact that the difference between a clandestine literature and no literature equals the difference between one and zero.

Furthermore, the very fact that members of the intellectual opposition can have a trial (though not an open one), can make themselves heard in the courtroom and count upon support outside it, do not confess to anything but plead not guilty, demonstrates that we deal here no longer with total domination. What happened to Sinyavsky and Daniel, the two writers who in February 1966 were tried for having published works abroad which could not have been published in the

Soviet Union and who were sentenced to seven and five years of hard labor respectively, was certainly outrageous by all standards of justice in constitutional government; but what they had to say was heard around the world and is not likely to be forgotten. They did not disappear in the hole of oblivion which totalitarian rulers prepare for their opponents. Less well known but perhaps even more convincing is that Khrushchev's own and most ambitious attempt at reversing the process of detotalitarization turned into a complete failure. In 1957, he introduced a new 'law against social parasites,' which would have enabled the regime to reintroduce mass deportations, re-establish slave labor on a large scale, and – most importantly for total domination – to let loose another flood of mass denunciations; for 'parasites' were supposed to be selected by the people themselves in mass meetings. The 'law,' however, met with the opposition of Soviet jurists and was dropped before it could even be tried out.[27] In other words, the people of the Soviet Union have emerged from the nightmare of totalitarian rule to the manifold hardships, dangers, and injustices of one-party dictatorship; and while it is entirely true that this modern form of tyranny offers none of the guarantees of constitutional government, that 'even accepting the presuppositions of Communist ideology, all power in the USSR is ultimately illegitimate,'[28] and that the country therefore can relapse into totalitarianism between one day and another without major upheavals, it is also true that the most horrible of all new forms of government, whose elements and historical origins I set out to analyze, came no less to an end in Russia with the death of Stalin than totalitarianism came to an end in Germany with the death of Hitler.

This book deals with totalitarianism, its origins and its elements, whereas its aftermath in either Germany or Russia is pertinent to its considerations only insofar as it is likely to throw light on what happened before. Hence, not the period after Stalin's death but rather the postwar era of his rule is of relevance in our context. And these eight years, from 1945 to 1953, confirm and spin out, they don't either contradict or add new elements to what had been manifest since the middle

27  See *ibid.*, p. 325.
28  *Ibid.*, pp. 339 ff.

thirties. The events that followed upon victory, the measures taken to reaffirm total domination after the temporary relaxation of the war period in the Soviet Union as well as those by which totalitarian rule was introduced in the satellite countries, were all in accord with the rules of the game as we had come to know it. The Bolshevization of the satellites started with popular-front tactics and a sham parliamentary system, proceeded quickly to the open establishment of one-party dictatorships in which the leaders and members of the formerly tolerated parties were liquidated, and then reached the last stage when the native Communist leaders, whom Moscow rightly or wrongly mistrusted, were brutally framed, humiliated in show trials, tortured, and killed under the rulership of the most corrupt and most despicable elements in the party, namely those who were primarily not Communists but agents of Moscow. It was as though Moscow repeated in great haste all the stages of the October Revolution up to the emergence of totalitarian dictatorship. The story therefore, while unspeakably horrible, is without much interest of its own and varies little: what happened in one satellite country happened at almost the same moment in all others from the Baltic Sea down to the Adriatic. Events differed in regions which were not included into the satellite system. The Baltic states were directly incorporated into the Soviet Union and fared considerably worse than the satellites: more than half a million people were deported from the three small countries and an 'enormous influx of Russian settlers' began to threaten the native populations with minority status in their own countries.[29] East Germany, on the other hand, is only now, after the erection of the Berlin Wall, slowly being incorporated into the satellite system, having been treated before rather as occupied territory with a Quisling government.

In our context, developments in the Soviet Union, especially after 1948 – the year of Zhdanov's mysterious death and the 'Leningrad affair' – are of greater importance. For the first time after the Great Purge, Stalin had a great number of high and highest officials executed, and we know for certain that this was planned as the beginning of another nationwide purge. This would have been touched off by the

---

29 See V. Stanley Vardys, 'How the Baltic Republics fare in the Soviet Union,' in *Foreign Affairs*, April, 1966.

'Doctors' plot' had Stalin's death not intervened. A group of mostly Jewish physicians were accused of having plotted 'to wipe out the leading cadres of the USSR.'[30] Everything that went on in Russia between 1948 and January 1953, when the 'Doctors' plot' was being 'discovered,' bore a striking and ominous similarity to the preparations of the Great Purge during the thirties: the death of Zhdanov and the Leningrad purge corresponded to Kirov's no less mysterious death in 1934 which was immediately followed by a kind of preparatory purge 'of all former oppositionists who remained in the Party.'[31] Moreover, the very content of the absurd accusation against the physicians, that they would kill off people in leading positions all over the country, must have filled with fearful forebodings all those who were acquainted with Stalin's method of accusing a fictitious enemy of the crime he himself was about to commit. (The best known example is of course his accusation that Tukhachevski conspired with Germany at the very moment when Stalin was contemplating an alliance with the Nazis.) Obviously, in 1952 Stalin's entourage was much wiser to what his words actually meant than they could have been in the thirties, and the very wording of the accusation must have spread panic among all higher officials of the regime. This panic may still be the most plausible explanation of Stalin's death, the mysterious circumstances surrounding it, and the swift closing of ranks in the higher echelons of the party, notoriously ridden by strife and intrigues, during the first months of the succession crisis. However little we know of the details of this story, we know more than enough to support my original conviction that such 'wrecking operations' as the Great Purge were not isolated episodes, not excesses of the regime provoked by extraordinary circumstances, but that they were an institution of terror and to be expected at regular intervals – unless, of course, the nature of the regime itself was changed.

The most dramatic new element in this last purge, which Stalin planned in the last years of his life, was a decisive shift in ideology, the introduction of a Jewish world conspiracy. For years, the ground for this change had been carefully laid in a number of trials in the

30 Armstrong, *op. cit.,* pp. 235 ff.
31 Fainsod, *op. cit.,* p. 56.

satellite countries – the Rajk trial in Hungary, the Ana Pauker affair in Rumania, and, in 1952, the Slansky trial in Czechoslovakia. In these preparatory measures, high party officials were singled out because of their 'Jewish bourgeois' origins and accused of Zionism; this accusation was gradually changed to implicate notoriously non-Zionist agencies (especially the American Jewish Joint Distribution Committee), in order to indicate that all Jews were Zionists and all Zionist groups 'hirelings of American imperialism.' [32] There was of course nothing new in the 'crime' of Zionism, but as the campaign progressed and began to center on Jews in the Soviet Union, another significant change took place: Jews now stood accused of 'cosmopolitanism' rather than Zionism, and the pattern of accusations that developed out of this slogan followed ever more closely the Nazi pattern of a Jewish world conspiracy in the sense of the Elders of Zion. It now became startlingly clear how deep an impression this mainstay of Nazi ideology must have made on Stalin – the first indications of this had been in evidence ever since the Hitler-Stalin pact – partly, to be sure, because of its obvious propaganda value in Russia as in all of the satellite countries, where anti-Jewish feeling was widespread and anti-Jewish propaganda had always enjoyed great popularity, but partly also because this type of a fictitious world conspiracy provided an ideologically more suitable background for totalitarian claims to world rule than Wall Street, capitalism, and imperialism. The open, unashamed adoption of what had become to the whole world the most prominent sign of Nazism was the last compliment Stalin paid to his late colleague and rival in total domination with whom, much to his chagrin, he had not been able to come to a lasting agreement.

Stalin, like Hitler, died in the midst of a horrifying unfinished business. And when this happened, the story this book has to tell, and the events it tries to understand and to come to terms with, came to an at least provisional end.

Hannah Arendt
June 1966

32  Armstrong, *op. cit.*, p. 236.

# PART ONE

## Antisemitism

*This is a remarkable century which opened with the Revolution and ended with the Affaire! Perhaps it will be called the century of rubbish.*

Roger Martin Du Gard

# CHAPTER ONE

## *Antisemitism as an Outrage to Common Sense*

Many still consider it an accident that Nazi ideology centered around antisemitism and that Nazi policy, consistently and uncompromisingly, aimed at the persecution and finally the extermination of the Jews. Only the horror of the final catastrophe, and even more the homelessness and uprootedness of the survivors, made the 'Jewish question' so prominent in our everyday political life. What the Nazis themselves claimed to be their chief discovery – the role of the Jewish people in world politics – and their chief interest – persecution of Jews all over the world – have been regarded by public opinion as a pretext for winning the masses or an interesting device of demagogy.

The failure to take seriously what the Nazis themselves said is comprehensible enough. There is hardly an aspect of contemporary history more irritating and mystifying than the fact that of all the great unsolved political questions of our century, it should have been this seemingly small and unimportant Jewish problem that had the dubious honor of setting the whole infernal machine in motion. Such discrepancies between cause and effect outrage our common sense, to say nothing of the historian's sense of balance and harmony. Compared with the events themselves, all explanations of antisemitism look as if they had been hastily and hazardously contrived, to cover up an issue which so gravely threatens our sense of proportion and our hope for sanity.

One of these hasty explanations has been the identification of antisemitism with rampant nationalism and its xenophobic outbursts. Unfortunately, the fact is that modern antisemitism grew in proportion as traditional nationalism declined, and reached its climax at the exact moment when the European system of nation-states and its precarious balance of power crashed.

It has already been noticed that the Nazis were not simple nationalists. Their nationalist propaganda was directed toward their fellow-
travelers and not their convinced members; the latter, on the contrary,
were never allowed to lose sight of a consistently supranational
approach to politics. Nazi 'nationalism' had more than one aspect in
common with the recent nationalistic propaganda in the Soviet Union,
which is also used only to feed the prejudices of the masses. The Nazis
had a genuine and never revoked contempt for the narrowness of
nationalism, the provincialism of the nation-state, and they repeated
time and again that their 'movement,' international in scope like the
Bolshevik movement, was more important to them than any state,
which would necessarily be bound to a specific territory. And not only
the Nazis, but fifty years of antisemitic history, stand as evidence
against the identification of antisemitism with nationalism. The first
antisemitic parties in the last decades of the nineteenth century were
also among the first that banded together internationally. From the
very beginning, they called international congresses and were concerned with a co-ordination of international, or at least inter-European,
activities.

General trends, like the coincident decline of the nation-state and
the growth of antisemitism, can hardly ever be explained satisfactor-
ily by one reason or by one cause alone. The historian is in most such
cases confronted with a very complex historical situation where he is
almost at liberty, and that means at a loss, to isolate one factor as the
'spirit of the time.' There are, however, a few helpful general rules.
Foremost among them for our purpose is Tocqueville's great discovery (in *L'Ancien Régime et la Révolution*, Book II, chap. 1) of the motives
for the violent hatred felt by the French masses for the aristocracy at
the outbreak of the Revolution – a hatred which stimulated Burke to
remark that the revolution was more concerned with 'the condition of
a gentleman' than with the institution of a king. According to Tocqueville, the French people hated aristocrats about to lose their power
more than it had ever hated them before, precisely because their rapid
loss of real power was not accompanied by any considerable decline
in their fortunes. As long as the aristocracy held vast powers of jurisdiction, they were not only tolerated but respected. When noblemen
lost their privileges, among others the privilege to exploit and oppress,

the people felt them to be parasites, without any real function in the rule of the country. In other words, neither oppression nor exploitation as such is ever the main cause for resentment; wealth without visible function is much more intolerable because nobody can understand why it should be tolerated.

Antisemitism reached its climax when Jews had similarly lost their public functions and their influence, and were left with nothing but their wealth. When Hitler came to power, the German banks were already almost *judenrein* (and it was here that Jews had held key positions for more than a hundred years) and German Jewry as a whole, after a long steady growth in social status and numbers, was declining so rapidly that statisticians predicted its disappearance in a few decades. Statistics, it is true, do not necessarily point to real historical processes; yet it is noteworthy that to a statistician Nazi persecution and extermination could look like a senseless acceleration of a process which would probably have come about in any case.

The same holds true for nearly all Western European countries. The Dreyfus Affair exploded not under the Second Empire, when French Jewry was at the height of its prosperity and influence, but under the Third Republic when Jews had all but vanished from important positions (though not from the political scene). Austrian antisemitism became violent not under the reign of Metternich and Franz Joseph, but in the postwar Austrian Republic when it was perfectly obvious that hardly any other group had suffered the same loss of influence and prestige through the disappearance of the Hapsburg monarchy.

Persecution of powerless or power-losing groups may not be a very pleasant spectacle, but it does not spring from human meanness alone. What makes men obey or tolerate real power and, on the other hand, hate people who have wealth without power, is the rational instinct that power has a certain function and is of some general use. Even exploitation and oppression still make society work and establish some kind of order. Only wealth without power or aloofness without a policy are felt to be parasitical, useless, revolting, because such conditions cut all the threads which tie men together. Wealth which does not exploit lacks even the relationship which exists between exploiter and exploited; aloofness without policy does not imply even the minimum concern of the oppressor for the oppressed.

The general decline of Western and Central European Jewry, however, constitutes merely the atmosphere in which the subsequent events took place. The decline itself explains them as little as the mere loss of power by the aristocracy would explain the French Revolution. To be aware of such general rules is important only in order to refute those recommendations of common sense which lead us to believe that violent hatred or sudden rebellion spring necessarily from great power and great abuses, and that consequently organized hatred of the Jews cannot but be a reaction to their importance and power.

More serious, because it appeals to much better people, is another common-sense fallacy: the Jews, because they were an entirely powerless group caught up in the general and insoluble conflicts of the time, could be blamed for them and finally be made to appear the hidden authors of all evil. The best illustration – and the best refutation – of this explanation, dear to the hearts of many liberals, is in a joke which was told after the first World War. An antisemite claimed that the Jews had caused the war; the reply was: Yes, the Jews and the bicyclists. Why the bicyclists? asks the one. Why the Jews? asks the other.

The theory that the Jews are always the scapegoat implies that the scapegoat might have been anyone else as well. It upholds the perfect innocence of the victim, an innocence which insinuates not only that no evil was done but that nothing at all was done which might possibly have a connection with the issue at stake. It is true that the scapegoat theory in its purely arbitrary form never appears in print. Whenever, however, its adherents painstakingly try to explain why a specific scapegoat was so well suited to his role, they show that they have left the theory behind them and have got themselves involved in the usual historical research – where nothing is ever discovered except that history is made by many groups and that for certain reasons one group was singled out. The so-called scapegoat necessarily ceases to be the innocent victim whom the world blames for all its sins and through whom it wishes to escape punishment; it becomes one group of people among other groups, all of which are involved in the business of this world. And it does not simply cease to be coresponsible because it became the victim of the world's injustice and cruelty.

Until recently the inner inconsistency of the scapegoat theory was sufficient reason to discard it as one of many theories which are motivated by escapism. But the rise of terror as a major weapon of government has lent it a credibility greater than it ever had before.

A fundamental difference between modern dictatorships and all other tyrannies of the past is that terror is no longer used as a means to exterminate and frighten opponents, but as an instrument to rule masses of people who are perfectly obedient. Terror as we know it today strikes without any preliminary provocation, its victims are innocent even from the point of view of the persecutor. This was the case in Nazi Germany when full terror was directed against Jews, *i.e.*, against people with certain common characteristics which were independent of their specific behavior. In Soviet Russia the situation is more confused, but the facts, unfortunately, are only too obvious. On the one hand, the Bolshevik system, unlike the Nazi, never admitted theoretically that it could practice terror against innocent people, and though in view of certain practices this may look like hypocrisy, it makes quite a difference. Russian practice, on the other hand, is even more 'advanced' than the German in one respect: arbitrariness of terror is not even limited by racial differentiation, while the old class categories have long since been discarded, so that anybody in Russia may suddenly become a victim of the police terror. We are not concerned here with the ultimate consequence of rule by terror – namely, that nobody, not even the executors, can ever be free of fear; in our context we are dealing merely with the arbitrariness by which victims are chosen, and for this it is decisive that they are objectively innocent, that they are chosen regardless of what they may or may not have done.

At first glance this may look like a belated confirmation of the old scapegoat theory, and it is true that the victim of modern terror does show all the characteristics of the scapegoat: he is objectively and absolutely innocent because nothing he did or omitted to do matters or has any connection with his fate.

There is, therefore, a temptation to return to an explanation which automatically discharges the victim of responsibility: it seems quite adequate to a reality in which nothing strikes us more forcefully than the utter innocence of the individual caught in the horror machine and his utter inability to change his fate. Terror, however, is only in the last instance of its development a mere form of government. In order to establish a totalitarian regime, terror must be presented as an instrument for carrying out a specific ideology; and that ideology must have won the adherence of many, and even a majority, before terror can be stabilized. The point for the historian is that the Jews, before becoming the main victims of modern terror, were the center of Nazi ideology. And an ideology which has to persuade and mobilize people cannot choose its victim arbitrarily. In other words, if a patent forgery like the 'Protocols of the Elders of Zion' is believed by so many people that it can become the text of a whole political movement, the task of the historian is no longer to discover a forgery. Certainly it is not to invent explanations which dismiss the chief political and historical fact of the matter: that the forgery is being believed. This fact is more important than the (historically speaking, secondary) circumstance that it is forgery.

The scapegoat explanation therefore remains one of the principal attempts to escape the seriousness of antisemitism and the significance of the fact that the Jews were driven into the storm center of events. Equally widespread is the opposite doctrine of an 'eternal antisemitism' in which Jew-hatred is a normal and natural reaction to which history gives only more or less opportunity. Outbursts need no special explanation because they are natural consequences of an eternal problem. That this doctrine was adopted by professional antisemites is a matter of course; it gives the best possible alibi for all horrors. If it is true that mankind has insisted on murdering Jews for more than two thousand years, then Jew-killing is a normal, and even human, occupation and Jew-hatred is justified beyond the need of argument.

The more surprising aspect of this explanation, the assumption of an eternal antisemitism, is that it has been adopted by a great many unbiased historians and by an even greater number of Jews. It is this odd coincidence which makes the theory so very dangerous and confusing. Its escapist basis is in both instances the same: just as antisemites understandably desire to escape responsibility for their deeds, so Jews, attacked and on the defensive, even more understandably do not wish under any circumstances to discuss their share of responsibility. In the case of Jewish, and frequently of Christian, adherents of this doctrine, however, the escapist tendencies of official apologetics are based upon more important and less rational motives.

The birth and growth of modern antisemitism has been accompanied by and interconnected with Jewish assimilation, the secularization and withering away of the old religious and spiritual values of Judaism. What actually happened was that great parts of the Jewish people were at the same time threatened by physical extinction from without and dissolution from within. In this situation, Jews concerned with the survival of their people would, in a curious desperate misinterpretation, hit on the consoling idea that antisemitism, after all, might be an excellent means for keeping the people together, so that the assumption of eternal antisemitism would even imply an eternal guarantee of Jewish existence. This superstition, a secularized travesty of the idea of eternity inherent in a faith in chosenness and a Messianic hope, has been strengthened through the fact that for many centuries the Jews experienced the Christian brand of hostility which was indeed a powerful agent of preservation, spiritually as well as politically. The Jews mistook modern anti-Christian antisemitism for the old religious Jew-hatred – and this all the more innocently because their assimilation had by-passed Christianity in its religious and cultural aspect. Confronted with an obvious symptom of the decline of Christianity, they could therefore imagine in all ignorance that this was some revival of the so-called 'Dark Ages.' Ignorance or misunderstanding of their own past were partly responsible for their fatal underestimation of the actual and unprecedented dangers which lay ahead. But one should also bear in mind that lack of political ability and judgment have been caused by the very nature of Jewish history, the history of a people without a government, without a country, and without a language. Jewish history offers the extraordinary spectacle of a people, unique in this respect, which began its history with a well-defined concept of history and an almost conscious resolution to achieve a well-circumscribed plan on earth and then, without giving up this concept, avoided all political action for two thousand years. The result was that the political history of the Jewish people became even more dependent upon unforeseen, accidental factors than the history of other nations, so that the Jews stumbled from one role to the other and accepted responsibility for none.

In view of the final catastrophe, which brought the Jews so near to complete annihilation, the thesis of eternal antisemitism has become more dangerous than ever. Today it would absolve Jew-haters of crimes greater than anybody had ever believed possible. Antisemitism, far from being a mysterious guarantee of the survival of the Jewish people, has been clearly revealed as a threat of its extermination. Yet this explanation of antisemitism, like the scapegoat theory and for similar reasons, has outlived its refutation by reality. It stresses, after all, with different arguments but equal stubbornness, that complete and inhuman innocence which so strikingly characterizes victims of modern terror, and therefore seems confirmed by the events. It even has the advantage over the scapegoat theory that somehow it answers the uncomfortable question: Why the Jews of all people? – if only with the question begging reply: Eternal hostility.

It is quite remarkable that the only two doctrines which at least attempt to explain the political significance of the antisemitic movement deny all specific Jewish responsibility and refuse to discuss matters in specific historical terms. In this inherent negation of the significance of human behavior, they bear a terrible resemblance to those modern practices and forms of government which, by means of arbitrary terror, liquidate the very possibility of human activity. Somehow in the extermination camps Jews were murdered as if in accordance with the explanation these doctrines had given of why they were hated: regardless of what they had done or omitted to do, regardless of vice or virtue. Moreover, the murderers themselves, only obeying orders and proud of their passionless efficiency, uncannily resembled the 'innocent' instruments of an inhuman impersonal course of events which the doctrine of eternal antisemitism had considered them to be.

Such common denominators between theory and practice are by themselves no indication of historical truth, although they are an indication of the 'timely' character of such opinions and explain why they sound so plausible to the multitude. The historian is concerned with them only insofar as they are themselves part of his history and because they stand in the way of his search for truth. Being a contemporary, he is as likely to succumb to their persuasive force as anybody else. Caution in handling generally accepted opinions that claim to explain whole trends of history is especially important for the historian of modern times, because the last century has produced an abundance of ideologies that pretend to be keys to history but are actually nothing but desperate efforts to escape responsibility.

Plato, in his famous fight against the ancient Sophists, discovered that their 'universal art of enchanting the mind by arguments' (*Phaedrus* 261) had nothing to do with truth but aimed at opinions which by their very nature are changing, and which are valid only 'at the time of the agreement and as long as the agreement lasts' (*Theaetetus* 172). He also discovered the very insecure position of truth in the world, for from 'opinions comes persuasion and not from truth' (*Phaedrus* 260). The most striking difference between ancient and modern sophists is that the ancients were satisfied with a passing victory of the argument at the expense of truth, whereas the moderns want a more lasting victory at the expense of reality. In other words, one destroyed the dignity of human thought whereas the others destroy the dignity of human action. The old manipulators of logic were the concern of the philosopher, whereas the modern manipulators of facts stand in the way of the historian. For history itself is destroyed, and its comprehensibility – based upon the fact that it is enacted by men and therefore can be understood by men – is in danger, whenever facts are no longer held to be part and parcel of the past and present world, and are misused to prove this or that opinion.

There are, to be sure, few guides left through the labyrinth of inarticulate facts if opinions are discarded and tradition is no longer accepted as unquestionable. Such perplexities of historiography, however, are very minor consequences, considering the profound upheavals of our time and their effect upon the historical structures of Western mankind. Their immediate result has been to expose all those components of our history which up to now had been hidden from our view. This does not mean that what came crashing down in this crisis (perhaps the most profound crisis in Western history since the downfall of the Roman Empire) was mere façade, although many things have been revealed as façade that only a few decades ago we thought were indestructible essences.

The simultaneous decline of the European nation-state and growth of antisemitic movements, the coincident downfall of nationally organized Europe and the extermination of Jews, which was prepared for by the victory of antisemitism over all competing isms in the preceding struggle for persuasion of public opinion, have to be taken as a serious indication of the source of antisemitism. Modern antisemitism must be seen in the more general framework of the development of the nation-state, and at the same time its source must be found in certain aspects of Jewish history and specifically Jewish functions during the last centuries. If, in the final stage of disintegration, antisemitic slogans proved the most effective means of inspiring and organizing great masses of people for imperialist expansion and destruction of the old forms of government, then the previous history of the relationship between Jews and the state must contain elementary clues to the growing hostility between certain groups of society and the Jews. We shall show this development in the next chapter.

If, furthermore, the steady growth of the modern mob – that is, of the *déclassés* of all classes – produced leaders who, undisturbed by the question of whether the Jews were sufficiently important to be made the focus of a political ideology, repeatedly saw in them the 'key to history' and the central cause of all evils, then the previous history of the relationship between Jews and society must contain the elementary indications of the hostile relationship between the mob and the Jews. We shall deal with the relationship between Jews and society in the third chapter.

The fourth chapter deals with the Dreyfus Affair, a kind of dress rehearsal for the performance of our own time. Because of the peculiar opportunity it offers of seeing, in a brief historical moment, the otherwise hidden potentialities of antisemitism as a major political weapon within the framework of nineteenth-century politics and its relatively well-balanced sanity, this case has been treated in full detail.

The following three chapters, to be sure, analyze only the preparatory elements, which were not fully realized until the decay of the nation-state and the development of imperialism reached the foreground of the political scene.

# CHAPTER TWO

# The Jews, the Nation-State, and the Birth of Antisemitism

## I: The Equivocalities of Emancipation and the Jewish State Banker

At the height of its development in the nineteenth century, the nation-state granted its Jewish inhabitants equality of rights. Deeper, older, and more fateful contradictions are hidden behind the abstract and palpable inconsistency that Jews received their citizenship from governments which in the process of centuries had made nationality a prerequisite for citizenship and homogeneity of population the outstanding characteristic of the body politic.

The series of emancipation edicts which slowly and hesitantly followed the French edict of 1792 had been preceded and were accompanied by an equivocal attitude toward its Jewish inhabitants on the part of the nation-state. The breakdown of the feudal order had given rise to the new revolutionary concept of equality, according to which a 'nation within the nation' could no longer be tolerated. Jewish restrictions and privileges had to be abolished together with all other special rights and liberties. This growth of equality, however, depended largely upon the growth of an independent state machine which, either as an enlightened despotism or as a constitutional government above all classes and parties, could, in splendid isolation, function, rule, and represent the interests of the nation as a whole. Therefore, beginning with the late seventeenth century, an unprecedented need arose for state credit and a new expansion of the state's sphere of economic and business interest, while no group among the European populations was prepared to grant credit to the state or take an active part in the development of state business. It was only natural that the Jews, with their age-old experience as moneylenders and their connections with European nobility – to whom they frequently owed local protection and for whom they used to handle financial matters – would be called upon for help; it was clearly in the interest of the new state business to grant the Jews certain privileges and to treat them as a separate group. Under no circumstances could the state afford to see them wholly assimilated into the rest of the population, which refused credit to the state, was reluctant to enter and to develop businesses owned by the state, and followed the routine pattern of private capitalistic enterprise.

Emancipation of the Jews, therefore, as granted by the national state system in Europe during the nineteenth century, had a double origin and an ever-present equivocal meaning. On the one hand it was due to the political and legal structure of a new body politic which could function only under the conditions of political and legal equality. Governments, for their own sake, had to iron out the inequalities of the old order as completely and as quickly as possible. On the other hand, it was the clear result of a gradual extension of specific Jewish privileges, granted originally only to individuals, then through them to a small group of well-to-do Jews; only when this limited group could no longer handle by themselves the ever-growing demands of state business, were these privileges finally extended to the whole of Western and Central European Jewry.[1]

Thus, at the same time and in the same countries, emancipation meant equality *and* privileges, the destruction of the old Jewish

[1] To the modern historian rights and liberties granted the court Jews during the seventeenth and eighteenth centuries may appear to be only the forerunners of equality: court Jews could live wherever they liked, they were permitted to travel freely within the realm of their sovereign, they were allowed to bear arms and had rights to special protection from local authorities. Actually these court Jews, characteristically called *Generalprivilegierte Juden* in Prussia, not only enjoyed better living conditions than their fellow Jews who still lived under almost medieval restrictions, but they were better off than their non-Jewish neighbors. Their standard of living was much higher than that of the contemporary middle class, their privileges in most cases were greater than those granted to the merchants. Nor did this situation escape the attention of their contemporaries. Christian Wilhelm Dohm, the outstanding advocate of Jewish emancipation in eighteenth-century Prussia, complained of the practice, in force since the time of Frederick William I, which granted rich Jews 'all sorts of favors and support' often 'at the expense of, and with neglect of diligent legal [that is, non-Jewish] citizens.' In *Denkwürdigkeiten meiner Zeit*, Lemgo, 1814–1819, IV, 487.

community autonomy *and* the conscious preservation of the Jews as a separate group in society, the abolition of special restrictions and special rights *and* the extension of such rights to a growing group of individuals. Equality of condition for all nationals had become the premise of the new body politic, and while this equality had actually been carried out at least to the extent of depriving the old ruling classes of their privilege to govern and the old oppressed classes of their right to be protected, the process coincided with the birth of the class society which again separated the nationals, economically and socially, as efficiently as the old regime. Equality of condition, as the Jacobins had understood it in the French Revolution, became a reality only in America, whereas on the European continent it was at once replaced by a mere formal equality before the law.

The fundamental contradiction between a political body based on equality before the law and a society based on the inequality of the class system prevented the development of functioning republics as well as the birth of a new political hierarchy. An insurmountable inequality of social condition, the fact that class membership on the Continent was bestowed upon the individual and, up to the first World War, almost guaranteed to him by birth, could nevertheless exist side by side with political equality. Only politically backward countries, like Germany, had retained a few feudal remnants. There members of the aristocracy, which on the whole was well on its way to transforming itself into a class, had a privileged political status, and thus could preserve as a group a certain special relationship to the state. But these were remnants. The fully developed class system meant invariably that the status of the individual was defined by his membership in his own class and his relationship to another, and not by his position in the state or within its machinery.

The only exceptions to this general rule were the Jews. They did not form a class of their own and they did not belong to any of the classes in their countries. As a group, they were neither workers, middle-class people, landholders, nor peasants. Their wealth seemed to make them part of the middle class, but they did not share in its capitalist development; they were scarcely represented in industrial enterprise and if, in the last stages of their history in Europe, they became employers on a large scale, they employed white-collar personnel and not workers. In other words, although their status was defined through their being Jews, it was not defined through their relationship to another class. Their special protection from the state (whether in the old form of open privileges, or a special emancipation edict which no other group needed and which frequently had to be reinforced against the hostility of society) and their special services to the governments prevented their submersion in the class system as well as their own establishment as a class.[2] Whenever, therefore, they were admitted to and entered society, they became a well-defined, self-preserving group within one of the classes, the aristocracy or the bourgeoisie.

There is no doubt that the nation-state's interest in preserving the Jews as a special group and preventing their assimilation into class society coincided with the Jewish interest in self-preservation and group survival. It is also more than probable that without this coincidence the governments' attempts would have been in vain; the powerful trends toward equalization of all citizens from the side of the state and incorporation of each individual into a class from the side of society, both clearly implying complete Jewish assimilation, could be frustrated only through a combination of government intervention and voluntary co-operation. Official policies for the Jews were, after all, not always so consistent and unwavering as we may believe if we consider only the final results.[3] It is indeed surprising to see how consistently Jews neglected their chances for normal capitalist enterprise and business.[4] But without the interests and practices of the governments, the Jews could hardly have preserved their group identity.

2 Jacob Lestschinsky, in an early discussion of the Jewish problem, pointed out that Jews did not belong to any social class, and spoke of a *'Klasseneinschiebsel'* (in *Weltwirtschafts-Archiv*, 1929, Band 30, 123 ff.), but saw only the disadvantages of this situation in Eastern Europe, not its great advantages in Western and Central European countries.

3 For example, under Frederick II after the Seven Years' War, a decided effort was made in Prussia to incorporate the Jews into a kind of mercantile system. The older general *Juden-reglement* of 1750 was supplanted by a system of regular permits issued only to those inhabitants who invested a considerable part of their fortune in new manufacturing enterprises. But here, as everywhere else, such government attempts failed completely.

4 Felix Priebatsch ('Die Judenpolitik des fürstlichen Absolutismus im 17. und 18. Jahrhundert,' in *Forschungen und Versuche zur Geschichte des Mittelalters und der Neuzeit*, 1915)

In contrast to all other groups, the Jews were defined and their position determined by the body politic. Since, however, this body politic had no other social reality, they were, socially speaking, in the void. Their social inequality was quite different from the inequality of the class system; it was again mainly the result of their relationship to the state, so that, in society, the very fact of being born a Jew would either mean that one was overprivileged – under special protection of the government – or underprivileged, lacking certain rights and opportunities which were withheld from the Jews in order to prevent their assimilation.

The schematic outline of the simultaneous rise and decline of the European nation-state system and European Jewry unfolds roughly in the following stages:

1. The seventeenth and eighteenth centuries witnessed the slow development of nation-states under the tutelage of absolute monarchs. Individual Jews everywhere rose out of deep obscurity into the sometimes glamorous, and always influential, position of court Jews who financed state affairs and handled the financial transactions of their princes. This development affected the masses who continued to live in a more or less feudal order as little as it affected the Jewish people as a whole.

---

cites a typical example from the early eighteenth century: 'When the mirror factory in Neuhaus, Lower Austria, which was subsidized by the administration, did not produce, the Jew Wertheimer gave the Emperor money to buy it. When asked to take over the factory he refused, stating that his time was taken up with his financial transactions.'

See also Max Köhler, 'Beiträge zur neueren jüdischen Wirtschaftsgeschichte. Die Juden in Halberstadt und Umgebung,' in *Studien zur Geschichte der Wirtschaft und Geisteskultur*, 1927, Band 3.

In this tradition, which kept rich Jews from real positions of power in capitalism, is the fact that in 1911 the Paris Rothschilds sold their share in the oil wells of Baku to the Royal Shell group, after having been, with the exception of Rockefeller, the world's biggest petroleum tycoons. This incident is reported in Richard Lewinsohn, *Wie sie gross und reich wurden*, Berlin, 1927.

André Sayou's statement ('Les Juifs' in *Revue Economique Internationale*, 1932) in his polemic against Werner Sombart's identification of Jews with capitalist development, may be taken as a general rule: 'The Rothschilds and other Israelites who were almost exclusively engaged in launching state loans and in the international movement of capital, did not try at all . . . to create great industries.'

2. After the French Revolution, which abruptly changed political conditions on the whole European continent, nation-states in the modern sense emerged whose business transactions required a considerably larger amount of capital and credit than the court Jews had ever been asked to place at a prince's disposal. Only the combined wealth of the wealthier strata of Western and Central European Jewry, which they entrusted to some prominent Jewish bankers for such purposes, could suffice to meet the new enlarged governmental needs. This period brought with it the granting of privileges, which up to then had been necessary only for court Jews, to the larger wealthy class, which had managed to settle in the more important urban and financial centers in the eighteenth century. Finally emancipation was granted in all full-fledged nation-states and withheld only in those countries where Jews, because of their numbers and the general backwardness of these regions, had not been able to organize themselves into a special separate group whose economic function was financial support of their government.

3. Since this intimate relationship between national government and Jews had rested on the indifference of the bourgeoisie to politics in general and state finance in particular, this period came to an end with the rise of imperialism at the end of the nineteenth century when capitalist business in the form of expansion could no longer be carried out without active political help and intervention by the state. Imperialism, on the other hand, undermined the very foundations of the nation-state and introduced into the European comity of nations the competitive spirit of business concerns. In the early decades of this development, Jews lost their exclusive position in state business to imperialistically minded businessmen; they declined in importance as a group, although individual Jews kept their influence as financial advisers and as inter-European middlemen. These Jews, however – in contrast to the nineteenth-century state bankers – had even less need of the Jewish community at large, notwithstanding its wealth, than the court Jews of the seventeenth and eighteenth centuries, and therefore they frequently cut themselves off completely from the Jewish community. The Jewish communities were no longer financially organized, and although individual Jews in high positions remained representative of Jewry as a

whole in the eyes of the Gentile world, there was little if any material reality behind this.

4. As a group, Western Jewry disintegrated together with the nation-state during the decades preceding the outbreak of the first World War. The rapid decline of Europe after the war found them already deprived of their former power, atomized into a herd of wealthy individuals. In an imperialist age, Jewish wealth had become insignificant; to a Europe with no sense of balance of power between its nations and of inter-European solidarity, the non-national, inter-European Jewish element became an object of universal hatred because of its useless wealth, and of contempt because of its lack of power.

The first governments to need regular income and secure finances were the absolute monarchies under which the nation-state came into being. Feudal princes and kings also had needed money, and even credit, but for specific purposes and temporary operations only; even in the sixteenth century, when the Fuggers put their own credit at the disposal of the state, they were not yet thinking of establishing a special state credit. The absolute monarchs at first provided for their financial needs partly through the old method of war and looting, and partly through the new device of tax monopoly. This undermined the power and ruined the fortunes of the nobility without assuaging the growing hostility of the population.

For a long time the absolute monarchies looked about society for a class upon which to rely as securely as the feudal monarchy had upon the nobility. In France an incessant struggle between the guilds and the monarchy, which wanted to incorporate them into the state system, had been going on since the fifteenth century. The most interesting of these experiments were doubtless the rise of mercantilism and the attempts of the absolute state to get an absolute monopoly over national business and industry. The resulting disaster, and the bankruptcy brought about by the concerted resistance of the rising bourgeoisie, are sufficiently well known.[5]

5 The influence, however, of mercantile experiments on future developments can hardly be overrated. France was the only country where the mercantile system was tried consistently and resulted in an early flourishing of manufactures which owed

Before the emancipation edicts, every princely household and every monarch in Europe already had a court Jew to handle financial business. During the seventeenth and eighteenth centuries, these court Jews were always single individuals who had inter-European connections and inter-European credit at their disposal, but did not form an international financial entity.[6] Characteristic of these times, when Jewish individuals and the first small wealthy Jewish communities were more powerful than at any time in the nineteenth century,[7] was the frankness with which their privileged status and their right to it was discussed, and the careful testimony of the authorities to the importance of their services to the state. There was not the slightest doubt or ambiguity about the connection between services rendered and privileges granted. Privileged Jews received noble titles almost as

their existence to state interference; she never quite recovered from the experience. In the era of free enterprise, her bourgeoisie shunned unprotected investment in native industries while her bureaucracy, also a product of the mercantile system, survived its collapse. Despite the fact that the bureaucracy also lost all its productive functions, it is even today more characteristic of the country and a greater impediment to her recovery than the bourgeoisie.

6 This had been the case in England since Queen Elizabeth's Marrano banker and the Jewish financiers of Cromwell's armies, until one of the twelve Jewish brokers admitted to the London Stock Exchange was said to have handled one-quarter of all government loans of his day (see Salo W. Baron, *A Social and Religious History of the Jews*, 1937, Vol. II: *Jews and Capitalism*); in Austria, where in only forty years (1695–1739), the Jews credited the government with more than 35 million florins and where the death of Samuel Oppenheimer in 1703 resulted in a grave financial crisis for both state and Emperor; in Bavaria, where in 1808 80 per cent of all government loans were endorsed and negotiated by Jews (see M. Grunwald, *Samuel Oppenheimer und sein Kreis*, 1913); in France, where mercantile conditions were especially favorable for the Jews, Colbert already praised their great usefulness to the state (Baron, *op. cit.*, *loc. cit.*), and where in the middle of the eighteenth century the German Jew, Liefman Calmer, was made a baron by a grateful king who appreciated services and loyalty to 'Our state and Our person' (Robert Anchel, 'Un Baron Juif Français au 18e siècle, Liefman Calmer,' in *Souvenir et Science*, I, pp. 52–55); and also in Prussia where Frederick II's *Münzjuden* were titled and where, at the end of the eighteenth century, 400 Jewish families formed one of the wealthiest groups in Berlin. (One of the best descriptions of Berlin and the role of the Jews in its society at the turn of the eighteenth century is to be found in Wilhelm Dilthey, *Das Leben Schleiermachers*, 1870, pp. 182 ff.).

7 Early in the eighteenth century, Austrian Jews succeeded in banishing Eisemenger's *Entdecktes Judentum*, 1703, and at the end of it, *The Merchant of Venice* could be played in Berlin only with a little prologue apologizing to the (not emancipated) Jewish audience.

a matter of course in France, Bavaria, Austria and Prussia, so that even outwardly they were more than just wealthy men. The fact that the Rothschilds had such a hard time getting their application for a title approved by the Austrian government (they succeeded in 1817), was the signal that a whole period had come to an end.

By the end of the eighteenth century it had become clear that none of the estates or classes in the various countries was willing or able to become the new ruling class, that is to identify itself with the government as the nobility had done for centuries.[8] The failure of the absolute monarchy to find a substitute within society led to the full development of the nation-state and its claim to be above all classes, completely independent of society and its particular interests, the true and only representative of the nation as a whole. It resulted, on the other side, in a deepening of the split between state and society upon which the body politic of the nation rested. Without it, there would have been no need – or even any possibility – of introducing the Jews into European history on equal terms.

When all attempts to ally itself with one of the major classes in society had failed, the state chose to establish itself as a tremendous business concern. This was meant to be for administrative purposes only, to be sure, but the range of interests, financial and otherwise, and the costs were so great that one cannot but recognize the existence of a special sphere of state business from the eighteenth century on. The independent growth of state business was caused by a conflict with the financially powerful forces of the time, with the bourgeoisie which went the way of private investment, shunned all state intervention, and refused active financial participation in what appeared to be an 'unproductive' enterprise. Thus the Jews were the only part of the population willing to finance the state's beginnings and to tie their destinies to its further development. With their credit and international connections, they were in an excellent position to help the

---

8 The only, and irrelevant, exception might be those tax collectors, called *fermiers-généraux*, in France, who rented from the state the right to collect taxes by guaranteeing a fixed amount to the government. They earned their great wealth from and depended directly upon the absolute monarchy, but were too small a group and too isolated a phenomenon to be economically influential by themselves.

nation-state to establish itself among the biggest enterprises and employers of the time.[9]

Great privileges, decisive changes in the Jewish condition, were necessarily the price of the fulfillment of such services, and, at the same time, the reward for great risks. The greatest privilege was equality. When the *Münzjuden* of Frederick of Prussia or the court Jews of the Austrian Emperor received through 'general privileges' and 'patents' the same status which half a century later all Prussian Jews received under the name of emancipation and equal rights; when, at the end of the eighteenth century and at the height of their wealth, the Berlin Jews managed to prevent an influx from the Eastern provinces because they did not care to share their 'equality' with poorer brethren whom they did not recognize as equals; when, at the time of the French National Assembly, the Bordeaux and Avignon Jews protested violently against the French government's granting equality to Jews of the Eastern provinces – it became clear that at least the Jews were not thinking in terms of equal rights but of privileges and special liberties. And it is really not surprising that privileged Jews, intimately linked to the businesses of their governments and quite aware of the nature and conditions of their status, were reluctant to accept for all Jews this gift of a freedom which they themselves possessed as the price for services, which they knew had been calculated as such and therefore could hardly become a right for all.[10]

Only at the end of the nineteenth century, with the rise of imperialism, did the owning classes begin to change their original

9 The urgencies compelling the ties between government business and the Jews may be gauged by those cases in which decidedly anti-Jewish officials had to carry out the policies. So Bismarck, in his youth, made a few antisemitic speeches only to become, as chancellor of the Reich, a close friend of Bleichroeder and a reliable protector of the Jews against Court Chaplain Stoecker's antisemitic movement in Berlin. William II, although as Crown Prince and a member of the anti-Jewish Prussian nobility very sympathetic to all antisemitic movements in the eighties, changed his antisemitic convictions and deserted his antisemitic protégés overnight when he inherited the throne.
10 As early as the eighteenth century, wherever whole Jewish groups got wealthy enough to be useful to the state, they enjoyed collective privileges and were separated as a group from their less wealthy and useful brethren, even in the same country. Like the *Schutzjuden* in Prussia, the Bordeaux and Bayonne Jews in France enjoyed equality long before the French Revolution and were even invited to present their complaints and propositions along with the other General Estates in the *Convocation des Etats Généraux* of 1787.

estimate of the unproductivity of state business. Imperialist expansion, together with the growing perfection of the instruments of violence and the state's absolute monopoly of them, made the state an interesting business proposition. This meant, of course, that the Jews gradually but automatically lost their exclusive and unique position.

But the good fortune of the Jews, their rise from obscurity to political significance, would have come to an even earlier end if they had been confined to a mere business function in the growing nation-states. By the middle of the last century some states had won enough confidence to get along without Jewish backing and financing of government loans.[11] The nationals' growing consciousness, moreover, that their private destinies were becoming more and more dependent upon those of their countries made them ready to grant the governments more of the necessary credit. Equality itself was symbolized in the availability to all of government bonds which were finally even considered the most secure form of capital investment simply because the state, which could wage national wars, was the only agency which actually could protect its citizens' properties. From the middle of the nineteenth century on, the Jews could keep their prominent position only because they had still another more important and fateful role to play, a role also intimately linked to their participation in the destinies of the state. Without territory and without a government of their own, the Jews had always been an inter-European element; this international status the nation-state necessarily preserved because the Jews' financial services rested on it. But even when their economic usefulness had exhausted itself, the inter-European status of the Jews

---

11 Jean Capefigue (*Histoire des grandes opérations financières*, Tome III: *Banque, Bourses, Emprunts*, 1855) pretends that during the July Monarchy only the Jews, and especially the house of Rothschild, prevented a sound state credit based upon the Banque de France. He also claims that the events of 1848 made the activities of the Rothschilds superfluous. Raphael Strauss ('The Jews in the Economic Evolution of Central Europe' in *Jewish Social Studies*, III, 1, 1941) also remarks that after 1830 'public credit already became less of a risk so that Christian banks began to handle this business in increasing measure.' Against these interpretations stands the fact that excellent relations prevailed between the Rothschilds and Napoleon III, although there can be no doubt as to the general trend of the time.

remained of great national importance in times of national conflicts and wars.

While the need of the nation-states for Jewish services developed slowly and logically, growing out of the general context of European history, the rise of the Jews to political and economic significance was sudden and unexpected to themselves as well as their neighbors. By the later Middle Ages the Jewish moneylender had lost all his former importance, and in the early sixteenth century Jews had already been expelled from cities and trade centers into villages and countryside, thereby exchanging a more uniform protection from remote higher authorities for an insecure status granted by petty local nobles.[12] The turning point had been in the seventeenth century when, during the Thirty Years' War, precisely because of their dispersion these small, insignificant moneylenders could guarantee the necessary provisions to the mercenary armies of the war-lords in far-away lands and with the aid of small peddlers buy victuals in entire provinces. Since these wars remained half-feudal, more or less private affairs of the princes, involving no interest of other classes and enlisting no help from the people, the Jews' gain in status was very limited and hardly visible. But the number of court Jews increased because now every feudal household needed the equivalent of the court Jew.

As long as these court Jews served small feudal lords who, as members of the nobility, did not aspire to represent any centralized authority, they were the servants of only one group in society. The property they handled, the money they lent, the provisions they bought up, all were considered the private property of their master, so that such activities could not involve them in political matters. Hated or favored, Jews could not become a political issue of any importance.

When, however, the function of the feudal lord changed, when he developed into a prince or king, the function of his court Jew changed too. The Jews, being an alien element, without much interest in such changes in their environment, were usually the last to become aware of their heightened status. As far as they were concerned, they went on handling private business, and their loyalty remained a personal affair unrelated to political considerations. Loyalty meant honesty; it did not

12 See Priebatsch, *op. cit.*

mean taking sides in a conflict or remaining true for political reasons. To buy up provisions, to clothe and feed an army, to lend currency for the hiring of mercenaries, meant simply an interest in the well-being of a business partner.

This kind of relationship between Jews and aristocracy was the only one that ever tied a Jewish group to another stratum in society. After it disappeared in the early nineteenth century, it was never replaced. Its only remnant for the Jews was a penchant for aristocratic titles (especially in Austria and France), and for the non-Jews a brand of liberal antisemitism which lumped Jews and nobility together and pretended that they were in some kind of financial alliance against the rising bourgeoisie. Such argumentation, current in Prussia and France, had a certain amount of plausibility as long as there was no general emancipation of the Jews. The privileges of the court Jews had indeed an obvious similarity to the rights and liberties of the nobility, and it was true that the Jews were as much afraid of losing their privileges and used the same arguments against equality as members of the aristocracy. The plausibility became even greater in the eighteenth century when most privileged Jews were given minor titles, and at the opening of the nineteenth century when wealthy Jews who had lost their ties with the Jewish communities looked for new social status and began to model themselves on the aristocracy. But all this was of little consequence, first because it was quite obvious that the nobility was on the decline and that the Jews, on the contrary, were continually gaining in status, and also because the aristocracy itself, especially in Prussia, happened to become the first class that produced an antisemitic ideology.

The Jews had been the purveyors in wars and the servants of kings, but they did not and were not expected to engage in the conflicts themselves. When these conflicts enlarged into national wars, they still remained an international element whose importance and usefulness lay precisely in their not being bound to any national cause. No longer state bankers and purveyors in wars (the last war financed by a Jew was the Prussian-Austrian war of 1866, when Bleichroeder helped Bismarck after the latter had been refused the necessary credits by the Prussian Parliament), the Jews had become the financial advisers and assistants in peace treaties and, in a less organized and more indefinite way, the providers of news. The last peace treaties drawn up without Jewish assistance were those of the Congress of Vienna, between the Continental powers and France. Bleichroeder's role in the peace negotiations between Germany and France in 1871 was already more significant than his help in war,[13] and he rendered even more important services in the late seventies when, through his connections with the Rothschilds, he provided Bismarck with an indirect news channel to Benjamin Disraeli. The peace treaties of Versailles were the last in which Jews played a prominent role as advisers. The last Jew who owed his prominence on the national scene to his international Jewish connection was Walter Rathenau, the ill-fated foreign minister of the Weimar Republic. He paid with his life for having (as one of his colleagues put it after his death) donated his prestige in the international world of finance and the support of Jews everywhere in the world[14] to the ministers of the new Republic, who were completely unknown on the international scene.

That antisemitic governments would not use Jews for the business of war and peace is obvious. But the elimination of Jews from the international scene had a more general and deeper significance than antisemitism. Just because the Jews had been used as a non-national element, they could be of value in war and peace only as long as during the war everybody tried consciously to keep the possibilities of peace intact, only as long as everybody's aim was a peace of compromise and the re-establishment of a *modus vivendi*. As soon as 'victory or death' became a determining policy, and war actually aimed at the complete annihilation of the enemy, the Jews could no longer be of any use. This policy spelled destruction of their collective existence in any case, although the disappearance from the political scene and even

13 According to an anecdote, faithfully reported by all his biographers, Bismarck said immediately after the French defeat in 1871: 'First of all, Bleichroeder has got to go to Paris, to get together with his fellow Jews and to talk it (the five billion francs for reparations) over with the bankers.' (See Otto Joehlinger, *Bismarck und die Juden*, Berlin, 1921.)

14 See Walter Frank, 'Walter Rathenau und die blonde Rasse,' in *Forschungen zur Judenfrage*, Band IV, 1940. Frank, in spite of his official position under the Nazis, remained somewhat careful about his sources and methods. In this article he quotes from the obituaries on Rathenau in the *Israelitisches Familienblatt* (Hamburg, July 6, 1922), *Die Zeit* (June, 1922), and *Berliner Tageblatt* (May 31, 1922).

extinction of a specific group-life would by no means necessarily have led to their physical extermination. The frequently repeated argument, however, that the Jews would have become Nazis as easily as their German fellow-citizens if only they had been permitted to join the movement, just as they had enlisted in Italy's Fascist party before Italian Fascism introduced race legislation, is only half true. It is true only with respect to the psychology of individual Jews, which of course did not greatly differ from the psychology of their environment. It is patently false in a historical sense. Nazism, even without antisemitism, would have been the deathblow to the existence of the Jewish people in Europe; to consent to it would have meant suicide, not necessarily for individuals of Jewish origin, but for the Jews as a people.

To the first contradiction, which determined the destiny of European Jewry during the last centuries, that is, the contradiction between equality and privilege (rather of equality granted in the form and for the purpose of privilege) must be added a second contradiction: the Jews, the only non-national European people, were threatened more than any other by the sudden collapse of the system of nation-states. This situation is less paradoxical than it may appear at first glance. Representatives of the nation, whether Jacobins from Robespierre to Clemenceau, or representatives of Central European reactionary governments from Metternich to Bismarck, had one thing in common: they were all sincerely concerned with the 'balance of power' in Europe. They tried, of course, to shift this balance to the advantage of their respective countries, but they never dreamed of seizing a monopoly over the continent or of annihilating their neighbors completely. The Jews could not only be used in the interest of this precarious balance, they even became a kind of symbol of the common interest of the European nations.

It is therefore more than accidental that the catastrophic defeats of the peoples of Europe began with the catastrophe of the Jewish people. It was particularly easy to begin the dissolution of the precarious European balance of power with the elimination of the Jews, and particularly difficult to understand that more was involved in this elimination than an unusually cruel nationalism or an ill-timed revival of 'old prejudices.' When the catastrophe came, the fate of the Jewish people was considered a 'special case' whose history follows exceptional laws, and whose destiny was therefore of no general relevance.

This breakdown of European solidarity was at once reflected in the breakdown of Jewish solidarity all over Europe. When the persecution of German Jews began, Jews of other European countries discovered that German Jews constituted an exception whose fate could bear no resemblance to their own. Similarly, the collapse of German Jewry was preceded by its split into innumerable factions, each of which believed and hoped that its basic human rights would be protected by special privileges – the privilege of having been a veteran of World War I, the child of a veteran, the proud son of a father killed in action. It looked as though the annihilation of all individuals of Jewish origin was being preceded by the bloodless destruction and self-dissolution of the Jewish people, as though the Jewish people had owed its existence exclusively to other peoples and their hatred.

It is still one of the most moving aspects of Jewish history that the Jews' active entry into European history was caused by their being an inter-European, non-national element in a world of growing or existing nations. That this role proved more lasting and more essential than their function as state bankers is one of the material reasons for the new modern type of Jewish productivity in the arts and sciences. It is not without historical justice that their downfall coincided with the ruin of a system and a political body which, whatever its other defects, had needed and could tolerate a purely European element.

The grandeur of this consistently European existence should not be forgotten because of the many undoubtedly less attractive aspects of Jewish history during the last centuries. The few European authors who have been aware of this aspect of the 'Jewish question' had no special sympathies for the Jews, but an unbiased estimate of the whole European situation. Among them was Diderot, the only eighteenth-century French philosopher who was not hostile to the Jews and who recognized in them a useful link between Europeans of different nationalities; Wilhelm von Humboldt who, witnessing their emancipation through the French Revolution, remarked that the Jews would lose their universality when they were changed into Frenchmen;[15] and finally Friedrich Nietzsche, who out of disgust with Bismarck's Ger-

15 Wilhelm von Humboldt, *Tagebücher*, ed. by Leitzmann, Berlin, 1916–1918, I, 475. – The article 'Juif' of the *Encyclopédie*, 1751–1765, Vol. IX, which was probably written by Diderot: 'Thus dispersed in our time ... [the Jews] have become instruments of

man Reich coined the word 'good European,' which made possible his correct estimate of the significant role of the Jews in European history, and saved him from falling into the pitfalls of cheap philosemitism or patronizing 'progressive' attitudes.

This evaluation, though quite correct in the description of a surface phenomenon, overlooks the most serious paradox embodied in the curious political history of the Jews. Of all European peoples, the Jews had been the only one without a state of their own and had been, precisely for this reason, so eager and so suitable for alliances with governments and states as such, no matter what these governments or states might represent. On the other hand, the Jews had no political tradition or experience, and were as little aware of the tension between society and state as they were of the obvious risks and power-possibilities of their new role. What little knowledge or traditional practice they brought to politics had its source first in the Roman Empire, where they had been protected, so to speak, by the Roman soldier, and later, in the Middle Ages, when they sought and received protection against the population and the local rulers from remote monarchical and Church authorities. From these experiences, they had somehow drawn the conclusion that authority, and especially high authority, was favorable to them and that lower officials, and especially the common people, were dangerous. This prejudice, which expressed a definite historical truth but no longer corresponded to new circumstances, was as deeply rooted in and as unconsciously shared by the vast majority of Jews as corresponding prejudices about Jews were commonly accepted by Gentiles.

The history of the relationship between Jews and governments is rich in examples of how quickly Jewish bankers switched their allegiance from one government to the next even after revolutionary changes. It took the French Rothschilds in 1848 hardly twenty-four hours to transfer their services from the government of Louis Philippe to the new short-lived French Republic and again to Napoleon III. The same process repeated itself, at a slightly slower pace, after the

---

communication between the most distant countries. They are like the cogs and nails needed in a great building in order to join and hold together all other parts.'

downfall of the Second Empire and the establishment of the Third Republic. In Germany this sudden and easy change was symbolized, after the revolution of 1918, in the financial policies of the Warburgs on one hand and the shifting political ambitions of Walter Rathenau on the other.[16]

More is involved in this type of behavior than the simple bourgeois pattern which always assumes that nothing succeeds like success.[17] Had the Jews been bourgeois in the ordinary sense of the word, they might have gauged correctly the tremendous power-possibilities of their new functions, and at least have tried to play that fictitious role of a secret world power which makes and unmakes governments, which antisemites assigned to them anyway. Nothing, however, could be farther from the truth. The Jews, without knowledge of or interest in power, never thought of exercising more than mild pressure for minor purposes of self-defense. This lack of ambition was later sharply resented by the more assimilated sons of Jewish bankers and business-men. While some of them dreamed, like Disraeli, of a secret Jewish society to which they might belong and which never existed, others, like Rathenau, who happened to be better informed, indulged in half-antisemitic tirades against the wealthy traders who had neither power nor social status.

This innocence has never been quite understood by non-Jewish statesmen or historians. On the other hand, their detachment from power was so much taken for granted by Jewish representatives or writers that they hardly ever mentioned it except to express their surprise at the absurd suspicions leveled against them. In the memoirs of statesmen of the last century many remarks occur to the effect that there won't be a war because Rothschild in London or

16 Walter Rathenau, foreign minister of the Weimar Republic in 1921 and one of the outstanding representatives of Germany's new will to democracy, had proclaimed as late as 1917 his 'deep monarchical convictions,' according to which only an 'anointed' and no 'upstart of a lucky career' should lead a country. See *Von kommenden Dingen*, 1917, p. 247.

17 This bourgeois pattern, however, should not be forgotten. If it were only a matter of individual motives and behavior patterns, the methods of the house of Rothschild certainly did not differ much from those of their Gentile colleagues. For instance, Napoleon's banker, Ouvrard, after having provided the financial means for Napoleon's hundred days' war, immediately offered his services to the returning Bourbons.

Paris or Vienna does not want it. Even so sober and reliable a historian as J. A. Hobson could state as late as 1905: 'Does any one seriously suppose that a great war could be undertaken by any European state, or a great state loan subscribed, if the House of Rothschild and its connexions set their face against it?'[18] This misjudgment is as amusing in its naïve assumption that everyone is like oneself, as Metternich's sincere belief that 'the house of Rothschild played a greater role in France than any foreign government,' or his confident prediction to the Viennese Rothschilds shortly before the Austrian revolution in 1848: 'If I should go to the dogs, you would go with me.' The truth of that matter was that the Rothschilds had as little political idea as other Jewish bankers of what they wanted to carry out in France, to say nothing of a well-defined purpose which would even remotely suggest a war. On the contrary, like their fellow Jews they never allied themselves with any specific government, but rather with governments, with authority as such. If at this time and later they showed a marked preference for monarchical governments as against republics, it was only because they rightly suspected that republics were based to a greater extent on the will of the people, which they instinctively mistrusted.

How deep the Jews' faith in the state was, and how fantastic their ignorance of actual conditions in Europe, came to light in the last years of the Weimar Republic when, already reasonably frightened about the future, the Jews for once tried their hand in politics. With the help of a few non-Jews, they then founded that middle-class party which they called 'State-party' (*Staatspartei*), the very name a contradiction in terms. They were so naïvely convinced that their 'party,' supposedly representing them in political and social struggle, ought to be the state itself, that the whole relationship of the party to the state never dawned upon them. If anybody had bothered to take seriously this party of respectable and bewildered gentlemen, he could only have concluded that loyalty at any price was a façade behind which sinister forces plotted to take over the state.

Just as the Jews ignored completely the growing tension between state and society, they were also the last to be aware that circumstances

18 J. H. Hobson, *Imperialism*, 1905, p. 57 of unrevised 1938 edition.

had forced them into the center of the conflict. They therefore never knew how to evaluate antisemitism, or rather never recognized the moment when social discrimination changed into a political argument. For more than a hundred years, antisemitism had slowly and gradually made its way into almost all social strata in almost all European countries until it emerged suddenly as the one issue upon which an almost unified opinion could be achieved. The law according to which this process developed was simple: each class of society which came into a conflict with the state as such became antisemitic because the only social group which seemed to represent the state were the Jews. And the only class which proved almost immune from antisemitic propaganda were the workers who, absorbed in the class struggle and equipped with a Marxist explanation of history, never came into direct conflict with the state but only with another class of society, the bourgeoisie, which the Jews certainly did not represent, and of which they were never a significant part.

The political emancipation of the Jews at the turn of the eighteenth century in some countries, and its discussion in the rest of Central and Western Europe, resulted first of all in a decisive change in their attitude toward the state, which was somehow symbolized in the rise of the house of Rothschild. The new policy of these court Jews, who were the first to become full-fledged state bankers, came to light when they were no longer content to serve one particular prince or government through their international relationships with court Jews of other countries, but decided to establish themselves internationally and serve simultaneously and concurrently the governments in Germany, France, Great Britain, Italy and Austria. To a large extent, this unprecedented course was a reaction of the Rothschilds to the dangers of real emancipation, which, together with equality, threatened to nationalize the Jewries of the respective countries, and to destroy the very inter-European advantages on which the position of Jewish bankers had rested. Old Meyer Amschel Rothschild, the founder of the house, must have recognized that the inter-European status of Jews was no longer secure and that he had better try to realize this unique international position in his own family. The establishment of his five sons in the five financial capitals of Europe – Frankfurt, Paris, London,

Naples and Vienna – was his ingenious way out of the embarrassing emancipation of the Jews.[19]

The Rothschilds had entered upon their spectacular career as the financial servants of the Kurfürst of Hessen, one of the outstanding moneylenders of his time, who taught them business practice and provided them with many of their customers. Their great advantage was that they lived in Frankfurt, the only great urban center from which Jews had never been expelled and where they formed nearly 10 per cent of the city's population at the beginning of the nineteenth century. The Rothschilds started as court Jews without being under the jurisdiction of either a prince or the Free City, but directly under the authority of the distant Emperor in Vienna. They thus combined all the advantages of the Jewish status in the Middle Ages with those of their own times, and were much less dependent upon nobility or other local authorities than any of their fellow court Jews. The later financial activities of the house, the tremendous fortune they amassed, and their even greater symbolic fame since the early nineteenth century, are sufficiently well known.[20] They entered the scene of big business during the last years of the Napoleonic wars when – from 1811 to 1816 – almost half the English subventions to the Continental powers went through their hands. When after the defeat of Napoleon the Continent needed great government loans everywhere for the reorganization of its state machines and the erection of financial structures on the model of the Bank of England, the Rothschilds enjoyed almost a monopoly in the handling of state loans. This lasted for three generations during which they succeeded in defeating all Jewish and non-Jewish competitors in the field. 'The House of Rothschild became,' as Capefigue put it,[21] 'the chief treasurer of the Holy Alliance.'

The international establishment of the house of Rothschild and its

19 How well the Rothschilds knew the sources of their strength is shown in their early house law according to which daughters and their husbands were eliminated from the business of the house. The girls were allowed, and after 1871, even encouraged, to marry into the non-Jewish aristocracy; the male descendants had to marry Jewish girls exclusively, and if possible (in the first generation this was generally the case) members of the family.

20 See especially Egon Cesar Conte Corti, *The Rise of the House of Rothschild*, New York, 1927.

21 Capefigue, *op. cit.*

sudden rise above all other Jewish bankers changed the whole structure of Jewish state business. Gone was the accidental development, unplanned and unorganized, when individual Jews shrewd enough to take advantage of a unique opportunity frequently rose to the heights of great wealth and fell to the depths of poverty in one man's lifetime; when such a fate hardly touched the destinies of the Jewish people as a whole except insofar as such Jews sometimes had acted as protectors and petitioners for distant communities; when, no matter how numerous the wealthy moneylenders or how influential the individual court Jews, there was no sign of the development of a well-defined Jewish group which collectively enjoyed specific privileges and rendered specific services. It was precisely the Rothschilds' monopoly on the issuance of government loans which made it possible and necessary to draw on Jewish capital at large, to direct a great percentage of Jewish wealth into the channels of state business, and which thereby provided the natural basis for a new inter-European cohesiveness of Central and Western European Jewry. What in the seventeenth and eighteenth centuries had been an unorganized connection among individual Jews of different countries, now became the more systematic disposition of these scattered opportunities by a single firm, physically present in all important European capitals, in constant contact with all sections of the Jewish people, and in complete possession of all pertinent information and all opportunities for organization.[22]

The exclusive position of the house of Rothschild in the Jewish world replaced to a certain extent the old bonds of religious and spiritual tradition whose gradual loosening under the impact of Western culture for the first time threatened the very existence of the Jewish people. To the outer world, this one family also became a symbol of the working reality of Jewish internationalism in a world of nation-states and nationally organized peoples. Where, indeed, was there better proof of the fantastic concept of a Jewish world government than in this one family, nationals of five different countries, prominent everywhere, in close co-operation with at least three different governments (the French, the Austrian, and the British), whose frequent

[22] It has never been possible to ascertain the extent to which the Rothschilds used Jewish capital for their own business transactions and how far their control of Jewish bankers went. The family has never permitted a scholar to work in its archives.

conflicts never for a moment shook the solidarity of interest of their state bankers? No propaganda could have created a symbol more effective for political purpose than the reality itself.

The popular notion that the Jews – in contrast to other peoples – were tied together by the supposedly closer bonds of blood and family ties, was to a large extent stimulated by the reality of this one family, which virtually represented the whole economic and political significance of the Jewish people. The fateful consequence was that when, for reasons which had nothing to do with the Jewish question, race problems came to the foreground of the political scene, the Jews at once fitted all ideologies and doctrines which defined a people by blood ties and family characteristics.

Yet another, less accidental, fact accounts for this image of the Jewish people. In the preservation of the Jewish people the family had played a far greater role than in any Western political or social body except the nobility. Family ties were among the most potent and stubborn elements with which the Jewish people resisted assimilation and dissolution. Just as declining European nobility strengthened its marriage and house laws, so Western Jewry became all the more family-conscious in the centuries of their spiritual and religious dissolution. Without the old hope for Messianic redemption and the firm ground of traditional folkways, Western Jewry became over-conscious of the fact that their survival had been achieved in an alien and often hostile environment. They began to look upon the inner family circle as a kind of last fortress and to behave toward members of their own group as though they were members of a big family. In other words, the antisemitic picture of the Jewish people as a family closely knit by blood ties had something in common with the Jews' own picture of themselves.

This situation was an important factor in the early rise and continuous growth of antisemitism in the nineteenth century. Which group of people would turn antisemitic in a given country at a given historical moment depended exclusively upon general circumstances which made them ready for a violent antagonism to their government. But the remarkable similarity of arguments and images which time and again were spontaneously reproduced have an intimate relationship with the truth they distort. We find the Jews always represented as an international trade organization, a world-wide family concern with identical interests everywhere, a secret force behind the throne which degrades all visible governments into mere façade, or into marionettes whose strings are manipulated from behind the scenes. Because of their close relationship to state sources of power, the Jews were invariably identified with power, and because of their aloofness from society and concentration upon the closed circle of the family, they were invariably suspected of working for the destruction of all social structures.

## II: Early Antisemitism

It is an obvious, if frequently forgotten, rule that anti-Jewish feeling acquires political relevance only when it can combine with a major political issue, or when Jewish group interests come into open conflict with those of a major class in society. Modern antisemitism, as we know it from Central and Western European countries, had political rather than economic causes, while complicated class conditions produced the violent popular hatred of Jews in Poland and Rumania. There, due to the inability of the governments to solve the land question and give the nation-state a minimum of equality through liberation of the peasants, the feudal aristocracy succeeded not only in maintaining its political dominance but also in preventing the rise of a normal middle class. The Jews of these countries, strong in number and weak in every other respect, seemingly fulfilled some of the functions of the middle class, because they were mostly shopkeepers and traders and because as a group they stood between the big landowners and the propertyless classes. Small property holders, however, can exist as well in a feudal as in a capitalist economy. The Jews, here as elsewhere, were unable or unwilling to develop along industrial capitalist lines, so that the net result of their activities was a scattered, inefficient organization of consumption without an adequate system of production. The Jewish positions were an obstacle for a normal capitalistic development because they looked as though they were the only ones from which economic advancement might be expected without being capable of fulfilling this expectation. Because of their appearance, Jewish interests were felt to be in conflict with those sections of the population from which a middle class could normally have developed. The governments, on the other hand, tried halfheartedly to encourage a middle class without liquidating the nobility and big landowners. Their only serious attempt was economic liquidation of the Jews – partly as a concession to public opinion, and partly because the Jews were actually still a part of the old feudal order. For centuries they had been middlemen between the nobility and peasantry; now they formed a middle class without fulfilling its productive functions and were indeed one of the elements that stood in the way of industrialization and capitalization.[23] These Eastern European conditions, however, although they constituted the essence of the Jewish mass question, are of little importance in our context. Their political significance was limited to backward countries where the ubiquitous hatred of Jews made it almost useless as a weapon for specific purposes.

Antisemitism first flared up in Prussia immediately after the defeat by Napoleon in 1807, when the 'Reformers' changed the political structure so that the nobility lost its privileges and the middle classes won their freedom to develop. This reform, a 'revolution from above,' changed the half-feudal structure of Prussia's enlightened despotism into a more or less modern nation-state whose final stage was the German Reich of 1871.

Although a majority of the Berlin bankers of the time were Jews, the Prussian reforms did not require any considerable financial help from them. The outspoken sympathies of the Prussian reformers, their advocacy of Jewish emancipation, was the consequence of the new equality of all citizens, the abolition of privilege, and the introduction of free trade. They were not interested in the preservation of Jews as Jews for special purposes. Their reply to the argument that under conditions of equality 'the Jews might cease to exist' would always have been: 'Let them. How does this matter to a government which asks only that they become good citizens?'[24] Emancipation, moreover, was relatively inoffensive, for Prussia had just lost the

23 James Parkes, *The Emergence of the Jewish Problem, 1878–1939*, 1946, discusses these conditions briefly and without bias in chapters iv and vi.
24 Christian Wilhelm Dohm, *Über die bürgerliche Verbesserung der Juden*, Berlin and Stettin, 1781, I, 174.

eastern provinces which had a large and poor Jewish population. The emancipation decree of 1812 concerned only those wealthy and useful Jewish groups who were already privileged with most civic rights and who, through the general abolition of privileges, would have suffered a severe loss in civil status. For these groups, emancipation meant not much more than a general legal affirmation of the status quo.

But the sympathies of the Prussian reformers for the Jews were more than the logical consequence of their general political aspirations. When, almost a decade later and in the midst of rising antisemitism, Wilhelm von Humboldt declared: 'I love the Jews really only *en masse*; *en détail* I rather avoid them,'[25] he stood of course in open opposition to the prevailing fashion, which favored individual Jews and despised the Jewish people. A true democrat, he wanted to liberate an oppressed people and not bestow privileges upon individuals. But this view was also in the tradition of the old Prussian government officials, whose consistent insistence throughout the eighteenth century upon better conditions and improved education for Jews has frequently been recognized. Their support was not motivated by economic or state reasons alone, but by a natural sympathy for the only social group that also stood outside the social body and within the sphere of the state, albeit for entirely different reasons. The education of a civil service whose loyalty belonged to the state and was independent of change in government, and which had severed its class ties, was one of the outstanding achievements of the old Prussian state. These officials were a decisive group in eighteenth-century Prussia, and the actual predecessors of the Reformers; they remained the backbone of the state machine all through the nineteenth century, although they lost much of their influence to the aristocracy after the Congress of Vienna.[26]

Through the attitude of the Reformers and especially through the emancipation edict of 1812, the special interests of the state in the Jews

25 *Wilhelm und Caroline von Humboldt in ihren Briefen*, Berlin, 1900, V, 236.
26 For an excellent description of these civil servants who were not essentially different in different countries, see Henri Pirenne, *A History of Europe from the Invasions to the XVI Century*, London, 1939, pp. 361–362: 'Without class prejudices and hostile to the privileges of the great nobles who despised them . . . it was not the King who spoke through them, but the anonymous monarchy, superior to all, subduing all to its power.'

became manifest in a curious way. The old frank recognition of their usefulness as Jews (Frederick II of Prussia exclaimed, when he heard of possible mass-conversion: 'I hope they won't do such a devilish thing!')[27] was gone. Emancipation was granted in the name of a principle, and any allusion to special Jewish services would have been sacrilege, according to the mentality of the time. The special conditions which had led to emancipation, though well known to everybody concerned, were now hidden as if they were a great and terrible secret. The edict itself, on the other hand, was conceived as the last and, in a sense, the most shining achievement of change from a feudal state into a nation-state and a society where henceforth there would be no special privileges whatsoever.

Among the naturally bitter reactions of the aristocracy, the class that was hardest hit, was a sudden and unexpected outburst of antisemitism. Its most articulate spokesman, Ludwig von der Marwitz (prominent among the founders of a conservative ideology), submitted a lengthy petition to the government in which he said that the Jews would now be the only group enjoying special advantages, and spoke of the 'transformation of the old awe-inspiring Prussian monarchy into a new-fangled Jew-state.' The political attack was accompanied by a social boycott which changed the face of Berlin society almost overnight. For aristocrats had been among the first to establish friendly social relationships with Jews and had made famous those salons of Jewish hostesses at the turn of the century, where a truly mixed society gathered for a brief time. To a certain extent, it is true, this lack of prejudice was the result of the services rendered by the Jewish moneylender who for centuries had been excluded from all greater business transactions and found his only opportunity in the economically unproductive and insignificant but socially important loans to people who had a tendency to live beyond their means. Nevertheless, it is remarkable that social relationships survived when the absolute monarchies with their greater financial possibilities had made the private loan business and the individual small court Jew a thing of the past. A nobleman's natural resentment against losing a valuable source of help in emergencies made him want to marry a Jewish girl with a rich father rather than hate the Jewish people.

27  See *Kleines Jahrbuch des Nützlichen und Angenehmen für Israeliten*, 1847.

Nor was the outburst of aristocratic antisemitism the result of a closer contact between Jews and nobility. On the contrary, they had in common an instinctive opposition to the new values of the middle classes, and one that sprang from very similar sources. In Jewish as well as in noble families, the individual was regarded first of all as a member of a family; his duties were first of all determined by the family which transcended the life and importance of the individual. Both were a-national and inter-European, and each understood the other's way of life in which national allegiance was secondary to loyalty to a family which more often than not was scattered all over Europe. They shared a conception that the present is nothing more than an insignificant link in the chain of past and future generations. Anti-Jewish liberal writers did not fail to point out this curious similarity of principles, and they concluded that perhaps one could get rid of nobility only by first getting rid of the Jews, and this not because of their financial connections but because both were considered to be a hindrance to the true development of that 'innate personality,' that ideology of self-respect, which the liberal middle classes employed in their fight against the concepts of birth, family, and heritage.

These pro-Jewish factors make it all the more significant that the aristocrats started the long line of antisemitic political argumentation. Neither economic ties nor social intimacy carried any weight in a situation where aristocracy openly opposed the egalitarian nation-state. Socially, the attack on the state identified the Jews with the government; despite the fact that the middle classes, economically and socially, reaped the real gains in the reforms, politically they were hardly blamed and suffered the old contemptuous aloofness.

After the Congress of Vienna, when during the long decades of peaceful reaction under the Holy Alliance, Prussian nobility had won back much of its influence on the state and temporarily become even more prominent than it had ever been in the eighteenth century, aristocratic antisemitism changed at once into mild discrimination without further political significance.[28] At the same time, with the help of the romantic intellectuals, conservatism reached its full development as

28 When the Prussian Government submitted a new emancipation law to the *Vereinigte Landtage* in 1847, nearly all members of the high aristocracy favored complete Jewish emancipation. See I. Elbogen, *Geschichte der Juden in Deutschland*, Berlin, 1935, p. 244.

one of the political ideologies which in Germany adopted a very characteristic and ingeniously equivocal attitude toward the Jews. From then on the nation-state, equipped with conservative arguments, drew a distinct line between Jews who were needed and wanted and those who were not. Under the pretext of the essential Christian character of the state – what could have been more alien to the enlightened despots! – the growing Jewish intelligentsia could be openly discriminated against without harming the affairs of bankers and businessmen. This kind of discrimination which tried to close the universities to Jews by excluding them from the civil services had the double advantage of indicating that the nation-state valued special services higher than equality, and of preventing, or at least postponing, the birth of a new group of Jews who were of no apparent use to the state and even likely to be assimilated into society.[29] When, in the eighties, Bismarck went to considerable trouble to protect the Jews against Stoecker's antisemitic propaganda, he said *expressis verbis* that he wanted to protest only against the attacks upon 'moneyed Jewry . . . whose interests are tied to the conservation of our state institutions' and that his friend Bleichroeder, the Prussian banker, did not complain about attacks on Jews in general (which he might have overlooked) but on rich Jews.[30]

The seeming equivocation with which government officials on the one hand protested against equality (especially professional equality) for the Jews, or complained somewhat later about Jewish influence in the press and yet, on the other, sincerely 'wished them well in every respect,'[31] was much more suited to the interests of the state than the earlier zeal of the reformer. After all, the Congress of Vienna had

29 This was the reason why Prussian kings were so very much concerned with the strictest conservation of Jewish customs and religious rituals. In 1823 Frederick William III prohibited 'the slightest renovations,' and his successor, Frederick William IV, openly declared that 'the state must not do anything which could further an amalgamation between the Jews and the other inhabitants' of his kingdom. Elbogen, *op. cit.*, pp. 223, 234.

30 In a letter to *Kultusminister* v. Puttkammer in October, 1880. See also Herbert von Bismarck's letter of November, 1880, to Tiedemann. Both letters in Walter Frank, *Hofprediger Adolf Stoecker und die christlich-soziale Bewegung*, 1928, pp. 304, 305.

31 August Varnhagen comments on a remark made by Frederick William IV. 'The king was asked what he intended to do with the Jews. He replied: "I wish them well in every respect, but I want them to feel that they are Jews." These words provide a key to many things.' *Tagebücher*, Leipzig, 1861, II, 113.

returned to Prussia the provinces in which the poor Jewish masses had lived for centuries, and nobody but a few intellectuals who dreamed of the French Revolution and the Rights of Man had ever thought of giving them the same status as their wealthy brethren – who certainly were the last to clamor for an equality by which they could only lose.[32] They knew as well as anybody else that 'every legal or political measure for the emancipation of the Jews must necessarily lead to a deterioration of their civic and social situation.'[33] And they knew better than anybody else how much their power depended upon their position and prestige within the Jewish communities. So they could hardly adopt any other policy but to 'endeavor to get more influence for themselves, and keep their fellow Jews in their national isolation, pretending that this separation is part of their religion. Why? . . . Because the others should depend upon them even more, so that they, as *unsere Leute*, could be used exclusively by those in power.'[34] And it did turn out that in the twentieth century, when emancipation was for the first time an accomplished fact for the Jewish masses, the power of the privileged Jews had disappeared.

Thus a perfect harmony of interests was established between the powerful Jews and the state. Rich Jews wanted and obtained control over their fellow Jews and segregation from non-Jewish society; the state could combine a policy of benevolence toward rich Jews with legal discrimination against the Jewish intelligentsia and furtherance of social segregation, as expressed in the conservative theory of the Christian essence of the state.

While antisemitism among the nobility remained without political consequence and subsided quickly in the decades of the Holy Alliance,

32 That Jewish emancipation would have to be carried out against the desires of Jewish representatives was common knowledge in the eighteenth century. Mirabeau argued before the *Assemblée Nationale* in 1789: 'Gentlemen, is it because the Jews don't want to be citizens that you don't proclaim them citizens? In a government like the one you now establish, all men must be men; you must expel all those who are not or who refuse to become men.' The attitude of German Jews in the early nineteenth century is reported by J. M. Jost, *Neuere Geschichte der Israeliten, 1815–1845*, Berlin, 1846, Band 10.

33 Adam Mueller (see *Ausgewählte Abhandlungen*, ed. by J. Baxa, Jena, 1921, p. 215) in a letter to Metternich in 1815.

34 H. E. G. Paulus, *Die jüdische Nationalabsonderung nach Ursprung, Folgen und Besserungsmitteln*, 1831.

liberals and radical intellectuals inspired and led a new movement immediately after the Congress of Vienna. Liberal opposition to Metternich's police regime on the Continent and bitter attacks on the reactionary Prussian government led quickly to antisemitic outbursts and a veritable flood of anti-Jewish pamphlets. Precisely because they were much less candid and outspoken in their opposition to the government than the nobleman Marwitz had been a decade before, they attacked the Jews more than the government. Concerned mainly with equal opportunity and resenting most of all the revival of aristocratic privileges which limited their admission to the public services, they introduced into the discussion the distinction between individual Jews, 'our brethren,' and Jewry as a group, a distinction which from then on was to become the trademark of leftist antisemitism. Although they did not fully understand why and how the government, in its enforced independence from society, preserved and protected the Jews as a separate group, they knew well enough that some political connection existed and that the Jewish question was more than a problem of individual Jews and human tolerance. They coined the new nationalist phrases 'state within the state,' and 'nation within the nation.' Certainly wrong in the first instance, because the Jews had no political ambitions of their own and were merely the only social group that was unconditionally loyal to the state, they were half right in the second, because the Jews, taken as a social and not as a political body, actually did form a separate group within the nation.[35]

In Prussia, though not in Austria or in France, this radical antisemitism was almost as short-lived and inconsequential as the earlier antisemitism of nobility. The radicals were more and more absorbed by the liberalism of the economically rising middle classes, which all over Germany some twenty years later clamored in their diets for Jewish emancipation and for realization of political equality. It established, however, a certain theoretical and even literary tradition whose influence can be recognized in the famous anti-Jewish writings of the young Marx, who so frequently and unjustly has been accused of antisemitism. That the Jew, Karl Marx, could write the same way these anti-Jewish

---

35 For a clear and reliable account of German antisemitism in the nineteenth century see Waldemar Gurian, 'Antisemitism in Modern Germany,' in *Essays on Anti-Semitism*, ed. by K. S. Pinson, 1946.

radicals did is only proof of how little this kind of anti-Jewish argument had in common with full-fledged antisemitism. Marx as an individual Jew was as little embarrassed by these arguments against 'Jewry' as, for instance, Nietzsche was by his arguments against Germany. Marx, it is true, in his later years never wrote or uttered an opinion on the Jewish question; but this is hardly due to any fundamental change of mind. His exclusive preoccupation with class struggle as a phenomenon inside society, with the problems of capitalist production in which Jews were not involved as either buyers or sellers of labor, and his utter neglect of political questions, automatically prevented his further inspection of the state structure, and thereby of the role of the Jews. The strong influence of Marxism on the labor movement in Germany is among the chief reasons why German revolutionary movements showed so few signs of anti-Jewish sentiment.[36] The Jews were indeed of little or no importance for the social struggles of the time.

The beginnings of the modern antisemitic movement date back everywhere to the last third of the nineteenth century. In Germany, it began rather unexpectedly once more among the nobility, whose opposition to the state was again aroused by the transformation of the Prussian monarchy into a fell-fledged nation-state after 1871. Bismarck, the actual founder of the German Reich, had maintained close relations with Jews ever since he became Prime Minister; now he was denounced for being dependent upon and accepting bribes from the Jews. His attempt and partial success in abolishing most feudal remnants in the government inevitably resulted in conflict with the aristocracy; in their attack on Bismarck they represented him as either an innocent victim or a paid agent of Bleichroeder. Actually the relationship was the very opposite; Bleichroeder was undoubtedly a highly esteemed and well-paid agent of Bismarck.[37]

Feudal aristocracy, however, though still powerful enough to

36 The only leftist German antisemite of any importance was E. Duehring who, in a confused way, invented a naturalistic explanation of a 'Jewish race' in his *Die Judenfrage als Frage der Rassenschädlichkeit für Existenz, Sitte und Cultur der Völker mit einer weltgeschichtlichen Antwort*, 1880.

37 For antisemitic attacks on Bismarck see Kurt Wawrzinek, *Die Entstehung der deutschen Antisemitenparteien, 1873–1890*, Historische Studien, Heft 168, 1927.

influence public opinion, was in itself neither strong nor important enough to start a real antisemitic movement like the one that began in the eighties. Their spokesman, Court Chaplain Stoecker, himself a son of lower middle-class parents, was a much less gifted representative of conservative interests than his predecessors, the romantic intellectuals who had formulated the main tenets of a conservative ideology some fifty years earlier. Moreover, he discovered the usefulness of antisemitic propaganda not through practical or theoretical considerations but by accident, when he, with the help of a great demagogic talent, found out it was highly useful for filling otherwise empty halls. But not only did he fail to understand his own sudden successes; as court chaplain and employee of both the royal family and the government, he was hardly in a position to use them properly. His enthusiastic audiences were composed exclusively of lower middle-class people, small shopkeepers and tradesmen, artisans and old-fashioned craftsmen. And the anti-Jewish sentiments of these people were not yet, and certainly not exclusively, motivated by a conflict with the state.

## III: The First Antisemitic Parties

The simultaneous rise of antisemitism as a serious political factor in Germany, Austria, and France in the last twenty years of the nineteenth century was preceded by a series of financial scandals and fraudulent affairs whose main source was an overproduction of ready capital. In France a majority of Parliament members and an incredible number of government officials were soon so deeply involved in swindle and bribery that the Third Republic was never to recover the prestige it lost during the first decades of its existence; in Austria and Germany the aristocracy was among the most compromised. In all three countries, Jews acted only as middlemen, and not a single Jewish house emerged with permanent wealth from the frauds of the Panama Affair and the *Gründungsschwindel*.

However, another group of people besides noblemen, government officials, and Jews were seriously involved in these fantastic investments whose promised profits were matched by incredible losses. This group consisted mainly of the lower middle classes, which now suddenly turned antisemitic. They had been more seriously hurt than any of the other groups: they had risked small savings and had been permanently ruined. There were important reasons for their gullibility. Capitalist expansion on the domestic scene tended more and more to liquidate small property-holders, to whom it had become a question of life or death to increase quickly the little they had, since they were only too likely to lose all. They were becoming aware that if they did not succeed in climbing upward into the bourgeoisie, they might sink down into the proletariat. Decades of general prosperity slowed down this development so considerably (though it did not change its trend) that their panic appears rather premature. For the time being, however, the anxiety of the lower middle classes corresponded exactly to Marx's prediction of their rapid dissolution.

The lower middle classes, or petty bourgeoisie, were the descendants of the guilds of artisans and tradesmen who for centuries had been protected against the hazards of life by a closed system which outlawed competition and was in the last instance under the protection of the state. They consequently blamed their misfortune upon the Manchester system, which had exposed them to the hardships of a competitive society and deprived them of all special protection and privileges granted by public authorities. They were, therefore, the first to clamor for the 'welfare state,' which they expected not only to shield them against emergencies but to keep them in the professions and callings they had inherited from their families. Since an outstanding characteristic of the century of free trade was the access of the Jews to all professions, it was almost a matter of course to think of the Jews as the representatives of the 'applied system of Manchester carried out to the extreme,'[38] even though nothing was farther from the truth.

This rather derivative resentment, which we find first in certain conservative writers who occasionally combined an attack on the bourgeoisie with an attack on Jews, received a great stimulus when those who had hoped for help from the government or gambled on miracles had to accept the rather dubious help of bankers. To the small shopkeeper the banker appeared to be the same kind of exploiter as

38  Otto Glagau, *Der Bankrott des Nationalliberalismus und die Reaktion*, Berlin, 1878. The same author's *Der Boersen- und Gruendungsschwindel*, 1876, is one of the most important antisemitic pamphlets of the time.

the owner of a big industrial enterprise was to the worker. But while the European workers, from their own experience and a Marxist education in economics, knew that the capitalist filled the double function of exploiting them and giving them the opportunity to produce, the small shopkeeper had found nobody to enlighten him about his social and economic destiny. His predicament was even worse than the worker's and on the basis of his experience he considered the banker a parasite and usurer whom he had to make his silent partner, even though this banker, in contrast to the manufacturer, had nothing whatsoever to do with his business. It is not difficult to comprehend that a man who put his money solely and directly to the use of begetting more money can be hated more bitterly than the one who gets his profit through a lengthy and involved process of production. Since at that time nobody asked for credit if he could possibly help it – certainly not small tradesmen – bankers looked like the exploiters not of working power and productive capacity, but of misfortune and misery.

Many of these bankers were Jews and, even more important, the general figure of the banker bore definite Jewish traits for historical reasons. Thus the leftist movement of the lower middle class and the entire propaganda against banking capital turned more or less antisemitic, a development of little importance in industrial Germany but of great significance in France and, to a lesser extent, in Austria. For a while it looked as though the Jews had indeed for the first time come into direct conflict with another class without interference from the state. Within the framework of the nation-state, in which the function of the government was more or less defined by its ruling position above competing classes, such a clash might even have been a possible, if dangerous, way to normalize the Jewish position.

To this social-economic element, however, another was quickly added which in the long run proved to be more ominous. The position of the Jews as bankers depended not upon loans to small people in distress, but primarily on the issuance of state loans. Petty loans were left to the small fellows, who in this way prepared themselves for the more promising careers of their wealthier and more honorable brethren. The social resentment of the lower middle classes against the Jews turned into a highly explosive political element, because these bitterly hated Jews were thought to be well on their way to political power. Were they not only too well known for their relationship with the government in other respects? Social and economic hatred, on the other hand, reinforced the political argument with that driving violence which up to then it had lacked completely.

Friedrich Engels once remarked that the protagonists of the antisemitic movement of his time were noblemen, and its chorus the howling mob of the petty bourgeoisie. This is true not only for Germany, but also for Austria's Christian Socialism and France's Anti-Dreyfusards. In all these cases, the aristocracy, in a desperate last struggle, tried to ally itself with the conservative forces of the churches – the Catholic Church in Austria and France, the Protestant Church in Germany – under the pretext of fighting liberalism with the weapons of Christianity. The mob was only a means to strengthen their position, to give their voices a greater resonance. Obviously they neither could nor wanted to organize the mob, and would dismiss it once their aim was achieved. But they discovered that antisemitic slogans were highly effective in mobilizing large strata of the population.

The followers of Court Chaplain Stoecker did not organize the first antisemitic parties in Germany. Once the appeal of antisemitic slogans had been demonstrated, radical antisemites at once separated themselves from Stoecker's Berlin movement, went into a full-scale fight against the government, and founded parties whose representatives in the Reichstag voted in all major domestic issues with the greatest opposition party, the Social Democrats.[39] They quickly got rid of the compromising initial alliance with the old powers; Boeckel, the first antisemitic member of Parliament, owed his seat to votes of the Hessian peasants whom he defended against 'Junkers and Jews,' that is against the nobility which owned too much land and against the Jews upon whose credit the peasants depended.

Small as these first antisemitic parties were, they at once distinguished themselves from all other parties. They made the original claim that they were not a party among parties but a party 'above all parties.' In the class- and party-ridden nation-state, only the state and the

39 See Wawrzinek, *op. cit.* An instructive account of all these events, especially with respect to Court Chaplain Stoecker, in Frank, *op. cit.*

government had ever claimed to be above all parties and classes, to represent the nation as a whole. Parties were admittedly groups whose deputies represented the interests of their voters. Even though they fought for power, it was implicitly understood that it was up to the government to establish a balance between the conflicting interests and their representatives. The antisemitic parties' claim to be 'above all parties' announced clearly their aspiration to become the representative of the whole nation, to get exclusive power, to take possession of the state machinery, to substitute themselves for the state. Since, on the other hand, they continued to be organized as a party, it was also clear that they wanted state power as a party, so that their voters would actually dominate the nation.

The body politic of the nation-state came into existence when no single group was any longer in a position to wield exclusive political power, so that the government assumed actual political rule which no longer depended upon social and economic factors. The revolutionary movements of the left, which fought for a radical change of social conditions, had never directly touched this supreme political authority. They had challenged only the power of the bourgeoisie and its influence upon the state, and were therefore always ready to submit to government guidance in foreign affairs, where the interests of an assumedly unified nation were at stake. The numerous programs of the antisemitic groups, on the other hand, were, from the beginning, chiefly concerned with foreign affairs; their revolutionary impulse was directed against the government rather than a social class, and they actually aimed to destroy the political pattern of the nation-state by means of a party organization.

The claim of a party to be beyond all parties had other, more significant, implications than antisemitism. If it had been only a question of getting rid of the Jews, Fritsch's proposal, at one of the early antisemitic congresses,[40] not to create a new party but rather to disseminate antisemitism until finally all existing parties were hostile to Jews, would have brought much quicker results. As it was, Fritsch's proposal went unheeded because antisemitism was then already an instrument

40 This proposition was made in 1886 in Cassel, where the *Deutsche Antisemitische Vereinigung* was founded.

for the liquidation not only of the Jews but of the body politic of the nation-state as well.

Nor was it an accident that the claim of the antisemitic parties coincided with the early stages of imperialism and found exact counterparts in certain trends in Great Britain which were free of antisemitism and in the highly antisemitic pan-movements on the Continent.[41] Only in Germany did these new trends spring directly from antisemitism as such, and antisemitic parties preceded and survived the formation of purely imperialist groups such as the Alldeutscher Verband and others, all of which also claimed to be more than and above party groups.

The fact that similar formations without active antisemitism – which avoided the charlatan aspect of the antisemitic parties and therefore seemed at first to have far better chances for final victory – were finally submerged or liquidated by the antisemitic movement is a good index to the importance of the issue. The antisemites' belief that their claim to exclusive rule was no more than what the Jews had in fact achieved, gave them the advantage of a domestic program, and conditions were such that one had to enter the arena of social struggle in order to win political power. They could pretend to fight the Jews exactly as the workers were fighting the bourgeoisie. Their advantage was that by attacking the Jews, who were believed to be the secret power behind governments, they could openly attack the state itself, whereas the imperialist groups, with their mild and secondary antipathy against Jews, never found the connection with the important social struggles of the times.

The second highly significant characteristic of the new antisemitic parties was that they started at once a supranational organization of all antisemitic groups in Europe, in open contrast to, and in defiance of, current nationalistic slogans. By introducing this supranational element, they clearly indicated that they aimed not only at political rule over the nation but had already planned a step further for an inter-European government 'above all nations.' [42] This second revolu-

41 For an extensive discussion of the 'parties above parties' and the pan-movements see chapter viii.

42 The first international anti-Jewish congress took place in 1882 in Dresden, with about 3,000 delegates from Germany, Austria-Hungary, and Russia; during the discussions, Stoecker was defeated by the radical elements who met one year later in

tionary element meant the fundamental break with the status quo; it has been frequently overlooked because the antisemites themselves, partly because of traditional habits and partly because they consciously lied, used the language of the reactionary parties in their propaganda.

The intimate relationship between the peculiar conditions of Jewish existence and the ideology of such groups is even more evident in the organization of a group beyond nations than in the creation of a party beyond parties. The Jews very clearly were the only inter-European element in a nationalized Europe. It seemed only logical that their enemies had to organize on the same principle, if they were to fight those who were supposed to be the secret manipulators of the political destiny of all nations.

While this argument was sure to be convincing as propaganda, the success of supranational antisemitism depended upon more general considerations. Even at the end of the last century, and especially since the Franco-Prussian War, more and more people felt that the national organization of Europe was antiquated because it could no longer adequately respond to new economic challenges. This feeling had been a powerful supporting argument for the international organization of socialism and had, in turn, been strengthened by it. The conviction that identical interests existed all over Europe was spreading through the masses.[43] Whereas the international socialist organizations remained passive and uninterested in all foreign policy issues (that is in precisely those questions where their internationalism might have been tested), the antisemites started with problems of foreign policy and even promised solution of domestic problems on a supranational basis. To take ideologies less at their face value and to look more closely at the actual programs of the respective parties is to discover

---

Chemnitz and founded the Alliance Antijuive Universelle. A good account of these meetings and congresses, their programs and discussions, is to be found in Wawrz-inek, *op. cit.*

43 The international solidarity of the workers' movements was, as far as it went, an inter-European matter. Their indifference to foreign policy was also a kind of self-protection against both active participation in or struggle against the contemporary imperialist policies of their respective countries. As far as economic interests were concerned, it was all too obvious that everybody in the French or British or Dutch nation would feel the full impact of the fall of their empires, and not just capitalists and bankers.

that the socialists, who were more concerned with domestic issues, fitted much better into the nation-state than the antisemites.

Of course this does not mean that the socialists' internationalist convictions were not sincere. These were, on the contrary, stronger and, incidentally, much older than the discovery of class interests which cut across the boundaries of national states. But the very awareness of the all-importance of class struggle induced them to neglect that heritage which the French Revolution had bequeathed to the workers' parties and which alone might have led them to an articulate political theory. The socialists kept implicitly intact the original concept of a 'nation among nations,' all of which belong to the family of mankind, but they never found a device by which to transform this idea into a working concept in the world of sovereign states. Their internationalism, consequently, remained a personal conviction shared by everybody, and their healthy disinterest in national sovereignty turned into a quite unhealthy and unrealistic indifference to foreign politics. Since the parties of the left did not object to nation-states on principle, but only to the aspect of national sovereignty; since, moreover, their own inarticulate hopes for federalist structures with eventual integration of all nations on equal terms somehow presupposed national liberty and independence of all oppressed peoples, they could operate within the framework of the nation-state and even emerge, in the time of decay of its social and political structure, as the only group in the population that did not indulge in expansionist fantasies and in thoughts of destroying other peoples.

The supranationalism of the antisemites approached the question of international organization from exactly the opposite point of view. Their aim was a dominating superstructure which would destroy all home-grown national structures alike. They could indulge in hypernationalistic talk even as they prepared to destroy the body politic of their own nation, because tribal nationalism, with its immoderate lust for conquest, was one of the principal powers by which to force open the narrow and modest limits of the nation-state and its sovereignty.[44] The more effective the chauvinistic propaganda, the easier it was to persuade public opinion of the necessity for a supranational structure

44 Compare chapter viii.

which would rule from above and without national distinctions by a universal monopoly of power and the instruments of violence.

There is little doubt that the special inter-European condition of the Jewish people could have served the purposes of socialist federalism at least as well as it was to serve the sinister plots of supranationalists. But socialists were so concerned with class struggle and so neglectful of the political consequences of their own inherited concepts that they became aware of the existence of the Jews as a political factor only when they were already confronted with full-blown antisemitism as a serious competitor on the domestic scene. Then they were not only unprepared to integrate the Jewish issue into their theories, but actually afraid to touch the question at all. Here as in other international issues, they left the field to the supranationalists who could then seem to be the only ones who knew the answers to world problems.

By the turn of the century, the effects of the swindles in the seventies had run their course and an era of prosperity and general well-being, especially in Germany, put an end to the premature agitations of the eighties. Nobody could have predicted that this end was only a temporary respite, that all unsolved political questions, together with all unappeased political hatreds, were to redouble in force and violence after the first World War. The antisemitic parties in Germany, after initial successes, fell back into insignificance; their leaders, after a brief stirring of public opinion, disappeared through the back door of history into the darkness of crackpot confusion and cure-all charlatanry.

## IV: Leftist Antisemitism

Were it not for the frightful consequences of antisemitism in our own time, we might have given less attention to its development in Germany. As a political movement, nineteenth-century antisemitism can be studied best in France, where for almost a decade it dominated the political scene. As an ideological force, competing with other more respectable ideologies for the acceptance of public opinion, it reached its most articulate form in Austria.

Nowhere had the Jews rendered such great services to the state as in Austria, whose many nationalities were kept together only by the

Dual Monarchy of the House of Hapsburg, and where the Jewish state banker, in contrast to all other European countries, survived the downfall of the monarchy. Just as at the beginning of this development in the early eighteenth century, Samuel Oppenheimer's credit had been identical with the credit of the House of Hapsburg, so 'in the end Austrian credit was that of the *Creditanstalt*' – a Rothschild banking house.[45] Although the Danube monarchy had no homogeneous population, the most important prerequisite for evolution into a nation-state, it could not avoid the transformation of an enlightened despotism into a constitutional monarchy and the creation of modern civil services. This meant that it had to adopt certain institutions of the nation-state. For one thing, the modern class system grew along nationality lines, so that certain nationalities began to be identified with certain classes or at least professions. The German became the dominating nationality in much the same sense as the bourgeoisie became the dominating class in the nation-states. The Hungarian landed aristocracy played a role that was even more pronounced than, but essentially similar to, that played by the nobility in other countries. The state machinery itself tried its best to keep the same absolute distance from society, to rule above all nationalities, as the nation-state with respect to its classes. The result for the Jews was simply that the Jewish nationality could not merge with the others and could not become a nationality itself, just as it had not merged with other classes in the nation-state, or become a class itself. As the Jews in nation-states had differed from all classes of society through their special relationship to the state, so they differed from all other nationalities in Austria through their special relationship to the Hapsburg monarchy. And just as everywhere else each class that came into open conflict with the state turned antisemitic, so in Austria each nationality that not only engaged in the all-pervading struggle of the nationalities but came into open conflict with the monarchy itself, started its fight with an attack upon the Jews. But there was a marked difference between these conflicts in Austria, and those in Germany and France. In Austria they were not only sharper, but at the outbreak of the first World War

45 See Paul H. Emden, 'The Story of the Vienna *Creditanstalt*,' in *Menorah Journal*, XXVIII, 1, 1940.

every single nationality, and that meant every stratum of society, was in opposition to the state, so that more than anywhere else in Western or Central Europe the population was imbued with active antisemitism.

Outstanding among these conflicts was the continuously rising state hostility of the German nationality, which accelerated after the foundation of the Reich and discovered the usefulness of antisemitic slogans after the financial crash of 1873. The social situation at that moment was practically the same as in Germany, but the social propaganda to catch the middle-class vote immediately indulged in a much more violent attack on the state, and a much more outspoken confession of nonloyalty to the country. Moreover, the German Liberal Party, under the leadership of Schoenerer, was from the beginning a lower middle-class party without connections or restraints from the side of the nobility, and with a decidedly left-wing outlook. It never achieved a real mass basis, but it was remarkably successful in the universities during the eighties where it organized the first closely knit students' organization on the basis of open antisemitism. Schoenerer's antisemitism, at first almost exclusively directed against the Rothschilds, won him the sympathies of the labor movement, which regarded him as a true radical gone astray.[46] His main advantage was that he could base his antisemitic propaganda on demonstrable facts: as a member of the Austrian Reichsrat he had fought for nationalization of the Austrian railroads, the major part of which had been in the hands of the Rothschilds since 1836 due to a state license which expired in 1886. Schoenerer succeeded in gathering 40,000 signatures against its renewal, and in placing the Jewish question in the limelight of public interest. The close connection between the Rothschilds and the financial interests of the monarchy became very obvious when the government tried to extend the license under conditions which were patently to the disadvantage of the state as well as the public.

46  See F. A. Neuschaefer, *Georg Ritter von Schoenerer*, Hamburg, 1935, and Eduard Pichl, *Georg Schoenerer*, 1938, 6 vols. Even in 1912, when the Schoenerer agitation had long lost all significance, the Viennese *Arbeiterzeitung* cherished very affectionate feelings for the man of whom it could think only in the words Bismarck had once uttered about Lassalle: 'And if we exchanged shots, justice would still demand that we admit even during the shooting: He is a man; and the others are old women.' (Neuschaefer, p. 33.)

Schoenerer's agitation in this matter became the actual beginning of an articulate antisemitic movement in Austria.[47] The point is that this movement, in contrast to the German Stoecker agitation, was initiated and led by a man who was sincere beyond doubt, and therefore did not stop at the use of antisemitism as a propaganda weapon, but developed quickly that Pan-German ideology which was to influence Nazism more deeply than any other German brand of antisemitism.

Though victorious in the long run, the Schoenerer movement was temporarily defeated by a second antisemitic party, the Christian-Socials under the leadership of Lueger. While Schoenerer had attacked the Catholic Church and its considerable influence on Austrian politics almost as much as he had the Jews, the Christian-Socials were a Catholic party who tried from the outset to ally themselves with those reactionary conservative forces which had proved so helpful in Germany and France. Since they made more social concessions, they were more successful than in Germany or in France. They, together with the Social Democrats, survived the downfall of the monarchy and became the most influential group in postwar Austria. But long before the establishment of an Austrian Republic, when, in the nineties, Lueger had won the Mayoralty of Vienna by an antisemitic campaign, the Christian-Socials already adopted that typically equivocal attitude toward the Jews in the nation-state – hostility to the intelligentsia and friendliness toward the Jewish business class. It was by no means an accident that, after a bitter and bloody contest for power with the socialist workers' movement, they took over the state machinery when Austria, reduced to its German nationality, was established as a nation-state. They turned out to be the only party which was prepared for exactly this role and, even under the old monarchy, had won popularity because of their nationalism. Since the Hapsburgs were a German house and had granted their German subjects a certain predominance, the Christian-Socials never attacked the monarchy. Their function was rather to win large parts of the German nationality for the support of an essentially unpopular government. Their antisemitism remained without consequence; the decades when Lueger ruled Vienna were actually a kind of golden age for the Jews. No matter how

47 See Neuschaefer, *op. cit.*, pp. 22 ff., and Pichl, *op. cit.*, I, 236 ff.

far their propaganda occasionally went in order to get votes, they never could have proclaimed with Schoenerer and the Pan-Germanists that 'they regarded antisemitism as the mainstay of our national ideology, as the most essential expression of genuine popular conviction and thus as the major national achievement of the century.' [48] And although they were as much under the influence of clerical circles as was the antisemitic movement in France, they were of necessity much more restrained in their attacks on the Jews because they did not attack the monarchy as the antisemites in France attacked the Third Republic.

The successes and failures of the two Austrian antisemitic parties show the scant relevance of social conflicts to the long-range issues of the time. Compared with the mobilization of all opponents to the government as such, the capturing of lower middle-class votes was a temporary phenomenon. Indeed, the backbone of Schoenerer's movement was in those German-speaking provinces without any Jewish population at all, where competition with Jews or hatred of Jewish bankers never existed. The survival of the Pan-Germanist movement and its violent antisemitism in these provinces, while it subsided in the urban centers, was merely due to the fact that these provinces were never reached to the same extent by the universal prosperity of the pre-war period which reconciled the urban population with the government.

The complete lack of loyalty to their own country and its government, for which the Pan-Germanists substituted an open loyalty to Bismarck's Reich, and the resulting concept of nationhood as something independent of state and territory, led the Schoenerer group to a veritable imperialist ideology in which lies the clue to its temporary weakness and its final strength. It is also the reason why the Pan-German party in Germany (the Alldeutschen), which never overstepped the limits of ordinary chauvinism, remained so extremely suspicious and reluctant to take the outstretched hands of their Austrian Germanist brothers. This Austrian movement aimed at more than rise to power as a party, more than the possession of the state machinery. It wanted a revolutionary reorganization of Central

48 Quoted from Pichl, *op. cit.*, I, p. 26.

Europe in which the Germans of Austria, together with and strength-ened by the Germans of Germany, would become the ruling people, in which all other peoples of the area would be kept in the same kind of semiservitude as the Slavonic nationalities in Austria. Because of this close affinity to imperialism and the fundamental change it brought to the concept of nationhood, we shall have to postpone the discussion of the Austrian Pan-Germanist movement. It is no longer, at least in its consequences, a mere nineteenth-century preparatory movement; it belongs, more than any other brand of antisemitism, to the course of events of our own century.

The exact opposite is true of French antisemitism. The Dreyfus Affair brings into the open all other elements of nineteenth-century anti-semitism in its mere ideological and political aspects; it is the culmination of the antisemitism which grew out of the special con-ditions of the nation-state. Yet its violent form foreshadowed future developments, so that the main actors of the Affair sometimes seem to be staging a huge dress rehearsal for a performance that had to be put off for more than three decades. It drew together all the open or sub-terranean, political or social sources which had brought the Jewish question into a predominant position in the nineteenth century; its premature outburst, on the other hand, kept it within the framework of a typical nineteenth-century ideology which, although it survived all French governments and political crises, never quite fitted into twentieth-century political conditions. When, after the 1940 defeat, French antisemitism got its supreme chance under the Vichy govern-ment, it had a definitely antiquated and, for major purposes, rather useless character, which German Nazi writers never forgot to point out.[49] It had no influence on the formation of Nazism and remains more significant in itself than as an active historical factor in the final catastrophe.

The principal reason for these wholesome limitations was that France's antisemitic parties, though violent on the domestic scene, had no supranational aspirations. They belonged after all to the oldest and

49 See especially Walfried Vernunft, 'Die Hintergründe des französischen Antisem-itismus,' in *Nationalsozialistische Monatshefte*, June, 1939.

most fully developed nation-state in Europe. None of the antisemites ever tried seriously to organize a 'party above parties' or to seize the state as a party and for no other purpose but party interests. The few attempted *coups d'état* which might be credited to the alliance between antisemites and higher army officers were ridiculously inadequate and obviously contrived.[50] In 1898 some nineteen members of Parliament were elected through antisemitic campaigns, but this was a peak which was never reached again and from which the decline was rapid.

It is true, on the other hand, that this was the earliest instance of the success of antisemitism as a catalytic agent for all other political issues. This can be attributed to the lack of authority of the Third Republic, which had been voted in with a very slight majority. In the eyes of the masses, the state had lost its prestige along with the monarchy, and attacks on the state were no longer a sacrilege. The early outburst of violence in France bears a striking resemblance to similar agitation in the Austrian and German Republics after the first World War. The Nazi dictatorship has been so frequently connected with so-called 'state-worship' that even historians have become somewhat blind to the truism that the Nazis took advantage of the complete breakdown of state worship, originally prompted by the worship of a prince who sits on the throne by the grace of God, and which hardly ever occurs in a Republic. In France, fifty years before Central European countries were affected by this universal loss of reverence, state worship had suffered many defeats. It was much easier to attack the Jews and the government together there than in Central Europe where the Jews were attacked in order to attack the government.

French antisemitism, moreover, is as much older than its European counterparts as is French emancipation of the Jews, which dates back to the end of the eighteenth century. The representatives of the Age of Enlightenment who prepared the French Revolution despised the Jews as a matter of course; they saw in them the backward remnants of the Dark Ages, and they hated them as the financial agents of the aristocracy. The only articulate friends of the Jews in France were conservative writers who denounced anti-Jewish attitudes as 'one of the

50  See Chapter iv.

favorite theses of the eighteenth century.' [51] For the more liberal or radical writer it had become almost a tradition to warn against the Jews as barbarians who still lived in the patriarchal form of government and recognized no other state.[52] During and after the French Revolution, the French clergy and French aristocrats added their voices to the general anti-Jewish sentiment, though for other and more material reasons. They accused the revolutionary government of having ordered the sale of clerical property to pay 'the Jews and merchants to whom the government is indebted.' [53] These old arguments, somehow kept alive through the never-ending struggle between Church and State in France, supported the general violence and embitterment which had been touched off by other and more modern forces at the end of the century.

Mainly because of the strong clerical support of antisemitism, the French socialist movement finally decided to take a stand against antisemitic propaganda in the Dreyfus Affair. Until then, however, nineteenth-century French leftist movements had been outspoken in their antipathy to the Jews. They simply followed the tradition of eighteenth-century enlightenment which was the source of French liberalism and radicalism, and they considered anti-Jewish attitudes an integral part of anticlericalism. These sentiments on the left were strengthened first by the fact that the Alsatian Jews continued to live from lending money to peasants, a practice which had already prompted Napoleon's decree of 1808. After conditions had changed in Alsace, leftist antisemitism found a new source of strength in the financial policies of the house of Rothschild, which played a large part in the financing of the Bourbons, maintained close connections with Louis Philippe, and flourished under Napoleon III.

Behind these obvious and rather superficial incentives to anti-Jewish attitudes there was a deeper cause, which was crucial to the

---

51 See J. de Maistre, *Les Soirées de St. Petersburg*, 1821, II, 55.

52 Charles Fourier, *Nouveau Monde Industriel*, 1829, Vol. V of his *Oeuvres Complètes*, 1841, p. 421. For Fourier's anti-Jewish doctrines, see also Edmund Silberner, 'Charles Fourier on the Jewish Question' in *Jewish Social Studies*, October, 1946.

53 See the newspaper *Le Patriote Français*, No. 457, November 8, 1790. Quoted from Clemens August Hoberg, 'Die geistigen Grundlagen des Antisemitismus im modernen Frankreich,' in *Forschungen zur Judenfrage*, 1940, Vol. IV.

whole structure of the specifically French brand of radicalism, and which almost succeeded in turning the whole French leftist movement against the Jews. Bankers were much stronger in the French economy than in other capitalist countries, and France's industrial development, after a brief rise during the reign of Napoleon III, lagged so far behind other nations' that pre-capitalist socialist tendencies continued to exert considerable influence. The lower middle classes which in Germany and Austria became antisemitic only during the seventies and eighties, when they were already so desperate that they could be used for reactionary politics as well as for the new mob policies, had been antisemitic in France some fifty years earlier, when, with the help of the working class, they carried the revolution of 1848 to a brief victory. In the forties, when Toussenel published his *Les Juifs, Rois de l'Epoque*, the most important book in a veritable flood of pamphlets against the Rothschilds, it was enthusiastically received by the entire left-wing press, which at the time was the organ of the revolutionary lower middle classes. Their sentiments, as expressed by Toussenel, though less articulate and less sophisticated, were not very different from those of the young Marx, and Toussenel's attack on the Rothschilds was only a less gifted and more elaborate variation of the letters from Paris which Boerne had written fifteen years before.[54] These Jews, too, mistook the Jewish banker for a central figure in the capitalist system, an error which has exerted a certain influence on the municipal and lower government bureaucracy in France up to our own time.[55]

54  Marx's essay on the Jewish question is sufficiently well known not to warrant quotation. Since Boerne's utterances, because of their merely polemical and untheoretical character, are being forgotten today, we quote from the 72nd letter from Paris (January, 1832): 'Rothschild kissed the Pope's hand . . . At last the order has come which God had planned when he created the world. A poor Christian kisses the Pope's feet, and a rich Jew kisses his hand. If Rothschild had gotten his Roman loan at 60 per cent, instead of 65, and could have sent the cardinal-chamberlain more than ten thousand ducats, they would have allowed him to embrace the Holy Father . . . Would it not be the greatest luck for the world if all kings were deposed and the Rothschild family placed on the throne?' *Briefe aus Paris, 1830–1833*.

55  This attitude is well described in the preface by the municipal councilor Paul Brousse to Cesare Lombroso's famous work on antisemitism (1899). The characteristic part of the argument is contained in the following: 'The small shopkeeper needs credit, and we know how badly organized and how expensive credit is these days. Here too

However this outburst of popular anti-Jewish feeling, nourished by an economic conflict between Jewish bankers and their desperate clientele, lasted no longer as an important factor in politics than similar outbursts with purely economic or social causes. The twenty years of Napoleon III's rule over a French Empire were an age of prosperity and security for French Jewry much like the two decades before the outbreak of the first World War in Germany and Austria.

The only brand of French antisemitism which actually remained strong, and outlasted social antisemitism as well as the contemptuous attitudes of anticlerical intellectuals, was tied up with a general xenophobia. Especially after the first World War, foreign Jews became the stereotypes for all foreigners. A differentiation between native Jews and those who 'invaded' the country from the East has been made in all Western and Central European countries. Polish and Russian Jews were treated exactly the same way in Germany and Austria as Rumanian and German Jews were treated in France, just as Jews from Posen in Germany or from Galicia in Austria were regarded with the same snobbish contempt as Jews from Alsace were in France. But only in France did this differentiation assume such importance on the domestic scene. And this is probably due to the fact that the Rothschilds, who more than anywhere else were the butt of anti-Jewish attacks, had immigrated into France from Germany, so that up to the outbreak of the second World War it became natural to suspect the Jews of sympathies with the national enemy.

Nationalistic antisemitism, harmless when compared with modern movements, was never a monopoly of reactionaries and chauvinists in France. On this point, the writer Jean Giraudoux, the propaganda minister in Daladier's war cabinet, was in complete agreement[56] with

the small merchant places the responsibility on the Jewish banker. All the way down to the worker – *i.e.* only those workers who have no clear notion of scientific socialism – everybody thinks the revolution is being advanced if the general expropriation of capitalists is preceded by the expropriation of Jewish capitalists, who are the most typical and whose names are the most familiar to the masses.'

56 For the surprising continuity in French antisemitic arguments, compare, for instance, Charles Fourier's picture of the Jew 'Iscariote' who arrives in France with 100,000 pounds, establishes himself in a town with six competitors in his field, crushes all the competing houses, amasses a great fortune, and returns to Germany (in *Théorie des quatre mouvements*, 1808, *Oeuvres Complètes*, 88 ff.) with Giraudoux's picture of 1939: 'By an infiltration whose secret I have tried in vain to detect, hundreds of thousands of

Pétain and the Vichy government, which also, no matter how hard it tried to please the Germans, could not break through the limitations of this outmoded antipathy for Jews. The failure was all the more conspicuous since the French had produced an outstanding antisemite who realized the full range and possibilities of the new weapon. That this man should be a prominent novelist is characteristic of conditions in France, where antisemitism in general had never fallen into the same social and intellectual disrepute as in other European countries.

Louis Ferdinand Céline had a simple thesis, ingenious and containing exactly the ideological imagination that the more rational French antisemitism had lacked. He claimed that the Jews had prevented the evolution of Europe into a political entity, had caused all European wars since 843, and had plotted the ruin of both France and Germany by inciting their mutual hostility. Céline proposed this fantastic explanation of history in his *Ecole des Cadavres*, written at the time of the Munich pact and published during the first months of the war. An earlier pamphlet on the subject, *Bagatelle pour un Massacre* (1938), although it did not include the new key to European history, was already remarkably modern in its approach; it avoided all restricting differentiations between native and foreign Jews, between good and bad ones, and did not bother with elaborate legislative proposals (a particular characteristic of French antisemitism), but went straight to the core of the matter and demanded the massacre of all Jews.

Céline's first book was very favorably received by France's leading intellectuals, who were half pleased by the attack on the Jews and half convinced that it was nothing more than an interesting new literary fancy.[57] For exactly the same reasons French home-grown Fascists did not take Céline seriously, despite the fact that the Nazis always knew he was the only true antisemite in France. The inherent good sense of

Ashkenasim, who escaped from the Polish and Rumanian Ghettos, have entered our country . . . eliminating our fellow citizens and, at the same time, ruining their professional customs and traditions . . . and defying all investigations of census, taxes and labor.' In *Pleins Pouvoirs*, 1939.

57 See especially the critical discussion in the *Nouvelle Revue Française* by Marcel Arland (February, 1938) who claims that Céline's position is essentially '*solide*.' André Gide (April, 1938) thinks that Céline in depicting only the Jewish '*spécialité*,' has succeeded in painting not the reality but the very hallucination which reality provokes.

French politicians and their deep-rooted respectability prevented their accepting a charlatan and crackpot. The result was that even the Germans, who knew better, had to continue to use such inadequate supporters as Doriot, a follower of Mussolini, and Pétain, an old French chauvinist with no comprehension whatever of modern problems, in their vain efforts to persuade the French people that extermination of the Jews would be a cure for everything under the sun. The way this situation developed during the years of French official, and even unofficial, readiness to co-operate with Nazi Germany, clearly indicates how ineffective nineteenth-century antisemitism was to the new political purposes of the twentieth, even in a country where it had reached its fullest development and had survived all other changes in public opinion. It did not matter that able nineteenth-century journalists like Edouard Drumont, and even great contemporary writers like Georges Bernanos, contributed to a cause that was much more adequately served by crackpots and charlatans.

That France, for various reasons, never developed a full-fledged imperialist party turned out to be the decisive element. As many French colonial politicians have pointed out,[58] only a French-German alliance would have enabled France to compete with England in the division of the world and to join successfully in the scramble for Africa. Yet France somehow never let herself be tempted into this competition, despite all her noisy resentment and hostility against Great Britain. France was and remained – though declining in importance – the *nation par excellence* on the Continent, and even her feeble imperialist attempts usually ended with the birth of new national independence movements. Since, moreover, her antisemitism had been nourished principally by the purely national French-German conflict, the Jewish issue was almost automatically kept from playing much of a role in imperialist policies, despite the conditions in Algeria, whose mixed population of native Jews and Arabs would have offered an excellent opportunity.[59] The simple and brutal destruction of the French nation-state by German aggression, the mockery of a German-French alliance on the basis of German occupation and

58  See for instance René Pinon, *France et Allemagne*, 1912.
59  Some aspects of the Jewish question in Algeria are treated in the author's article, 'Why the Crémieux Decree was Abrogated,' in *Contemporary Jewish Record*, April, 1943.

French defeat, may have proved how little strength of her own the *nation par excellence* had carried into our times from a glorious past; it did not change her essential political structure.

## V: The Golden Age of Security

Only two decades separated the temporary decline of the antisemitic movements from the outbreak of the first World War. This period has been adequately described as a 'Golden Age of Security' [60] because only a few who lived in it felt the inherent weakness of an obviously outmoded political structure which, despite all prophecies of imminent doom, continued to function in spurious splendor and with inexplicable, monotonous stubbornness. Side by side, and apparently with equal stability, an anachronistic despotism in Russia, a corrupt bureaucracy in Austria, a stupid militarism in Germany and a half-hearted Republic in continual crisis in France – all of them still under the shadow of the world-wide power of the British Empire – managed to carry on. None of these governments was especially popular, and all faced growing domestic opposition; but nowhere did there seem to exist an earnest political will for radical change in political conditions. Europe was much too busy expanding economically for any nation or social stratum to take political questions seriously. Everything could go on because nobody cared. Or, in the penetrating words of Chesterton, 'everything is prolonging its existence by denying that it exists.' [61]

The enormous growth of industrial and economic capacity produced a steady weakening of purely political factors, while at the same time economic forces became dominant in the international play of power. Power was thought to be synonymous with economic capacity before people discovered that economic and industrial capacity are only its modern prerequisites. In a sense, economic power could bring governments to heel because they had the same faith in economics as

60 The term is Stefan Zweig's, who thus named the period up to the first World War in *The World of Yesterday: An Autobiography*, 1943.
61 For a wonderful description of the British state of affairs, see G. K. Chesterton, *The Return of Don Quixote*, which did not appear until 1927 but was 'planned and partly written before the War.'

the plain businessmen who had somehow convinced them that the state's means of violence had to be used exclusively for protection of business interests and national property. For a very brief time, there was some truth in Walter Rathenau's remark that 300 men, who all know each other, held the destinies of the world in their hands. This odd state of affairs lasted exactly until 1914 when, through the very fact of war, the confidence of the masses in the providential character of economic expansion fell apart.

The Jews were more deluded by the appearances of the golden age of security than any other section of the European peoples. Antisemitism seemed to be a thing of the past; the more the governments lost in power and prestige, the less attention was paid to the Jews. While the state played an ever narrower and emptier representative role, political representation tended to become a kind of theatrical performance of varying quality until in Austria the theater itself became the focus of national life, an institution whose public significance was certainly greater than that of Parliament. The theatrical quality of the political world had become so patent that the theater could appear as the realm of reality.

The growing influence of big business on the state and the state's declining need for Jewish services threatened the Jewish banker with extinction and forced certain shifts in Jewish occupations. The first sign of the decline of the Jewish banking houses was their loss of prestige and power within the Jewish communities. They were no longer strong enough to centralize and, to a certain extent, monopolize the general Jewish wealth. More and more Jews left state finance for independent business. Out of food and clothing deliveries to armies and governments grew the Jewish food and grain commerce, and the garment industries in which they soon acquired a prominent position in all countries; pawnshops and general stores in small country towns were the predecessors of department stores in the cities. This does not mean that the relationship between Jews and governments ceased to exist, but fewer individuals were involved, so that at the end of this period we have almost the same picture as at the beginning: a few Jewish individuals in important financial positions with little or no connection with the broader strata of the Jewish middle class.

More important than the expansion of the independent Jewish business class was another shift in the occupational structure. Central and

Western European Jewries had reached a saturation point in wealth and economic fortune. This might have been the moment for them to show that they actually wanted money for money's or for power's sake. In the former case, they might have expanded their businesses and handed them down to their descendants; in the latter they might have entrenched themselves more firmly in state business and fought the influence of big business and industry on governments. But they did neither. On the contrary, the sons of the well-to-do businessmen and, to a lesser extent, bankers, deserted their fathers' careers for the liberal professions or purely intellectual pursuits they had not been able to afford a few generations before. What the nation-state had once feared so much, the birth of a Jewish intelligentsia, now proceeded at a fantastic pace. The crowding of Jewish sons of well-to-do parents into the cultural occupations was especially marked in Germany and Austria, where a great proportion of cultural institutions, like newspapers, publishing, music, and theater, became Jewish enterprises.

What had been made possible through the traditional Jewish preference and respect for intellectual occupations resulted in a real break with tradition and the intellectual assimilation and nationalization of important strata of Western and Central European Jewry. Politically, it indicated emancipation of Jews from state protection, growing consciousness of a common destiny with their fellow-citizens, and a considerable loosening of the ties that had made Jews an inter-European element. Socially, the Jewish intellectuals were the first who, as a group, needed and wanted admittance to non-Jewish society. Social discrimination, a small matter to their fathers who had not cared for social intercourse with Gentiles, became a paramount problem for them.

Searching for a road into society, this group was forced to accept social behavior patterns set by individual Jews who had been admitted into society during the nineteenth century as exceptions to the rule of discrimination. They quickly discovered the force that would open all doors, the 'radiant Power of Fame' (Stefan Zweig), which a hundred years' idolatry of genius had made irresistible. What distinguished the Jewish pursuit of fame from the general fame idolatry of the time was that Jews were not primarily interested in it for themselves. To live in the aura of fame was more important than to become famous; thus they became outstanding reviewers, critics, collectors, and organizers of what was famous. The 'radiant power' was a very real social force by which the socially homeless were able to establish a home. The Jewish intellectuals, in other words, tried, and to a certain extent succeeded, in becoming the living tie binding famous individuals into a society of the renowned, an international society by definition, for spiritual achievement transcends national boundaries. The general weakening of political factors, for two decades having brought about a situation in which reality and appearance, political reality and theatrical performance could easily parody each other, now enabled them to become the representatives of a nebulous international society in which national prejudices no longer seemed valid. And paradoxically enough, this international society seemed to be the only one that recognized the nationalization and assimilation of its Jewish members; it was far easier for an Austrian Jew to be accepted as an Austrian in France than in Austria. The spurious world citizenship of this generation, this fictitious nationality which they claimed as soon as their Jewish origin was mentioned, in part already resembled those passports which later granted their owner the right to sojourn in every country except the one that issued it.

By their very nature, these circumstances could not but bring Jews into prominence just when their activities, their satisfaction and happiness in the world of appearance, proved that, as a group, they wanted in fact neither money nor power. While serious statesmen and publicists now bothered with the Jewish question less than at any time since the emancipation, and while antisemitism almost entirely disappeared from the open political scene, Jews became the symbols of Society as such and the objects of hatred for all those whom society did not accept. Antisemitism, having lost its ground in the special conditions that had influenced its development during the nineteenth century, could be freely elaborated by charlatans and crackpots into that weird mixture of half-truths and wild superstitions which emerged in Europe after 1914, the ideology of all frustrated and resentful elements.

Since the Jewish question in its social aspect turned into a catalyst of social unrest, until finally a disintegrated society recrystallized ideologically around a possible massacre of Jews, it is necessary to outline some of the main traits of the social history of emancipated Jewry in the bourgeois society of the last century.

# CHAPTER THREE

## The Jews and Society

The Jews' political ignorance, which fitted them so well for their special role and for taking roots in the state's sphere of business, and their prejudices against the people and in favor of authority, which blinded them to the political dangers of antisemitism, caused them to be oversensitive toward all forms of social discrimination. It was difficult to see the decisive difference between political argument and mere antipathy when the two developed side by side. The point, however, is that they grew out of exactly opposite aspects of emancipation: political antisemitism developed because the Jews were a separate body, while social discrimination arose because of the growing equality of Jews with all other groups.

Equality of condition, though it is certainly a basic requirement for justice, is nevertheless among the greatest and most uncertain ventures of modern mankind. The more equal conditions are, the less explanation there is for the differences that actually exist between people; and thus all the more unequal do individuals and groups become. This perplexing consequence came fully to light as soon as equality was no longer seen in terms of an omnipotent being like God or an unavoidable common destiny like death. Whenever equality becomes a mundane fact in itself, without any gauge by which it may be measured or explained, then there is one chance in a hundred that it will be recognized simply as a working principle of a political organization in which otherwise unequal people have equal rights; there are ninety-nine chances that it will be mistaken for an innate quality of every individual, who is 'normal' if he is like everybody else and 'abnormal' if he happens to be different. This perversion of equality from a political into a social concept is all the more dangerous when a society leaves but little space for special groups and individuals, for then their differences become all the more conspicuous.

The great challenge to the modern period, and its peculiar danger, has been that in it man for the first time confronted man without the protection of differing circumstances and conditions. And it has been precisely this new concept of equality that has made modern race relations so difficult, for there we deal with natural differences which by no possible and conceivable change of conditions can become less conspicuous. It is because equality demands that I recognize each and every individual as my equal, that the conflicts between different groups, which for reasons of their own are reluctant to grant each other this basic equality, take on such terribly cruel forms.

Hence the more equal the Jewish condition, the more surprising were Jewish differences. This new awareness led to social resentment against the Jews and at the same time to a peculiar attraction toward them; the combined reactions determined the social history of Western Jewry. Discrimination, however, as well as attraction, were politically sterile. They neither produced a political movement against the Jews nor served in any way to protect them against their enemies. They did succeed, though, in poisoning the social atmosphere, in perverting all social intercourse between Jews and Gentiles, and had a definite effect on Jewish behavior. The formation of a Jewish type was due to both – to special discrimination and to special favor.

Social antipathy for Jews, with its varying forms of discrimination, did no great political harm in European countries, for genuine social and economic equality was never achieved. To all appearances new classes developed as groups to which one belonged by birth. There is no doubt that it was only in such a framework that society could suffer the Jews to establish themselves as a special clique.

The situation would have been entirely different if, as in the United States, equality of condition had been taken for granted; if every member of society – from whatever stratum – had been firmly convinced that by ability and luck he might become the hero of a success story. In such a society, discrimination becomes the only means of distinction, a kind of universal law according to which groups may find themselves outside the sphere of civic, political, and economic equality. Where discrimination is not tied up with the Jewish issue only, it can become a crystallization point for a political movement that wants to solve all the natural difficulties and conflicts of a multinational country by violence, mob rule, and the sheer vulgarity of race concepts. It is one of the most promising and dangerous paradoxes of the American Republic that it dared to realize equality on the basis of the most unequal population in the world, physically and historically. In the United States, social antisemitism may one day become the very dangerous nucleus for a political movement.[1] In Europe, however, it had little influence on the rise of political antisemitism.

## I: Between Pariah and Parvenu

The precarious balance between society and state, upon which the nation-state rested socially and politically, brought about a peculiar law governing Jewish admission to society. During the 150 years when Jews truly lived amidst, and not just in the neighborhood of, Western European peoples, they always had to pay with political misery for social glory and with social insult for political success. Assimilation, in the sense of acceptance by non-Jewish society, was granted them only as long as they were clearly distinguished exceptions from the Jewish masses even though they still shared the same restricted and humiliating political conditions, or later only when, after an accomplished emancipation and resulting social isolation, their political status was already challenged by antisemitic movements. Society, confronted with political, economic, and legal equality for Jews, made it quite

---

1 Although Jews stood out more than other groups in the homogeneous populations of European countries, it does not follow that they are more threatened by discrimination than other groups in America. In fact, up to now, not the Jews but the Negroes – by nature and history the most unequal among the peoples of America – have borne the burden of social and economic discrimination.

This could change, however, if a political movement ever grew out of this merely social discrimination. Then Jews might very suddenly become the principal objects of hatred for the simple reason that they, alone among all other groups, have themselves, within their history and their religion, expressed a well-known principle of separation. This is not true of the Negroes or Chinese, who are therefore less endangered politically, even though they may differ more from the majority than the Jews.

clear that none of its classes was prepared to grant them social equality, and that only exceptions from the Jewish people would be received. Jews who heard the strange compliment that they were exceptions, exceptional Jews, knew quite well that it was this very ambiguity – that they were Jews and yet presumably not *like* Jews – which opened the doors of society to them. If they desired this kind of intercourse, they tried, therefore, 'to be and yet not to be Jews.'[2]

The seeming paradox had a solid basis in fact. What non-Jewish society demanded was that the newcomer be as 'educated' as itself, and that, although he not behave like an 'ordinary Jew,' he be and produce something out of the ordinary, since, after all, he was a Jew. All advocates of emancipation called for assimilation, that is, adjustment to and reception by, society, which they considered either a preliminary condition to Jewish emancipation or its automatic consequence. In other words, whenever those who actually tried to improve Jewish conditions attempted to think of the Jewish question from the point of view of the Jews themselves, they immediately approached it merely in its social aspect. It has been one of the most unfortunate facts in the history of the Jewish people that only its enemies, and almost never its friends, understood that the Jewish question was a political one.

The defenders of emancipation tended to present the problem as one of 'education,' a concept which originally applied to Jews as well as non-Jews.[3] It was taken for granted that the vanguard in both camps would consist of specially 'educated,' tolerant, cultured persons. It followed, of course, that the particularly tolerant, educated and cultured non-Jews could be bothered socially only with exceptionally educated Jews. As a matter of course, the demand, among the educated, for the abolition of prejudice was very quickly to become a rather one-sided affair, until only the Jews, finally, were urged to educate themselves.

This, however, is only one side of the matter. Jews were exhorted to

2 This surprisingly apt observation was made by the liberal Protestant theologian H. E. G. Paulus in a valuable little pamphlet, *Die jüdische Nationalabsonderung nach Ursprung, Folgen und Besserungsmitteln*, 1831. Paulus, much attacked by Jewish writers of the time, advocated a gradual individual emancipation on the basis of assimilation.

3 This attitude is expressed in Wilhelm v. Humboldt's 'Expert Opinion' of 1809: 'The state should not exactly teach respect for the Jews, but should abolish an inhuman and prejudiced way of thinking etc. . . .' In Ismar Freund, *Die Emancipation der Juden in Preussen*, Berlin, 1912, II, 270.

become educated enough not to behave like ordinary Jews, but they were, on the other hand, accepted only because they were Jews, because of their foreign, exotic appeal. In the eighteenth century, this had its source in the new humanism which expressly wanted 'new specimens of humanity' (Herder), intercourse with whom would serve as an example of possible intimacy with all types of mankind. To the enlightened Berlin of Mendelssohn's time, the Jews served as living proof that all men are human. For this generation, friendship with Mendelssohn or Markus Herz was an ever-renewed demonstration of the dignity of man. And because Jews were a despised and oppressed people, they were for it an even purer and more exemplary model of mankind. It was Herder, an outspoken friend of the Jews, who first used the later misused and misquoted phrase, 'strange people of Asia driven into our regions.' [4] With these words, he and his fellow-humanists greeted the 'new specimens of humanity' for whom the eighteenth century had 'searched the earth,' [5] only to find them in their age-old neighbors. Eager to stress the basic unity of mankind, they wanted to show the origins of the Jewish people as more alien, and hence more exotic, than they actually were, so that the demonstration of humanity as a universal principle might be more effective.

For a few decades at the turn of the eighteenth century, when French Jewry already enjoyed emancipation and German Jewry had almost no hope or desire for it, Prussia's enlightened intelligentsia made 'Jews all over the world turn their eyes to the Jewish community in Berlin' [6] (and not in Paris!). Much of this was due to the success of Lessing's *Nathan the Wise*, or to its misinterpretation, which held that the 'new specimens of humanity,' because they had become examples of mankind, must also be more intensely human individuals.[7] Mirabeau was strongly

4 J. G. Herder, 'Über die politische Bekehrung der Juden' in *Adrastea und das 18. Jahrhundert*, 1801–03.

5 Herder, *Briefe zur Beförderung der Humanität* (1793–97), 40. Brief.

6 Felix Priebatsch, 'Die Judenpolitik des fürstlichen Absolutismus im 17. und 18. Jahrhundert,' in *Forschungen und Versuche zur Geschichte des Mittelalters und der Neuzeit*, 1915, p. 646.

7 Lessing himself had no such illusions. His last letter to Moses Mendelssohn expressed most clearly what he wanted: 'the shortest and safest way to that European country without either Christians or Jews.' For Lessing's attitude toward Jews, see Franz Mehring, *Die Lessinglegende*, 1906.

influenced by this idea and used to cite Mendelssohn as his example.[8] Herder hoped that educated Jews would show a greater freedom from prejudice because 'the Jew is free of certain political judgments which it is very hard or impossible for us to abandon.' Protesting against the habit of the time of granting 'concessions of new mercantile advantages,' he proposed education as the true road to emancipation of Jews from Judaism, from 'the old and proud national prejudices . . . customs that do not belong to our age and constitutions,' so that Jews could become 'purely humanized,' and of service to 'the development of the sciences and the entire culture of mankind.'[9] At about the same time, Goethe wrote in a review of a book of poems that their author, a Polish Jew, did 'not achieve more than a Christian *étudiant en belles lettres*,' and complained that where he had expected something genuinely new, some force beyond shallow convention, he had found ordinary mediocrity.[10]

One can hardly overestimate the disastrous effect of this exaggerated good will on the newly Westernized, educated Jews and the impact it had on their social and psychological position. Not only were they faced with the demoralizing demand that they be exceptions to their own people, recognize 'the sharp difference between them and the others,' and ask that such 'separation . . . be also legalized' by the governments;[11] they were expected even to become exceptional specimens of humanity. And since this, and not Heine's conversion, constituted the true 'ticket of admission' into cultured European society, what else could these and future generations of Jews do but try desperately not to disappoint anybody?[12]

8 See Honoré Q. R. de Mirabeau, *Sur Moses Mendelssohn*, London, 1788.

9 J. G. Herder, 'Ueber die politische Bekehrung der Juden,' *op. cit.*

10 Johann Wolfgang v. Goethe's review of Isachar Falkensohn Behr, *Gedichte eines polnischen Juden*, Mietau and Leipzig, 1772, in *Frankfurter Gelehrte Anzeigen*.

11 Friedrich Schleiermacher, *Briefe bei Gelegenheit der politisch theologischen Aufgabe und des Sendschreibens jüdischer Hausväter*, 1799, in *Werke*, 1846, Abt. I, Band V, 34.

12 This does not, however, apply to Moses Mendelssohn, who hardly knew the thoughts of Herder, Goethe, Schleiermacher, and other members of the younger generation. Mendelssohn was revered for his uniqueness. His firm adherence to his Jewish religion made it impossible for him to break ultimately with the Jewish people, which his successors did as a matter of course. He felt he was 'a member of an oppressed people who must beg for the good will and protection of the governing nation' (see his 'Letter to Lavater,' 1770, in *Gesammelte Schriften*, Vol. VII, Berlin, 1930); that is, he always knew that the extraordinary esteem for his person paralleled an extraordinary

In the early decades of this entry into society, when assimilation had not yet become a tradition to follow, but something achieved by few and exceptionally gifted individuals, it worked very well indeed. While France was the land of political glory for the Jews, the first to recognize them as citizens, Prussia seemed on the way to becoming the country of social splendor. Enlightened Berlin, where Mendelssohn had established close connections with many famous men of his time, was only a beginning. His connections with non-Jewish society still had much in common with the scholarly ties that had bound Jewish and Christian learned men together in nearly all periods of European history. The new and surprising element was that Mendelssohn's friends used these relationships for nonpersonal, ideological, or even political purposes. He himself explicitly disavowed all such ulterior motives and expressed time and again his complete satisfaction with the conditions under which he had to live, as though he had foreseen that his exceptional social status and freedom had something to do with the fact that he still belonged to 'the lowliest inhabitants of the (Prussian king's) domain.'[13]

This indifference to political and civil rights survived Mendelssohn's innocent relationships with the learned and enlightened men of his time; it was carried later into the salons of those Jewish women who gathered together the most brilliant society Berlin was ever to see. Not until after the Prussian defeat of 1806, when the introduction of Napoleonic legislation into large regions of Germany put the

---

contempt for his people. Since he, unlike Jews of following generations, did not share this contempt, he did not consider himself an exception.

13 The Prussia which Lessing had described as 'Europe's most enslaved country' was to Mendelssohn 'a state in which one of the wisest princes who ever ruled men has made the arts and sciences flourish, has made national freedom of thought so general that its beneficent effects reach even the lowliest inhabitants of his domain.' Such humble contentment is touching and surprising if one realizes that the 'wisest prince' had made it very hard for the Jewish philosopher to get permission to sojourn in Berlin and, at a time when his *Münzjuden* enjoyed all privileges, did not even grant him the regular status of a 'protected Jew.' Mendelssohn was even aware that he, the friend of all educated Germany, would be subject to the same tax levied upon an ox led to the market if ever he decided to visit his friend Lavater in Leipzig, but no political conclusion regarding the improvement of such conditions ever occurred to him. (See the 'Letter to Lavater,' *op. cit.*, and his preface to his translation of Menasseh Ben Israel in *Gesammelte Schriften*, Vol. III, Leipzig, 1843–45.)

question of Jewish emancipation on the agenda of public discussion, did this indifference change into outright fear. Emancipation would liberate the educated Jews, together with the 'backward' Jewish people, and their equality would wipe out that precious distinction, upon which, as they were very well aware, their social status was based. When the emancipation finally came to pass, most assimilated Jews escaped into conversion to Christianity, characteristically finding it bearable and not dangerous to be Jews before emancipation, but not after.

Most representative of these salons, and the genuinely mixed society they brought together in Germany, was that of Rahel Varnhagen. Her original, unspoiled, and unconventional intelligence, combined with an absorbing interest in people and a truly passionate nature, made her the most brilliant and the most interesting of these Jewish women. The modest but famous soirées in Rahel's 'garret' brought together 'enlightened' aristocrats, middle-class intellectuals, and actors – that is, all those who, like the Jews, did not belong to respectable society. Thus Rahel's salon, by definition and intentionally, was established on the fringe of society, and did not share any of its conventions or prejudices.

It is amusing to note how closely the assimilation of Jews into society followed the precepts Goethe had proposed for the education of his *Wilhelm Meister*, a novel which was to become the great model of middle-class education. In this book the young burgher is educated by noblemen and actors, so that he may learn how to present and represent his individuality, and thereby advance from the modest status of a burgher's son into a nobleman. For the middle classes and for the Jews, that is, for those who were actually outside of high aristocratic society, everything depended upon 'personality' and the ability to express it. To know how to play the role of what one actually was, seemed the most important thing. The peculiar fact that in Germany the Jewish question was held to be a question of education was closely connected with this early start and had its consequence in the educational philistinism of both the Jewish and non-Jewish middle classes, and also in the crowding of Jews into the liberal professions.

The charm of the early Berlin salons was that nothing really mattered but personality and the uniqueness of character, talent, and expression. Such uniqueness, which alone made possible an almost unbounded communication and unrestricted intimacy, could be replaced neither by rank, money, success, nor literary fame. The brief encounter of true personalities, which joined a Hohenzollern prince, Louis Ferdinand, to the banker Abraham Mendelssohn; or a political publicist and diplomat, Friedrich Gentz, to Friedrich Schlegel, a writer of the then ultramodern romantic school – these were a few of the more famous visitors at Rahel's 'garret' – came to an end in 1806 when, according to their hostess, this unique meeting place 'foundered like a ship containing the highest enjoyment of life.' Along with the aristocrats, the romantic intellectuals became antisemitic, and although this by no means meant that either group gave up all its Jewish friends, the innocence and splendor were gone.

The real turning point in the social history of German Jews came not in the year of the Prussian defeat, but two years later, when, in 1808, the government passed the municipal law giving full civic, though not political, rights to the Jews. In the peace treaty of 1807, Prussia had lost with her eastern provinces the majority of her Jewish population; the Jews left within her territory were 'protected Jews' in any event, that is, they already enjoyed civic rights in the form of individual privileges. The municipal emancipation only legalized these privileges, and outlived the general emancipation decree of 1812; Prussia, having regained Posen and its Jewish masses after the defeat of Napoleon, practically rescinded the decree of 1812, which now would have meant political rights even for poor Jews, but left the municipal law intact.

Though of little political importance so far as the actual improvement of the Jews' status is concerned, these final emancipation decrees together with the loss of the provinces in which the majority of Prussian Jews lived, had tremendous social consequences. Before 1807, the protected Jews of Prussia had numbered only about 20 per cent of the total Jewish population. By the time the emancipation decree was issued, protected Jews formed the majority in Prussia, with only 10 per cent of 'foreign Jews' left for contrast. Now the dark poverty and backwardness against which 'exception Jews' of wealth and education had stood out so advantageously was no longer there. And this background, so essential as a basis of comparison for social success and psychological self-respect, never again became what it had been before Napoleon. When the Polish provinces were regained in 1816, the formerly 'protected Jews' (now registered as Prussian citizens of Jewish faith) still numbered above 60 per cent.[14]

Socially speaking, this meant that the remaining Jews in Prussia had lost the native background against which they had been measured as exceptions. Now they themselves composed such a background, but a contracted one, against which the individual had to strain doubly in order to stand out at all. 'Exception Jews' were once again simply Jews, not exceptions from but representatives of a despised people. Equally bad was the social influence of governmental interference. Not only the classes antagonistic to the government and therefore openly hostile to the Jews, but all strata of society, became more or less aware that Jews of their acquaintance were not so much individual exceptions as members of a group in whose favor the state was ready to take exceptional measures. And this was precisely what the 'exception Jews' had always feared.

Berlin society left the Jewish salons with unmatched rapidity, and by 1808 these meeting-places had already been supplanted by the houses of the titled bureaucracy and the upper middle class. One can see, from any of the numerous correspondences of the time, that the intellectuals as well as the aristocrats now began to direct their contempt for the Eastern European Jews, whom they hardly knew, against the educated Jews of Berlin, whom they knew very well. The latter would never again achieve the self-respect that springs from a collective consciousness of being exceptional; henceforth, each one of them had to prove that although he was a Jew, yet he was not a Jew. No longer would it suffice to distinguish oneself from a more or less unknown mass of 'backward brethren'; one had to stand out – as an individual who could be congratulated on being an exception – from 'the Jew,' and thus from the people as a whole.

Social discrimination, and not political antisemitism, discovered the phantom of 'the Jew.' The first author to make the distinction between the Jewish individual and 'the Jew in general, the Jew everywhere and nowhere' was an obscure publicist who had, in 1802,

---

14 See Heinrich Silbergleit, *Die Bevölkerungs- und Berufsverhältnisse der Juden im Deutschen Reich*, Vol. I, Berlin, 1930.

written a biting satire on Jewish society and its hunger for education, the magic wand for general social acceptance. Jews were depicted as a 'principle' of philistine and upstart society.[15] This rather vulgar piece of literature not only was read with delight by quite a few prominent members of Rahel's salon, but even indirectly inspired a great romantic poet, Clemens von Brentano, to write a very witty paper in which again the philistine was identified with the Jew.[16]

With the early idyll of a mixed society something disappeared which was never, in any other country and at any other time, to return. Never again did any social group accept Jews with a free mind and heart. It would be friendly with Jews either because it was excited by its own daring and 'wickedness' or as a protest against making pariahs of fellow-citizens. But social pariahs the Jews did become wherever they had ceased to be political and civil outcasts.

It is important to bear in mind that assimilation as a group phenomenon really existed only among Jewish intellectuals. It is no accident that the first educated Jew, Moses Mendelssohn, was also the first who, despite his low civic status, was admitted to non-Jewish society. The court Jews and their successors, the Jewish bankers and businessmen in the West, were never socially acceptable, nor did they care to leave the very narrow limits of their invisible ghetto. In the beginning they were proud, like all unspoiled upstarts, of the dark background of misery and poverty from which they had risen; later, when they were attacked from all sides, they had a vested interest in the poverty and even backwardness of the masses because it became an argument, a token of their own security. Slowly, and with misgivings, they were forced away from the more rigorous demands of Jewish law – they never left religious traditions altogether – yet demanded all the more

15 C. W. F. Grattenauer's widely read pamphlet *Wider die Juden* of 1802 had been preceded as far back as 1791 by another, *Ueber die physische und moralische Verfassung der heutigen Juden* in which the growing influence of the Jews in Berlin was already pointed out. Although the early pamphlet was reviewed in the *Allgemeine Deutsche Bibliothek*, 1792, Vol. CXII, almost nobody ever read it.

16 Clemens Brentano's *Der Philister vor, in und nach der Geschichte* was written for and read to the so-called *Christlich-Deutsche Tischgesellschaft*, a famous club of writers and patriots, founded in 1808 for the struggle against Napoleon.

orthodoxy from the Jewish masses.[17] The dissolution of Jewish communal autonomy made them that much more eager not only to protect Jewish communities against the authorities, but also to rule over them with the help of the state, so that the phrase denoting the 'double dependence' of poor Jews on 'both the government and their wealthy brethren' only reflected reality.[18]

The Jewish notables (as they were called in the nineteenth century) ruled the Jewish communities, but they did not belong to them socially or even geographically. They stood, in a sense, as far outside Jewish society as they did outside Gentile society. Having made brilliant individual careers and been granted considerable privileges by their masters, they formed a kind of community of exceptions with extremely limited social opportunities. Naturally despised by court society, lacking business connections with the non-Jewish middle class, their social contacts were as much outside the laws of society as their economic rise had been independent of contemporary economic conditions. This isolation and independence frequently gave them a feeling of power and pride, illustrated by the following anecdote told in the beginning eighteenth century: 'A certain Jew . . . when gently reproached by a noble and cultured physician with (the Jewish) pride although they had no princes among them and no part in

17 Thus the Rothschilds in the 1820's withdrew a large donation from their native community of Frankfurt, in order to counteract the influence of reformers who wanted Jewish children to receive a general education. See Isaak Markus Jost, *Neuere Geschichte der Israeliten*, 1846, X, 102.

18 *Op. cit.*, IX, 38. – The court Jews and the rich Jewish bankers who followed in their footsteps never wanted to leave the Jewish community. They acted as its representatives and protectors against public authorities; they were frequently granted official power over communities which they ruled from afar so that the old autonomy of Jewish communities was undermined and destroyed from within long before it was abolished by the nation-state. The first court Jew with monarchical aspirations in his own 'nation' was a Jew of Prague, a purveyor of supplies to the Elector Maurice of Saxony in the sixteenth century. He demanded that all rabbis and community heads be selected from members of his family. (See Bondy-Dworsky, *Geschichte der Juden in Boehmen, Maehren und Schlesien*, Prague, 1906, II, 727.) The practice of installing court Jews as dictators in their communities became general in the eighteenth century and was followed by the rule of 'notables' in the nineteenth century.

government . . . replied with insolence: We are not princes, but we govern them.'[19]

Such pride is almost the opposite of class arrogance, which developed but slowly among the privileged Jews. Ruling as absolute princes among their own people, they still felt themselves to be *primi inter pares*. They were prouder of being a 'privileged Rabbi of all Jewry' or a 'Prince of the Holy Land' than of any titles their masters might offer them.[20] Until the middle of the eighteenth century, they would all have agreed with the Dutch Jew who said: '*Neque in toto orbi alicui natione inservimus*,' and neither then nor later would they have understood fully the answer of the 'learned Christian' who replied: 'But this means happiness only for a few. The people considered as a *corpo (sic)* is hunted everywhere, has no self-government, is subject to foreign rule, has no power and no dignity, and wanders all over the world, a stranger everywhere.'[21]

Class arrogance came only when business connections were established among state bankers of different countries; intermarriage between leading families soon followed, and culminated in a real international caste system, unknown thus far in Jewish society. This was all the more glaring to non-Jewish observers, since it took place when the old feudal estates and castes were rapidly disappearing into new classes. One concluded, very wrongly, that the Jewish people were a remnant of the Middle Ages and did not see that this new caste was of quite recent birth. It was completed only in the nineteenth century and comprised numerically no more than perhaps a hundred families. But since these were in the limelight, the Jewish people as a whole came to be regarded as a caste.[22]

Great, therefore, as the role of the court Jews had been in political history and for the birth of antisemitism, social history might easily neglect them were it not for the fact that they had certain

19 Johann Jacob Schudt, *Jüdische Merkwürdigkeiten*, Frankfurt a.M., 1715–1717, IV, Annex, 48.

20 Selma Stern, *Jud Suess*, Berlin, 1929, pp. 18 f.

21 Schudt, *op. cit.*, I, 19.

22 Christian Friedrich Ruehs defines the whole Jewish people as a 'caste of merchants.' 'Ueber die Ansprüche der Juden an das deutsche Bürgerrecht,' in *Zeitschrift für die neueste Geschichte*, 1815.

psychological traits and behavior patterns in common with Jewish intellectuals who were, after all, usually the sons of businessmen. The Jewish notables wanted to dominate the Jewish people and therefore had no desire to leave it, while it was characteristic of Jewish intellectuals that they wanted to leave their people and be admitted to society; they both shared the feeling that they were exceptions, a feeling perfectly in harmony with the judgment of their environment. The 'exception Jews' of wealth felt like exceptions from the common destiny of the Jewish people and were recognized by the governments as exceptionally useful; the 'exception Jews' of education felt themselves exceptions from the Jewish people and also exceptional human beings, and were recognized as such by society.

Assimilation, whether carried to the extreme of conversion or not, never was a real menace to the survival of the Jews.[23] Whether they were welcomed or rejected, it was because they were Jews, and they were well aware of it. The first generations of educated Jews still wanted sincerely to lose their identity as Jews, and Boerne wrote with a great deal of bitterness, 'Some reproach me with being a Jew, some praise me because of it, some pardon me for it, but all think of it.'[24] Still brought up on eighteenth-century ideas, they longed for a country without either Christians or Jews; they had devoted themselves to science and the arts, and were greatly hurt when they found out that governments which would give every privilege and honor to a Jewish banker, condemned Jewish intellectuals to starvation.[25] The conversions which, in the early nineteenth century, had been prompted by fear of being lumped together with the Jewish masses, now became a necessity for daily bread. Such a premium on lack of character forced a whole generation of Jews into bitter opposition against state and

23 A remarkable, though little-known, fact is that assimilation as a program led much more frequently to conversion than to mixed marriage. Unfortunately statistics cover up rather than reveal this fact because they consider all unions between converted and nonconverted Jewish partners to be mixed marriages. We know, however, that there were quite a number of families in Germany who had been baptized for generations and yet remained purely Jewish. That the converted Jew only rarely left his family and even more rarely left his Jewish surroundings altogether, accounts for this. The Jewish family, at any rate, proved to be a more conserving force than Jewish religion.
24 *Briefe aus Paris*, 74th Letter, February, 1832.
25 *Ibid.*, 72nd Letter.

society. The 'new specimens of humanity,' if they were worth their salt, all became rebels, and since the most reactionary governments of the period were supported and financed by Jewish bankers, their rebellion was especially violent against the official representatives of their own people. The anti-Jewish denunciations of Marx and Boerne cannot be properly understood except in the light of this conflict between rich Jews and Jewish intellectuals.

This conflict, however, existed in full vigor only in Germany and did not survive the antisemitic movement of the century. In Austria, there was no Jewish intelligentsia to speak of before the end of the nineteenth century, when it felt immediately the whole impact of antisemitic pressure. These Jews, like their wealthy brethren, preferred to trust themselves to the Hapsburg monarchy's protection, and became socialist only after the first World War, when the Social Democratic party came to power. The most significant, though not the only, exception to this rule was Karl Kraus, the last representative of the tradition of Heine, Boerne, and Marx. Kraus's denunciations of Jewish businessmen on one hand, and Jewish journalism as the organized cult of fame on the other, were perhaps even more bitter than those of his predecessors because he was so much more isolated in a country where no Jewish revolutionary tradition existed. In France, where the emancipation decree had survived all changes of governments and regimes, the small number of Jewish intellectuals were neither the forerunners of a new class nor especially important in intellectual life. Culture as such, education as a program, did not form Jewish behavior patterns as it did in Germany.

In no other country had there been anything like the short period of true assimilation so decisive for the history of German Jews, when the real vanguard of a people not only accepted Jews, but was even strangely eager to associate with them. Nor did this attitude ever completely disappear from German society. To the very end, traces of it could easily be discerned, which showed, of course, that relations with Jews never came to be taken for granted. At best it remained a program, at worst a strange and exciting experience. Bismarck's well-known remark about 'German stallions to be paired off with Jewish mares,' is but the most vulgar expression of a prevalent point of view.

It is only natural that this social situation, though it made rebels out of the first educated Jews, would in the long run produce a specific kind of conformism rather than an effective tradition of rebellion.[26] Conforming to a society which discriminated against 'ordinary' Jews and in which, at the same time, it was generally easier for an educated Jew to be admitted to fashionable circles than for a non-Jew of similar condition, Jews had to differentiate themselves clearly from the 'Jew in general,' and just as clearly to indicate that they were Jews; under no circumstances were they allowed simply to disappear among their neighbors. In order to rationalize an ambiguity which they themselves did not fully understand, they might pretend to 'be a man in the street and a Jew at home.'[27] This actually amounted to a feeling of being different from other men in the street because they were Jews, and different from other Jews at home because they were not like 'ordinary Jews.'

The behavior patterns of assimilated Jews, determined by this continuous concentrated effort to distinguish themselves, created a Jewish type that is recognizable everywhere. Instead of being defined by nationality or religion, Jews were being transformed into a social group whose members shared certain psychological attributes and reactions, the sum total of which was supposed to constitute 'Jewishness.' In other words, Judaism became a psychological quality and the Jewish question became an involved personal problem for every individual Jew.

In his tragic endeavor to conform through differentiation and distinction, the new Jewish type had as little in common with the feared 'Jew in general' as with that abstraction, the 'heir of the prophets and eternal promoter of justice on earth,' which Jewish apologetics conjured up whenever a Jewish journalist was being attacked. The Jew of the apologists was endowed with attributes that are indeed the privileges of pariahs, and which certain Jewish rebels living on the fringe of society did possess – humanity, kindness, freedom from prejudice,

26 The 'conscious pariah' (Bernard Lazare) was the only tradition of rebellion which established itself, although those who belonged to it were hardly aware of its existence. See the author's 'The Jew as Pariah. A Hidden Tradition,' in *Jewish Social Studies*, Vol. VI, No. 2 (1944).

27 It is not without irony that this excellent formula, which may serve as a motto for Western European assimilation, was propounded by a Russian Jew and first published in Hebrew. It comes from Judah Leib Gordon's Hebrew poem, *Hakitzah ami*, 1863. See S. M. Dubnow, *History of the Jews in Russia and Poland*, 1918, II, 228 f.

sensitiveness to injustice. The trouble was that these qualities had nothing to do with the prophets and that, worse still, these Jews usually belonged neither to Jewish society nor to fashionable circles of non-Jewish society. In the history of assimilated Jewry, they played but an insignificant role. The 'Jew in general,' on the other hand, as described by professional Jew-haters, showed those qualities which the parvenu must acquire if he wants to arrive – inhumanity, greed, insolence, cringing servility, and determination to push ahead. The trouble in this case was that these qualities have also nothing to do with national attributes and that, moreover, these Jewish business-class types showed little inclination for non-Jewish society and played almost as small a part in Jewish social history. As long as defamed peoples and classes exist, parvenu- and pariah-qualities will be produced anew by each generation with incomparable monotony, in Jewish society and everywhere else.

For the formation of a social history of the Jews within nineteenth-century European society, it was, however, decisive that to a certain extent every Jew in every generation had somehow at some time to decide whether he would remain a pariah and stay out of society altogether, or become a parvenu, or conform to society on the demoralizing condition that he not so much hide his origin as 'betray with the secret of his origin the secret of his people as well.' [28] The latter road was difficult, indeed, as such secrets did not exist and had to be made up. Since Rahel Varnhagen's unique attempt to establish a social life outside of official society had failed, the way of the pariah and the parvenu were equally ways of extreme solitude, and the way of conformism one of constant regret. The so-called complex psychology of the average Jew, which in a few favored cases developed into a very modern sensitiveness, was based on an ambiguous situation. Jews felt simultaneously the pariah's regret at not having become a parvenu and the parvenu's bad conscience at having betrayed his people and exchanged equal rights for personal privileges. One thing was certain: if one wanted to avoid all ambiguities of social existence, one had to resign oneself to the fact that to be a Jew meant to belong either to an

---

28  This formulation was made by Karl Kraus around 1912. See *Untergang der Welt durch schwarze Magie*, 1925.

overprivileged upper class or to an underprivileged mass which, in Western and Central Europe, one could belong to only through an intellectual and somewhat artificial solidarity.

The social destinies of average Jews were determined by their eternal lack of decision. And society certainly did not compel them to make up their minds, for it was precisely this ambiguity of situation and character that made the relationship with Jews attractive. The majority of assimilated Jews thus lived in a twilight of favor and misfortune and knew with certainty only that both success and failure were inextricably connected with the fact that they were Jews. For them the Jewish question had lost, once and for all, all political significance; but it haunted their private lives and influenced their personal decisions all the more tyrannically. The adage, 'a man in the street and a Jew at home,' was bitterly realized: political problems were distorted to the point of pure perversion when Jews tried to solve them by means of inner experience and private emotions; private life was poisoned to the point of inhumanity – for example in the question of mixed marriages – when the heavy burden of unsolved problems of public significance was crammed into that private existence which is much better ruled by the unpredictable laws of passion than by considered policies.

It was by no means easy not to resemble the 'Jew in general' and yet remain a Jew; to pretend not to be like Jews and still show with sufficient clarity that one was Jewish. The average Jew, neither a parvenu nor a 'conscious pariah' (Bernard Lazare), could only stress an empty sense of difference which continued to be interpreted, in all its possible psychological aspects and variations from innate strangeness to social alienation. As long as the world was somewhat peaceful, this attitude did not work out badly and for generations even became a *modus vivendi*. Concentration on an artificially complicated inner life helped Jews to respond to the unreasonable demands of society, to be strange and exciting, to develop a certain immediacy of self-expression and presentation which were originally the attributes of the actor and the virtuoso, people whom society has always half denied and half admired. Assimilated Jews, half proud and half ashamed of their Jewishness, clearly were in this category.

The process by which bourgeois society developed out of the ruins of its revolutionary traditions and memories added the black ghost of boredom to economic saturation and general indifference to political questions. Jews became people with whom one hoped to while away some time. The less one thought of them as equals, the more attractive and entertaining they became. Bourgeois society, in its search for entertainment and its passionate interest in the individual, insofar as he differed from the norm that is man, discovered the attraction of everything that could be supposed to be mysteriously wicked or secretly vicious. And precisely this feverish preference opened the doors of society to Jews; for within the framework of this society, Jewishness, after having been distorted into a psychological quality, could easily be perverted into a vice. The Enlightenment's genuine tolerance and curiosity for everything human was being replaced by a morbid lust for the exotic, abnormal, and different as such. Several types in society, one after the other, represented the exotic, the anomalous, the different, but none of them was in the least connected with political questions. Thus only the role of Jews in this decaying society could assume a stature that transcended the narrow limits of a society affair.

Before we follow the strange ways which led the 'exception Jews,' famous and notorious strangers, into the salons of the Faubourg St. Germain in *fin-de-siècle* France, we must recall the only great man whom the elaborate self-deception of the 'exception Jews' ever produced. It seems that every commonplace idea gets one chance in at least one individual to attain what used to be called historical greatness. The great man of the 'exception Jews' was Benjamin Disraeli.

## II: The Potent Wizard[29]

Benjamin Disraeli, whose chief interest in life was the career of Lord Beaconsfield, was distinguished by two things: first, the gift of the gods which we moderns banally call luck, and which other periods revered as a goddess named Fortune, and second, more intimately and more wondrously connected with Fortune than one may be able to

29 The title phrase is taken from a sketch of Disraeli by Sir John Skelton in 1867. See W. F. Monypenny and G. E. Buckle, *The Life of Benjamin Disraeli, Earl of Beaconsfield*, New York, 1929, II, 292–93.

explain, the great carefree innocence of mind and imagination which makes it impossible to classify the man as a careerist, though he never thought seriously of anything except his career. His innocence made him recognize how foolish it would be to feel *déclassé* and how much more exciting it would be for himself and for others, how much more useful for his career, to accentuate the fact that he was a Jew 'by dressing differently, combing his hair oddly, and by queer manners of expression and verbiage.'[30] He cared for admission to high and highest society more passionately and shamelessly than any other Jewish intellectual did; but he was the only one of them who discovered the secret of how to preserve luck, that natural miracle of pariahdom, and who knew from the beginning that one never should bow down in order to 'move up from high to higher.'

He played the game of politics like an actor in a theatrical performance, except that he played his part so well that he was convinced by his own make-believe. His life and his career read like a fairy-tale, in which he appeared as the prince – offering the blue flower of the romantics, now the primrose of imperialist England, to his princess, the Queen of England. The British colonial enterprise was the fairyland upon which the sun never sets and its capital the mysterious Asiatic Delhi whence the prince wanted to escape with his princess from foggy prosaic London. This may have been foolish and childish; but when a wife writes to her husband as Lady Beaconsfield wrote to hers: 'You know you married me for money, and I know that if you had to do it again you would do it for love,'[31] one is silenced before a happiness that seemed to be against all the rules. Here was one who started out to sell his soul to the devil, but the devil did not want the soul and the gods gave him all the happiness of this earth.

Disraeli came from an entirely assimilated family; his father, an enlightened gentleman, baptized the son because he wanted him to have the opportunities of ordinary mortals. He had few connections with Jewish society and knew nothing of Jewish religion or customs. Jewishness, from the beginning, was a fact of origin which he was at liberty to embellish, unhindered by actual knowledge. The

---

30 Morris S. Lazaron, *Seed of Abraham*, New York, 1930, 'Benjamin Disraeli,' pp. 260 ff.
31 Horace B. Samuel, 'The Psychology of Disraeli,' in *Modernities*, London, 1914.

result was that somehow he looked at this fact much in the same way as a Gentile would have looked at it. He realized much more clearly than other Jews that being a Jew could be as much an opportunity as a handicap. And since, unlike his simple and modest father, he wanted nothing less than to become an ordinary mortal and nothing more than 'to distinguish himself above all his contemporaries,' [32] he began to shape his 'olive complexion and coal-black eyes' until he with 'the mighty dome of his forehead – no Christian temple, to be sure – (was) unlike any living creature one has met.' [33] He knew instinctively that everything depended upon the 'division between him and mere mortals,' upon an accentuation of his lucky 'strangeness.'

All this demonstrates a unique understanding of society and its rules. Significantly, it was Disraeli who said, 'What is a crime among the multitude is only a vice among the few' [34] – perhaps the most profound insight into the very principle by which the slow and insidious decline of nineteenth-century society into the depth of mob and underworld morality took place. Since he knew this rule, he knew also that Jews would have no better chances anywhere than in circles which pretended to be exclusive and to discriminate against them; for inasmuch as these circles of the few, together with the multitude, thought of Jewishness as a crime, this 'crime' could be transformed at any moment into an attractive 'vice.' Disraeli's display of exoticism, strangeness, mysteriousness, magic, and power drawn from secret sources, was aimed correctly at this disposition in society. And it was his virtuosity at the social game which made him choose the Conservative Party, won him a seat in Parliament, the post of Prime Minister, and, last but not least, the lasting admiration of society and the friendship of a Queen.

One of the reasons for his success was the sincerity of his play. The impression he made on his more unbiased contemporaries was a

---

32 J. A. Froude thus closes his biography of *Lord Beaconsfield*, 1890: 'The aim with which he started in life was to distinguish himself above all his contemporaries, and wild as such an ambition must have appeared, he at last won the stake for which he played so bravely.'

33 Sir John Skelton, *op. cit.*

34 In his novel *Tancred*, 1847.

curious mixture of acting and 'absolute sincerity and unreserve.' [35] This could only be achieved by a genuine innocence that was partly due to an upbringing from which all specific Jewish influence had been excluded.[36] But Disraeli's good conscience was also due to his having been born an Englishman. England did not know Jewish masses and Jewish poverty, as she had admitted them centuries after their expulsion in the Middle Ages; the Portuguese Jews who settled in England in the eighteenth century were wealthy and educated. Not until the end of the nineteenth century, when the pogroms in Russia initiated the modern Jewish emigrations, did Jewish poverty enter London, and along with it the difference between the Jewish masses and their well-to-do brethren. In Disraeli's time the Jewish question, in its Continental form, was quite unknown, because only Jews welcome to the state lived in England. In other words, the English 'exception Jews' were not so aware of being exceptions as their Continental brothers were. When Disraeli scorned the 'pernicious doctrine of modern times, the natural equality of men,' [37] he consciously followed in the footsteps of Burke who had 'preferred the rights of an Englishman to the Rights of Man,' but ignored the actual situation in which privileges for the few had been substituted for rights for all. He was so ignorant of the real conditions among the Jewish people, and so convinced of 'the influence of the Jewish race upon modern communities,' that he frankly demanded that the Jews 'receive all that honour and favour from the northern and western races, which, in civilized and refined nations, should be the lot of those who charm the public taste and elevate the public feeling.' [38] Since political influence of Jews in England centered around the English branch of the Rothschilds, he felt very proud about the Rothschilds' help in defeating Napoleon and did not see any reason why he should not be outspoken in his political opinions as a Jew.[39] As a baptized Jew, he was of course never an official

35 Sir John Skelton, *op. cit.*

36 Disraeli himself reported: 'I was not bred among my race and was nourished in great prejudice against them.' For his family background, see especially Joseph Caro, 'Benjamin Disraeli, Juden und Judentum,' in *Monatsschrift für Geschichte und Wissenschaft des Judentums*, 1932, Jahrgang 76.

37 *Lord George Bentinck. A Political Biography*, London, 1852, 496.

38 *Ibid.*, p. 491.

39 *Ibid.*, pp. 497 ff.

spokesman for any Jewish community, but it remains true that he was the only Jew of his kind and his century who tried as well as he knew to represent the Jewish people politically.

Disraeli, who never denied that 'the fundamental fact about (him) was that he was a Jew,' [40] had an admiration for all things Jewish that was matched only by his ignorance of them. The mixture of pride and ignorance in these matters, however, was characteristic of all the newly assimilated Jews. The great difference is that Disraeli knew even a little less of Jewish past and present and therefore dared to speak out openly what others betrayed in the half-conscious twilight of behavior patterns dictated by fear and arrogance.

The political result of Disraeli's ability to gauge Jewish possibilities by the political aspirations of a normal people was more serious; he almost automatically produced the entire set of theories about Jewish influence and organization that we usually find in the more vicious forms of antisemitism. First of all, he actually thought of himself as the 'chosen man of the chosen race.' [41] What better proof was there than his own career: a Jew without name and riches, helped only by a few Jewish bankers, was carried to the position of the first man in England; one of the less liked men of Parliament became Prime Minister and earned genuine popularity among those who for a long time had 'regarded him as a charlatan and treated him as a pariah.' [42] Political success never satisfied him. It was more difficult and more important to be admitted to London's society than to conquer the House of Commons, and it was certainly a greater triumph to be elected a member of Grillion's dining club – 'a select coterie of which it has been customary to make rising politicians of both parties, but from which the socially objectionable are rigorously excluded' [43] – than to be Her Majesty's Minister. The delightfully unexpected climax of all these sweet triumphs was the sincere friendship of the Queen, for if the monarchy in England had lost most of its political prerogatives in a strictly controlled, constitutional nation-state, it had won and retained undisputed primacy in English society. In measuring the

40 Monypenny and Buckle, *op. cit.*, p. 1507.
41 Horace S. Samuel, *op. cit.*
42 Monypenny and Buckle, *op. cit.*, p. 147.
43 *Ibid.*

greatness of Disraeli's triumph, one should remember that Lord Robert Cecil, one of his eminent colleagues in the Conservative Party, could still, around 1850, justify a particularly bitter attack by stating that he was only 'plainly speaking out what every one is saying of Disraeli in private and no one will say in public.' [44] Disraeli's greatest victory was that finally nobody said in private what would not have flattered and pleased him if it had been said in public. It was precisely this unique rise to genuine popularity which Disraeli had achieved through a policy of seeing only the advantages, and preaching only the privileges, of being born a Jew.

Part of Disraeli's good fortune is the fact that he always fitted his time, and that consequently his numerous biographers understood him more completely than is the case with most great men. He was a living embodiment of ambition, that powerful passion which had developed in a century seemingly not allowing for any distinctions and differences. Carlyle, at any rate, who interpreted the whole world's history according to a nineteenth-century ideal of the hero, was clearly in the wrong when he refused a title from Disraeli's hands. [45] No other man among his contemporaries corresponded to Carlyle's heroes as well as Disraeli, with his concept of greatness as such, emptied of all specific achievements; no other man fulfilled so exactly the demands of the late nineteenth century for genius in the flesh as this charlatan who took his role seriously and acted the great part of the Great Man with genuine naïveté and an overwhelming display of fantastic tricks and entertaining artistry. Politicians fell in love with the charlatan who transformed boring business transactions into dreams with an oriental flavor; and when society sensed an aroma of black magic in Disraeli's shrewd dealings, the 'potent wizard' had actually won the heart of his time.

Disraeli's ambition to distinguish himself from other mortals and his longing for aristocratic society were typical of the middle classes of his time and country. Neither political reasons nor economic motives, but

44 Robert Cecil's article appeared in the most authoritative organ of the Tories, the *Quarterly Review*. See Monypenny and Buckle, *op. cit.*, pp. 19–22.
45 This happened as late as 1874. Carlyle is reported to have called Disraeli 'a cursed Jew,' 'the worst man who ever lived.' See Caro, *op. cit.*

the impetus of his social ambition, made him join the Conservative Party and follow a policy that would always 'select the Whigs for hostility and the Radicals for alliance.' [46] In no European country did the middle classes ever achieve enough self-respect to reconcile their intelligentsia with their social status, so that aristocracy could continue to determine the social scale when it had already lost all political significance. The unhappy German philistine discovered his 'innate personality' in his desperate struggle against caste arrogance, which had grown out of the decline of nobility and the necessity to protect aristocratic titles against bourgeois money. Vague blood theories and strict control of marriages are rather recent phenomena in the history of European aristocracy. Disraeli knew much better than the German philistines what was required to meet the demands of aristocracy. All attempts of the bourgeoisie to attain social status failed to convince aristocratic arrogance because they reckoned with individuals and lacked the most important element of caste conceit, the pride in privilege without individual effort and merit, simply by virtue of birth. The 'innate personality' could never deny that its development demanded education and special effort of the individual. When Disraeli 'summoned up a pride of race to confront a pride of caste,' [47] he knew that the social status of the Jews, whatever else might be said of it, at least depended solely on the fact of birth and not on achievement.

Disraeli went even a step further. He knew that the aristocracy, which year after year had to see quite a number of rich middle-class men buy titles, was haunted by very serious doubts of its own value. He therefore defeated them at their game by using his rather trite and popular imagination to describe fearlessly how the Englishmen 'came from a parvenu and hybrid race, while he himself was sprung from the purest blood in Europe,' how 'the life of a British peer (was) mainly regulated by Arabian laws and Syrian customs,' how 'a Jewess is the queen of heaven' or that 'the flower of the Jewish race is even now sitting on the right hand of the Lord God of Sabaoth.' [48] And when he finally wrote that 'there is no longer in fact an aristocracy in England, for the superiority of the animal man is an essential quality of

46 Lord Salisbury in an article in the *Quarterly Review*, 1869.

47 E. T. Raymond, *Disraeli, The Alien Patriot*, London, 1925, p. 1.

48 H. B. Samuel, *op. cit.*, Disraeli, *Tancred*, and *Lord George Bentinck*, respectively.

aristocracy,'[49] he had in fact touched the weakest point of modern aristocratic race theories, which were later to be the point of departure for bourgeois and upstart race opinions.

Judaism, and belonging to the Jewish people, degenerated into a simple fact of birth only among assimilated Jewry. Originally it had meant a specific religion, a specific nationality, the sharing of specific memories and specific hopes, and, even among the privileged Jews, it meant at least still sharing specific economic advantages. Secularization and assimilation of the Jewish intelligentsia had changed self-consciousness and self-interpretation in such a way that nothing was left of the old memories and hopes but the awareness of belonging to a chosen people. Disraeli, though certainly not the only 'exception Jew' to believe in his own chosenness without believing in Him who chooses and rejects, was the only one who produced a full-blown race doctrine out of this empty concept of a historic mission. He was ready to assert that the Semitic principle 'represents all that is spiritual in our nature,' that 'the vicissitudes of history find their main solution – all is race,' which is 'the key to history' regardless of 'language and religion,' for 'there is only one thing which makes a race and that is blood' and there is only one aristocracy, the 'aristocracy of nature' which consists of 'an unmixed race of a first-rate organization.'[50]

The close relationship of this to more modern race ideologies need not be stressed, and Disraeli's discovery is one more proof of how well they serve to combat feelings of social inferiority. For if race doctrines finally served much more sinister and immediately political purposes, it is still true that much of their plausibility and persuasiveness lay in the fact that they helped anybody feel himself an aristocrat who had been selected by birth on the strength of 'racial' qualification. That these new selected ones did not belong to an elite, to a selected few – which, after all, had been inherent in the pride of a nobleman – but had to share chosenness with an ever-growing mob, did no essential harm to the doctrine, for those who did not belong to the chosen race grew numerically in the same proportion.

Disraeli's race doctrines, however, were as much the result of his

49  In his novel *Coningsby*, 1844.
50  See *Lord George Bentinck* and the novels *Endymion*, 1881, and *Coningsby*.

extraordinary insight into the rules of society as the outgrowth of the specific secularization of assimilated Jewry. Not only was the Jewish intelligentsia caught up in the general secularization process, which in the nineteenth century had already lost the revolutionary appeal of the Enlightenment along with the confidence in an independent, self-reliant humanity and therefore remained without any protection against transformation of formerly genuine religious beliefs into superstitions. The Jewish intelligentsia was exposed also to the influences of the Jewish reformers who wanted to change a national religion into a religious denomination. To do so, they had to transform the two basic elements of Jewish piety – the Messianic hope and the faith in Israel's chosenness, and they deleted from Jewish prayer-books the visions of an ultimate restoration of Zion, along with the pious anticipation of the day at the end of days when the segregation of the Jewish people from the nations of the earth would come to an end. Without the Messianic hope, the idea of chosenness meant eternal segregation; without faith in chosenness, which charged one specific people with the redemption of the world, Messianic hope evaporated into the dim cloud of general philanthropy and universalism which became so characteristic of specifically Jewish political enthusiasm.

The most fateful element in Jewish secularization was that the concept of chosenness was being separated from the Messianic hope, whereas in Jewish religion these two elements were two aspects of God's redemptory plan for mankind. Out of Messianic hope grew that inclination toward final solutions of political problems which aimed at nothing less than establishing a paradise on earth. Out of the belief in chosenness by God grew that fantastic delusion, shared by unbelieving Jews and non-Jews alike, that Jews are by nature more intelligent, better, healthier, more fit for survival – the motor of history and the salt of the earth. The enthusiastic Jewish intellectual dreaming of the paradise on earth, so certain of freedom from all national ties and prejudices, was in fact farther removed from political reality than his fathers, who had prayed for the coming of Messiah and the return of the people to Palestine. The assimilationists, on the other hand, who without any enthusiastic hope had persuaded themselves that they were the salt of the earth, were more effectively separated from the nations by this unholy conceit than their fathers had been by the fence of the Law, which, as it was faithfully believed, separated Israel from the Gentiles but would be destroyed in the days of the Messiah. It was this conceit of the 'exception Jews,' who were too 'enlightened' to believe in God and, on the grounds of their exceptional position everywhere, superstitious enough to believe in themselves, that actually tore down the strong bonds of pious hope which had tied Israel to the rest of mankind.

Secularization, therefore, finally produced that paradox, so decisive for the psychology of modern Jews, by which Jewish assimilation – in its liquidation of national consciousness, its transformation of a national religion into a confessional denomination, and its meeting of the half-hearted and ambiguous demands of state and society by equally ambiguous devices and psychological tricks – engendered a very real Jewish chauvinism, if by chauvinism we understand the perverted nationalism in which (in the words of Chesterton) 'the individual is himself the thing to be worshipped; the individual is his own ideal and even his own idol.' From now on, the old religious concept of chosenness was no longer the essence of Judaism; it became instead the essence of Jewishness.

This paradox has found its most powerful and charming embodiment in Disraeli. He was an English imperialist and a Jewish chauvinist; but it is not difficult to pardon a chauvinism which was rather a play of imagination because, after all, 'England was the Israel of his imagination';[51] and it is not difficult, either, to pardon his English imperialism, which had so little in common with the single-minded resoluteness of expansion for expansion's sake, since he was, after all, 'never a thorough Englishman and was proud of the fact.'[52] All those curious contradictions which indicate so clearly that the potent wizard never took himself quite seriously and always played a role to win society and to find popularity, add up to a unique charm, they introduce into all his utterances an element of charlatan enthusiasm and day-dreaming which makes him utterly different from his imperialist followers. He was lucky enough to do his dreaming and acting in a time when Manchester and the businessmen had not yet taken over

51  Sir John Skelton, *op. cit.*
52  Horace B. Samuel, *op. cit.*

the imperial dream and were even in sharp and furious opposition to 'colonial adventures.' His superstitious belief in blood and race – into which he mixed old romantic folk credulities about a powerful supra-national connection between gold and blood – carried no suspicion of possible massacres, whether in Africa, Asia, or Europe proper. He began as a not too gifted writer and remained an intellectual whom chance made a member of Parliament, leader of his party, Prime Minister, and a friend of the Queen of England.

Disraeli's notion of the Jews' role in politics dates back to the time when he was still simply a writer and had not yet begun his political career. His ideas on the subject were therefore not the result of actual experience, but he clung to them with remarkable tenacity throughout his later life.

In his first novel, *Alroy* (1833), Disraeli evolved a plan for a Jewish Empire in which Jews would rule as a strictly separated class. The novel shows the influence of current illusions about Jewish power-possibilities as well as the young author's ignorance of the actual power conditions of his time. Eleven years later, political experience in Parliament and intimate intercourse with prominent men taught Disraeli that 'the aims of the Jews, whatever they may have been before and since, were, in his day, largely divorced from the assertion of political nationality in any form.' [53] In a new novel, *Coningsby*, he abandoned the dream of a Jewish Empire and unfolded a fantastic scheme according to which Jewish money dominates the rise and fall of courts and empires and rules supreme in diplomacy. Never in his life did he give up this second notion of a secret and mysterious influence of the chosen men of the chosen race, with which he replaced his earlier dream of an openly constituted, mysterious ruler caste. It became the pivot of his political philosophy. In contrast to his much-admired Jewish bankers who granted loans to governments and earned commissions, Disraeli looked at the whole affair with the outsider's incomprehension that such power-possibilities could be handled day after day by people who were not ambitious for power. What he could not understand was that a Jewish banker was even less interested in politics than his non-Jewish

53 Monypenny and Buckle, *op. cit.*, p. 882.

colleagues; to Disraeli, at any rate, it was a matter of course that Jewish wealth was only a means for Jewish politics. The more he learned about the Jewish bankers' well-functioning organization in business matters and their international exchange of news and information, the more convinced he became that he was dealing with something like a secret society which, without anybody knowing it, had the world's destinies in its hands.

It is well known that the belief in a Jewish conspiracy that was kept together by a secret society had the greatest propaganda value for antisemitic publicity, and by far outran all traditional European superstitions about ritual murder and well-poisoning. It is of great significance that Disraeli, for exactly opposite purposes and at a time when nobody thought seriously of secret societies, came to identical conclusions, for it shows clearly to what extent such fabrications were due to social motives and resentments and how much more plausibly they explained events or political and economic activities than the more trivial truth did. In Disraeli's eyes, as in the eyes of many less well-known and reputable charlatans after him, the whole game of politics was played between secret societies. Not only the Jews, but every other group whose influence was not politically organized or which was in opposition to the whole social and political system, became for him powers behind the scenes. In 1863, he thought he witnessed 'a struggle between the secret societies and the European millionaires; Rothschild hitherto has won.' [54] But also 'the natural equality of men and the abrogation of property are proclaimed by secret societies';[55] as late as 1870, he could still talk seriously of forces 'beneath the surface' and believe sincerely that 'secret societies and their international energies, the Church of Rome and her claims and methods, the eternal conflict between science and faith' were at work to determine the course of human history.[56]

Disraeli's unbelievable naïveté made him connect all these 'secret' forces with the Jews. 'The first Jesuits were Jews; that mysterious Russian diplomacy which so alarms Western Europe is organized and principally carried on by Jews; that mighty revolution which is at this

54  *Ibid.*, p. 73. In a letter to Mrs. Brydges Williams of July 21, 1863.
55  *Lord George Bentinck*, p. 497.
56  In his novel *Lothair*, 1870.

moment preparing in Germany and which will be in fact a second and greater Reformation . . . is entirely developing under the auspices of Jews,' 'men of Jewish race are found at the head of every one of (communist and socialist groups). The people of God co-operates with atheists; the most skilful accumulators of property ally themselves with communists, the peculiar and chosen race touch the hands of the scum and low castes of Europe! And all this because they wish to destroy that ungrateful Christendom which owes them even its name and whose tyranny they can no longer endure.' [57] In Disraeli's imagination, the world had become Jewish.

In this singular delusion, even that most ingenious of Hitler's publicity stunts, the cry of a secret alliance between the Jewish capitalist and the Jewish socialist, was already anticipated. Nor can it be denied that the whole scheme, imaginary and fantastic as it was, had a logic of its own. If one started, as Disraeli did, from the assumption that Jewish millionaires were makers of Jewish politics, if one took into account the insults Jews had suffered for centuries (which were real enough, but still stupidly exaggerated by Jewish apologetic propaganda), if one had seen the not infrequent instances when the son of a Jewish millionaire became a leader of the workers' movement and knew from experience how closely knit Jewish family ties were as a rule, Disraeli's image of a calculated revenge upon the Christian peoples was not so far-fetched. The truth was, of course, that the sons of Jewish millionaires inclined toward leftist movements precisely because their banker fathers had never come into an open class conflict with workers. They therefore completely lacked that class consciousness that the son of any ordinary bourgeois family would have had as a matter of course, while, on the other side, and for exactly the same reasons, the workers did not harbor those open or hidden antisemitic sentiments which every other class showed the Jews as a matter of course. Obviously leftist movements in most countries offered the only true possibilities for assimilation.

Disraeli's persistent fondness for explaining politics in terms of secret societies was based on experiences which later convinced many lesser European intellectuals. His basic experience had been that a

57 *Lord George Bentinck.*

place in English society was much more difficult to win than a seat in Parliament. English society of his time gathered in fashionable clubs which were independent of party distinctions. The clubs, although they were extremely important in the formation of a political elite, escaped public control. To an outsider they must have looked very mysterious indeed. They were secret insofar as not everybody was admitted to them. They became mysterious only when members of other classes asked admittance and were either refused or admitted after a plethora of incalculable, unpredictable, apparently irrational difficulties. There is no doubt that no political honor could replace the triumphs that intimate association with the privileged could give. Disraeli's ambitions, significantly enough, did not suffer even at the end of his life when he experienced severe political defeats, for he remained 'the most commanding figure of London society.'[58]

In his naïve certainty of the paramount importance of secret societies, Disraeli was a forerunner of those new social strata who, born outside the framework of society, could never understand its rules properly. They found themselves in a state of affairs where the distinctions between society and politics were constantly blurred and where, despite seemingly chaotic conditions, the same narrow class interest always won. The outsider could not but conclude that a consciously established institution with definite goals achieved such remarkable results. And it is true that this whole society game needed only a resolute political will to transform its half-conscious play of interests and essentially purposeless machinations into a definite policy. This is what occurred briefly in France during the Dreyfus Affair, and again in Germany during the decade preceding Hitler's rise to power.

Disraeli, however, was not only outside of English, he was outside of Jewish, society as well. He knew little of the mentality of the Jewish

---

58 Monypenny and Buckle, *op. cit.*, p. 1470. This excellent biography gives a correct evaluation of Disraeli's triumph. After having quoted Tennyson's *In Memoriam*, canto 64, it continues as follows: 'In one respect Disraeli's success was more striking and complete than that suggested in Tennyson's lines; he not only scaled the political ladder to the topmost rung and "shaped the whisper of the throne"; he also conquered Society. He dominated the dinner-tables and what we would call the salons of Mayfair . . . and his social triumph, whatever may be thought by philosophers of its intrinsic value, was certainly not less difficult of achievement for a despised outsider than his political, and was perhaps sweeter to his palate' (p. 1506).

bankers whom he so deeply admired, and he would have been disappointed indeed had he realized that these 'exception Jews,' despite exclusion from bourgeois society (they never really tried to be admitted), shared its foremost political principle that political activity centers around protection of property and profits. Disraeli saw, and was impressed by, only a group with no outward political organization, whose members were still connected by a seeming infinity of family and business connections. His imagination went to work whenever he had to deal with them and found everything 'proved' – when, for instance, the shares of the Suez Canal were offered the English government through the information of Henry Oppenheim (who had learned that the Khedive of Egypt was anxious to sell) and the sale was carried through with the help of a four million sterling loan from Lionel Rothschild.

Disraeli's racial convictions and theories about secret societies sprang, in the last analysis, from his desire to explain something apparently mysterious and in fact chimerical. He could not make a political reality out of the chimerical power of 'exception Jews'; but he could, and did, help transform chimeras into public fears and to entertain a bored society with highly dangerous fairy-tales.

With the consistency of most race fanatics, Disraeli spoke only with contempt of the 'modern newfangled sentimental principle of nationality.' [59] He hated the political equality at the basis of the nation-state and he feared for the survival of the Jews under its conditions. He fancied that race might give a social as well as political refuge against equalization. Since he knew the nobility of his time far better than he ever came to know the Jewish people, it is not surprising that he modeled the race concept after aristocratic caste concepts.

No doubt these concepts of the socially underprivileged could have gone far, but they would have had little significance in European politics had they not met with real political necessities when, after the scramble for Africa, they could be adapted to political purposes. This willingness to believe on the part of bourgeois society gave Disraeli, the only Jew of the nineteenth century, his share of genuine popularity. In the end, it was not his fault that the same trend that accounted

59 *Ibid.*, Vol. I, Book 3.

for his singular great good fortune finally led to the great catastrophe of his people.

## III: Between Vice and Crime

Paris has rightly been called *la capitale du dixneuvième siècle* (Walter Benjamin). Full of promise, the nineteenth century had started with the French Revolution, for more than one hundred years witnessed the vain struggle against the degeneration of the *citoyen* into the *bourgeois*, reached its nadir in the Dreyfus Affair, and was given another fourteen years of morbid respite. The first World War could still be won by the Jacobin appeal of Clemenceau, France's last son of the Revolution, but the glorious century of the *nation par excellence* was at an end[60] and Paris was left, without political significance and social splendor, to the intellectual avant-garde of all countries. France played a very small part in the twentieth century, which started, immediately after Disraeli's death, with the scramble for Africa and the competition for imperialist domination in Europe. Her decline, therefore, caused partly by the economic expansion of other nations, and partly by internal disintegration, could assume forms and follow laws which seemed inherent in the nation-state.

To a certain extent, what happened in France in the eighties and nineties happened thirty and forty years later in all European nation-states. Despite chronological distances, the Weimar and Austrian Republics had much in common historically with the Third Republic, and certain political and social patterns in the Germany and Austria of the twenties and thirties seemed almost consciously to follow the model of France's *fin-de-siècle*.

Nineteenth-century antisemitism, at any rate, reached its climax in France and was defeated because it remained a national domestic issue without contact with imperialist trends, which did not exist there. The main features of this kind of antisemitism reappeared in

---

60 Yves Simon, *La Grande Crise de la République Française*, Montreal, 1941, p. 20: 'The spirit of the French Revolution survived the defeat of Napoleon for more than a century. . . . It triumphed but only to fade unnoticed on November 11, 1918. The French Revolution? Its dates must surely be set at 1789-1918.'

Germany and Austria after the first World War, and its social effect on the respective Jewries was almost the same, although less sharp, less extreme, and more disturbed by other influences.[61]

The chief reason, however, for the choice of the salons of the Faubourg Saint-Germain as an example of the role of Jews in non-Jewish society is that nowhere else is there an equally grand society or a more truthful record of it. When Marcel Proust, himself half Jewish and in emergencies ready to identify himself as a Jew, set out to search for 'things past,' he actually wrote what one of his admiring critics has called an *apologia pro vita sua*. The life of this greatest writer of twentieth-century France was spent exclusively in society; all events appeared to him as they are reflected in society and reconsidered by the individual, so that reflections and reconsiderations constitute the specific reality and texture of Proust's world.[62] Throughout the *Remembrance of Things Past*, the individual and his reconsiderations belong to society, even when he retires into the mute and uncommunicative solitude in which Proust himself finally disappeared when he had decided to write his work. There his inner life, which insisted on transforming all worldly happenings into inner experience, became like a mirror in whose reflection truth might appear. The contemplator of inner experience resembles the onlooker in society insofar as neither has an immediate approach to life but perceives reality only if it is reflected. Proust, born on the fringe of society, but still rightfully belonging to it though an outsider, enlarged this inner experience until it included the whole range of aspects as they appeared to and were reflected by all members of society.

There is no better witness, indeed, of this period when society had emancipated itself completely from public concerns, and when politics

61 The fact that certain psychological phenomena did not come out as sharply in German and Austrian Jews, may partly be due to the strong hold of the Zionist movement on Jewish intellectuals in these countries. Zionism in the decade after the first World War, and even in the decade preceding it, owed its strength not so much to political insight (and did not produce political convictions), as it did to its critical analysis of psychological reactions and sociological facts. Its influence was mainly pedagogical and went far beyond the relatively small circle of actual members of the Zionist movement.

62 Compare the interesting remarks on this subject by E. Levinas, 'L'Autre dans Proust' in *Deucalion*, No. 2, 1947.

itself was becoming a part of social life. The victory of bourgeois values over the citizen's sense of responsibility meant the decomposition
of political issues into their dazzling, fascinating reflections in society.
It must be added that Proust himself was a true exponent of this society, for he was involved in both of its most fashionable 'vices,' which
he, 'the greatest witness of dejudaized Judaism' interconnected in the
'darkest comparison which ever has been made on behalf of Western
Judaism':[63] the 'vice' of Jewishness and the 'vice' of homosexuality, and
which in their reflection and individual reconsideration became very
much alike indeed.[64]

It was Disraeli who had discovered that vice is but the corresponding reflection of crime in society. Human wickedness, if accepted by
society, is changed from an act of will into an inherent, psychological
quality which man cannot choose or reject but which is imposed upon
him from without, and which rules him as compulsively as the drug
rules the addict. In assimilating crime and transforming it into vice,
society denies all responsibility and establishes a world of fatalities in
which men find themselves entangled. The moralistic judgment as a
crime of every departure from the norm, which fashionable circles
used to consider narrow and philistine, if demonstrative of inferior
psychological understanding, at least showed greater respect for
human dignity. If crime is understood to be a kind of fatality, natural
or economic, everybody will finally be suspected of some special predestination to it. 'Punishment is the right of the criminal,' of which he
is deprived if (in the words of Proust) 'judges assume and are more
inclined to pardon murder in inverts and treason in Jews for reasons
derived from . . . racial predestination.' It is an attraction to murder
and treason which hides behind such perverted tolerance, for in a
moment it can switch to a decision to liquidate not only all actual
criminals but all who are 'racially' predestined to commit certain
crimes. Such changes take place whenever the legal and political

---

63 J. E. van Praag, 'Marcel Proust, Témoin du Judaisme déjudaizé' in *Revue Juive de
Genève*, 1937, Nos. 48, 49, 50.

A curious coincidence (or is it more than a coincidence?) occurs in the moving-picture
*Crossfire* which deals with the Jewish question. The story was taken from Richard
Brooks's *The Brick Foxhole*, in which the murdered Jew of *Crossfire* was a homosexual.
64 For the following see especially *Cities of the Plain*, Part I, pp. 20–45.

machine is not separated from society so that social standards can penetrate into it and become political and legal rules. The seeming broadmindedness that equates crime and vice, if allowed to establish its own code of law, will invariably prove more cruel and inhuman than laws, no matter how severe, which respect and recognize man's independent responsibility for his behavior.

The Faubourg Saint-Germain, however, as Proust depicts it, was in the early stages of this development. It admitted inverts because it felt attracted by what it judged to be a vice. Proust describes how Monsieur de Charlus, who had formerly been tolerated, 'notwithstanding his vice,' for his personal charm and old name, now rose to social heights. He no longer needed to lead a double life and hide his dubious acquaintances, but was encouraged to bring them into the fashionable houses. Topics of conversation which he formerly would have avoided – love, beauty, jealousy – lest somebody suspect his anomaly, were now welcomed avidly 'in view of the experience, strange, secret, refined and monstrous upon which he founded' his views.[65]

Something very similar happened to the Jews. Individual exceptions, ennobled Jews, had been tolerated and even welcomed in the society of the Second Empire, but now Jews as such were becoming increasingly popular. In both cases, society was far from being prompted by a revision of prejudices. They did not doubt that homosexuals were 'criminals' or that Jews were 'traitors'; they only revised their attitude toward crime and treason. The trouble with their new broadmindedness, of course, was not that they were no longer horrified by inverts but that they were no longer horrified by crime. They did not in the least doubt the conventional judgment. The best-hidden disease of the nineteenth century, its terrible boredom and general weariness, had burst like an abscess. The outcasts and the pariahs upon whom society called in its predicament were, whatever else they might have been, at least not plagued by ennui and, if we are to trust Proust's judgment, were the only ones in *fin-de-siècle* society who were still capable of passion. Proust leads us through the labyrinth of social connections and ambitions only by the thread of man's capacity for love, which is presented in the perverted passion of Monsieur de

65 *Cities of the Plain*, Part II, chapter iii.

Charlus for Morel, in the devastating loyalty of the Jew Swann to his courtesan and in the author's own desperate jealousy of Albertine, herself the personification of vice in the novel. Proust made it very clear that he regarded the outsiders and newcomers, the inhabitants of 'Sodome et Ghomorre,' not only as more human but as more normal.

The difference between the Faubourg Saint-Germain, which had suddenly discovered the attractiveness of Jews and inverts, and the mob which cried 'Death to the Jews' was that the salons had not yet associated themselves openly with crime. This meant that on the one hand they did not yet want to participate actively in the killing, and on the other, still professed openly an antipathy toward Jews and a horror of inverts. This in turn resulted in that typically equivocal situation in which the new members could not confess their identity openly, and yet could not hide it either. Such were the conditions from which arose the complicated game of exposure and concealment, of half-confessions and lying distortions, of exaggerated humility and exaggerated arrogance, all of which were consequences of the fact that only one's Jewishness (or homosexuality) had opened the doors of the exclusive salons, while at the same time they made one's position extremely insecure. In this equivocal situation, Jewishness was for the individual Jew at once a physical stain and a mysterious personal privilege, both inherent in a 'racial predestination.'

Proust describes at great length how society, constantly on the lookout for the strange, the exotic, the dangerous, finally identifies the refined with the monstrous and gets ready to admit monstrosities – real or fancied – such as the strange, unfamiliar 'Russian or Japanese play performed by native actors';[66] the 'painted, paunchy, tightly buttoned personage [of the invert], reminding one of a box of exotic and dubious origin from which escapes the curious odor of fruits the mere thought of tasting which stirs the heart';[67] the 'man of genius' who is supposed to emanate a 'sense of the supernatural' and around whom society will 'gather as though around a turning-table, to learn the secret of the Infinite.'[68] In the atmosphere of this 'necromancy,' a

66  Ibid.
67  Ibid.
68  The Guermantes Way, Part I, chapter i.

Jewish gentleman or a Turkish lady might appear 'as if they really were creatures evoked by the effort of a medium.' [69]

Obviously the role of the exotic, the strange, and the monstrous could not be played by those individual 'exception Jews' who, for almost a century, had been admitted and tolerated as 'foreign upstarts' and on 'whose friendship nobody would ever have dreamed of priding himself.' [70] Much better suited of course were those whom nobody had ever known, who, in the first stage of their assimilation, were not identified with, and were not representative of, the Jewish community, for such identification with well-known bodies would have limited severely society's imagination and expectations. Those who, like Swann, had an unaccountable flair for society and taste in general were admitted; but more enthusiastically embraced were those who, like Bloch, belonged to 'a family of little repute, [and] had to support, as on the floor of the ocean, the incalculable pressure of what was imposed on him not only by the Christians upon the surface but by all the intervening layers of Jewish castes superior to his own, each of them crushing with its contempt the one that was immediately beneath it.' Society's willingness to receive the utterly alien and, as it thought, utterly vicious, cut short that climb of several generations by which newcomers had 'to carve their way through to the open air by raising themselves from Jewish family to Jewish family.' [71] It was no accident that this happened shortly after native French Jewry, during the Panama scandal, had given way before the initiative and unscrupulousness of some German Jewish adventurers; the individual exceptions, with or without title, who more than ever before sought the society of antisemitic and monarchist salons where they could dream of the good old days of the Second Empire, found themselves in the same category as Jews whom they would never have invited to their houses. If Jewishness as exceptionalness was the reason for admitting Jews, then those were preferred who were clearly 'a solid troop, homogeneous within itself and utterly dissimilar to the people

69 *Ibid.*
70 *Ibid.*
71 *Within a Budding Grove*, Part II, 'Placenames: The Place.'

who watched them go past,' those who had not yet 'reached the same stage of assimilation' as their upstart brethren.[72]

Although Benjamin Disraeli was still one of those Jews who were admitted to society because they were exceptions, his secularized self-representation as a 'chosen man of the chosen race' foreshadowed and outlined the lines along which Jewish self-interpretation was to take place. If this, fantastic and crude as it was, had not been so oddly similar to what society expected of Jews, Jews would never have been able to play their dubious role. Not, of course, that they consciously adopted Disraeli's convictions or purposely elaborated the first timid, perverted self-interpretation of their Prussian predecessors of the beginning of the century; most of them were blissfully ignorant of all Jewish history. But wherever Jews were educated, secularized, and assimilated under the ambiguous conditions of society and state in Western and Central Europe, they lost that measure of political responsibility which their origin implied and which the Jewish notables had still felt, albeit in the form of privilege and rulership. Jewish origin, without religious and political connotation, became everywhere a psychological quality, was changed into 'Jewishness,' and from then on could be considered only in the categories of virtue or vice. If it is true that 'Jewishness' could not have been perverted into an interesting vice without a prejudice which considered it a crime, it is also true that such perversion was made possible by those Jews who considered it an innate virtue.

Assimilated Jewry has been reproached with alienation from Judaism, and the final catastrophe brought upon it is frequently thought to have been a suffering as senseless as it was horrible, since it had lost the old value of martyrdom. This argument overlooks the fact that as far as the old ways of faith and life are concerned, 'alienation' was equally apparent in Eastern European countries. But the usual notion of the Jews of Western Europe as 'dejudaized' is misleading for another reason. Proust's picture, in contrast to the all too obviously interested utterances of official Judaism, shows that never did the fact of Jewish birth play such a decisive role in private life and everyday existence as

72 *Ibid.*

among the assimilated Jews. The Jewish reformer who changed a national religion into a religious denomination with the understanding that religion is a private affair, the Jewish revolutionary who pretended to be a world citizen in order to rid himself of Jewish nationality, the educated Jew, 'a man in the street and a Jew at home' – each one of these succeeded in converting a national quality into a private affair. The result was that their private lives, their decisions and sentiments, became the very center of their 'Jewishness.' And the more the fact of Jewish birth lost its religious, national, and social-economic significance, the more obsessive Jewishness became; Jews were obsessed by it as one may be by a physical defect or advantage, and addicted to it as one may be to a vice.

Proust's 'innate disposition' is nothing but this personal, private obsession, which was so greatly justified by a society where success and failure depended upon the fact of Jewish birth. Proust mistook it for 'racial predestination,' because he saw and depicted only its social aspect and individual reconsiderations. And it is true that to the recording onlooker the behavior of the Jewish clique showed the same obsession as the behavior patterns followed by inverts. Both felt either superior or inferior, but in any case proudly different from other normal beings; both believed their difference to be a natural fact acquired by birth; both were constantly justifying, not what they did, but what they were; and both, finally, always wavered between such apologetic attitudes and sudden, provocative claims that they were an elite. As though their social position were forever frozen by nature, neither could move from one clique into another. The need to belong existed in other members of society too – 'the question is not as for Hamlet, to be or not to be, but to belong or not to belong' [73] – but not to the same extent. A society disintegrating into cliques and no longer tolerating outsiders, Jews or inverts, as individuals but because of the special circumstances of their admission, looked like the embodiment of this clannishness.

Each society demands of its members a certain amount of acting, the ability to present, represent, and act what one actually is. When society disintegrates into cliques such demands are no longer made of

[73] *Cities of the Plain*, Part II, chapter iii.

the individual but of members of cliques. Behavior then is controlled by silent demands and not by individual capacities, exactly as an actor's performance must fit into the ensemble of all other roles in the play. The salons of the Faubourg Saint-Germain consisted of such an ensemble of cliques, each of which presented an extreme behavior pattern. The role of the inverts was to show their abnormality, of the Jews to represent black magic ('necromancy'), of the artists to manifest another form of supranatural and superhuman contact, of the aristocrats to show that they were not like ordinary ('bourgeois') people. Despite their clannishness, it is true, as Proust observed, that 'save on the days of general disaster when the majority rally round the victim as the Jews rallied round Dreyfus,' all these newcomers shunned intercourse with their own kind. The reason was that all marks of distinction were determined only by the ensemble of the cliques, so that Jews or inverts felt that they would lose their distinctive character in a society of Jews or inverts, where Jewishness or homosexuality would be the most natural, the most uninteresting, and the most banal thing in the world. The same, however, held true of their hosts who also needed an ensemble of counterparts before whom they could be different, nonaristocrats who would admire aristocrats as these admired the Jews or the homosexuals.

Although these cliques had no consistency in themselves and dissolved as soon as no members of other cliques were around, their members used a mysterious sign-language as though they needed something strange by which to recognize each other. Proust reports at length the importance of such signs, especially for newcomers. While, however, the inverts, masters at sign-language, had at least a real secret, the Jews used this language only to create the expected atmosphere of mystery. Their signs mysteriously and ridiculously indicated something universally known: that in the corner of the salon of the Princess So-and-So sat another Jew who was not allowed openly to admit his identity but who without this meaningless quality would never have been able to climb into that corner.

It is noteworthy that the new mixed society at the end of the nineteenth century, like the first Jewish salons in Berlin, again centered around nobility. Aristocracy by now had all but lost its eagerness for culture and its curiosity about 'new specimens of humanity,' but it retained its old scorn of bourgeois society. An urge for social distinction was its answer to political equality and the loss of political position and privilege which had been affirmed with the establishment of the Third Republic. After a short and artificial rise during the Second Empire, French aristocracy maintained itself only by social clannishness and half-hearted attempts to reserve the higher positions in the army for its sons. Much stronger than political ambition was an aggressive contempt for middle-class standards, which undoubtedly was one of the strongest motives for the admission of individuals and whole groups of people who had belonged to socially unacceptable classes. The same motive that had enabled Prussian aristocrats to meet socially with actors and Jews finally led in France to the social prestige of inverts. The middle classes, on the other hand, had not acquired social self-respect, although they had in the meantime risen to wealth and power. The absence of a political hierarchy in the nation-state and the victory of equality rendered 'society secretly more hierarchical as it became outwardly more democratic.'[74] Since the principle of hierarchy was embodied in the exclusive social circles of the Faubourg Saint-Germain, each society in France 'reproduced the characteristics more or less modified, more or less in caricature of the society of the Faubourg Saint-Germain which it sometimes pretended . . . to hold in contempt, no matter what status or what political ideas its members might hold.' Aristocratic society was a thing of the past in appearance only; actually it pervaded the whole social body (and not only of the people of France) by imposing 'the key and the grammar of fashionable social life.'[75] When Proust felt the need for an *apologia pro vita sua* and reconsidered his own life spent in aristocratic circles, he gave an analysis of society as such.

The main point about the role of Jews in this *fin-de-siècle* society is that it was the antisemitism of the Dreyfus Affair which opened society's doors to Jews, and that it was the end of the Affair, or rather the discovery of Dreyfus' innocence, that put an end to their social glory.[76]

74 *The Guermantes Way*, Part II, chapter ii.

75 Ramon Fernandez, 'La vie sociale dans l'oeuvre de Marcel Proust,' in *Les Cahiers Marcel Proust*, No. 2, 1927.

76 'But this was the moment when from the effects of the Dreyfus case there had arisen an antisemitic movement parallel to a more abundant movement towards the

In other words, no matter what the Jews thought of themselves or of Dreyfus, they could play the role society had assigned them only as long as this same society was convinced that they belonged to a race of traitors. When the traitor was discovered to be the rather stupid victim of an ordinary frame-up, and the innocence of the Jews was established, social interest in Jews subsided as quickly as did political antisemitism. Jews were again looked upon as ordinary mortals and fell into the insignificance from which the supposed crime of one of their own had raised them temporarily.

It was essentially the same kind of social glory that the Jews of Germany and Austria enjoyed under much more severe circumstances immediately after the first World War. Their supposed crime then was that they had been guilty of the war, a crime which, no longer identified with a single act of a single individual, could not be refuted, so that the mob's evaluation of Jewishness as a crime remained undisturbed and society could continue to be delighted and fascinated by its Jews up to the very end. If there is any psychological truth in the scapegoat theory, it is as the effect of this social attitude toward Jews; for when antisemitic legislation forced society to oust the Jews, these 'philosemites' felt as though they had to purge themselves of secret viciousness, to cleanse themselves of a stigma which they had mysteriously and wickedly loved. This psychology, to be sure, hardly explains why these 'admirers' of Jews finally became their murderers, and it may even be doubted that they were prominent among those who ran the death factories, although the percentage of the so-called educated classes among the actual killers is amazing. But it does explain the incredible disloyalty of precisely those strata of society which had known Jews most intimately and had been most delighted and charmed by Jewish friends.

As far as the Jews were concerned, the transformation of the 'crime' of Judaism into the fashionable 'vice' of Jewishness was dangerous in the extreme. Jews had been able to escape from Judaism into conversion; from Jewishness there was no escape. A crime, moreover, is met

---

penetration of society by Israelites. The politicians had not been wrong in thinking that the discovery of the judicial error would deal a fatal blow to antisemitism. But provisionally at least a social antisemitism was on the contrary enhanced and exacerbated by it.' See *The Sweet Cheat Gone*, chapter ii.

with punishment; a vice can only be exterminated. The interpretation given by society to the fact of Jewish birth and the role played by Jews in the framework of social life are intimately connected with the catastrophic thoroughness with which antisemitic devices could be put to work. The Nazi brand of antisemitism had its roots in these social conditions as well as in political circumstances. And though the concept of race had other and more immediately political purposes and functions, its application to the Jewish question in its most sinister aspect owed much of its success to social phenomena and convictions which virtually constituted a consent by public opinion.

The deciding forces in the Jews' fateful journey to the storm center of events were without doubt political; but the reactions of society to antisemitism and the psychological reflections of the Jewish question in the individual had something to do with the specific cruelty, the organized and calculated assault upon every single individual of Jewish origin, that was already characteristic of the antisemitism of the Dreyfus Affair. This passion-driven hunt of the 'Jew in general,' the 'Jew everywhere and nowhere,' cannot be understood if one considers the history of antisemitism as an entity in itself, as a mere political movement. Social factors, unaccounted for in political or economic history, hidden under the surface of events, never perceived by the historian and recorded only by the more penetrating and passionate force of poets or novelists (men whom society had driven into the desperate solitude and loneliness of the *apologia pro vita sua*) changed the course that mere political antisemitism would have taken if left to itself, and which might have resulted in anti-Jewish legislation and even mass expulsion but hardly in wholesale extermination.

Ever since the Dreyfus Affair and its political threat to the rights of French Jewry had produced a social situation in which Jews enjoyed an ambiguous glory, antisemitism appeared in Europe as an insoluble mixture of political motives and social elements. Society always reacted first to a strong antisemitic movement with marked preference for Jews, so that Disraeli's remark that 'there is no race at this present . . . that so much delights and fascinates and elevates and ennobles Europe as the Jewish,' became particularly true in times of danger. Social 'philosemitism' always ended by adding to political antisemitism that mysterious fanaticism without which antisemitism could hardly have become the best slogan for organizing the masses. All the *déclassés* of capitalist society were finally ready to unite and establish mob organizations of their own; their propaganda and their attraction rested on the assumption that a society which had shown its willingness to incorporate crime in the form of vice into its very structure would by now be ready to cleanse itself of viciousness by openly admitting criminals and by publicly committing crimes.

# CHAPTER FOUR

# The Dreyfus Affair

## I: The Facts of the Case

It happened in France at the end of the year 1894. Alfred Dreyfus, a Jewish officer of the French General Staff, was accused and convicted of espionage for Germany. The verdict, lifelong deportation to Devil's Island, was unanimously adopted. The trial took place behind closed doors. Out of an allegedly voluminous dossier of the prosecution, only the so-called 'bordereau' was shown. This was a letter, supposedly in Dreyfus' handwriting, addressed to the German military attaché, Schwartzkoppen. In July, 1895, Colonel Picquart became head of the Information Division of the General Staff. In May, 1896, he told the chief of the General Staff, Boisdeffre, that he had convinced himself of Dreyfus' innocence and of the guilt of another officer, Major Walsin-Esterhazy. Six months later, Picquart was removed to a dangerous post in Tunisia. At the same time, Bernard Lazare, on behalf of Dreyfus' brothers, published the first pamphlet of the Affair: *Une erreur judiciaire; la vérité sur l'affaire Dreyfus*. In June, 1897, Picquart informed Scheurer-Kestner, Vice-President of the Senate, of the facts of the trials and of Dreyfus' innocence. In November, 1897, Clemenceau started his fight for re-examination of the case. Four weeks later Zola joined the ranks of the Dreyfusards. *J'Accuse* was published by Clemenceau's newspaper in January, 1898. At the same time, Picquart was arrested. Zola, tried for calumny of the army, was convicted by both the ordinary tribunal and the Court of Appeal. In August, 1898, Esterhazy was dishonorably discharged because of embezzlement. He at once hurried to a British journalist and told him that he – and not Dreyfus – was the author of the 'bordereau,' which he had forged in Dreyfus' handwriting on orders from Colonel Sandherr, his superior and former chief of the counterespionage division. A few days later Colonel Henry, another member of the same department, confessed forgeries of several other pieces of the secret Dreyfus dossier and committed suicide. Thereupon the Court of Appeal ordered an investigation of the Dreyfus case.

In June, 1899, the Court of Appeal annulled the original sentence against Dreyfus of 1894. The revision trial took place in Rennes in August. The sentence was made ten years' imprisonment because of 'alleviating circumstances.' A week later Dreyfus was pardoned by the President of the Republic. The World Exposition opened in Paris in April, 1900. In May, when the success of the Exposition was guaranteed, the Chamber of Deputies, with overwhelming majority, voted against any further revision of the Dreyfus case. In December of the same year all trials and lawsuits connected with the affair were liquidated through a general amnesty.

In 1903 Dreyfus asked for a new revision. His petition was neglected until 1906, when Clemenceau had become Prime Minister. In July, 1906, the Court of Appeal annulled the sentence of Rennes and acquitted Dreyfus of all charges. The Court of Appeal, however, had no authority to acquit; it should have ordered a new trial. Another revision before a military tribunal would, in all probability and despite the overwhelming evidence in favor of Dreyfus, have led to a new conviction. Dreyfus, therefore, was never acquitted in accordance with the law,[1] and the Dreyfus case was never really settled. The reinstatement of the accused was never recognized by the French people, and the passions that were originally aroused never entirely subsided. As late as 1908, nine years after the pardon and two years after Dreyfus was cleared, when, at Clemenceau's instance, the body of Emile Zola was transferred to the Pantheon, Alfred Dreyfus was openly attacked in the street. A Paris court acquitted his assailant and indicated that it 'dissented' from the decision which had cleared Dreyfus.

[1] The most extensive and still indispensable work on the subject is that of Joseph Reinach, *L'Affaire Dreyfus*, Paris, 1903–11, 7 vols. The most detailed among recent studies, written from a socialist viewpoint, is by Wilhelm Herzog, *Der Kampf einer Republik*, Zürich, 1933. Its exhaustive chronological tables are very valuable. The best political and historical evaluation of the affair is to be found in D. W. Brogan, *The Development of Modern France*, 1940, Books VI and VII. Brief and reliable is G. Charensol, *L'Affaire Dreyfus et la Troisième République*, 1930.

Even stranger is the fact that neither the first nor the second World War has been able to bury the affair in oblivion. At the behest of the Action Française, the *Précis de l'Affaire Dreyfus*[2] was republished in 1924 and has since been the standard reference manual of the Anti-Dreyfusards. At the premiere of *L'Affaire Dreyfus* (a play written by Rehfisch and Wilhelm Herzog under the pseudonym of René Kestner) in 1931, the atmosphere of the nineties still prevailed with quarrels in the auditorium, stink-bombs in the stalls, the shock troops of the Action Française standing around to strike terror into actors, audience and bystanders. Nor did the government – Laval's government – act in any way differently than its predecessors some thirty years before: it gladly admitted it was unable to guarantee a single undisturbed performance, thereby providing a new late triumph for the Anti-Dreyfusards. The play had to be suspended. When Dreyfus died in 1935, the general press was afraid to touch the issue[3] while the leftist papers still spoke in the old terms of Dreyfus' innocence and the right wing of Dreyfus' guilt. Even today, though to a lesser extent, the Dreyfus Affair is still a kind of shibboleth in French politics. When Pétain was condemned the influential provincial newspaper *Voix du Nord* (of Lille) linked the Pétain case to the Dreyfus case and maintained that 'the country remains divided as it was after the Dreyfus case,' because the verdict of the court could not settle a political conflict and 'bring to all the French peace of mind or of heart.'[4]

While the Dreyfus Affair in its broader political aspects belongs to the twentieth century, the Dreyfus case, the various trials of the Jewish Captain Alfred Dreyfus, are quite typical of the nineteenth century, when men followed legal proceedings so keenly because each instance afforded a test of the century's greatest achievement, the complete impartiality of the law. It is characteristic of the period that a miscarriage of justice could arouse such political passions and inspire such an endless succession of trials and retrials, not to speak of duels and fisticuffs. The doctrine of equality before the law was still so firmly

2 Written by two officers and published under the pseudonym Henri Dutrait-Crozon.
3 The *Action Française* (July 19, 1935) praised the restraint of the French press while voicing the opinion that 'the famous champions of justice and truth of forty years ago have left no disciples.'
4 See G. H. Archambault in *New York Times*, August 18, 1945, p. 5.

implanted in the conscience of the civilized world that a single miscarriage of justice could provoke public indignation from Moscow to
New York. Nor was anyone, except in France itself, so 'modern' as to
associate the matter with political issues.[5] The wrong done to a single
Jewish officer in France was able to draw from the rest of the world a
more vehement and united reaction than all the persecutions of German Jews a generation later. Even Czarist Russia could accuse France
of barbarism while in Germany members of the Kaiser's entourage
would openly express an indignation matched only by the radical
press of the 1930's.[6]

The *dramatis personae* of the case might have stepped out of the pages
of Balzac: on the one hand, the class-conscious generals frantically covering up for the members of their own clique and, on the other, their
antagonist, Picquart, with his calm, clear-eyed and slightly ironical honesty. Beside them stand the nondescript crowd of the men in Parliament,
each terrified of what his neighbor might know; the President of the
Republic, notorious patron of the Paris brothels, and the examining
magistrates, living solely for the sake of social contacts. Then there is
Dreyfus himself, actually a parvenu, continually boasting to his colleagues of his family fortune which he spent on women; his brothers,
pathetically offering their entire fortune, and then reducing the offer to
150,000 francs, for the release of their kinsman, never quite sure whether
they wished to make a sacrifice or simply to suborn the General Staff;
and the lawyer Démange, really convinced of his client's innocence but
basing the defense on an issue of doubt so as to save himself from attacks
and injury to his personal interests. Lastly, there is the adventurer

5 The sole exceptions, the Catholic journals, most of which agitated in all countries
against Dreyfus, will be discussed below. American public opinion was such that in
addition to protests an organized boycott of the Paris World Exposition scheduled for
1900 was begun. On the effect of this threat see below. For a comprehensive study see
the master's essay on file at Columbia University by Rose A. Halperin, 'The American
Reaction to the Dreyfus Case,' 1941. The author wishes to thank Professor S. W. Baron
for his kindness in placing this study at her disposal.

6 Thus, for example, H. B. von Buelow, the German chargé d'affaires at Paris, wrote
to Reichchancellor Hohenlohe that the verdict at Rennes was a 'mixture of vulgarity
and cowardice, the surest signs of barbarism,' and that France 'has therewith shut herself out of the family of civilized nations,' cited by Herzog, *op. cit.*, under date of
September 12, 1899. In the opinion of von Buelow the *Affaire* was the 'shibboleth' of
German liberalism; see his *Denkwürdigkeiten*, Berlin, 1930–31, I, 428.

Esterhazy, he of the ancient escutcheon, so utterly bored by this bourgeois world as to seek relief equally in heroism and knavery. An erstwhile
second lieutenant of the Foreign Legion, he impressed his colleagues
greatly by his superior boldness and impudence. Always in trouble, he
lived by serving as duelist's second to Jewish officers and by blackmailing their wealthy coreligionists. Indeed, he would avail himself of the
good offices of the chief rabbi himself in order to obtain the requisite
introductions. Even in his ultimate downfall he remained true to the
Balzac tradition. Not treason nor wild dreams of a great orgy in which a
hundred thousand besotted Prussian Uhlans would run berserk through
Paris[7] but a paltry embezzlement of a relative's cash sent him to his
doom. And what shall we say of Zola, with his impassioned moral fervor, his somewhat empty pathos, and his melodramatic declaration, on
the eve of his flight to London, that he had heard the voice of Dreyfus
begging him to bring this sacrifice?[8]

All this belongs typically to the nineteenth century and by itself
would never have survived two World Wars. The old-time enthusiasm
of the mob for Esterhazy, like its hatred of Zola, have long since died
down to embers, but so too has that fiery passion against aristocracy
and clergy which had once inflamed Jaurès and which had alone
secured the final release of Dreyfus. As the Cagoulard affair was to
show, officers of the General Staff no longer had to fear the wrath of
the people when they hatched their plots for a *coup d'état*. Since the
separation of Church and State, France, though certainly no longer
clerical-minded, had lost a great deal of her anticlerical feeling, just as
the Catholic Church had itself lost much of its political aspiration.
Pétain's attempt to convert the republic into a Catholic state was
blocked by the utter indifference of the people and by the lower
clergy's hostility to clerico-fascism.

The Dreyfus Affair in its political implications could survive
because two of its elements grew in importance during the twentieth
century. The first is hatred of the Jews; the second, suspicion of the
republic itself, of Parliament, and the state machine. The larger
section of the public could still go on thinking the latter, rightly or

7  Théodore Reinach, *Histoire sommaire de l'Affaire Dreyfus*, Paris, 1924, p. 96.
8  Reported by Joseph Reinach, as cited by Herzog, *op. cit.*, under date of June 18, 1898.

wrongly, under the influence of the Jews and the power of the banks. Down to our times the term Anti-Dreyfusard can still serve as a recognized name for all that is antirepublican, antidemocratic, and antisemitic. A few years ago it still comprised everything, from the monarchism of the Action Française to the National Bolshevism of Doriot and the social Fascism of Déat. It was not, however, to these Fascist groups, numerically unimportant as they were, that the Third Republic owed its collapse. On the contrary, the plain, if paradoxical, truth is that their influence was never so slight as at the moment when the collapse actually took place. What made France fall was the fact that she had no more true Dreyfusards, no one who believed that democracy and freedom, equality and justice could any longer be defended or realized under the republic.[9] At long last the republic fell like overripe fruit into the lap of that old Anti-Dreyfusard clique[10] which had always formed the kernel of her army, and this at a time when she had few enemies but almost no friends. How little the Pétain clique was a product of German Fascism was shown clearly by its slavish adherence to the old formulas of forty years before.

While Germany shrewdly truncated her and ruined her entire economy through the demarcation line, France's leaders in Vichy tinkered with the old Barrès formula of 'autonomous provinces,' thereby crippling her all the more. They introduced anti-Jewish legislation more promptly than any Quisling, boasting all the while that they had no need to import antisemitism from Germany and that their law

9 That even Clemenceau no longer believed in it toward the end of his life is shown clearly by the remark quoted in René Benjamin, *Clémenceau dans la retraite*, Paris, 1930, p. 249: 'Hope? Impossible! How can I go on hoping when I no longer believe in that which roused me, namely, democracy?'

10 Weygand, a known adherent of the Action Française, was in his youth an Anti-Dreyfusard. He was one of the subscribers to the 'Henry Memorial' established by the *Libre Parole* in honor of the unfortunate Colonel Henry, who paid with suicide for his forgeries, while on the General Staff. The list of subscribers was later published by Quillard, one of the editors of *L'Aurore* (Clemenceau's paper), under the title of *Le Monument Henry*, Paris, 1899. As for Pétain, he was on the general staff of the military government of Paris from 1895 to 1899, at a time when nobody but a proven Anti-Dreyfusard would have been tolerated. See Contamine de Latour, 'Le Maréchal Pétain,' in *Revue de Paris*, I, 57–69. D. W. Brogan, *op. cit.*, p. 382, pertinently observes that of the five World War I marshals, four (Foch, Pétain, Lyautey, and Fayolle) were bad republicans, while the fifth, Joffre, had well-known clerical leanings.

governing the Jews differed in essential points from that of the Reich.[11] They sought to mobilize the Catholic clergy against the Jews, only to give proof that the priests have not only lost their political influence but are not actually antisemites. On the contrary, it was the very bishops and synods which the Vichy regime wanted to turn once more into political powers who voiced the most emphastic protest against the persecution of the Jews.

Not the Dreyfus case with its trials but the Dreyfus Affair in its entirety offers a foregleam of the twentieth century. As Bernanos pointed out in 1931,[12] 'The Dreyfus affair already belongs to that tragic era which certainly was not ended by the last war. The affair reveals the same inhuman character, preserving amid the welter of unbridled passions and the flames of hate an inconceivably cold and callous heart.' Certainly it was not in France that the true sequel to the affair was to be found, but the reason why France fell an easy prey to Nazi aggression is not far to seek. Hitler's propaganda spoke a language long familiar and never quite forgotten. That the 'Caesarism'[13] of the *Action Française* and the nihilistic nationalism of Barrès and Maurras never succeeded in their original form is due to a variety of causes, all of them negative. They lacked social vision and were unable to translate into popular terms those mental phantasmagoria which their contempt for the intellect had engendered.

We are here concerned essentially with the political bearings of the Dreyfus Affair and not with the legal aspects of the case. Sharply outlined in it are a number of traits characteristic of the twentieth century. Faint and barely distinguishable during the early decades of the century, they have at last emerged into full daylight and stand revealed as

11 The myth that Pétain's anti-Jewish legislation was forced upon him by the Reich, which took in almost the whole of French Jewry, has been exploded on the French side itself. See especially Yves Simon, *La Grande crise de la République Française: observations sur la vie politique des français de 1918 à 1938*, Montreal, 1941.

12 Cf. Georges Bernanos, *La grande peur des bien-pensants, Edouard Drumont*, Paris, 1931, p. 262.

13 Waldemar Gurian, *Der integrale Nationalismus in Frankreich: Charles Maurras und die Action Française*, Frankfurt-am-Main, 1931, p. 92, makes a sharp distinction between the monarchist movement and other reactionary tendencies. The same author discusses the Dreyfus case in his *Die politischen und sozialen Ideen des französischen Katholizismus*, M. Gladbach, 1929.

belonging to the main trends of modern times. After thirty years of a mild, purely social form of anti-Jewish discrimination, it had become a little difficult to remember that the cry, 'Death to the Jews,' had echoed through the length and breadth of a modern state once before when its domestic policy was crystallized in the issue of antisemitism. For thirty years the old legends of world conspiracy had been no more than the conventional stand-by of the tabloid press and the dime novel and the world did not easily remember that not long ago, but at a time when the 'Protocols of the Elders of Zion' were still unknown, a whole nation had been racking its brains trying to determine whether 'secret Rome' or 'secret Judah' held the reins of world politics.[14]

Similarly, the vehement and nihilistic philosophy of spiritual self-hatred[15] suffered something of an eclipse when a world at temporary peace with itself yielded no crop of outstanding criminals to justify the exaltation of brutality and unscrupulousness. The Jules Guérins had to wait nearly forty years before the atmosphere was ripe again for quasi-military storm troops. The *déclassés*, produced through the nineteenth-century economy, had to grow numerically until they were strong minorities of the nations, before that *coup d'état*, which had remained but a grotesque plot[16] in France, could achieve reality in Germany almost without effort. The prelude to Nazism was played over the entire European stage. The Dreyfus case, therefore, is more than a bizarre, imperfectly solved 'crime,'[17] an affair of staff officers

---

14 For the creation of such myths on both sides, Daniel Halévy, 'Apologie pour notre passé,' in *Cahiers de la quinzaine*, Series XL, No. 10, 1910.

15 A distinctly modern note is struck in Zola's *Letter to France* of 1898: 'We hear on all sides that the concept of liberty has gone bankrupt. When the Dreyfus business cropped up, this prevalent hatred of liberty found a golden opportunity ... Don't you see that the only reason why Scheurer-Kestner has been attacked with such fury is that he belongs to a generation which believed in liberty and worked for it? Today one shrugs one's shoulders at such things ... "Old greybeards," one laughs, "outmoded greathearts."' Herzog, *op. cit.*, under date of January 6, 1898.

16 The farcical nature of the various attempts made in the nineties to stage a *coup d'état* was clearly analyzed by Rosa Luxemburg in her article, 'Die soziale Krise in Frankreich,' in *Die Neue Zeit*, Vol. I, 1901.

17 Whether Colonel Henry forged the *bordereau* on orders from the chief of staff or upon his own initiative, is still unknown. Similarly, the attempted assassination of Labori, counsel for Dreyfus at the Rennes tribunal, has never been properly cleared up. Cf. Emile Zola, *Correspondance: lettres à Maître Labori*, Paris, 1929, p. 32, n. 1.

disguised by false beards and dark glasses, peddling their stupid forgeries by night in the streets of Paris. Its hero is not Dreyfus but Clemenceau and it begins not with the arrest of a Jewish staff officer but with the Panama scandal.

## II: The Third Republic and French Jewry

Between 1880 and 1888 the Panama Company, under the leadership of de Lesseps, who had constructed the Suez Canal, was able to make but little practical progress. Nevertheless, within France itself it succeeded during this period in raising no less than 1,335,538,454 francs in private loans.[18] This success is the more significant when one considers the carefulness of the French middle class in money matters. The secret of the company's success lies in the fact that its several public loans were invariably backed by Parliament. The building of the Canal was generally regarded as a public and national service rather than as a private enterprise. When the company went bankrupt, therefore, it was the foreign policy of the republic that really suffered the blow. Only after a few years did it become clear that even more important was the ruination of some half-million middle-class Frenchmen. Both the press and the Parliamentary Commission of Inquiry came to roughly the same conclusion: the company had already been bankrupt for several years. De Lesseps, they contended, had been living in hopes of a miracle, cherishing the dream that new funds would be somehow forthcoming to push on with the work. In order to win sanction for the new loans he had been obliged to bribe the press, half of Parliament, and all of the higher officials. This, however, had called for the employment of middlemen and these in turn had commanded exorbitant commissions. Thus, the very thing which had originally inspired public confidence in the enterprise, namely, Parliament's backing of the loans, proved in the end the factor which converted a not too sound private business into a colossal racket.

There were no Jews either among the bribed members of Parliament or on the board of the company. Jacques Reinach and Cornélius

18 Cf. Walter Frank, *Demokratie und Nationalismus in Frankreich*, Hamburg, 1933, p. 273.

Herz, however, vied for the honor of distributing the baksheesh among the members of the Chamber, the former working on the right wing of the bourgeois parties and the latter on the radicals (the anti-clerical parties of the petty bourgeoisie).[19] Reinach was the secret financial counsellor of the government during the eighties[20] and there-fore handled its relations with the Panama Company, while Herz's role was a double one. On the one hand he served Reinach as liaison with the radical wings of Parliament, to which Reinach himself had no access; on the other this office gave him such a good insight into the extent of the corruption that he was able constantly to blackmail his boss and to involve him ever deeper in the mess.[21]

Naturally there were quite a number of smaller Jewish business-men working for both Herz and Reinach. Their names, however, may well repose in the oblivion into which they have deservedly fallen. The more uncertain the situation of the company, the higher, natu-rally, was the rate of commission, until in the end the company itself received but little of the moneys advanced to it. Shortly before the crash Herz received for a single intra-parliamentary transaction an advance of no less than 600,000 francs. The advance, however, was premature. The loan was not taken up and the shareholders were simply 600,000 francs out of pocket.[22] The whole ugly racket ended disastrously for Reinach. Harassed by the blackmail of Herz he finally committed suicide.[23]

Shortly before his death, however, he had taken a step the conse-quences of which for French Jewry can scarcely be exaggerated. He had given the *Libre Parole*, Edouard Drumont's antisemitic daily, his list of suborned members of Parliament, the so-called 'remittance

19  Cf. Georges Suarez, *La Vie orgueilleuse de Clémenceau*, Paris, 1930, p. 156.

20  Such, for instance, was the testimony of the former minister, Rouvier, before the Commission of Inquiry.

21  Barrès (quoted by Bernanos, *op. cit.*, p. 271) puts the matter tersely: 'Whenever Rein-ach had swallowed something, it was Cornélius Herz who knew how to make him disgorge it.'

22  Cf. Frank, *op. cit.*, in the chapter headed 'Panama'; cf. Suarez, *op. cit.*, p. 155.

23  The quarrel between Reinach and Herz lends to the Panama scandal an air of gang-sterism unusual in the nineteenth century. In his resistance to Herz's blackmail Reinach went so far as to recruit the aid of former police inspectors in placing a price of ten thousand francs on the head of his rival; cf. Suarez, *op. cit.*, p. 157.

men,' imposing as the sole condition that the paper should cover up for him personally when it published its exposure. The *Libre Parole* was transformed overnight from a small and politically insignificant sheet into one of the most influential papers in the country, with a 300,000 circulation. The golden opportunity proffered by Reinach was handled with consummate care and skill. The list of culprits was published in small installments so that hundreds of politicians had to live on tenterhooks morning after morning. Drumont's journal, and with it the entire antisemitic press and movement, emerged at last as a dangerous force in the Third Republic.

The Panama scandal, which, in Drumont's phrase, rendered the invisible visible, brought with it two revelations. First, it disclosed that the members of Parliament and civil servants had become businessmen. Secondly, it showed that the intermediaries between private enterprise (in this case, the company) and the machinery of the state were almost exclusively Jews.[24] What was most surprising was that all these Jews who worked in such an intimate relationship with the state machinery were newcomers. Up to the establishment of the Third Republic, the handling of the finances of the state had been pretty well monopolized by the Rothschilds. An attempt by their rivals, Péreires Brothers, to wrest part of it from their hands by establishing the Crédit Mobilier had ended in a compromise. And in 1882, the Rothschild group was still powerful enough to drive into bankruptcy the Catholic Union Générale, the real purpose of which had been to ruin Jewish bankers.[25] Immediately after the conclusion of the peace treaty of 1871, whose financial provisions had been handled on the French side by Rothschild and on the German side by Bleichroeder, a former agent of the house, the Rothschilds embarked on an unprecedented policy: they came out openly for the monarchists and against the republic.[26] What was new in this was not the monarchist trend but the fact that

24 Cf. Levaillant, 'La Genèse de l'antisémitisme sous la Troisième République,' in *Revue des études juives*, Vol. LIII (1907), p. 97.

25 See Bernard Lazare, *Contre l'Antisémitisme: histoire d'une polémique*, Paris, 1896.

26 On the complicity of the Haute Banque in the Orleanist movement see G. Charensol, *op. cit.* One of the spokesmen of this powerful group was Arthur Meyer, publisher of the *Gaulois*. A baptized Jew, Meyer belonged to the most virulent section of the Anti-Dreyfusards. See Clemenceau, 'Le spectacle du jour,' in *L'Iniquité*, 1899; see also the entries in Hohenlohe's diary, in Herzog, *op. cit.*, under date of June 11, 1898.

for the first time an important Jewish financial power set itself in opposition to the current regime. Up to that time the Rothschilds had accommodated themselves to whatever political system was in power. It seemed, therefore, that the republic was the first form of government that really had no use for them.

Both the political influence and the social status of the Jews had for centuries been due to the fact that they were a closed group who worked directly for the state and were directly protected by it on account of their special services. Their close and immediate connection with the machinery of government was possible only so long as the state remained at a distance from the people, while the ruling classes continued to be indifferent to its management. In such circumstances the Jews were, from the state's point of view, the most dependable element in society just because they did not really belong to it. The parliamentary system allowed the liberal bourgeoisie to gain control of the state machine. To this bourgeoisie, however, the Jews had never belonged and they therefore regarded it with a not unwarranted suspicion. The regime no longer needed the Jews as much as before, since it was now possible to achieve through Parliament a financial expansion beyond the wildest dreams of the former more or less absolute or constitutional monarchs. Thus the leading Jewish houses gradually faded from the scene of finance politics and betook themselves more and more to the antisemitic salons of the aristocracy, there to dream of financing reactionary movements designed to restore the good old days.[27] Meanwhile, however, other Jewish circles, newcomers among Jewish plutocrats, were beginning to take an increasing part in the commercial life of the Third Republic. What the Rothschilds had almost forgotten and what had nearly cost them their power was the simple fact that once they withdrew, even for a moment, from active interest in a regime, they immediately lost their influence not only upon cabinet circles but upon the Jews. The Jewish immigrants were the first to see their chance.[28] They realized only too well that the republic, as it had developed, was

27 On current leanings toward Bonapartism see Frank, *op. cit.*, p. 419. based upon unpublished documents taken from the archives of the German ministry of foreign affairs.

28 Jacques Reinach was born in Germany, received an Italian barony and was naturalized in France. Cornélius Herz was born in France, the son of Bavarian parents.

not the logical sequel of a united people's uprising. Out of the slaughter of some 20,000 Communards, out of military defeat and economic collapse, what had in fact emerged was a regime whose capacity for government had been doubtful from its inception. So much, indeed, was this the case that within three years a society brought to the brink of ruin was clamoring for a dictator. And when it got one in President General MacMahon (whose only claim to distinction was his defeat at Sedan), that individual had promptly turned out to be a parliamentarian of the old school and after a few years (1879) resigned. Meanwhile, however, the various elements in society, from the opportunists to the radicals and from the coalitionists to the extreme right, had made up their minds what kind of policies they required from their representatives and what methods they ought to employ. The right policy was defense of vested interests and the right method was corruption.[29] After 1881, swindle (to quote Léon Say) became the only law.

It has been justly observed that at this period of French history every political party had its Jew, in the same way that every royal household once had its court Jew.[30] The difference, however, was profound. Investment of Jewish capital in the state had helped to give the Jews a productive role in the economy of Europe. Without their assistance the eighteenth-century development of the nation-state and its independent civil service would have been inconceivable. It was, after all, to these court Jews that Western Jewry owed its emancipation. The shady transactions of Reinach and his confederates did not even lead to

---

Migrating to America in early youth, he acquired citizenship and amassed a fortune there. For further details, cf. Brogan, *op. cit.*, pp. 268 ff.

Characteristic of the way in which native Jews disappeared from public office is the fact that as soon as the affairs of the Panama Company began to go badly, Lévy-Crémieux, its original financial adviser, was replaced by Reinach; see Brogan, *op. cit.*, Book VI, chapter 2.

29 Georges Lachapelle, *Les Finances de la Troisième République*, Paris, 1937, pp. 54 ff., describes in detail how the bureaucracy gained control of public funds and how the Budget Commission was governed entirely by private interests.

With regard to the economic status of members of Parliament cf. Bernanos, *op. cit.*, p. 192: 'Most of them, like Gambetta, lacked even a change of underclothes.'

30 As Frank remarks (*op. cit.*, pp. 321 ff.), the right had its Arthur Meyer, Boulangerism its Alfred Naquet, the opportunists their Reinachs, and the Radicals their Dr. Cornélius Herz.

permanent riches.[31] All they did was to shroud in even deeper darkness the mysterious and scandalous relations between business and politics. These parasites upon a corrupt body served to provide a thoroughly decadent society with an exceedingly dangerous alibi. Since they were Jews it was possible to make scapegoats of them when public indignation had to be allayed. Afterwards things could go on the same old way. The antisemites could at once point to the Jewish parasites on a corrupt society in order to 'prove' that all Jews everywhere were nothing but termites in the otherwise healthy body of the people. It did not matter to them that the corruption of the body politic had started without the help of Jews; that the policy of businessmen (in a bourgeois society to which Jews had not belonged) and their ideal of unlimited competition had led to the disintegration of the state in party politics; that the ruling classes had proved incapable any longer of protecting their own interests, let alone those of the country as a whole. The antisemites who called themselves patriots introduced that new species of national feeling which consists primarily in a complete whitewash of one's own people and a sweeping condemnation of all others.

The Jews could remain a separate group outside of society only so long as a more or less homogeneous and stable state machine had a use for them and was interested in protecting them. The decay of the state machine brought about the dissolution of the closed ranks of Jewry, which had so long been bound up with it. The first sign of this appeared in the affairs conducted by newly naturalized French Jews over whom their native-born brethren had lost control in much the same way as occurred in the Germany of the inflation period. The newcomers filled the gaps between the commercial world and the state.

Far more disastrous was another process which likewise began at this time and which was imposed from above. The dissolution of the state into factions, while it disrupted the closed society of the Jews, did not force them into a vacuum in which they could go on vegetating outside of state and society. For that the Jews were too rich and, at a

31 To these newcomers Drumont's charge applies (*Les Trétaux du succès*, Paris, 1901. p. 237): 'Those great Jews who start from nothing and attain everything . . . they come from God knows where, live in a mystery, die in a guess . . . They don't arrive, they jump up . . . They don't die, they fade out.'

time when money was one of the salient requisites of power, too powerful. Rather did they tend to become absorbed into the variety of social 'sets,' in accordance with their political leanings or, more frequently, their social connections. This, however, did not lead to their disappearance. On the contrary, they maintained certain relations with the state machine and continued, albeit in a crucially different form, to manipulate the business of the state. Thus, despite their known opposition to the Third Republic, it was none other than the Rothschilds who undertook the placement of the Russian loan while Arthur Meyer, though baptized and an avowed monarchist, was among those involved in the Panama scandal. This meant that the newcomers in French Jewry who formed the principal links between private commerce and the machinery of government were followed by the native-born. But if the Jews had previously constituted a strong, close-knit group, whose usefulness for the state was obvious, they were now split up into cliques, mutually antagonistic but all bent on the same purpose of helping society to batten on the state.

## III: Army and Clergy Against the Republic

Seemingly removed from all such factors, seemingly immune from all corruption, stood the army, a heritage from the Second Empire. The republic had never dared to dominate it, even when monarchistic sympathies and intrigues came to open expression in the Boulanger crisis. The officer class consisted then as before of the sons of those old aristocratic families whose ancestors, as emigrés, had fought against their fatherland during the revolutionary wars. These officers were strongly under the influence of the clergy who ever since the Revolution had made a point of supporting reactionary and antirepublican movements. Their influence was perhaps equally strong over those officers who were of somewhat lower birth but who hoped, as a result of the Church's old practice of marking talent without regard to pedigree, to gain promotion with the help of the clergy.

In contrast to the shifting and fluid cliques of society and Parliament, where admission was easy and allegiance fickle, stood the rigorous exclusiveness of the army, so characteristic of the caste system. It was neither military life, professional honor, nor *esprit de corps* that held its officers together to form a reactionary bulwark against the republic and against all democratic influences; it was simply the tie of caste.[32] The refusal of the state to democratize the army and to subject it to the civil authorities entailed remarkable consequences. It made the army an entity outside of the nation and created an armed power whose loyalties could be turned in directions which none could foretell. That this caste-ridden power, if but left to itself, was neither for nor against anyone is shown clearly by the story of the almost burlesque *coups d'état* in which, despite statements to the contrary, it was really unwilling to take part. Even its notorious monarchism was, in the final analysis, nothing but an excuse for preserving itself as an independent interest-group, ready to defend its privileges 'without regard to and in despite of, even against the republic.' [33] Contemporary journalists and later historians have made valiant efforts to explain the conflict between military and civil powers during the Dreyfus Affair in terms of an antagonism between 'businessmen and soldiers.' [34] We know today, however, how unjustified is this indirectly antisemitic interpretation. The intelligence department of the General Staff were themselves reasonably expert at business. Were they not trafficking as openly in forged *bordereaux* and selling them as nonchalantly to foreign military attachés as a leather merchant might traffic in skins and then become President of the Republic, or the son-in-law of the President traffic in honors and distinctions?[35] Indeed, the zeal of Schwartzkoppen, the German attaché, who was anxious to discover more military secrets than France had to hide, must have been a positive source of

32 See the excellent anonymous article, 'The Dreyfus Case: A Study of French Opinion,' in *The Contemporary Review*, Vol. LXXIV (October, 1898).

33 See Luxemburg, *loc. cit.*: 'The reason the army was reluctant to make a move was that it wanted to show its opposition to the civil power of the republic, without at the same time losing the force of that opposition by committing itself to a monarchy.'

34 It is under this caption that Maximilian Harden (a German Jew) described the Dreyfus case in *Die Zukunft* (1898). Walter Frank, the antisemitic historian, employs the same slogan in the heading of his chapter on Dreyfus while Bernanos (*op. cit.*, p. 413) remarks in the same vein that 'rightly or wrongly, democracy sees in the military its most dangerous rival.'

35 The Panama scandal was preceded by the so-called 'Wilson affair.' The President's son-in-law was found conducting an open traffic in honors and decorations.

embarrassment to these gentlemen of the counterespionage service who, after all, could sell no more than they produced.

It was the great mistake of Catholic politicians to imagine that, in pursuit of their European policy, they could make use of the French army simply because it appeared to be antirepublican. The Church was, in fact, slated to pay for this error with the loss of its entire political influence in France.[36] When the department of intelligence finally emerged as a common fake factory, as Esterhazy, who was in a position to know, described the Deuxième Bureau,[37] no one in France, not even the army, was so seriously compromised as the Church. Toward the end of the last century the Catholic clergy had been seeking to recover its old political power in just those quarters where, for one or another reason, secular authority was on the wane among the people. Cases in point were those of Spain, where a decadent feudal aristocracy had brought about the economic and cultural ruin of the country, and Austria-Hungary, where a conflict of nationalities was threatening daily to disrupt the state. And such too was the case in France, where the nation appeared to be sinking fast into the slough of conflicting interests.[38] The army – left in a political vacuum by the Third Republic – gladly accepted the guidance of the Catholic clergy which at least provided for civilian leadership without which the military lose their 'raison d'être (which) is to defend the principle embodied in civilian society' – as Clemenceau put it.

The Catholic Church then owed its popularity to the widespread popular skepticism which saw in the republic and in democracy the loss of all order, security, and political will. To many the hierarchic system of the Church seemed the only escape from chaos. Indeed, it was this, rather than any religious revivalism, which caused the clergy to be held in respect.[39] As a matter of fact, the staunchest supporters of the Church

36 See Father Edouard Lecanuet, *Les Signes avant-coureurs de la séparation, 1894–1910*, Paris, 1930.

37 See Bruno Weil, *L'Affaire Dreyfus*, Paris, 1930, p. 169.

38 Cf. Clemenceau, 'La Croisade,' *op. cit.*: 'Spain is writhing under the yoke of the Roman Church. Italy appears to have succumbed. The only countries left are Catholic Austria, already in her death-struggle, and the France of the Revolution, against which the papal hosts are even now deployed.'

39 Cf. Bernanos, *op. cit.*, p. 152: 'The point cannot be sufficiently repeated: the real beneficiaries of that movement of reaction which followed the fall of the empire and

at that period were the exponents of that so-called 'cerebral' Catholicism, the 'Catholics without faith,' who were henceforth to dominate the entire monarchist and extreme nationalist movement. Without believing in their other-worldly basis, these 'Catholics' clamored for more power to all authoritarian institutions. This, indeed, had been the line first laid down by Drumont and later endorsed by Maurras.[40]

The large majority of the Catholic clergy, deeply involved in political maneuvers, followed a policy of accommodation. In this, as the Dreyfus Affair makes clear, they were conspicuously successful. Thus, when Victor Basch took up the cause for a retrial his house at Rennes was stormed under the leadership of three priests,[41] while no less distinguished a figure than the Dominican Father Didon called on the students of the Collège D'Arcueil to 'draw the sword, terrorize, cut off heads and run amok.'[42] Similar too was the outlook of the three hundred lesser clerics who immortalized themselves in the 'Henry Memorial,' as the *Libre Parole's* list of subscribers to a fund for the benefit of Madame Henry (widow of the Colonel who had committed suicide while in prison[43]) was called, and which certainly is a monument for all time to the shocking corruption of the upper classes of the French people at that date. During the period of the Dreyfus crisis it was not her regular clergy, not her ordinary religious orders, and certainly not her *homines religiosi* who influenced the political line of the Catholic Church. As far as Europe was concerned, her reactionary policies in France, Austria, and Spain, as well as her support of antisemitic trends in Vienna, Paris, and Algiers were probably an immediate consequence of Jesuit influence. It was the Jesuits who had always best represented, both in the written and spoken word, the antisemitic school of the Catholic clergy.[44] This is largely the consequence of their

---

the defeat were the clergy. Thanks to them national reaction assumed after 1873 the character of a religious revival.'

40 On Drumont and the origin of 'cerebral Catholicism,' see Bernanos, *op. cit.*, pp. 127 ff.

41 Cf. Herzog, *op. cit.*, under date of January 21, 1898.

42 See Lecanuet, *op. cit.*, p. 182.

43 See above, note 10.

44 The Jesuits' magazine *Civiltà Cattolica* was for decades the most outspokenly antisemitic and one of the most influential Catholic magazines in the world. It carried anti-Jewish propaganda long before Italy went Fascist, and its policy was not affected

statutes according to which each novice must prove that he has no Jewish blood back to the fourth generation.[45] And since the beginning of the nineteenth century the direction of the Church's international policy had passed into their hands.[46]

We have already observed how the dissolution of the state machinery facilitated the entry of the Rothschilds into the circles of the antisemitic aristocracy. The fashionable set of Faubourg Saint-Germain opened its doors not only to a few ennobled Jews, but their baptized sycophants, the antisemitic Jews, were also suffered to drift in as well as complete newcomers.[47] Curiously enough, the Jews of Alsace, who like the Dreyfus family had moved to Paris following the cession of that territory, took an especially prominent part in this social climb. Their exaggerated patriotism came out most markedly in the way they strove to dissociate themselves from Jewish immigrants. The Dreyfus family belonged to that section of French Jewry which sought to assimilate by adopting its own brand of antisemitism.[48] This

---

by the anti-Christian attitude of the Nazis. See Joshua Starr, 'Italy's Antisemites,' in *Jewish Social Studies*, 1939.

According to L. Koch, S.J.: 'Of all orders, the Society of Jesus through its constitution is best protected against any Jewish influences.' In *Jesuiten-Lexikon*, Paderborn, 1934, article 'Juden.'

45 Originally, according to the Convention of 1593, all Christians of Jewish descent were excluded. A decree of 1608 stipulated reinvestigations back to the fifth generation; the last provision of 1923 reduced this to four generations. These requirements can be waived by the chief of the order in individual cases.

46 Cf. H. Boehmer, *Les Jésuites*, translated from the German, Paris, 1910, p. 284: 'Since 1820 . . . no such thing as independent national churches able to resist the Jesuit-dictated orders of the Pope has existed. The higher clergy of our day have pitched their tents in front of the Holy See and the Church has become what Bellarmin, the great Jesuit controversialist, always demanded it should become, an absolute monarchy whose policies can be directed by the Jesuits and whose development can be determined by pressing a button.'

47 Cf. Clemenceau, 'Le spectacle du jour,' in *op. cit.*: 'Rothschild, friend of the entire antisemitic nobility . . . of a piece with Arthur Meyer, who is more papist than the Pope.'

48 On the Alisatian Jews, to whom Dreyfus belonged, see André Foucault, *Un nouvel aspect de l'Affaire Dreyfus*, in Les Oeuvres Libres, 1938, p. 310: 'In the eyes of the Jewish bourgeoisie of Paris they were the incarnation of nationalist *raideur* . . . that attitude of distant disdain which the gentry affects towards its parvenu co-religionists. Their desire to assimilate completely to Gallic modes, to live on intimate terms with our old-established families, to occupy the most distinguished positions in the state, and the contempt which they showed for the commercial elements of Jewry, for the

adjustment to the French aristocracy had one inevitable result: the Jews tried to launch their sons upon the same higher military careers as were pursued by those of their new-found friends. It was here that the first cause of friction arose. The admission of the Jews into high society had been relatively peaceful. The upper classes, despite their dreams of a restored monarchy, were a politically spineless lot and did not bother unduly one way or the other. But when the Jews began seeking equality in the army, they came face to face with the determined opposition of the Jesuits who were not prepared to tolerate the existence of officers immune to the influence of the confessional.[49] Moreover, they came up against an inveterate caste spirit, which the easy atmosphere of the salons had led them to forget, a caste spirit which, already strengthened by tradition and calling, was still further fortified by uncompromising hostility to the Third Republic and to the civil administration.

A modern historian has described the struggle between Jews and Jesuits as a 'struggle between two rivals,' in which the 'higher Jesuit clergy and the Jewish plutocracy stood facing one another in the middle of France like two invisible lines of battle.'[50] The description is true insofar as the Jews found in the Jesuits their first unappeasable foes, while the latter came promptly to realize how powerful a weapon antisemitism could be. This was the first attempt and the only one prior to Hitler to exploit the 'major political concept'[51] of antisemitism on a Pan-European scale. On the other hand, however, if it is assumed that the struggle was one of two equally matched 'rivals' the description is palpably false. The Jews sought no higher degree of power than was being wielded by any of the other cliques into which the republic had split. All they desired at the time was sufficient influence to pursue

---

recently naturalized "Polaks" of Galicia, gave them almost the appearance of traitors against their own race . . . The Dreyfuses of 1894? Why, they were antisemites!'

49  Cf. 'K.V.T.' in *The Contemporary Review,* LXXIV, 598: 'By the will of the democracy all Frenchmen are to be soldiers; by the will of the Church Catholics only are to hold the chief commands.'

50  Herzog, *op. cit.,* p. 35.

51  Cf. Bernanos, *op. cit.,* p. 151: 'So, shorn of ridiculous hyperbole, antisemitism showed itself for what it really is: not a mere piece of crankiness, a mental quirk, but a major political concept.'

their social and business interests. They did not aspire to a political share in the management of the state. The only organized group who sought that were the Jesuits. The trial of Dreyfus was preceded by a number of incidents which show how resolutely and energetically the Jews tried to gain a place in the army and how common, even at that time, was the hostility toward them. Constantly subjected to gross insult, the few Jewish officers there were were obliged always to fight duels while Gentile comrades were unwilling to act as their seconds. It is, indeed, in this connection that the infamous Esterhazy first comes upon the scene as an exception to the rule.[52]

It has always remained somewhat obscure whether the arrest and condemnation of Dreyfus was simply a judicial error which just happened by chance to light up a political conflagration, or whether the General Staff deliberately planted the forged *bordereau* for the express purpose of at last branding a Jew as a traitor. In favor of the latter hypothesis is the fact that Dreyfus was the first Jew to find a post on the General Staff and under existing conditions this could only have aroused not merely annoyance but positive fury and consternation. In any case anti-Jewish hatred was unleashed even before the verdict was returned. Contrary to custom, which demanded the withholding of all information in a spy case still *sub iudice*, officers of the General Staff cheerfully supplied the *Libre Parole* with details of the case and the name of the accused. Apparently they feared lest Jewish influence with the government lead to a suppression of the trial and a stifling of the whole business. Some show of plausibility was afforded these fears by the fact that certain circles of French Jewry were known at the time

52 See Esterhazy's letter of July, 1894, to Edmond de Rothschild, quoted by J. Reinach, *op. cit.*, II, 53 ff.: 'I did not hesitate when Captain Crémieux could find no Christian officer to act as his second.' Cf. T. Reinach, *Histoire sommaire de l'Affaire Dreyfus*, pp. 60 ff. See also Herzog, *op. cit.*, under date of 1892 and June, 1894, where these duels are listed in detail and all of Esterhazy's intermediaries named. The last occasion was in September, 1896, when he received 10,000 francs. This misplaced generosity was later to have disquieting results. When, from the comfortable security of England, Esterhazy at length made his revelations and thereby compelled a revision of the case, the antisemitic press naturally suggested that he had been paid by the Jews for his self-condemnation. The idea is still advanced as a major argument in favor of Dreyfus' guilt.

to be seriously concerned about the precarious situation of Jewish officers.

It must also be remembered that the Panama scandal was then fresh in the public mind and that following the Rothschild loan to Russia distrust of the Jews had grown considerably.[53] War Minister Mercier was not only lauded by the bourgeois press at every fresh turn of the trial but even Jaurès' paper, the organ of the socialists, congratulated him on 'having opposed the formidable pressure of corrupt politicians and high finance.' [54] Characteristically this encomium drew from the *Libre Parole* the unstinted commendation, 'Bravo, Jaurès!' Two years later, when Bernard Lazare published his first pamphlet on the miscarriage of justice, Jaurès' paper carefully refrained from discussing its contents but charged the socialist author with being an admirer of Rothschild and probably a paid agent.[55] Similarly, as late as 1897, when the fight for Dreyfus' reinstatement had already begun, Jaurès could see nothing in it but the conflict of two bourgeois groups, the opportunists and the clerics. Finally, even after the Rennes retrial Wilhelm Liebknecht, the German Social Democrat, still believed in the guilt of Dreyfus because he could not imagine that a member of the upper classes could ever be the victim of a false verdict.[56]

The skepticism of the radical and socialist press, strongly colored as it was by anti-Jewish feelings, was strengthened by the bizarre tactics of the Dreyfus family in its attempt to secure a retrial. In trying to save an innocent man they employed the very methods usually adopted in the case of a guilty one. They stood in mortal terror of publicity and

53 Herzog, *op. cit.*, under date of 1892 shows at length how the Rothschilds began to adapt themselves to the republic. Curiously enough the papal policy of coalitionism, which represents an attempt at rapprochement by the Catholic Church, dates from precisely the same year. It is therefore not impossible that the Rothschild line was influenced by the clergy. As for the loan of 500 million francs to Russia, Count Münster pertinently observed: 'Speculation is dead in France . . . The capitalists can find no way of negotiating their securities . . . and this will contribute to the success of the loan . . . The big Jews believe that if they make money they will best be able to help their small-time brethren. The result is that, though the French market is glutted with Russian securities, Frenchmen are still giving good francs for bad roubles'; Herzog, *ibid.*

54 Cf. J. Reinach, *op. cit.*, I, 471.

55 Cf. Herzog, *op. cit.*, p. 212.

56 Cf. Max J. Kohler, 'Some New Light on the Dreyfus Case,' in *Studies in Jewish Bibliography and Related Subjects in Memory of A. S. Freidus*, New York, 1929.

relied exclusively on back-door maneuvers.[57] They were lavish with their cash and treated Lazare, one of their most valuable helpers and one of the greatest figures in the case, as if he were their paid agent.[58] Clemenceau, Zola, Picquart, and Labori – to name but the more active of the Dreyfusards – could in the end only save their good names by dissociating their efforts, with greater or less fuss and publicity, from the more concrete aspects of the issue.[59]

There was only one basis on which Dreyfus could or should have been saved. The intrigues of a corrupt Parliament, the dry rot of a collapsing society, and the clergy's lust for power should have been met squarely with the stern Jacobin concept of the nation based upon human rights – that republican view of communal life which asserts that (in the words of Clemenceau) by infringing on the rights of one you infringe on the rights of all. To rely on Parliament or on society was to lose the fight before beginning it. For one thing the resources of Jewry were in no way superior to those of the rich Catholic bourgeoisie; for another all of the higher strata of society, from the clerical and aristocratic families of the Faubourg Saint-Germain to the anticlerical and radical petty bourgeoisie, were only too willing to see the Jews formally removed from the body politic. In this way, they

---

57 The Dreyfus family, for instance, summarily rejected the suggestion of Arthur Lévy, the writer, and Lévy-Bruhl, the scholar, that they should circulate a petition of protest among all leading figures of public life. Instead they embarked on a series of personal approaches to any politician with whom they happened to have contact; cf. Dutrait-Crozon, *op. cit.*, p. 51. See also Foucault, *op. cit.*, p. 309: 'At this distance, one may wonder at the fact that the French Jews, instead of working on the papers secretly, did not give adequate and open expression to their indignation.'

58 Cf. Herzog, *op. cit.*, under date of December, 1894 and January, 1898. See also Charensol, *op. cit.*, p. 79, and Charles Péguy, 'Le Portrait de Bernard Lazare,' in *Cahiers de la quinzaine*, Series XI, No. 2 (1910).

59 Labori's withdrawal, after Dreyfus' family had hurriedly withdrawn the brief from him while the Rennes tribunal was still sitting, caused a major scandal. An exhaustive, if greatly exaggerated, account will be found in Frank, *op. cit.*, p. 432. Labori's own statement, which speaks eloquently for his nobility of character, appeared in *La Grande Revue* (February, 1900). After what had happened to his counsel and friend Zola at once broke relations with the Dreyfus family. As for Picquart, the *Echo de Paris* (November 30, 1901) reported that after Rennes he had nothing more to do with the Dreyfuses. Clemenceau in face of the fact that the whole of France, or even the whole world, grasped the real meaning of the trials better than the accused or his family, was more inclined to consider the incident humorous; cf. Weil, *op. cit.*, pp. 307–8.

reckoned, they would be able to purge themselves of possible taint. The loss of Jewish social and commercial contacts seemed to them a price well worth paying. Similarly, as the utterances of Jaurès indicate, the Affair was regarded by Parliament as a golden opportunity for rehabilitating, or rather regaining, its time-honored reputation for incorruptibility. Last, but by no means least, in the countenancing of such slogans as 'Death to the Jews' or 'France for the French' an almost magic formula was discovered for reconciling the masses to the existent state of government and society.

## IV: The People and the Mob

If it is the common error of our time to imagine that propaganda can achieve all things and that a man can be talked into anything provided the talking is sufficiently loud and cunning, in that period it was commonly believed that the 'voice of the people was the voice of God,' and that the task of a leader was, as Clemenceau so scornfully expressed it,[60] to follow that voice shrewdly. Both views go back to the same fundamental error of regarding the mob as identical with rather than as a caricature of the people.

The mob is primarily a group in which the residue of all classes are represented. This makes it so easy to mistake the mob for the people, which also comprises all strata of society. While the people in all great revolutions fight for true representation, the mob always will shout for the 'strong man,' the 'great leader.' For the mob hates society from which it is excluded, as well as Parliament where it is not represented. Plebiscites, therefore, with which modern mob leaders have obtained such excellent results, are an old concept of politicians who rely upon the mob. One of the more intelligent leaders of the Anti-Dreyfusards, Déroulède, clamored for a 'Republic through plebiscite.'

High society and politicians of the Third Republic had produced the French mob in a series of scandals and public frauds. They now felt a tender sentiment of parental familiarity with their offspring, a

60 Cf. Clemenceau's article, February 2, 1898, in *op. cit.* On the futility of trying to win the workers with antisemitic slogans and especially on the attempts of Léon Daudet, see the Royalist writer Dimier, *Vingt ans d'Action Française*, Paris, 1926.

feeling mixed with admiration and fear. The least society could do for its offspring was to protect it verbally. While the mob actually stormed Jewish shops and assailed Jews in the streets, the language of high society made real, passionate violence look like harmless child's play.[61] The most important of the contemporary documents in this respect is the 'Henry Memorial' and the various solutions it proposed to the Jewish question: Jews were to be torn to pieces like Marsyas in the Greek myth; Reinach ought to be boiled alive; Jews should be stewed in oil or pierced to death with needles; they should be 'circumcised up to the neck.' One group of officers expressed great impatience to try out a new type of gun on the 100,000 Jews in the country. Among the subscribers were more than 1,000 officers, including four generals in active service, and the minister of war, Mercier. The relatively large number of intellectuals[62] and even of Jews in the list is surprising. The upper classes knew that the mob was flesh of their flesh and blood of their blood. Even a Jewish historian of the time, although he had seen with his own eyes that Jews are no longer safe when the mob rules the street, spoke with secret admiration of the 'great collective movement.'[63] This only shows how deeply most Jews were rooted in a society which was attempting to eliminate them.

If Bernanos, with reference to the Dreyfus Affair, describes anti-semitism as a major political concept, he is undoubtedly right with respect to the mob. It had been tried out previously in Berlin and Vienna, by Ahlwardt and Stoecker, by Schoenerer and Lueger, but nowhere was its efficacy more clearly proved than in France. There can be no doubt that in the eyes of the mob the Jews came to serve as an object lesson for all the things they detested. If they hated society

61 Very characteristic in this respect are the various depictions of contemporary society in J. Reinach, *op. cit.*, I, 233 ff.; III, 141: 'Society hostesses fell in step with Guérin. Their language (which scarcely outran their thoughts) would have struck horror in the Amazon of Damohey . . .' Of special interest in this connection is an article by André Chevrillon, 'Huit Jours à Rennes,' in *La Grande Revue*, February, 1900. He relates, *inter alia*, the following revealing incident: 'A physician speaking to some friends of mine about Dreyfus, chanced to remark, "I'd like to torture him." "And I wish," rejoined one of the ladies, "that he were innocent. Then he'd suffer more."'

62 The intellectuals include, strangely enough, Paul Valéry, who contributed three francs '*non sans réflexion.*'

63 J. Reinach, *op. cit.*, I, 233.

they could point to the way in which the Jews were tolerated within it; and if they hated the government they could point to the way in which the Jews had been protected by or were identifiable with the state. While it is a mistake to assume that the mob preys only on Jews, the Jews must be accorded first place among its favorite victims.

Excluded as it is from society and political representation, the mob turns of necessity to extraparliamentary action. Moreover, it is inclined to seek the real forces of political life in those movements and influences which are hidden from view and work behind the scenes. There can be no doubt that during the nineteenth century Jewry fell into this category, as did Freemasonry (especially in Latin countries) and the Jesuits.[64] It is, of course, utterly untrue that any of these groups really constituted a secret society bent on dominating the world by means of a gigantic conspiracy. Nevertheless, it is true that their influence, however overt it may have been, was exerted beyond the formal realm of politics, operating on a large scale in lobbies, lodges, and the confessional. Ever since the French Revolution these three groups have shared the doubtful honor of being, in the eyes of the European mob, the pivotal point of world politics. During the Dreyfus crisis each was able to exploit this popular notion by hurling at the other charges of conspiring to world domination. The slogan, 'secret Judah,' is due, no doubt, to the inventiveness of certain Jesuits, who chose to see in the first Zionist Congress (1897) the core of a Jewish world conspiracy.[65] Similarly, the concept of 'secret Rome' is due to the anticlerical Freemasons and perhaps to the indiscriminate slanders of some Jews as well.

The fickleness of the mob is proverbial, as the opponents of Dreyfus were to learn to their sorrow when, in 1899, the wind changed and the small group of true republicans, headed by Clemenceau, suddenly realized, with mixed feelings, that a section of the mob had rallied to

64 A study of European superstition would probably show that Jews became objects of this typically nineteenth-century brand of superstition fairly late. They were preceded by the Rosicrucians, Templars, Jesuits, and Freemasons. The treatment of nineteenth-century history suffers greatly from the lack of such a study.

65 See 'Il caso Dreyfus,' in *Civiltà Cattolica* (February 5, 1898). – Among the exceptions to the foregoing statement the most notable is the Jesuit Pierre Charles Louvain, who has denounced the 'Protocols.'

their side.[66] In some eyes the two parties to the great controversy now seemed like 'two rival gangs of charlatans squabbling for recognition by the rabble'[67] while actually the voice of the Jacobin Clemenceau had succeeded in bringing back one part of the French people to their greatest tradition. Thus the great scholar, Emile Duclaux, could write: 'In this drama played before a whole people and so worked up by the press that the whole nation ultimately took part in it, we see the chorus and anti-chorus of the ancient tragedy railing at each other. The scene is France and the theater is the world.'

Led by the Jesuits and aided by the mob the army at last stepped into the fray confident of victory. Counterattack from the civil power had been effectively forestalled. The antisemitic press had stopped men's mouths by publishing Reinach's lists of the deputies involved in the Panama scandal.[68] Everything suggested an effortless triumph. The society and the politicians of the Third Republic, its scandals and affairs, had created a new class of *déclassés*; they could not be expected to fight against their own product; on the contrary, they were to adopt the language and outlook of the mob. Through the army the Jesuits would gain the upper hand over the corrupt civil power and the way would thus be paved for a bloodless *coup d'état*.

So long as there was only the Dreyfus family trying with bizarre methods to rescue their kinsman from Devil's Island, and so long as there were only Jews concerned about their standing in the antisemitic salons and the still more antisemitic army, everything certainly pointed that way. Obviously there was no reason to expect an attack on the army or on society from *that* quarter. Was not the sole desire of the Jews to continue to be accepted in society and suffered in the armed forces? No one in military or civilian circles needed to suffer a

66 Cf. Martin du Gard, *Jean Barois*, pp. 272 ff., and Daniel Halévy, in *Cahiers de la quin-zaine,* Series XI, cahier 10, Paris, 1910.

67 Cf. Georges Sorel, *La Revolution dreyfusienne*, Paris, 1911, pp. 70–71.

68 To what extent the hands of members of Parliament were tied is shown by the case of Scheurer-Kestner, one of their better elements and vice-president of the senate. No sooner had he entered his protest against the trial than *Libre Parole* proclaimed the fact that his son-in-law had been involved in the Panama scandal. See Herzog, *op. cit.,* under date of November, 1897.

sleepless night on *their* account.[69] It was disconcerting, therefore, when it transpired that in the intelligence office of the General Staff there sat a high officer, who, though possessed of a good Catholic background, excellent military prospects, and the 'proper' degree of antipathy toward the Jews, had yet not adopted the principle that the end justifies the means. Such a man, utterly divorced from social clannishness or professional ambition, was Picquart, and of this simple, quiet, politically disinterested spirit the General Staff was soon to have its fill. Picquart was no hero and certainly no martyr. He was simply that common type of citizen with an average interest in public affairs who in the hour of danger (though not a minute earlier) stands up to defend his country in the same unquestioning way as he discharges his daily duties.[70] Nevertheless, the cause only grew serious when, after several delays and hesitations, Clemenceau at last became convinced that Dreyfus was innocent and the republic in danger. At the beginning of the struggle only a handful of well-known writers and scholars rallied to the cause, Zola, Anatole France, E. Duclaux, Gabriel Monod, the historian, and Lucien Herr, librarian of the Ecole Normale. To these must be added the small and then insignificant circle of young intellectuals who were later to make history in the *Cahiers de la quinzaine*.[71] That, however, was the full roster of Clemenceau's allies. There was no political group, not a single politician of repute, ready to stand at his side. The greatness of Clemenceau's approach lies in the fact that it was not directed against a particular miscarriage of justice, but was based upon such 'abstract' ideas as justice, liberty, and civic virtue. It was based, in short, on those very concepts which had formed the

---

69 Cf. Brogan, *op. cit.*, Book VII, ch. 1: 'The desire to let the matter rest was not uncommon among French Jews, especially among the richer French Jews.'

70 Immediately after he had made his discoveries Picquart was banished to a dangerous post in Tunis. Thereupon he made his will, exposed the whole business, and deposited a copy of the document with his lawyer. A few months later, when it was discovered that he was still alive, a deluge of mysterious letters came pouring in, compromising him and accusing him of complicity with the 'traitor' Dreyfus. He was treated like a gangster who had threatened to 'squeal.' When all this proved of no avail, he was arrested, drummed out of the army, and divested of his decorations, all of which he endured with quiet equanimity.

71 To this group, led by Charles Péguy, belonged the youthful Romain Rolland, Suarez, Georges Sorel, Daniel Halévy, and Bernard Lazare.

staple of old-time Jacobin patriotism and against which much mud and abuse had already been hurled. As time wore on and Clemenceau continued, unmoved by threats and disappointments, to enunciate the same truths and to embody them in demands, the more 'concrete' nationalists lost ground. Followers of men like Barrès, who had accused the supporters of Dreyfus of losing themselves in a 'welter of metaphysics,' came to realize that the abstractions of the 'Tiger' were actually nearer to political realities than the limited intelligence of ruined businessmen or the barren traditionalism of fatalistic intellectuals.[72] Where the concrete approach of the realistic nationalists eventually led them is illustrated by the priceless story of how Charles Maurras had 'the honor and pleasure,' after the defeat of France, of falling in during his flight to the south with a female astrologer who interpreted to him the political meaning of recent events and advised him to collaborate with the Nazis.[73]

Although antisemitism had undoubtedly gained ground during the three years following the arrest of Dreyfus, before the opening of Clemenceau's campaign, and although the anti-Jewish press had attained a circulation comparable to that of the chief papers, the streets had remained quiet. It was only when Clemenceau began his articles in *L'Aurore*, when Zola published his *J'Accuse*, and when the Rennes tribunal set off the dismal succession of trials and retrials that the mob stirred into action. Every stroke of the Dreyfusards (who were known to be a small minority) was followed by a more or less violent disturbance on the streets.[74] The organization of the mob by the General Staff was remarkable. The trail leads straight from the army to the *Libre Parole* which, directly or indirectly, through its articles or the personal intervention of its editors, mobilized students, monarchists, adventurers, and plain gangsters and pushed them into

---

72 Cf. M. Barrès, *Scènes et doctrines du nationalisme*, Paris, 1899.

73 See Yves Simon, *op. cit.*, pp. 54–55.

74 The faculty rooms of Rennes University were wrecked after five professors had declared themselves in favor of a retrial. After the appearance of Zola's first article Royalist students demonstrated outside the offices of *Figaro*, after which the paper desisted from further articles of the same type. The publisher of the pro-Dreyfus *La Bataille* was beaten up on the street. The judges of the Court of Cassation, which finally set aside the verdict of 1894, reported unanimously that they had been threatened with 'unlawful assault.' Examples could be multiplied.

the streets. If Zola uttered a word, at once his windows were stoned. If Scheurer-Kestner wrote to the colonial minister, he was at once beaten up on the streets while the papers made scurrilous attacks on his private life. And all accounts agree that if Zola, when once charged, had been acquitted he would never have left the courtroom alive.

The cry, 'Death to the Jews,' swept the country. In Lyon, Rennes, Nantes, Tours, Bordeaux, Clermont-Ferrant, and Marseille – everywhere, in fact – antisemitic riots broke out and were invariably traceable to the same source. Popular indignation broke out everywhere on the same day and at precisely the same hour.[75] Under the leadership of Guérin the mob took on a military complexion. Antisemitic shock troops appeared on the streets and made certain that every pro-Dreyfus meeting should end in bloodshed. The complicity of the police was everywhere patent.[76]

The most modern figure on the side of the Anti-Dreyfusards was probably Jules Guérin. Ruined in business, he had begun his political career as a police stool pigeon, and acquired that flair for discipline and organization which invariably marks the underworld. This he was later able to divert into political channels, becoming the founder and head of the Ligue Antisémite. In him high society found its first criminal hero. In its adulation of Guérin bourgeois society showed clearly that in its code of morals and ethics it had broken for good with its own standards. Behind the Ligue stood two members of the aristocracy, the Duke of Orléans and the Marquis de Morès. The latter had lost his fortune in America and became famous for organizing the butchers of Paris into a manslaughtering brigade.

Most eloquent of these modern tendencies was the farcical siege of the so-called Fort Chabrol. It was here, in this first of 'Brown Houses,' that the cream of the Ligue Antisémite foregathered when the police decided at last to arrest their leader. The installations were the acme of technical perfection. 'The windows were protected by iron shutters.

75  On January 18, 1898, antisemitic demonstrations took place at Bordeaux, Marseille, Clermont-Ferrant, Nantes, Rouen, and Lyon. On the following day student riots broke out in Rouen, Toulouse, and Nantes.
76  The crudest instance was that of the police prefect of Rennes, who advised Professor Victor Basch, when the latter's house was stormed by a mob 2,000 strong, that he ought to hand in his resignation, as he could no longer guarantee his safety.

There was a system of electric bells and telephones from cellar to roof. Five yards or so behind the massive entrance, itself always kept locked and bolted, there was a tall grill of cast iron. On the right, between the grill and the main entrance was a small door, likewise iron-plated, behind which sentries, handpicked from the butcher legions, mounted guard day and night.'[77] Max Régis, instigator of the Algerian pogroms, is another who strikes a modern note. It was this youthful Régis who once called upon a cheering Paris rabble to 'water the tree of freedom with the blood of the Jews.' Régis represented that section of the movement which hoped to achieve power by legal and parliamentary methods. In accordance with this program he had himself elected mayor of Algiers and utilized his office to unleash the pogroms in which several Jews were killed, Jewish women criminally assaulted and Jewish-owned stores looted. It was to him also that the polished and cultured Edouard Drumont, that most famous French antisemite, owed his seat in Parliament.

What was new in all this was not the activity of the mob; for that there were abundant precedents. What was new and surprising at the time – though all too familiar to us – was the organization of the mob and the hero-worship enjoyed by its leaders. The mob became the direct agent of that 'concrete' nationalism espoused by Barrès, Maurras, and Daudet, who together formed what was undoubtedly a kind of elite of the younger intellectuals. These men, who despised the people and who had themselves but recently emerged from a ruinous and decadent cult of estheticism, saw in the mob a living expression of virile and primitive 'strength.' It was they and their theories which first identified the mob with the people and converted its leaders into national heroes.[78] It was their philosophy of pessimism and their delight in doom that was the first sign of the imminent collapse of the European intelligentsia.

Even Clemenceau was not immune from the temptation to identify the mob with the people. What made him especially prone to this error was the consistently ambiguous attitude of the Labor party

77 Cf. Bernanos, *op. cit.*, p. 346.

78 For these theories see especially Charles Maurras, *Au Signe de Flore; souvenirs de la vie politique; l'Affaire Dreyfus et la fondation de l'Action Française*, Paris, 1931; M. Barrès, *op. cit.*; Léon Daudet, *Panorama de la Troisième République*, Paris, 1936.

toward the question of 'abstract' justice. No party, including the socialists, was ready to make an issue of justice per se, 'to stand, come what may, for justice, the sole unbreakable bond of union between civilized men.'[79] The socialists stood for the interests of the workers, the opportunists for those of the liberal bourgeoisie, the coalitionists for those of the Catholic higher classes, and the radicals for those of the anticlerical petty bourgeoisie. The socialists had the great advantage of speaking in the name of a homogeneous and united class. Unlike the bourgeois parties they did not represent a society which had split into innumerable cliques and cabals. Nevertheless, they were concerned primarily and essentially with the interests of their class. They were not troubled by any higher obligation toward human solidarity and had no conception of what communal life really meant. Typical of their attitude was the observation of Jules Guesde, the counterpart of Jaurès in the French party, that 'law and honor are mere words.'

The nihilism which characterized the nationalists was no monopoly of the Anti-Dreyfusards. On the contrary, a large proportion of the socialists and many of those who championed Dreyfus, like Guesde, spoke the same language. If the Catholic *La Croix* remarked that 'it is no longer a question whether Dreyfus is innocent or guilty but only of who will win, the friends of the army or its foes,' the corresponding sentiment might well have been voiced, *mutatis mutandis*, by the partisans of Dreyfus.[80] Not only the mob but a considerable section of the French people declared itself, at best, quite uninterested in whether one group of the population was or was not to be excluded from the law.

As soon as the mob began its campaign of terror against the partisans of Dreyfus, it found the path open before it. As Clemenceau attests, the workers of Paris cared little for the whole affair. If the various elements of the bourgeoisie squabbled among themselves, that, they thought, scarcely affected their own interests. 'With the open consent of the people,' wrote Clemenceau, 'they have proclaimed before the world the failure of their "democracy." Through them a

79 Cf. Clemenceau, 'A la dérive,' in *op. cit.*
80 It was precisely this which so greatly disillusioned the champions of Dreyfus, especially the circle around Charles Péguy. This disturbing similarity between Dreyfusards and Anti-Dreyfusards is the subject matter of the instructive novel by Martin du Gard, *Jean Barois*, 1913.

sovereign people shows itself thrust from its throne of justice, shorn of its infallible majesty. For there is no denying that this evil has befallen us with the full complicity of the people itself . . . The people is not God. Anyone could have foreseen that this new divinity would some day topple to his fall. A collective tyrant, spread over the length and breadth of the land, is no more acceptable than a single tyrant ensconced upon his throne.' [81]

At last Clemenceau convinced Jaurès that an infringement of the rights of one man was an infringement of the rights of all. But in this he was successful only because the wrongdoers happened to be the inveterate enemies of the people ever since the Revolution, namely, the aristocracy and the clergy. It was *against* the rich and the clergy, not *for* the republic, not *for* justice and freedom that the workers finally took to the streets. True, both the speeches of Jaurès and the articles of Clemenceau are redolent of the old revolutionary passion for human rights. True, also, that this passion was strong enough to rally the people to the struggle, but first they had to be convinced that not only justice and the honor of the republic were at stake but also their own class 'interests.' As it was, a large number of socialists, both inside and outside the country, still regarded it as a mistake to meddle (as they put it) in the internecine quarrels of the bourgeoisie or to bother about saving the republic.

The first to wean the workers, at least partially, from this mood of indifference was that great lover of the people, Emile Zola. In his famous indictment of the republic he was also, however, the first to deflect from the presentation of precise political facts and to yield to the passions of the mob by raising the bogy of 'secret Rome.' This was a note which Clemenceau adopted only reluctantly, though Jaurès did with enthusiasm. The real achievement of Zola, which is hard to detect from his pamphlets, consists in the resolute and dauntless courage with which this man, whose life and works had exalted the people to a point 'bordering on idolatry,' stood up to challenge, combat, and finally conquer the masses, in whom, like Clemenceau, he could all the time scarcely distinguish the mob from the people. 'Men have been found to resist the most powerful monarchs and to refuse to bow

81 Preface to *Contre la Justice*, 1900.

down before them, but few indeed have been found to resist the crowd, to stand up alone before misguided masses, to face their implacable frenzy without weapons and with folded arms to dare a no when a yes is demanded. Such a man was Zola!' [82]

Scarcely had *J'Accuse* appeared when the Paris socialists held their first meeting and passed a resolution calling for a revision of the Dreyfus case. But only five days later some thirty-two socialist officials promptly came out with a declaration that the fate of Dreyfus, 'the class enemy,' was no concern of theirs. Behind this declaration stood large elements of the party in Paris. Although a split in its ranks continued throughout the Affair, the party numbered enough Dreyfusards to prevent the Ligue Antisémite from thenceforth controlling the streets. A socialist meeting even branded antisemitism 'a new form of reaction.' Yet a few months later when the parliamentary elections took place, Jaurès was not returned, and shortly afterwards, when Cavaignac, the minister of war, treated the Chamber to a speech attacking Dreyfus and commending the army as indispensable, the delegates resolved, with only two dissenting votes, to placard the walls of Paris with the text of that address. Similarly, when the great Paris strike broke out in October of the same year, Münster, the German ambassador, was able reliably and confidentially to inform Berlin that 'as far as the broad masses are concerned, this is in no sense a political issue. The workers are simply out for higher wages and these they are bound to get in the end. As for the Dreyfus case, they have never bothered their heads about it.' [83]

Who then, in broad terms, were the supporters of Dreyfus? Who were the 300,000 Frenchmen who so eagerly devoured Zola's *J'Accuse* and who followed religiously the editorials of Clemenceau? Who were the men who finally succeeded in splitting every class, even every family, in France into opposing factions over the Dreyfus issue? The answer is that they formed no party or homogeneous group. Admittedly they were recruited more from the lower than from the upper classes, as they comprised, characteristically enough, more physicians than lawyers or civil servants. By and large, however, they were a

82 Clemenceau, in a speech before the Senate several years later; cf. Weil, *op. cit.*, pp. 112–13.
83 See Herzog, *op. cit.*, under date of October 10, 1898.

mixture of diverse elements: men as far apart as Zola and Péguy or Jaurès and Picquart, men who on the morrow would part company and go their several ways. 'They come from political parties and religious communities who have nothing in common, who are even in conflict with each other . . . Those men do not know each other. They have fought and on occasion will fight again. Do not deceive yourselves; those are the "elite" of the French democracy.' [84]

Had Clemenceau possessed enough self-confidence at that time to consider only those who heeded him the true people of France, he would not have fallen prey to that fatal pride which marked the rest of his career. Out of his experiences in the Dreyfus Affair grew his despair of the people, his contempt for men, finally his belief that he and he alone would be able to save the republic. He could never stoop to play the claque to the antics of the mob. Therefore, once he began to identify the mob with the people, he did indeed cut the ground from under his feet, and forced himself into that grim aloofness which thereafter distinguished him.

The disunity of the French people was apparent in each family. Characteristically enough, it found political expression only in the ranks of the Labor party. All others, as well as all parliamentary groups, were solidly against Dreyfus at the beginning of the campaign for a retrial. All this means, however, is that the bourgeois parties no longer represented the true feelings of the electorate, for the same disunity that was so patent among the socialists obtained among almost all sections of the populace. Everywhere a minority existed which took up Clemenceau's plea for justice, and this heterogeneous minority made up the Dreyfusards. Their fight against the army and the corrupt complicity of the republic which backed it was the dominating factor in French internal politics from the end of 1897 until the opening of the Exposition in 1900. It also exerted an appreciable influence on the nation's foreign policy. Nevertheless, this entire struggle, which was to result eventually in at least a partial triumph, took place exclusively outside of Parliament. In that so-called representative assembly, comprising as it did a full 600 delegates drawn from every shade and color both of labor and of the bourgeoisie, there were in

84 'K.V.T.,' *op. cit.*, p. 608.

1898 but two supporters of Dreyfus and one of them, Jaurès, was not re-elected.

The disturbing thing about the Dreyfus Affair is that it was not only the mob which had to work along extraparliamentary lines. The entire minority, fighting as it was for Parliament, democracy, and the republic, was likewise constrained to wage its battle outside the Chamber. The only difference between the two elements was that while the one used the streets, the other resorted to the press and the courts. In other words, the whole of France's political life during the Dreyfus crisis was carried on outside Parliament. Nor do the several parliamentary votes in favor of the army and against a retrial in any way invalidate this conclusion. It is significant to remember that when parliamentary feeling began to turn, shortly before the opening of the Paris Exposition, Minister of War Gallifet was able to declare truthfully that this in no wise represented the mood of the country.[85] On the other hand the vote against a retrial must not be construed as an endorsement of the *coup d'état* policy which the Jesuits and certain radical antisemites were trying to introduce with the help of the army.[86] It was due, rather, to plain resistance against any change in the status quo. As a matter of fact, an equally overwhelming majority of the Chamber would have rejected a military-clerical dictatorship.

Those members of Parliament who had learned to regard politics as the professional representation of vested interests were naturally anxious to preserve that state of affairs upon which their 'calling' and their profits depended. The Dreyfus case revealed, moreover, that the people likewise wanted their representatives to look after their own special interests rather than to function as statesmen. It was distinctly

85  Gallifet, minister of war, wrote to Waldeck: 'Let us not forget that the great majority of people in France are antisemitic. Our position would be, therefore, that on the one side we would have the entire army and the majority of Frenchmen, not to speak of the civil service and the senators . . .' cf. J. Reinach, *op. cit.*, V, 579.

86  The best known of such attempts is that of Déroulède who sought, while attending the funeral of President Paul Faure, in February, 1899, to incite General Roget to mutiny. The German ambassadors and chargés d'affaires in Paris reported such attempts every few months. The situation is well summed up by Barrès, *op. cit.*, p. 4: 'In Rennes we have found our battlefield. All we need is soldiers or, more precisely, generals – or, still more precisely, *a* general.' Only it was no accident that this general was non-existent.

unwise to mention the case in election propaganda. Had this been due solely to antisemitism the situation of the Dreyfusards would certainly have been hopeless. In point of fact, during the elections they already enjoyed considerable support among the working class. Nevertheless even those who sided with Dreyfus did not care to see this political question dragged into the elections. It was, indeed, because he insisted on making it the pivot of his campaign that Jaurès lost his seat.

If Clemenceau and the Dreyfusards succeeded in winning over large sections of all classes to the demand of a retrial, the Catholics reacted as a bloc; among them there was no divergence of opinion. What the Jesuits did in steering the aristocracy and the General Staff, was done for the middle and lower classes by the Assumptionists, whose organ, *La Croix*, enjoyed the largest circulation of all Catholic journals in France.[87] Both centered their agitation against the republic around the Jews. Both represented themselves as defenders of the army and the commonweal against the machinations of 'international Jewry.' More striking, however, than the attitude of the Catholics in France was the fact that the Catholic press throughout the world was solidly against Dreyfus. 'All these journalists marched and are still marching at the word of command of their superiors.' [88] As the case progressed, it became increasingly clear that the agitation against the Jews in France followed an international line. Thus the *Civiltà Cattolica* declared that Jews must be excluded from the nation everywhere, in France, Germany, Austria, and Italy. Catholic politicians were among the first to realize that latter-day power politics must be based on the interplay of colonial ambitions. They were therefore the first to link antisemitism to imperialism, declaring that the Jews were agents of England and thereby identifying antagonism toward them with Anglophobia.[89] The Dreyfus case, in which Jews were the central figures, thus afforded them a welcome opportunity to play their game. If

87  Brogan goes so far as to blame the Assumptionists for the entire clerical agitation.
88  'K.V.T.,' *op. cit.*, p. 597.
89  'The initial stimulus in the Affair very probably came from London, where the Congo-Nile mission of 1896–1898 was causing some degree of disquietude'; thus Maurras in *Action Française* (July 14, 1935). The Catholic press of London defended the Jesuits; see 'The Jesuits and the Dreyfus Case,' in *The Month*, Vol. XVIII (1899).

England had taken Egypt from the French the Jews were to blame,[90] while the movement for an Anglo-American alliance was due, of course, to 'Rothschild imperialism.'[91] That the Catholic game was not confined to France became abundantly clear once the curtain was rung down on that particular scene. At the close of 1899, when Dreyfus had been pardoned and when French public opinion had turned round through fear of a projected boycott of the Exposition, only an interview with Pope Leo XIII was needed to stop the spread of antisemitism throughout the world.[92] Even in the United States, where championship of Dreyfus was particularly enthusiastic among the non-Catholics, it was possible to detect in the Catholic press after 1897 a marked resurgence of antisemitic feeling which, however, subsided overnight following the interview with Leo XIII.[93] The 'grand strategy' of using antisemitism as an instrument of Catholicism had proved abortive.

## V: The Jews and the Dreyfusards

The case of the unfortunate Captain Dreyfus had shown the world that in every Jewish nobleman and multimillionaire there still remained something of the old-time pariah, who has no country, for whom human rights do not exist, and whom society would gladly exclude from its privileges. No one, however, found it more difficult to grasp this fact than the emancipated Jews themselves. 'It isn't enough for them,' wrote Bernard Lazare, 'to reject any solidarity with their foreign-born brethren; they have also to go charging them with all the evils which their own cowardice engenders. They are not content with being more jingoist than the native Frenchmen; like all emancipated Jews everywhere, they have also of their own volition broken all ties of solidarity. Indeed, they go so far that for the three dozen or so men in France who are ready to defend one of their martyred brethren

---

90 *Civiltà Cattolica*, February 5, 1898.

91 See the particularly characteristic article of Rev. George McDermot, C.S.P., 'Mr. Chamberlain's Foreign Policy and the Dreyfus Case,' in the American monthly *Catholic World*, Vol. LXVII (September, 1898).

92 Cf. Lecanuet, *op. cit.*, p. 188.

93 Cf. Rose A. Halperin, *op. cit.*, pp. 59, 77 ff.

you can find some thousands ready to stand guard over Devil's Island, alongside the most rabid patriots of the country.'[94] Precisely because they had played so small a part in the political development of the lands in which they lived, they had come, during the course of the century, to make a fetish of legal equality. To them it was the unquestionable basis of eternal security. When the Dreyfus Affair broke out to warn them that their security was menaced, they were deep in the process of a disintegrating assimilation, through which their lack of political wisdom was intensified rather than otherwise. They were rapidly assimilating themselves to those elements of society in which all political passions are smothered beneath the dead weight of social snobbery, big business, and hitherto unknown opportunities for profit. They hoped to get rid of the antipathy which this tendency had called forth by diverting it against their poor and as yet unassimilated immigrant brethren. Using the same tactics as Gentile society had employed against them they took pains to dissociate themselves from the so-called *Ostjuden*. Political antisemitism, as it had manifested itself in the pogroms of Russia and Rumania, they dismissed airily as a survival from the Middle Ages, scarcely a reality of modern politics. They could never understand that more was at stake in the Dreyfus Affair than mere social status, if only because more than mere social antisemitism had been brought to bear.

These then are the reasons why so few wholehearted supporters of Dreyfus were to be found in the ranks of French Jewry. The Jews, including the very family of the accused, shrank from starting a political fight. On just these grounds, Labori, counsel for Zola, was refused the defense before the Rennes tribunal, while Dreyfus' second lawyer, Démange, was constrained to base his plea on the issue of doubt. It was hoped thereby to smother under a deluge of compliments any possible attack from the army or its officers. The idea was that the royal road to an acquittal was to pretend that the whole thing boiled down to the possibility of a judicial error, the victim of which just happened by chance to be a Jew. The result was a second verdict and Dreyfus, refusing to face the true issue, was induced to renounce a retrial and

94  Bernard Lazare, *Job's Dungheap*, New York, 1948, p. 97.

instead to petition for clemency, that is, to plead guilty.[95] The Jews failed to see that what was involved was an organized fight against them on a political front. They therefore resisted the co-operation of men who were prepared to meet the challenge on this basis. How blind their attitude was is shown clearly by the case of Clemenceau. Clemenceau's struggle for justice as the foundation of the state certainly embraced the restoration of equal rights to the Jews. In an age, however, of class struggle on the one hand and rampant jingoism on the other, it would have remained a political abstraction had it not been conceived, at the same time, in actual terms of the oppressed fighting their oppressors. Clemenceau was one of the few true friends modern Jewry has known just because he recognized and proclaimed before the world that Jews were one of the oppressed peoples of Europe. The antisemite tends to see in the Jewish parvenu an upstart pariah; consequently in every huckster he fears a Rothschild and in every *shnorrer* a parvenu. But Clemenceau, in his consuming passion for justice, still saw the Rothschilds as members of a downtrodden people. His anguish over the national misfortune of France opened his eyes and his heart even to those 'unfortunates, who pose as leaders of their people and promptly leave them in the lurch,' to those cowed and subdued elements who, in their ignorance, weakness and fear, have been so much bedazzled by admiration of the stronger as to exclude them from partnership in any active struggle and who are able to 'rush to the aid of the winner' only when the battle has been won.[96]

## VI: The Pardon and Its Significance

That the Dreyfus drama was a comedy became apparent only in its final act. The *deus ex machina* who united the disrupted country,

95 Cf. Fernand Labori, 'Le mal politique et les partis,' in *La Grande Revue* (October–December, 1901): 'From the moment at Rennes when the accused pleaded guilty and the defendant renounced recourse to a retrial in the hope of gaining a pardon, the Dreyfus case as a great, universal human issue was definitely closed.' In his article entitled 'Le Spectacle du jour,' Clemenceau speaks of the Jews of Algiers 'in whose behalf Rothschild will not voice the least protest.'

96 See Clemenceau's articles entitled 'Le Spectacle du jour,' 'Et les Juifs!' 'La Farce du syndicat,' and 'Encore les juifs!' in *L'Iniquité*.

turned Parliament in favor of a retrial and eventually reconciled the disparate elements of the people from the extreme right to the socialists, was nothing other than the Paris Exposition of 1900. What Clemenceau's daily editorials, Zola's pathos, Jaurès' speeches, and the popular hatred of clergy and aristocracy had failed to achieve, namely, a change of parliamentary feeling in favor of Dreyfus, was at last accomplished by the fear of a boycott. The same Parliament that a year before had unanimously rejected a retrial, now by a two-thirds majority passed a vote of censure on an Anti-Dreyfus government. In July, 1899, the Waldeck-Rousseau cabinet came to power. President Loubet pardoned Dreyfus and liquidated the entire affair. The Exposition was able to open under the brightest of commercial skies and general fraternization ensued: even socialists became eligible for government posts; Millerand, the first socialist minister in Europe, received the portfolio of commerce.

Parliament became the champion of Dreyfus! That was the upshot. For Clemenceau, of course, it was a defeat. To the bitter end he denounced the ambiguous pardon and the even more ambiguous amnesty. 'All it has done,' wrote Zola, 'is to lump together in a single stinking pardon men of honor and hoodlums. All have been thrown into one pot.' [97] Clemenceau remained, as at the beginning, utterly alone. The socialists, above all, Jaurès, welcomed both pardon and amnesty. Did it not insure them a place in the government and a more extensive representation of their special interests? A few months later, in May, 1900, when the success of the Exposition was assured, the real truth at last emerged. All these appeasement tactics were to be at the expense of the Dreyfusards. The motion for a further retrial was defeated 425 to 60, and not even Clemenceau's own government in 1906 could change the situation; it did not dare to entrust the retrial to a normal court of law. The (illegal) acquittal through the Court of Appeals was a compromise. But defeat for Clemenceau did not mean victory for the Church and the army. The separation of Church and State and the ban on parochial education brought to an end the political influence of Catholicism in France. Similarly, the subjection of the intelligence service to the ministry of war, *i.e.*, to the civil authority,

97 Cf. Zola's letter dated September 13, 1899, in *Correspondance: lettres à Maître Labori.*

robbed the army of its blackmailing influence on cabinet and Chamber and deprived it of any justification for conducting police inquiries on its own account.

In 1909 Drumont stood for the Academy. Once his antisemitism had been lauded by the Catholics and acclaimed by the people. Now, however, the 'greatest historian since Fustel' (Lemaître) was obliged to yield to Marcel Prévost, author of the somewhat pornographic *Demi-Vierges,* and the new 'immortal' received the congratulations of the Jesuit Father Du Lac.[98] Even the Society of Jesus had composed its quarrel with the Third Republic. The close of the Dreyfus case marked the end of clerical antisemitism. The compromise adopted by the Third Republic cleared the defendant without granting him a regular trial, while it restricted the activities of Catholic organizations. Whereas Bernard Lazare had asked equal rights for both sides, the state had allowed one exception for the Jews and another which threatened the freedom of conscience of Catholics.[99] The parties which were really in conflict were both placed outside the law, with the result that the Jewish question on the one hand and political Catholicism on the other were banished thenceforth from the arena of practical politics.

Thus closes the only episode in which the subterranean forces of the nineteenth century enter the full light of recorded history. The only visible result was that it gave birth to the Zionist movement – the only political answer Jews have ever found to antisemitism and the only ideology in which they have ever taken seriously a hostility that would place them in the center of world events.

---

98 Cf. Herzog, *op. cit.,* p. 97.
99 Lazare's position in the Dreyfus Affair is best described by Charles Péguy, 'Notre Jeunesse,' in *Cahiers de la quinzaine,* Paris, 1910. Regarding him as the true representative of Jewish interests, Péguy formulates Lazare's demands as follows: 'He was a partisan of the impartiality of the law. Impartiality of law in the Dreyfus case, impartial law in the case of the religious orders. This seems like a trifle; this can lead far. This led him to isolation in death.' (Translation quoted from Introduction to Lazare's *Job's Dungheap.*) Lazare was one of the first Dreyfusards to protest against the law governing congregations.

# PART TWO

## Imperialism

*I would annex the planets if I could.*

Cecil Rhodes

# CHAPTER FIVE

# The Political Emancipation
of the Bourgeoisie

The three decades from 1884 to 1914 separate the nineteenth century, which ended with the scramble for Africa and the birth of the pan-movements, from the twentieth, which began with the first World War. This is the period of Imperialism, with its stagnant quiet in Europe and breath-taking developments in Asia and Africa.[1] Some of the fundamental aspects of this time appear so close to totalitarian phenomena of the twentieth century that it may be justifiable to consider the whole period a preparatory stage for coming catastrophes. Its quiet, on the other hand, makes it appear still very much a part of the nineteenth century. We can hardly avoid looking at this close and yet distant past with the too-wise eyes of those who know the end of the story in advance, who know it led to an almost complete break in the continuous flow of Western history as we had known it for more than two thousand years. But we must also admit a certain nostalgia for what can still be called a 'golden age of security,' for an age, that is, when even horrors were still marked by a certain moderation and controlled by respectability, and therefore could be related to the general appearance of sanity. In other words, no matter how close to us this past is, we are perfectly aware that our experience of concentration camps and death factories is as remote from its general atmosphere as it is from any other period in Western history.

The central inner-European event of the imperialist period was the political emancipation of the bourgeoisie, which up to then had been the first class in history to achieve economic pre-eminence without

---

1 J. A. Hobson, *Imperialism*, London, 1905, 1938, p. 19: 'Though, for convenience, the year 1870 has been taken as indicative of the beginning of a conscious policy of Imperialism, it will be evident that the movement did not attain its full impetus until the middle of the eighties . . . from about 1884.'

aspiring to political rule. The bourgeoisie had developed within, and together with, the nation-state, which almost by definition ruled over and beyond a class-divided society. Even when the bourgeoisie had already established itself as the ruling class, it had left all political decisions to the state. Only when the nation-state proved unfit to be the framework for the further growth of capitalist economy did the latent fight between state and society become openly a struggle for power. During the imperialist period neither the state nor the bourgeoisie won a decisive victory. National institutions resisted throughout the brutality and megalomania of imperialist aspirations, and bourgeois attempts to use the state and its instruments of violence for its own economic purposes were always only half successful. This changed when the German bourgeoisie staked everything on the Hitler movement and aspired to rule with the help of the mob, but then it turned out to be too late. The bourgeoisie succeeded in destroying the nation-state but won a Pyrrhic victory; the mob proved quite capable of taking care of politics by itself and liquidated the bourgeoisie along with all other classes and institutions.

## I: Expansion and the Nation-State

'Expansion is everything,' said Cecil Rhodes, and fell into despair, for every night he saw overhead 'these stars . . . these vast worlds which we can never reach. I would annex the planets if I could.'[2] He had discovered the moving principle of the new, the imperialist era (within less than two decades, British colonial possessions increased by 4½ million square miles and 66 million inhabitants, the French nation gained 3½ million square miles and 26 million people, the Germans won a new empire of a million square miles and 13 million natives, and Belgium through her king acquired 900,000 square miles with 8½ million population[3]); and yet in a flash of wisdom Rhodes recognized at the same moment its inherent insanity and its contradiction to the

2 S. Gertrude Millin, *Rhodes*, London, 1933, p. 138.
3 These figures are quoted by Carlton J. H. Hayes, *A Generation of Materialism*, New York, 1941, p. 237, and cover the period from 1871–1900. – See also Hobson, *op. cit.*, p. 19: 'Within 15 years some 3¾ millions of square miles were added to the British Empire,

human condition. Naturally, neither insight nor sadness changed his policies. He had no use for the flashes of wisdom that led him so far beyond the normal capacities of an ambitious businessman with a marked tendency toward megalomania.

'World politics is for a nation what megalomania is for an individual,'[4] said Eugen Richter (leader of the German progressive party) at about the same historical moment. But his opposition in the Reichstag to Bismarck's proposal to support private companies in the foundation of trading and maritime stations, showed clearly that he understood the economic needs of a nation in his time even less than Bismarck himself. It looked as though those who opposed or ignored imperialism – like Eugen Richter in Germany, or Gladstone in England, or Clemenceau in France – had lost touch with reality and did not realize that trade and economics had already involved every nation in world politics. The national principle was leading into provincial ignorance and the battle fought by sanity was lost.

Moderation and confusion were the only rewards of any statesman's consistent opposition to imperialist expansion. Thus Bismarck, in 1871, rejected the offer of French possessions in Africa in exchange for Alsace-Lorraine, and twenty years later acquired Heligoland from Great Britain in return for Uganda, Zanzibar, and Vitu – two kingdoms for a bathtub, as the German imperialists told him, not without justice. Thus in the eighties Clemenceau opposed the imperialist party in France when they wanted to send an expeditionary force to Egypt against the British, and thirty years later he surrendered the Mosul oil fields to England for the sake of a French-British alliance. Thus Gladstone was being denounced by Cromer in Egypt as 'not a man to whom the destinies of the British Empire could safely be entrusted.'

That statesmen, who thought primarily in terms of the established national territory, were suspicious of imperialism was justified enough, except that more was involved than what they called 'overseas adventures.' They knew by instinct rather than by insight that this new expansion movement, in which 'patriotism . . . is best

---

1 million square miles with 14 millions inhabitants to the German, 3½ millions square miles with 37 millions inhabitants to the French.'

4 See Ernst Hasse, *Deutsche Weltpolitik*, Flugschriften des Alldeutschen Verbandes, No. 5, 1897, p. 1.

expressed in money-making' (Huebbe-Schleiden) and the national flag is a 'commercial asset' (Rhodes), could only destroy the political body of the nation-state. Conquest as well as empire building had fallen into disrepute for very good reasons. They had been carried out successfully only by governments which, like the Roman Republic, were based primarily on law, so that conquest could be followed by integration of the most heterogeneous peoples by imposing upon them a common law. The nation-state, however, based upon a homogeneous population's active consent to its government ('*le plébiscite de tous les jours*' [5]), lacked such a unifying principle and would, in the case of conquest, have to assimilate rather than to integrate, to enforce consent rather than justice, that is, to degenerate into tyranny. Robespierre was already well aware of this when he exclaimed: '*Périssent les colonies si elles nous en coûtent l'honneur, la liberté.*'

Expansion as a permanent and supreme aim of politics is the central political idea of imperialism. Since it implies neither temporary looting nor the more lasting assimilation of conquest, it is an entirely new concept in the long history of political thought and action. The reason for this surprising originality – surprising because entirely new concepts are very rare in politics – is simply that this concept is not really political at all, but has its origin in the realm of business speculation, where expansion meant the permanent broadening of industrial production and economic transactions characteristic of the nineteenth century.

In the economic sphere, expansion was an adequate concept because industrial growth was a working reality. Expansion meant increase in actual production of goods to be used and consumed. The processes of production are as unlimited as the capacity of man to produce for, establish, furnish, and improve on the human world. When production and economic growth slowed down, their limits were not so much economic as political, insofar as production

5 Ernest Renan in his classical essay *Qu'est-ce qu'une nation?*, Paris, 1882, stressed 'the actual consent, the desire to live together, the will to preserve worthily the undivided inheritance which has been handed down' as the chief elements which keep the members of a people together in such a way that they form a nation. Translation quoted from *The Poetry of the Celtic Races, and other Studies*, London, 1896.

depended on, and products were shared by, many different peoples who were organized in widely differing political bodies.

Imperialism was born when the ruling class in capitalist production came up against national limitations to its economic expansion. The bourgeoisie turned to politics out of economic necessity; for if it did not want to give up the capitalist system whose inherent law is constant economic growth, it had to impose this law upon its home governments and to proclaim expansion to be an ultimate political goal of foreign policy.

With the slogan 'expansion for expansion's sake,' the bourgeoisie tried and partly succeeded in persuading their national governments to enter upon the path of world politics. The new policy they proposed seemed for a moment to find its natural limitations and balances in the very fact that several nations started their expansions simultaneously and competitively. Imperialism in its initial stages could indeed still be described as a struggle of 'competing empires' and distinguished from the 'idea of empire in the ancient and medieval world (which) was that of a federation of States, under a hegemony, covering . . . the entire recognized world.' [6] Yet such a competition was only one of the many remnants of a past era, a concession to that still prevailing national principle according to which mankind is a family of nations vying for excellence, or to the liberal belief that competition will automatically set up its own stabilizing predetermined limits before one competitor has liquidated all the others. This happy balance, however, had hardly been the inevitable outcome of mysterious economic laws, but had relied heavily on political, and even more on police institutions that prevented competitors from using revolvers. How a competition between fully armed business concerns – 'empires' – could end in anything but victory for one and death for the others is difficult to understand. In other words, competition is no more a principle of politics than expansion, and needs political power just as badly for control and restraint.

In contrast to the economic structure, the political structure cannot be expanded indefinitely, because it is not based upon the productivity of man, which is, indeed, unlimited. Of all forms of

6 Hobson, *op. cit.*

government and organizations of people, the nation-state is least suited for unlimited growth because the genuine consent at its base cannot be stretched indefinitely, and is only rarely, and with difficulty, won from conquered peoples. No nation-state could with a clear conscience ever try to conquer foreign peoples, since such a conscience comes only from the conviction of the conquering nation that it is imposing a superior law upon barbarians.[7] The nation, however, conceived of its law as an outgrowth of a unique national substance which was not valid beyond its own people and the boundaries of its own territory.

Wherever the nation-state appeared as conqueror, it aroused national consciousness and desire for sovereignty among the conquered people, thereby defeating all genuine attempts at empire building. Thus the French incorporated Algeria as a province of the mother country, but could not bring themselves to impose their own laws upon an Arab people. They continued rather to respect Islamic law and granted their Arab citizens 'personal status,' producing the nonsensical hybrid of a nominally French territory, legally as much a part of France as the Département de la Seine, whose inhabitants are not French citizens.

The early British 'empire builders,' putting their trust in conquest as a permanent method of rule, were never able to incorporate their nearest neighbors, the Irish, into the far-flung structure either of the British Empire or the British Commonwealth of Nations; but when, after the last war, Ireland was granted dominion status and welcomed as a full-fledged member of the British Commonwealth, the failure was just as real, if less palpable. The oldest 'possession' and newest dominion unilaterally denounced its dominion status (in 1937) and severed all ties with the English nation when it refused to participate in the war. England's rule by permanent conquest, since it 'simply failed to destroy' Ireland (Chesterton), had not so much aroused her own

7 This bad conscience springing from the belief in consent as the basis of all political organization is very well described by Harold Nicolson, *Curzon: The Last Phase 1919–1925*, Boston–New York, 1934, in the discussion of British policy in Egypt: 'The justification of our presence in Egypt remains based, not upon the defensible right of conquest, or on force, but upon our own belief in the element of consent. That element, in 1919, did not in any articulate form exist. It was dramatically challenged by the Egyptian outburst of March 1919.'

'slumbering genius of imperialism'[8] as it had awakened the spirit of national resistance in the Irish.

The national structure of the United Kingdom had made quick assimilation and incorporation of the conquered peoples impossible; the British Commonwealth was never a 'Commonwealth of Nations' but the heir of the United Kingdom, *one* nation dispersed throughout the world. Dispersion and colonization did not expand, but transplanted, the political structure, with the result that the members of the new federated body remained closely tied to their common mother country for sound reasons of common past and common law. The Irish example proves how ill fitted the United Kingdom was to build an imperial structure in which many different peoples could live contentedly together.[9] The British nation proved to be adept not at the Roman art of empire building but at following the Greek model of colonization. Instead of conquering and imposing their own law upon foreign peoples, the English colonists settled on newly won territory in the four corners of the world and remained members of the same British nation.[10] Whether the federated structure of the

---

8 As Lord Salisbury put it, rejoicing over the defeat of Gladstone's first Home Rule Bill. During the following twenty years of Conservative – and that was at that time imperialist – rule (1885–1905), the English-Irish conflict was not only not solved but became much more acute. See also Gilbert K. Chesterton, *The Crimes of England*, 1915, pp. 57 ff.

9 Why in the initial stages of national development the Tudors did not succeed in incorporating Ireland into Great Britain as the Valois had succeeded in incorporating Brittany and Burgundy into France, is still a riddle. It may be, however, that a similar process was brutally interrupted by the Cromwell regime, which treated Ireland as one great piece of booty to be divided among its servants. After the Cromwell revolution, at any rate, which was as crucial for the formation of the British nation as the French Revolution became for the French, the United Kingdom had already reached that stage of maturity that is always accompanied by a loss of the power of assimilation and integration which the body politic of the nation possesses only in its initial stages. What then followed was, indeed, one long sad story of 'coercion [that] was not imposed that the people might live quietly but that people might die quietly' (Chesterton, *op. cit.*, p. 60).

For a historical survey of the Irish question that includes the latest developments, compare the excellent unbiased study of Nicholas Mansergh, *Britain and Ireland* (in *Longman's Pamphlets on the British Commonwealth*, London, 1942).

10 Very characteristic is the following statement of J. A. Froude made shortly before the beginning of the imperialist era: 'Let it be once established that an Englishman emigrating to Canada or the Cape, or Australia, or New Zealand did not forfeit his

Commonwealth, admirably built on the reality of one nation dispersed over the earth, will be sufficiently elastic to balance the nation's inherent difficulties in empire building and to admit permanently non-British peoples as full-fledged 'partners in the concern' of the Commonwealth, remains to be seen. The present dominion status of India – a status, by the way, flatly refused by Indian nationalists during the war – has frequently been considered to be a temporary and transitory solution.[11]

The inner contradiction between the nation's body politic and conquest as a political device has been obvious since the failure of the Napoleonic dream. It is due to this experience and not to humanitarian considerations that conquest has since been officially condemned and has played a minor role in the adjustment of borderline conflicts. The Napoleonic failure to unite Europe under the French flag was a clear indication that conquest by a nation led either to the full awakening of the conquered people's national consciousness and to consequent rebellion against the conqueror, or to tyranny. And though tyranny, because it needs no consent, may successfully rule over foreign peoples, it can stay in power only if it destroys first of all the national institutions of its own people.

The French, in contrast to the British and all other nations in Europe, actually tried in recent times to combine *ius* with *imperium* and to build an empire in the old Roman sense. They alone at least attempted to develop the body politic of the nation into an imperial

---

nationality, that he was still on English soil as much as if he was in Devonshire or Yorkshire, and would remain an Englishman while the English Empire lasted; and if we spent a quarter of the sums which were sunk in the morasses at Balaclava in sending out and establishing two millions of our people in those colonies, it would contribute more to the essential strength of the country than all the wars in which we have been entangled from Agincourt to Waterloo.' Quoted from Robert Livingston Schuyler, *The Fall of the Old Colonial System*, New York, 1945, pp. 280–81.

11 The eminent South African writer, Jan Disselboom, expressed very bluntly the attitude of the Commonwealth peoples on this question: 'Great Britain is merely a partner in the concern . . . all descended from the same closely allied stock . . . Those parts of the Empire which are not inhabited by races of which this is true, were never partners in the concern. They were the private property of the predominant partner . . . You can have the white dominion, or you can have the Dominion of India, but you cannot have both.' (Quoted from A. Carthill, *The Lost Dominion*, 1924.)

political structure, believed that 'the French nation (was) marching . . . to spread the benefits of French civilization'; they wanted to incorporate overseas possessions into the national body by treating the conquered peoples as 'both . . . brothers and . . . subjects – brothers in the fraternity of a common French civilization, and subjects in that they are disciples of French light and followers of French leading.' [12] This was partly carried out when colored delegates took their seats in the French Parliament and when Algeria was declared to be a department of France.

The result of this daring enterprise was a particularly brutal exploitation of overseas possessions for the sake of the nation. All theories to the contrary, the French Empire actually was evaluated from the point of view of national defense,[13] and the colonies were considered lands of soldiers which could produce a *force noire* to protect the inhabitants of France against their national enemies. Poincaré's famous phrase in 1923, 'France is not a country of forty millions; she is a country of one hundred millions,' pointed simply to the discovery of an 'economical form of gunfodder, turned out by mass-production methods.' [14] When Clemenceau insisted at the peace table in 1918 that he cared about nothing but 'an unlimited right of levying black troops to assist in the defense of French territory in Europe if France were attacked in the future by Germany,' [15] he did not save the French nation from German aggression, as we are now unfortunately in a position to know, although his plan was carried out by the General Staff; but he dealt a death-blow to the still dubious possibility of a French Empire.[16]

12 Ernest Barker, *Ideas and Ideals of the British Empire*, Cambridge, 1941, p. 4.

See also the very good introductory remarks on the foundations of the French Empire in *The French Colonial Empire* (in *Information Department Papers* No. 25, published by The Royal Institute of International Affairs, London, 1941), pp. 9 ff. 'The aim is to assimilate colonial peoples to the French people, or, where this is not possible in more primitive communities, to "associate" them, so that more and more the difference between *la France métropole* and *la France d'outremer* shall be a geographical difference and not a fundamental one.'

13 See Gabriel Hanotaux, 'Le Général Mangin' in *Revue des Deux Mondes* (1925), Tome 27.

14 W. P. Crozier, 'France and her "Black Empire"' in *New Republic*, January 23, 1924.

15 David Lloyd George, *Memoirs of the Peace Conference*, New Haven, 1939, I, 362 ff.

16 A similar attempt at brutal exploitation of overseas possessions for the sake of the nation was made by the Netherlands in the Dutch East Indies after the defeat of

Compared with this blind desperate nationalism, British imperialists compromising on the mandate system looked like guardians of the self-determination of peoples. And this despite the fact that they started at once to misuse the mandate system by 'indirect rule,' a method which permits the administrator to govern a people 'not directly but through the medium of their own tribal and local authorities.'[17]

The British tried to escape the dangerous inconsistency inherent in the nation's attempt at empire building by leaving the conquered peoples to their own devices as far as culture, religion, and law were concerned, by staying aloof and refraining from spreading British law and culture. This did not prevent the natives from developing national consciousness and from clamoring for sovereignty and independence – though it may have retarded the process somewhat. But it has strengthened tremendously the new imperialist consciousness of a fundamental, and not just a temporary, superiority of man over man, of the 'higher' over the 'lower breeds.' This in turn exacerbated

---

Napoleon had restored the Dutch colonies to the much impoverished mother country. By means of compulsory cultivation the natives were reduced to slavery for the benefit of the government in Holland. Multatuli's *Max Havelaar*, first published in the sixties of the last century, was aimed at the government at home and not at the services abroad. (See de Kat Angelino, *Colonial Policy*, Vol. II, *The Dutch East Indies*, Chicago, 1931, p. 45.)

This system was quickly abandoned and the Netherlands Indies, for a while, became 'the admiration of all colonizing nations.' (Sir Hesketh Bell, former Governor of Uganda, Northern Nigeria, etc., *Foreign Colonial Administration in the Far East*, 1928, Part I). The Dutch methods have many similarities with the French: the granting of European status to deserving natives, introduction of a European school system, and other devices of gradual assimilation. The Dutch thereby achieved the same result: a strong national independence movement among the subject people.

In the present study Dutch and Belgian imperialism are being neglected. The first is a curious and changing mixture of French and English methods; the second is the story not of the expansion of the Belgian nation or even the Belgian bourgeoisie, but of the expansion of the Belgian king personally, unchecked by any government, unconnected with any other institution. Both the Dutch and the Belgian forms of imperialism are atypical. The Netherlands did not expand during the eighties, but only consolidated and modernized their old possessions. The unequalled atrocities committed in the Belgian Congo, on the other hand, would offer too unfair an example for what was generally happening in overseas possessions.

17 Ernest Barker, *op. cit.*, p. 69.

the subject peoples' fight for freedom and blinded them to the unquestionable benefits of British rule. From the very aloofness of their administrators who, 'despite their genuine respect for the natives as a people, and in some cases even their love for them . . . almost to a man, do not believe that they are or ever will be capable of governing themselves without supervision,'[18] the 'natives' could not but conclude that they were being excluded and separated from the rest of mankind forever.

Imperialism is not empire building and expansion is not conquest. The British conquerors, the old 'breakers of law in India' (Burke), had little in common with the exporters of British money or the administrators of the Indian peoples. If the latter had changed from applying decrees to the making of laws, they might have become empire builders. The point, however, is that the English nation was not interested in this and would hardly have supported them. As it was, the imperialist-minded businessmen were followed by civil servants who wanted 'the African to be left an African,' while quite a few, who had not yet outgrown what Harold Nicolson once called their 'boyhood-ideals,'[19] wanted to help them to 'become a better African'[20] – whatever that may mean. In no case were they 'disposed to apply the administrative and political system of their own country to the government of backward populations,'[21] and to tie the far-flung possessions of the British Crown to the English nation.

In contrast to true imperial structures, where the institutions of the mother country are in various ways integrated into the empire, it is characteristic of imperialism that national institutions remain separate from the colonial administration although they are allowed to exercise control. The actual motivation for this separation was a curious mixture of arrogance and respect: the new arrogance of the administrators abroad who faced 'backward populations' or 'lower breeds' found its correlative in the respect of old-fashioned statesmen

18  Selwyn James, *South of the Congo*, New York, 1943, p. 326.
19  About these boyhood ideals and their role in British imperialism, see chapter vii. How they were developed and cultivated is described in Rudyard Kipling's *Stalky and Company*.
20  Ernest Barker, *op. cit.*, p. 150.
21  Lord Cromer, 'The Government of Subject Races,' in *Edinburgh Review*, January, 1908.

at home who felt that no nation had the right to impose its law upon a foreign people. It was in the very nature of things that the arrogance turned out to be a device for rule, while the respect, which remained entirely negative, did not produce a new way for peoples to live together, but managed only to keep the ruthless imperialist rule by decree within bounds. To the salutary restraint of national institutions and politicians we owe whatever benefits the non-European peoples have been able, after all and despite everything, to derive from Western domination. But the colonial services never ceased to protest against the interference of the 'inexperienced majority' – the nation – that tried to press the 'experienced minority' – the imperialist administrators – 'in the direction of imitation,' [22] namely, of government in accordance with the general standards of justice and liberty at home.

That a movement of expansion for expansion's sake grew up in nation-states which more than any other political bodies were defined by boundaries and the limitations of possible conquest, is one example of the seemingly absurd disparities between cause and effect which have become the hallmark of modern history. The wild confusion of modern historical terminology is only a by-product of these disparities. By comparisons with ancient Empires, by mistaking expansion for conquest, by neglecting the difference between Commonwealth and Empire (which pre-imperialist historians called the difference between plantations and possessions, or colonies and dependencies, or, somewhat later, colonialism and imperialism[23]), by

22 *Ibid.*
23 The first scholar to use the term imperialism to differentiate clearly between the 'Empire' and the 'Commonwealth' was J. A Hobson. But the essential difference was always well known. The principle of 'colonial freedom' for instance, cherished by all liberal British statesmen after the American Revolution, was held valid only insofar as the colony was 'formed of the British people or . . . such admixture of the British population as to make it safe to introduce representative institutions.' See Robert Livingston Schuyler, *op. cit.*, pp. 236 ff.

In the nineteenth century, we must distinguish three types of overseas possessions within the British Empire: the settlements or plantations or colonies, like Australia and other dominions; the trade stations and possessions like India; and the maritime and military stations like the Cape of Good Hope, which were held for the sake of the

neglecting, in other words, the difference between export of (British) people and export of (British) money,[24] historians tried to dismiss the disturbing fact that so many of the important events in modern history look as though molehills had labored and had brought forth mountains.

Contemporary historians, confronted with the spectacle of a few capitalists conducting their predatory searches round the globe for new investment possibilities and appealing to the profit motives of the much-too-rich and the gambling instincts of the much-too-poor, want to clothe imperialism with the old grandeur of Rome and Alexander the Great, a grandeur which would make all following events more humanly tolerable. The disparity between cause and effect was betrayed in the famous, and unfortunately true, remark that the British Empire was acquired in a fit of absent-mindedness; it became cruelly obvious in our own time when a World War was needed to get rid of Hitler, which was shameful precisely because it was also comic. Something similar was already apparent during the Dreyfus Affair when the best elements in the nation were needed to conclude a struggle which had started as a grotesque conspiracy and ended as a farce.

The only grandeur of imperialism lies in the nation's losing battle against it. The tragedy of this half-hearted opposition was not that many national representatives could be bought by the new imperialist businessmen; worse than corruption was the fact that the incorruptible were convinced that imperialism was the only way to conduct world politics. Since maritime stations and access to raw materials were really necessary for all nations, they came to believe that annexation and expansion worked for the salvation of the nation. They were the first to fail to understand the fundamental difference between the old foundation of trade and maritime stations for the sake of trade and the new policy of expansion. They believed Cecil Rhodes when he told them to 'wake up to the fact that you cannot live unless you have the trade of the world,' 'that your trade is the world, and your life is the

---

former. All these possessions underwent a change in government and political significance in the era of imperialism.

24 Ernest Barker, *op. cit.*

world, and not England,' and that therefore they 'must deal with these questions of expansion and retention of the world.' [25] Without wanting to, sometimes even without knowing it, they not only became accomplices in imperialist politics, but were the first to be blamed and exposed for their 'imperialism.' Such was the case of Clemenceau who, because he was so desperately worried about the future of the French nation, turned 'imperialist' in the hope that colonial manpower would protect French citizens against aggressors.

The conscience of the nation, represented by Parliament and a free press, functioned, and was resented by colonial administrators, in all European countries with colonial possessions – whether England, France, Belgium, Germany, or Holland. In England, in order to distinguish between the imperial government seated in London and controlled by Parliament and colonial administrators, this influence was called the 'imperial factor,' thereby crediting imperialism with the merits and remnants of justice it so eagerly tried to eliminate.[26] The 'imperial factor' was expressed politically in the concept that the natives were not only protected but in a way represented by the British, the 'Imperial Parliament.' [27] Here the English came very close to the French experiment in empire building, although they never went

---

25 Millin, *op. cit.*, p. 175.

26 The origin of this misnomer probably lies in the history of British rule in South Africa, and goes back to the times when the local governors, Cecil Rhodes and Jameson, involved the 'Imperial Government' in London, much against its intentions, in the war against the Boers. 'In fact Rhodes, or rather Jameson, was absolute ruler of a territory three times the size of England, which could be administered "without waiting for the grudging assent or polite censure of the High Commissioner"' who was the representative of an Imperial Government that retained only 'nominal control.' (Reginal Ivan Lovell, *The Struggle for South Africa, 1875–1899*, New York, 1934, p. 194.) And what happens in territories in which the British government has resigned its jurisdiction to the local European population that lacks all traditional and constitutional restraint of nation-states, can best be seen in the tragic story of the South African Union since its independence, that is, since the time when the 'Imperial Government' no longer had any right to interfere.

27 The discussion in the House of Commons in May, 1908, between Charles Dilke and the Colonial Secretary is interesting in this respect. Dilke warned against giving self-government to the Crown colonies because this would result in rule of the white planters over their colored workers. He was told that the natives too had a representation in the English House of Commons. See G. Zoepfl, 'Kolonien und Kolonialpolitik' in *Handwörterbuch der Staatswissenschaften*.

so far as to give actual representation to subject peoples. Nevertheless, they obviously hoped that the nation as a whole could act as a kind of trustee for its conquered peoples, and it is true that it invariably tried its best to prevent the worst.

The conflict between the representatives of the 'imperial factor' (which should rather be called the national factor) and the colonial administrators runs like a red thread through the history of British imperialism. The 'prayer' which Cromer addressed to Lord Salisbury during his administration of Egypt in 1896, 'save me from the English Departments,' [28] was repeated over and over again, until in the twenties of this century the nation and everything it stood for were openly blamed by the extreme imperialist party for the threatened loss of India. The imperialists had always been deeply resentful that the government of India should have 'to justify its existence and its policy before public opinion in England'; this control now made it impossible to proceed to those measures of 'administrative massacres' [29] which, immediately after the close of the first World War, had been tried occasionally elsewhere as a radical means of pacification,[30] and which indeed might have prevented India's independence.

A similar hostility prevailed in Germany between national representatives and colonial administrators in Africa. In 1897, Carl Peters was removed from his post in German Southeast Africa and had to resign from the government service because of atrocities against the natives. The same thing happened to Governor Zimmerer. And in 1905, the tribal chiefs for the first time addressed their complaints to

---

28 Lawrence J. Zetland, *Lord Cromer*, 1923, p. 224.

29 A. Carthill, *The Lost Dominion*, 1924, pp. 41–42, 93.

30 An instance of 'pacification' in the Near East was described at great length by T. E. Lawrence in an article 'France, Britain and the Arabs' written for *The Observer* (1920): 'There is a preliminary Arab success, the British reinforcements go out as a punitive force. They fight their way . . . to their objective, which is meanwhile bombarded by artillery, aeroplanes, or gunboats. Finally perhaps a village is burnt and the district pacified. It is odd that we don't use poison gas on these occasions. Bombing the houses is a patchy way of getting the women and children . . . By gas attacks the whole population of offending districts could be wiped out neatly; and as a method of government it would be no more immoral than the present system.' See his *Letters*, edited by David Garnett, New York, 1939, pp. 311 ff.

the Reichstag, with the result that when the colonial administrators threw them into jail, the German Government intervened.[31]

The same was true of French rule. The governors general appointed by the government in Paris were either subject to powerful pressure from French colonials as in Algeria, or simply refused to carry out reforms in the treatment of natives, which were allegedly inspired by 'the weak democratic principles of (their) government.'[32] Everywhere imperialist administrators felt that the control of the nation was an unbearable burden and threat to domination.

And the imperialists were perfectly right. They knew the conditions of modern rule over subject peoples better than those who on the one hand protested against government by decree and arbitrary bureaucracy and on the other hoped to retain their possessions forever for the greater glory of the nation. The imperialists knew better than nationalists that the body politic of the nation is not capable of empire building. They were perfectly aware that the march of the nation and its conquest of peoples, if allowed to follow its own inherent law, ends with the peoples' rise to nationhood and the defeat of the conqueror. French methods, therefore, which always tried to combine national aspirations with empire building, were much less successful than British methods, which, after the eighties of the last century, were openly imperialistic, although restrained by a mother country that retained its national democratic institutions.

## II: Power and the Bourgeoisie

What imperialists actually wanted was expansion of political power without the foundation of a body politic. Imperialist expansion had been touched off by a curious kind of economic crisis, the overproduction of capital and the emergence of 'superfluous' money, the result of

---

31 In 1910, on the other hand, the Colonial Secretary B. Dernburg had to resign because he had antagonized the colonial planters by protecting the natives. See Mary E. Townsend, *Rise and Fall of Germany's Colonial Empire*, New York, 1930, and P. Leutwein, *Kämpfe um Afrika*, Luebeck, 1936.
32 In the words of Léon Cayla, former Governor General of Madagascar and friend of Pétain.

oversaving, which could no longer find productive investment within the national borders. For the first time, investment of power did not pave the way for investment of money, but export of power followed meekly in the train of exported money, since uncontrollable investments in distant countries threatened to transform large strata of society into gamblers, to change the whole capitalist economy from a system of production into a system of financial speculation, and to replace the profits of production with profits in commissions. The decade immediately before the imperialist era, the seventies of the last century, witnessed an unparalleled increase in swindles, financial scandals, and gambling in the stock market.

The pioneers in this pre-imperialist development were those Jewish financiers who had earned their wealth outside the capitalist system and had been needed by the growing nation-states for internationally guaranteed loans.[33] With the firm establishment of the tax system that provided for sounder government finances, this group had every reason to fear complete extinction. Having earned their money for centuries through commissions, they were naturally the first to be tempted and invited to serve in the placement of capital which could no longer be invested profitably in the domestic market. The Jewish international financiers seemed indeed especially suited for such essentially international business operations.[34] What is more, the

33 For this and the following compare chapter ii.

34 It is interesting that all early observers of imperialist developments stress this Jewish element very strongly while it hardly plays any role in more recent literature. Especially noteworthy, because very reliable in observation and very honest in analysis, is J. A. Hobson's development in this respect. In the first essay which he wrote on the subject, 'Capitalism and Imperialism in South Africa' (in *Contemporary Review*, 1900), he said: 'Most of (the financiers) were Jews, for the Jews are par excellence the international financiers, and, though English-speaking, most of them are of continental origin . . . They went there (Transvaal) for money, and those who came early and made most have commonly withdrawn their persons, leaving their economic fangs in the carcass of their prey. They fastened on the Rand . . . as they are prepared to fasten upon any other spot upon the globe . . . Primarily, they are financial speculators taking their gains not out of the genuine fruits of industry, even the industry of others, but out of construction, promotion and financial manipulation of companies.' In Hobson's later study *Imperialism*, however, the Jews are not even mentioned; it had become obvious in the meantime that their influence and role had been temporary and somewhat superficial.

For the role of Jewish financiers in South Africa, see chapter vii.

governments themselves, whose assistance in some form was needed for investments in faraway countries, tended in the beginning to prefer the well-known Jewish financiers to newcomers in international finance, many of whom were adventurers.

After the financiers had opened the channels of capital export to the superfluous wealth, which had been condemned to idleness within the narrow framework of national production, it quickly became apparent that the absentee shareholders did not care to take the tremendous risks which corresponded to their tremendously enlarged profits. Against these risks, the commission-earning financiers, even with the benevolent assistance of the state, did not have enough power to insure them: only the material power of a state could do that.

As soon as it became clear that export of money would have to be followed by export of government power, the position of financiers in general, and Jewish financiers in particular, was considerably weakened, and the leadership of imperialist business transactions and enterprise was gradually taken over by members of the native bourgeoisie. Very instructive in this respect is the career of Cecil Rhodes in South Africa, who, an absolute newcomer, in a few years could supplant the all-powerful Jewish financiers in first place. In Germany, Bleichroeder, who in 1885 had still been a co-partner in the founding of the *Ostafrikanische Gesellschaft*, was superseded along with Baron Hirsch when Germany began the construction of the Bagdad railroad, fourteen years later, by the coming giants of imperialist enterprise, Siemens and the Deutsche Bank. Somehow the government's reluctance to yield real power to Jews and the Jews' reluctance to engage in business with political implication coincided so well that, despite the great wealth of the Jewish group, no actual struggle for power ever developed after the initial stage of gambling and commission-earning had come to an end.

The various national governments looked with misgiving upon the growing tendency to transform business into a political issue and to identify the economic interests of a relatively small group with national interests as such. But it seemed that the only alternative to export of power was the deliberate sacrifice of a great part of the national wealth. Only through the expansion of the national instruments of violence could the foreign-investment movement be rationalized, and the wild speculations with super-fluous capital, which had provoked gambling of all savings, be reintegrated into the economic system of the nation. The state expanded its power because, given the choice between greater losses than the economic body of any country could sustain and greater gains than any people left to its own devices would have dreamed of, it could only choose the latter.

The first consequence of power export was that the state's instru-ments of violence, the police and the army, which in the framework of the nation existed beside, and were controlled by, other national institutions, were separated from this body and promoted to the posi-tion of national representatives in uncivilized or weak countries. Here, in backward regions without industries and political organiza-tion, where violence was given more latitude than in any Western country, the so-called laws of capitalism were actually allowed to cre-ate realities. The bourgeoisie's empty desire to have money beget money as men beget men had remained an ugly dream so long as money had to go the long way of investment in production; not money had begotten money, but men had made things and money. The secret of the new happy fulfillment was precisely that economic laws no longer stood in the way of the greed of the owning classes. Money could finally beget money because power, with complete disregard for all laws – economic as well as ethical – could appropriate wealth. Only when exported money succeeded in stimulating the export of power could it accomplish its owners' designs. Only the unlimited accumula-tion of power could bring about the unlimited accumulation of capital.

Foreign investments, capital export which had started as an emergency measure, became a permanent feature of all economic systems as soon as it was protected by export of power. The imperial-ist concept of expansion, according to which expansion is an end in itself and not a temporary means, made its appearance in political thought when it had become obvious that one of the most important permanent functions of the nation-state would be expansion of power. The state-employed administrators of violence soon formed a new class within the nations and, although their field of activity was far away from the mother country, wielded an important influence on the body politic at home. Since they were actually nothing but functionaries of violence they could only think in terms of power politics. They were the first who, as a class and supported by their everyday experience, would claim that power is the essence of every political structure.

The new feature of this imperialist political philosophy is not the predominant place it gave violence, nor the discovery that power is one of the basic political realities. Violence has always been the *ultima ratio* in political action and power has always been the visible expression of rule and government. But neither had ever before been the conscious aim of the body politic or the ultimate goal of any definite policy. For power left to itself can achieve nothing but more power, and violence administered for power's (and not for law's) sake turns into a destructive principle that will not stop until there is nothing left to violate.

This contradiction, inherent in all ensuing power politics, however, takes on an appearance of sense if one understands it in the context of a supposedly permanent process which has no end or aim but itself. Then the test of achievement can indeed become meaningless and power can be thought of as the never-ending, self-feeding motor of all political action that corresponds to the legendary unending accumulation of money that begets money. The concept of unlimited expansion that alone can fulfill the hope for unlimited accumulation of capital, and brings about the aimless accumulation of power, makes the foundation of new political bodies – which up to the era of imperialism always had been the upshot of conquest – well-nigh impossible. In fact, its logical consequence is the destruction of all living communities, those of the conquered peoples as well as of the people at home. For every political structure, new or old, left to itself develops stabilizing forces which stand in the way of constant transformation and expansion. Therefore all political bodies appear to be temporary obstacles when they are seen as part of an eternal stream of growing power.

While the administrators of permanently increasing power in the past era of moderate imperialism did not even try to incorporate conquered territories, and preserved existing backward political communities like empty ruins of bygone life, their totalitarian successors dissolved and destroyed all politically stabilized structures, their own as well as those of other peoples. The mere export of violence made the servants into masters without giving them the master's prerogative: the possible creation of something new. Monopolistic concentration and tremendous accumulation of violence at home made the servants active agents in the destruction, until finally totalitarian expansion became a nation- and a people-destroying force.

Power became the essence of political action and the center of political thought when it was separated from the political community which it should serve. This, it is true, was brought about by an economic factor. But the resulting introduction of power as the only content of politics, and of expansion as its only aim, would hardly have met with such universal applause, nor would the resulting dissolution of the nation's body politic have met with so little opposition, had it not so perfectly answered the hidden desires and secret convictions of the economically and socially dominant classes. The bourgeoisie, so long excluded from government by the nation-state and by their own lack of interest in public affairs, was politically emancipated by imperialism.

Imperialism must be considered the first stage in political rule of the bourgeoisie rather than the last stage of capitalism. It is well known how little the owning classes had aspired to government, how well contented they had been with every type of state that could be trusted with protection of property rights. For them, indeed, the state had always been only a well-organized police force. This false modesty, however, had the curious consequence of keeping the whole bourgeois class out of the body politic; before they were subjects in a monarchy or citizens in a republic, they were essentially private persons. This privateness and primary concern with money-making had developed a set of behavior patterns which are expressed in all those proverbs – 'nothing succeeds like success,' 'might is right,' 'right is expediency,' etc. – that necessarily spring from the experience of a society of competitors.

When, in the era of imperialism, businessmen became politicians and were acclaimed as statesmen, while statesmen were taken seriously only if they talked the language of successful businessmen and 'thought in continents,' these private practices and devices were gradually transformed into rules and principles for the conduct of public affairs. The significant fact about this process of revaluation, which began at the end of the last century and is still in effect, is that it began with the application of bourgeois convictions to foreign affairs and only slowly was extended to domestic politics. Therefore, the nations concerned were hardly aware that the recklessness that had prevailed in private life, and against which the public body always had to defend itself and its individual citizens, was about to be elevated to the one publicly honored political principle.

It is significant that modern believers in power are in complete accord with the philosophy of the only great thinker who ever attempted to derive public good from private interest and who, for the sake of private good, conceived and outlined a Commonwealth whose basis and ultimate end is accumulation of power. Hobbes, indeed, is the only great philosopher to whom the bourgeoisie can rightly and exclusively lay claim, even if his principles were not recognized by the bourgeois class for a long time. Hobbes's *Leviathan*[35] exposed the only political theory according to which the state is based not on some kind of constituting law – whether divine law, the law of nature, or the law of social contract – which determines the rights and wrongs of the individual's interest with respect to public affairs, but on the individual interests themselves, so that 'the private interest is the same with the publique.'[36]

There is hardly a single bourgeois moral standard which has not been anticipated by the unequaled magnificence of Hobbes's logic. He gives an almost complete picture, not of Man but of the bourgeois man, an analysis which in three hundred years has neither been outdated nor excelled. 'Reason . . . is nothing but Reckoning'; 'a free

35 All quotes in the following if not annotated are from the *Leviathan*.
36 The coincidence of this identification with the totalitarian pretense of having abolished the contradictions between individual and public interests is significant enough (see chapter xii). However, one should not overlook the fact that Hobbes wanted most of all to protect private interests by pretending that, rightly understood, they were the interests of the body politic as well, while on the contrary totalitarian regimes proclaim the nonexistence of privacy.

Subject, a free Will . . . [are] words . . . without meaning; that is to say, Absurd.' A being without reason, without the capacity for truth, and without free will – that is, without the capacity for responsibility – man is essentially a function of society and judged therefore according to his 'value or worth . . . his price; that is to say so much as would be given for the use of his power.' This price is constantly evaluated and re-evaluated by society, the 'esteem of others,' depending upon the law of supply and demand.

Power, according to Hobbes, is the accumulated control that permits the individual to fix prices and regulate supply and demand in such a way that they contribute to his own advantage. The individual will consider his advantage in complete isolation, from the point of view of an absolute minority, so to speak; he will then realize that he can pursue and achieve his interest only with the help of some kind of majority. Therefore, if man is actually driven by nothing but his individual interests, desire for power must be the fundamental passion of man. It regulates the relations between individual and society, and all other ambitions as well, for riches, knowledge, and honor follow from it.

Hobbes points out that in the struggle for power, as in their native capacities for power, all men are equal; for the equality of men is based on the fact that each has by nature enough power to kill another. Weakness can be compensated for by guile. Their equality as potential murderers places all men in the same insecurity, from which arises the need for a state. The *raison d'être* of the state is the need for some security of the individual, who feels himself menaced by all his fellow-men.

The crucial feature in Hobbes's picture of man is not at all the realistic pessimism for which it has been praised in recent times. For if it were true that man is a being such as Hobbes would have him, he would be unable to found any body politic at all. Hobbes, indeed, does not succeed, and does not even want to succeed, in incorporating this being definitely into a political community. Hobbes's Man owes no loyalty to his country if it has been defeated and he is excused for every treachery if he happens to be taken prisoner. Those who live outside the Commonwealth (for instance, slaves) have no further obligation toward their fellow-men but are permitted to kill as many as they can;

while, on the contrary, 'to resist the Sword of the Commonwealth in defence of another man, guilty or innocent, no man hath Liberty,' which means that there is neither fellowship nor responsibility between man and man. What holds them together is a common interest which may be 'some Capitall crime, for which every one of them expecteth death'; in this case they have the right to 'resist the Sword of the Commonwealth,' to 'joyn together, and assist, and defend one another . . . For they but defend their lives.'

Thus membership in any form of community is for Hobbes a temporary and limited affair which essentially does not change the solitary and private character of the individual (who has 'no pleasure, but on the contrary a great deale of griefe in keeping company, where there is no power to overawe them all') or create permanent bonds between him and his fellow-men. It seems as though Hobbes's picture of man defeats his purpose of providing the basis for a Commonwealth and gives instead a consistent pattern of attitudes through which every genuine community can easily be destroyed. This results in the inherent and admitted instability of Hobbes's Commonwealth, whose very conception includes its own dissolution – 'when in a warre (forraign, or intestine,) the enemies get a final Victory . . . then is the Commonwealth dissolved, and every man at liberty to protect himself' – an instability that is all the more striking as Hobbes's primary and frequently repeated aim was to secure a maximum of safety and stability.

It would be a grave injustice to Hobbes and his dignity as a philosopher to consider this picture of man an attempt at psychological realism or philosophical truth. The fact is that Hobbes is interested in neither, but concerned exclusively with the political structure itself, and he depicts the features of man according to the needs of the Leviathan. For argument's and conviction's sake, he presents his political outline as though he started from a realistic insight into man, a being that 'desires power after power,' and as though he proceeded from this insight to a plan for a body politic best fitted for this power-thirsty animal. The actual process, *i.e.*, the only process in which his concept of man makes sense and goes beyond the obvious banality of an assumed human wickedness, is precisely the opposite.

This new body politic was conceived for the benefit of the new bourgeois society as it emerged in the seventeenth century and this picture of man is a sketch for the new type of Man who would fit into it. The Commonwealth is based on the delegation of power, and not of rights. It acquires a monopoly on killing and provides in exchange a conditional guarantee against being killed. Security is provided by the law, which is a direct emanation from the power monopoly of the state (and is not established by man according to human standards of right and wrong). And as this law flows directly from absolute power, it represents absolute necessity in the eyes of the individual who lives under it. In regard to the law of the state – that is, the accumulated power of society as monopolized by the state – there is no question of right or wrong, but only absolute obedience, the blind conformism of bourgeois society.

Deprived of political rights, the individual, to whom public and official life manifests itself in the guise of necessity, acquires a new and increased interest in his private life and his personal fate. Excluded from participation in the management of public affairs that involve all citizens, the individual loses his rightful place in society and his natural connection with his fellow-men. He can now judge his individual private life only by comparing it with that of others, and his relations with his fellow-men inside society take the form of competition. Once public affairs are regulated by the state under the guise of necessity, the social or public careers of the competitors come under the sway of chance. In a society of individuals, all equipped by nature with equal capacity for power and equally protected from one another by the state, only chance can decide who will succeed.[37]

37 The elevation of chance to the position of final arbiter over the whole of life was to reach its full development in the nineteenth century. With it came a new genre of literature, the novel, and the decline of the drama. For the drama became meaningless in a world without action, while the novel could deal adequately with the destinies of human beings who were either the victims of necessity or the favorites of luck. Balzac showed the full range of the new genre and even presented human passions as man's fate, containing neither virtue nor vice, neither reason nor free will. Only the novel in its full maturity, having interpreted and re-interpreted the entire scale of human matters, could preach the new gospel of infatuation with one's own fate that has played such a great role among nineteenth-century intellectuals. By means of such infatuation the artist and intellectual tried to draw a line between themselves and the philistines, to protect themselves against the inhumanity of good or bad luck, and they developed all the gifts of modern sensitivity – for suffering, for understanding, for

According to bourgeois standards, those who are completely unlucky and unsuccessful are automatically barred from competition, which is the life of society. Good fortune is identified with honor, and bad luck with shame. By assigning his political rights to the state the individual also delegates his social responsibilities to it: he asks the state to relieve him of the burden of caring for the poor precisely as he asks for protection against criminals. The difference between pauper and criminal disappears – both stand outside society. The unsuccessful are robbed of the virtue that classical civilization left them; the unfortunate can no longer appeal to Christian charity.

Hobbes liberates those who are excluded from society – the unsuccessful, the unfortunate, the criminal – from every obligation toward society and state if the state does not take care of them. They may give free rein to their desire for power and are told to take advantage of their elemental ability to kill, thus restoring that natural equality which society conceals only for the sake of expediency. Hobbes foresees and justifies the social outcasts' organization into a gang of murderers as a logical outcome of the bourgeoisie's moral philosophy.

Since power is essentially only a means to an end a community based solely on power must decay in the calm of order and stability; its complete security reveals that it is built on sand. Only by acquiring more power can it guarantee the status quo; only by constantly extending its authority and only through the process of power accumulation can it remain stable. Hobbes's Commonwealth is a vacillating structure and must always provide itself with new props from the outside; otherwise it would collapse overnight into the aimless, senseless chaos of the private interests from which it sprang. Hobbes embodies the necessity of power accumulation in the theory of the state of nature, the 'condition of perpetual war' of all against all, in which the various single states still remain vis-à-vis each other like their individual subjects before they submitted to the authority of a Commonwealth.[38] This ever-present possibility of war guarantees the

---

playing a prescribed role – which are so desperately needed by human dignity, which demands of a man that he at least be a willing victim if nothing else.

38 The presently popular liberal notion of a World Government is based, like all liberal notions of political power, on the same concept of individuals submitting to a

Commonwealth a prospect of permanence because it makes it possible for the state to increase its power at the expense of other states.

It would be erroneous to take at its face value the obvious inconsistency between Hobbes's plea for security of the individual and the inherent instability of his Commonwealth. Here again he tries to persuade, to appeal to certain basic instincts for security which he knew well enough could survive in the subjects of the *Leviathan* only in the form of absolute submission to the power which 'over-awes them all,' that is, in an all-pervading, overwhelming fear – not exactly the basic sentiment of a safe man. What Hobbes actually starts from is an unmatched insight into the political needs of the new social body of the rising bourgeoisie, whose fundamental belief in an unending process of property accumulation was about to eliminate all individual safety. Hobbes drew the necessary conclusions from social and economic behavior patterns when he proposed his revolutionary changes in political constitution. He outlined the only new body politic which could correspond to the new needs and interests of a new class. What he actually achieved was a picture of man as he ought to become and ought to behave if he wanted to fit into the coming bourgeois society.

Hobbes's insistence on power as the motor of all things human and divine (even God's reign over men is 'derived not from Creating them . . . but from the Irresistible Power') sprang from the theoretically indisputable proposition that a never-ending accumulation of property must be based on a never-ending accumulation of power. The philosophical correlative of the inherent instability of a community founded on power is the image of an endless process of history which, in order to be consistent with the constant growth of power, inexorably catches up with individuals, peoples, and finally all mankind. The limitless process of capital accumulation needs the political structure of so 'unlimited a Power' that it can protect growing property by constantly growing more powerful. Granted the fundamental dynamism of the new social class, it is perfectly true that 'he cannot

---

central authority which 'overawes them all,' except that nations are now taking the place of individuals. The World Government is to overcome and eliminate authentic politics, that is, different peoples getting along with each other in the full force of their power.

assure the power and means to live well, which he hath at present, without the acquisition of more.' The consistency of this conclusion is in no way altered by the remarkable fact that for some three hundred years there was neither a sovereign who would 'convert this Truth of Speculation into the Utility of Practice,' nor a bourgeoisie politically conscious and economically mature enough openly to adopt Hobbes's philosophy of power.

This process of never-ending accumulation of power necessary for the protection of a never-ending accumulation of capital determined the 'progressive' ideology of the late nineteenth century and foreshadowed the rise of imperialism. Not the naïve delusion of a limitless growth of property, but the realization that power accumulation was the only guarantee for the stability of so-called economic laws, made progress irresistible. The eighteenth-century notion of progress, as conceived in pre-revolutionary France, intended criticism of the past to be a means of mastering the present and controlling the future; progress culminated in the emancipation of man. But this notion had little to do with the endless progress of bourgeois society, which not only did not want the liberty and autonomy of man, but was ready to sacrifice everything and everybody to supposedly superhuman laws of history. 'What we call progress is [the] wind . . . [that] drives [the angel of history] irresistibly into the future to which he turns his back while the pile of ruins before him towers to the skies.' [39] Only in Marx's dream of a classless society which, in Joyce's words, was to awaken mankind from the nightmare of history, does a last, though utopian, trace of the eighteenth-century concept appear.

The imperialist-minded businessman, whom the stars annoyed because he could not annex them, realized that power organized for its own sake would beget more power. When the accumulation of capital had reached its natural, national limits, the bourgeoisie

[39] Walter Benjamin, 'Über den Begriff der Geschichte,' *Institut für Sozialforschung*, New York, 1942, mimeographed. – The imperialists themselves were quite aware of the implications of their concept of progress. Said the very representative author from the Civil Services in India who wrote under the pseudonym A. Carthill: 'One must always feel sorry for those persons who are crushed by the triumphal car of progress' (*op. cit.*, p. 209).

understood that only with an 'expansion is everything' ideology, and only with a corresponding power-accumulating process, would it be possible to set the old motor into motion again. At the same moment, however, when it seemed as though the true principle of perpetual motion had been discovered, the specifically optimistic mood of the progress ideology was shaken. Not that anybody began to doubt the irresistibility of the process itself, but many people began to see what had frightened Cecil Rhodes: that the human condition and the limitations of the globe were a serious obstacle to a process that was unable to stop and to stabilize, and could therefore only begin a series of destructive catastrophes once it had reached these limits.

In the imperialistic epoch a philosophy of power became the philosophy of the elite, who quickly discovered and were quite ready to admit that the thirst for power could be quenched only through destruction. This was the essential cause of their nihilism (especially conspicuous in France at the turn, and in Germany in the twenties, of this century) which replaced the superstition of progress with the equally vulgar superstition of doom, and preached automatic annihilation with the same enthusiasm that the fanatics of automatic progress had preached the irresistibility of economic laws. It had taken Hobbes, the great idolator of Success, three centuries to succeed. This was partly because the French Revolution, with its conception of man as lawmaker and *citoyen*, had almost succeeded in preventing the bourgeoisie from fully developing its notion of history as a necessary process. But it was also partly because of the revolutionary implications of the Commonwealth, its fearless breach with Western tradition, which Hobbes did not fail to point out.

Every man and every thought which does not serve and does not conform to the ultimate purpose of a machine whose only purpose is the generation and accumulation of power is a dangerous nuisance. Hobbes judged that the books of the 'ancient Greeks and Romans' were as 'prejudicial' as the teaching of a Christian 'Summum bonum . . . as [it] is spoken of in the Books of the old Morall Philosophers' or the doctrine that 'whatsoever a man does against his Conscience, is Sinne' and that 'Lawes are the Rules of Just and Unjust.' Hobbes's deep distrust of the whole Western tradition of political thought will not surprise us if we remember that he wanted nothing more nor less than the justification of Tyranny which, though it has occurred many times in Western history, has never been honored with a philosophical foundation. That the Leviathan actually amounts to a permanent government of tyranny, Hobbes is proud to admit: 'the name of Tyranny signifieth nothing more nor lesse than the name of Soveraignty . . . I think the toleration of a professed hatred of Tyranny, is a Toleration of hatred to Commonwealth in generall . . .'

Since Hobbes was a philosopher, he could already detect in the rise of the bourgeoisie all those antitraditionalist qualities of the new class which would take more than three hundred years to develop fully. His *Leviathan* was not concerned with idle speculation about new political principles or the old search for reason as it governs the community of men; it was strictly a 'reckoning of the consequences' that follow from the rise of a new class in society whose existence is essentially tied up with property as a dynamic, new property-producing device. The so-called accumulation of capital which gave birth to the bourgeoisie changed the very conception of property and wealth: they were no longer considered to be the results of accumulation and acquisition but their beginnings; wealth became a never-ending process of getting wealthier. The classification of the bourgeoisie as an owning class is only superficially correct, for a characteristic of this class has been that everybody could belong to it who conceived of life as a process of perpetually becoming wealthier, and considered money as something sacrosanct which under no circumstances should be a mere commodity for consumption.

Property by itself, however, is subject to use and consumption and therefore diminishes constantly. The most radical and the only secure form of possession is destruction, for only what we have destroyed is safely and forever ours. Property owners who do not consume but strive to enlarge their holdings continually find one very inconvenient limitation, the unfortunate fact that men must die. Death is the real reason why property and acquisition can never become a true political principle. A social system based essentially on property cannot possibly proceed toward anything but the final destruction of all property. The finiteness of personal life is as serious a challenge to property as the foundation of society, as the limits of the globe are a challenge to expansion as the foundation of the body politic. By transcending the limits of human life in planning for an automatic continuous growth of wealth beyond all personal needs and possibilities of consumption, individual property is made a public affair and taken out of the sphere of mere private life. Private interests which by their very nature are temporary, limited by man's natural span of life, can now escape into the sphere of public affairs and borrow from them that infinite length of time which is needed for continuous accumulation. This seems to create a society very similar to that of the ants and bees where 'the Common good differeth not from the Private; and being by nature enclined to their private, they procure thereby the common benefit.'

Since, however, men are neither ants nor bees, the whole thing is a delusion. Public life takes on the deceptive aspect of a total of private interests as though these interests could create a new quality through sheer addition. All the so-called liberal concepts of politics (that is, all the pre-imperialist political notions of the bourgeoisie) – such as unlimited competition regulated by a secret balance which comes mysteriously from the sum total of competing activities, the pursuit of 'enlightened self-interest' as an adequate political virtue, unlimited progress inherent in the mere succession of events – have this in common: they simply add up private lives and personal behavior patterns and present the sum as laws of history, or economics, or politics. Liberal concepts, however, while they express the bourgeoisie's instinctive distrust of and its innate hostility to public affairs, are only a temporary compromise between the old standards of Western culture and the new class's faith in property as a dynamic, self-moving principle. The old standards give way to the extent that automatically growing wealth actually replaces political action.

Hobbes was the true, though never fully recognized, philosopher of the bourgeoisie because he realized that acquisition of wealth conceived as a never-ending process can be guaranteed only by the seizure of political power, for the accumulating process must sooner or later force open all existing territorial limits. He foresaw that a society which had entered the path of never-ending acquisition had to engineer a dynamic political organization capable of a corresponding never-ending process of power generation. He even, through sheer force of imagination, was able to outline the main psychological traits of the new type of man who would fit into such a society and its tyrannical body politic. He foresaw the necessary idolatry of power itself by this new human type, that he would be flattered at being called a power-thirsty animal, although actually society would force him to surrender all his natural forces, his virtues and his vices, and would make him the poor meek little fellow who has not even the right to rise against tyranny, and who, far from striving for power, submits to any existing government and does not stir even when his best friend falls an innocent victim to an incomprehensible *raison d'état*.

For a Commonwealth based on the accumulated and monopolized power of all its individual members necessarily leaves each person powerless, deprived of his natural and human capacities. It leaves him degraded into a cog in the power-accumulating machine, free to console himself with sublime thoughts about the ultimate destiny of this machine, which itself is constructed in such a way that it can devour the globe simply by following its own inherent law.

The ultimate destructive purpose of this Commonwealth is at least indicated in the philosophical interpretation of human equality as an 'equality of ability' to kill. Living with all other nations 'in the condition of a perpetuall war, and upon the confines of battle, with their frontiers armed, and canons planted against their neighbours round about,' it has no other law of conduct but the 'most conducing to [its] benefit' and will gradually devour weaker structures until it comes to a last war 'which provideth for every man, by Victory, or Death.'

By 'Victory or Death,' the Leviathan can indeed overcome all political limitations that go with the existence of other peoples and can envelop the whole earth in its tyranny. But when the last war has come and every man has been provided for, no ultimate peace is established on earth: the power-accumulating machine, without which continual expansion would not have been achieved, needs more material to devour in its never-ending process. If the last victorious Commonwealth cannot proceed to 'annex the planets,' it can only proceed to destroy itself in order to begin anew the never-ending process of power generation.

## III: The Alliance Between Mob and Capital

When imperialism entered the scene of politics with the scramble for Africa in the eighties, it was promoted by businessmen, opposed fiercely by the governments in power, and welcomed by a surprisingly large section of the educated classes.[40] To the last it seemed to be God-sent, a cure for all evils, an easy panacea for all conflicts. And it is true that imperialism in a sense did not disappoint these hopes. It gave a new lease on life to political and social structures which were quite obviously threatened by new social and political forces and which, under other circumstances, without the interference of imperialist developments, would hardly have needed two world wars to disappear.

As matters stood, imperialism spirited away all troubles and produced that deceptive feeling of security, so universal in pre-war Europe, which deceived all but the most sensitive minds. Péguy in France and Chesterton in England knew instinctively that they lived in a world of hollow pretense and that its stability was the greatest pretense of all. Until everything began to crumble, the stability of obviously outdated political structures was a fact, and their stubborn unconcerned longevity seemed to give the lie to those who felt the ground tremble under their feet. The solution of the riddle was imperialism. The answer to the fateful question: why did the European comity of nations allow this evil to spread until everything was destroyed, the good as well as the bad, is that all governments knew very well that their countries were secretly disintegrating, that the body politic was being destroyed from within, and that they lived on borrowed time.

Innocently enough, expansion appeared first as the outlet for excess

---

40 'The Services offer the cleanest and most natural support to an aggressive foreign policy; expansion of the empire appeals powerfully to the aristocracy and the professional classes by offering new and ever-growing fields for the honorable and profitable employment of their sons' (J. A. Hobson, 'Capitalism and Imperialism in South Africa,' *op. cit.*). It was 'above all . . . patriotic professors and publicists regardless of political affiliation and unmindful of personal economic interest' who sponsored 'the outward imperialistic thrusts of the '70ies and early '80ies' (Hayes, *op. cit.*, p. 220).

capital production and offered a remedy, capital export.[41] The tremendously increased wealth produced by capitalist production under a social system based on maldistribution had resulted in 'oversaving' – that is, the accumulation of capital which was condemned to idleness within the existing national capacity for production and consumption. This money was actually superfluous, needed by nobody though owned by a growing class of somebodies. The ensuing crises and depressions during the decades preceding the era of imperialism[42] had impressed upon the capitalists the thought that their whole economic system of production depended upon a supply and demand that from now on must come from 'outside of capitalist society.'[43] Such supply and demand came from inside the nation, so long as the capitalist system did not control all its classes together with its entire productive capacity. When capitalism had pervaded the entire economic structure and all social strata had come into the orbit of its production and consumption system, capitalists clearly had to decide either to see the whole system collapse or to find new markets, that is, to penetrate new countries which were not yet subject to capitalism and therefore could provide a new noncapitalistic supply and demand.

The decisive point about the depressions of the sixties and seventies, which initiated the era of imperialism, was that they forced the bourgeoisie to realize for the first time that the original sin of simple robbery, which centuries ago had made possible the 'original

41 For this and the following see J. A. Hobson, *Imperialism*, who as early as 1905 gave a masterly analysis of the driving economic forces and motives as well as of some of its political implications. When, in 1938, his early study was republished, Hobson could rightly state in his introduction to an unchanged text that his book was real proof 'that the chief perils and disturbances . . . of today . . . were all latent and discernible in the world of a generation ago . . .'

42 The obvious connection between the severe crises in the sixties in England and the seventies on the Continent and imperialism is mentioned in Hayes, *op. cit.*, in a footnote only (on p. 219), and in Schuyler, *op. cit.*, who believes that 'a revival of interest in emigration was an important factor in the beginnings of the imperial movement' and that this interest had been caused by 'a serious depression in British trade and industry' toward the close of the sixties (p. 280). Schuyler also describes at some length the strong 'anti-imperial sentiment of the mid-Victorian era.' Unfortunately, Schuyler makes no differentiation between the Commonwealth and the Empire proper, although the discussion of pre-imperialist material might easily have suggested such a differentiation.

43 Rosa Luxemburg, *Die Akkumulation des Kapitals*, Berlin, 1923, p. 273.

accumulation of capital' (Marx) and had started all further accumulation, had eventually to be repeated lest the motor of accumulation suddenly die down.[44] In the face of this danger, which threatened not only the bourgeoisie but the whole nation with a catastrophic breakdown in production, capitalist producers understood that the forms and laws of their production system 'from the beginning had been calculated for the whole earth.'[45]

The first reaction to the saturated home market, lack of raw materials, and growing crises, was export of capital. The owners of superfluous wealth first tried foreign investment without expansion and without political control, which resulted in an unparalleled orgy of swindles, financial scandals, and stock-market speculation, all the more alarming since foreign investments grew much more rapidly than domestic ones.[46] Big money resulting from oversaving paved the way for little money, the product of the little fellow's work. Domestic enterprises, in order to keep pace with high profits from foreign investment, turned likewise to fraudulent methods and attracted an increasing number of people who, in the hope of miraculous returns, threw their money out of the window. The Panama scandal in France, the *Gründungsschwindel* in Germany and Austria, became classic examples. Tremendous losses resulted from the promises of tremendous profits. The owners of little money lost so much so quickly that the

---

44 Rudolf Hilferding, *Das Finanzkapital*, Wien, 1910, p. 401, mentions – but does not analyze the implications of – the fact that imperialism 'suddenly uses again the methods of the original accumulation of capitalistic wealth.'

45 According to Rosa Luxemburg's brilliant insight into the political structure of imperialism (*op. cit.*, pp. 273 ff., pp. 361 ff.), the 'historical process of the accumulation of capital depends in all its aspects upon the existence of noncapitalist social strata,' so that 'imperialism is the political expression of the accumulation of capital in its competition for the possession of the remainders of the noncapitalistic world.' This essential dependence of capitalism upon a noncapitalistic world lies at the basis of all other aspects of imperialism, which then may be explained as the results of oversaving and maldistribution (Hobson, *op. cit.*), as the result of overproduction and the consequent need for new markets (Lenin, *Imperialism, the Last Stage of Capitalism*, 1917), as the result of an undersupply of raw material (Hayes, *op. cit.*), or as capital export in order to equalize the national profit rate (Hilferding, *op. cit.*).

46 According to Hilferding, *op. cit.*, p. 409, note, the British income from foreign investment increased ninefold while national income doubled from 1865 to 1898. He assumes a similar though probably less marked increase for German and French foreign investments.

owners of superfluous big capital soon saw themselves left alone in what was, in a sense, a battlefield. Having failed to change the whole society into a community of gamblers they were again superfluous, excluded from the normal process of production to which, after some turmoil, all other classes returned quietly, if somewhat impoverished and embittered.[47]

Export of money and foreign investment as such are not imperialism and do not necessarily lead to expansion as a political device. As long as the owners of superfluous capital were content with investing 'large portions of their property in foreign lands,' even if this tendency ran 'counter to all past traditions of nationalism,'[48] they merely confirmed their alienation from the national body on which they were parasites anyway. Only when they demanded government protection of their investments (after the initial stage of swindle had opened their eyes to the possible use of politics against the risks of gambling) did they re-enter the life of the nation. In this appeal, however, they followed the established tradition of bourgeois society, always to consider political institutions exclusively as an instrument for the protection of individual property.[49] Only the fortunate coincidence of the rise of a

47 For France see George Lachapelle, *Les Finances de la Troisième République*, Paris, 1937, and D. W. Brogan, *The Development of Modern France*, New York, 1941. For Germany, compare the interesting contemporary testimonies like Max Wirth, *Geschichte der Handelskrisen*, 1873, chapter 15, and A. Schaeffle, 'Der "grosse Boersenkrach" des Jahres 1873' in *Zeitschrift für die gesamte Staatswissenschaft*, 1874, Band 30.

48 J. A. Hobson, 'Capitalism and Imperialism,' *op. cit.*

49 See Hilferding, *op. cit.*, p. 406. 'Hence the cry for strong state power by all capitalists with vested interests in foreign countries . . . Exported capital feels safest when the state power of its own country rules the new domain completely . . . Its profits should be guaranteed by the state if possible. Thus, exportation of capital favors an imperialist policy.' P. 423: 'It is a matter of course that the attitude of the bourgeoisie toward the state undergoes a complete change when the political power of the state becomes a competitive instrument for the finance capital in the world market. The bourgeoisie had been hostile to the state in its fight against economic mercantilism and political absolutism . . . Theoretically at least, economic life was to be completely free of state intervention; the state was to confine itself politically to the safeguarding of security and the establishment of civil equality.' P. 426: 'However, the desire for an expansionist policy causes a revolutionary change in the mentality of the bourgeoisie. It ceases to be pacifist and humanist.' P. 470: 'Socially, expansion is a vital condition for the preservation of capitalist society; economically, it is the condition for the preservation of, and temporary increase in, the profit rate.'

new class of property holders and the industrial revolution had made the bourgeoisie producers and stimulators of production. As long as it fulfilled this basic function in modern society, which is essentially a community of producers, its wealth had an important function for the nation as a whole. The owners of superfluous capital were the first section of the class to want profits without fulfilling some real social function – even if it was the function of an exploiting producer – and whom, consequently, no police could ever have saved from the wrath of the people.

Expansion then was an escape not only for superfluous capital. More important, it protected its owners against the menacing prospect of remaining entirely superfluous and parasitical. It saved the bourgeoisie from the consequences of maldistribution and revitalized its concept of ownership at a time when wealth could no longer be used as a factor in production within the national framework and had come into conflict with the production ideal of the community as a whole.

Older than the superfluous wealth was another by-product of capitalist production: the human debris that every crisis, following invariably upon each period of industrial growth, eliminated permanently from producing society. Men who had become permanently idle were as superfluous to the community as the owners of superfluous wealth. That they were an actual menace to society had been recognized throughout the nineteenth century and their export had helped to populate the dominions of Canada and Australia as well as the United States. The new fact in the imperialist era is that these two superfluous forces, superfluous capital and superfluous working power, joined hands and left the country together. The concept of expansion, the export of government power and annexation of every territory in which nationals had invested either their wealth or their work, seemed the only alternative to increasing losses in wealth and population. Imperialism and its idea of unlimited expansion seemed to offer a permanent remedy for a permanent evil.[50]

50 These motives were especially outspoken in German imperialism. Among the first activities of the Alldeutsche Verband (founded in 1891) were efforts to prevent German emigrants from changing their citizenship, and the first imperialist speech of William II, on the occasion of the twenty-fifth anniversary of the foundation of the Reich, contained the following typical passage: 'The German Empire has become a World

Ironically enough, the first country in which superfluous wealth and superfluous men were brought together was itself becoming superfluous. South Africa had been in British possession since the beginning of the century because it assured the maritime road to India. The opening of the Suez Canal, however, and the subsequent administrative conquest of Egypt, lessened considerably the importance of the old trade station on the Cape. The British would, in all probability, have withdrawn from Africa just as all European nations had done whenever their possessions and trade interests in India were liquidated.

The particular irony and, in a sense, symbolical circumstance in the unexpected development of South Africa into the 'culture-bed of Imperialism'[51] lies in the very nature of its sudden attractiveness when it had lost all value for the Empire proper: diamond fields were discovered in the seventies and large gold mines in the eighties. The new desire for profit-at-any-price converged for the first time with the old fortune hunt. Prospectors, adventurers, and the scum of the big cities emigrated to the Dark Continent along with capital from industrially developed countries. From now on, the mob, begotten by the monstrous accumulation of capital, accompanied its begetter on those voyages of discovery where nothing was discovered but new possibilities for investment. The owners of superfluous wealth were the only men who could use the superfluous men who came from the four corners of the earth. Together they established the first paradise of parasites whose lifeblood was gold. Imperialism, the product of superfluous money and superfluous men, began its startling career by producing the most superfluous and unreal goods.

It may still be doubtful whether the panacea of expansion would have become so great a temptation for non-imperialists if it had offered its dangerous solutions only for those superfluous forces which, in any case, were already outside the nation's body corporate. The complicity

---

Empire. Thousands of our compatriots live everywhere, in distant parts of the earth . . . Gentlemen, it is your solemn duty to help me unite this greater German Empire with our native country.' Compare also J. A. Froude's statement in note 10.

51 E. H. Dance, *The Victorian Illusion*, London, 1928, p. 164: 'Africa, which had been included neither in the itinerary of Saxondom nor in the professional philosophers of imperial history, became the culture-bed of British imperialism.'

of all parliamentary parties in imperialist programs is a matter of record. The history of the British Labor Party in this respect is an almost unbroken chain of justifications of Cecil Rhodes' early prediction: 'The workmen find that although the Americans are exceedingly fond of them, and are just now exchanging the most brotherly sentiments with them, yet they are shutting out their goods. The workmen also find that Russia, France and Germany locally are doing the same, and the workmen see that if they do not look out they will have no place in the world to trade at all. And so the workmen have become Imperialist and the Liberal Party are following.' [52] In Germany, the liberals (and not the Conservative Party) were the actual promoters of that famous naval policy which contributed so heavily to the outbreak of the first World War.[53] The Socialist Party wavered between active support of the imperialist naval policy (it repeatedly voted funds for the building of a German navy after 1906) and complete neglect of all questions of foreign policy. Occasional warnings against the *Lumpenproletariat*, and the possible bribing of sections of the working class with crumbs from the imperialist table, did not lead to a deeper understanding of the great appeal which the imperialist programs had to the rank and file of the party. In Marxist terms the new phenomenon of an alliance between mob and capital seemed so unnatural, so obviously in conflict with the doctrine of class struggle, that the actual dangers of the imperialist attempt – to divide mankind into master races and slave races, into higher and lower breeds, into colored peoples and white men, all of which were attempts to unify the people on the basis of the mob – were completely overlooked. Even the breakdown of international solidarity at the outbreak of the first World War did not disturb the complacency of the socialists and their faith in the proletariat as such. Socialists were still probing the economic laws of imperialism when imperialists had long since stopped obeying them,

52 Quoted from Millin, *op. cit.*

53 'The liberals, and not the Right of Parliament, were the supporters of the naval policy.' Alfred von Tirpitz, *Erinnerungen*, 1919. See also Daniel Frymann (pseud. for Heinrich Class), *Wenn ich der Kaiser wär*, 1912: 'The true imperial party is the National Liberal Party.' Frymann, a prominent German chauvinist during the first World War, even adds with respect to the conservatives: 'The aloofness of conservative milieus with regard to race doctrines is also worthy of note.'

when in overseas countries these laws had been sacrificed to the 'imperial factor' or to the 'race factor,' and when only a few elderly gentlemen in high finance still believed in the inalienable rights of the profit rate.

The curious weakness of popular opposition to imperialism, the numerous inconsistencies and outright broken promises of liberal statesmen, frequently ascribed to opportunism or bribery, have other and deeper causes. Neither opportunism nor bribery could have persuaded a man like Gladstone to break his promise, as the leader of the Liberal Party, to evacuate Egypt when he became Prime Minister. Half consciously and hardly articulately, these men shared with the people the conviction that the national body itself was so deeply split into classes, that class struggle was so universal a characteristic of modern political life, that the very cohesion of the nation was jeopardized. Expansion again appeared as a lifesaver, if and insofar as it could provide a common interest for the nation as a whole, and it is mainly for this reason that imperialists were allowed to become 'parasites upon patriotism.'[54]

Partly, of course, such hopes still belonged with the old vicious practice of 'healing' domestic conflicts with foreign adventures. The difference, however, is marked. Adventures are by their very nature limited in time and space; they may succeed temporarily in overcoming conflicts, although as a rule they fail and tend rather to sharpen them. From the very beginning the imperialist adventure of expansion appeared to be an eternal solution, because expansion was conceived as unlimited. Furthermore, imperialism was not an adventure in the usual sense, because it depended less on nationalist slogans than on the seemingly solid basis of economic interests. In a society of clashing interests, where the common good was identified with the sum total of individual interests, expansion as such appeared to be a possible common interest of the nation as a whole. Since the owning and dominant classes had convinced everybody that economic interest and the passion for ownership are a sound basis for the body politic, even non-imperialist statesmen were easily persuaded to yield when a common economic interest appeared on the horizon.

These then are the reasons why nationalism developed so clear a tendency toward imperialism, the inner contradiction of the two

54 Hobson, *op. cit.*, p. 61.

principles notwithstanding.[55] The more ill-fitted nations were for the incorporation of foreign peoples (which contradicted the constitution of their own body politic), the more they were tempted to oppress them. In theory, there is an abyss between nationalism and imperialism; in practice, it can and has been bridged by tribal nationalism and outright racism. From the beginning, imperialists in all countries preached and boasted of their being 'beyond the parties,' and the only ones to speak for the nation as a whole. This was especially true of the Central and Eastern European countries with few or no overseas holdings; there the alliance between mob and capital took place at home and resented even more bitterly (and attacked much more violently) the national institutions and all national parties.[56]

The contemptuous indifference of imperialist politicians to domestic issues was marked everywhere, however, and especially in England. While 'parties above parties' like the Primrose League were of secondary influence, imperialism was the chief cause of the degeneration of the two-party system into the Front Bench system, which led to a 'diminution of the power of opposition' in Parliament and to a growth of 'power of the Cabinet as against the House of Commons.'[57] Of course this was also carried through as a policy beyond the strife of parties and particular interests, and by men who claimed to speak for the nation as a whole. Such language was bound to attract and delude precisely those persons who still retained a spark of political idealism. The cry for unity resembled exactly the battle cries which had always led peoples to war; and yet, nobody detected in the universal and permanent instrument of unity the germ of universal and permanent war.

Government officials engaged more actively than any other group in

---

55 Hobson, *op. cit.*, was the first to recognize both the fundamental opposition of imperialism and nationalism and the tendency of nationalism to become imperialist. He called imperialism a perversion of nationalism 'in which nations . . . transform the wholesome stimulative rivalry of various national types into the cut-throat struggle of competing empires' (p. 9).

56 See chapter viii.

57 Hobson, *op. cit.*, pp. 146 ff. – 'There can be no doubt that the power of the Cabinet as against the House of Commons has grown steadily and rapidly and it appears to be still growing,' noticed Bryce in 1901, in *Studies in History and Jurisprudence*, 1901, I, 177. For the working of the Front Bench system see also Hilaire Belloc and Cecil Chesterton, *The Party System*, London, 1911.

the nationalist brand of imperialism and were chiefly responsible for the confusion of imperialism with nationalism. The nation-states had created and depended upon the civil services as a permanent body of officials who served regardless of class interest and governmental changes. Their professional honor and self-respect – especially in England and Germany – derived from their being servants of the nation as a whole. They were the only group with a direct interest in supporting the state's fundamental claim to independence of classes and factions. That the authority of the nation-state itself depended largely on the economic independence and political neutrality of its civil servants becomes obvious in our time; the decline of nations has invariably started with the corruption of its permanent administration and the general conviction that civil servants are in the pay, not of the state, but of the owning classes. At the close of the century the owning classes had become so dominant that it was almost ridiculous for a state employee to keep up the pretense of serving the nation. Division into classes left them outside the social body and forced them to form a clique of their own. In the colonial services they escaped the actual disintegration of the national body. In ruling foreign peoples in faraway countries, they could much better pretend to be heroic servants of the nation, 'who by their services had glorified the British race,' [58] than if they had stayed at home. The colonies were no longer simply 'a vast system of outdoor relief for the upper classes' as James Mill could still describe them; they were to become the very backbone of British nationalism, which discovered in the domination of distant countries and the rule over strange peoples the only way to serve British, and nothing but British, interests. The services actually believed that 'the peculiar genius of each nation shows itself nowhere more clearly than in their system of dealing with subject races.' [59]

The truth was that only far from home could a citizen of England, Germany, or France be nothing but an Englishman or German or

58 Lord Curzon at the unveiling of Lord Cromer's memorial tablet. See Lawrence J. Zetland, *Lord Cromer*, 1932, p. 362.

59 Sir Hesketh Bell, *op. cit.*, Part I, p. 300.

The same sentiment prevailed in the Dutch colonial services. 'The highest task, the task without precedent is that which awaits the East Indian Civil Service official . . . it should be considered as the highest honor to serve in its ranks . . . the select body which fulfills the mission of Holland overseas.' See De Kat Angelino, *Colonial Policy*, Chicago, 1931, II, 129.

Frenchman. In his own country he was so entangled in economic interests or social loyalties that he felt closer to a member of his class in a foreign country than to a man of another class in his own. Expansion gave nationalism a new lease on life and therefore was accepted as an instrument of national politics. The members of the new colonial societies and imperialist leagues felt 'far removed from the strife of parties,' and the farther away they moved the stronger their belief that they 'represented only a national purpose.' [60] This shows the desperate state of the European nations before imperialism, how fragile their institutions had become, how outdated their social system proved in the face of man's growing capacity to produce. The means for preservation were desperate too, and in the end the remedy proved worse than the evil – which, incidentally, it did not cure.

The alliance between capital and mob is to be found at the genesis of every consistently imperialist policy. In some countries, particularly in Great Britain, this new alliance between the much-too-rich and the much-too-poor was and remained confined to overseas possessions. The so-called hypocrisy of British policies was the result of the good sense of English statesmen who drew a sharp line between colonial methods and normal domestic policies, thereby avoiding with considerable success the feared boomerang effect of imperialism upon the homeland. In other countries, particularly in Germany and Austria, the alliance took effect at home in the form of pan-movements, and to a lesser extent in France, in a so-called colonial policy. The aim of these 'movements' was, so to speak, to imperialize the whole nation (and not only the 'superfluous' part of it), to combine domestic and foreign policy in such a way as to organize the nation for the looting of foreign territories and the permanent degradation of alien peoples.

The rise of the mob out of the capitalist organization was observed early, and its growth carefully and anxiously noted by all great historians of the nineteenth century. Historical pessimism from Burckhardt to Spengler springs essentially from this consideration. But what the

---

60 The President of the German 'Kolonialverein,' Hohenlohe-Langenburg, in 1884. See Mary E. Townsend, *Origin of Modern German Colonialism, 1871–1885,* 1921.

historians, sadly preoccupied with the phenomenon in itself, failed to grasp was that the mob could not be identified with the growing industrial working class, and certainly not with the people as a whole, but that it was composed actually of the refuse of all classes. This composition made it seem that the mob and its representatives had abolished class differences, that those standing outside the class-divided nation were the people itself (the *Volksgemeinschaft*, as the Nazis would call it) rather than its distortion and caricature. The historical pessimists understood the essential irresponsibility of this new social stratum, and they also correctly foresaw the possibility of converting democracy into a despotism whose tyrants would rise from the mob and lean on it for support. What they failed to understand was that the mob is not only the refuse but also the by-product of bourgeois society, directly produced by it and therefore never quite separable from it. They failed for this reason to notice high society's constantly growing admiration for the underworld, which runs like a red thread through the nineteenth century, its continuous step-by-step retreat on all questions of morality, and its growing taste for the anarchical cynicism of its offspring. At the turn of the century, the Dreyfus Affair showed that underworld and high society in France were so closely bound together that it was difficult definitely to place any of the 'heroes' among the Anti-Dreyfusards in either category.

This feeling of kinship, the joining together of begetter and offspring, already classically expressed in Balzac's novels, antedates all practical economic, political, or social considerations and recalls those fundamental psychological traits of the new type of Western man that Hobbes outlined three hundred years ago. But it is true that it was mainly due to the insights acquired by the bourgeoisie during the crises and depressions which preceded imperialism that high society finally admitted its readiness to accept the revolutionary change in moral standards which Hobbes's 'realism' had proposed, and which was now being proposed anew by the mob and its leaders. The very fact that the 'original sin' of 'original accumulation of capital' would need additional sins to keep the system going was far more effective in persuading the bourgeoisie to shake off the restraints of Western tradition than either its philosopher or its underworld. It finally induced the German bourgeoisie to throw off the mask of hypocrisy and openly confess its relationship to the mob, calling on it expressly to champion its property interests.

It is significant that this should have happened in Germany. In England and Holland the development of bourgeois society had progressed relatively quietly and the bourgeoisie of these countries enjoyed centuries of security and freedom from fear. Its rise in France, however, was interrupted by a great popular revolution whose consequences interfered with the bourgeoisie's enjoyment of supremacy. In Germany, moreover, where the bourgeoisie did not reach full development until the latter half of the nineteenth century, its rise was accompanied from the start by the growth of a revolutionary working-class movement with a tradition nearly as old as its own. It was a matter of course that the less secure a bourgeois class felt in its own country, the more it would be tempted to shed the heavy burden of hypocrisy. High society's affinity with the mob came to light in France earlier than in Germany, but was in the end equally strong in both countries. France, however, because of her revolutionary traditions and her relative lack of industrialization, produced only a relatively small mob, so that her bourgeoisie was finally forced to look for help beyond the frontiers and to ally itself with Hitler Germany.

Whatever the precise nature of the long historical evolution of the bourgeoisie in the various European countries, the political principles of the mob, as encountered in imperialist ideologies and totalitarian movements, betray a surprisingly strong affinity with the political attitudes of bourgeois society, if the latter are cleansed of hypocrisy and untainted by concessions to Christian tradition. What more recently made the nihilistic attitudes of the mob so intellectually attractive to the bourgeoisie is a relationship of principle that goes far beyond the actual birth of the mob.

In other words, the disparity between cause and effect which characterized the birth of imperialism has its reasons. The occasion – superfluous wealth created by overaccumulation, which needed the mob's help to find safe and profitable investment – set in motion a force that had always lain in the basic structure of bourgeois society, though it had been hidden by nobler traditions and by that blessed hypocrisy which La Rochefoucauld called the compliment vice pays to virtue. At the same time, completely unprincipled power politics could not be played until a mass of people was available who were free of all principles and so large numerically that they surpassed the ability of state and society to take care of them. The fact that this mob could be used only by imperialist politicians and inspired only by racial doctrines made it appear as though imperialism alone were able to settle the grave domestic, social, and economic problems of modern times.

The philosophy of Hobbes, it is true, contains nothing of modern race doctrines, which not only stir up the mob, but in their totalitarian form outline very clearly the forms of organization through which humanity could carry the endless process of capital and power accumulation through to its logical end in self-destruction. But Hobbes at least provided political thought with the prerequisite for all race doctrines, that is, the exclusion in principle of the idea of humanity which constitutes the sole regulating idea of international law. With the assumption that foreign politics is necessarily outside of the human contract, engaged in the perpetual war of all against all, which is the law of the 'state of nature,' Hobbes affords the best possible theoretical foundation for those naturalistic ideologies which hold nations to be tribes, separated from each other by nature, without any connection whatever, unconscious of the solidarity of mankind and having in common only the instinct for self-preservation which man shares with the animal world. If the idea of humanity, of which the most conclusive symbol is the common origin of the human species, is no longer valid, then nothing is more plausible than a theory according to which brown, yellow, or black races are descended from some other species of apes than the white race, and that all together are predestined by nature to war against each other until they have disappeared from the face of the earth.

If it should prove to be true that we are imprisoned in Hobbes's endless process of power accumulation, then the organization of the mob will inevitably take the form of transformation of nations into races, for there is, under the conditions of an accumulating society, no other unifying bond available between individuals who in the very process of power accumulation and expansion are losing all natural connections with their fellow-men.

Racism may indeed carry out the doom of the Western world and, for that matter, of the whole of human civilization. When Russians have become Slavs, when Frenchmen have assumed the role of commanders of a *force noire*, when Englishmen have turned into 'white men,' as already for a disastrous spell all Germans became Aryans, then this change will itself signify the end of Western man. For no matter what learned scientists may say, race is, politically speaking, not the beginning of humanity but its end, not the origin of peoples but their decay, not the natural birth of man but his unnatural death.

# CHAPTER SIX

# Race-Thinking Before Racism

If race-thinking were a German invention, as it has been sometimes asserted, then 'German thinking' (whatever that may be) was victorious in many parts of the spiritual world long before the Nazis started their ill-fated attempt at world conquest. Hitlerism exercised its strong international and inter-European appeal during the thirties because racism, although a state doctrine only in Germany, had been a powerful trend in public opinion everywhere. The Nazi political war machine had long been in motion when in 1939 German tanks began their march of destruction, since – in political warfare – racism was calculated to be a more powerful ally than any paid agent or secret organization of fifth columnists. Strengthened by the experiences of almost two decades in the various capitals, the Nazis were confident that their best 'propaganda' would be their racial policy itself, from which, despite many other compromises and broken promises, they had never swerved for expediency's sake.[1] Racism was neither a new nor a secret weapon, though never before had it been used with this thoroughgoing consistency.

The historical truth of the matter is that race-thinking, with its roots deep in the eighteenth century, emerged simultaneously in all Western countries during the nineteenth century. Racism has been the powerful ideology of imperialistic policies since the turn of our century. It certainly has absorbed and revived all the old patterns of race opinions which, however, by themselves would hardly have been able to create or, for that matter, to degenerate into racism as a *Weltanschauung* or an ideology. In the middle of the last century, race opinions were

1 During the German-Russian pact, Nazi propaganda stopped all attacks on 'Bolshevism' but never gave up the race-line.

still judged by the yardstick of political reason: Tocqueville wrote to Gobineau about the latter's doctrines, 'They are probably wrong and certainly pernicious.'[2] Not until the end of the century were dignity and importance accorded race-thinking as though it had been one of the major spiritual contributions of the Western world.[3]

Until the fateful days of the 'scramble for Africa,' race-thinking had been one of the many free opinions which, within the general framework of liberalism, argued and fought each other to win the consent of public opinion.[4] Only a few of them became full-fledged ideologies, that is, systems based upon a single opinion that proved strong enough to attract and persuade a majority of people and broad enough to lead them through the various experiences and situations of an average modern life. For an ideology differs from a simple opinion in that it claims to possess either the key to history, or the solution for all the 'riddles of the universe,' or the intimate knowledge of the hidden universal laws which are supposed to rule nature and man. Few ideologies have won enough prominence to survive the hard competitive struggle of persuasion, and only two have come out on top and essentially defeated all others: the ideology which interprets history as an economic struggle of classes, and the other that interprets history as a natural fight of races. The appeal of both to large masses was so strong that they were able to enlist state support and establish themselves as official national doctrines. But far beyond the boundaries within which race-thinking and class-thinking have developed into obligatory patterns of thought, free public opinion has adopted them to such an extent that not only intellectuals but great masses of people will no longer accept a presentation of past or present facts that is not in agreement with either of these views.

The tremendous power of persuasion inherent in the main ideologies of our times is not accidental. Persuasion is not possible without appeal to either experiences or desires, in other words to immediate political needs. Plausibility in these matters comes neither from

2 'Lettres de Alexis de Tocqueville et de Arthur de Gobineau,' in *Revue des Deux Mondes*, 1907, Tome 199, Letter of November 17, 1853.
3 The best historical account of race-thinking in the pattern of a 'history of ideas' is Erich Voegelin, *Rasse und Staat*, Tuebingen, 1933.
4 For the host of nineteenth-century conflicting opinions see Carlton J. H. Hayes, *A Generation of Materialism*, New York, 1941, pp. 111–122.

scientific facts, as the various brands of Darwinists would like us to believe, nor from historical laws, as the historians pretend, in their efforts to discover the law according to which civilizations rise and fall. Every full-fledged ideology has been created, continued and improved as a political weapon and not as a theoretical doctrine. It is true that sometimes – and such is the case with racism – an ideology has changed its original political sense, but without immediate contact with political life none of them could be imagined. Their scientific aspect is secondary and arises first from the desire to provide watertight arguments, and second because their persuasive power also got hold of scientists, who no longer were interested in the result of their research but left their laboratories and hurried off to preach to the multitude their new interpretations of life and world.[5] We owe it to these 'scientific' preachers rather than to any scientific findings that today no single science is left into whose categorical system race-thinking has not deeply penetrated. This again has made historians, some of whom have been tempted to hold science responsible for race-thinking, mistake certain either philological or biological research results for causes instead of consequences of race-thinking.[6]

5 'Huxley neglected scientific research of his own from the '70's onward, so busy was he in the role of "Darwin's bulldog" barking and biting at theologians' (Hayes, *op. cit.*, p. 126). Ernst Haeckel's passion for popularizing scientific results which was at least as strong as his passion for science itself, has been stressed recently by an applauding Nazi writer, H. Bruecher, 'Ernst Haeckel, Ein Wegbereiter biologischen Staatsdenkens.' In *Nationalsozialistische Monatshefte*, 1935, Heft 69.

Two rather extreme examples may be quoted to show what scientists are capable of. Both were scholars of good standing, writing during World War I. The German historian of art, Josef Strzygowski, in his *Altai, Iran und Völkerwanderung* (Leipzig, 1917) discovered the Nordic race to be composed of Germans, Ukrainians, Armenians, Persians, Hungarians, Bulgars and Turks (pp. 306–307). The Society of Medicine of Paris not only published a report on the discovery of 'polychesia' (excessive defecation) and 'bromidrosis' (body odor) in the German race, but proposed urinalysis for the detection of German spies; German urine was 'found' to contain 20 per cent non-uric nitrogen as against 15 per cent for other races. See Jacques Barzun, *Race*, New York, 1937, p. 239.

6 This *quid pro quo* was partly the result of the zeal of students who wanted to put down every single instance in which race has been mentioned. Thereby they mistook relatively harmless authors, for whom explanation by race was a possible and sometimes fascinating opinion, for full-fledged racists. Such opinions, in themselves harmless, were advanced by the early anthropologists as starting points of their

The opposite would have come closer to the truth. As a matter of fact, the doctrine that Might is Right needed several centuries (from the seventeenth to the nineteenth) to conquer natural science and produce the 'law' of the survival of the fittest. And if, to take another instance, the theory of de Maistre and Schelling about savage tribes as the decaying residues of former peoples had suited the nineteenth-century political devices as well as the theory of progress, we would probably never have heard much of 'primitives' and no scientist would have wasted his time looking for the 'missing link' between ape and man. The blame is not to be laid on any science as such, but rather on certain scientists who were no less hypnotized by ideologies than their fellow-citizens.

The fact that racism is the main ideological weapon of imperialistic politics is so obvious that it seems as though many students prefer to avoid the beaten track of truism. Instead, an old misconception of racism as a kind of exaggerated nationalism is still given currency. Valuable works of students, especially in France, who have proved that racism is not only a quite different phenomenon but tends to destroy the body politic of the nation, are generally overlooked. Witnessing the gigantic competition between race-thinking and class-thinking for dominion over the minds of modern men, some have been inclined to see in the one the expression of national and in

---

investigations. A typical instance is the naïve hypothesis of Paul Broca, noted French anthropologist of the middle of the last century, who assumed that 'the brain has something to do with race and the measured shape of the skull is the best way to get at the contents of the brain' (quoted after Jacques Barzun, *op. cit.*, p. 162). It is obvious that this assertion, without the support of a conception of the nature of man, is simply ridiculous.

As for the philologists of the early nineteenth century, whose concept of 'Aryanism' has seduced almost every student of racism to count them among the propagandists or even inventors of race-thinking, they are as innocent as innocent can be. When they overstepped the limits of pure research it was because they wanted to include in the same cultural brotherhood as many nations as possible. In the words of Ernest Seillière, *La Philosophie de l'Impérialisme*, 4 vols., 1903–1906: 'There was a kind of intoxication: modern civilization believed it had recovered its pedigree ... and an organism was born which embraced in one and the same fraternity all nations whose language showed some affinity with Sanskrit.' (Préface, Tome I, p. xxxv.) In other words, these men were still in the humanistic tradition of the eighteenth century and shared its enthusiasm about strange people and exotic cultures.

the other the expression of international trends, to believe the one to be the mental preparation for national wars and the other to be the ideology for civil wars. This has been possible because of the first World War's curious mixture of old national and new imperialistic conflicts, a mixture in which old national slogans proved still to possess a far greater appeal to the masses of all countries involved than any imperialistic aims. The last war, however, with its Quislings and collaborationists everywhere, should have proved that racism can stir up civil conflicts in every country, and is one of the most ingenious devices ever invented for preparing civil war.

For the truth is that race-thinking entered the scene of active politics the moment the European peoples had prepared, and to a certain extent realized, the new body politic of the nation. From the very beginning, racism deliberately cut across all national boundaries, whether defined by geographical, linguistic, traditional, or any other standards, and denied national-political existence as such. Race-thinking, rather than class-thinking, was the ever-present shadow accompanying the development of the comity of European nations, until it finally grew to be the powerful weapon for the destruction of those nations. Historically speaking, racists have a worse record of patriotism than the representatives of all other international ideologies together, and they were the only ones who consistently denied the great principle upon which national organizations of peoples are built, the principle of equality and solidarity of all peoples guaranteed by the idea of mankind.

## I: A 'Race' of Aristocrats Against a 'Nation' of Citizens

A steadily rising interest in the most different, strange, and even savage peoples was characteristic of France during the eighteenth century. This was the time when Chinese paintings were admired and imitated, when one of the most famous works of the century was named *Lettres Persanes*, and when travelers' reports were the favorite reading of society. The honesty and simplicity of savage and uncivilized peoples were opposed to the sophistication and frivolity of culture. Long before the nineteenth century with its tremendously enlarged opportunities for travel brought the non-European world into the home of every average citizen, eighteenth-century French society had tried to grasp spiritually the content of cultures and countries that lay far beyond European boundaries. A great enthusiasm for 'new specimens of mankind' (Herder) filled the hearts of the heroes of the French Revolution who together with the French nation liberated every people of every color under the French flag. This enthusiasm for strange and foreign countries culminated in the message of fraternity, because it was inspired by the desire to prove in every new and surprising 'specimen of mankind' the old saying of La Bruyère: '*La raison est de tous les climats.*'

Yet it is this nation-creating century and humanity-loving country to which we must trace the germs of what later proved to become the nation-destroying and humanity-annihilating power of racism.[7] It is a remarkable fact that the first author who assumed the coexistence of different peoples with different origins in France, was at the same time the first to elaborate definite class-thinking. The Comte de Boulainvilliers, a French nobleman who wrote at the beginning of the eighteenth century and whose works were published after his death, interpreted the history of France as the history of two different nations of which the one, of Germanic origin, had conquered the older inhabitants, the 'Gaules,' had imposed its laws upon them, had taken their lands, and had settled down as the ruling class, the 'peerage' whose supreme rights rested upon the 'right of conquest' and the 'necessity of obedience always due to the strongest.' [8] Engaged chiefly in finding arguments against the rising political power of the *Tiers Etat* and their spokesmen, the '*nouveau corps*' formed by '*gens de lettres et de lois*,' Boulainvilliers had to fight the monarchy too because the French king wanted no longer to represent the peerage as *primus inter pares*

---

7 François Hotman, French sixteenth-century author of *Franco-Gallia*, is sometimes held to be a forerunner of eighteenth-century racial doctrines, as by Ernest Seillière, *op. cit.* Against this misconception, Théophile Simar has rightly protested: 'Hotman appears, not as an apologist for the Teutons, but as the defender of the people which was oppressed by the monarchy' (*Etude Critique sur la Formation de la doctrine des Races au 18e et son expansion au 19e siècle*, Bruxelles, 1922, p. 20).

8 *Histoire de l'Ancien Gouvernement de la France*, 1727, Tome I, p. 33.

but the nation as a whole; in him, for a while, the new rising class found its most powerful protector. In order to regain uncontested primacy for the nobility, Boulainvilliers proposed that his fellow-noblemen deny a common origin with the French people, break up the unity of the nation, and claim an original and therefore eternal distinction.[9] Much bolder than most of the later defenders of nobility, Boulainvilliers denied any predestined connection with the soil; he conceded that the 'Gaules' had been in France longer, that the 'Francs' were strangers and barbarians. He based his doctrine solely on the eternal right of conquest and found no difficulty in asserting that 'Friesland . . . has been the true cradle of the French nation.' Centuries before the actual development of imperialistic racism, following only the inherent logic of his concept, he considered the original inhabitants of France natives in the modern sense, or in his own terms 'subjects' – not of the king – but of all those whose advantage was descent from the conquering people, who by right of birth were to be called 'Frenchmen.'

Boulainvilliers was deeply influenced by the seventeenth-century might-right doctrines and he certainly was one of the most consistent contemporary disciples of Spinoza, whose *Ethics* he translated and whose *Traité théologico-politique* he analyzed. In his reception and application of Spinoza's political ideas, might was changed into conquest and conquest acted as a kind of unique judgment on the natural qualities and human privileges of men and nations. In this we may detect the first traces of later naturalistic transformations the might-right doctrine was to go through. This view is really corroborated by the fact that Boulainvilliers was one of the outstanding freethinkers of his time, and that his attacks on the Christian Church were hardly motivated by anticlericalism alone.

Boulainvilliers' theory, however, still deals with peoples and not with races; it bases the right of the superior people on a historical deed, conquest, and not on a physical fact – although the historical deed already has a certain influence on the natural qualities of the conquered people. It invents two different peoples within France in order

9  That the Comte de Boulainvilliers' history was meant as a political weapon against the *Tiers Etat* was stated by Montesquieu, *Esprit des Lois*, 1748, XXX, chap. x.

to counteract the new national idea, represented as it was to a certain extent by the absolute monarchy in alliance with the *Tiers Etat*. Boulainvilliers is antinational at a time when the idea of nationhood was felt to be new and revolutionary, but had not yet shown, as it did in the French Revolution, how closely it was connected with a democratic form of government. Boulainvilliers prepared his country for civil war without knowing what civil war meant. He is representative of many of the nobles who did not regard themselves as representative of the nation, but as a separate ruling caste which might have much more in common with a foreign people of the 'same society and condition' than with its compatriots. It has been, indeed, these antinational trends that exercised their influence in the milieu of the *émigrés* and finally were absorbed by new and outspoken racial doctrines late in the nineteenth century.

Not until the actual outbreak of the Revolution forced great numbers of the French nobility to seek refuge in Germany and England did Boulainvilliers' ideas show their usefulness as a political weapon. In the meantime, his influence upon the French aristocracy was kept alive, as can be seen in the works of another Comte, the Comte Dubuat-Nançay,[10] who wanted to tie French nobility even closer to its Continental brothers. On the eve of the Revolution, this spokesman of French feudalism felt so insecure that he hoped for 'the creation of a kind of *Internationale* of aristocracy of barbarian origin,'[11] and since the German nobility was the only one whose help could eventually be expected, here too the true origin of the French nation was supposed to be identical with that of the Germans and the French lower classes, though no longer slaves, were not free by birth but by '*affranchissement*,' by grace of those who were free by birth, of the nobility. A few years later the French exiles actually tried to form an *internationale* of aristocrats in order to stave off the revolt of those they considered to be a foreign enslaved people. And although the more practical side of these attempts suffered the spectacular disaster of Valmy, *émigrés* like Charles François Dominique de Villiers, who in about 1800 opposed the '*Gallo-Romains*' to the Germanics, or like William Alter who a

10 *Les Origines de l'Ancien Gouvernement de la France, de l'Allemagne et de l'Italie,* 1789.
11 Seillière, *op. cit.,* p. xxxii.

decade later dreamed of a federation of all Germanic peoples,[12] did not admit defeat. It probably never occurred to them that they were actually traitors, so firmly were they convinced that the French Revolution was a 'war between foreign peoples' – as François Guizot much later put it.

While Boulainvilliers, with the calm fairness of a less disturbed time, based the rights of nobility solely on the rights of conquest without directly depreciating the very nature of the other conquered nation, the Comte de Montlosier, one of the rather dubious personages among the French exiles, openly expressed his contempt for this 'new people risen from slaves . . . (a mixture) of all races and all times.'[13] Times obviously had changed and noblemen who no longer belonged to an unconquered race also had to change. They gave up the old idea, so dear to Boulainvilliers and even to Montesquieu, that conquest alone, *fortune des armes*, determined the destinies of men. The Valmy of noble ideologies came when the Abbé Siéyès in his famous pamphlet told the *Tiers Etat* to 'send back into the forests of Franconia all those families who preserve the absurd pretension of being descended from the conquering race and of having succeeded to their rights.'[14]

It is rather curious that from these early times when French noblemen in their class struggle against the bourgeoisie discovered that they belonged to another nation, had another genealogical origin, and were more closely tied to an international caste than to the soil of France, all French racial theories have supported the Germanism or at least the superiority of the Nordic peoples as against their own countrymen. For if the men of the French Revolution identified themselves mentally with Rome, it was not because they opposed to the 'Germanism' of their nobility a 'Latinism' of the *Tiers Etat*, but because they felt they were the spiritual heirs of Roman Republicans. This historical

---

12 See René Maunier, *Sociologie Coloniale*, Paris, 1932, Tome II, p. 115.

13 Montlosier, even in exile, was closely connected with the French chief of police, Fouché, who helped him improve the sad financial conditions of a refugee. Later, he served as a secret agent for Napoleon in French society. See Joseph Brugerette, *Le Comte de Montlosier*, 1931, and Simar, *op. cit.*, p. 71.

14 *Qu'est-ce-que le Tiers Etat?* (1789) published shortly before the outbreak of the Revolution. Translation quoted after J. H. Clapham, *The Abbé Siéyès*, London, 1912, p. 62.

claim, in contrast to the tribal identification of the nobility, might have been among the causes that prevented 'Latinism' from emerging as a racial doctrine of its own. In any event, paradoxical as it sounds, the fact is that Frenchmen were to insist earlier than Germans or Englishmen on this *idée fixe* of Germanic superiority.[15] Nor did the birth of German racial consciousness after the Prussian defeat of 1806, directed as it was against the French, change the course of racial ideologies in France. In the forties of the last century, Augustin Thierry still adhered to the identification of classes and races and distinguished between a 'Germanic nobility' and a 'celtic bourgeoisie,'[16] and again a nobleman, the Comte de Rémusat, proclaimed the Germanic origin of the European aristocracy. Finally, the Comte de Gobineau developed an opinion already generally accepted among the French nobility into a full-fledged historical doctrine, claiming to have detected the secret law of the fall of civilizations and to have exalted history to the dignity of a natural science. With him race-thinking completed its first stage, and began its second stage whose influences were to be felt until the twenties of our century.

## II: Race Unity as a Substitute for National Emancipation

Race-thinking in Germany did not develop before the defeat of the old Prussian army by Napoleon. It owed its rise to the Prussian patriots and political romanticism, rather than to the nobility and their spokesmen. In contrast to the French brand of race-thinking as a weapon for civil war and for splitting the nation, German race-thinking was invented in an effort to unite the people against foreign domination. Its authors did not look for allies beyond the frontiers but wanted to awaken in the people a consciousness of common origin. This actually excluded the nobility with their notoriously cosmopolitan relations – which, however, were less characteristic of the Prussian Junkers than of the rest of the European nobility; at any rate, it excluded the

15 'Historical Aryanism has its origin in 18th century feudalism and was supported by 19th century Germanism' observes Seillière, *op. cit.*, p. ii.
16 *Lettres sur l'histoire de France* (1840).

possibility of this race-thinking basing itself on the most exclusive class of the people.

Since German race-thinking accompanied the long frustrated attempts to unite the numerous German states, it remained so closely connected, in its early stages, with more general national feelings that it is rather difficult to distinguish between mere nationalism and clear-cut racism. Harmless national sentiments expressed themselves in what we know today to be racial terms, so that even historians who identify the twentieth-century German brand of racism with the peculiar language of German nationalism have strangely been led into mistaking Nazism for German nationalism, thereby helping to under-estimate the tremendous international appeal of Hitler's propaganda. These particular conditions of German nationalism changed only when, after 1870, the unification of the nation actually had taken place and German racism, together with German imperialism, fully developed. From these early times, however, not a few characteristics survived which have remained significant for the specifically German brand of race-thinking.

In contrast to France, Prussian noblemen felt their interests to be closely connected with the position of the absolute monarchy and, at least since the time of Frederick II, they sought recognition as the legitimate representatives of the nation as a whole. With the exception of the few years of Prussian reforms (from 1808–1812), the Prussian nobility was not frightened by the rise of a bourgeois class that might have wanted to take over the government, nor did they have to fear a coalition between the middle classes and the ruling house. The Prussian king, until 1809 the greatest landlord of the country, remained *primus inter pares* despite all efforts of the Reformers. Race-thinking, therefore, developed outside the nobility, as a weapon of certain nationalists who wanted the union of all German-speaking peoples and therefore insisted on a common origin. They were liberals in the sense that they were rather opposed to the exclusive rule of the Prussian Junkers. As long as this common origin was defined by common language, one can hardly speak of race-thinking.[17]

17 This is the case for instance in Friedrich Schlegel's *Philosophische Vorlesungen aus den Jahren 1804–1806*, II, 357. The same holds true for Ernst Moritz Arndt. See Alfred P. Pundt, *Arndt and the National Awakening in Germany*, New York, 1935, pp. 116 f. Even

It is noteworthy that only after 1814 is this common origin described frequently in terms of 'blood relationship,' of family ties, of tribal unity, of unmixed origin. These definitions, which appear almost simultaneously in the writings of the Catholic Josef Goerres and nationalistic liberals like Ernst Moritz Arndt or F. L. Jahn, bear witness to the utter failure of the hopes of rousing true national sentiments in the German people. Out of the failure to raise the people to nationhood, out of the lack of common historical memories and the apparent popular apathy to common destinies in the future, a naturalistic appeal was born which addressed itself to tribal instincts as a possible substitute for what the whole world had seen to be the glorious power of French nationhood. The organic doctrine of a history for which 'every race is a separate, complete whole'[18] was invented by men who needed ideological definitions of national unity as a substitute for political nationhood. It was a frustrated nationalism that led to Arndt's statement that Germans – who apparently were the last to develop an organic unity – had the luck to be of pure, unmixed stock, a 'genuine people.'[19]

Organic naturalistic definitions of peoples are an outstanding characteristic of German ideologies and German historism. They nevertheless are not yet actual racism, for the same men who speak in these 'racial' terms still uphold the central pillar of genuine nationhood, the equality of all peoples. Thus, in the same article in which Jahn compares the laws of peoples with the laws of animal life, he insists on the genuine equal plurality of peoples in whose complete multitude alone mankind can be realized.[20] And Arndt, who later was to express strong sympathies with the national liberation movements

---

Fichte, the favorite modern scapegoat for German race-thinking, hardly ever went beyond the limits of nationalism.

18 Joseph Goerres, in *Rheinischer Merkur*, 1814, No. 25.

19 In *Phantasien zur Berichtigung der Urteile über künftige deutsche Verfassungen*, 1815.

20 'Animals of mixed stock have no real generative power; similarly, hybrid peoples have no folk propagation of their own . . . The ancestor of humanity is dead, the original race is extinct. That is why each dying people is a misfortune for humanity . . . Human nobility cannot express itself in one people alone.' In *Deutsches Volkstum*, 1810.

The same instance is expressed by Goerres, who despite his naturalistic definition of people ('all members are united by a common tie of blood'), follows a true national principle when he states: 'No branch has a right to dominate the other' (*op. cit.*).

of the Poles and the Italians, exclaimed: 'Cursed be anyone who would subjugate and rule foreign peoples.' [21] Insofar as German national feelings had not been the fruit of a genuine national development but rather the reaction to foreign occupation,[22] national doctrines were of a peculiar negative character, destined to create a wall around the people, to act as substitutes for frontiers which could not be clearly defined either geographically or historically.

If, in the early form of French aristocracy, race-thinking had been invented as an instrument of internal division and had turned out to be a weapon for civil war, this early form of German race-doctrine was invented as a weapon of internal national unity and turned out to be a weapon for national wars. As the decline of the French nobility as an important class in the French nation would have made this weapon useless if the foes of the Third Republic had not revived it, so upon the accomplishment of German national unity the organic doctrine of history would have lost its meaning had not modern imperialistic schemers wanted to revive it, in order to appeal to the people and to hide their hideous faces under the respectable cover of nationalism. The same does not hold true for another source of German racism which, though seemingly more remote from the scene of politics, had a far stronger genuine bearing upon later political ideologies.

Political romanticism has been accused of inventing race-thinking, as it has been and could be accused of inventing every other possible irresponsible opinion. Adam Mueller and Friedrich Schlegel are symptomatic in the highest degree of a general playfulness of modern thought in which almost any opinion can gain ground temporarily. No real thing, no historical event, no political idea was safe from the all-embracing and all-destroying mania by which these first literati could always find new and original opportunities for new and fascinating opinions. 'The world must be romanticized,' as Novalis put it, wanting 'to bestow a high sense upon the common, a mysterious appearance upon the ordinary, the dignity of the unknown upon the

---

21 *Blick aus der Zeit auf die Zeit*, 1814. – Translation quoted from Alfred P. Pundt, *op. cit.*
22 'Not until Austria and Prussia had fallen after a vain struggle did I really begin to love Germany . . . as Germany succumbed to conquest and subjection it became to me one and indissoluble,' writes E. M. Arndt in his *Erinnerungen aus Schweden*, 1818, p. 82. Translation quoted from Pundt, *op. cit.*, p. 151.

well-known.'[23] One of these romanticized objects was the people, an object that could be changed at a moment's notice into the state, or the family, or nobility, or anything else that either – in the earlier days – happened to cross the minds of one of these intellectuals or – later when, growing older, they had learned the reality of daily bread – happened to be asked for by some paying patron.[24] Therefore it is almost impossible to study the development of any of the free competing opinions of which the nineteenth century is so amazingly full, without coming across romanticism in its German form.

What these first modern intellectuals actually prepared was not so much the development of any single opinion but the general mentality of modern German scholars; these latter have proved more than once that hardly an ideology can be found to which they would not willingly submit if the only reality – which even a romantic can hardly afford to overlook – is at stake, the reality of their position. For this peculiar behavior, romanticism provided the most excellent pretext in its unlimited idolization of the 'personality' of the individual, whose very arbitrariness became the proof of genius. Whatever served the so-called productivity of the individual, namely, the entirely arbitrary game of his 'ideas,' could be made the center of a whole outlook on life and world.

This inherent cynicism of romantic personality-worship has made possible certain modern attitudes among intellectuals. They were fairly well represented by Mussolini, one of the last heirs of this movement, when he described himself as at the same time 'aristocrat and democrat, revolutionary and reactionary, proletarian and antiproletarian, pacifist and antipacifist.' The ruthless individualism of romanticism never meant anything more serious than that 'everybody is free to create for himself his own ideology.' What was new in Mussolini's experiment was the 'attempt to carry it out with all possible energy.'[25]

Because of this inherent 'relativism' the direct contribution of

23 'Neue Fragmentensammlung' (1798) in *Schriften*, Leipzig, 1929, Tome II, p. 335.
24 For the romantic attitude in Germany see Carl Schmitt, *Politische Romantik*, München, 1925.
25 Mussolini, 'Relativismo e Fascismo,' in *Diuturna*, Milano, 1924. The translation quoted from F. Neumann, *Behemoth*, 1942, pp. 462–463.

romanticism to the development of race-thinking can almost be neglected. In the anarchic game whose rules entitle everybody at any given time to at least one personal and arbitrary opinion, it is almost a matter of course that every conceivable opinion should be formulated and duly printed. Much more characteristic than this chaos was the fundamental belief in personality as an ultimate aim in itself. In Germany, where the conflict between the nobility and the rising middle class was never fought out on the political scene, personality worship developed as the only means of gaining at least some kind of social emancipation. The governing class of the country frankly showed its traditional contempt for business and its dislike for association with merchants in spite of the latter's growing wealth and importance, so that it was not easy to find the means of winning some kind of self-respect. The classic German *Bildungsroman, Wilhelm Meister,* in which the middle-class hero is educated by noblemen and actors because the bourgeois in his own social sphere is without 'personality,' is evidence enough of the hopelessness of the situation.

German intellectuals, though they hardly promoted a political fight for the middle classes to which they belonged, fought an embittered and, unfortunately, highly successful battle for social status. Even those who had written in defense of nobility still felt their own interests at stake when it came to social ranks. In order to enter competition with rights and qualities of birth, they formulated the new concept of the 'innate personality' which was to win general approval within bourgeois society. Like the title of the heir of an old family, the 'innate personality' was given by birth and not acquired by merit. Just as the lack of common history for the formation of the nation had been artificially overcome by the naturalistic concept of organic development, so, in the social sphere, nature itself was supposed to supply a title when political reality had refused it. Liberal writers soon boasted of 'true nobility' as opposed to the shabby titles of Baron or others which could be given and taken away, and asserted, by implication, that their natural privileges, like 'force or genius,' could not be retraced to any human deed.[26]

The discriminatory point of this new social concept was

26 See the very interesting pamphlet against the nobility by the liberal writer Buchholz, *Untersuchungen ueber den Geburtsadel*, Berlin, 1807, p. 68: 'True nobility . . . cannot be given or taken away; for, like power and genius, it sets itself and exists by itself.'

immediately affirmed. During the long period of mere social antisemitism, which introduced and prepared the discovery of Jew-hating as a
political weapon, it was the lack of 'innate personality,' the innate lack
of tact, the innate lack of productivity, the innate disposition for trading, etc., which separated the behavior of his Jewish colleague from
that of the average businessman. In its feverish attempt to summon up
some pride of its own against the caste arrogance of the Junkers, without, however, daring to fight for political leadership, the bourgeoisie
from the very beginning wanted to look down not so much on other
lower classes of their own, but simply on other peoples. Most significant for these attempts is the small literary work of Clemens Brentano[27]
which was written for and read in the ultranationalistic club of
Napoleon-haters that gathered together in 1808 under the name of 'Die
Christlich-Deutsche Tischgesellschaft.' In his highly sophisticated and
witty manner, Brentano points out the contrast between the 'innate
personality,' the genial individual, and the 'philistine' whom he immediately identifies with Frenchmen and Jews. Thereafter, the German
bourgeois would at least try to attribute to other peoples all the qualities which the nobility despised as typically bourgeois – at first to the
French, later to the English, and always to the Jews. As for the mysterious qualities which an 'innate personality' received at birth, they were
exactly the same as those the real Junkers claimed for themselves.

Although in this way standards of nobility contributed to the rise of
race-thinking, the Junkers themselves did hardly anything for the
shaping of this mentality. The only Junker of this period to develop a
political theory of his own, Ludwig von der Marwitz, never used racial
terms. According to him, nations were separated by language – a
spiritual and not a physical difference – and although he was violently
opposed to the French Revolution, he spoke like Robespierre when it
came to the possible aggression of one nation against another: 'Who
aims at expanding his frontiers should be considered a disloyal betrayer
among the whole European republic of states.'[28] It was Adam Mueller
who insisted on purity of descent as a test of nobility, and it was Haller

27 Clemens Brentano, *Der Philister vor, in und nach der Geschichte*, 1811.
28 'Entwurf eines Friedenspaktes.' In Gerhard Ramlow, *Ludwig von der Marwitz und
die Anfänge konservativer Politik und Staatsauffassung in Preussen*, Historische Studien,
Heft 185, p. 92.

who went beyond the obvious fact that the powerful rule those deprived of power by stating it as a natural law that the weak should be dominated by the strong. Noblemen, of course, applauded enthusiastically when they learned that their usurpation of power was not only legal but in accordance with natural laws, and it was a consequence of bourgeois definitions that during the course of the nineteenth century they avoided *'mesalliances'* more carefully than ever before.[29]

This insistence on common tribal origin as an essential of nationhood, formulated by German nationalists during and after the war of 1814, and the emphasis laid by the romantics on the innate personality and natural nobility prepared the way intellectually for race-thinking in Germany. From the former sprang the organic doctrine of history with its natural laws; from the latter arose at the end of the century the grotesque homunculus of the superman whose natural destiny it is to rule the world. As long as these trends ran side by side, they were but temporary means of escape from political realities. Once welded together, they formed the very basis for racism as a full-fledged ideology. This, however, did not happen first in Germany, but in France, and was not accomplished by middle-class intellectuals but by a highly gifted and frustrated nobleman, the Comte de Gobineau.

## III: The New Key to History

In 1853, Count Arthur de Gobineau published his *Essai sur l'Inégalité des Races Humaines* which, only some fifty years later, at the turn of the century, was to become a kind of standard work for race theories in history. The first sentence of the four-volume work – 'The fall of civilization is the most striking and, at the same time, the most obscure of all phenomena of history'[30] – indicates clearly the essentially new and modern interest of its author, the new pessimistic mood which pervades his work and which is the ideological force that was capable of uniting all

29 See Sigmund Neumann, *Die Stufen des preussischen Konservatismus*, Historische Studien, Heft 190, Berlin, 1930. Especially pp. 48, 51, 64, 82. For Adam Mueller, see *Elemente der Staatskunst*, 1809.

30 Translation quoted from *The Inequality of Human Races*, translated by Adrien Collins, 1915.

previous factors and conflicting opinions. True, from time immemorial, mankind has wanted to know as much as possible about past cultures, fallen empires, extinct peoples; but nobody before Gobineau thought of finding one single reason, one single force according to which civilization always and everywhere rises and falls. Doctrines of decay seem to have some very intimate connection with race-thinking. It certainly is no coincidence that another early 'believer in race,' Benjamin Disraeli, was equally fascinated by the fall of cultures, while on the other hand Hegel, whose philosophy was concerned in great part with the dialectical law of development in history, was never interested in the rise and fall of cultures as such or in any law which would explain the death of nations: Gobineau demonstrated precisely such a law. Without Darwinism or any other evolutionist theory to influence him, this historian boasted of having introduced history into the family of natural sciences, detected the natural law of all courses of events, reduced all spiritual utterances or cultural phenomena to something 'that by virtue of exact science our eyes can see, our ears can hear, our hands can touch.'

The most surprising aspect of the theory, set forth in the midst of the optimistic nineteenth century, is the fact that the author is fascinated by the fall and hardly interested in the rise of civilizations. At the time of writing the *Essai* Gobineau gave but little thought to the possible use of his theory as a weapon in actual politics, and therefore had the courage to draw the inherent sinister consequences of his law of decay. In contrast to Spengler, who predicts only the fall of Western culture, Gobineau foresees with 'scientific' precision nothing less than the definite disappearance of Man – or, in his words, of the human race – from the face of the earth. After four volumes of rewriting human history, he concludes: 'One might be tempted to assign a total duration of 12 to 14 thousand years to human rule over the earth, which era is divided into two periods: the first has passed away and possessed the youth . . . the second has begun and will witness the declining course down toward decrepitude.'

It has rightly been observed that Gobineau, thirty years before Nietzsche, was concerned with the problem of '*décadence*.' [31] There is,

31 See Robert Dreyfus, 'La vie et les prophéties du Comte de Gobineau,' Paris, 1905, in *Cahiers de la quinzaine*, Ser. 6, Cah. 16, p. 56.

however, this difference, that Nietzsche possessed the basic experience of European decadence, writing as he did during the climax of
this movement with Baudelaire in France, Swinburne in England, and
Wagner in Germany, whereas Gobineau was hardly aware of the variety of the modern *taedium vitae*, and must be regarded as the last heir
of Boulainvilliers and the French exiled nobility who, without psychological complications, simply (and rightly) feared for the fate of
aristocracy as a caste. With a certain naïveté he accepted almost literally the eighteenth-century doctrines about the origin of the French
people: the bourgeois are the descendants of Gallic-Roman slaves,
noblemen are Germanic.[32] The same is true for his insistence on the
international character of nobility. A more modern aspect of his theories is revealed in the fact that he possibly was an impostor (his French
title being more than dubious), that he exaggerated and overstrained
the older doctrines until they became frankly ridiculous – he claimed
for himself a genealogy which led over a Scandinavian pirate to Odin:
'I, too, am of the race of Gods.'[33] But his real importance is that in the
midst of progress-ideologies he prophesied doom, the end of mankind
in a slow natural catastrophe. When Gobineau started his work, in the
days of the bourgeois king, Louis Philippe, the fate of nobility appeared
sealed. Nobility no longer needed to fear the victory of the *Tiers Etat*,
it had already occurred and they could only complain. Their distress,
as expressed by Gobineau, sometimes comes very near to the great
despair of the poets of decadence who, a few decades later, sang the
frailty of all things human – *les neiges d'antan*, the snows of yesteryear.
As far as Gobineau himself was concerned, this affinity is rather
incidental; but it is interesting to note that once this affinity was
established, nothing could prevent very respectable intellectuals at the
turn of the century, like Robert Dreyfus in France or Thomas Mann in
Germany, from taking this descendant of Odin seriously. Long before
the horrible and the ridiculous had merged into the humanly incomprehensible mixture that is the hallmark of our century, the ridiculous
had lost its power to kill.

It is also to the peculiar pessimistic mood, to the active despair of

32  *Essai*, Tome II, Book IV, p. 445, and the article 'Ce qui est arrivé à la France en 1870,'
in *Europe*, 1923.
33  J. Duesberg, 'Le Comte de Gobineau,' in *Revue Générale*, 1939.

the last decades of the century that Gobineau owed his belated fame. This, however, does not necessarily mean that he himself was a forerunner of the generation of 'the merry dance of death and trade' (Joseph Conrad). He was neither a statesman who believed in business nor a poet who praised death. He was only a curious mixture of frustrated nobleman and romantic intellectual who invented racism almost by accident. This was when he saw that he could not simply accept the old doctrines of the two peoples within France and that, in view of changed circumstances, he had to revise the old line that the best men necessarily are at the top of society. In sad contrast to his teachers, he had to explain why the best men, noblemen, could not even hope to regain their former position. Step by step, he identified the fall of his caste with the fall of France, then of Western civilization, and then of the whole of mankind. Thus he made that discovery, for which he was so much admired by later writers and biographers, that the fall of civilizations is due to a degeneration of race and the decay of race is due to a mixture of blood. This implies that in every mixture the lower race is always dominant. This kind of argumentation, almost commonplace after the turn of the century, did not fit in with the progress-doctrines of Gobineau's contemporaries, who soon acquired another *idée fixe,* the 'survival of the fittest.' The liberal optimism of the victorious bourgeoisie wanted a new edition of the might-right theory, not the key to history or the proof of inevitable decay. Gobineau tried in vain to get a wider audience by taking a side in the American slave issue and by conveniently building his whole system on the basic conflict between white and black. He had to wait almost fifty years to become a success among the elite, and not until the first World War with its wave of death-philosophies could his works claim wide popularity.[34]

What Gobineau was actually looking for in politics was the definition and creation of an 'elite' to replace the aristocracy. Instead of

34 See the Gobineau memorial issue of the French review *Europe*, 1923. Especially the article of Clément Serpeille de Gobineau, 'Le Gobinisme et la pensée moderne.' 'Yet it was not until . . . the middle of the war that I thought the *Essai sur les Races* was inspired by a productive hypothesis, the only one that could explain certain events happening before our eyes . . . I was surprised to note that this opinion was almost unanimously shared. After the war, I noticed that for nearly the whole younger generation the works of Gobineau had become a revelation.'

princes, he proposed a 'race of princes,' the Aryans, who he said were in danger of being submerged by the lower non-Aryan classes through democracy. The concept of race made it possible to organize the 'innate personalities' of German romanticism, to define them as members of a natural aristocracy destined to rule over all others. If race and mixture of races are the all-determining factors for the individual – and Gobineau did not assume the existence of 'pure' breeds – it is possible to pretend that physical superiorities might evolve in every individual no matter what his present social situation, that every exceptional man belongs to the 'true surviving sons of . . . the Merovings,' the 'sons of kings.' Thanks to race, an 'elite' would be formed which could lay claim to the old prerogatives of feudal families, and this only by asserting that they felt like noblemen; the acceptance of the race ideology as such would become conclusive proof that an individual was 'well-bred,' that 'blue blood' ran through his veins and that a superior origin implied superior rights. From one political event, therefore, the decline of the nobility, the Count drew two contradictory consequences – the decay of the human race and the formation of a new natural aristocracy. But he did not live to see the practical application of his teachings which resolved their inherent contradictions – the new race-aristocracy actually began to effect the 'inevitable' decay of mankind in a supreme effort to destroy it.

Following the example of his forerunners, the exiled French noblemen, Gobineau saw in his race-elite not only a bulwark against democracy but also against the 'Canaan monstrosity' of patriotism.[35] And since France still happened to be the *'patrie' par excellence*, for her government – whether kingdom or Empire or Republic – was still based upon the essential equality of men, and since, worst of all, she was the only country of his time in which even people with black skin could enjoy civil rights, it was natural for Gobineau to give allegiance not to the French people, but to the English, and later, after the French defeat of 1871, to the Germans.[36] Nor can this lack of dignity be called

---

35 *Essai*, Tome II, Book IV, p. 440 and note on p. 445: 'The word *patrie* . . . has regained its significance only since the Gallo-Roman strata rose and assumed a political role. With their triumph, patriotism has again become a virtue.'

36 See Seillière, *op. cit.*, Tome I: *Le Comte de Gobineau et l'Aryanisme historique*, p. 32: 'In the *Essai* Germany is hardly Germanic, Great Britain is Germanic to a much higher

accidental and this opportunism an unhappy coincidence. The old saying that nothing succeeds like success reckons with people who are used to various and arbitrary opinions. Ideologists who pretend to possess the key to reality are forced to change and twist their opinions about single cases according to the latest events and can never afford to come into conflict with their ever-changing deity, reality. It would be absurd to ask people to be reliable who by their very convictions must justify any given situation.

It must be conceded that up to the time when the Nazis, in establishing themselves as a race-elite, frankly bestowed their contempt on all peoples, including the German, French racism was the most consistent, for it never fell into the weakness of patriotism. (This attitude did not change even during the last war; true, the '*essence aryenne*' no longer was a monopoly of the Germans but rather of the Anglo-Saxons, the Swedes, and the Normans, but nation, patriotism, and law were still considered to be 'prejudices, fictitious and nominal values.')[37] Even Taine believed firmly in the superior genius of the 'Germanic nation,'[38] and Ernest Renan was probably the first to oppose the 'Semites' to the 'Aryans' in a decisive '*division du genre humain*,' although he held civilization to be the great superior force which destroys local originalities as well as original race differences.[39] All the loose race talk that is so characteristic of French writers after 1870,[40] even if they are not racists in any strict sense of the word, follows antinational, pro-Germanic lines.

If the consistent antinational trend of Gobinism served to equip the enemies of French democracy and, later, of the Third Republic, with

degree . . . Certainly, Gobineau later changed his mind, but under the influence of success.' It is interesting to note that for Seillière who during his studies became an ardent adherent of Gobinism – 'the intellectual climate to which probably the lungs of the 20th century will have to adapt themselves' – success appeared as quite a sufficient reason for Gobineau's suddenly revised opinion.

37 Examples could be multiplied. The quotation is taken from Camille Spiess, *Impérialismes Gobinisme en France*, Paris, 1917.

38 For Taine's stand see John S. White, 'Taine on Race and Genius,' in *Social Research*, February, 1943.

39 In Gobineau's opinion, the Semites were a white hybrid race bastardized by a mixture with blacks. For Renan see *Histoire Générale et Système comparé des Langues*, 1863, Part I, pp. 4, 503, and *passim*. The same distinction in his *Langues Sémitiques*, I, 15.

40 This has been very well exposed by Jacques Barzun, *op. cit.*

real or fictitious allies beyond the frontiers of their country, the specific amalgamation of the race and 'elite' concepts equipped the international intelligentsia with new and exciting psychological toys to play with on the great playground of history. Gobineau's *'fils des rois'* were close relatives of the romantic heroes, saints, geniuses and supermen of the late nineteenth century, all of whom can hardly hide their German romantic origin. The inherent irresponsibility of romantic opinions received a new stimulant from Gobineau's mixture of races, because this mixture showed a historical event of the past which could be traced in the depths of one's own self. This meant that inner experiences could be given historical significance, that one's own self had become the battlefield of history. 'Since I read the *Essai*, every time some conflict stirred up the hidden sources of my being, I have felt that a relentless battle went on in my soul, the battle between the black, the yellow, the Semite and the Aryans.'[41] Significant as this and similar confessions may be of the state of mind of modern intellectuals, who are the true heirs of romanticism whatever opinion they happen to hold, they nevertheless indicate the essential harmlessness and political innocence of people who probably could have been forced into line by each and every ideology.

## IV: The 'Rights of Englishmen' vs. the Rights of Men

While the seeds of German race-thinking were planted during the Napoleonic wars, the beginnings of the later English development appeared during the French Revolution and may be traced back to the man who violently denounced it as the 'most astonishing [crisis] that has hitherto happened in the world' – to Edmund Burke.[42] The tremendous influence his work has exercised not only on English but also on German political thought is well known. The fact, however, must be stressed because of resemblances between German and English

41 This surprising gentleman is none other than the well-known writer and historian Elie Faure, 'Gobineau et le Problème des Races,' in *Europe*, 1923.
42 *Reflections on the Revolution in France*, 1790, Everyman's Library Edition, New York, p. 8.

race-thinking as contrasted with the French brand. These resemblances stem from the fact that both countries had defeated the Tricolor and therefore showed a certain tendency to discriminate against the ideas of *Liberté-Egalité-Fraternité* as foreign inventions. Social inequality being the basis of English society, British Conservatives felt not a little uncomfortable when it came to the 'rights of men.' According to opinions widely held by nineteenth-century Tories, inequality belonged to the English national character. Disraeli found 'something better than the Rights of Men in the rights of Englishmen' and to Sir James Stephen 'few things in history [seemed] so beggarly as the degree to which the French allowed themselves to be excited about such things.' [43] This is one of the reasons why they could afford to develop race-thinking along national lines until the end of the nineteenth century, whereas the same opinions in France showed their true antinational face from the very beginning.

Burke's main argument against the 'abstract principles' of the French Revolution is contained in the following sentence: 'It has been the uniform policy of our constitution to claim and assert our liberties, as an *entailed inheritance* derived to us from our forefathers, and to be transmitted to our posterity; as an estate specially belonging to the people of this kingdom, without any reference whatever to any other more general or prior right.' The concept of inheritance, applied to the very nature of liberty, has been the ideological basis from which English nationalism received its curious touch of race-feeling ever since the French Revolution. Formulated by a middle-class writer, it signified the direct acceptance of the feudal concept of liberty as the sum total of privileges inherited together with title and land. Without encroaching upon the rights of the privileged class within the English nation, Burke enlarged the principle of these privileges to include the whole English people, establishing them as a kind of nobility among nations. Hence he drew his contempt for those who claimed their franchise as the rights of men, rights which he saw fit to claim only as 'the rights of Englishmen.'

In England nationalism developed without serious attacks on the

---

43 *Liberty, Equality, Fraternity*, 1873, p. 254. For Lord Beaconsfield see Benjamin Disraeli, *Lord George Bentinck*, 1853, p. 184.

old feudal classes. This has been possible because the English gentry, from the seventeenth century on and in ever-increasing numbers, had assimilated the higher ranks of the bourgeoisie, so that sometimes even the common man could attain the position of a lord. By this process much of the ordinary caste arrogance of nobility was taken away and a considerable sense of responsibility for the nation as a whole was created; but by the same token, feudal concepts and mentality could influence the political ideas of the lower classes more easily than elsewhere. Thus, the concept of inheritance was accepted almost unchanged and applied to the entire British 'stock.' The consequence of this assimilation of noble standards was that the English brand of race-thinking was almost obsessed with inheritance theories and their modern equivalent, eugenics.

Ever since the European peoples made practical attempts to include all the peoples of the earth in their conception of humanity, they have been irritated by the great physical differences between themselves and the peoples they found on other continents.[44] The eighteenth-century enthusiasm for the diversity in which the all-present identical nature of man and reason could find expression provided a rather thin cover of argument to the crucial question, whether the Christian tenet of the unity and equality of all men, based upon common descent from one original set of parents, would be kept in the hearts of men who were faced with tribes which, as far as we know, never had found by themselves any adequate expression of human reason or human passion in either cultural deeds or popular customs, and which had developed human institutions only to a very low level. This new problem which appeared on the historical scene of Europe and America with the more intimate knowledge of African tribes had already caused, and this especially in America and some British possessions, a relapse into forms of social organization which were thought to have been definitely liquidated by Christianity. But even slavery, though actually established on a strict racial basis, did not make the

---

44 A significant if moderate echo of this inner bewilderment can be found in many an eighteenth-century traveling report. Voltaire thought it important enough to make a special note in his *Dictionnaire Philosophique*: 'We have seen, moreover, how different the races are who inhabit this globe, and how great must have been the surprise of the first Negro and the first white man who met' (Article: *Homme*).

slave-holding peoples race-conscious before the nineteenth century. Throughout the eighteenth century, American slave-holders themselves considered it a temporary institution and wanted to abolish it gradually. Most of them probably would have said with Jefferson: 'I tremble when I think that God is just.'

In France, where the problem of black tribes had been met with the desire to assimilate and educate, the great scientist Leclerc de Buffon had given a first classification of races which, based upon the European peoples and classifying all others by their differences, had taught equality by strict juxtaposition.[45] The eighteenth century, to use Tocqueville's admirably precise phrase, 'believed in the variety of races but in the unity of the human species.' [46] In Germany, Herder had refused to apply the 'ignoble word' race to men, and even the first cultural historian of mankind to make use of the classification of different species, Gustav Klemm,[47] still respected the idea of mankind as the general framework for his investigations.

But in America and England, where people had to solve a problem of living together after the abolition of slavery, things were considerably less easy. With the exception of South Africa – a country which influenced Western racism only after the 'scramble for Africa' in the eighties – these nations were the first to deal with the race problem in practical politics. The abolition of slavery sharpened inherent conflicts instead of finding a solution for existing serious difficulties. This was especially true in England where the 'rights of Englishmen' were not replaced by a new political orientation which might have declared the rights of men. The abolition of slavery in the British possessions in 1834 and the discussion preceding the American Civil War, therefore, found in England a highly confused public opinion which was fertile soil for the various naturalistic doctrines which arose in those decades.

The first of these was represented by the polygenists who, challenging the Bible as a book of pious lies, denied any relationship between human 'races'; their main achievement was the destruction of the idea of the natural law as the uniting link between all men and

45 *Histoire Naturelle*, 1769–89.
46 *Op. cit.*, letter of May 15, 1852.
47 *Allgemeine Kulturgeschichte der Menschheit*, 1843–1852.

all peoples. Although it did not stipulate predestined racial superiority, polygenism arbitrarily isolated all peoples from one another by the deep abyss of the physical impossibility of human understanding and communication. Polygenism explains why 'East is East and West is West; And never the twain shall meet,' and helped much to prevent intermarriage in the colonies and to promote discrimination against individuals of mixed origin. According to polygenism, these people are not true human beings; they belong to no single race, but are a kind of monster whose 'every cell is the theater of a civil war.' [48]

Lasting as the influence of polygenism on English race-thinking proved to be in the long run, in the nineteenth century it was soon to be beaten in the field of public opinion by another doctrine. This doctrine also started from the principle of inheritance but added to it the political principle of the nineteenth century, progress, whence it arrived at the opposite but far more convincing conclusion that man is related not only to man but to animal life, that the existence of lower races shows clearly that gradual differences alone separate man and beast and that a powerful struggle for existence dominates all living things. Darwinism was especially strengthened by the fact that it followed the path of the old might-right doctrine. But while this doctrine when used exclusively by aristocrats, had spoken the proud language of conquest, it was now translated into the rather bitter language of people who had known the struggle for daily bread and fought their way to the relative security of upstarts.

Darwinism met with such overwhelming success because it provided, on the basis of inheritance, the ideological weapons for race as well as class rule and could be used for, as well as against, race discrimination. Politically speaking, Darwinism as such was neutral, and it has led, indeed, to all kinds of pacifism and cosmopolitanism as well as to the sharpest forms of imperialistic ideologies. [49] In the seventies and eighties of the last century, Darwinism was still almost exclusively in the hands of the utilitarian anticolonial party in England. And the first philosopher of evolution, Herbert Spencer, who treated sociology as part of biology, believed natural selection to benefit the

---

48 A. Carthill, *The Lost Dominion*, 1924, p. 158.

49 See Friedrich Brie, *Imperialistische Strömungen in der englischen Literatur*, Halle, 1928.

evolution of mankind and to result in everlasting peace. For political discussion, Darwinism offered two important concepts: the struggle for existence with optimistic assertion of the necessary and automatic 'survival of the fittest,' and the indefinite possibilities which seemed to lie in the evolution of man out of animal life and which started the new 'science' of eugenics.

The doctrine of the necessary survival of the fittest, with its implication that the top layers in society eventually are the 'fittest,' died as the conquest doctrine had died, namely, at the moment when the ruling classes in England or the English domination in colonial possessions were no longer absolutely secure, and when it became highly doubtful whether those who were 'fittest' today would still be the fittest tomorrow. The other part of Darwinism, the genealogy of man from animal life, unfortunately survived. Eugenics promised to overcome the troublesome uncertainties of the survival doctrine according to which it was impossible either to predict who would turn out to be the fittest or to provide the means for the nations to develop everlasting fitness. This possible consequence of applied eugenics was stressed in Germany in the twenties as a reaction to Spengler's *Decline of the West*.[50] The process of selection had only to be changed from a natural necessity which worked behind the backs of men into an 'artificial,' consciously applied physical tool. Bestiality had always been inherent in eugenics, and Ernst Haeckel's early remark that mercy-death would save 'useless expenses for family and state' is quite characteristic.[51] Finally the last disciples of Darwinism in Germany decided to leave the field of scientific research altogether, to forget about the search for the missing link between man and ape, and started instead their practical efforts to change man into what the Darwinists thought an ape is.

But before Nazism, in the course of its totalitarian policy, attempted to change man into a beast, there were numerous efforts to develop him on a strictly hereditary basis into a god.[52] Not only Herbert

50 See, for instance, Otto Bangert, *Gold oder Blut*, 1927. 'Therefore a civilization can be eternal,' p. 17.
51 In *Lebenswunder*, 1904, pp. 128 ff.
52 Almost a century before evolutionism had donned the cloak of science, warning voices foretold the inherent consequences of a madness that was then merely in the stage of pure imagination. Voltaire, more than once, had played with evolutionary

Spencer, but all the early evolutionists and Darwinists 'had as strong a faith in humanity's angelic future as in man's simian origin.'[53] Selected inheritance was believed to result in 'hereditary genius,'[54] and again aristocracy was held to be the natural outcome, not of politics, but of natural selection, of pure breeding. To transform the whole nation into a natural aristocracy from which choice exemplars would develop into geniuses and supermen, was one of the many 'ideas' produced by frustrated liberal intellectuals in their dreams of replacing the old governing classes by a new 'elite' through nonpolitical means. At the end of the century, writers treated political topics in terms of biology and zoology as a matter of course, and zoologists wrote 'Biological Views of our Foreign Policy' as though they had detected an infallible guide for statesmen.[55] All of them put forward new ways to control and

---

opinions – see chiefly 'Philosophie Générale: Métaphysique, Morale et Théologie,' *Oeuvres Complètes*, 1785, Tome 40, pp. 16 ff. – In his *Dictionnaire Philosophique*, Article 'Chaîne des Etres Créés,' he wrote: 'At first, our imagination is pleased at the imperceptible transition of crude matter to organized matter, of plants to zoophytes, of these zoophytes to animals, of these to man, of man to spirits, of these spirits clothed with a small aerial body to immaterial substances; and . . . to God Himself . . . But the most perfect spirit created by the Supreme Being, can he become God? Is there not an infinity between God and him? . . . Is there not obviously a void between the monkey and man?'

53 Hayes, *op. cit.*, p. 11. Hayes rightly stresses the strong practical morality of all these early materialists. He explains 'this curious divorce of morals from beliefs' by 'what later sociologists have described as a time lag' (p. 130). This explanation, however, appears rather weak if one recalls that other materialists who, like Haeckel in Germany or Vacher de Lapouge in France, had left the calm of studies and research for propaganda activities, did not greatly suffer from such a time lag; that, on the other hand, their contemporaries who were not tinged by their materialistic doctrines, such as Barrès and Co. in France, were very practical adherents of the perverse brutality which swept France during the Dreyfus Affair. The sudden decay of morals in the Western world seems to be caused less by an autonomous development of certain 'ideas' than by a series of new political events and new political and social problems which confronted a bewildered and confused humanity.

54 Such was the title of the widely read book of Fr. Galton, published in 1869, which caused a flood of literature about the same topic in the following decades.

55 'A Biological View of Our Foreign Policy' was published by P. Charles Michel in *Saturday Review*, London, February, 1896. The most important works of this kind are: Thomas Huxley, *The Struggle for Existence in Human Society*, 1888. His main thesis: The fall of civilizations is necessary only as long as birthrate is uncontrolled. Benjamin Kidd, *Social Evolution*, 1894. John B. Crozier, *History of Intellectual Development on the Lines of Modern Evolution*, 1897–1901. Karl Pearson (*National Life*, 1901), Professor of

regulate the 'survival of the fittest' in accordance with the national interests of the English people.[56]

The most dangerous aspect of these evolutionist doctrines is that they combined the inheritance concept with the insistence on personal achievement and individual character which had been so important for the self-respect of the nineteenth-century middle class. This middle class wanted scientists who could prove that the great men, not the aristocrats, were the true representatives of the nation, in whom the 'genius of the race' was personified. These scientists provided an ideal escape from political responsibility when they 'proved' the early statement of Benjamin Disraeli that the great man is 'the personification of race, its choice exemplar.' The development of this 'genius' found its logical end when another disciple of evolutionism simply declared: 'The Englishman is the Overman and the history of England is the history of his evolution.'[57]

It is as significant for English as it was for German race-thinking that it originated among middle-class writers and not the nobility, that it was born of the desire to extend the benefits of noble standards to all classes and that it was nourished by true national feelings. In this respect, Carlyle's ideas on the genius and hero were really more the weapons of a 'social reformer' than the doctrines of the 'Father of British Imperialism,' a very unjust accusation, indeed.[58] His hero worship which earned him wide audiences in both England and in Germany, had the same sources as the personality worship of German romanticism. It was the same assertion and glorification of the innate greatness of the individual character independent of his social environment. Among the men who influenced the colonial movement from the middle of the nineteenth century until the outbreak of actual imperialism

---

Eugenics at London University, was among the first to describe progress as a kind of impersonal monster which devours everything that happens to be in its way. Charles H. Harvey, *The Biology of British Politics*, 1904, argues that by strict control of the 'struggle for life' within the nation, a nation could become all-powerful for the inevitable fight with other people for existence.

56 See especially K. Pearson, *op. cit.*, But Fr. Galton had already stated: 'I wish to emphasize the fact that the improvement of the natural gifts of future generations of the human race is largely under our control' (*op. cit.*, ed. 1892, p. xxvi).

57 *Testament of John Davidson*, 1908.

58 C. A. Bodelsen, *Studies in Mid-Victorian Imperialism*, 1924, pp. 22 ff.

at its end, not one has escaped the influence of Carlyle, but not one can be accused of preaching outspoken racism. Carlyle himself, in his essay on the 'Nigger Question' is concerned with means to help the West Indies produce 'heroes.' Charles Dilke, whose *Greater Britain* (1869) is sometimes taken as the beginning of imperialism,[59] was an advanced radical who glorified the English colonists as being part of the British nation, as against those who would look down upon them and their lands as mere colonies. J. R. Seeley, whose *Expansion of England* (1883) sold 80,000 copies in less than two years, still respects the Hindus as a foreign people and distinguishes them clearly from 'barbarians.' Even Froude, whose admiration for the Boers, the first white people to be converted clearly to the tribal philosophy of racism, might appear suspect, opposed too many rights for South Africa because 'self-government in South Africa meant the government of the natives by the European colonists and that is not self-government.'[60]

Very much as in Germany, English nationalism was born and stimulated by a middle class which had never entirely emancipated itself from the nobility and therefore bore the first germs of race-thinking. But unlike Germany, whose lack of unity made necessary an ideological wall to substitute for historical or geographical facts, the British Isles were completely separated from the surrounding world by natural frontiers and England as a nation had to devise a theory of unity among people who lived in far-flung colonies beyond the seas, separated from the mother country by thousands of miles. The only link between them was common descent, common origin, common language. The separation of the United States had shown that these links in themselves do not guarantee domination; and not only America, other colonies too, though not with the same violence, showed strong tendencies toward developing along different constitutional lines from the mother country. In order to save these former British nationals, Dilke, influenced by Carlyle, spoke of 'Saxondom,' a word that seemed able to win back even the people of the United States, to whom one-third of his book is devoted. Being a radical, Dilke could act as though the War of Independence had not been a war between two nations, but the English form of eighteenth-century civil

59 E. H. Dance, *The Victorian Illusion*, 1928. 'Imperialism began with a book . . . Dilke's *Greater Britain*.'
60 'Two Lectures on South Africa,' in *Short Studies on Great Subjects*, 1867–1882.

war, in which he belatedly sided with the Republicans. For here lies one of the reasons for the surprising fact that social reformers and radicals were the promoters of nationalism in England: they wanted to keep the colonies not only because they thought they were necessary outlets for the lower classes; they actually wanted to retain the influence on the mother country which these more radical sons of the British Isles exercised. This motif is strong with Froude, who wished 'to retain the colonies because he thought it possible to reproduce in them a simpler state of society and a nobler way of life than were possible in industrial England,'[61] and it had a definite impact on Seeley's *Expansion of England*: 'When we have accustomed ourselves to contemplate the whole Empire together and we call it *all* England we shall see that there too is a United States.' Whatever later political writers may have used 'Saxondom' for, in Dilke's work it had a genuine political meaning for a nation that was no longer held together by a limited country. 'The idea which in all the length of my travels has been at once my fellow and my guide – the key wherewith to unlock the hidden things of strange new lands – is the conception . . . of the grandeur of our race already girdling the earth, which it is destined perhaps, eventually to overspread' (Preface). For Dilke, common origin, inheritance, 'grandeur of race' were neither physical facts nor the key to history but a much-needed guide in the present world, the only reliable link in a boundless space.

Because English colonists had spread all over the earth, it happened that the most dangerous concept of nationalism, the idea of 'national mission,' was especially strong in England. Although national mission as such developed for a long while untinged by racial influences in all countries where peoples aspired to nationhood, it proved finally to have a peculiarly close affinity to race-thinking. The above-quoted English nationalists may be considered borderline cases in the light of later experience. In themselves, they were not more harmful than, for example, Auguste Comte in France when he expressed the hope for a united, organized, regenerated humanity under the leadership – *présidence* – of France.[62] They do not give up the idea of mankind, though they think England is the supreme guarantee for humanity.

61 C. A. Bodelsen, *op. cit.*, p. 199.
62 In his *Discours sur l'Ensemble du Positivisme*, 1848, pp. 384 ff.

They could not help but overstress this nationalistic concept because of its inherent dissolution of the bond between soil and people implied in the mission idea, a dissolution which for English politics was not a propagated ideology but an established fact with which every statesman had to reckon. What separates them definitely from later racists is that none of them was ever seriously concerned with discrimination against other peoples as lower races, if only for the reason that the countries they were talking about, Canada and Australia, were almost empty and had no serious population problem.

It is, therefore, not by accident that the first English statesman who repeatedly stressed his belief in races and race superiority as a determining factor of history and politics was a man who without particular interest in the colonies and the English colonists – 'the colonial deadweight which we do not govern' – wanted to extend British imperial power to Asia and, indeed, forcefully strengthened the position of Great Britain in the only colony with a grave population and cultural problem. It was Benjamin Disraeli who made the Queen of England the Empress of India; he was the first English statesman who regarded India as the cornerstone of an Empire and who wanted to cut the ties which linked the English people to the nations of the Continent.[63] Thereby he laid one of the foundation stones for a fundamental change in British rule in India. This colony had been governed with the usual ruthlessness of conquerors – men whom Burke had called 'the breakers of the law in India.' It was now to receive a carefully planned administration which aimed at the establishment of a permanent government by administrative measures. This experiment has brought England very close to the danger against which Burke had warned, that the 'breakers of the law in India' might become 'the makers of law for England.'[64] For all those, to whom there was 'no transaction in the

63 'Power and influence we should exercise in Asia; consequently in Western Europe' (W. F. Monypenny and G. E. Buckle, *The Life of Benjamin Disraeli, Earl of Beaconsfield*, New York, 1929, II, 210). But 'If ever Europe by her shortsightedness falls into an inferior and exhausted state, for England there will remain an illustrious future' (*Ibid.*, I, Book IV, ch. 2). For 'England is no longer a mere European power . . . she is really more an Asiatic power than a European' (*Ibid.*, II, 201).

64 Burke, *op. cit.*, pp. 42–43: 'The power of the House of Commons . . . is indeed great; and long may it be able to preserve its greatness . . . and it will do so, as long as it can keep the breaker of the law in India from becoming the maker of law for England.'

history of England of which we have more just cause to be proud . . . than the establishment of the Indian Empire,' held liberty and equality to be 'big names for a small thing.' [65]

The policy introduced by Disraeli signified the establishment of an exclusive caste in a foreign country whose only function was rule and not colonization. For the realization of this conception which Disraeli did not live to see accomplished, racism would indeed be an indispensable tool. It foreshadowed the menacing transformation of the people from a nation into an 'unmixed race of a first-rate organization' that felt itself to be 'the aristocracy of nature' – to repeat in Disraeli's own words quoted above.[66]

What we have followed so far is the story of an opinion in which we see only now, after all the terrible experiences of our times, the first dawn of racism. But although racism has revived elements of race-thinking in every country, it is not the history of an idea endowed by some 'immanent logic' with which we were concerned. Race-thinking was a source of convenient arguments for varying political conflicts, but it never possessed any kind of monopoly over the political life of the respective nations; it sharpened and exploited existing conflicting interests or existing political problems, but it never created new conflicts or produced new categories of political thinking. Racism sprang from experiences and political constellations which were still unknown and would have been utterly strange even to such devoted defenders of 'race' as Gobineau or Disraeli. There is an abyss between the men of brilliant and facile conceptions and men of brutal deeds and active bestiality which no intellectual explanation is able to bridge. It is highly probable that the thinking in terms of race would have disappeared in due time together with other irresponsible opinions of the nineteenth century, if the 'scramble for Africa' and the new era of imperialism had not exposed Western humanity to new and shocking experiences. Imperialism would have necessitated the invention of racism as the only possible 'explanation' and excuse for its deeds, even if no race-thinking had ever existed in the civilized world.

65 Sir James F. Stephen, *op. cit.*, p. 253, and *passim*; see also his 'Foundations of the Government of India,' 1883, in *The Nineteenth Century*, LXXX.
66 For Disraeli's racism, compare chapter iii.

Since, however, race-thinking did exist, it proved to be a powerful help to racism. The very existence of an opinion which could boast of a certain tradition served to hide the destructive forces of the new doctrine which, without this appearance of national respectability or the seeming sanction of tradition, might have disclosed its utter incompatibility with all Western political and moral standards of the past, even before it was allowed to destroy the comity of European nations.

# CHAPTER SEVEN

# Race and Bureaucracy

Two new devices for political organization and rule over foreign peoples were discovered during the first decades of imperialism. One was race as a principle of the body politic, and the other bureaucracy as a principle of foreign domination. Without race as a substitute for the nation, the scramble for Africa and the investment fever might well have remained the purposeless 'dance of death and trade' (Joseph Conrad) of all gold rushes. Without bureaucracy as a substitute for government, the British possession of India might well have been left to the recklessness of the 'breakers of law in India' (Burke) without changing the political climate of an entire era.

Both discoveries were actually made on the Dark Continent. Race was the emergency explanation of human beings whom no European or civilized man could understand and whose humanity so frightened and humiliated the immigrants that they no longer cared to belong to the same human species. Race was the Boers' answer to the overwhelming monstrosity of Africa – a whole continent populated and overpopulated by savages – an explanation of the madness which grasped and illuminated them like 'a flash of lightning in a serene sky: "Exterminate all the brutes."' [1] This answer resulted in the most terrible massacres in recent history, the Boers' extermination of Hottentot tribes, the wild murdering by Carl Peters in German Southeast Africa, the decimation of the peaceful Congo population – from 20 to 40 million reduced to 8 million people; and finally, perhaps worst of all, it resulted in the triumphant introduction of such means of pacification into ordinary, respectable foreign policies. What head of a civilized

---

1 Joseph Conrad, 'Heart of Darkness' in *Youth and Other Tales*, 1902, is the most illuminating work on actual race experience in Africa.

state would ever before have uttered the exhortation of William II to a German expeditionary contingent fighting the Boxer insurrection in 1900: 'Just as the Huns a thousand years ago, under the leadership of Attila, gained a reputation by virtue of which they still live in history, so may the German name become known in such a manner in China that no Chinese will ever again dare to look askance at a German.'[2]

While race, whether as a home-grown ideology in Europe or an emergency explanation for shattering experiences, has always attracted the worst elements in Western civilization, bureaucracy was discovered by and first attracted the best, and sometimes even the most clear-sighted, strata of the European intelligentsia. The administrator who ruled by reports[3] and decrees in more hostile secrecy than any oriental despot grew out of a tradition of military discipline in the midst of ruthless and lawless men; for a long time he had lived by the honest, earnest boyhood ideals of a modern knight in shining armor sent to protect helpless and primitive people. And he fulfilled this task, for better or worse, as long as he moved in a world dominated by the old 'trinity – war, trade and piracy' (Goethe), and not in a complicated game of far-reaching investment policies which demanded the domination of one people, not as before for the sake of its own riches, but for the sake of another country's wealth. Bureaucracy was the organization of the great game of expansion in which every area was considered a stepping-stone to further involvements and every people an instrument for further conquest.

Although in the end racism and bureaucracy proved to be interrelated in many ways, they were discovered and developed independently. No one who in one way or the other was implicated in their perfection ever came to realize the full range of potentialities of power accumulation and destruction that this combination alone provided. Lord Cromer, who in Egypt changed from an ordinary British chargé d'affaires into an imperialist bureaucrat, would no more have dreamed

---

2 Quoted from Carlton J. Hayes, *A Generation of Materialism*, New York, 1941, p. 338. – An even worse case is of course that of Leopold II of Belgium, responsible for the blackest pages in the history of Africa. 'There was only one man who could be accused of the outrages which reduced the native population [of the Congo] from between 20 to 40 million in 1890 to 8,500,000 in 1911 – Leopold II.' See Selwyn James, *South of the Congo*, New York, 1943, p. 305.

3 See A. Carthill's description of the 'Indian system of government by reports' in *The Lost Dominion*, 1924, p. 70.

of combining administration with massacre ('administrative massacres' as Carthill bluntly put it forty years later), than the race fanatics of South Africa thought of organizing massacres for the purpose of establishing a circumscribed, rational political community (as the Nazis did in the extermination camps).

## I: The Phantom World of the Dark Continent

Up to the end of the last century, the colonial enterprises of the seafaring European peoples produced two outstanding forms of achievement: in recently discovered and sparsely populated territories, the founding of new settlements which adopted the legal and political institutions of the mother country; and in well-known though exotic countries in the midst of foreign peoples, the establishment of maritime and trade stations whose only function was to facilitate the never very peaceful exchange of the treasures of the world. Colonization took place in America and Australia, the two continents that, without a culture and a history of their own, had fallen into the hands of Europeans. Trade stations were characteristic of Asia where for centuries Europeans had shown no ambition for permanent rule or intentions of conquest, decimation of the native population, and permanent settlement.[4] Both forms of overseas enterprise evolved in a long steady process which extended over almost four centuries, during which the settlements gradually achieved independence, and the possession of trade stations shifted among the nations according to their relative weakness or strength in Europe.

The only continent Europe had not touched in the course of its colonial history was the Dark Continent of Africa. Its northern shores, populated by Arabic peoples and tribes, were well known and had

4 It is important to bear in mind that colonization of America and Australia was accompanied by comparatively short periods of cruel liquidation because of the natives' numerical weakness, whereas 'in understanding the genesis of modern South African society it is of the greatest importance to know that the land beyond the Cape's borders was not the open land which lay before the Australian squatter. It was already an area of settlement, of settlement by a great Bantu population.' See C. W. de Kiewiet, *A History of South Africa, Social and Economic* (Oxford, 1941), p. 59.

belonged to the European sphere of influence in one way or another since the days of antiquity. Too well populated to attract settlers, and too poor to be exploited, these regions suffered all kinds of foreign rule and anarchic neglect, but oddly enough never – after the decline of the Egyptian Empire and the destruction of Carthage – achieved authentic independence and reliable political organization. European countries tried time and again, it is true, to reach beyond the Mediterranean to impose their rule on Arabic lands and their Christianity on Moslem peoples, but they never attempted to treat North African territories like overseas possessions. On the contrary, they frequently aspired to incorporate them into the respective mother country. This age-old tradition, still followed in recent times by Italy and France, was broken in the eighties when England went into Egypt to protect the Suez Canal without any intention either of conquest or incorporation. The point is not that Egypt was wronged but that England (a nation that did not lie on the shores of the Mediterranean) could not possibly have been interested in Egypt as such, but needed her only because there were treasures in India.

While imperialism changed Egypt from a country occasionally coveted for her own sake into a military station for India and a stepping-stone for further expansion, the exact opposite happened to South Africa. Since the seventeenth century, the significance of the Cape of Good Hope had depended upon India, the center of colonial wealth; any nation that established trade stations there needed a maritime station on the Cape, which was then abandoned when trade in India was liquidated. At the end of the eighteenth century, the British East India Company defeated Portugal, Holland, and France and won a trade monopoly in India; the occupation of South Africa followed as a matter of course. If imperialism had simply continued the old trends of colonial trade (which is so frequently mistaken for imperialism), England would have liquidated her position in South Africa with the opening of the Suez Canal in 1869.[5] Although today South Africa belongs to the Commonwealth, it was always different from the other dominions; fertility and sparseness of population, the main prerequi-

5 'As late as 1884 the British Government had still been willing to diminish its authority and influence in South Africa' (De Kiewiet, *op. cit.*, p. 113).

sites for definite settlement, were lacking, and a single effort to settle 5,000 unemployed Englishmen at the beginning of the nineteenth century proved a failure. Not only did the streams of emigrants from the British Isles consistently avoid South Africa throughout the nineteenth century, but South Africa is the only dominion from which a steady stream of emigrants has gone back to England in recent times.[6] South Africa, which became the 'culture-bed of Imperialism' (Dance), was never claimed by England's most radical defenders of 'Saxondom' and it did not figure in the visions of her most romantic dreamers of an Asiatic Empire. This in itself shows how small the real influence of pre-imperialist colonial enterprise and overseas settlement was on the development of imperialism itself. If the Cape colony had remained within the framework of pre-imperialist policies, it would have been abandoned at the exact moment when it actually became all-important.

Although the discoveries of gold mines and diamond fields in the seventies and eighties would have had little consequence in themselves if they had not accidentally acted as a catalytic agent for imperialist forces, it remains remarkable that the imperialists' claim to have found a permanent solution to the problem of superfluity was initially motivated by a rush for the most superfluous raw material on earth. Gold hardly has a place in human production and is of no importance compared with iron, coal, oil, and rubber; instead, it is the most

6 The following table of British immigration to and emigration from South Africa between 1924 and 1928 shows that Englishmen had a stronger inclination to leave the country than other immigrants and that, with one exception, each year showed a greater number of British people leaving the country than coming in:

| Year | British Immigration | Total Immigration | British Emigration | Total Emigration |
|---|---|---|---|---|
| 1924 | 3.724 | 5.265 | 5.275 | 5.857 |
| 1925 | 2.400 | 5.426 | 4.019 | 4.483 |
| 1926 | 4.094 | 6.575 | 3.512 | 3.799 |
| 1927 | 3.681 | 6.595 | 3.717 | 3.988 |
| 1928 | 3.285 | 7.050 | 3.409 | 4.127 |
| Total | 17.184 | 30.911 | 19.932 | 22.254 |

These figures are quoted from Leonard Barnes, *Caliban in Africa. An Impression of Colour Madness*, Philadelphia, 1931, p. 59, note.

ancient symbol of mere wealth. In its uselessness in industrial production it bears an ironical resemblance to the superfluous money that financed the digging of gold and to the superfluous men who did the digging. To the imperialists' pretense of having discovered a permanent savior for a decadent society and antiquated political organization, it added its own pretense of apparently eternal stability and independence of all functional determinants. It was significant that a society about to part with all traditional absolute values began to look for an absolute value in the world of economics where, indeed, such a thing does not and cannot exist, since everything is functional by definition. This delusion of an absolute value has made the production of gold since ancient times the business of adventurers, gamblers, criminals, of elements outside the pale of normal, sane society. The new turn in the South African gold rush was that here the luck-hunters were not distinctly outside civilized society but, on the contrary, very clearly a by-product of this society, an inevitable residue of the capitalist system and even the representatives of an economy that relentlessly produced a superfluity of men and capital.

The superfluous men, 'the Bohemians of the four continents'[7] who came rushing down to the Cape, still had much in common with the old adventurers. They too felt 'Ship me somewheres east of Suez where the best is like the worst, / Where there aren't no Ten Commandments, an' a man can raise a thirst.' The difference was not their morality or immorality, but rather that the decision to join this crowd 'of all nations and colors'[8] was no longer up to them; that they had not stepped out of society but had been spat out by it; that they were not enterprising beyond the permitted limits of civilization but simply victims without use or function. Their only choice had been a negative one, a decision against the workers' movements, in which the best of the superfluous men or of those who were threatened with superfluity established a kind of countersociety through which men could find their way back into a human world of fellowship and purpose. They were nothing of their own making, they were like living symbols of what had happened to them, living abstractions and witnesses of the

7 J. A. Froude, 'Leaves from a South African Journal' (1874), in *Short Studies on Great Subjects*, 1867–1882, Vol. IV.
8 *Ibid.*

absurdity of human institutions. They were not individuals like the old adventurers, they were the shadows of events with which they had nothing to do.

Like Mr. Kurtz in Conrad's 'Heart of Darkness,' they were 'hollow to the core,' 'reckless without hardihood, greedy without audacity and cruel without courage.' They believed in nothing and 'could get (themselves) to believe anything – anything.' Expelled from a world with accepted social values, they had been thrown back upon themselves and still had nothing to fall back upon except, here and there, a streak of talent which made them as dangerous as Kurtz if they were ever allowed to return to their homelands. For the only talent that could possibly burgeon in their hollow souls was the gift of fascination which makes a 'splendid leader of an extreme party.' The more gifted were walking incarnations of resentment like the German Carl Peters (possibly the model for Kurtz), who openly admitted that he 'was fed up with being counted among the pariahs and wanted to belong to a master race.'[9] But gifted or not, they were all 'game for anything from pitch and toss to wilful murder' and to them their fellow-men were 'no more one way or another than that fly there.' Thus they brought with them, or they learned quickly, the code of manners which befitted the coming type of murderer to whom the only unforgivable sin is to lose his temper.

There were, to be sure, authentic gentlemen among them, like Mr. Jones of Conrad's *Victory*, who out of boredom were willing to pay any price to inhabit the 'world of hazard and adventure,' or like Mr. Heyst, who was drunk with contempt for everything human until he drifted 'like a detached leaf . . . without ever catching on to anything.' They were irresistibly attracted by a world where everything was a joke, which could teach them 'the Great Joke' that is 'the mastery of despair.' The perfect gentleman and the perfect scoundrel came to know each other well in the 'great wild jungle without law,' and they found themselves 'well-matched in their enormous dissimilarity, identical souls in different disguises.' We have seen the behavior of high society during the Dreyfus Affair and watched Disraeli discover the social relationship between vice and crime;

9 Quoted from Paul Ritter, *Kolonien im deutschen Schrifttum*, 1936, Preface.

here, too, we have essentially the same story of high society falling in love with its own underworld, and of the criminal feeling elevated when by civilized coldness, the avoidance of 'unnecessary exertion,' and good manners he is allowed to create a vicious, refined atmosphere around his crimes. This refinement, the very contrast between the brutality of the crime and the manner of carrying it out, becomes the bridge of deep understanding between himself and the perfect gentleman. But what, after all, took decades to achieve in Europe, because of the delaying effect of social ethical values, exploded with the suddenness of a short circuit in the phantom world of colonial adventure.

Outside all social restraint and hypocrisy, against the backdrop of native life, the gentleman and the criminal felt not only the closeness of men who share the same color of skin, but the impact of a world of infinite possibilities for crimes committed in the spirit of play, for the combination of horror and laughter, that is for the full realization of their own phantom-like existence. Native life lent these ghostlike events a seeming guarantee against all consequences because anyhow it looked to these men like a 'mere play of shadows. A play of shadows, the dominant race could walk through unaffected and disregarded in the pursuit of its incomprehensible aims and needs.'

The world of native savages was a perfect setting for men who had escaped the reality of civilization. Under a merciless sun, surrounded by an entirely hostile nature, they were confronted with human beings who, living without the future of a purpose and the past of an accomplishment, were as incomprehensible as the inmates of a madhouse. 'The prehistoric man was cursing us, praying to us, welcoming us – who could tell? We were cut off from the comprehension of our surroundings; we glided past like phantoms, wondering and secretly appalled, as sane men would be, before an enthusiastic outbreak in a madhouse. We could not understand because we were too far and could not remember, because we were traveling in the night of first ages, of those ages that are gone leaving hardly a sign – and no memories. The earth seemed unearthly . . . and the men . . . No, they were not inhuman. Well, you know, that was the worst of it – this suspicion of their not being inhuman. It would come slowly to one. They howled and leaped, and spun, and made horrid faces; but what thrilled you was just the thought of their humanity – like yours – the thought of your remote kinship with this wild and passionate uproar' ('Heart of Darkness').

It is strange that, historically speaking, the existence of 'prehistoric men' had so little influence on Western man before the scramble for Africa. It is, however, a matter of record that nothing much had happened as long as savage tribes, outnumbered by European settlers, had been exterminated, as long as shiploads of Negroes were imported as slaves into the Europe-determined world of the United States, or even as long as only individuals had drifted into the interior of the Dark Continent where the savages were numerous enough to constitute a world of their own, a world of folly, to which the European adventurer added the folly of the ivory hunt. Many of these adventurers had gone mad in the silent wilderness of an overpopulated continent where the presence of human beings only underlined utter solitude, and where an untouched, overwhelmingly hostile nature that nobody had ever taken the trouble to change into human landscape seemed to wait in sublime patience 'for the passing away of the fantastic invasion' of man. But their madness had remained a matter of individual experience and without consequences.

This changed with the men who arrived during the scramble for Africa. These were no longer lonely individuals; 'all Europe had contributed to the making of (them).' They concentrated on the southern part of the continent where they met the Boers, a Dutch splinter group which had been almost forgotten by Europe, but which now served as a natural introduction to the challenge of new surroundings. The response of the superfluous men was largely determined by the response of the only European group that ever, though in complete isolation, had to live in a world of black savages.

The Boers are descended from Dutch settlers who in the middle of the seventeenth century were stationed at the Cape to provide fresh vegetables and meat for ships on their voyage to India. A small group of French Huguenots was all that followed them in the course of the next century, so that it was only with the help of a high birthrate that the little Dutch splinter grew into a small people. Completely isolated from the current of European history, they set out on a path such 'as few nations have trod before them, and scarcely one trod with success.' [10]

The two main material factors in the development of the Boer people were the extremely bad soil which could be used only for extensive cattle-raising, and the very large black population which was organized in tribes and lived as nomad hunters. [11] The bad soil made close settlement impossible and prevented the Dutch peasant settlers from following the village organization of their homeland. Large families, isolated from each other by broad spaces of wilderness, were forced into a kind of clan organization and only the ever-present threat of a common foe, the black tribes which by far outnumbered the white settlers, deterred these clans from active war against each other. The solution to the double problem of lack of fertility and abundance of natives was slavery. [12]

Slavery, however, is a very inadequate word to describe what actually happened. First of all, slavery, though it domesticated a certain part of the savage population, never got hold of all of them, so the Boers were never able to forget their first horrible fright before a species of men whom human pride and the sense of human dignity could not allow them to accept as fellow-men. This fright of something like oneself that still under no circumstances ought to be like oneself remained at the basis of slavery and became the basis for a race society.

Mankind remembers the history of peoples but has only legendary knowledge of prehistoric tribes. The word 'race' has a precise meaning only when and where peoples are confronted with such tribes of which they have no historical record and which do not know any

10 Lord Selbourne in 1907: 'The white people of South Africa are committed to such a path as few nations have trod before them, and scarcely one trod with success.' See Kiewiet, *op. cit.*, chapter 6.

11 See especially chapter iii of Kiewiet, *op. cit.*

12 'Slaves and Hottentots together provoked remarkable changes in the thought and habits of the colonists, for climate and geography were not alone in forming the distinctive traits of the Boer race. Slaves and droughts, Hottentots and isolation, cheap labor and land, combined to create the institutions and habits of South African society. The sons and daughters born to sturdy Hollanders and Huguenots learned to look upon the labour of the field and upon all hard physical toil as the functions of a servile race' (Kiewiet, *op. cit.*, p. 21).

history of their own. Whether these represent 'prehistoric man,' the accidentally surviving specimens of the first forms of human life on earth, or whether they are the 'posthistoric' survivors of some unknown disaster which ended a civilization we do not know. They certainly appeared rather like the survivors of one great catastrophe which might have been followed by smaller disasters until catastrophic monotony seemed to be a natural condition of human life. At any rate, races in this sense were found only in regions where nature was particularly hostile. What made them different from other human beings was not at all the color of their skin but the fact that they behaved like a part of nature, that they treated nature as their undisputed master, that they had not created a human world, a human reality, and that therefore nature had remained, in all its majesty, the only overwhelming reality – compared to which they appeared to be phantoms, unreal and ghostlike. They were, as it were, 'natural' human beings who lacked the specifically human character, the specifically human reality, so that when European men massacred them they somehow were not aware that they had committed murder.

Moreover, the senseless massacre of native tribes on the Dark Continent was quite in keeping with the traditions of these tribes themselves. Extermination of hostile tribes had been the rule in all African native wars, and it was not abolished when a black leader happened to unite several tribes under his leadership. King Tchaka, who at the beginning of the nineteenth century united the Zulu tribes in an extraordinarily disciplined and warlike organization, established neither a people nor a nation of Zulus. He only succeeded in exterminating more than one million members of weaker tribes.[13] Since discipline and military organization by themselves cannot establish a political body, the destruction remained an unrecorded episode in an unreal, incomprehensible process which cannot be accepted by man and therefore is not remembered by human history.

Slavery in the case of the Boers was a form of adjustment of a European people to a black race,[14] and only superficially resembled those historical instances when it had been a result of conquest or slave

13  See James, *op. cit.*, p. 28.
14  'The true history of South African colonization describes the growth, not of a settlement of Europeans, but of a totally new and unique society of different races and

trade. No body politic, no communal organization kept the Boers together, no territory was definitely colonized, and the black slaves did not serve any white civilization. The Boers had lost both their peasant relationship to the soil and their civilized feeling for human fellowship. 'Each man fled the tyranny of his neighbor's smoke'[15] was the rule of the country, and each Boer family repeated in complete isolation the general pattern of Boer experience among black savages and ruled over them in absolute lawlessness, unchecked by 'kind neighbors ready to cheer you or to fall on you, stepping delicately between the butcher and the policeman, in the holy terror of scandal and gallows and lunatic asylums' (Conrad). Ruling over tribes and living parasitically from their labor, they came to occupy a position very similar to that of the native tribal leaders whose domination they had liquidated. The natives, at any rate, recognized them as a higher form of tribal leadership, a kind of natural deity to which one has to submit; so that the divine role of the Boers was as much imposed by their black slaves as assumed freely by themselves. It is a matter of course that to these white gods of black slaves each law meant only deprivation of freedom, government only restriction of the wild arbitrariness of the clan.[16] In the natives the Boers discovered the only 'raw material' which Africa provided in abundance and they used them not for the production of riches but for the mere essentials of human existence.

The black slaves in South Africa quickly became the only part of the population that actually worked. Their toil was marked by all the known disadvantages of slave labor, such as lack of initiative, laziness, neglect of tools, and general inefficiency. Their work therefore barely sufficed to keep their masters alive and never reached the comparative abundance which nurtures civilization. It was this absolute dependence on the work of others and complete contempt for labor and productivity in any form that transformed the Dutchman into the Boer and gave his concept of race a distinctly economic meaning.[17]

---

colours and cultural attainments, fashioned by conflicts of racial heredity and the oppositions of unequal social groups' (Kiewiet, *op. cit.*, p. 19).

15 Kiewiet, *op. cit.*, p. 19.

16 '[The Boers'] society was rebellious, but it was not revolutionary' (*ibid.*, p. 58).

17 'Little effort was made to raise the standard of living or increase the opportunities of the class of slaves and servants. In this manner, the limited wealth of the Colony

The Boers were the first European group to become completely alienated from the pride which Western man felt in living in a world created and fabricated by himself.[18] They treated the natives as raw material and lived on them as one might live on the fruits of wild trees. Lazy and unproductive, they agreed to vegetate on essentially the same level as the black tribes had vegetated for thousands of years. The great horror which had seized European men at their first confrontation with native life was stimulated by precisely this touch of inhumanity among human beings who apparently were as much a part of nature as wild animals. The Boers lived on their slaves exactly the way natives had lived on an unprepared and unchanged nature. When the Boers, in their fright and misery, decided to use these savages as though they were just another form of animal life, they embarked upon a process which could only end with their own degeneration into a white race living beside and together with black races from whom in the end they would differ only in the color of their skin.

The poor whites in South Africa, who in 1923 formed 10 per cent of the total white population[19] and whose standard of living does not differ much from that of the Bantu tribes, are today a warning example of this possibility. Their poverty is almost exclusively the consequence of their contempt for work and their adjustment to the way of life of black tribes. Like the blacks, they deserted the soil if the most primitive cultivation no longer yielded the little that was necessary or if

---

became the privilege of its white population . . . Thus early did South Africa learn that a self-conscious group may escape the worst effects of life in a poor and unprosperous land by turning distinctions of race and colour into devices for social and economic discrimination' (*ibid.*, p. 22).

18  The point is that, for instance, in 'the West Indies such a large proportion of slaves as were held at the Cape would have been a sign of wealth and a source of prosperity'; whereas 'at the Cape slavery was the sign of an unenterprising economy . . . whose labour was wastefully and inefficiently used' (*ibid.*). It was chiefly this that led Barnes (*op. cit.*, p. 107) and many other observers to the conclusion: 'South Africa is thus a foreign country, not only in the sense that its standpoint is definitely un-British, but also in the much more radical sense that its very *raison d'etre*, as an attempt at an organised society, is in contradiction to the principles on which the states of Christendom are founded.'

19  This corresponded to as many as 160,000 individuals (Kiewiet, *op. cit.*, p. 181). James (*op. cit.*, p. 43) estimated the number of poor whites in 1943 at 500,000 which would correspond to about 20 per cent of the white population.

they had exterminated the animals of the region.[20] Together with their former slaves, they came to the gold and diamond centers, abandoning their farms whenever the black workers departed. But in contrast to the natives who were immediately hired as cheap unskilled labor, they demanded and were granted charity as the right of a white skin, having lost all consciousness that normally men do not earn a living by the color of their skin.[21] Their race consciousness today is violent not only because they have nothing to lose save their membership in the white community, but also because the race concept seems to define their own condition much more adequately than it does that of their former slaves, who are well on the way to becoming workers, a normal part of human civilization.

Racism as a ruling device was used in this society of whites and blacks before imperialism exploited it as a major political idea. Its basis, and its excuse, were still experience itself, a horrifying experience of something alien beyond imagination or comprehension; it was tempting indeed simply to declare that these were not human beings. Since, however, despite all ideological explanations the black men stubbornly insisted on retaining their human features, the 'white men' could not but reconsider their own humanity and decide that they themselves were more than human and obviously chosen by God to be the gods of black men. This conclusion was logical and unavoidable if one wanted to deny radically all common bonds with savages; in practice it meant that Christianity for the first time could not act as a decisive curb on the dangerous perversions of human self-consciousness, a premonition of its essential ineffectiveness in other more recent race societies.[22] The Boers simply denied the Christian

20 'The poor white Afrikaaner population, living on the same subsistence level as the Bantus, is primarily the result of the Boers' inability or stubborn refusal to learn agricultural science. Like the Bantu, the Boer likes to wander from one area to another, tilling the soil until it is no longer fertile, shooting the wild game until it ceases to exist' (*ibid.*).

21 'Their race was their title of superiority over the natives, and to do manual labour conflicted with the dignity conferred upon them by their race . . . Such an aversion degenerated, in those who were most demoralized, into a claim to charity as a right' (Kiewiet, *op. cit.*, p. 216).

22 The Dutch Reformed Church has been in the forefront of the Boers' struggle against the influence of Christian missionaries on the Cape. In 1944, however, they

doctrine of the common origin of men and changed those passages of the Old Testament which did not yet transcend the limits of the old Israelite national religion into a superstition which could not even be called a heresy.[23] Like the Jews, they firmly believed in themselves as the chosen people,[24] with the essential difference that they were chosen not for the sake of divine salvation of mankind, but for the lazy domination over another species that was condemned to an equally lazy drudgery.[25] This was God's will on earth as the Dutch Reformed Church proclaimed it and still proclaims it today in sharp and hostile contrast to the missionaries of all other Christian denominations.[26]

Boer racism, unlike the other brands, has a touch of authenticity and, so to speak, of innocence. A complete lack of literature and other intellectual achievement is the best witness to this statement.[27] It was and remains a desperate reaction to desperate living conditions which was inarticulate and inconsequential as long as it was left alone. Things began to happen only with the arrival of the British, who showed little interest in their newest colony which in 1849 was still called a military station (as opposed to either a colony or a plantation). But their mere presence – that is, their contrasting attitude toward the

---

went one step farther and adopted 'without a single voice of dissent' a motion opposing the marriage of Boers with English-speaking citizens. (According to the Cape *Times*, editorial of July 18, 1944. Quoted from *New Africa*, Council on African Affairs, Monthly Bulletin, October, 1944.)

23 Kiewiet (*op. cit.*, p. 181) mentions 'the doctrine of racial superiority which was drawn from the Bible and reinforced by the popular interpretation which the nineteenth century placed upon Darwin's theories.'

24 'The God of the Old Testament has been to them almost as much a national figure as He has been to the Jews . . . I recall a memorable scene in a Cape Town club, where a bold Briton, dining by chance with three or four Dutchmen, ventured to observe that Christ was a non-European and that, legally speaking, he would have been a prohibited immigrant in the Union of South Africa. The Dutchmen were so electrified at the remark that they nearly fell off their chairs' (Barnes, *op. cit.*, p. 33).

25 'For the Boer farmer the separation and the degradation of the natives are ordained by God, and it is crime and blasphemy to argue to the contrary' (Norman Bentwich, 'South Africa. Dominion of Racial Problems.' In *Political Quarterly*, 1939, Vol. X, No. 3).

26 'To this day the missionary is to the Boer the fundamental traitor, the white man who stands for black against white' (S. Gertrude Millin, *Rhodes*, London, 1933, p. 38).

27 'Because they had little art, less architecture, and no literature, they depended upon their farms, their Bibles, and their blood to set them off sharply against the native and the outlander' (Kiewiet, *op. cit.*, p. 121).

natives whom they did not consider a different animal species, their later attempts (after 1834) to abolish slavery, and above all their efforts to impose fixed boundaries upon landed property – provoked the stagnant Boer society into violent reactions. It is characteristic of the Boers that these reactions followed the same, repeated pattern throughout the nineteenth century: Boer farmers escaped British law by treks into the interior wilderness of the country, abandoning without regret their homes and their farms. Rather than accept limitations upon their possessions, they left them altogether.[28] This does not mean that the Boers did not feel at home wherever they happened to be; they felt and still feel much more at home in Africa than any subsequent immigrants, but in Africa and not in any specific limited territory. Their fantastic treks, which threw the British administration into consternation, showed clearly that they had transformed themselves into a tribe and had lost the European's feeling for a territory, a *patria* of his own. They behaved exactly like the black tribes who had also roamed the Dark Continent for centuries – feeling at home wherever the horde happened to be, and fleeing like death every attempt at definite settlement.

Rootlessness is characteristic of all race organizations. What the European 'movements' consciously aimed at, the transformation of the people into a horde, can be watched like a laboratory test in the Boers' early and sad attempt. While rootlessness as a conscious aim was based primarily upon hatred of a world that had no place for

28 'The true Vortrekker hated a boundary. When the British Government insisted on fixed boundaries for the Colony and for farms within it, something was taken from him . . . It was best surely to betake themselves across the border where there were water and free land and no British Government to disallow Vagrancy Laws and where white men could not be haled to court to answer the complaints of their servants' (*Ibid.*, pp. 54–55). 'The Great Trek, a movement unique in the history of colonization' (p. 58) 'was the defeat of the policy of more intensive settlement. The practice which required the area of an entire Canadian township for the settlement of ten families was extended through all of South Africa. It made for ever impossible the segregation of white and black races in separate areas of settlement . . . By taking the Boers beyond the reach of British law, the Great Trek enabled them to establish "proper" relations with the native population' (p. 56). 'In later years, the Great Trek was to become more than a protest; it was to become a rebellion against the British administration, and the foundation stone of the Anglo-Boer racialism of the twentieth century' (James, *op. cit.*, p. 28).

'superfluous' men, so that its destruction could become a supreme political goal, the rootlessness of the Boers was a natural result of early emancipation from work and complete lack of a human-built world. The same striking similarity prevails between the 'movements' and the Boers' interpretation of 'chosenness.' But while the Pan-German, Pan-Slav, or Polish Messianic movements' chosenness was a more or less conscious instrument for domination, the Boers' perversion of Christianity was solidly rooted in a horrible reality in which miserable 'white men' were worshipped as divinities by equally unfortunate 'black men.' Living in an environment which they had no power to transform into a civilized world, they could discover no higher value than themselves. The point, however, is that no matter whether racism appears as the natural result of a catastrophe or as the conscious instrument for bringing it about, it is always closely tied to contempt for labor, hatred of territorial limitation, general rootlessness, and an activistic faith in one's own divine chosenness.

Early British rule in South Africa, with its missionaries, soldiers, and explorers, did not realize that the Boers' attitudes had some basis in reality. They did not understand that absolute European supremacy – in which they, after all, were as interested as the Boers – could hardly be maintained except through racism because the permanent European settlement was so hopelessly outnumbered;[29] they were shocked 'if Europeans settled in Africa were to act like savages themselves because it was the custom of the country,'[30] and to their simple utilitarian minds it seemed folly to sacrifice productivity and profit to the phantom world of white gods ruling over black shadows. Only with the settlement of Englishmen and other Europeans during the gold rush did they gradually adjust to a population which could not be lured back into European civilization even by profit motives, which had lost contact even with the lower incentives of European man when it had cut itself off from his higher motives,

---

29  In 1939, the total population of the Union of South Africa amounted to 9,500,000 of whom 7,000,000 were natives and 2,500,000 Europeans. Of the latter, more than 1,250,000 were Boers, about one-third were British, and 100,000 were Jews. See Norman Bentwich, *op. cit.*

30  J. A. Froude, *op. cit.*, p. 375.

because both lose their meaning and appeal in a society where nobody wants to achieve anything and everyone has become a god.

## II: Gold and Race

The diamond fields of Kimberley and the gold mines of the Witwatersrand happened to lie in this phantom world of race, and 'a land that had seen boat-load after boat-load of emigrants for New Zealand and Australia pass it unheeding by now saw men tumbling on to its wharves and hurrying up country to the mines. Most of them were English, but among them was more than a sprinkling from Riga and Kiev, Hamburg and Frankfort, Rotterdam and San Francisco.' [31] All of them belonged to 'a class of persons who prefer adventure and speculation to settled industry, and who do not work well in the harness of ordinary life . . . [There were] diggers from America and Australia, German speculators, traders, saloonkeepers, professional gamblers, barristers . . . ex-officers of the army and navy, younger sons of good families . . . a marvelous motley assemblage among whom money flowed like water from the amazing productiveness of the mine.' They were joined by thousands of natives who first came to 'steal diamonds and to lag their earnings out in rifles and powder,' [32] but quickly started to work for wages and became the seemingly inexhaustible cheap labor supply when the 'most stagnant of colonial regions suddenly exploded into activity.' [33]

The abundance of natives, of cheap labor, was the first and perhaps most important difference between this gold rush and others of its type. It was soon apparent that the mob from the four corners of the earth would not even have to do the digging; at any rate, the permanent attraction of South Africa, the permanent resource that tempted the adventurers to permanent settlement, was not the gold but this human raw material which promised a permanent emancipation from work. [34] The Europeans served solely as supervisors and did not even

---

31 Kiewiet, *op. cit.*, p. 119.
32 Froude, *op. cit.*, p. 400.
33 Kiewiet, *op. cit.*, p. 119.
34 'What an abundance of rain and grass was to New Zealand mutton, what a plenty of cheap grazing land was to Australian wool, what the fertile prairie acres were to

produce skilled labor and engineers, both of which had constantly to be imported from Europe.

Second in importance only, for the ultimate outcome, was the fact that this gold rush was not simply left to itself but was financed, organized, and connected with the ordinary European economy through the accumulated superfluous wealth and with the help of Jewish financiers. From the very beginning 'a hundred or so Jewish merchants who have gathered like eagles over their prey' [35] actually acted as middlemen through whom European capital was invested in the gold mining and diamond industries.

The only section of the South African population that did not have and did not want to have a share in the suddenly exploding activities of the country were the Boers. They hated all these *uitlanders*, who did not care for citizenship but who needed and obtained British protection, thereby seemingly strengthening British government influence on the Cape. The Boers reacted as they had always reacted, they sold their diamond-laden possessions in Kimberley and their farms with gold mines near Johannesburg and trekked once more into the interior wilderness. They did not understand that this new influx was different from the British missionaries, government officials, or ordinary settlers, and they realized only when it was too late and they had already lost their share in the riches of the gold hunt that the new idol of Gold was not at all irreconcilable with their idol of Blood, that the new mob was as unwilling to work and as unfit to establish a civilization as they were themselves, and would therefore spare them the British officials' annoying insistence on law and the Christian missionaries' irritating concept of human equality.

The Boers feared and fled what actually never happened, namely, the industrialization of the country. They were right insofar as normal production and civilization would indeed have destroyed automatically the way of life of a race society. A normal market for labor and merchandise would have liquidated the privileges of race. But gold and diamonds, which soon provided a living for half of South Africa's population, were not merchandise in the same sense and were not

Canadian wheat, cheap native labour was to South African mining and industrial enterprise' (Kiewiet, *op. cit.*, p. 96).

35 J. A. Froude, *ibid*.

produced in the same way as wool in Australia, meat in New Zealand, or wheat in Canada. The irrational, non-functional place of gold in the economy made it independent of rational production methods which, of course, could never have tolerated the fantastic disparities between black and white wages. Gold, an object for speculation and essentially dependent in value upon political factors, became the 'lifeblood' of South Africa[36] but it could not and did not become the basis of a new economic order.

The Boers also feared the mere presence of the *uitlanders* because they mistook them for British settlers. The *uitlanders*, however, came solely in order to get rich quickly, and only those remained who did not quite succeed or who, like the Jews, had no country to return to. Neither group cared very much to establish a community after the model of European countries, as British settlers had done in Australia, Canada, and New Zealand. It was Barnato who happily discovered that 'the Transvaal Government is like no other government in the world. It is indeed not a government at all, but an unlimited company of some twenty thousand shareholders.'[37] Similarly, it was more or less a series of misunderstandings which finally led to the British-Boer war, which the Boers wrongly believed to be 'the culmination of the British Government's lengthy quest for a united South Africa,' while it was actually prompted mainly by investment interests.[38] When the Boers lost the war, they lost no more than they had already deliberately abandoned, that is, their share in the riches; but they definitely won the consent of all other European elements, including the British government, to the lawlessness of a race society.[39] Today, all sections

36 'The goldmines are the life-blood of the Union . . . one half of the population obtained their livelihood directly or indirectly from the goldmining industry, and . . . one half of the finances of the government were derived directly or indirectly from gold mining' (Kiewiet, *op. cit.*, p. 155).

37 See Paul H. Emden, *Jews of Britain, A Series of Biographies*, London, 1944, chapter 'From Cairo to the Cape.'

38 Kiewiet (*op. cit.*, pp. 138–39) mentions, however, also another 'set of circumstances': 'Any attempt by the British Government to secure concessions or reforms from the Transvaal Government made it inevitably the agent of the mining magnates . . . Great Britain gave its support, whether this was clearly realized in Downing Street or not, to capital and mining investments.'

39 'Much of the hesitant and evasive conduct of British statesmanship in the generation before the Boer War could be attributed to the indecision of the British Government

of the population, British or Afrikander, organized workers or capitalists, agree on the race question,[40] and whereas the rise of Nazi Germany and its conscious attempt to transform the German people into a race strengthened the political position of the Boers considerably, Germany's defeat has not weakened it.

The Boers hated and feared the financiers more than the other foreigners. They somehow understood that the financier was a key figure in the combination of superfluous wealth and superfluous men, that it was his function to turn the essentially transitory gold hunt into a much broader and more permanent business.[41] The war with the British, moreover, soon demonstrated an even more decisive aspect; it was quite obvious that it had been prompted by foreign investors who demanded the government's protection of their tremendous profits in faraway countries as a matter of course – as though armies engaged in a war against foreign peoples were nothing but native police forces involved in a fight with native criminals. It made little difference to the Boers that the men who introduced this kind of violence into the shadowy affairs of the gold and diamond production were no longer the financiers, but those who somehow had risen from the mob itself and, like Cecil Rhodes, believed less in profits than in expansion for expansion's sake.[42] The financiers, who were mostly Jews and only the

---

between its obligation to the natives and its obligation to the white communities . . . Now, however, the Boer War compelled a decision on native policy. In the terms of the peace the British Government promised that no attempt would be made to alter the political status of the natives before self-government had been granted to the ex-Republics. In that epochal decision the British Government receded from its humanitarian position and enabled the Boer leaders to win a signal victory in the peace negotiations which marked their military defeat. Great Britain abandoned the effort to exercise a control over the vital relations between white and black. Downing Street had surrendered to the frontiers' (Kiewiet, *op. cit.*, pp. 143–44).

40 'There is . . . an entirely erroneous notion that the Africaaners and the English-speaking people of South Africa still disagree on how to treat the natives. On the contrary, it is one of the few things on which they do agree' (James, *op. cit.*, p. 47).

41 This was mostly due to the methods of Alfred Beit who had arrived in 1875 to buy diamonds for a Hamburg firm. 'Till then only speculators had been share-holders in mining ventures . . . Beit's method attracted the genuine investor also' (Emden, *op. cit.*).

42 Very characteristic in this respect was Barnato's attitude when it came to the amalgamation of his business with the Rhodes group. 'For Barnato the amalgamation was nothing but a financial transaction in which he wanted to make money . . . He

representatives, not the owners, of the superfluous capital, had neither the necessary political influence nor enough economic power to introduce political purposes and the use of violence into speculation and gambling.

Without doubt the financiers, though finally not the decisive factor in imperialism, were remarkably representative of it in its initial period.[43] They had taken advantage of the overproduction of capital and its accompanying complete reversal of economic and moral values. Instead of mere trade in goods and mere profit from production, trade in capital itself emerged on an unprecedented scale. This alone would have given them a prominent position; in addition profits from investments in foreign countries soon increased at a much more rapid rate than trade profits, so that traders and merchants lost their primacy to the financier.[44] The main economic characteristic of the financier is that he earns his profits not from production and exploitation or exchange of merchandise or normal banking, but solely through commissions. This is important in our context because it gives him that touch of unreality, of phantom-like existence and essential futility even in a normal economy, that are typical of so many South African events. The financiers certainly did not exploit anybody and they had least control over the course of their business ventures, whether these turned out to be common swindles or sound enterprises belatedly confirmed.

It is also significant that it was precisely the mob element among the Jewish people who turned into financiers. It is true that the discovery of gold mines in South Africa had coincided with the first modern

---

therefore desired that the company should have nothing to do with politics. Rhodes however was not merely a business man . . .' This shows how very wrong Barnato was when he thought that 'if I had received the education of Cecil Rhodes there would not have been a Cecil Rhodes' (*ibid.*).

43 Compare chapter v, note 34.

44 The increase in profits from foreign investment and a relative decrease of foreign trade profits characterizes the economic side of imperialism. In 1899, it was estimated that Great Britain's whole foreign and colonial trade had brought her an income of only 18 million pounds, while in the same year profits from foreign investment amounted to 90 or 100 million pounds. See J. A. Hobson, *Imperialism*, London, 1938, pp. 53 ff. It is obvious that investment demanded a much more conscious long-range policy of exploitation than mere trade.

pogroms in Russia, so that a trickle of Jewish emigrants went to South Africa. There, however, they would hardly have played a role in the international crowd of desperadoes and fortune hunters if a few Jewish financiers had not been there ahead of them and taken an immediate interest in the newcomers who clearly could represent them in the population.

The Jewish financiers came from practically every country on the continent where they had been, in terms of class, as superfluous as the other South African immigrants. They were quite different from the few established families of Jewish notables whose influence had steadily decreased after 1820, and into whose ranks they could therefore no longer be assimilated. They belonged in that new caste of Jewish financiers which, from the seventies and eighties on, we find in all European capitals, where they had come, mostly after having left their countries of origin, in order to try their luck in the international stock-market gamble. This they did everywhere to the great dismay of the older Jewish families, who were too weak to stop the unscrupulousness of the newcomers and therefore only too glad if the latter decided to transfer the field of their activities overseas. In other words, the Jewish financiers had become as superfluous in legitimate Jewish banking as the wealth they represented had become superfluous in legitimate industrial enterprise and the fortune hunters in the world of legitimate labor. In South Africa itself, where the merchant was about to lose his status within the country's economy to the financier, the new arrivals, the Barnatos, Beits, Sammy Marks, removed the older Jewish settlers from first position much more easily than in Europe.[45] In South Africa, though hardly anywhere else, they were the third factor in the initial alliance between capital and mob; to a large extent, they set the alliance into motion, handled the influx of capital and its investment in the gold mines and diamond fields, and soon became more conspicuous than anybody else.

45 Early Jewish settlers in South Africa in the eighteenth and the first part of the nineteenth century were adventurers; traders and merchants followed them after the middle of the century, among whom the most prominent turned to industries such as fishing, sealing, and whaling (De Pass Brothers) and ostrich breeding (the Mosenthal family). Later, they were almost forced into the Kimberley diamond industries where, however, they never achieved such pre-eminence as Barnato and Beit.

The fact of their Jewish origin added an undefinable symbolic flavor to the role of the financiers – a flavor of essential homelessness and rootlessness – and thus served to introduce an element of mystery, as well as to symbolize the whole affair. To this must be added their actual international connections, which naturally stimulated the general popular delusions concerning Jewish political power all over the world. It is quite comprehensible that all the fantastic notions of a secret international Jewish power – notions which originally had been the result of the closeness of Jewish banking capital to the state's sphere of business – became even more virulent here than on the European continent. Here, for the first time Jews were driven into the midst of a race society and almost automatically singled out by the Boers from all other 'white' people for special hatred, not only as the representatives of the whole enterprise, but as a different 'race,' the embodiment of a devilish principle introduced into the normal world of 'blacks' and 'whites.' This hatred was all the more violent as it was partly caused by the suspicion that the Jews with their own older and more authentic claim would be harder than anyone else to convince of the Boers' claim to chosenness. While Christianity simply denied the principle as such, Judaism seemed a direct challenge and rival. Long before the Nazis consciously built up an antisemitic movement in South Africa, the race issue had invaded the conflict between the *uitlander* and the Boers in the form of antisemitism,[46] which is all the more noteworthy since the importance of Jews in the South African gold and diamond economy did not survive the turn of the century.

As soon as the gold and diamond industries reached the stage of imperialist development where absentee shareholders demand their governments' political protection, it turned out that the Jews could not hold their important economic position. They had no home government to turn to and their position in South African society was so insecure that much more was at stake for them than a mere decrease in influence. They could preserve economic security and permanent settlement in South Africa, which they needed more than any other group of *uitlanders*, only if they achieved some status in

46 Ernst Schultze, 'Die Judenfrage in Sued-Afrika,' in *Der Weltkampf*, October, 1938, Vol. XV, No. 178.

society – which in this case meant admission to exclusive British clubs. They were forced to trade their influence against the position of a gentleman, as Cecil Rhodes very bluntly put it when he bought his way into the Barnato Diamond Trust, after having amalgamated his De Beers Company with Alfred Beit's Company.[47] But these Jews had more to offer than just economic power; it was thanks to them that Cecil Rhodes, as much a newcomer and adventurer as they, was finally accepted by England's respectable banking business with which the Jewish financiers after all had better connections than anybody else.[48] 'Not one of the English banks would have lent a single shilling on the security of gold shares. It was the unbounded confidence of these diamond men from Kimberley that operated like a magnet upon their co-religionists at home.'[49]

The gold rush became a full-fledged imperialist enterprise only after Cecil Rhodes had dispossessed the Jews, taken investment policies from England's into his own hands, and had become the central figure on the Cape. Seventy-five per cent of the dividends paid to shareholders went abroad, and a large majority of them to Great Britain. Rhodes succeeded in interesting the British government in his business affairs, persuaded them that expansion and export of the instruments of violence was necessary to protect investments, and that such a policy was a holy duty of every national government. On the other hand, he introduced on the Cape itself that typically imperialist economic policy of neglecting all industrial enterprises which were not owned by absentee shareholders, so that finally not only the gold mining companies but the government itself discouraged the exploitation of abundant base metal deposits and the production of consumers' goods.[50] With the initiation of this policy, Rhodes

47 Barnato sold his shares to Rhodes in order to be introduced to the Kimberley Club. 'This is no mere money transaction,' Rhodes is reported to have told Barnato, 'I propose to make a gentleman of you.' Barnato enjoyed his life as a gentleman for eight years and then committed suicide. See Millin, *op. cit.*, pp. 14, 85.

48 'The path from one Jew [in this case, Alfred Beit from Hamburg] to another is an easy one. Rhodes went to England to see Lord Rothschild and Lord Rothschild approved of him' (*ibid.*).

49 Emden, *op. cit.*

50 'South Africa concentrated almost all its peacetime industrial energy on the production of gold. The average investor put his money into gold because it offered the

introduced the most potent factor in the eventual appeasement of the Boers; the neglect of all authentic industrial enterprise was the most solid guarantee for the avoidance of normal capitalist development and thus against a normal end of race society.

It took the Boers several decades to understand that imperialism was nothing to be afraid of, since it would neither develop the country as Australia and Canada had been developed, nor draw profits from the country at large, being quite content with a high turnover of investments in one specific field. Imperialism therefore was willing to abandon the so-called laws of capitalist production and their egalitarian tendencies, so long as profits from specific investments were safe. This led eventually to the abolition of the law of mere profitableness and South Africa became the first example of a phenomenon that occurs whenever the mob becomes the dominant factor in the alliance between mob and capital.

In one respect, the most important one, the Boers remained the undisputed masters of the country: whenever rational labor and production policies came into conflict with race considerations, the latter won. Profit motives were sacrificed time and again to the demands of a race society, frequently at a terrific price. The rentability of the railroads was destroyed overnight when the government dismissed 17,000 Bantu employees and paid whites wages that amounted to 200 per cent more;[51] expenses for municipal government became prohibitive when native municipal employees were replaced with whites; the Color Bar Bill finally excluded all black workers from mechanical jobs and forced industrial enterprise to a tremendous increase of production costs. The race world of the Boers had nobody to fear any more, least of all

---

quickest and biggest returns. But South Africa also has tremendous deposits of iron ore, copper, asbestos, manganese, tin, lead, platinum, chrome, mica and graphite. These, along with the coal mines and the handful of factories producing consumer goods, were known as "secondary" industries. The investing public's interest in them was limited. And development of these secondary industries was discouraged by the gold-mining companies and to a large extent by the government' (James, *op. cit.*, p. 333).

51 James, *op. cit.*, pp. 111–112. 'The Government reckoned that this was a good example for private employers to follow ... and public opinion soon forced changes in the hiring policies of many employers.'

white labor, whose trade unions complained bitterly that the Color Bar Bill did not go far enough.[52]

At first glance, it is surprising that a violent antisemitism survived the disappearance of the Jewish financiers as well as the successful indoctrination with racism of all parts of the European population. The Jews were certainly no exception to this rule; they adjusted to racism as well as everybody else and their behavior toward black people was beyond reproach.[53] Yet they had, without being aware of it and under pressure of special circumstances, broken with one of the most powerful traditions of the country.

The first sign of 'anormal' behavior came immediately after the Jewish financiers had lost their position in the gold and diamond industries. They did not leave the country but settled down permanently[54] into a unique position for a white group: they neither belonged to the 'lifeblood' of Africa nor to the 'poor white trash.' Instead they started almost immediately to build up those industries and professions which according to South African opinion are 'secondary' because they are not connected with gold.[55] Jews became manufacturers of furniture and clothes, shopkeepers and members of the professions, physicians, lawyers, and journalists. In other words, no

52 James, *op. cit.*, p. 108.

53 Here again, a definite difference between the earlier settlers and the financiers can be recognized until the end of the nineteenth century. Saul Salomon, for instance, a Negrophilist member of the Cape Parliament, was a descendant of a family which had settled in South Africa in the early nineteenth century. Emden, *op. cit.*

54 Between 1924 and 1930, 12,319 Jews immigrated to South Africa while only 461 left the country. These figures are very striking if one considers that the total immigration for the same period after deduction of emigrants amounted to 14,241 persons. (See Schultze, *op. cit.*) If we compare these figures with the immigration table of note 6, it follows that Jews constituted roughly one-third of the total immigration to South Africa in the twenties, and that they, in sharp contrast to all other categories of *uitlanders*, settled there permanently; their share in the annual emigration is less than 2 per cent.

55 'Rabid Afrikaaner nationalist leaders have deplored the fact that there are 102,000 Jews in the Union; most of them are white-collar workers, industrial employers, shopkeepers, or members of the professions. The Jews did much to build up the secondary industries of South Africa – *i.e.*, industries other than gold and diamond mining – concentrating particularly on the manufacture of clothes and furniture' (James, *op. cit.*, p. 46).

matter how well they thought they were adjusted to the mob conditions of the country and its race attitude, Jews had broken its most
important pattern by introducing into South African economy a factor
of normalcy and productivity, with the result that when Mr. Malan
introduced into Parliament a bill to expel all Jews from the Union he
had the enthusiastic support of all poor whites and of the whole
Afrikander population.[56]

This change in the economic function, the transformation of South
African Jewry from representing the most shadowy characters in the
shadow world of gold and race into the only productive part of the
population, came like an oddly belated confirmation of the original
fears of the Boers. They had hated the Jews not so much as the middlemen of superfluous wealth or the representatives of the world of gold;
they had feared and despised them as the very image of the *uitlanders*
who would try to change the country into a normal producing part of
Western civilization, whose profit motives, at least, would mortally
endanger the phantom world of race. And when the Jews were finally
cut off from the golden lifeblood of the *uitlanders* and could not leave
the country as all other foreigners would have done in similar circumstances, developing 'secondary' industries instead, the Boers turned
out to be right. The Jews, entirely by themselves and without being
the image of anything or anybody, had become a real menace to race
society. As matters stand today, the Jews have against them the concerted hostility of all those who believe in race or gold – and that is
practically the whole European population in South Africa. Yet they
cannot and will not make common cause with the only other group
which slowly and gradually is being won away from race society: the
black workers who are becoming more and more aware of their
humanity under the impact of regular labor and urban life. Although
they, in contrast to the 'whites,' do have a genuine race origin, they
have made no fetish of race, and the abolition of race society means
only the promise of their liberation.

In contrast to the Nazis, to whom racism and antisemitism were
major political weapons for the destruction of civilization and the setting up of a new body politic, racism and antisemitism are a matter of

56  *Ibid.*, pp. 67–68.

course and a natural consequence of the status quo in South Africa. They did not need Nazism in order to be born and they influenced Nazism only in an indirect way.

There were, however, real and immediate boomerang effects of South Africa's race society on the behavior of European peoples: since cheap Indian and Chinese labor had been madly imported to South Africa whenever her interior supply was temporarily halted,[57] a change of attitude toward colored people was felt immediately in Asia where, for the first time, people were treated in almost the same way as those African savages who had frightened Europeans literally out of their wits. The difference was only that there could be no excuse and no humanly comprehensible reason for treating Indians and Chinese as though they were not human beings. In a certain sense, it is only here that the real crime began, because here everyone ought to have known what he was doing. It is true that the race notion was somewhat modified in Asia; 'higher and lower breeds,' as the 'white man' would say when he started to shoulder his burden, still indicate a scale and the possibility of gradual development, and the idea somehow escapes the concept of two entirely different species of animal life. On the other hand, since the race principle supplanted the older notion of alien and strange peoples in Asia, it was a much more consciously applied weapon for domination and exploitation than in Africa.

Less immediately significant but of greater importance for totalitarian governments was the other experience in Africa's race society, that profit motives are not holy and can be overruled, that societies can function according to principles other than economic, and that such circumstances may favor those who under conditions of rationalized production and the capitalist system would belong to the underprivileged. South Africa's race society taught the mob the great lesson of which it had always had a confused premonition, that through sheer violence an underprivileged group could create a class

57 More than 100,000 Indian coolies were imported to the sugar plantations of Natal in the nineteenth century. These were followed by Chinese laborers in the mines who numbered about 55,000 in 1907. In 1910, the British government ordered the repatriation of all Chinese mine laborers, and in 1913 it prohibited any further immigration from India or any other part of Asia. In 1931, 142,000 Asiatics were still in the Union and treated like African natives. (See also Schultze, *op. cit.*)

lower than itself, that for this purpose it did not even need a revolution but could band together with groups of the ruling classes, and that foreign or backward peoples offered the best opportunities for such tactics.

The full impact of the African experience was first realized by leaders of the mob, like Carl Peters, who decided that they too had to belong to a master race. African colonial possessions became the most fertile soil for the flowering of what later was to become the Nazi elite. Here they had seen with their own eyes how peoples could be converted into races and how, simply by taking the initiative in this process, one might push one's own people into the position of the master race. Here they were cured of the illusion that the historical process is necessarily 'progressive,' for if it was the course of older colonization to trek to something, the 'Dutchman trekked away from everything,'[58] and if 'economic history once taught that man had developed by gradual steps from a life of hunting to pastoral pursuits and finally to a settled and agricultural life,' the story of the Boers clearly demonstrated that one could also come 'from a land that had taken the lead in a thrifty and intensive cultivation ... [and] gradually become a herdsman and a hunter.'[59] These leaders understood very well that precisely because the Boers had sunk back to the level of savage tribes they remained their undisputed masters. They were perfectly willing to pay the price, to recede to the level of a race organization, if by so doing they could buy lordship over other 'races.' And they knew from their experiences with people gathered from the four corners of the earth in South Africa that the whole mob of the Western civilized world would be with them.[60]

---

58  Barnes, *op. cit.*, p. 13.

59  Kiewiet, *op. cit.*, p. 13.

60  'When economists declared that higher wages were a form of bounty, and that protected labour was uneconomical, the answer was given that the sacrifice was well made if the unfortunate elements in the white population ultimately found an assured footing in modern life.' 'But it has not been in South Africa alone that the voice of the conventional economist has gone unheeded since the end of the Great War ... In a generation which saw England abandon free trade, America leave the gold standard, the Third Reich embrace autarchy ... South Africa's insistence that its economic life must be organized to secure the dominant position of the white race is not seriously out of place' (Kiewiet, *op. cit.*, pp. 224 and 245).

## III: The Imperialist Character

Of the two main political devices of imperialist rule, race was discovered in South Africa and bureaucracy in Algeria, Egypt, and India; the former was originally the barely conscious reaction to tribes of whose humanity European man was ashamed and frightened, whereas the latter was a consequence of that administration by which Europeans had tried to rule foreign peoples whom they felt to be hopelessly their inferiors and at the same time in need of their special protection. Race, in other words, was an escape into an irresponsibility where nothing human could any longer exist, and bureaucracy was the result of a responsibility that no man can bear for his fellow-man and no people for another people.

The exaggerated sense of responsibility in the British administrators of India who succeeded Burke's 'breakers of law' had its material basis in the fact that the British Empire had actually been acquired in a 'fit of absent-mindedness.' Those, therefore, who were confronted with the accomplished fact and the job of keeping what had become theirs through an accident, had to find an interpretation that could change the accident into a kind of willed act. Such historical changes of fact have been carried through by legends since ancient times, and legends dreamed up by the British intelligentsia have played a decisive role in the formation of the bureaucrat and the secret agent of the British services.

Legends have always played a powerful role in the making of history. Man, who has not been granted the gift of undoing, who is always an unconsulted heir of other men's deeds, and who is always burdened with a responsibility that appears to be the consequence of an unending chain of events rather than conscious acts, demands an explanation and interpretation of the past in which the mysterious key to his future destiny seems to be concealed. Legends were the spiritual foundations of every ancient city, empire, people, promising safe guidance through the limitless spaces of the future. Without ever relating facts reliably, yet always expressing their true significance, they offered a truth beyond realities, a remembrance beyond memories.

Legendary explanations of history always served as belated corrections of facts and real events, which were needed precisely because history itself would hold man responsible for deeds he had not done and for consequences he had never foreseen. The truth of the ancient legends – what gives them their fascinating actuality many centuries after the cities and empires and peoples they served have crumbled to dust – was nothing but the form in which past events were made to fit the human condition in general and political aspirations in particular. Only in the frankly invented tale about events did man consent to assume his responsibility for them, and to consider past events *his* past. Legends made him master of what he had not done, and capable of dealing with what he could not undo. In this sense, legends are not only among the first memories of mankind, but actually the true beginning of human history.

The flourishing of historical and political legends came to a rather abrupt end with the birth of Christianity. Its interpretation of history, from the days of Adam to the Last Judgment, as one single road to redemption and salvation, offered the most powerful and all-inclusive legendary explanation of human destiny. Only after the spiritual unity of Christian peoples gave way to the plurality of nations, when the road to salvation became an uncertain article of individual faith rather than a universal theory applicable to all happenings, did new kinds of historical explanations emerge. The nineteenth century has offered us the curious spectacle of an almost simultaneous birth of the most varying and contradictory ideologies, each of which claimed to know the hidden truth about otherwise incomprehensible facts. Legends, however, are not ideologies; they do not aim at universal explanation but are always concerned with concrete facts. It seems rather significant that the growth of national bodies was nowhere accompanied by a foundation legend, and that a first unique attempt in modern times was made precisely when the decline of the national body had become obvious and imperialism seemed to take the place of old-fashioned nationalism.

The author of the imperialist legend is Rudyard Kipling, its topic is the British Empire, its result the imperialist character (imperialism was the only school of character in modern politics). And while the legend of the British Empire has little to do with the realities of British imperialism, it forced or deluded into its services the best sons of Eng-land. For legends attract the very best in our times, just as ideologies attract the average, and the whispered tales of gruesome secret pow-ers behind the scenes attract the very worst. No doubt, no political structure could have been more evocative of legendary tales and justi-fications than the British Empire, than the British people's drifting from the conscious founding of colonies into ruling and dominating foreign peoples all over the world.

The foundation legend, as Kipling tells it, starts from the funda-mental reality of the people of the British Isles.[61] Surrounded by the sea, they need and win the help of the three elements of Water, Wind, and Sun through the invention of the Ship. The ship made the always dangerous alliance with the elements possible and made the English-man master of the world. 'You'll win the world,' says Kipling, 'without anyone *caring* how you did it: you'll keep the world without anyone *knowing* how you did it: and you'll carry the world on your backs with-out anyone *seeing* how you did it. But neither you nor your sons will get anything out of that little job except Four Gifts – one for the Sea, one for the Wind, one for the Sun and one for the Ship that carries you . . . For, winning the world, and keeping the world, and carrying the world on their backs – on land, or on sea, or in the air – your sons will always have the Four Gifts. Long-headed and slow-spoken and heavy – damned heavy – in the hand, will they be; and always a little bit to windward of every enemy – that they may be a safeguard to all who pass on the seas on their lawful occasions.'

What brings the little tale of the 'First Sailor' so close to ancient foundation legends is that it presents the British as the only politically mature people, caring for law and burdened with the welfare of the world, in the midst of barbarian tribes who neither care nor know what keeps the world together. Unfortunately this presentation lacked the innate truth of ancient legends; the world cared and knew and saw how they did it and no such tale could ever have convinced the world that they did not 'get anything out of that little job.' Yet there was a certain reality in England herself which corresponded to Kipling's leg-end and made it at all possible, and that was the existence of such

61 Rudyard Kipling, 'The First Sailor,' in *Humorous Tales*, 1891.

virtues as chivalry, nobility, bravery, even though they were utterly out of place in a political reality ruled by Cecil Rhodes or Lord Curzon.

The fact that the 'white man's burden' is either hypocrisy or racism has not prevented a few of the best Englishmen from shouldering the burden in earnest and making themselves the tragic and quixotic fools of imperialism. As real in England as the tradition of hypocrisy is another less obvious one which one is tempted to call a tradition of dragon-slayers who went enthusiastically into far and curious lands to strange and naïve peoples to slay the numerous dragons that had plagued them for centuries. There is more than a grain of truth in Kipling's other tale, 'The Tomb of His Ancestor,'[62] in which the Chinn family 'serve India generation after generation, as dolphins follow in line across the open sea.' They shoot the deer that steals the poor man's crop, teach him the mysteries of better agricultural methods, free him from some of his more harmful superstitions and kill lions and tigers in grand style. Their only reward is indeed a 'tomb of ancestors' and a family legend, believed by the whole Indian tribe, according to which 'the revered ancestor . . . has a tiger of his own – a saddle tiger that he rides round the country whenever he feels inclined.' Unfortunately, this riding around the countryside is 'a sure sign of war or pestilence or – or something,' and in this particular case it is a sign of vaccination. So that Chinn the Youngest, a not very important underling in the hierarchy of the Army Services, but all-important as far as the Indian tribe is concerned, has to shoot the beast of his ancestor so that people can be vaccinated without fear of 'war or pestilence or something.'

As modern life goes, the Chinns indeed 'are luckier than most folks.' Their chance is that they were born into a career that gently and naturally leads them to the realization of the best dreams of youth. When other boys have to forget 'noble dreams,' they happen to be just old enough to translate them into action. And when after thirty years of service they retire, their steamer will pass 'the outward bound troopship, carrying his son eastward to the family duty,' so that the power of old Mr. Chinn's existence as a government-appointed and

62  In *The Day's Work*, 1898.

army-paid dragon-slayer can be imparted to the next generation. No doubt, the British government pays them for their services, but it is not at all clear in whose service they eventually land. There is a strong possibility that they really serve this particular Indian tribe, generation after generation, and it is consoling all around that at least the tribe itself is convinced of this. The fact that the higher services know hardly anything of little Lieutenant Chinn's strange duties and adventures, that they are hardly aware of his being a successful reincarnation of his grandfather, gives his dreamlike double existence an undisturbed basis in reality. He is simply at home in two worlds, separated by water- and gossip-tight walls. Born in 'the heart of the scrubby tigerish country' and educated among his own people in peaceful, well-balanced, ill-informed England, he is ready to live permanently with two peoples and is rooted in and well acquainted with the tradition, language, superstition, and prejudices of both. At a moment's notice he can change from the obedient underling of one of His Majesty's soldiers into an exciting and noble figure in the natives' world, a well-beloved protector of the weak, the dragon-slayer of old tales.

The point is that these queer quixotic protectors of the weak who played their role behind the scenes of official British rule were not so much the product of a primitive people's naïve imagination as of dreams which contained the best of European and Christian traditions, even when they had already deteriorated into the futility of boyhood ideals. It was neither His Majesty's soldier nor the British higher official who could teach the natives something of the greatness of the Western world. Only those who had never been able to outgrow their boyhood ideals and therefore had enlisted in the colonial services were fit for the task. Imperialism to them was nothing but an accidental opportunity to escape a society in which a man had to forget his youth if he wanted to grow up. English society was only too glad to see them depart to faraway countries, a circumstance which permitted the toleration and even the furtherance of boyhood ideals in the public school system; the colonial services took them away from England and prevented, so to speak, their converting the ideals of their boyhood into the mature ideas of men. Strange and curious lands attracted the best of England's youth since the end of the nineteenth century, deprived her society of the most honest and the most dangerous elements, and guaranteed, in addition to this bliss, a certain conservation, or perhaps petrification, of boyhood noblesse which preserved *and* infantilized Western moral standards.

Lord Cromer, secretary to the Viceroy and financial member in the pre-imperialist government of India, still belonged in the category of British dragon-slayers. Led solely by 'the sense of sacrifice' for backward populations and 'the sense of duty' [63] to the glory of Great Britain that 'has given birth to a class of officials who have both the desire and the capacity to govern,' [64] he declined in 1894 the post of Viceroy and refused ten years later the position of Secretary of State for Foreign Affairs. Instead of such honors, which would have satisfied a lesser man, he became the little-publicized and all-powerful British Consul General in Egypt from 1883 to 1907. There he became the first imperialist administrator, certainly 'second to none among those who by their services have glorified the British race';[65] perhaps the last to die in undisturbed pride: 'Let these suffice for Britain's meed – / No nobler price was ever won, / The blessings of a people freed / The consciousness of duty done.' [66]

Cromer went to Egypt because he realized that 'the Englishman straining far over to hold his loved India [has to] plant a firm foot on the banks of the Nile.' [67] Egypt was to him only a means to an end, a necessary expansion for the sake of security for India. At almost the same moment it happened that another Englishman set foot on the African continent, though at its opposite end and for opposite reasons: Cecil Rhodes went to South Africa and saved the Cape colony after it had lost all importance for the Englishman's 'loved India.' Rhodes's ideas on expansion were far more advanced than those of his more respectable colleague in the north; to him expansion did not need to be justified by such sensible motives as the holding of what one already

---

63  Lawrence J. Zetland, *Lord Cromer*, 1932, p. 16.

64  Lord Cromer, 'The Government of Subject Races' in *Edinburgh Review*, January, 1908.

65  Lord Curzon at the unveiling of the memorial tablet for Cromer. See Zetland, *op. cit.*, p. 362.

66  Quoted from a long poem by Cromer. See Zetland, *op. cit.*, pp. 17–18.

67  From a letter Lord Cromer wrote in 1882. *Ibid.*, p. 87.

possessed. 'Expansion was everything' and India, South Africa, and Egypt were equally important or unimportant as stepping-stones in an expansion limited only by the size of the earth. There certainly was an abyss between the vulgar megalomaniac and the educated man of sacrifice and duty; yet they arrived at roughly identical results and were equally responsible for the 'Great Game' of secrecy, which was no less insane and no less detrimental to politics than the phantom world of race.

The outstanding similarity between Rhodes's rule in South Africa and Cromer's domination of Egypt was that both regarded the countries not as desirable ends in themselves but merely as means for some supposedly higher purpose. They were similar therefore in their indifference and aloofness, in their genuine lack of interest in their subjects, an attitude which differed as much from the cruelty and arbitrariness of native despots in Asia as from the exploiting carelessness of conquerors, or the insane and anarchic oppression of one race tribe through another. As soon as Cromer started to rule Egypt for the sake of India, he lost his role of protector of 'backward peoples' and could no longer sincerely believe that 'the self-interest of the subject-races is the principal basis of the whole Imperial fabric.' [68]

Aloofness became the new attitude of all members of the British services; it was a more dangerous form of governing than despotism and arbitrariness because it did not even tolerate that last link between the despot and his subjects, which is formed by bribery and gifts. The very integrity of the British administration made despotic government more inhuman and inaccessible to its subjects than Asiatic rulers or reckless conquerors had ever been.[69] Integrity and aloofness were symbols for an absolute division of interests to the point where they are not even permitted to conflict. In comparison, exploitation, oppression, or corruption look like safeguards of human dignity, because exploiter and exploited, oppressor and oppressed, corruptor and corrupted still live in the same world, still share the same goals, fight each other for the possession of the same things; and it is this

---

68 Lord Cromer, *op. cit.*
69 Bribery 'was perhaps the most human institution among the barbed-wire entanglements of the Russian order.' Moissaye J. Olgin, *The Soul of the Russian Revolution*, New York, 1917.

*tertium comparationis* which aloofness destroyed. Worst of all was the fact that the aloof administrator was hardly aware that he had invented a new form of government but actually believed that his attitude was conditioned by 'the forcible contact with a people living on a lower plane.' So, instead of believing in his individual superiority with some degree of essentially harmless vanity, he felt that he belonged to 'a nation which had reached a comparatively high plane of civilization' [70] and therefore held his position by right of birth, regardless of personal achievements.

Lord Cromer's career is fascinating because it embodies the very turning point from the older colonial to imperialist services. His first reaction to his duties in Egypt was a marked uneasiness and concern about a state of affairs which was not 'annexation' but a 'hybrid form of government to which no name can be given and for which there is no precedent.' [71] In 1885, after two years of service, he still harbored serious doubts about a system in which he was the nominal British Consul General and the actual ruler of Egypt and wrote that a 'highly delicate mechanism [whose] efficient working depends very greatly on the judgment and ability of a few individuals . . . can . . . be justified [only] if we are able to keep before our eyes the possibility of evacuation . . . If that possibility becomes so remote as to be of no practical account . . . it would be better for us . . . to arrange . . . with the other Powers that we should take over the government of the country, guarantee its debt, etc.' [72] No doubt Cromer was right, and either, occupation or evacuation, would have normalized matters. But that 'hybrid form of government' without precedent was to become characteristic of all imperialist enterprise, with the result that a few decades afterwards everybody had lost Cromer's early sound judgment about possible and impossible forms of government, just as there was lost Lord Selbourne's early insight that a race society as a way of life was unprecedented. Nothing could better characterize the initial stage of imperialism than the combination of these two judgments on conditions in Africa: a way of life without precedent in the south, a government without precedent in the north.

70 Zetland, *op. cit.*, p. 89.
71 From a letter Lord Cromer wrote in 1884. *Ibid.*, p. 117.
72 In a letter to Lord Granville, a member of the Liberal Party, in 1885. *Ibid.*, p. 219.

In the following years, Cromer reconciled himself to the 'hybrid form of government'; in his letters he began to justify it and to expound the need for the government without name and precedent. At the end of his life, he laid down (in his essay on 'The Government of Subject Races') the main lines of what one may well call a philosophy of the bureaucrat.

Cromer started by recognizing that 'personal influence' without a legal or written political treaty could be enough for 'sufficiently effective supervision over public affairs'[73] in foreign countries. This kind of informal influence was preferable to a well-defined policy because it could be altered at a moment's notice and did not necessarily involve the home government in case of difficulties. It required a highly trained, highly reliable staff whose loyalty and patriotism were not connected with personal ambition or vanity and who would even be required to renounce the human aspiration of having their names connected with their achievements. Their greatest passion would have to be for secrecy ('the less British officials are talked about the better'),[74] for a role behind the scenes; their greatest contempt would be directed at publicity and people who love it.

Cromer himself possessed all these qualities to a very high degree; his wrath was never more strongly aroused than when he was 'brought out of [his] hiding place,' when 'the reality which before was only known to a few behind the scenes [became] patent to all the world.'[75] His pride was indeed to 'remain more or less hidden [and] to pull the strings.'[76] In exchange, and in order to make his work possible at all, the bureaucrat has to feel safe from control – the praise as well as the blame, that is – of all public institutions, either Parliament, the 'English Departments,' or the press. Every growth of democracy or even the simple functioning of existing democratic institutions can only be a danger, for it is impossible to govern 'a people by a people – the people of India by the people of England.'[77] Bureaucracy is always a government of experts, of an 'experienced minority' which has to resist as well as it knows how the constant

---

73 From a letter to Lord Rosebery in 1886. *Ibid.*, p. 134.
74 *Ibid.*, p. 352.
75 From a letter to Lord Rosebery in 1893. *Ibid.*, pp. 204–205.
76 From a letter to Lord Rosebery in 1893. *Ibid.*, p. 192.
77 From a speech by Cromer in Parliament after 1904. *Ibid.*, p. 311.

pressure from 'the inexperienced majority.' Each people is fundamentally an inexperienced majority and can therefore not be trusted with such a highly specialized matter as politics and public affairs. Bureaucrats, moreover, are not supposed to have general ideas about political matters at all; their patriotism should never lead them so far astray that they believe in the inherent goodness of political principles in their own country; that would only result in their cheap 'imitative' application 'to the government of backward populations,' which, according to Cromer, was the principal defect of the French system.[78]

Nobody will ever pretend that Cecil Rhodes suffered from a lack of vanity. According to Jameson, he expected to be remembered for at least four thousand years. Yet, despite all his appetite for self-glorification, he hit upon the same idea of rule through secrecy as the overmodest Lord Cromer. Extremely fond of drawing up wills, Rhodes insisted in all of them (over the course of two decades of his public life) that his money should be used to found 'a secret society . . . to carry out his scheme,' which was to be 'organized like Loyola's, supported by the accumulated wealth of those whose aspiration is a desire to do something,' so that eventually there would be 'between two and three thousand men in the prime of life scattered all over the world, each one of whom would have had impressed upon his mind in the most susceptible period of his life the dream of the Founder, each one of whom, moreover, would have been especially – mathematically – selected towards the Founder's purpose.'[79] More farsighted than Cromer, Rhodes opened the society at once to all members of the 'Nordic race'[80] so that the aim was not so much the growth and glory

78 During the negotiations and considerations of the administrative pattern for the annexation of the Sudan, Cromer insisted on keeping the whole matter outside the sphere of French influence; he did this not because he wanted to secure a monopoly in Africa for England but much rather because he had 'the utmost want of confidence in their administrative system as applied to subject races' (from a letter to Salisbury in 1899, *Ibid.*, p. 248).

79 Rhodes drew up six wills (the first was already composed in 1877), all of which mention the 'secret society.' For extensive quotes, see Basil Williams, *Cecil Rhodes*, London, 1921, and Millin, *op. cit.*, pp. 128 and 331. The citations are upon the authority of W. T. Stead.

80 It is well known that Rhodes's 'secret society' ended as the very respectable Rhodes Scholarship Association to which even today not only Englishmen but members of all 'Nordic races,' such as Germans, Scandinavians, and Americans, are admitted.

of Great Britain – her occupation of the 'entire continent of Africa, the Holy Land, the valley of the Euphrates, the islands of Cyprus and Candia, the whole of South America, the islands of the Pacific . . . the whole of the Malay Archipelago, the seaboards of China and Japan [and] the ultimate recovery of the United States'[81] – as the expansion of the 'Nordic race' which, organized in a secret society, would establish a bureaucratic government over all peoples of the earth.

What overcame Rhodes's monstrous innate vanity and made him discover the charms of secrecy was the same thing that overcame Cromer's innate sense of duty: the discovery of an expansion which was not driven by the specific appetite for a specific country but conceived as an endless process in which every country would serve only as stepping-stone for further expansion. In view of such a concept, the desire for glory can no longer be satisfied by the glorious triumph over a specific people for the sake of one's own people, nor can the sense of duty be fulfilled through the consciousness of specific services and the fulfillment of specific tasks. No matter what individual qualities or defects a man may have, once he has entered the maelstrom of an unending process of expansion, he will, as it were, cease to be what he was and obey the laws of the process, identify himself with anonymous forces that he is supposed to serve in order to keep the whole process in motion; he will think of himself as mere function, and eventually consider such functionality, such an incarnation of the dynamic trend, his highest possible achievement. Then, as Rhodes was insane enough to say, he could indeed 'do nothing wrong, what he did became right. It was his duty to do what he wanted. He felt himself a god – nothing less.'[82] But Lord Cromer sanely pointed out the same phenomenon of men degrading themselves voluntarily into mere instruments or mere functions when he called the bureaucrats 'instruments of incomparable value in the execution of a policy of Imperialism.'[83]

It is obvious that these secret and anonymous agents of the force of expansion felt no obligation to man-made laws. The only 'law' they obeyed was the 'law' of expansion, and the only proof of their

81 Basil Williams, op. cit., p. 51.
82 Millin, op. cit., p. 92.
83 Cromer, op. cit.

'lawfulness' was success. They had to be perfectly willing to disappear into complete oblivion once failure had been proved, if for any reason they were no longer 'instruments of incomparable value.' As long as they were successful, the feeling of embodying forces greater than themselves made it relatively easy to resign and even to despise applause and glorification. They were monsters of conceit in their success and monsters of modesty in their failure.

At the basis of bureaucracy as a form of government, and of its inherent replacement of law with temporary and changing decrees, lies this superstition of a possible and magic identification of man with the forces of history. The ideal of such a political body will always be the man behind the scenes who pulls the strings of history. Cromer finally shunned every 'written instrument, or, indeed, anything which is tangible' [84] in his relationships with Egypt – even a proclamation of annexation – in order to be free to obey only the law of expansion, without obligation to a man-made treaty. Thus does the bureaucrat shun every general law, handling each situation separately by decree, because a law's inherent stability threatens to establish a permanent community in which nobody could possibly be a god because all would have to obey a law.

The two key figures in this system, whose very essence is aimless process, are the bureaucrat on one side and the secret agent on the other. Both types, as long as they served only British imperialism, never quite denied that they were descended from dragon-slayers and protectors of the weak and therefore never drove bureaucratic regimes to their inherent extremes. A British bureaucrat almost two decades after Cromer's death knew 'administrative massacres' could keep India within the British Empire, but he knew also how utopian it would be to try to get the support of the hated 'English Departments' for an otherwise quite realistic plan. [85] Lord Curzon, Viceroy of India,

---

84 From a letter of Lord Cromer to Lord Rosebery in 1886. Zetland, *op. cit.*, p. 134.
85 'The Indian system of government by reports was . . . suspect [in England]. There was no trial by jury in India and the judges were all paid servants of the Crown, many of them removable at pleasure . . . Some of the men of formal law felt rather uneasy as to the success of the Indian experiment. "If," they said, "despotism and bureaucracy work so well in India, may not that be perhaps at some time used as an argument for

showed nothing of Cromer's noblesse and was quite characteristic of a society that increasingly inclined to accept the mob's race standards if they were offered in the form of fashionable snobbery.[86] But snobbery is incompatible with fanaticism and therefore never really efficient.

The same is true of the members of the British Secret Service. They too are of illustrious origin – what the dragon-slayer was to the bureaucrat, the adventurer is to the secret agent – and they too can rightly lay claim to a foundation legend, the legend of the Great Game as told by Rudyard Kipling in *Kim*.

Of course every adventurer knows what Kipling means when he praises Kim because 'what he loved was the game for its own sake.' Every person still able to wonder at 'this great and wonderful world' knows that it is hardly an argument against the game when 'missionaries and secretaries of charitable societies could not see the beauty of it.' Still less, it seems, have those a right to speak who think it 'a sin to kiss a white girl's mouth and a virtue to kiss a black man's shoe.'[87] Since life itself ultimately has to be lived and loved for its own sake, adventure and love of the game for its own sake easily appear to be a most intensely human symbol of life. It is this underlying passionate humanity that makes *Kim* the only novel of the imperialist era in which a genuine brotherhood links together the 'higher and lower breeds,' in which Kim, 'a Sahib and the son of a Sahib,' can rightly talk of 'us' when he talks of the 'chain-men,' 'all on one lead-rope.' There is more to this 'we' – strange in the mouth of a believer in imperialism – than the all-enveloping anonymity of men who are proud to have 'no name, but only a number and a letter,' more than the common pride of

---

introducing something of the same system here?"' The government of India, at any rate, 'knew well enough that it would have to justify its existence and its policy before public opinion in England, and it well knew that that public opinion would never tolerate oppression' (A. Carthill, *op. cit.*, pp. 70 and 41–42).

86 Harold Nicolson in his *Curzon: The Last Phase 1919–1925*, Boston–New York, 1934, tells the following story: 'Behind the lines in Flanders was a large brewery in the vats of which the private soldiers would bathe on returning from the trenches. Curzon was taken to see this dantesque exhibit. He watched with interest those hundred naked figures disporting themselves in the steam. "Dear me!," he said, "I had no conception that the lower classes had such white skins." Curzon would deny the authenticity of this story but loved it none the less' (pp. 47–48).

87 Carthill, *op. cit.*, p. 88.

having 'a price upon [one's] head.' What makes them comrades is the common experience of being – through danger, fear, constant surprise, utter lack of habits, constant preparedness to change their identities – symbols of life itself, symbols, for instance, of happenings all over India, immediately sharing the life of it all as 'it runs like a shuttle throughout all Hind,' and therefore no longer 'alone, one person, in the middle of it all,' trapped, as it were, by the limitations of one's own individuality or nationality. Playing the Great Game, a man may feel as though he lives the only life worth while because he has been stripped of everything which may still be considered to be accessory. Life itself seems to be left, in a fantastically intensified purity, when man has cut himself off from all ordinary social ties, family, regular occupation, a definite goal, ambitions, and the guarded place in a community to which he belongs by birth. 'When every one is dead the Great Game is finished. Not before.' When one is dead, life is finished, not before, not when one happens to achieve whatever he may have wanted. That the game has no ultimate purpose makes it so dangerously similar to life itself.

Purposelessness is the very charm of Kim's existence. Not for the sake of England did he accept his strange duties, nor for the sake of India, nor for any other worthy or unworthy cause. Imperialist notions like expansion for expansion's or power for power's sake might have suited him, but he would not have cared particularly and certainly would not have constructed any such formula. He stepped into his peculiar way of 'theirs not to reason why, theirs but to do and die' without even asking the first question. He was tempted only by the basic endlessness of the game and by secrecy as such. And secrecy again seems like a symbol of the basic mysteriousness of life.

Somehow it was not the fault of the born adventurers, of those who by their very nature dwelt outside society and outside all political bodies, that they found in imperialism a political game that was endless by definition; they were not supposed to know that in politics an endless game can end only in catastrophe and that political secrecy hardly ever ends in anything nobler than the vulgar duplicity of a spy. The joke on these players of the Great Game was that their employers knew what they wanted and used their passion for anonymity for ordinary spying. But this triumph of the profit-hungry investors was temporary, and they were duly cheated when a few decades later they met the players of the game of totalitarianism, a game played without ulterior motives like profit and therefore played with such murderous efficiency that it devoured even those who financed it.

Before this happened, however, the imperialists had destroyed the best man who ever turned from an adventurer (with a strong mixture of dragon-slayer) into a secret agent, Lawrence of Arabia. Never again was the experiment of secret politics made more purely by a more decent man. Lawrence experimented fearlessly upon himself, and then came back and believed that he belonged to the 'lost generation.' He thought this was because 'the old men came out again and took from us our victory' in order to 're-make [the world] in the likeness of the former world they knew.' [88] Actually the old men were quite in-efficient even in this, and handed their victory, together with their power, down to other men of the same 'lost generation,' who were neither older nor so dissimilar to Lawrence. The only difference was that Lawrence still clung fast to a morality which, however, had already lost all objective bases and consisted only of a kind of private and necessarily quixotic attitude of chivalry.

Lawrence was seduced into becoming a secret agent in Arabia because of his strong desire to leave the world of dull respectability whose conti-nuity had become simply meaningless, because of his disgust with the world as well as with himself. What attracted him most in Arab civiliza-tion was its 'gospel of bareness . . . [which] involves apparently a sort of moral bareness too,' which 'has refined itself clear of household gods.' [89] What he tried to avoid most of all after he had returned to English civil-ization was living a life of his own, so that he ended with an apparently incomprehensible enlistment as a private in the British army, which obvi-ously was the only institution in which a man's honor could be identified with the loss of his individual personality.

When the outbreak of the first World War sent T. E. Lawrence to the Arabs of the Near East with the assignment to rouse them into a rebellion against their Turkish masters and make them fight on the

88  T. E. Lawrence, *Seven Pillars of Wisdom*, Introduction (first edition, 1926) which was omitted on the advice of George Bernard Shaw from the later edition. See T. E. Law-rence, *Letters*, edited by David Garnett, New York, 1939, pp. 262 ff.

89  From a letter written in 1918. *Letters*, p. 244.

British side, he came into the very midst of the Great Game. He could achieve his purpose only if a national movement was stirred up among Arab tribes, a national movement that ultimately was to serve British imperialism. Lawrence had to behave as though the Arab national movement were his prime interest, and he did it so well that he came to believe in it himself. But then again he did not belong, he was ultimately unable 'to think their thought' and to 'assume their character.'[90] Pretending to be an Arab, he could only lose his 'English self'[91] and was fascinated by the complete secrecy of self-effacement rather than fooled by the obvious justifications of benevolent rule over backward peoples that Lord Cromer might have used. One generation older and sadder than Cromer, he took great delight in a role that demanded a reconditioning of his whole personality until he fitted into the Great Game, until he became the incarnation of the force of the Arab national movement, until he lost all natural vanity in his mysterious alliance with forces necessarily bigger than himself, no matter how big he could have been, until he acquired a deadly 'contempt, not for other men, but for all they do' on their own initiative and not in alliance with the forces of history.

When, at the end of the war, Lawrence had to abandon the pretenses of a secret agent and somehow recover his 'English self,'[92] he 'looked at the West and its conventions with new eyes: they destroyed it all for me.'[93] From the Great Game of incalculable bigness, which no publicity had glorified or limited and which had elevated him, in his twenties, above kings and prime ministers because he had 'made 'em or played with them,'[94] Lawrence came home with an obsessive desire

90 T. E. Lawrence, *Seven Pillars of Wisdom*, Garden City, 1938, chapter i.
91 *Ibid.*
92 How ambiguous and how difficult a process this must have been is illustrated by the following anecdote: 'Lawrence had accepted an invitation to dinner at Claridge's and a party afterwards at Mrs. Harry Lindsay's. He shirked the dinner, but came to the party in Arab dresses.' This happened in 1919. *Letters*, p. 272, note 1.
93 Lawrence, *op. cit.*, ch. i.
94 Lawrence wrote in 1929: 'Anyone who had gone up so fast as I went . . . and had seen so much of the inside of the top of the world might well lose his aspirations, and get weary of the ordinary motives of action, which had moved him till he reached the top. I wasn't King or Prime Minister, but I made 'em, or played with them, and after that there wasn't much more, in that direction, for me to do' (*Letters*, p. 653).

for anonymity and the deep conviction that nothing he could possibly still do with his life would ever satisfy him. This conclusion he drew from his perfect knowledge that it was not he who had been big, but only the role he had aptly assumed, that his bigness had been the result of the Game and not a product of himself. Now he did not 'want to be big any more' and, determined that he was not 'going to be respectable again,' he thus was indeed 'cured . . . of any desire ever to do anything for myself.'[95] He had been the phantom of a force, and he became a phantom among the living when the force, the function, was taken away from him. What he was frantically looking for was another role to play, and this incidentally was the 'game' about which George Bernard Shaw inquired so kindly but uncomprehendingly, as though he spoke from another century, not understanding why a man of such great achievements should not own up to them.[96] Only another role, another function would be strong enough to prevent himself and the world from identifying him with his deeds in Arabia, from replacing his old self with a new personality. He did not want to become 'Lawrence of Arabia,' since, fundamentally, he did not want to regain a new self after having lost the old. His greatness was that he was passionate enough to refuse cheap compromises and easy roads into reality and respectability, that he never lost his awareness that he had been only a function and had played a role and therefore 'must not benefit in any way from what he had done in Arabia. The honors which he had won were refused. The jobs offered on account of his reputation had to be declined nor would he allow himself to exploit his success by profiting from writing a single paid piece of journalism under the name of Lawrence.'[97]

The story of T. E. Lawrence in all its moving bitterness and greatness was not simply the story of a paid official or a hired spy, but precisely the story of a real agent or functionary, of somebody who actually believed he had entered – or been driven into – the stream of

95 *Ibid.*, pp. 244, 447, 450. Compare especially the letter of 1918 (p. 244) with the two letters to George Bernard Shaw of 1923 (p. 447) and 1928 (p. 616).
96 George Bernard Shaw, asking Lawrence in 1928 'What is your game *really?*', suggested that his role in the army or his looking for a job as a night-watchman (for which he could 'get good references') were not authentic.
97 Garnett, *op. cit.*, p. 264.

historical necessity and become a functionary or agent of the secret forces which rule the world. 'I had pushed my go-cart into the eternal stream, and so it went faster than the ones that are pushed cross-stream or up-stream. I did not believe finally in the Arab movement: but thought it necessary in its time and place.'[98] Just as Cromer had ruled Egypt for the sake of India, or Rhodes South Africa for the sake of further expansion, Lawrence had acted for some ulterior unpredictable purpose. The only satisfaction he could get out of this, lacking the calm good conscience of some limited achievement, came from the sense of functioning itself, from being embraced and driven by some big movement. Back in London and in despair, he would try to find some substitute for this kind of 'self-satisfaction' and would 'only get it out of hot speed on a motor-bike.'[99] Although Lawrence had not yet been seized by the fanaticism of an ideology of movement, probably because he was too well educated for the superstitions of his time, he had already experienced that fascination, based on despair of all possible human responsibility, which the eternal stream and its eternal movement exert. He drowned himself in it and nothing was left of him but some inexplicable decency and a pride in having 'pushed the right way.' 'I am still puzzled as to how far the individual counts: a lot, I fancy, if he pushes the right way.'[100] This, then, is the end of the real pride of Western man who no longer counts as an end in himself, no longer does 'a thing of himself nor a thing so clean as to be his own'[101] by giving laws to the world, but has a chance only 'if he pushes the right way,' in alliance with the secret forces of history and necessity – of which he is but a function.

When the European mob discovered what a 'lovely virtue' a white skin could be in Africa,[102] when the English conqueror in India became an administrator who no longer believed in the universal validity of law, but was convinced of his own innate capacity to rule and dominate, when the dragon-slayers turned into either 'white men' of 'higher

98  *Letters*, in 1930, p. 693.
99  *Ibid.*, in 1924, p. 456.
100  *Ibid.*, p. 693.
101  Lawrence, *op. cit.*, chapter i.
102  Millin, *op. cit.*, p. 15.

breeds' or into bureaucrats and spies, playing the Great Game of endless ulterior motives in an endless movement; when the British Intelligence Services (especially after the first World War) began to attract England's best sons, who preferred serving mysterious forces all over the world to serving the common good of their country, the stage seemed to be set for all possible horrors. Lying under anybody's nose were many of the elements which gathered together could create a totalitarian government on the basis of racism. 'Administrative massacres' were proposed by Indian bureaucrats while African officials declared that 'no ethical considerations such as the rights of man will be allowed to stand in the way' of white rule.[103]

The happy fact is that although British imperialist rule sank to some level of vulgarity, cruelty played a lesser role between the two World Wars than ever before and a minimum of human rights was always safeguarded. It is this moderation in the midst of plain insanity that paved the way for what Churchill has called 'the liquidation of His Majesty's Empire' and that eventually may turn out to mean the transformation of the English nation into a Commonwealth of English peoples.

---

103 As put by Sir Thomas Watt, a citizen of South Africa, of British descent. See Barnes, *op. cit.*, p. 230.

# CHAPTER EIGHT

# Continental Imperialism: the Pan-Movements

Nazism and Bolshevism owe more to Pan-Germanism and Pan-Slavism (respectively) than to any other ideology or political movement. This is most evident in foreign policies, where the strategies of Nazi Germany and Soviet Russia have followed so closely the well-known programs of conquest outlined by the pan-movements before and during the first World War that totalitarian aims have frequently been mistaken for the pursuance of some permanent German or Russian interests. While neither Hitler nor Stalin has ever acknowledged his debt to imperialism in the development of his methods of rule, neither has hesitated to admit his indebtedness to the pan-movements' ideology or to imitate their slogans.[1]

The birth of the pan-movements did not coincide with the birth of imperialism; around 1870, Pan-Slavism had already outgrown the vague and confused theories of the Slavophiles,[2] and Pan-German sentiment was current in Austria as early as the middle of the nineteenth century. They crystallized into movements, however, and captured

---

1 Hitler wrote in *Mein Kampf* (New York, 1939): In Vienna, 'I laid the foundations for a world concept in general and a way of political thinking in particular which I had later only to complete in detail, but which never afterward forsook me' (p. 129). – Stalin came back to Pan-Slav slogans during the last war. The 1945 Pan-Slav Congress in Sofia, which had been called by the victorious Russians, adopted a resolution pronouncing it 'not only an international political necessity to declare Russian its language of general communication and the official language of all Slav countries, but a moral necessity.' (See *Aufbau*, New York, April 6, 1945.) Shortly before, the Bulgarian radio had broadcast a message by the Metropolitan Stefan, vicar of the Holy Bulgarian Synod, in which he called upon the Russian people 'to remember their messianic mission' and prophesied the coming 'unity of the Slav people.' (See *Politics*, January, 1945.)

2 For an exhaustive presentation and discussion of the Slavophiles see Alexandre Koyré, *La philosophie et le problème national en Russie au début du 19e siècle* (Institut Français de Leningrad, Bibliothèque Vol. X, Paris, 1929).

the imagination of broader strata only with the triumphant imperialist expansion of the Western nations in the eighties. The Central and Eastern European nations, which had no colonial possessions and little hope for overseas expansion, now decided that they 'had the same right to expand as other great peoples and that if [they were] not granted this possibility overseas, [they would] be forced to do it in Europe.'[3] Pan-Germans and Pan-Slavs agreed that, living in 'continental states' and being 'continental peoples,' they had to look for colonies on the continent,[4] to expand in geographic continuity from a center of power,[5] that against 'the idea of England . . . expressed by the words: I want to rule the sea, [stands] the idea of Russia [expressed] by the words: I want to rule the land,'[6] and that eventually the 'tremendous superiority of the land to the sea . . . the superior significance of land power to sea power . . . ,' would become apparent.[7]

The chief importance of continental, as distinguished from overseas, imperialism lies in the fact that its concept of cohesive expansion does not allow for any geographic distance between the methods and institutions of colony and of nation, so that it did not require boomerang effects in order to make itself and all its consequences felt in

3 Ernst Hasse, *Deutsche Politik*, 4. Heft: *Die Zukunft des deutschen Volkstums*, 1907, p. 132.
4 *Ibid.*, 3. Heft. *Deutsche Grenzpolitik*, pp. 167–168. Geopolitical theories of this kind were current among the Alldeutschen, the members of the Pan-German League. They always compared Germany's geopolitical needs with those of Russia. Austrian Pan-Germans characteristically never drew such a parallel.
5 The Slavophile writer Danilewski, whose *Russia and Europe* (1871) became the standard work of Pan-Slavism, praised the Russians' 'political capacity' because of their 'tremendous thousand-year-old state that still grows and whose power does not expand like the European power in a colonial way but remains always concentrated around its nucleus, Moscow.' See K. Staehlin, *Geschichte Russlands von den Anfängen bis zur Gegenwart*, 1923–1939, 5 vols., IV/I, 274.
6 The quotation is from J. Slowacki, a Polish publicist who wrote in the forties. See N. O. Lossky, *Three Chapters from the History of Polish Messianism*, Prague, 1936, in International Philosophical Library, II, 9.
Pan-Slavism, the first of the pan-isms (see Hoetzsch, *Russland*, Berlin, 1913, p. 439), expressed these geopolitical theories almost forty years before Pan-Germanism began to 'think in continents.' The contrast between English sea power and continental land power was so conspicuous that it would be far-fetched to look for influences.
7 Reismann-Grone, *Ueberseepolitik oder Festlandspolitik?*, 1905, in Alldeutsche Flugschriften, No. 22, p. 17.

Europe. Continental imperialism truly begins at home.[8] If it shared
with overseas imperialism the contempt for the narrowness of the
nation-state, it opposed to it not so much economic arguments, which
after all quite frequently expressed authentic national needs, as an
'enlarged tribal consciousness'[9] which was supposed to unite all
people of similar folk origin, independent of history and no matter
where they happened to live.[10] Continental imperialism, therefore,
started with a much closer affinity to race concepts, enthusiastically
absorbed the tradition of race-thinking,[11] and relied very little on specific experiences. Its race concepts were completely ideological in basis
and developed much more quickly into a convenient political weapon
than similar theories expressed by overseas imperialists which could
always claim a certain basis in authentic experience.

The pan-movements have generally been given scant attention in the
discussion of imperialism. Their dreams of continental empires were
overshadowed by the more tangible results of overseas expansion, and

8 Ernst Hasse of the Pan-German League proposed to treat certain nationalities
(Poles, Czechs, Jews, Italians, etc.) in the same way as overseas imperialism treated
natives in non-European continents. See *Deutsche Politik*, 1. Heft: *Das Deutsche Reich als
Nationalstaat*, 1905, p. 62. This is the chief difference between the Pan-German League,
founded in 1886, and earlier colonial societies such as the Central-Verein für Handelsgeographie (founded in 1863). A very reliable description of the activities of the
Pan-German League is given in Mildred S. Wertheimer, *The Pan-German League*,
*1890–1914*, 1924.

9 Emil Deckert, *Panlatinismus, Panslawismus und Panteutonismus in ihrer Bedeutung für
die politische Weltlage*, Frankfurt a/M, 1914, p. 4.

10 Pan-Germans already talked before the first World War of the distinction between
'Staatsfremde,' people of Germanic origin who happened to live under the authority of
another country, and 'Volksfremde,' people of non-Germanic origin who happened to
live in Germany. See Daniel Frymann (pseud. for Heinrich Class), *Wenn ich der Kaiser
wär. Politische Wahrheiten und Notwendigkeiten*, 1912.

When Austria was incorporated into the Third Reich, Hitler addressed the German
people of Austria with typically Pan-German slogans. 'Wherever we may have been
born,' he told them, we are all 'the sons of the German people.' *Hitler's Speeches*, ed. by
N. H. Baynes, 1942, II, 1408.

11 Th. G. Masaryk, *Zur russischen Geschichts- und Religionsphilosophie* (1913), describes
the 'zoological nationalism' of the Slavophiles since Danilewski (p. 257). Otto Bonhard,
official historian of the Pan-German League, stated the close relationship between its
ideology and the racism of Gobineau and H. S. Chamberlain. See *Geschichte des alldeutschen Verbandes*, 1920, p. 95.

their lack of interest in economics[12] stood in ridiculous contrast to the tremendous profits of early imperialism. Moreover, in a period when almost everybody had come to believe that politics and economics were more or less the same thing, it was easy to overlook the similarities as well as the significant differences between the two brands of imperialism. The protagonists of the pan-movements share with Western imperialists that awareness of all foreign-policy issues which had been forgotten by the older ruling groups of the nation-state.[13] Their influence on intellectuals was even more pronounced – the Russian intelligentsia, with only a few exceptions, was Pan-Slavic, and Pan-Germanism started in Austria almost as a students' movement.[14] Their chief difference from the more respectable imperialism of the Western nations was the lack of capitalist support; their attempts to expand were not and could not be preceded by export of superfluous money and superfluous men, because Europe did not offer colonial opportunities for either. Among their leaders, we find therefore almost no businessmen and few adventurers, but many members of the free professions, teachers, and civil servants.[15]

While overseas imperialism, its antinational tendencies notwithstanding, succeeded in giving a new lease on life to the antiquated institutions of the nation-state, continental imperialism was and remained unequivocally hostile to all existing political bodies. Its

12 An exception is Friedrich Naumann, *Central Europe* (London, 1916), who wanted to replace the many nationalities in Central Europe with one united 'economic people' (*Wirtschaftsvolk*) under German leadership. Although his book was a bestseller throughout the first World War, it influenced only the Austrian Social Democratic Party; see Karl Renner, *Oesterreichs Erneuerung. Politisch-programmatische Aufsätze*, Vienna, 1916, pp. 37 ff.

13 'At least before the war, the interest of the great parties in foreign affairs had been completely overshadowed by domestic issues. The Pan-German League's attitude is different and this is undoubtedly a propaganda asset' (Martin Wenck, *Alldeutsche Taktik*, 1917).

14 See Paul Molisch, *Geschichte der deutschnationalen Bewegung in Oesterreich*, Jena, 1926, p. 90: It is a fact 'that the student body does not at all simply mirror the general political constellation; on the contrary, strong Pan-German opinions have largely originated in the student body and thence found their way into general politics.'

15 Useful information about the social composition of the membership of the Pan-German League, its local and executive officers, can be found in Wertheimer, *op. cit.* See also Lothar Werner, *Der alldeutsche Verband, 1890–1918*, Historische Studien, Heft 278, Berlin, 1935, and Gottfried Nippold, *Der deutsche Chauvinismus*, 1913, pp. 179 ff.

general mood, therefore, was far more rebellious and its leaders far more adept at revolutionary rhetoric. While overseas imperialism had offered real enough panaceas for the residues of all classes, continental imperialism had nothing to offer except an ideology and a movement. Yet this was quite enough in a time which preferred a key to history to political action, when men in the midst of communal disintegration and social atomization wanted to belong at any price. Similarly, the visible distinction of a white skin, whose advantages in a black or brown environment are easily understood, could be matched success-fully by a purely imaginary distinction between an Eastern and a Western, or an Aryan and a non-Aryan soul. The point is that a rather complicated ideology and an organization which furthered no imme-diate interest proved to be more attractive than tangible advantages and commonplace convictions.

Despite their lack of success, with its proverbial appeal to the mob, the pan-movements exerted from the beginning a much stronger attraction than overseas imperialism. This popular appeal, which withstood tangible failures and constant changes of program, fore-shadowed later totalitarian groups which were similarly vague as to actual goals and subject to day-to-day changes of political lines. What held the pan-movements' membership together was much more a general mood than a clearly defined aim. It is true that overseas imper-ialism also placed expansion as such above any program of conquest and therefore took possession of every territory that offered itself as an easy opportunity. Yet, however capricious the export of superfluous money may have been, it served to delimit the ensuing expansion; the aims of the pan-movements lacked even this rather anarchic element of human planning and geographic restraint. Yet, though they had no specific programs for world conquest, they generated an all-embracing mood of total predominance, of touching and embracing all human issues, of 'pan-humanism,' as Dostoevski once put it.[16]

In the imperialist alliance between mob and capital, the initiative lay mostly with the representatives of business – except in the case of South Africa, where a clear-cut mob policy developed very early. In the pan-movements, on the other hand, the initiative always lay exclusively

16 Quoted from Hans Kohn, 'The Permanent Mission' in *The Review of Politics*, July, 1948.

with the mob, which was led then (as today) by a certain brand of intellectuals. They still lacked the ambition to rule the globe, and they did not even dream of the possibilities of total domination. But they did know how to organize the mob, and they were aware of the organizational, not merely ideological or propaganda, uses to which race concepts can be put. Their significance is only superficially grasped in the relatively modest theories of foreign policy – a Germanized Central Europe or a Russianized Eastern and Southern Europe – which served as starting points for the world-conquest programs of Nazism and Bolshevism.[17] The 'Germanic peoples' outside the Reich and 'our minor Slavonic brethren' outside Holy Russia generated a comfortable smoke screen of national rights to self-determination, easy stepping-stones to further expansion. Yet, much more essential was the fact that the totalitarian governments inherited an aura of holiness: they had only to invoke the past of 'Holy Russia' or 'the Holy Roman Empire' to arouse all kinds of superstitions in Slav or German intellectuals.[18] Pseudomystical nonsense, enriched by countless and arbitrary historical memories, provided an emotional appeal that seemed to transcend, in depth and breadth, the limitations of nationalism. Out of it, at any rate, grew that new kind of nationalist feeling whose violence proved an excellent motor to set mob masses in motion and quite adequate to replace the older national patriotism as an emotional center.

This new type of tribal nationalism, more or less characteristic of all Central and Eastern European nations and nationalities, was quite different in content and significance – though not in violence – from Western nationalist excesses. Chauvinism – now usually thought of in connection with the *'nationalisme intégral'* of Maurras and Barrès around the turn of the century, with its romantic glorification of the past and its morbid cult of the dead – even in its most wildly fantastic

17 Danilewski, *op. cit.*, included in a future Russian empire all Balkan countries, Turkey, Hungary, Czechoslovakia, Galicia, and Istria with Trieste.
18 The Slavophile K. S. Aksakow, writing in the middle of the nineteenth century, took the official name 'Holy Russia' quite literally, as did later Pan-Slavs. See Th. G. Masaryk, *op. cit.*, pp. 234 ff. – Very characteristic of the vague nonsense of Pan-Germanism is Moeller van den Bruck, *Germany's Third Empire* (New York, 1934), in which he proclaims: 'There is only One Empire, as there is only One Church. Anything else that claims the title may be a state or a community or a sect. There exists only The Empire' (p. 263).

manifestations, did not hold that men of French origin, born and raised in another country, without any knowledge of French language or culture, would be 'born Frenchmen' thanks to some mysterious qualities of body or soul. Only with the 'enlarged tribal consciousness' did that peculiar identification of nationality with one's own soul emerge, that turned-inward pride that is no longer concerned only with public affairs but pervades every phase of private life until, for example, 'the private life of each true Pole . . . is a public life of Polishness.'[19]

In psychological terms, the chief difference between even the most violent chauvinism and this tribal nationalism is that the one is extroverted, concerned with visible spiritual and material achievements of the nation, whereas the other, even in its mildest forms (for example, the German youth movement) is introverted, concentrates on the individual's own soul which is considered as the embodiment of general national qualities. Chauvinist mystique still points to something that really existed in the past (as in the case of the *nationalisme intégral*) and merely tries to elevate this into a realm beyond human control; tribalism, on the other hand, starts from non-existent pseudomystical elements which it proposes to realize fully in the future. It can be easily recognized by the tremendous arrogance, inherent in its self-concentration, which dares to measure a people, its past and present, by the yardstick of exalted inner qualities and inevitably rejects its visible existence, tradition, institutions, and culture.

Politically speaking, tribal nationalism always insists that its own people is surrounded by 'a world of enemies,' 'one against all,' that a fundamental difference exists between this people and all others. It claims its people to be unique, individual, incompatible with all others, and denies theoretically the very possibility of a common mankind long before it is used to destroy the humanity of man.

## I: Tribal Nationalism

Just as continental imperialism sprang from the frustrated ambitions of countries which did not get their share in the sudden expansion of

19  George Cleinow, *Die Zukunft Polens*, Leipzig, 1914, II, 93 ff.

the eighties, so tribalism appeared as the nationalism of those peoples who had not participated in national emancipation and had not achieved the sovereignty of a nation-state. Wherever the two frustrations were combined, as in multinational Austria-Hungary and Russia, the pan-movements naturally found their most fertile soil. Moreover, since the Dual Monarchy harbored both Slavic and German irredentist nationalities, Pan-Slavism and Pan-Germanism concentrated from the beginning on its destruction, and Austria-Hungary became the real center of pan-movements. Russian Pan-Slavs claimed as early as 1870 that the best possible starting point for a Pan-Slav empire would be the disintegration of Austria,[20] and Austrian Pan-Germans were so violently aggressive against their own government that even the Alldeutsche Verband in Germany complained frequently about the 'exaggerations' of the Austrian brother movement.[21] The German-conceived blueprint for the economic union of Central Europe under German leadership, along with all similar continental-empire projects of the German Pan-Germans, changed at once, when Austrian Pan-Germans got hold of it, into a structure that would become 'the center of German life all over the earth and be allied with all other Germanic states.'[22]

It is self-evident that the expansionist tendencies of Pan-Slavism were as embarrassing to the Czar as the Austrian Pan-Germans' unsolicited professions of loyalty to the Reich and disloyalty to Austria were to Bismarck.[23] For no matter how high national feelings

20  During the Crimean War (1853–1856) Michael Pagodin, a Russian folklorist and philologist, wrote a letter to the Czar in which he called the Slav peoples Russia's only reliable powerful allies (Staehlin, *op. cit.*, p. 35); shortly thereafter General Nikolai Muravyev-Amursky, 'one of the great Russian empire-builders,' hoped for 'the liberation of the Slavs from Austria and Turkey' (Hans Kohn, *op. cit.*); and as early as 1870 a military pamphlet appeared which demanded the 'destruction of Austria as a necessary condition for a Pan-Slav federation' (see Staehlin, *op. cit.*, p. 282).

21  See Otto Bonhard, *op. cit.*, pp. 58 ff., and Hugo Grell, *Der alldeutsche Verband, seine Geschichte, seine Bestrebungen, seine Erfolge*, 1898, in Alldeutsche Flugschriften, No. 8.

22  According to the Austrian Pan-German program of 1913, quoted from Eduard Pichl (al. Herwig), *Georg Schoenerer*, 1938, 6 vols., VI, 375.

23  When Schoenerer, with his admiration for Bismarck, declared in 1876 that 'Austria as a great power must cease' (Pichl, *op. cit.*, I, 90), Bismarck thought and told his Austrian admirers that 'a powerful Austria is a vital necessity to Germany.' See F. A. Neuschaefer, *Georg Ritter von Schoenerer* (Dissertation), Hamburg, 1935. The Czar's

occasionally ran, or how ridiculous nationalistic claims might become in times of emergency, as long as they were bound to a defined national territory and controlled by pride in a limited nation-state they remained within limits which the tribalism of the pan-movements overstepped at once.

The modernity of the pan-movements may best be gauged from their entirely new position on antisemitism. Suppressed minorities like the Slavs in Austria and the Poles in Czarist Russia were more likely, because of their conflict with the government, to discover the hidden connections between the Jewish communities and the European nation-states, and this discovery could easily lead to more fundamental hostility. Wherever antagonism to the state was not identified with lack of patriotism, as in Poland, where it was a sign of Polish loyalty to be disloyal to the Czar, or in Austria, where Germans looked upon Bismarck as their great national figure, this antisemitism assumed more violent forms because the Jews then appeared as agents not only of an oppressive state machine but of a foreign oppressor. But the fundamental role of antisemitism in the pan-movements is explained as little by the position of minorities as by the specific experiences which Schoenerer, the protagonist of Austrian Pan-Germanism, had had in his earlier career when, still a member of the Liberal Party, he became aware of the connections between the Hapsburg monarchy and the Rothschilds' domination of Austria's railroad system.[24] This by itself would hardly have made him announce that 'we Pan-Germans regard antisemitism as the mainstay of our national ideology,'[25] nor could anything similar have induced the Pan-Slav Russian writer Rozanov to pretend that 'there is no problem in Russian life in which like a "comma" there is not also the question: How to cope with the Jew.'[26]

---

attitude toward Pan-Slavism was much more equivocal because the Pan Slav conception of the state included strong popular support for despotic government. Yet even under such tempting circumstances, the Czar refused to support the expansionist demand of the Slavophiles and their successors. See Staehlin, *op. cit.*, pp. 30 ff

24 See chapter ii.

25 Pichl, *op. cit.*, I, 26. The translation is quoted from the excellent article by Oscar Karbach, 'The Founder of Modern Political Antisemitism: Georg von Schoenerer,' in *Jewish Social Studies*, Vol. VII, No. 1, January, 1945.

26 Vassiliff Rozanov, *Fallen Leaves*, 1929, pp. 163–164.

The clue to the sudden emergence of antisemitism as the center of a whole outlook on life and the world – as distinguished from its mere political role in France during the Dreyfus Affair or its role as an instrument of propaganda in the German Stoecker movement – lies in the nature of tribalism rather than in political facts and circumstances. The true significance of the pan-movements' antisemitism is that hatred of the Jews was, for the first time, severed from all actual experience concerning the Jewish people, political, social, or economic, and followed only the peculiar logic of an ideology.

Tribal nationalism, the driving force behind continental imperialism, had little in common with the nationalism of the fully developed Western nation-state. The nation-state, with its claim to popular representation and national sovereignty, as it had developed since the French Revolution through the nineteenth century, was the result of a combination of two factors that were still separate in the eighteenth century and remained separate in Russia and Austria-Hungary: nationality and state. Nations entered the scene of history and were emancipated when peoples had acquired a consciousness of themselves as cultural and historical entities, and of their territory as a permanent home, where history had left its visible traces, whose cultivation was the product of the common labor of their ancestors and whose future would depend upon the course of a common civilization. Wherever nation-states came into being, migrations came to an end, while, on the other hand, in the Eastern and Southern European regions the establishment of nation-states failed because they could not fall back upon firmly rooted peasant classes.[27] Sociologically the nation-state was the body politic of the European emancipated peasant classes, and this is the reason why national armies could keep their permanent position within these states only up to the end of the last century, that is, only as long as they were truly representative of the rural class. 'The Army,' as Marx has pointed out, 'was the "point of honor" with the allotment farmers: it was themselves turned into masters, defending abroad their newly established property . . . The uniform was their state costume, war was their poetry; the allotment

27  See C. A. Macartney, *National States and National Minorities*, London, 1934, pp. 432 ff.

was the fatherland, and patriotism became the ideal form of property.'[28] The Western nationalism which culminated in general conscription was the product of firmly rooted *and* emancipated peasant classes.

While consciousness of nationality is a comparatively recent development, the structure of the state was derived from centuries of monarchy and enlightened despotism. Whether in the form of a new republic or of a reformed constitutional monarchy, the state inherited as its supreme function the protection of all inhabitants in its territory no matter what their nationality, and was supposed to act as a supreme legal institution. The tragedy of the nation-state was that the people's rising national consciousness interfered with these functions. In the name of the will of the people the state was forced to recognize only 'nationals' as citizens, to grant full civil and political rights only to those who belonged to the national community by right of origin and fact of birth. This meant that the state was partly transformed from an instrument of the law into an instrument of the nation.

The conquest of the state by the nation[29] was greatly facilitated by the downfall of the absolute monarchy and the subsequent new development of classes. The absolute monarch was supposed to serve the interests of the nation as a whole, to be the visible exponent and proof of the existence of such a common interest. The enlightened despotism was based on Rohan's 'kings command the peoples and interest commands the king';[30] with the abolition of the king and sovereignty of the people, this common interest was in constant danger of being replaced by a permanent conflict among class interests and struggle for control of the state machinery, that is, by a permanent civil war. The only remaining bond between the citizens of a nation-state without a monarch to symbolize their essential community, seemed to be national, that is, common origin. So that in a century when every class and section in the population was dominated by class or group interest, the interest of the nation as a whole was supposedly guaranteed in a common origin, which sentimentally expressed itself in nationalism.

28 Karl Marx, *The Eighteenth Brumaire of Louis Bonaparte*, English translation by De Leon, 1898.
29 See J. T. Delos, *La Nation*, Montreal, 1944, an outstanding study on the subject.
30 See the Duc de Rohan, *De l'Intérêt des Princes et Etats de la Chrétienté*, 1638, dedicated to the Cardinal Richelieu.

The secret conflict between state and nation came to light at the very birth of the modern nation-state, when the French Revolution combined the declaration of the Rights of Man with the demand for national sovereignty. The same essential rights were at once claimed as the inalienable heritage of all human beings *and* as the specific heritage of specific nations; the same nation was at once declared to be subject to laws, which supposedly would flow from the Rights of Man, *and* sovereign, that is, bound by no universal law and acknowledging nothing superior to itself.[31] The practical outcome of this contradiction was that from then on human rights were protected and enforced only as national rights and that the very institution of a state, whose supreme task was to protect and guarantee man his rights as man, as citizen and as national, lost its legal, rational appearance and could be interpreted by the romantics as the nebulous representative of a 'national soul' which through the very fact of its existence was supposed to be beyond or above the law. National sovereignty, accordingly, lost its original connotation of freedom of the people and was being surrounded by a pseudomystical aura of lawless arbitrariness.

Nationalism is essentially the expression of this perversion of the state into an instrument of the nation and the identification of the citizen with the member of the nation. The relationship between state and society was determined by the fact of class struggle, which had supplanted the former feudal order. Society was pervaded by liberal individualism which wrongly believed that the state ruled over mere individuals, when in reality it ruled over classes, and which saw in the state a kind of supreme individual before which all others had to bow. It seemed to be the will of the nation that the state protect it from the consequences of its social atomization and, at the same time, guarantee its possibility of remaining in a state of atomization. To be equal to this task, the state had to enforce all earlier tendencies toward centralization; only a strongly centralized administration which monopolized all instruments of violence and power-possibilities could counterbalance the centrifugal forces constantly produced in a class-ridden society. Nationalism, then, became the precious cement

31 One of the most illuminating discussions of the principle of sovereignty is still Jean Bodin, *Six Livres de la République*, 1576. For a good report and discussion of Bodin's main theories, see George H. Sabine, *A History of Political Theory*, 1937.

for binding together a centralized state and an atomized society, and it actually proved to be the only working, live connection between the individuals of the nation-state.

Nationalism always preserved this initial intimate loyalty to the government and never quite lost its function of preserving a precarious balance between nation and state on one hand, between the nationals of an atomized society on the other. Native citizens of a nation-state frequently looked down upon naturalized citizens, those who had received their rights by law and not by birth, from the state and not from the nation; but they never went so far as to propose the Pan-German distinction between '*Staatsfremde*,' aliens of the state, and '*Volksfremde*,' aliens of the nation, which was later incorporated into Nazi legislation. Insofar as the state, even in its perverted form, remained a legal institution, nationalism was controlled by some law, and insofar as it had sprung from the identification of nationals with their territory, it was limited by definite boundaries.

Quite different was the first national reaction of peoples for whom nationality had not yet developed beyond the inarticulateness of ethnic consciousness, whose languages had not yet outgrown the dialect stage through which all European languages went before they became suited for literary purposes, whose peasant classes had not struck deep roots in the country and were not on the verge of emancipation, and to whom, consequently, their national quality appeared to be much more a portable private matter, inherent in their very personality, than a matter of public concern and civilization.[32] If they wanted to match the national pride of Western nations, they had no country, no state, no historic achievement to show but could only point to themselves, and that meant, at best, to their language – as though language by itself were already an achievement – at worst, to their Slavic, or Germanic, or God-knows-what soul. Yet in a century which naïvely

---

32 Interesting in this context are the socialist propositions of Karl Renner and Otto Bauer in Austria to separate nationality entirely from its territorial basis and to make it a kind of personal status; this of course corresponded to a situation in which ethnic groups were dispersed all over the empire without losing any of their national character. See Otto Bauer, *Die Nationalitätenfrage und die österreichische Sozialdemokratie*, Vienna, 1907, on the personal (as opposed to the territorial) principle, pp. 332 ff., 353 ff. 'The personal principle wants to organize nations not as territorial bodies but as mere associations of persons.'

assumed that all peoples were virtually nations there was hardly anything else left to the oppressed peoples of Austria-Hungary, Czarist Russia, or the Balkan countries, where no conditions existed for the realization of the Western national trinity of people-territory-state, where frontiers had changed constantly for many centuries and populations had been in a stage of more or less continuous migration. Here were masses who had not the slightest idea of the meaning of *patria* and patriotism, not the vaguest notion of responsibility for a common, limited community. This was the trouble with the 'belt of mixed populations' (Macartney) that stretched from the Baltic to the Adriatic and found its most articulate expression in the Dual Monarchy.

Tribal nationalism grew out of this atmosphere of rootlessness. It spread widely not only among the peoples of Austria-Hungary but also, though on a higher level, among members of the unhappy intelligentsia of Czarist Russia. Rootlessness was the true source of that 'enlarged tribal consciousness' which actually meant that members of these peoples had no definite home but felt at home wherever other members of their 'tribe' happened to live. 'It is our distinction,' said Schoenerer, '. . . that we do not gravitate toward Vienna but gravitate to whatever place Germans may live in.'[33] The hallmark of the pan-movements was that they never even tried to achieve national emancipation, but at once, in their dreams of expansion, transcended the narrow bounds of a national community and proclaimed a folk community that would remain a political factor even if its members were dispersed all over the earth. Similarly, and in contrast to the true national liberation movements of small peoples, which always began with an exploration of the national past, they did not stop to consider history but projected the basis of their community into a future toward which the movement was supposed to march.

Tribal nationalism, spreading through all oppressed nationalities in Eastern and Southern Europe, developed into a new form of organization, the pan-movements, among those peoples who combined some kind of national home country, Germany and Russia, with a large, dispersed irredenta, Germans and Slavs abroad.[34] In contrast to

---

33 Pichl, *op. cit.*, I, 152.
34 No full-fledged pan-movement ever developed except under these conditions. Pan-Latinism was a misnomer for a few abortive attempts of the Latin nations to make

overseas imperialism, which was content with relative superiority, a national mission, or a white man's burden, the pan-movements started with absolute claims to chosenness. Nationalism has been frequently described as an emotional surrogate of religion, but only the tribalism of the pan-movements offered a new religious theory and a new concept of holiness. It was not the Czar's religious function and position in the Greek Church that led Russian Pan-Slavs to the affirmation of the Christian nature of the Russian people, of their being, according to Dostoevski, the 'Christopher among the nations' who carry God directly into the affairs of this world.[35] It was because of claims to being 'the true divine people of modern times'[36] that the Pan-Slavs abandoned their earlier liberal tendencies and, notwithstanding governmental opposition and occasionally even persecution, became staunch defenders of Holy Russia.

Austrian Pan-Germans laid similar claims to divine chosenness even though they, with a similar liberal past, remained anticlerical and became anti-Christians. When Hitler, a self-confessed disciple of Schoenerer, stated during the last war: 'God the Almighty has made our nation. We are defending His work by defending its very existence,'[37] the reply from the other side, from a follower of Pan-Slavism, was equally true to type: 'The German monsters are not only our foes, but God's foes.'[38] These recent formulations were not born of

---

some kind of alliance against the German danger, and even Polish Messianism never claimed more than what at some time might conceivably have been Polish-dominated territory. See also Deckert, *op. cit.*, who stated in 1914: 'that Pan-Latinism has declined more and more, and that nationalism and state consciousness have become stronger and retained a greater potential there than anywhere else in Europe' (p. 7).

35  Nicolas Berdyaev, *The Origin of Russian Communism*, 1937, p. 102. – K. S. Aksakow called the Russian people the 'only Christian people on earth' in 1855 (see Hans Ehrenberg and N. V. Bubnoff, *Oestliches Christentum*, Bd. I, pp. 92 ff.), and the poet Tyutchev asserted at the same time that 'the Russian people is Christian not only through the Orthodoxy of its faith but by something more intimate. It is Christian by that faculty of renunciation and sacrifice which is the foundation of its moral nature.' Quoted from Hans Kohn, *op. cit.*

36  According to Chaadayev whose *Philosophical Letters*, *1829–1831* constituted the first systematic attempt to see world history centered around the Russian people. See Ehrenberg, *op. cit.*, I, 5 ff.

37  Speech of January 30, 1945, as recorded in the New York *Times*, January 31.

38  The words of Luke, the Archbishop of Tambov, as quoted in *The Journal of the Moscow Patriarchate*, No. 2, 1944.

propaganda needs of the moment, and this kind of fanaticism does not simply abuse religious language; behind it lies a veritable theology which gave the earlier pan-movements their momentum and retained a considerable influence on the development of modern totalitarian movements.

The pan-movements preached the divine origin of their own people as against the Jewish-Christian faith in the divine origin of Man. According to them, man, belonging inevitably to some people, received his divine origin only indirectly through membership in a people. The individual, therefore, has his divine value only as long as he belongs to the people singled out for divine origin. He forfeits this whenever he decides to change his nationality, in which case he severs all bonds through which he was endowed with divine origin and falls, as it were, into metaphysical homelessness. The political advantage of this concept was twofold. It made nationality a permanent quality which no longer could be touched by history, no matter what happened to a given people – emigration, conquest, dispersion. Of even more immediate impact, however, was that in the absolute contrast between the divine origin of one's own people and all other nondivine peoples all differences between the individual members of the people disappeared, whether social or economic or psychological. Divine origin changed the people into a uniform 'chosen' mass of arrogant robots.[39]

The untruth of this theory is as conspicuous as its political usefulness. God created neither men – whose origin clearly is procreation – nor peoples – who came into being as the result of human organization. Men are unequal according to their natural origin, their different organization, and fate in history. Their equality is an equality of rights only, that is, an equality of human purpose; yet behind this equality of human purpose lies, according to Jewish-Christian tradition, another equality, expressed in the concept of one common origin beyond

39 This was already recognized by the Russian Jesuit, Prince Ivan S. Gagarin, in his pamphlet *La Russie sera-t-elle catholique?* (1856) in which he attacked the Slavophiles because 'they wish to establish the most complete religious, political, and national uniformity. In their foreign policy, they wish to fuse all Orthodox Christians of whatever nationality, and all Slavs of whatever religion, in a great Slav and orthodox empire.' (Quoted from Hans Kohn, *op. cit.*)

human history, human nature, and human purpose – the common origin in the mythical, unidentifiable Man who alone is God's creation. This divine origin is the metaphysical concept on which the political equality of purpose may be based, the purpose of establishing mankind on earth. Nineteenth-century positivism and progressivism perverted this purpose of human equality when they set out to demonstrate what cannot be demonstrated, namely, that men are equal by nature and different only by history and circumstances, so that they can be equalized not by rights, but by circumstances and education. Nationalism and its concept of a 'national mission' perverted the national concept of mankind as a family of nations into a hierarchical structure where differences of history and organization were misinterpreted as differences between men, residing in natural origin. Racism, which denied the common origin of man and repudiated the common purpose of establishing humanity, introduced the concept of the divine origin of one people as contrasted with all others, thereby covering the temporary and changeable product of human endeavor with a pseudomystical cloud of divine eternity and finality.

This finality is what acts as the common denominator between the pan-movements' philosophy and race concepts, and explains their inherent affinity in theoretical terms. Politically, it is not important whether God or nature is thought to be the origin of a people; in both cases, no matter how exalted the claim for one's own people, peoples are transformed into animal species so that a Russian appears as different from a German as a wolf is from a fox. A 'divine people' lives in a world in which it is the born persecutor of all other weaker species, or the born victim of all other stronger species. Only the rules of the animal kingdom can possibly apply to its political destinies.

The tribalism of the pan-movements with its concept of the 'divine origin' of one people owed part of its great appeal to its contempt for liberal individualism,[40] the ideal of mankind and the dignity of man. No human dignity is left if the individual owes his value only to the fact that he happens to be born a German or a Russian; but there is, in its stead, a new coherence, a sense of mutual reliability among all

40 'People will recognize that man has no other destination in this world but to work for the destruction of his personality and its replacement through a social and unpersonal existence.' Chaadayev, *op. cit.* Quoted from Ehrenberg, *op. cit.*, p. 60.

members of the people which indeed was very apt to assuage the rightful apprehensions of modern men as to what might happen to them if, isolated individuals in an atomized society, they were not protected by sheer numbers and enforced uniform coherence. Similarly, the 'belt of mixed populations,' more exposed than other sections of Europe to the storms of history and less rooted in Western tradition, felt earlier than other European peoples the terror of the ideal of humanity and of the Judaeo-Christian faith in the common origin of man. They did not harbor any illusions about the 'noble savage,' because they knew something of the potentialities of evil without research into the habits of cannibals. The more peoples know about one another, the less they want to recognize other peoples as their equals, the more they recoil from the ideal of humanity.

The appeal of tribal isolation and master race ambitions was partly due to an instinctive feeling that mankind, whether a religious or humanistic ideal, implies a common sharing of responsibility.[41] The shrinking of geographic distances made this a political actuality of the first order.[42] It also made idealistic talk about mankind and the dignity of man an affair of the past simply because all these fine and dreamlike notions, with their time-honored traditions, suddenly assumed a terrifying timeliness. Even insistence on the sinfulness of all men, of course absent from the phraseology of the liberal protagonists of 'mankind,' by no means suffices for an understanding of the fact – which the people understood only too well – that the idea of humanity,

41  The following passage in Frymann, *op. cit.*, p. 186, is characteristic: 'We know our own people, its qualities and its shortcomings – mankind we do not know and we refuse to care or get enthusiastic about it. Where does it begin, where does it end, that we are supposed to love because it belongs to mankind . . . ? Are the decadent or half-bestial Russian peasant of the *mir*, the Negro of East-Africa, the half-breed of German South-West Africa, or the unbearable Jews of Galicia and Rumania all members of mankind? . . . One can believe in the solidarity of the Germanic peoples – whoever is outside this sphere does not matter to us.'

42  It was this shrinking of geographic distances that found an expression in Friedrich Naumann's *Central Europe*: 'The day is still distant when there shall be "one fold and one shepherd," but the days are past when shepherds without number, lesser or greater, drove their flocks unrestrained over the pastures of Europe. The spirit of large-scale industry and of super-national organisation has seized politics. People think, as Cecil Rhodes once expressed it, "in Continents."' These few sentences were quoted in innumerable articles and pamphlets of the time.

purged of all sentimentality, has the very serious consequence that in one form or another men must assume responsibility for all crimes committed by men, and that eventually all nations will be forced to answer for the evil committed by all others.

Tribalism and racism are the very realistic, if very destructive, ways of escaping this predicament of common responsibility. Their metaphysical rootlessness, which matched so well the territorial uprootedness of the nationalities it first seized, was equally well suited to the needs of the shifting masses of modern cities and was therefore grasped at once by totalitarianism; even the fanatical adoption by the Bolsheviks of the greatest antinational doctrine, Marxism, was counteracted and Pan-Slav propaganda reintroduced in Soviet Russia because of the tremendous isolating value of these theories in themselves.[43]

It is true that the system of rule in Austria-Hungary and Czarist Russia served as a veritable education in tribal nationalism, based as it was upon the oppression of nationalities. In Russia this oppression was the exclusive monopoly of the bureaucracy which also oppressed the Russian people with the result that only the Russian intelligentsia became Pan-Slav. The Dual Monarchy, on the contrary, dominated its troublesome nationalities by giving to them just enough freedom to oppress other nationalities, with the result that these became the real mass basis for the ideology of the pan-movements. The secret of the survival of the House of Hapsburg in the nineteenth century lay in careful balance and support of a supranational machinery by the mutual antagonism and exploitation of Czechs by Germans, of Slovaks by Hungarians, of Ruthenians by Poles, and so on. For all of them it became a matter of course that one might achieve nationhood at the expense of the others and that one would gladly be deprived of freedom if the oppression came from one's own national government.

The two pan-movements developed without any help from the Russian or German governments. This did not prevent their Austrian

43 Very interesting in this respect are the new theories of Soviet Russian genetics. Inheritance of acquired characteristics clearly means that populations living under unfavorable conditions pass on poorer hereditary endowment and *vice versa*. 'In a word, we should have innate master and subject races.' See H. S. Muller, 'The Soviet Master Race Theory,' in *New Leader*, July 30, 1949.

adherents from indulging in the delights of high treason against the Austrian government. It was this possibility of educating masses in the spirit of high treason which provided Austrian pan-movements with the sizable popular support they always lacked in Germany and Russia proper. It was as much easier to induce the German worker to attack the German bourgeoisie than the government, as it was easier in Russia 'to arouse the peasants against squires than against the Czar.'[44] The differences in the attitudes of German workers and Russian peasants were surely tremendous; the former looked upon a not too beloved monarch as the symbol of national unity, and the latter considered the head of their government to be the true representative of God on earth. These differences, however, mattered less than the fact that neither in Russia nor in Germany was the government so weak as in Austria, nor had its authority fallen into such disrepute that the pan-movements could make political capital out of revolutionary unrest. Only in Austria did the revolutionary impetus find its natural outlet in the pan-movements. The (not very ably carried out) device of *divide et impera* did little to diminish the centrifugal tendencies of national sentiments, but it succeeded quite well in inducing superiority complexes and a general mood of disloyalty.

Hostility to the state as an institution runs through the theories of all pan-movements. The Slavophiles' opposition to the state has been rightly described as 'entirely different from anything to be found in the system of official nationalism';[45] the state by its very nature was held to be alien to the people. Slav superiority was felt to lie in the Russian people's indifference to the state, in their keeping themselves as a *corpus separatum* from their own government. This is what the Slavophiles meant when they called the Russians a 'stateless people' and this made it possible for these 'liberals' to reconcile themselves to despotism; it was in accord with the demand of despotism that the people not 'interfere with state power,' that is, with the absoluteness of that power.[46] The Pan-Germans, who were more articulate politically,

44 G. Fedotov's 'Russia and Freedom,' in *The Review of Politics*, Vol. VIII, No. 1, January, 1946, is a veritable masterpiece of historical writing; it gives the gist of the whole of Russian history.

45 N. Berdyaev, *op. cit.*, p. 29.

46 K. S. Aksakov in Ehrenberg, *op. cit.*, p. 97.

always insisted on the priority of national over state interest[47] and usually argued that 'world politics transcends the framework of the state,' that the only permanent factor in the course of history was the people and not states; and that therefore national needs, changing with circumstances, should determine, at all times, the political acts of the state.[48] But what in Germany and Russia remained only high-sounding phrases up to the end of the first World War, had a real enough aspect in the Dual Monarchy whose decay generated a permanent spiteful contempt for the government.

It would be a serious error to assume that the leaders of the pan-movements were reactionaries or 'counter-revolutionaries.' Though as a rule not too interested in social questions, they never made the mistake of siding with capitalist exploitation and most of them had belonged, and quite a few continued to belong, to liberal, progressive parties. It is quite true, in a sense, that the Pan-German League 'embodied a real attempt at popular control in foreign affairs. It believed firmly in the efficiency of a strong nationally minded public opinion . . . and initiating national policies through force of popular demand.'[49] Except that the mob, organized in the pan-movements and inspired by race ideologies, was not at all the same people whose revolutionary actions had led to constitutional government and whose true representatives at that time could be found only in the workers' movements, but with its 'enlarged tribal consciousness' and its conspicuous lack of patriotism resembled much rather a 'race.'

Pan-Slavism, in contrast to Pan-Germanism, was formed by and permeated the whole Russian intelligentsia. Much less developed in organizational form and much less consistent in political programs, it maintained for a remarkably long time a very high level of literary sophistication and philosophical speculation. While Rozanov

47 See for instance Schoenerer's complaint that the Austrian '*Verfassungspartei*' still subordinated national interests to state interests (Pichl, *op. cit.*, I, 151). See also the characteristic passages in the Pan-German Graf E. Reventlow's *Judas Kampf und Niederlage in Deutschland*, 1937, pp. 39 ff. Reventlow saw National Socialism as the realization of Pan-Germanism because of its refusal to 'idolize' the state which is only one of the functions of folk life.

48 Ernst Hasse, *Deutsche Weltpolitik*, 1897, in Alldeutsche Flugschriften, No. 5, and *Deutsche Politik*, 1. Heft: *Das deutsche Reich als Nationalstaat*, 1905, p. 50.

49 Wertheimer, *op. cit.*, p. 209.

speculated about the mysterious differences between Jewish and Christian sex power and came to the surprising conclusion that the Jews are 'united with that power, Christians being separated from it,'[50] the leader of Austria's Pan-Germans cheerfully discovered devices to 'attract the interest of the little man by propaganda songs, post cards, Schoenerer beer mugs, walking sticks and matches.'[51] Yet eventually 'Schelling and Hegel were discarded and natural science was called upon to furnish the theoretical ammunition' by the Pan-Slavs as well.[52]

Pan-Germanism, founded by a single man, Georg von Schoenerer, and chiefly supported by German-Austrian students, spoke from the beginning a strikingly vulgar language, destined to appeal to much larger and different social strata. Schoenerer was consequently also 'the first to perceive the possibilities of antisemitism as an instrument for forcing the direction of foreign policy and disrupting . . . the internal structure of the state.'[53] Some of the reasons for the suitability of the Jewish people for this purpose are obvious: their very prominent position with respect to the Hapsburg monarchy together with the fact that in a multinational country they were more easily recognized as a separate nationality than in nation-states whose citizens, at least in theory, were of homogeneous stock. This, however, while it certainly explains the violence of the Austrian brand of antisemitism and shows how shrewd a politician Schoenerer was when he exploited the issue, does not help us understand the central ideological role of antisemitism in both pan-movements.

'Enlarged tribal consciousness' as the emotional motor of the pan-movements was fully developed before antisemitism became their central and centralizing issue. Pan-Slavism, with its longer and more respectable history of philosophic speculation and a more conspicuous political ineffectiveness, turned antisemitic only in the last decades of the nineteenth century; Schoenerer the Pan-German had already openly announced his hostility to state institutions when

50  Rozanov, *op. cit.*, pp. 56–57.

51  Oscar Karbach, *op. cit.*

52  Louis Levine, *Pan-Slavism and European Politics*, New York, 1914, describes this change from the older Slavophile generation to the new Pan-Slav movement.

53  Oscar Karbach, *op. cit.*

many Jews were still members of his party.[54] In Germany, where the Stoecker movement had demonstrated the usefulness of antisemitism as a political propaganda weapon, the Pan-German League started with a certain antisemitic tendency, but before 1918 it never went so far as to exclude Jews from membership.[55] The Slavophiles' occasional antipathy to Jews turned into antisemitism in the whole Russian intelligentsia when, after the assassination of the Czar in 1881, a wave of pogroms organized by the government brought the Jewish question into the focus of public attention.

Schoenerer, who discovered antisemitism at the same time, probably became aware of its possibilities almost by accident: since he wanted above all to destroy the Hapsburg empire, it was not difficult to calculate the effect of the exclusion of one nationality on a state structure that rested on a multitude of nationalities. The whole fabric of this peculiar constitution, the precarious balance of its bureaucracy could be shattered if the moderate oppression, under which all nationalities enjoyed a certain amount of equality, was undermined by popular movements. Yet, this purpose could have been equally well served by the Pan-Germans' furious hatred of the Slav nationalities, a hatred which had been well established long before the movement turned antisemitic and which had been approved by its Jewish members.

What made the antisemitism of the pan-movements so effective that it could survive the general decline of antisemitic propaganda during the deceptive quiet that preceded the outbreak of the first World War was its merger with the tribal nationalism of Eastern Europe. For there existed an inherent affinity between the pan-movements' theories about peoples and the rootless existence of the Jewish people. It seemed the Jews were the one perfect example of a people in the tribal sense, their organization the model the pan-movements were striving to emulate, their survival and their supposed power the best proof of the correctness of racial theories.

If other nationalities in the Dual Monarchy were but weakly rooted

54 The Linz Program, which remained the Pan-Germans' program in Austria, was originally phrased without its Jew paragraph; there were even three Jews on the drafting committee in 1882. The Jew paragraph was added in 1885. See Oscar Karbach, *op. cit.*

55 Otto Bonhard, *op. cit.*, p. 45.

in the soil and had little sense of the meaning of a common territory, the Jews were the example of a people who without any home at all had been able to keep their identity through the centuries and could therefore be cited as proof that no territory was needed to constitute a nationality.[56] If the pan-movements insisted on the secondary importance of the state and the paramount importance of the people, organized throughout countries and not necessarily represented in visible institutions, the Jews were a perfect model of a nation without a state and without visible institutions.[57] If tribal nationalities pointed to themselves as the center of their national pride, regardless of historical achievements and partnership in recorded events, if they believed that some mysterious inherent psychological or physical quality made them the incarnation not of Germany but Germanism, not of Russia, but the Russian soul, they somehow knew, even if they did not know how to express it, that the Jewishness of assimilated Jews was exactly the same kind of personal individual embodiment of Judaism and that the peculiar pride of secularized Jews, who had not given up the claim to chosenness, really meant that they believed they were different and better simply because they happened to be born as Jews, regardless of Jewish achievements and tradition.

It is true enough that this Jewish attitude, this, as it were, Jewish brand of tribal nationalism, had been the result of the abnormal position of the Jews in modern states, outside the pale of society and nation. But the position of these shifting ethnic groups, who became conscious of their nationality only through the example of other – Western – nations, and later the position of the uprooted masses of the big cities, which racism mobilized so efficiently, was in many ways very similar. They too were outside the pale of society, and they too were outside the political body of the nation-state which seemed to be the only satisfactory political organization of peoples. In the Jews they recognized at once their happier, luckier competitors because, as they

---

56  So by the certainly not antisemitic Socialist Otto Bauer, *op. cit.*, p. 373.

57  Very instructive for Jewish self-interpretation is A. S. Steinberg's essay 'Die weltanschaulichen Voraussetzungen der jüdischen Geschichtsschreibung,' in *Dubnov Festschrift*, 1930: 'If one . . . is convinced of the concept of life as expressed in Jewish history . . . then the state question loses its importance, no matter how one may answer it.'

saw it, the Jews had found a way of constituting a society of their own which, precisely because it had no visible representation and no normal political outlet, could become a substitute for the nation.

But what drove the Jews into the center of these racial ideologies more than anything else was the even more obvious fact that the pan-movements' claim to chosenness could clash seriously only with the Jewish claim. It did not matter that the Jewish concept had nothing in common with the tribal theories about the divine origin of one's own people. The mob was not much concerned with such niceties of historical correctness and was hardly aware of the difference between a Jewish mission in history to achieve the establishment of mankind and its own 'mission' to dominate all other peoples on earth. But the leaders of the pan-movements knew quite well that the Jews had divided the world, exactly as they had, into two halves – themselves and all the others.[58] In this dichotomy the Jews again appeared to be the luckier competitors who had inherited something, were recognized for something which Gentiles had to build from scratch.[59]

It is a 'truism' that has not been made truer by repetition that antisemitism is only a form of envy. But in relation to Jewish chosenness it is true enough. Whenever peoples have been separated from action and achievements, when these natural ties with the common world have broken or do not exist for one reason or another, they have been inclined to turn upon themselves in their naked natural givenness and to claim divinity and a mission to redeem the whole world. When this happens in Western civilization, such peoples will invariably find the age-old claim of the Jews in their way. This is what the spokesmen of pan-movements sensed, and this is why they remained so untroubled by the realistic question of whether the Jewish problem in terms of numbers and power was important enough to make hatred of Jews the

58 The closeness of these concepts to each other may be seen in the following coincidence to which many other examples could be added: Steinberg, *op. cit.*, says of the Jews: their history takes place outside all usual historical laws; Chaadayev calls the Russians an exception people. Berdyayev stated bluntly (*op. cit.*, p. 135): 'Russian Messianism is akin to Jewish Messianism.'

59 See the antisemite E. Reventlow, *op. cit.*, but also the philosemite Russian philosopher Vladimir Solovyov, *Judaism and the Christian Question* (1884): Between the two religious nations, the Russians and the Poles, history has introduced a third religious people, the Jews. See Ehrenberg, *op. cit.*, p. 314 ff. See also Cleinow, *op. cit.*, pp. 44 ff.

mainstay of their ideology. As their own national pride was independent of all achievements, so their hatred of the Jews had emancipated itself from all specific Jewish deeds and misdeeds. In this the pan-movements were in complete agreement, although neither knew how to utilize this ideological mainstay for purposes of political organization.

The time-lag between the formulation of the pan-movements' ideology and the possibility of its serious political application is demonstrated by the fact that the 'Protocols of the Elders of Zion' – forged around 1900 by agents of the Russian secret police in Paris upon the suggestion of Pobyedonostzev, the political adviser of Nicholas II, and the only Pan-Slav ever in an influential position – remained a half-forgotten pamphlet until 1919, when it began its veritably triumphal procession through all European countries and languages;[60] its circulation some thirty years later was second only to Hitler's *Mein Kampf.* Neither the forger nor his employer knew that a time would come when the police would be the central institution of a society and the whole power of a country organized according to the supposedly Jewish principles laid down in the Protocols. Perhaps it was Stalin who was the first to discover all the potentialities for rule that the police possessed; it certainly was Hitler who, shrewder than Schoenerer his spiritual father, knew how to use the hierarchical principle of racism, how to exploit the antisemitic assertion of the existence of a 'worst' people in order properly to organize the 'best' and all the conquered and oppressed in between, how to generalize the superiority complex of the pan-movements so that each people, with the necessary exception of the Jews, could look down upon one that was even worse off than itself.

Apparently a few more decades of hidden chaos and open despair were necessary before large strata of people happily admitted that they were going to achieve what, as they believed, only Jews in their innate devilishness had been able to achieve thus far. The leaders of the pan-movements, at any rate, though already vaguely aware of the social question, were very one-sided in their insistence on foreign policy. They therefore were unable to see that antisemitism could form the necessary link connecting domestic with external methods; they

---

60  See John S. Curtiss, *The Protocols of Zion*, New York, 1942.

did not know yet how to establish their 'folk community,' that is, the completely uprooted, racially indoctrinated horde.

That the pan-movements' fanaticism hit upon the Jews as the ideological center, which was the beginning of the end of European Jewry, constitutes one of the most logical and most bitter revenges history has ever taken. For of course there is some truth in 'enlightened' assertions from Voltaire to Renan and Taine that the Jews' concept of chosenness, their identification of religion and nationality, their claim to an absolute position in history and a singled-out relationship with God, brought into Western civilization an otherwise unknown element of fanaticism (inherited by Christianity with its claim to exclusive possession of Truth) on one side, and on the other an element of pride that was dangerously close to its racial perversion.[61] Politically, it was of no consequence that Judaism and an intact Jewish piety always were notably free of, and even hostile to, the heretical immanence of the Divine.

For tribal nationalism is the precise perversion of a religion which made God choose one nation, one's own nation; only because this ancient myth, together with the only people surviving from antiquity, had struck deep roots in Western civilization could the modern mob leader, with a certain amount of plausibility, summon up the impudence to drag God into the petty conflicts between peoples and to ask His consent to an election which the leader had already happily manipulated.[62] The hatred of the racists against the Jews sprang from a superstitious apprehension that it actually might be the Jews, and not themselves, whom God had chosen, to whom success was granted

61 See Berdyaev, *op. cit.*, p. 5: 'Religion and nationality in the Muscovite kingdom grew up together, as they did also in the consciousness of the ancient Hebrew people. And in the same way as Messianic consciousness was an attribute of Judaism, it was an attribute of Russian Orthodoxy also.'

62 A fantastic example of the madness in the whole business is the following passage in Léon Bloy – which fortunately is not characteristic of French nationalism: 'France is so much the first of the nations that all others, no matter who they are, must be honored if they are permitted to eat the bread of her dogs. If only France is happy, then the rest of the world can be satisfied even though they have to pay for France's happiness with slavery or destruction. But if France suffers, then God Himself suffers, the terrible God . . . This is as absolute and as inevitable as the secret of predestination.' Quoted from R. Nadolny, *Germanisierung oder Slavisierung?*, 1928, p. 55.

by divine providence. There was an element of feeble-minded resentment against a people who, it was feared, had received a rationally incomprehensible guarantee that they would emerge eventually, and in spite of appearances, as the final victors in world history.

For to the mentality of the mob the Jewish concept of a divine mission to bring about the kingdom of God could only appear in the vulgar terms of success and failure. Fear and hatred were nourished and somewhat rationalized by the fact that Christianity, a religion of Jewish origin, had already conquered Western mankind. Guided by their own ridiculous superstition, the leaders of the pan-movements found that little hidden cog in the mechanics of Jewish piety that made a complete reversion and perversion possible, so that chosenness was no longer the myth for an ultimate realization of the ideal of a common humanity – but for its final destruction.

## II: The Inheritance of Lawlessness

Open disregard for law and legal institutions and ideological justification of lawlessness has been much more characteristic of continental than of overseas imperialism. This is partly due to the fact that continental imperialists lacked the geographical distance to separate the illegality of their rule on foreign continents from the legality of their home countries' institutions. Of equal importance is the fact that the pan-movements originated in countries which had never known constitutional government, so that their leaders naturally conceived of government and power in terms of arbitrary decisions from above.

Contempt for law became characteristic of all movements. Though more fully articulated in Pan-Slavism than in Pan-Germanism it reflected the actual conditions of rule in both Russia and Austria-Hungary. To describe these two despotisms, the only ones left in Europe at the outbreak of the first World War, in terms of multinational states gives only one part of the picture. As much as for their rule over multinational territories they were distinguished from other governments in that they governed the peoples directly (and not only exploited them) by a bureaucracy; parties played insignificant roles, and parliaments had no legislative functions; the state ruled through an administration that applied decrees. The significance of Parliament for the Dual Monarchy was little more than that of a not too bright debating society. In Russia as well as pre-war Austria serious opposition could hardly be found there but was exerted by outside groups who knew that their entering the parliamentary system would only detract popular attention and support from them.

Legally, government by bureaucracy is government by decree, and this means that power, which in constitutional government only enforces the law, becomes the direct source of all legislation. Decrees moreover remain anonymous (while laws can always be traced to specific men or assemblies), and therefore seem to flow from some over-all ruling power that needs no justification. Pobyedonostzev's contempt for the 'snares' of the law was the eternal contempt of the administrator for the supposed lack of freedom of the legislator, who is hemmed in by principles, and for the inaction of the executors of law, who are restricted by its interpretation. The bureaucrat, who by merely administering decrees has the illusion of constant action, feels tremendously superior to these 'impractical' people who are forever entangled in 'legal niceties' and therefore stay outside the sphere of power which to him is the source of everything.

The administrator considers the law to be powerless because it is by definition separated from its application. The decree, on the other hand, does not exist at all except if and when it is applied; it needs no justification except applicability. It is true that decrees are used by all governments in times of emergency, but then the emergency itself is a clear justification and automatic limitation. In governments by bureaucracy decrees appear in their naked purity as though they were no longer issued by powerful men, but were the incarnation of power itself and the administrator only its accidental agent. There are no general principles which simple reason can understand behind the decree, but ever-changing circumstances which only an expert can know in detail. People ruled by decree never know what rules them because of the impossibility of understanding decrees in themselves and the carefully organized ignorance of specific circumstances and their practical significance in which all administrators keep their subjects. Colonial imperialism, which also ruled by decree and was sometimes even defined as the *'régime des décrets,'* [62a] was dangerous enough; yet the very fact that the administrators over native populations were imported and felt to be usurpers, mitigated its influence on the subject peoples. Only where, as in Russia and Austria, native rules and a native bureaucracy were accepted as the legitimate government, could rule by decree create the atmosphere of arbitrariness and secretiveness which effectively hid its mere expediency.

Rule by decree has conspicuous advantages for the domination of far-flung territories with heterogeneous populations and for a policy of oppression. Its efficiency is superior simply because it ignores all intermediary stages between issuance and application, and because it prevents political reasoning by the people through the withholding of information. It can easily overcome the variety of local customs and need not rely on the necessarily slow process of development of general law. It is most helpful for the establishment of a centralized administration because it overrides automatically all matters of local autonomy. If rule by good laws has sometimes been called the rule of wisdom, rule by appropriate decrees may rightly be called the rule of cleverness. For it is clever to reckon with ulterior motives and aims, and it is wise to understand and create by deduction from generally accepted principles.

Government by bureaucracy has to be distinguished from the mere outgrowth and deformation of civil services which frequently accompanied the decline of the nation-state – as, notably, in France. There the administration has survived all changes in regime since the Revolution, entrenched itself like a parasite in the body politic, developed its own class interests, and become a useless organism whose only purpose appears to be chicanery and prevention of normal economic and political development. There are of course many superficial similarities between the two types of bureaucracy, especially if one pays too much attention to the striking psychological similarity of petty officials. But if the French people have made the very serious mistake of accepting their administration as a necessary evil, they have never committed the fatal error of allowing it to rule the

---

62a See M. Larcher, *Traité Elémentaire de Législation Algérienne*, 1903, Vol. II, pp. 150–152: 'The *régime des décrets* is the government of all French colonies.'

country – even though the consequence has been that nobody rules it. The French atmosphere of government has become one of inefficiency and vexations; but it has not created an aura of pseudomysticism.

And it is this pseudomysticism that is the stamp of bureaucracy when it becomes a form of government. Since the people it dominates never really know why something is happening, and a rational interpretation of laws does not exist, there remains only one thing that counts, the brutal naked event itself. What happens to one then becomes subject to an interpretation whose possibilities are endless, unlimited by reason and unhampered by knowledge. Within the framework of such endless interpretative speculation, so characteristic of all branches of Russian pre-revolutionary literature, the whole texture of life and world assume a mysterious secrecy and depth. There is a dangerous charm in this aura because of its seemingly inexhaustible richness; interpretation of suffering has a much larger range than that of action for the former goes on in the inwardness of the soul and releases all the possibilities of human imagination, whereas the latter is constantly checked, and possibly led into absurdity, by outward consequence and controllable experience.

One of the most glaring differences between the old-fashioned rule by bureaucracy and the up-to-date totalitarian brand is that Russia's and Austria's pre-war rulers were content with an idle radiance of power and, satisfied to control its outward destinies, left the whole inner life of the soul intact. Totalitarian bureaucracy, with a more complete understanding of the meaning of absolute power, intruded upon the private individual and his inner life with equal brutality. The result of this radical efficiency has been that the inner spontaneity of people under its rule was killed along with their social and political activities, so that the merely political sterility under the older bureaucracies was followed by total sterility under totalitarian rule.

The age which saw the rise of the pan-movements, however, was still happily ignorant of total sterilization. On the contrary, to an innocent observer (as most Westerners were) the so-called Eastern soul appeared to be incomparably richer, its psychology more profound, its literature more meaningful than that of the 'shallow' Western democracies. This psychological and literary adventure into the 'depths' of suffering did not come to pass in Austria-Hungary because its literature was mainly German-language literature in general. Instead of inspiring profound humbug, Austrian bureaucracy rather caused its greatest modern writer to become the humorist and critic of the whole matter. Franz Kafka knew well enough the superstition of fate which possesses people who live under the perpetual rule of accidents, the inevitable tendency to read a special superhuman meaning into happenings whose rational significance is beyond the knowledge and understanding of the concerned. He was well aware of the weird attractiveness of such peoples, their melancholy and beautifully sad folk tales which seemed so superior to the lighter and brighter litera-ture of more fortunate peoples. He exposed the pride in necessity as such, even the necessity of evil, and the nauseating conceit which identifies evil and misfortune with destiny. The miracle is only that he could do this in a world in which the main elements of this atmos-phere were not fully articulated; he trusted his great powers of imagination to draw all the necessary conclusions and, as it were, to complete what reality had somehow neglected to bring into full focus.[63]

Only the Russian Empire of that time offered a complete picture of rule by bureaucracy. The chaotic conditions of the country – too vast to be ruled, populated by primitive peoples without experience in pol-itical organization of any kind, who vegetated under the incomprehensible overlordship of the Russian bureaucracy – conjured up an atmosphere of anarchy and hazard in which the conflicting whims of petty officials and the daily accidents of incompetence and inconsistency inspired a philosophy that saw in the Accident the true

---

63 See especially the magnificent story in *The Castle* (1930) of the Barnabases, which reads like a weird travesty of a piece of Russian literature. The family is living under a curse, treated as lepers till they feel themselves such, merely because one of their pretty daughters once dared to reject the indecent advances of an important official. The plain villagers, controlled to the last detail by a bureaucracy, and slaves even in their thoughts to the whims of their all-powerful officials, had long since come to real-ize that to be in the right or to be in the wrong was for them a matter of pure 'fate' which they could not alter. It is not, as K. naïvely assumes, the sender of an obscene letter who is exposed, but the recipient who becomes branded and tainted. This is what the villagers mean when they speak of their 'fate.' In K.'s view, 'it's unjust and mon-strous, but [he is] the only one in the village of that opinion.'

Lord of Life, something like the apparition of Divine Providence.[64] To the Pan-Slav who always insisted on the so much more 'interesting' conditions in Russia against the shallow boredom of civilized countries, it looked as though the Divine had found an intimate immanence in the soul of the unhappy Russian people, matched nowhere else on earth. In an unending stream of literary variations the Pan-Slavs opposed the profundity and violence of Russia to the superficial banality of the West, which did not know suffering or the meaning of sacrifice, and behind whose sterile civilized surface were hidden frivolity and triteness.[65] The totalitarian movements still owed much of their appeal to this vague and embittered anti-Western mood that was especially in vogue in pre-Hitler Germany and Austria, but had seized the general European intelligentsia of the twenties as well. Up to the moment of actual seizure of power, they could use this passion for the profound and rich 'irrational,' and during the crucial years when the exiled Russian intelligentsia exerted a not negligible influence upon the spiritual mood of an entirely disturbed Europe, this purely literary attitude proved to be a strong emotional factor in preparing the ground for totalitarianism.[66]

Movements, as contrasted to parties, did not simply degenerate

64 Deification of accidents serves of course as rationalization for every people that is not master of its own destiny. See for instance Steinberg, *op. cit.*: 'For it is Accident that has become decisive for the structure of Jewish history. And Accident . . . in the language of religion is called Providence' (p. 34).

65 A Russian writer once said that Pan-Slavism 'engenders an implacable hatred of the West, a morbid cult of everything Russian . . . the salvation of the universe is still possible, but it can come about only through Russia . . . The Pan-Slavists, seeing enemies of their idea everywhere, persecute everybody who does not agree with them . . .' (Victor Bérard, *L'Empire russe et le tsarisme*, 1905.) See also N. V. Bubnoff, *Kultur und Geschichte im russischen Denken der Gegenwart*, 1927, in Osteuropa: Quellen und Studien, Heft 2, Chapter v.

66 Ehrenberg, *op. cit.*, stresses this in his epilogue: The ideas of a Kirejewski, Chomjakow, Leontjew 'may have died out in Russia after the Revolution. But now they have spread all over Europe and live today in Sofia, Constantinople, Berlin, Paris, London. Russians, and precisely the disciples of these authors . . . publish books and edit magazines that are read in all European countries; through them, these ideas – the ideas of their spiritual fathers – are represented. The Russian spirit has become European' (p. 334).

into bureaucratic machines,[67] but saw in bureaucratic regimes possible models of organization. The admiration which inspired the Pan-Slav Pogodin's description of the machine of Czarist Russian bureaucracy would have been shared by them all: 'A tremendous machine, constructed after the simplest principles, guided by the hand of *one* man . . . which sets it in motion at every moment with a single movement, no matter which direction and speed he may choose. And this is not merely a mechanical motion, the machine is entirely animated by inherited emotions, which are subordination, limitless confidence and devotion to the Czar who is their God on earth. Who would dare to attack us and whom could we not force into obedience?'[68]

Pan-Slavists were less opposed to the state than their Pan-Germanist colleagues. They sometimes even tried to convince the Czar to become the head of the movement. The reason for this tendency is of course that the Czar's position differed considerably from that of any European monarch, the Emperor of Austria-Hungary not excluded, and that the Russian despotism never developed into a rational state in the Western sense but remained fluid, anarchic, and unorganized. Czarism, therefore, sometimes appeared to the Pan-Slavists as the symbol of a gigantic moving force surrounded by a halo of unique holiness.[69] Pan-Slavism, in contrast to Pan-Germanism, did not have to invent a new ideology to suit the needs of the Slavic soul and its movement, but could interpret – and make a mystery of – Czarism as the anti-Western, anticonstitutional, antistate expression of the movement itself. This mystification of anarchic power inspired Pan-Slavism with its most pernicious theories about the transcendent nature and inherent goodness of all power. Power was conceived as a divine emanation pervading all natural and human activity. It was no longer a

---

67 For the bureaucratization of party machines, Robert Michels, *Political Parties; a sociological study of the oligarchical tendencies of modern democracy* (English translation Glencoe, 1949, from the German edition of 1911), is still the standard work.

68 K. Staehlin, 'Die Entstehung des Panslawismus,' in *Germano-Slavica*, 1936, Heft 4.

69 M. N. Katkov: 'All power has its derivation from God; the Russian Czar, however, was granted a special significance distinguishing him from the rest of the world's rulers . . . He is a successor of the Caesars of the Eastern Empire . . . the founders of the very creed of the Faith of Christ . . . Herein lies the mystery of the deep distinction between Russia and all the nations of the world.' Quoted from Salo W. Baron, *Modern Nationalism and Religion*, 1947.

means to achieve something: it simply existed, men were dedicated to its service for the love of God, and any law that might regulate or restrain its 'limitless and terrible strength' was clearly sacrilege. In its complete arbitrariness, power as such was held to be holy, whether it was the power of the Czar or the power of sex. Laws were not only incompatible with it, they were sinful, man-made 'snares' that prevented the full development of the 'divine.'[70] The government, no matter what it did, was still the 'Supreme Power in action,'[71] and the Pan-Slav movement only had to adhere to this power and to organize its popular support, which eventually would permeate and therefore sanctify the whole people – a colossal herd, obedient to the arbitrary will of one man, ruled neither by law nor interest, but kept together solely by the cohesive force of their numbers and the conviction of their own holiness.

From the beginning, the movements lacking the 'strength of inherited emotions' had to differ from the model of the already existing Russian despotism in two respects. They had to make propaganda which the established bureaucracy hardly needed, and did this by

70 Pobyedonostzev in his *Reflections of a Russian Statesman*, London, 1898: 'Power exists not for itself alone but for the love of God. It is a service to which men are dedicated. Thence comes the limitless, terrible strength of power and its limitless and terrible burden' (p. 254). Or: 'The law becomes a snare not only to the people, but ... to the very authorities engaged in its administration ... if at every step the executor of the law finds in the law itself restrictive prescriptions ... then all authority is lost in doubt, weakened by the law ... and crushed by the fear of responsibility' (p. 88).

71 According to Katkov 'government in Russia means a thing totally different from what is understood by this term in other countries ... In Russia the government in the highest sense of the word, is the Supreme Power in action ...' Moissaye J. Olgin, *The Soul of the Russian Revolution*, New York, 1917, p. 57. – In a more rationalized form, we find the theory that 'legal guarantees were needed in states founded upon conquest and threatened by the conflict of classes and races; they were superfluous in a Russia with harmony of classes and friendship of races' (Hans Kohn, *op. cit.*).

Although idolization of power played a less articulate role in Pan-Germanism, there was always a certain antilegal tendency which for instance comes out clearly in Frymann, *op. cit.*, who as early as 1912 proposed the introduction of that 'protective custody' (*Sicherheitshaft*), that is, arrest without any legal reason, which the Nazis then used to fill concentration camps.

introducing an element of violence;[72] and they found a substitute for the role of 'inherited emotions' in the ideologies which Continental parties had already developed to a considerable extent. The difference in their use of ideology was that they not only added ideological justification to interest representation, but used ideologies as organizational principles. If the parties had been bodies for the organization of class interests, the movements became embodiments of ideologies. In other words, movements were 'charged with philosophy' and claimed they had set into motion 'the individualization of the moral universal within a collective.'[73]

It is true that concretization of ideas had first been conceived in Hegel's theory of state and history and had been further developed in Marx's theory of the proletariat as the protagonist of mankind. It is of course not accidental that Russian Pan-Slavism was as much influenced by Hegel as Bolshevism was influenced by Marx. Yet neither Marx nor Hegel assumed actual human beings and actual parties or countries to be ideas in the flesh; both believed in the process of history in which ideas could be concretized only in a complicated dialectical movement. It needed the vulgarity of mob leaders to hit upon the tremendous possibilities of such concretization for the organization of masses. These men began to tell the mob that each of its members could become such a lofty all-important walking embodiment of something ideal if he would only join the movement. Then he no longer had to be loyal or generous or courageous, he would automatically be the very incarnation of Loyalty, Generosity, Courage. Pan-Germanism showed itself somewhat superior in organizational theory, insofar as it shrewdly deprived the individual German of all these wondrous qualities if he did not adhere to the movement

---

72 There is of course a patent similarity between the French mob organization during the Dreyfus Affair (see p. 144) and Russian pogrom groups such as the 'Black Hundreds' in which the 'wildest and the least cultivated dregs of old Russia [were gathered and which] kept contact with the majority of the Orthodox episcopate' (Fedotow, *op. cit.*) – or the 'League of the Russian People' with its secret Fighting Squadrons recruited from the lower agents of the police, paid by the government, and led by intellectuals. See E. Cherikover, 'New Materials on the Pogroms in Russia at the Beginning of the Eighties' in *Historishe Schriften* (Vilna), II, 463; and N. M. Gelber, 'The Russian Pogroms in the Early Eighties in the Light of the Austrian Diplomatic Correspondence,' *ibid.*
73 Delos, *op. cit.*

(thereby foreshadowing the spiteful contempt which Nazism later expressed for the non-Party members of the German people), whereas Pan-Slavism, absorbed deeply in its limitless speculations about the Slav soul, assumed that every Slav consciously or unconsciously possessed such a soul no matter whether he was properly organized or not. It needed Stalin's ruthlessness to introduce into Bolshevism the same contempt for the Russian people that the Nazis showed toward the Germans.

It is this absoluteness of movements which more than anything else separates them from party structures and their partiality, and serves to justify their claim to overrule all objections of individual conscience. The particular reality of the individual person appears against the background of a spurious reality of the general and universal, shrinks into a negligible quantity or is submerged in the stream of dynamic movement of the universal itself. In this stream the difference between ends and means evaporates together with the personality, and the result is the monstrous immorality of ideological politics. All that matters is embodied in the moving movement itself; every idea, every value has vanished into a welter of superstitious pseudoscientific immanence.

## III: Party and Movement

The striking and fateful difference between continental and overseas imperialism has been that their initial successes and failures were in exact opposition. While continental imperialism, even in its beginnings, succeeded in realizing the imperialist hostility against the nation-state by organizing large strata of people outside the party system, and always failed to get results in tangible expansion, overseas imperialism, in its mad and successful rushes to annex more and more far-flung territories, was never very successful when it attempted to change the home countries' political structure. The nation-state system's ruin, having been prepared by its own overseas imperialism, was eventually carried out by those movements which had originated outside its own realm. And when it came to pass that movements began successfully to compete with the nation-state's

party system, it was also seen that they could undermine only countries with a multiparty system, that mere imperialist tradition was not
sufficient to give them mass appeal, and that Great Britain, the classic
country of two-party rule, did not produce a movement of either
Fascist or Communist orientation of any consequence outside her
party system.

The slogan 'above the parties,' the appeal to 'men of all parties,' and
the boast that they would 'stand far removed from the strife of parties
and represent only a national purpose' was equally characteristic of
all imperialist groups,[74] where it appeared as a natural consequence
of their exclusive interest in foreign policy in which the nation was
supposed to act as a whole in any event, independent of classes and
parties.[75] Since, moreover, in the Continental systems this representation of the nation as a whole had been the 'monopoly' of the state,[76]
it could even seem that the imperialists put the state's interests
above everything else, or that the interest of the nation as a whole had
found in them its long-sought popular support. Yet despite all such
claims to true popularity the 'parties above parties' remained
small societies of intellectuals and well-to-do people who, like the

74 As the President of the German Kolonialverein put it in 1884. See Mary E. Townsend,
*Origin of Modern German Colonialism: 1871–1885*, New York, 1921. The Pan-German
League always insisted on its being 'above the parties; this was and is a vital condition
for the League' (Otto Bonhard, *op. cit.*). The first real party that claimed to be more
than a party, namely an 'imperial party,' was the National-Liberal Party in Germany
under the leadership of Ernst Bassermann (Frymann, *op. cit.*).

In Russia, the Pan-Slavs needed only to pretend to be nothing more than popular
support for the government, in order to be removed from all competition with parties;
for the government as 'the Supreme Power in action ... cannot be understood as
related to parties.' Thus M. N. Katkov, close journalistic collaborator of Pobyedonostzev. See Olgin, *op. cit.*, p. 57.

75 This clearly was still the purpose of the early 'beyond party' groups among which
up to 1918 the Pan-German League must still be counted. 'Standing outside of all
organized political parties, we may go our purely national way. We do not ask: Are you
conservative? Are you liberal? ... The German nation is the meeting point upon which
all parties can make common cause.' Lehr, *Zwecke und Ziele des alldeutschen Verbandes*,
Flugschriften, No. 14. Translation quoted from Wertheimer, *op. cit.*, p. 110.

76 Carl Schmitt, *Staat, Bewegung, Volk* (1934), speaks of the 'monopoly of politics which
the state had acquired during the seventeenth and eighteenth centuries.'

Pan-German League, could hope to find a larger appeal only in times of national emergency.[77]

The decisive invention of the pan-movements, therefore, was not that they too claimed to be outside and above the party system, but that they called themselves 'movements,' their very name alluding to the profound distrust for all parties that was already widespread in Europe at the turn of the century and finally became so decisive that in the days of the Weimar Republic, for instance, 'each new group believed it could find no better legitimization and no better appeal to the masses than a clear insistence that it was not a "party" but a "movement." '[78]

It is true that the actual disintegration of the European party system was brought about, not by the pan- but by the totalitarian movements. The pan-movements, however, which found their place somewhere between the small and comparatively harmless imperialist societies and the totalitarian movements, were forerunners of the totalitarians, insofar as they had already discarded the element of snobbery so conspicuous in all imperialist leagues, whether the snobbery of wealth and birth in England or of education in Germany, and therefore could take advantage of the deep popular hatred for those institutions which were supposed to represent the people.[79] It is not surprising that the appeal of movements in Europe has not been hurt much by the defeat of Nazism and the growing fear of Bolshevism. As

77 Wertheimer, *op. cit.*, depicts the situation quite correctly when she says: 'That there was any vital connection before the war between the Pan-German League and the imperial government is entirely preposterous.' On the other hand, it was perfectly true that German policy during the first World War was decisively influenced by Pan-Germans because the higher officer corps had become Pan-German. See Hans Delbrück, *Ludendorffs Selbstportrait*, Berlin, 1922. Compare also his earlier article on the subject, 'Die Alldeutschen,' in *Preussische Jahrbücher*, 154, December, 1913.

78 Sigmund Neumann, *Die deutschen Parteien*, 1932, p. 99.

79 Moeller van den Bruck, *Das dritte Reich*, 1923, pp. vii–viii, describes the situation: 'When the World War ended in defeat . . . we met Germans everywhere who said they were outside all parties, who talked about "freedom from parties," who tried to find a point of view "above parties." . . . A complete lack of respect for Parliaments . . . which at no time have the faintest idea of what is really going on in the country . . . is very widespread among the people.'

matters stand now, the only country in Europe where Parliament is not despised and the party system not hated is Great Britain.[80]

Faced with the stability of political institutions in the British Isles and the simultaneous decline of all nation-states on the Continent, one can hardly avoid concluding that the difference between the Anglo-Saxon and the Continental party system must be an important factor. For the merely material differences between a greatly impoverished England and an undestroyed France were not great after the close of this war; unemployment, the greatest revolutionizing factor in prewar Europe, had hit England even harder than many Continental countries; and the shock to which England's political stability was being exposed right after the war through the Labor Government's liquidation of imperialist government in India and its tentative efforts to rebuild an English world policy along nonimperialist lines must have been tremendous. Nor does mere difference in social structure account for the relative strength of Great Britain; for the economic basis of her social system has been severely changed by the socialist Government without any decisive change in political institutions.

Behind the external difference between the Anglo-Saxon two-party and the Continental multiparty system lies a fundamental distinction between the party's function within the body politic, which has great consequences for the party's attitude to power, and the citizen's position in his state. In the two-party system one party always represents the government and actually rules the country, so that, temporarily, the party in power becomes identical with the state. The state, as a permanent guarantee of the country's unity, is represented only in the permanence of the office of the King[81] (for the permanent Undersecretaryship of the Foreign Office is only a matter of continuity). As the

---

80 British dissatisfaction with the Front Bench system has nothing to do with this anti-Parliamentarian sentiment, the British in this instance being opposed to something that prevents Parliament from functioning properly.

81 The British party system, the oldest of all, 'began to take shape . . . only when the affairs of state ceased to be exclusively the prerogative of the crown . . . ,' that is, after 1688. 'The King's role has been historically to represent the nation as a unity as against the factional strife of parties.' See article 'Political Parties' 3, 'Great Britain' by W. A. Rudlin in *Encyclopedia of the Social Sciences*.

two parties are planned and organized for alternate rule,[82] all branches of the administration are planned and organized for alternation. Since the rule of each party is limited in time, the opposition party exerts a control whose efficiency is strengthened by the certainty that it is the ruler of tomorrow. In fact, it is the opposition rather than the symbolic position of the King that guarantees the integrity of the whole against one-party dictatorship. The obvious advantages of this system are that there is no essential difference between government and state, that power as well as the state remain within the grasp of the citizens organized in the party, which represents the power and the state either of today or of tomorrow, and that consequently there is no occasion for indulgence in lofty speculations about Power and State as though they were something beyond human reach, metaphysical entities independent of the will and action of the citizens.

The Continental party system supposes that each party defines itself consciously as a part of the whole, which in turn is represented by a state above parties.[83] A one-party rule therefore can only signify the dictatorial domination of one part over all others. Governments formed by alliances between party leaders are always only party governments, clearly distinguished from the state which rests above and beyond them. One of the minor shortcomings of this system is that cabinet members cannot be chosen according to competence, for too many parties are represented, and ministers are necessarily chosen according to party alliances;[84] the British system, on the other hand,

82 In what seems to be the earliest history of the 'party,' George W. Cooke, *The History of Party*, London, 1836, in the preface defines the subject as a system by which 'two classes of statesmen . . . alternately govern a mighty empire.'

83 The best account of the essence of the Continental party system is given by the Swiss jurist Johann Caspar Bluntschli, *Charakter und Geist der politischen Parteien*, 1869. He states: 'It is true that a party is only part of a greater whole, never this whole itself . . . It must never identify itself with the whole, the people or the state . . . therefore a party may fight against other parties, but it must never ignore them and usually must not want to destroy them. No party can exist all by itself' (p. 3). The same idea is expressed by Karl Rosenkranz, a German Hegelian philosopher, whose book on political parties appeared before parties existed in Germany: *Ueber den Begriff der politischen Partei* (1843): 'Party is conscious partiality' (p. 9).

84 See John Gilbert Heinberg, *Comparative Major European Governments*, New York, 1937, chapters vii and viii. 'In England one political party usually has a majority in the House of Commons, and the leaders of the party are members of the Cabinet . . . In

permits a choice of the best men from the large ranks of one party. Much more relevant, however, is the fact that the multiparty system never allows any one man or any one party to assume full responsibility, with the natural consequence that no government, formed by party alliances, ever feels fully responsible. Even if the improbable happens and an absolute majority of one party dominates Parliament and results in one-party rule, this can only end either in dictatorship, because the system is not prepared for such government, or in the bad conscience of a still truly democratic leadership which, accustomed to thinking of itself only as part of the whole, will naturally be afraid of using its power. This bad conscience functioned in a well-nigh exemplary fashion when, after the first World War, the German and Austrian Social Democratic parties emerged for a short moment as absolute majority parties, yet repudiated the power which went with this position.[85]

Since the rise of the party systems it has been a matter of course to identify parties with particular interests, economic or others,[86] and all Continental parties, not only the labor groups, have been very frank in

France, no political party in practice ever has a majority of the members of the Chamber of Deputies, and, consequently, the Council of Ministers is composed of the leaders of a number of party groups' (p. 158).

85 See *Demokratie und Partei*, ed. by Peter R. Rohden, Vienna, 1932, Introduction: 'The distinguishing characteristic of German parties is . . . that all parliamentary groups are resigned not to represent the *volonté générale* . . . That is why the parties were so embarrassed when the November Revolution brought them to power. Each of them was so organized that it could only make a relative claim, *i.e.*, it always reckoned with the existence of other parties representing other partial interests and thus naurally limited its own ambitions' (pp. 13–14).

86 The Continental party system is of very recent date. With the exception of the French parties which date back to the French Revolution, no European country knew party representation prior to 1848. Parties came into being through formation of factions in Parliament. In Sweden, the Social Democratic Party was the first party (in 1889) with a fully formulated program (*Encyclopedia of Social Sciences, loc. cit.*). For Germany, see Ludwig Bergstraesser, *Geschichte der politischen Parteien*, 1921. All parties were frankly based upon protection of interests; the German Conservative Party for instance developed from the 'Association to protect the interests of big landed property' founded in 1848. Interests were not necessarily economic, however. The Dutch parties, for instance, were formed 'over the two questions that so largely dominate Dutch politics – the broadening of the franchise and the subsidizing of private [mainly denominational] education' (*Encyclopedia of the Social Sciences, loc. cit.*).

admitting this as long as they could be sure that a state above parties exerts its power more or less in the interest of all. The Anglo-Saxon party, on the contrary, founded on some 'particular principle' for the service of the 'national interest,'[87] is itself the actual or future state of the country; particular interests are represented in the party itself, as its right and left wing, and held in check by the very necessities of government. And since in the two-party system a party cannot exist for any length of time if it does not win enough strength to assume power, no theoretical justification is needed, no ideologies are developed, and the peculiar fanaticism of Continental party strife, which springs not so much from conflicting interests as from antagonistic ideologies, is completely absent.[88]

The trouble with the Continental parties, separated on principle from government and power, was not so much that they were trapped in the narrowness of particular interests as that they were ashamed of these interests and therefore developed those justifications which led each one into an ideology claiming that its particular interests coincided with the most general interests of humanity. The conservative party was not content to defend the interests of landed property but needed a philosophy according to which God had created man to till the soil by the sweat of his brow. The same is true for the progress ideology of the middle-class parties and for the labor parties' claim that the proletariat is the leader of mankind. This strange combination of lofty philosophy and down-to-earth interests is paradoxical only at first glance. Since these parties did not organize their members (or educate their leaders) for the purpose of handling public affairs, but represented them only as private individuals with private interests, they had to cater to all private needs, spiritual as well as material. In other words, the chief difference between the Anglo-Saxon and the Continental party is that the former is a political organization of

87 Edmund Burke's definition of party: 'Party is a body of men united for promoting, by their joint endeavor, the national interest, upon some particular principle in which they are all agreed' (*Upon Party*, 2nd edition, London, 1850).

88 Arthur N. Holcombe (*Encyclopedia of the Social Sciences, loc. cit.*) rightly stressed that in the double party system the principles of the two parties 'have tended to be the same. If they had not been substantially the same, submission to the victor would have been intolerable to the vanquished.'

citizens who need to 'act in concert' in order to act at all,[89] while the latter is the organization of private individuals who want their interests to be protected against interference from public affairs.

It is consistent with this system that the Continental state philosophy recognized men to be citizens only insofar as they were not party members, *i.e.*, in their individual unorganized relationship to the state (*Staatsbürger*) or in their patriotic enthusiasm in times of emergency (*citoyens*).[90] This was the unfortunate result of the transformation of the *citoyen* of the French Revolution into the *bourgeois* of the nineteenth century on one hand, and of the antagonism between state and society on the other. The Germans tended to consider patriotism an obedient self-oblivion before the authorities and the French an enthusiastic loyalty to the phantom of 'eternal France.' In both cases, patriotism meant an abandonment of one's party and partial interests in favor of the government and the national interest. The point is that such nationalistic deformation was almost inevitable in a system that created political parties out of private interests, so that the public good had to depend upon force from above and a vague generous self-sacrifice from below which could be achieved only by arousing nationalistic passions. In England, on the contrary, antagonism between private and national interest never played a decisive role in

---

89 Burke, *op. cit.*: 'They believed that no men could act with effect, who did not act in concert; that no men could act in concert, who did not act with confidence; that no men could act with confidence, who were not bound together by common opinions, common affections, and common interests.'

90 For the Central European concept of citizen (the *Staatsbürger*) as opposed to party member, see Bluntschli, *op. cit.*: 'Parties are not state institutions . . . not members of the state organism, but free social associations whose formations depend upon a changing membership united for common political action by a definite conviction.' The difference between state and party interest is stressed time and again: 'The party must never put itself above the state, must never put its party interest above the state interest' (pp. 9 and 10).

Burke, on the contrary, argues against the concept according to which party interests or party membership make a man a worse citizen. 'Commonwealths are made of families, free commonwealths of parties also; and we may as well affirm that our natural regards and ties of blood tend inevitably to make men bad citizens, as that the bonds of our party weaken those by which we are held to our country' (*op. cit.*). Lord John Russell, *On Party* (1850), even goes one step further when he asserts that the chief of the good effects of parties is 'that it gives a substance to the shadowy opinions of politicians, and attaches them to steady and lasting principles.'

politics. The more, therefore, the party system on the Continent corresponded to class interests, the more urgent was the need of the nation for nationalism, for some popular expression and support of national interests, a support which England with its direct government by party and opposition never needed so much.

If we consider the difference between the Continental multiparty and the British two-party system with regard to their predisposition to the rise of movements, it seems plausible that it should be easier for a one-party dictatorship to seize the state machinery in countries where the state is above the parties, and thereby above the citizens, than in those where the citizens by acting 'in concert,' *i.e.*, through party organization, can win power legally and feel themselves to be the proprietors of the state either of today or of tomorrow. It appears even more plausible that the mystification of power inherent in the movements should be more easily achieved the farther removed the citizens are from the sources of power – easier in bureaucratically ruled countries where power positively transcends the capacity to understand on the part of the ruled, than in constitutionally governed countries where the law is above power and power is only a means of its enforcement; and easier yet in countries where the state power is beyond the reach of the parties and therefore, even if it remains within the reach of the citizen's intelligence, is removed beyond the reach of his practical experience and action.

The alienation of the masses from government, which was the beginning of their eventual hatred of and disgust with Parliament, was different in France and other Western democracies on one hand, and in the Central European countries, Germany chiefly, on the other. In Germany, where the state was by definition above the parties, party leaders as a rule surrendered their party allegiance the moment they became ministers and were charged with official duties. Disloyalty to one's own party was the duty of everyone in public office.[91] In France,

91 Compare with this attitude the telling fact that in Great Britain Ramsay MacDonald was never able to live down his 'betrayal' of the Labor Party. In Germany the spirit of civil service asked of those in public office to be 'above the parties.' Against this spirit of the old Prussian civil service the Nazis asserted the priority of the Party, because they wanted dictatorship. Goebbels demanded explicitly: 'Each party member who becomes a state functionary has to remain a National Socialist first ... and to

ruled by party alliances, no real government has been possible since the establishment of the Third Republic and its fantastic record of cabinets. Her weakness was the opposite of the German one; she had liquidated the state which was above the parties and above Parliament without reorganizing her party system into a body capable of governing. The government necessarily became a ridiculous exponent of the ever-changing moods of Parliament and public opinion. The German system, on the other hand, made Parliament a more or less useful battlefield for conflicting interests and opinions whose main function was to influence the government but whose practical necessity in the handling of state affairs was, to say the least, debatable. In France, the parties suffocated the government; in Germany, the state emasculated the parties.

Since the end of the last century, the repute of these Continental parliaments and parties has constantly declined; to the people at large they looked like expensive and unnecessary institutions. For this reason alone each group that claimed to present something above party and class interests and started outside of Parliament had a great chance for popularity. Such groups seemed more competent, more sincere, and more concerned with public affairs. This, however, was so in appearance only, for the true goal of every 'party above parties' was to promote one particular interest until it had devoured all others, and to make one particular group the master of the state machine. This is what finally happened in Italy under Mussolini's Fascism, which up to 1938 was not totalitarian but just an ordinary nationalist dictatorship developed logically from a multiparty democracy. For there is indeed some truth in the old truism about the affinity between majority rule and dictatorship, but this affinity has nothing whatever to do with totalitarianism. It is obvious that, after many decades of inefficient and muddled multiparty rule, the seizure of the state for the advantage of one party can come as a great relief because it assures at least, though only for a limited time, some consistency, some permanence, and a little less contradiction.

The fact that the seizure of power by the Nazis was usually

---

co-operate closely with the party administration' (quoted from Gottfried Neesse, *Partei und Staat*, 1939, p. 28).

identified with such a one-party dictatorship merely showed how much political thinking was still rooted in the old established patterns, and how little the people were prepared for what really was to come. The only typically modern aspect of the Fascist party dictatorship is that here, too, the party insisted that it was a movement; that it was nothing of the kind, but merely usurped the slogan 'movement' in order to attract the masses, became evident as soon as it seized the state machine without drastically changing the power structure of the country, being content to fill all government positions with party members. It was precisely through the identification of the party with the state, which both the Nazis and the Bolsheviks have always carefully avoided, that the party ceased to be a 'movement' and became tied to the basically stable structure of the state.

Even though the totalitarian movements and their predecessors, the pan-movements, were not 'parties above parties' aspiring to seize the state machine but movements aiming at the destruction of the state, the Nazis found it very convenient to pose as such, that is, to pretend to follow faithfully the Italian model of Fascism. Thus they could win the help of those upper-class and business elite who mistook the Nazis for the older groups they had themselves frequently initiated and which had made only the rather modest pretense of conquering the state machine for one party.[92] The businessmen who helped Hitler into power naïvely believed that they were only supporting a dictator, and one of their own making, who would naturally rule to the advantage of their own class and the disadvantage of all others.

The imperialist-inspired 'parties above parties' had never known how to profit from popular hatred of the party system as such; Germany's frustrated pre-war imperialism, in spite of its dreams of continental expansion and its violent denunciation of the nation-state's democratic institutions, never reached the scope of a movement. It certainly was not sufficient to haughtily discard class interests, the very foundation of the nation's party system, for this left them less

92 Such as the Kolonialverein, the Centralverein für Handelsgeographie, the Flotten-verein, or even the Pan-German League, which however prior to the first World War had no connection whatsoever with big business. See Wertheimer, *op. cit.*, p. 73. Typical of this 'above parties' of the bourgeoisie were of course the Nationalliberalen; see note 74.

appeal than even the ordinary parties still enjoyed. What they conspicuously lacked, despite all high-sounding nationalist phrases, was a real nationalist or other ideology. After the first World War, when the German Pan-Germans, especially Ludendorff and his wife, recognized this error and tried to make up for it, they failed despite their remarkable ability to appeal to the most superstitious beliefs of the masses because they clung to an outdated nontotalitarian state worship and could not understand that the masses' furious interest in the so-called 'suprastate powers' (*überstaatliche Mächte*) – i.e., the Jesuits, the Jews, and the Freemasons – did not spring from nation or state worship but, on the contrary, from envy and the desire also to become a 'suprastate power.'[93]

The only countries where to all appearances state idolatry and nation worship were not yet outmoded and where nationalist slogans against the 'suprastate' forces were still a serious concern of the people were those Latin-European countries like Italy and, to a lesser degree, Spain and Portugal, which had actually suffered a definite hindrance to their full national development through the power of the Church. It was partly due to this authentic element of belated national development and partly to the wisdom of the Church, which very sagely recognized that Fascism was neither anti-Christian nor totalitarian in principle and only established a separation of Church and State which already existed in other countries, that the initial anticlerical flavor of Fascist nationalism subsided rather quickly and gave way to a *modus vivendi* as in Italy, or to a positive alliance, as in Spain and Portugal.

Mussolini's interpretation of the corporate state idea was an attempt to overcome the notorious national dangers in a class-ridden society with a new integrated social organization[94] and to solve the

---

93 Erich Ludendorff, *Die überstaatlichen Mächte im letzten Jahre des Weltkrieges*, Leipzig, 1927. See also *Feldherrnworte*, 1938, 2 vols.; I, 43, 55; II, 80.

94 The main purpose of the corporate state was 'that of correcting and neutralizing a condition brought about by the industrial revolution of the nineteenth century which dissociated capital and labor in industry, giving rise on the one hand to a capitalist class of employers of labor and on the other to a great propertyless class, the industrial proletariat. The juxtaposition of these classes inevitably led to the clash of their opposing interests' (*The Fascist Era*, published by the Fascist Confederation of Industrialists, Rome, 1939, chapter iii).

antagonism between state and society, on which the nation-state had rested, by the incorporation of the society into the state.[95] The Fascist movement, a 'party above parties,' because it claimed to represent the interest of the nation as a whole, seized the state machine, identified itself with the highest national authority, and tried to make the whole people 'part of the state.' It did not, however, think itself 'above the state,' and its leaders did not conceive of themselves as 'above the nation.'[96] As regards the Fascists, their movement had come to an end with the seizure of power, at least with respect to domestic policies; the movement could now maintain its motion only in matters of foreign policy, in the sense of imperialist expansion and typically imperialist adventures. Even before the seizure of power, the Nazis clearly kept aloof from this Fascist form of dictatorship, in which the 'movement' merely serves to bring the party to power, and consciously used the party 'to drive on the movement,' which, contrary to the party, must not have any 'definite, closely determined goals.'[97]

The difference between the Fascist and the totalitarian movements is best illustrated by their attitude toward the army, that is, toward the national institution *par excellence*. In contrast to the Nazis and the Bolsheviks, who destroyed the spirit of the army by subordinating it to the political commissars or totalitarian elite formations, the Fascists could use such intensely nationalist instruments as the army, with

95  'If the State is truly to represent the nation, then the people composing the nation must be part of the State.

'How is this to be secured?

'The Fascist answer is by organizing the people in groups according to their respective activities, groups which through their leaders . . . rise by stages as in a pyramid, at the base of which are the masses and at the apex the State.

'No group outside the State, no group against the State, all groups within the State . . . which . . . is the nation itself rendered articulate.' (*Ibid.*)

96  For the relationship between party and state in totalitarian countries and especially the incorporation of the Fascist party into the state of Italy, see Franz Neumann, *Behemoth*, 1942, chapter 1.

97  See the extremely interesting presentation of the relationship between party and movement in the 'Dienstvorschrift für die Parteiorganisation der NSDAP,' 1932, p. II ff., and the presentation by Werner Best in *Die deutsche Polizei*, 1941, p. 107, which has the same orientation: 'It is the task of the Party . . . to hold the movement together and give it support and direction.'

which they identified themselves as they had identified themselves with the state. They wanted a Fascist state and a Fascist army, but still an army and a state; only in Nazi Germany and Soviet Russia army and state became subordinated functions of the movement. The Fascist dictator – but neither Hitler nor Stalin – was the only true usurper in the sense of classical political theory, and his one-party rule was in a sense the only one still intimately connected with the multiparty system. He carried out what the imperialist-minded leagues, societies, and 'parties above parties' had aimed at, so that it is particularly Italian Fascism that has become the only example of a modern mass movement organized within the framework of an existing state, inspired solely by extreme nationalism, and which transformed the people permanently into such *Staatsbürger* or *patriotes* as the nation-state had mobilized only in times of emergency and *union sacrée*.[98]

There are no movements without hatred of the state, and this was virtually unknown to the German Pan-Germans in the relative stability of prewar Germany. The movements originated in Austria-Hungary, where hatred of the state was an expression of patriotism for the oppressed nationalities and where the parties – with the exception of the Social Democratic Party (next to the Christian-Social Party the only one sincerely loyal to Austria) – were formed along national, and not along class lines. This was possible because economic and national interests were almost identical here and because economic and social status depended largely on nationality; nationalism, therefore, which had been a unifying force in the nation-states, here became at once a principle of internal disruption, which resulted in a decisive difference in the structure of the parties as compared with those of nation-states. What held together the members of the parties in multinational Austria-Hungary was not a particular interest, as in the other Continental party systems, or a particular principle for organized action as in the Anglo-Saxon, but chiefly the sentiment of belonging to the same

98 Mussolini, in his speech of November 14, 1933, defends his one-party rule with arguments current in all nation-states during a war: A single political party is needed so 'that political discipline may exist . . . and that the bond of a common fate may unite everyone above contrasting interests' (Benito Mussolini, *Four Speeches on the Corporate State*, Rome, 1935).

nationality. Strictly speaking, this should have been and was a great weakness in the Austrian parties, because no definite goals or programs could be deduced from the sentiment of tribal belonging. The pan-movements made a virtue of this shortcoming by transforming parties into movements and by discovering that form of organization which, in contrast to all others, would never need a goal or program but could change its policy from day to day without harm to its membership. Long before Nazism proudly pronounced that though it had a program it did not need one, Pan-Germanism discovered how much more important for mass appeal a general mood was than laid-down outlines and platforms. For the only thing that counts in a movement is precisely that it keeps itself in constant movement.[99] The Nazis, therefore, used to refer to the fourteen years of the Weimar Republic as the 'time of the System' – *Systemzeit* – the implication being that this time was sterile, lacked dynamism, did not 'move,' and was followed by their 'era of the movement.'

The state, even as a one-party dictatorship, was felt to be in the way of the ever-changing needs of an ever-growing movement. There was no more characteristic difference between the imperialist 'above party group' of the Pan-German League in Germany itself and the Pan-German movement in Austria than their attitudes toward the state:[100] while the 'party above parties' wanted only to seize the state machine, the true movement aimed at its destruction; while the former still recognized the state as highest authority once its representation had fallen into the hands of the members of one party (as in Mussolini's Italy), the latter recognized the movement as independent of and superior in authority to the state.

The pan-movements' hostility to the party system acquired practical significance when, after the first World War, the party system ceased

99  The following anecdote recorded by Berdyaev is noteworthy: 'A Soviet young man went to France . . . [and] was asked what impression France left upon him. He answered: "There is no freedom in this country." . . . The young man expounded his idea of freedom: . . . The so-called [French] freedom was of the kind which leaves everything unchanged; every day was like its predecessors . . . and so the young man who came from Russia was bored in France' (*op. cit.*, pp. 182–183).

100  The Austrian state hostility sometimes occurred also among German Pan-Germans, especially if these were *Auslandsdeutsche*, like Moeller van den Bruck.

to be a working device and the class system of European society broke down under the weight of growing masses entirely declassed by events. What came to the fore then were no longer mere pan-movements but their totalitarian successors, which in a few years determined the politics of all other parties to such a degree that they became either anti-Fascist or anti-Bolshevik or both.[101] By this negative approach seemingly forced upon them from the outside, the older parties showed clearly that they too were no longer able to function as representatives of specific class interests but had become mere defenders of the status quo. The speed with which the German and Austrian Pan-Germans rallied to Nazism has a parallel in the much slower and more complicated course through which Pan-Slavs finally found out that the liquidation of Lenin's Russian Revolution had been thorough enough to make it possible for them to support Stalin wholeheartedly. That Bolshevism and Nazism at the height of their power outgrew mere tribal nationalism and had little use for those who were still actually convinced of it in principle, rather than as mere propaganda material, was neither the Pan-Germans' nor the Pan-Slavs' fault and hardly checked their enthusiasm.

The decay of the Continental party system went hand in hand with a decline of the prestige of the nation-state. National homogeneity was severely disturbed by migrations and France, the *nation par excellence*, became in a matter of years utterly dependent on foreign labor; a restrictive immigration policy, inadequate to new needs, was still truly 'national,' but made it all the more obvious that the nation-state was no longer capable of facing the major political issues of the time.[102] Even more serious was the ill-fated effort of the peace treaties of 1919 to introduce national state organizations into Eastern and Southern Europe where the state people frequently had only a relative majority and were outnumbered by the combined

---

101 Hitler described the situation correctly when he said during the elections of 1932: 'Against National Socialism there are only negative majorities in Germany' (quoted from Konrad Heiden, *Der Führer*, 1944, p. 564).

102 At the outbreak of the second World War, at least 10 per cent of France's population was foreign and not naturalized. Her mines in the north were chiefly worked by Poles and Belgians, her agriculture in the south by Spaniards and Italians. See Carr-Saunders, *World Population*, Oxford, 1936, pp. 145–158.

'minorities.' This new situation would have been sufficient in itself to undermine seriously the class basis of the party system; everywhere parties were now organized along national lines as though the liquidation of the Dual Monarchy had served only to enable a host of similar experiments to start on a dwarfed scale.[103] In other countries, where the nation-state and the class basis of its parties were not touched by migrations and heterogeneity of population, inflation and unemployment caused a similar breakdown; and it is obvious that the more rigid the country's class system, the more class-conscious its people had been, the more dramatic and dangerous was this breakdown.

This was the situation between the two wars when every movement had a greater chance than any party because the movement attacked the institution of the state and did not appeal to classes. Fascism and Nazism always boasted that their hatred was directed not against individual classes, but the class system as such, which they denounced as an invention of Marxism. Even more significant was the fact that the Communists also, notwithstanding their Marxist ideology, had to abandon the rigidity of their class appeal when, after 1935, under the pretext of enlarging their mass base, they formed Popular Fronts everywhere and began to appeal to the same growing masses outside all class strata which up to then had been the natural prey to Fascist movements. None of the old parties was prepared to receive these masses, nor did they gauge correctly the growing importance of their numbers and the growing political influence of their leaders. This error in judgment by the older parties can be explained by the fact that their secure position in Parliament and safe representation in the offices and institutions of the state made them feel much closer to the sources of power than to the masses; they thought the state would remain forever the undisputed master of all instruments of violence, and that the army, that supreme institution of the nation-state, would remain the decisive element in all domestic crises. They therefore felt free to ridicule the numerous paramilitary formations

103 'Since 1918 none of the [succession states] has produced . . . a party which might embrace more than one race, one religion, one social class or one region. The only exception is the Communist Party of Czechoslovakia' (*Encyclopedia of the Social Science*, *loc. cit.*).

which had sprung up without any officially recognized help. For the weaker the party system grew under the pressure of movements outside of Parliament and classes, the more rapidly all former antagonism of the parties to the state disappeared. The parties, laboring under the illusion of a 'state above parties,' misinterpreted this harmony as a source of strength, as a wondrous relationship to something of a higher order. But the state was as threatened as the party system by the pressure of revolutionary movements, and it could no longer afford to keep its lofty and necessarily unpopular position above internal domestic strife. The army had long since ceased to be a reliable bulwark against revolutionary unrest, not because it was in sympathy with the revolution but because it had lost its position. Twice in modern times, and both times in France, the *nation par excellence*, the army had already proved its essential unwillingness or incapacity to help those in power or to seize power by itself: in 1850, when it permitted the mob of the 'Society of December 10' to carry Napoleon III to power,[104] and again at the end of the nineteenth century, during the Dreyfus Affair, when nothing would have been easier than the establishment of a military dictatorship. The neutrality of the army, its willingness to serve every master, eventually left the state in a position of 'mediation between the organized party interests. It was no longer *above* but *between* the classes of society.' [105] In other words, the state and the parties together defended the status quo without realizing that this very alliance served as much as anything else to change the status quo.

The breakdown of the European party system occurred in a spectacular way with Hitler's rise to power. It is now often conveniently forgotten that at the moment of the outbreak of the second World War, the majority of European countries had already adopted some form of dictatorship and discarded the party system, and that this revolutionary change in government had been effected in most countries without revolutionary upheaval. Revolutionary action more often than not was a theatrical concession to the desires of violently discontented masses rather than an actual battle for power. After all, it did not make much

104 See Karl Marx, *op. cit.*
105 Carl Schmitt, *op. cit.*, p. 31.

difference if a few thousand almost unarmed people staged a march on Rome and took over the government in Italy, or whether in Poland (in 1934) a so-called 'partyless bloc,' with a program of support for a semi-fascist government and a membership drawn from the nobility and the poorest peasantry, workers and businessmen, Catholics and orthodox Jews, legally won two-thirds of the seats in Parliament.[106]

In France, Hitler's rise to power, accompanied by a growth of Communism and Fascism, quickly cancelled the other parties' original relationships to each other and changed time-honored party lines over-night. The French Right, up to then strongly anti-German and pro-war, after 1933 became the vanguard of pacifism and understanding with Germany. The Left switched with equal speed from pacifism at any price to a firm stand against Germany and was soon accused of being a party of warmongers by the same parties which only a few years before had denounced its pacifism as national treachery.[107] The years that followed Hitler's rise to power proved even more disastrous to the integrity of the French party system. In the Munich crisis each party, from Right to Left, split internally on the only relevant political issue: who was for, who was against war with Germany.[108] Each party harbored a peace faction and a war faction; none of them could remain united on major political decisions and none stood the test of Fascism and Nazism without splitting into anti-Fascist on one side, Nazi fellow-travelers on the other. That Hitler could choose freely from all parties for the erection of puppet regimes was the consequence of this pre-war situation, and not of an especially shrewd Nazi maneuver. There was not a single party in Europe that did not produce collaborators.

Against the disintegration of the older parties stood the clear-cut unity of the Fascist and Communist movements everywhere – the former, outside of Germany and Italy, loyally advocating peace even at the price of foreign domination, and the latter for a long while preaching war even at the price of national ruin. The point, however, is not so

---

106  Vaclav Fiala, 'Les Partis politiques polonais,' in *Monde Slave*, Février, 1935.

107  See the careful analysis by Charles A. Micaud, *The French Right and Nazi Germany, 1933–1939*, 1943.

108  The most famous instance was the split in the French socialist party in 1938 when Blum's faction remained in a minority against Déat's pro-Munich group during the party Congress of the Seine Department.

much that the extreme Right everywhere had abandoned its traditional nationalism in favor of Hitler's Europe and that the extreme Left had forgotten its traditional pacifism in favor of old nationalist slogans, but rather that both movements could count on the loyalty of a membership and leadership which would not be disturbed by a sudden switch in policy. This was dramatically exposed in the German-Russian non-aggression pact, when the Nazis had to drop their chief slogan against Bolshevism and the Communists had to return to a pacifism which they always had denounced as petty-bourgeois. Such sudden turns did not hurt them in the least. It is still well remembered how strong the Communists remained after their second *volte-face* less than two years later when the Soviet Union was attacked by Nazi Germany, and this in spite of the fact that both political lines had involved the rank and file in serious and dangerous political activities which demanded real sacrifices and constant action.

Different in appearance but much more violent in reality was the breakdown of the party system in pre-Hitler Germany. This came into the open during the last presidential elections in 1932 when entirely new and complicated forms of mass propaganda were adopted by all parties.

The choice of candidates was itself peculiar. While it was a matter of course that the two movements, which stood outside of and fought the parliamentary system from opposite sides, would present their own candidates (Hitler for the Nazis, and Thälmann for the Communists), it was rather surprising to see that all other parties could suddenly agree upon one candidate. That this candidate happened to be old Hindenburg who enjoyed the matchless popularity which, since the time of MacMahon, awaits the defeated general at home, was not just a joke; it showed how much the old parties wanted merely to identify themselves with the old-time state, the state above the parties whose most potent symbol had been the national army, to what an extent, in other words, they had already given up the party system itself. For in the face of the movements, the differences between the parties had indeed become quite meaningless; the existence of all of them was at stake and consequently they banded together and hoped to maintain a status quo that guaranteed their existence. Hindenburg became the symbol of the nation-state and the party system, while Hitler and Thälmann competed with each other to become the true symbol of the people.

As significant as the choice of candidates were the electoral posters. None of them praised its candidate for his own merits; the posters for Hindenburg claimed merely that 'a vote for Thälmann is a vote for Hitler' – warning the workers not to waste their votes on a candidate sure to be beaten (Thälmann) and thus put Hitler in the saddle. This was how the Social Democrats reconciled themselves to Hindenburg, who was not even mentioned. The parties of the Right played the same game and emphasized that 'a vote for Hitler is a vote for Thälmann.' Both, in addition, alluded quite clearly to the instances in which the Nazis and Communists had made common cause, in order to convince all loyal party members, whether Right or Left, that the preservation of the status quo demanded Hindenburg.

In contrast to the propaganda for Hindenburg that appealed to those who wanted the status quo at any price – and in 1932 that meant unemployment for almost half the German people – the candidates of the movements had to reckon with those who wanted change at any price (even at the price of destruction of all legal institutions), and these were at least as numerous as the ever-growing millions of unemployed and their families. The Nazis therefore did not wince at the absurdity that 'a vote for Thälmann is a vote for Hindenburg,' the Communists did not hesitate to reply that 'a vote for Hitler is a vote for Hindenburg,' both threatening their voters with the menace of the status quo in exactly the same way their opponents had threatened their members with the specter of the revolution.

Behind the curious uniformity of method used by the supporters of all the candidates lay the tacit assumption that the electorate would go to the polls because it was frightened – afraid of the Communists, afraid of the Nazis, or afraid of the status quo. In this general fear all class divisions disappeared from the political scene; while the party alliance for the defense of the status quo blurred the older class structure maintained in the separate parties, the rank and file of the movements was completely heterogeneous and as dynamic and fluctuating as unemployment itself.[109] While within the framework of the

109 The German socialist party underwent a typical change from the beginning of the century to 1933. Prior to the first World War only 10 per cent of its members did not belong to the working class whereas about 25 per cent of its votes came from the middle classes. In 1930, however, only 60 per cent of its members were workers

national institutions the parliamentary Left had joined the parliamentary Right, the two movements were busy organizing together the famous transportation strike on the streets of Berlin in November, 1932.

When one considers the extraordinarily rapid decline of the Continental party system, one should bear in mind the very short life span of the whole institution. It existed nowhere before the nineteenth century, and in most European countries the formation of political parties took place only after 1848, so that its reign as an unchallenged institution in national politics lasted hardly four decades. During the last two decades of the nineteenth century, all the significant political developments in France, as well as in Austria-Hungary, already took place outside of and in opposition to parliamentary parties, while everywhere smaller imperialist 'parties above parties' challenged the institution for the sake of popular support for an aggressive, expansionist foreign policy.

While the imperialist leagues set themselves above parties for the sake of identification with the nation-state, the pan-movements attacked these same parties as part and parcel of a general system which included the nation-state; they were not so much 'above parties' as 'above the state' for the sake of a direct identification with the people. The totalitarian movements eventually were led to discard the people also, whom, however, following closely in the footsteps of the pan-movements they used for propaganda purposes. The 'totalitarian state' is a state in appearance only, and the movement no longer truly identifies itself even with the needs of the people. The Movement by now is above state and people, ready to sacrifice both for the sake of its ideology: 'The Movement . . . is State as well as People, and neither the present state . . . nor the present German people can even be conceived without the Movement.'[110]

Nothing proves better the irreparable decay of the party system than the great efforts after this war to revive it on the Continent, their pitiful results, the enhanced appeal of movements after the defeat of Nazism, and the obvious threat of Bolshevism to national independence. The result of all efforts to restore the status quo has been only

---

and at least 40 per cent of its votes were middle-class votes. See Sigmund Neumann, *op. cit.*, pp. 28 ff.
110 Schmitt, *op. cit.*

the restoration of a political situation in which the destructive movements are the only 'parties' that function properly. Their leadership has maintained authority under the most trying circumstances and in spite of constantly changing party lines. In order to gauge correctly the chances for survival of the European nation-state, it would be wise not to pay too much attention to nationalist slogans which the movements occasionally adopt for purposes of hiding their true intentions, but rather to consider that by now everybody knows that they are regional branches of international organizations, that the rank and file is not disturbed in the least when it becomes obvious that their policy serves foreign-policy interests of another and even hostile power, and that denunciations of their leaders as fifth columnists, traitors to the country, etc., do not impress their members to any considerable degree. In contrast to the old parties, the movements have survived the last war and are today the only 'parties' which have remained alive and meaningful to their adherents.

# CHAPTER NINE

# The Decline of the Nation-State and the End of the Rights of Man

It is almost impossible even now to describe what actually happened in Europe on August 4, 1914. The days before and the days after the first World War are separated not like the end of an old and the beginning of a new period, but like the day before and the day after an explosion. Yet this figure of speech is as inaccurate as are all others, because the quiet of sorrow which settles down after a catastrophe has never come to pass. The first explosion seems to have touched off a chain reaction in which we have been caught ever since and which nobody seems to be able to stop. The first World War exploded the European comity of nations beyond repair, something which no other war had ever done. Inflation destroyed the whole class of small property owners beyond hope for recovery or new formation, something which no monetary crisis had ever done so radically before. Unemployment, when it came, reached fabulous proportions, was no longer restricted to the working class but seized with insignificant exceptions whole nations. Civil wars which ushered in and spread over the twenty years of uneasy peace were not only bloodier and more cruel than all their predecessors; they were followed by migrations of groups who, unlike their happier predecessors in the religious wars, were welcomed nowhere and could be assimilated nowhere. Once they had left their homeland they remained homeless, once they had left their state they became stateless; once they had been deprived of their human rights they were rightless, the scum of the earth. Nothing which was being done, no matter how stupid, no matter how many people knew and foretold the consequences, could be undone or prevented. Every event had the finality of a last judgment, a judgment that was passed neither by God nor by the devil, but looked rather like the expression of some unredeemably stupid fatality.

Before totalitarian politics consciously attacked and partially destroyed the very structure of European civilization, the explosion of 1914 and its severe consequences of instability had sufficiently shattered the façade of Europe's political system to lay bare its hidden frame. Such visible exposures were the sufferings of more and more groups of people to whom suddenly the rules of the world around them had ceased to apply. It was precisely the seeming stability of the surrounding world that made each group forced out of its protective boundaries look like an unfortunate exception to an otherwise sane and normal rule, and which filled with equal cynicism victims and observers of an apparently unjust and abnormal fate. Both mistook this cynicism for growing wisdom in the ways of the world, while actually they were more baffled and therefore became more stupid than they ever had been before. Hatred, certainly not lacking in the pre-war world, began to play a central role in public affairs everywhere, so that the political scene in the deceptively quiet years of the twenties assumed the sordid and weird atmosphere of a Strindbergian family quarrel. Nothing perhaps illustrates the general disintegration of political life better than this vague, pervasive hatred of everybody and everything, without a focus for its passionate attention, with nobody to make responsible for the state of affairs – neither the government nor the bourgeoisie nor an outside power. It consequently turned in all directions, haphazardly and unpredictably, incapable of assuming an air of healthy indifference toward anything under the sun.

This atmosphere of disintegration, though characteristic of the whole of Europe between the two wars, was more visible in the defeated than in the victorious countries, and it developed fully in the states newly established after the liquidation of the Dual Monarchy and the Czarist Empire. The last remnants of solidarity between the non-emancipated nationalities in the 'belt of mixed populations' evaporated with the disappearance of a central despotic bureaucracy which had also served to gather together and divert from each other the diffuse hatreds and conflicting national claims. Now everybody was against everybody else, and most of all against his closest neighbors – the Slovaks against the Czechs, the Croats against the Serbs, the Ukrainians against the Poles. And this was not the result of the conflict between nationalities and the state peoples (or minorities and majorities); the Slovaks not only constantly sabotaged the democratic Czech government in Prague, but at the same time persecuted the Hungarian minority on their own soil, while a similar hostility against the state people on one hand, and among themselves on the other, existed among the dissatisfied minorities in Poland.

At first glance these troubles in the old European trouble spot looked like petty nationalist quarrels without any consequence for the political destinies of Europe. Yet in these regions and out of the liquidation of the two multinational states of pre-war Europe, Russia and Austria-Hungary, two victim groups emerged whose sufferings were different from those of all others in the era between the wars; they were worse off than the dispossessed middle classes, the unemployed, the small *rentiers*, the pensioners whom events had deprived of social status, the possibility to work, and the right to hold property: they had lost those rights which had been thought of and even defined as inalienable, namely the Rights of Man. The stateless and the minorities, rightly termed 'cousins-germane,' [1] had no governments to represent and to protect them and therefore were forced to live either under the law of exception of the Minority Treaties, which all governments (except Czechoslovakia) had signed under protest and never recognized as law, or under conditions of absolute lawlessness.

With the emergence of the minorities in Eastern and Southern Europe and with the stateless people driven into Central and Western Europe, a completely new element of disintegration was introduced into postwar Europe. Denationalization became a powerful weapon of totalitarian politics, and the constitutional inability of European nation-states to guarantee human rights to those who had lost nationally guaranteed rights, made it possible for the persecuting governments to impose their standard of values even upon their opponents. Those whom the persecutor had singled out as scum of the earth – Jews, Trotskyites, etc. – actually were received as scum of the earth everywhere; those whom persecution had called undesirable became the *indésirables* of Europe. The official SS newspaper, the *Schwarze Korps*, stated explicitly in 1938 that if the world was not yet

1 By S. Lawford Childs, 'Refugees – a Permanent Problem in International Organization' in *War is not Inevitable. Problems of Peace*, 13th Series, London, 1938, published by the International Labor Office.

convinced that the Jews were the scum of the earth, it soon would be when unidentifiable beggars, without nationality, without money, and without passports crossed their frontiers.[2] And it is true that this kind of factual propaganda worked better than Goebbels' rhetoric, not only because it established the Jews as scum of the earth, but also because the incredible plight of an ever-growing group of innocent people was like a practical demonstration of the totalitarian movements' cynical claims that no such thing as inalienable human rights existed and that the affirmations of the democracies to the contrary were mere prejudice, hypocrisy, and cowardice in the face of the cruel majesty of a new world. The very phrase 'human rights' became for all concerned – victims, persecutors, and onlookers alike – the evidence of hopeless idealism or fumbling feeble-minded hypocrisy.

## I: The 'Nation of Minorities' and the Stateless People

Modern power conditions which make national sovereignty a mockery except for giant states, the rise of imperialism, and the pan-movements undermined the stability of Europe's nation-state system from the outside. None of these factors, however, had sprung directly from the tradition and the institutions of nation-states themselves. Their internal disintegration began only after the first World War, with the appearance of minorities created by the Peace Treaties

---

2  The early persecution of German Jews by the Nazis must be considered as an attempt to spread antisemitism among 'those peoples who are friendlily disposed to Jews, above all the Western democracies' rather than as an effort to get rid of the Jews. A circular letter from the Ministry of Foreign Affairs to all German authorities abroad shortly after the November pogroms of 1938, stated: 'The emigration movement of only about 100,000 Jews has already sufficed to awaken the interest of many countries in the Jewish danger . . . Germany is very interested in maintaining the dispersal of Jewry . . . the influx of Jews in all parts of the world invokes the opposition of the native population and thereby forms the best propaganda for the German Jewish policy . . . The poorer and therefore more burdensome the immigrating Jew is to the country absorbing him, the stronger the country will react.' See *Nazi Conspiracy and Aggression*, Washington, 1946, published by the U.S. Government, VI, 87 ff.

and of a constantly growing refugee movement, the consequence of revolutions.

The inadequacy of the Peace Treaties has often been explained by the fact that the peacemakers belonged to a generation formed by experiences in the pre-war era, so that they never quite realized the full impact of the war whose peace they had to conclude. There is no better proof of this than their attempt to regulate the nationality problem in Eastern and Southern Europe through the establishment of nation-states and the introduction of minority treaties. If the wisdom of the extension of a form of government which even in countries with old and settled national tradition could not handle the new problems of world politics had become questionable, it was even more doubtful whether it could be imported into an area which lacked the very conditions for the rise of nation-states: homogeneity of population and rootedness in the soil. But to assume that nation-states could be established by the methods of the Peace Treaties was simply preposterous. Indeed: 'One glance at the demographic map of Europe should be sufficient to show that the nation-state principle cannot be introduced into Eastern Europe.'[3] The Treaties lumped together many peoples in single states, called some of them 'state people' and entrusted them with the government, silently assumed that others (such as the Slovaks in Czechoslovakia, or the Croats and Slovenes in Yugoslavia) were equal partners in the government, which of course they were not,[4] and with equal arbitrariness created out of the remnant a third group of nationalities called 'minorities,' thereby adding to the many burdens of the new states the trouble of observing special regulations for part of the population.[5] The result was that those peoples to whom

3 Kurt Tramples, 'Völkerbund und Völkerfreiheit,' in *Süddeutsche Monatshefte*, 26, Jahrgang Juli 1929.

4 The struggle of the Slovaks against the 'Czech' government in Prague ended with the Hitler-supported independence of Slovakia; the Yugoslav constitution of 1921 was 'accepted' in Parliament against the votes of all Croat and Slovene representatives. For a good summary of Yugoslav history between the two wars, see *Propyläen Weltgeschichte. Das Zeitalter des Imperialismus*, 1933, Band 10, 471 ff.

5 Mussolini was quite right when he wrote after the Munich crisis: 'If Czechoslovakia finds herself today in what might be called a "delicate situation," it is because she was not just Czechoslovakia, but Czech-Germano-Polono-Magyaro-Rutheno-Rumano-Slovakia . . .' (Quoted from Hubert Ripka, *Munich: Before and After*, London, 1939, p. 117.)

states were not conceded, no matter whether they were official minorities or only nationalities, considered the Treaties an arbitrary game which handed out rule to some and servitude to others. The newly created states, on the other hand, which were promised equal status in national sovereignty with the Western nations, regarded the Minority Treaties as an open breach of promise and discrimination because only new states, and not even defeated Germany, were bound to them.

The perplexing power vacuum resulting from the dissolution of the Dual Monarchy and the liberation of Poland and the Baltic countries from Czarist despotism was not the only factor that had tempted the statesmen into this disastrous experiment. Much stronger was the impossibility of arguing away any longer the more than 100 million Europeans who had never reached the stage of national freedom and self-determination to which colonial peoples already aspired and which was being held out to them. It was indeed true that the role of the Western and Central European proletariat, the oppressed history-suffering group whose emancipation was a matter of life and death for the whole European social system, was played in the East by 'peoples without a history.' [6] The national liberation movements of the East were revolutionary in much the same way as the workers' movements in the West; both represented the 'unhistorical' strata of Europe's population and both strove to secure recognition and participation in public affairs. Since the object was to conserve the European status quo, the granting of national self-determination and sovereignty to all European peoples seemed indeed inevitable;

6 This term was first coined by Otto Bauer, *Die Nationalitätenfrage und die österreichische Sozialdemokratie*, Vienna, 1907.

Historical consciousness played a great role in the formation of national consciousness. The emancipation of nations from dynastic rule and the overlordship of an international aristocracy was accompanied by the emancipation of literature from the 'international' language of the learned (Latin first and later French) and the growth of national languages out of the popular vernacular. It seemed that peoples whose language was fit for literature had reached national maturity *per definitionem*. The liberation movements of Eastern European nationalities, therefore, started with a kind of philological revival (the results were sometimes grotesque and sometimes very fruitful) whose political function it was to prove that the people who possessed a literature and a history of their own, had the right to national sovereignty.

the alternative would have been to condemn them ruthlessly to the status of colonial peoples (something the pan-movements had always proposed) and to introduce colonial methods into European affairs.[7]

The point, of course, is that the European status quo could not be preserved and that it became clear only after the downfall of the last remnants of European autocracy that Europe had been ruled by a system which had never taken into account or responded to the needs of at least 25 percent of her population. This evil, however, was not cured with the establishment of the succession states, because about 30 per cent of their roughly 100 million inhabitants were officially recognized as exceptions who had to be specially protected by minority treaties. This figure, moreover, by no means tells the whole story; it only indicates the difference between peoples with a government of their own and those who supposedly were too small and too scattered to reach full nationhood. The Minority Treaties covered only those nationalities of whom there were considerable numbers in at least two of the succession states, but omitted from consideration all the other nationalities without a government of their own, so that in some of the succession states the nationally frustrated peoples constituted 50 per cent of the total population.[8] The worst factor in this situation was not even that it became a matter of course for the nationalities to be disloyal

7 Of course this was not always a clear-cut alternative. So far nobody has bothered to find out the characteristic similarities between colonial and minority exploitation. Only Jacob Robinson, 'Staatsbürgerliche und wirtschaftliche Gleichberechtigung' in *Süddeutsche Monatshefte*, 26, Jahrgang July 1929, remarks in passing: 'A peculiar economic protectionism appeared, not directed against other countries but against certain groups of the population. Surprisingly, certain methods of colonial exploitation could be observed in Central Europe.'

8 It has been estimated that prior to 1914 there were about 100 million people whose national aspirations had not been fulfilled. (See Charles Kingsley Webster, 'Minorities: History,' in *Encyclopedia Britannica*, 1929.) The population of minorities was estimated approximately between 25 and 30 millions. (P. de Azcarate, 'Minorities: League of Nations,' *ibid.*) The actual situation in Czechoslovakia and Yugoslavia was much worse. In the former, the Czech 'state people' constituted, with 7,200,000, about 50 per cent of the population, and in the latter 5,000,000 Serbs formed only 42 per cent of the total. See W. Winkler, *Statistisches Handbuch der europäischen Nationalitäten*, Vienna, 1931; Otto Junghann, *National Minorities in Europe*, 1932. Slightly different figures are given by Tramples, *op. cit.*

to their imposed government and for the governments to oppress their nationalities as efficiently as possible, but that the nationally frustrated population was firmly convinced – as was everybody else – that true freedom, true emancipation, and true popular sovereignty could be attained only with full national emancipation, that people without their own national government were deprived of human rights. In this conviction, which could base itself on the fact that the French Revolution had combined the declaration of the Rights of Man with national sovereignty, they were supported by the Minority Treaties themselves, which did not entrust the governments with the protection of different nationalities but charged the League of Nations with the safeguarding of the rights of those who, for reasons of territorial settlement, had been left without national states of their own.

Not that the minorities would trust the League of Nations any more than they had trusted the state peoples. The League, after all, was composed of national statesmen whose sympathies could not but be with the unhappy new governments which were hampered and opposed on principle by between 25 and 50 per cent of their inhabitants. Therefore the creators of the Minority Treaties were soon forced to interpret their real intentions more strictly and to point out the 'duties' the minorities owed to the new states;[9] it now developed that the Treaties had been conceived merely as a painless and humane method of assimilation, an interpretation which naturally enraged the minorities.[10] But nothing else could have been expected within a system of sovereign nation-states; if the Minority Treaties had been intended to be more than a

9 P. de Azcarate, *op. cit.*: 'The Treaties contain no stipulations regarding the "duties" of minorities towards the States of which they are a part. The Third Ordinary Assembly of the League, however, in 1922 . . . adopted . . . resolutions regarding the "duties of minorities" . . .'

10 The French and the British delegates were most outspoken in this respect. Said Briand: 'The process at which we should aim is not the disappearance of the minorities, but a kind of assimilation . . .' And Sir Austen Chamberlain, British representative, even claimed that 'the object of the Minority Treaties [is] . . . to secure . . . that measure of protection and justice which would gradually prepare them to be merged in the national community to which they belonged' (C. A. Macartney, *National States and National Minorities*, London, 1934, pp. 276, 277).

temporary remedy for a topsy-turvy situation, then their implied restriction on national sovereignty would have affected the national sovereignty of the older European powers. The representatives of the great nations knew only too well that minorities within nation-states must sooner or later be either assimilated or liquidated. And it did not matter whether they were moved by humanitarian considerations to protect splinter nationalities from persecution, or whether political considerations led them to oppose bilateral treaties between the concerned states and the majority countries of the minorities (after all, the Germans were the strongest of all the officially recognized minorities, both in numbers and economic position); they were neither willing nor able to overthrow the laws by which nation-states exist.[11]

Neither the League of Nations nor the Minority Treaties would have prevented the newly established states from more or less forcefully assimilating their minorities. The strongest factor against assimilation was the numerical and cultural weakness of the so-called state peoples. The Russian or the Jewish minority in Poland did not feel Polish culture to be superior to its own and neither was particularly impressed by the fact that Poles formed roughly 60 per cent of Poland's population.

The embittered nationalities, completely disregarding the League of Nations, soon decided to take matters into their own hands. They banded together in a minority congress which was remarkable in more than one respect. It contradicted the very idea behind the League treaties by calling itself officially the 'Congress of Organized National Groups in European States,' thereby nullifying the great labor spent during the peace negotiations to avoid the ominous word 'national.'[12]

---

11 It is true that some Czech statesmen, the most liberal and democratic of the leaders of national movements, once dreamed of making the Czechoslovak republic a kind of Switzerland. The reason why even Beneš never seriously attempted to effectuate such a solution to his harassing nationality problems was that Switzerland was not a model that could be imitated, but rather a particularly fortunate exception that proved an otherwise established rule. The newly established states did not feel secure enough to abandon a centralized state apparatus and could not create overnight those small self-administrative bodies of communes and cantons upon whose very extensive powers the Swiss system of federation is based.

12 Wilson notably, who had been a fervent advocate of granting 'racial, religious, and linguistic rights to the minorities,' 'feared that "national rights" would prove harmful

This had the important consequence that all 'nationalities,' and not just 'minorities,' would join and that the number of the 'nation of minorities' grew so considerably that the combined nationalities in the succession states outnumbered the state peoples. But in still another way the 'Congress of National Groups' dealt a decisive blow to the League treaties. One of the most baffling aspects of the Eastern European nationality problem (more baffling than the small size and great number of peoples involved, or the 'belt of mixed populations'[13]) was the interregional character of the nationalities which, in case they put their national interests above the interests of their respective governments, made them an obvious risk to the security of their countries.[14] The League treaties had attempted to ignore the interregional character of the minorities by concluding a separate treaty with each country, as though there were no Jewish or German minority beyond the borders of the respective states. The 'Congress of National Groups' not only sidestepped the territorial principle of the League; it was naturally dominated by the two nationalities which were represented in all succession states and were therefore in a position, if they wished, to make their weight felt all over Eastern and Southern Europe. These two groups were the Germans and the Jews. The German minorities in Rumania and Czechoslovakia voted of course with the German minorities in Poland and Hungary, and nobody could have expected the Polish Jews, for instance, to remain indifferent to discriminatory practices of the Rumanian government. In other words, national interests and not common interests of minorities as such formed the true basis of membership in the Congress,[15] and only

inasmuch as minority groups thus marked as separate corporate bodies would be rendered thereby "liable to jealousy and attack" ' (Oscar J. Janowsky, *The Jews and Minority Rights*, New York, 1933, p. 351). Macartney, *op. cit.*, p. 4, describes the situation and the 'prudent work of the Joint Foreign Committee' that labored to avoid the term 'national.'

13  The term is Macartney's, *op. cit.*, *passim*.

14  'The result of the Peace settlement was that every State in the belt of mixed population . . . now looked upon itself as a national state. But the facts were against them . . . Not one of these states was in fact uni-national, just as there was not, on the other hand, one nation all of whose members lived in a single state' (Macartney, *op. cit.*, p. 210).

15  In 1933 the chairman of the Congress expressly emphasized: 'One thing is certain: we do not meet in our congresses merely as members of abstract minorities; each of us belongs body and soul to a specific people, his own, and feels himself tied to the fate of

the harmonious relationship between the Jews and the Germans (the Weimar Republic had successfully played the role of special protector of minorities) kept it together. Therefore, in 1933 when the Jewish delegation demanded a protest against the treatment of Jews in the Third Reich (a move which they had no right to make, strictly speaking, because German Jews were no minority) and the Germans announced their solidarity with Germany and were supported by a majority (antisemitism was rife in all succession states), the Congress, after the Jewish delegation had left forever, sank into complete insignificance.

The real significance of the Minority Treaties lies not in their practical application but in the fact that they were guaranteed by an international body, the League of Nations. Minorities had existed before,[16] but the minority as a permanent institution, the recognition that millions of people lived outside normal legal protection and needed an additional guarantee of their elementary rights from an outside body, and the assumption that this state of affairs was not temporary but that the Treaties were needed in order to establish a lasting *modus vivendi* – all this was something new, certainly on such a scale, in European history. The Minority Treaties said in plain language what until then had been only implied in the working system of nation-states, namely, that only nationals could be citizens, only people of the same national origin could enjoy the full protection of legal institutions, that persons of different nationality needed some law of exception until or unless they were completely assimilated and divorced from their origin. The interpretative speeches on the League treaties by statesmen of countries without minority obligations spoke

---

that people for better or worse. Consequently, each of us stands here, if I may say so, as a full-blooded German or full-blooded Jew, as a full-blooded Hungarian or full-blooded Ukrainian.' See *Sitzungsbericht des Kongresses der organisierten nationalen Gruppen in den Staaten Europas*, 1933, p. 8.

16 The first minorities arose when the Protestant principle of freedom of conscience accomplished the suppression of the principle *cuius regio eius religio*. The Congress of Vienna in 1815 had already taken steps to secure certain rights to the Polish populations in Russia, Prussia, and Austria, rights that certainly were not merely 'religious'; it is, however, characteristic that all later treaties – the protocol guaranteeing the independence of Greece in 1830, the one guaranteeing the independence of Moldavia and Wallachia in 1856, and the Congress of Berlin in 1878 concerned with Rumania – speak of 'religious,' and not 'national' minorities, which were granted 'civil' but not 'political' rights.

an even plainer language: they took it for granted that the law of a country could not be responsible for persons insisting on a different nationality.[17] They thereby admitted – and were quickly given the opportunity to prove it practically with the rise of stateless people – that the transformation of the state from an instrument of the law into an instrument of the nation had been completed; the nation had conquered the state, national interest had priority over law long before Hitler could pronounce 'right is what is good for the German people.' Here again the language of the mob was only the language of public opinion cleansed of hypocrisy and restraint.

Certainly the danger of this development had been inherent in the structure of the nation-state since the beginning. But insofar as the establishment of nation-states coincided with the establishment of constitutional government, they always had represented and been based upon the rule of law as against the rule of arbitrary administration and despotism. So that when the precarious balance between nation and state, between national interest and legal institutions broke down, the disintegration of this form of government and of organization of peoples came about with terrifying swiftness. Its disintegration, curiously enough, started at precisely the moment when the right to national self-determination was recognized for all of Europe and when its essential conviction, the supremacy of the will of the nation over all legal and 'abstract' institutions, was universally accepted.

At the time of the Minority Treaties it could be, and was, argued in their favor, as it were as their excuse, that the older nations enjoyed constitutions which implicitly or explicitly (as in the case of France, the *nation par excellence*) were founded upon the Rights of Man, that even if there were other nationalities within their borders they needed no additional law for them, and that only in the newly established succession states was a temporary enforcement of human rights necessary

17  De Mello Franco, representative of Brazil on the Council of the League of Nations, put the problem very clearly: 'It seems to me obvious that those who conceived this system of protection did not dream of creating within certain States a group of inhabitants who would regard themselves as permanently foreign to the general organization of the country' (Macartney, *op. cit.*, p. 277).

as a compromise and exception.[18] The arrival of the stateless people brought an end to this illusion.

The minorities were only half stateless; *de jure* they belonged to some political body even though they needed additional protection in the form of special treaties and guarantees; some secondary rights, such as speaking one's own language and staying in one's own cultural and social milieu, were in jeopardy and were halfheartedly protected by an outside body; but other more elementary rights, such as the right to residence and to work, were never touched. The framers of the Minority Treaties did not foresee the possibility of wholesale population transfers or the problem of people who had become 'undeportable' because there was no country on earth in which they enjoyed the right to residence. The minorities could still be regarded as an exceptional phenomenon, peculiar to certain territories that deviated from the norm. This argument was always tempting because it left the system itself untouched; it has in a way survived the second World War whose peacemakers, convinced of the impracticability of minority treaties, began to 'repatriate' nationalities as much as possible in an effort to unscramble 'the belt of mixed populations.'[19] And this attempted large-scale repatriation was not the direct result of the catastrophic experiences following in the wake of the Minority Treaties; rather, it was hoped that such a step would finally solve a problem which, in the preceding decades, had assumed ever larger proportions

18 'The regime for the protection of minorities was designed to provide a remedy in cases where a territorial settlement was inevitably imperfect from the point of view of nationality' (Joseph Roucek, *The Minority Principle as a Problem of Political Science*, Prague, 1928, p. 29). The trouble was that imperfection of territorial settlement was the fault not only in the minority settlements but in the establishment of the succession states themselves, since there was no territory in this region to which several nationalities could not lay claim.

19 An almost symbolic evidence of this change of mind can be found in statements of President Eduard Beneš of Czechoslovakia, the only country that after the first World War had submitted with good grace to the obligations of the Minority Treaties. Shortly after the outbreak of World War II Beneš began to lend his support to the principle of transfer of populations, which finally led to the expulsion of the German minority and the addition of another category to the growing mass of Displaced Persons. For Beneš' stand, see Oscar I. Janowsky, *Nationalities and National Minorities*, New York, 1945, pp. 136 ff.

and for which an internationally recognized and accepted procedure simply did not exist – the problem of the stateless people.

Much more stubborn in fact and much more far-reaching in consequence has been statelessness, the newest mass phenomenon in contemporary history, and the existence of an ever-growing new people comprised of stateless persons, the most symptomatic group in contemporary politics.[20] Their existence can hardly be blamed on one factor alone, but if we consider the different groups among the stateless it appears that every political event since the end of the first World War inevitably added a new category to those who lived outside the pale of the law, while none of the categories, no matter how the original constellation changed, could ever be renormalized.[21]

20 'The problem of statelessness became prominent after the Great War. Before the war, provisions existed in some countries, notably in the United States, under which naturalization could be revoked in those cases in which the naturalized person ceased to maintain a genuine attachment to his adopted country. A person so denaturalized became stateless. During the war, the principal European States found it necessary to amend their laws of nationality so as to take power to cancel naturalization' (John Hope Simpson, *The Refugee Problem*, Institute of International Affairs, Oxford, 1939, p. 231). The class of stateless persons created through revocation of naturalization was very small; they established, however, an easy precedent so that, in the interwar period, naturalized citizens were as a rule the first section of a population that became stateless. Mass cancellation of naturalizations, such as the one introduced by Nazi Germany in 1933 against all naturalized Germans of Jewish origin, usually preceded denationalization of citizens by birth in similar categories, and the introduction of laws that made denaturalization possible through simple decree, like the ones in Belgium and other Western democracies in the thirties, usually preceded actual mass denaturalization; a good instance is the practice of the Greek government with respect to the Armenian refugees: of 45,000 Armenian refugees 1,000 were naturalized between 1923 and 1928. After 1928, a law which would have naturalized all refugees under twenty-two years of age was suspended, and in 1936, all naturalizations were canceled by the government. (See Simpson, *op. cit.*, p. 41.)

21 Twenty-five years after the Soviet regime had disowned one and a half million Russians, it was estimated that at least 350,000 to 450,000 were still stateless – which is a tremendous percentage if one considers that a whole generation had passed since the initial flight, that a considerable portion had gone overseas, and that another large part had acquired citizenship in different countries through marriage. (See Simpson, *op. cit.*, p. 559; Eugene M. Kulischer, *The Displacement of Population in Europe*, Montreal, 1943; Winifred N. Hadsel, 'Can Europe's Refugees Find New Homes?' in *Foreign Policy Reports*, August, 1943, Vol. X, no. 10.)

Among them, we still find that oldest group of stateless people, the *Heimatlosen* produced by the Peace Treaties of 1919, the dissolution of Austria-Hungary, and the establishment of the Baltic states. Sometimes their real origin could not be determined, especially if at the end of the war they happened not to reside in the city of their birth,[22] sometimes their place of origin changed hands so many times in the turmoil of postwar disputes that the nationality of its inhabitants changed from year to year (as in Vilna which a French official once termed *la capitale des apatrides*); more often than one would imagine, people took refuge in statelessness after the first World War in order to remain where they were and avoid being deported to a 'homeland' where they would be strangers (as in the case of many Polish and Rumanian Jews in France and Germany, mercifully helped by the antisemitic attitude of their respective consulates).

Unimportant in himself, apparently just a legal freak, the *apatride* received belated attention and consideration when he was joined in his legal status by the postwar refugees who had been forced out of their countries by revolutions, and were promptly denationalized by the victorious governments at home. To this group belong, in chronological order, millions of Russians, hundreds of thousands of Armenians, thousands of Hungarians, hundreds of thousands of Germans, and more than half a million Spaniards – to enumerate only the more important categories. The behavior of these governments may appear today to be the natural consequence of civil war; but at the time mass denationalizations were something entirely new and unforeseen. They presupposed a state structure which, if it was not yet fully totalitarian, at least would not tolerate any opposition and would rather

It is true that the United States has placed stateless immigrants on a footing of complete equality with other foreigners, but this has been possible only because this, the country *par excellence* of immigration, has always considered newcomers as prospective citizens of its own, regardless of their former national allegiances.

22 The *American Friends Service Bulletin* (General Relief Bulletin, March, 1943) prints the perplexed report of one of their field workers in Spain who had been confronted with the problem of 'a man who was born in Berlin, Germany, but who is of Polish origin because of his Polish parents and who is therefore . . . *apatride*, but is claiming Ukrainian nationality and has been claimed by the Russian government for repatriation and service in the Red Army.'

lose its citizens than harbor people with different views. They revealed, moreover, what had been hidden throughout the history of national sovereignty, that sovereignties of neighboring countries could come into deadly conflict not only in the extreme case of war but in peace. It now became clear that full national sovereignty was possible only as long as the comity of European nations existed; for it was this spirit of unorganized solidarity and agreement that prevented any government's exercise of its full sovereign power. Theoretically, in the sphere of international law, it had always been true that sovereignty is nowhere more absolute than in matters of 'emigration, naturalization, nationality, and expulsion';[23] the point, however, is that practical consideration and the silent acknowledgment of common interests restrained national sovereignty until the rise of totalitarian regimes. One is almost tempted to measure the degree of totalitarian infection by the extent to which the concerned governments use their sovereign right of denationalization (and it would be quite interesting then to discover that Mussolini's Italy was rather reluctant to treat its refugees this way[24]). But one should bear in mind at the same time that there was hardly a country left on the Continent that did not pass between the two wars some new legislation which, even if it did not use this right extensively, was always phrased to allow for getting rid of a great number of its inhabitants at any opportune moment.[25]

23 Lawrence Preuss, 'La Dénationalisation imposée pour des motifs politiques,' in *Revue Internationale Française du Droit des Gens*, 1937, Vol. IV, Nos. 1, 2, 5.

24 An Italian law of 1926 against 'abusive emigration' seemed to foreshadow denaturalization measures against anti-Fascist refugees; however, after 1929 the denaturalization policy was abandoned and Fascist organizations abroad were introduced. Of the 40,000 members of the Unione Popolare Italiana in France, at least 10,000 were authentic anti-Fascist refugees, but only 3,000 were without passports. See Simpson, *op. cit.*, pp. 122 ff.

25 The first law of this type was a French war measure in 1915 which concerned only naturalized citizens of enemy origin who had retained their original nationality; Portugal went much farther in a decree of 1916 which automatically denaturalized all persons born of a German father. Belgium issued a law in 1922 which canceled naturalization of persons who had committed antinational acts during the war, and reaffirmed it by a new decree in 1934 which in the characteristically vague manner of the time spoke of persons '*manquant gravement à leurs devoirs de citoyen belge.*' In Italy, since 1926, all persons could be denaturalized who were not 'worthy of Italian citizenship' or a menace to the public order. Egypt and Turkey in 1926 and 1928 respectively issued laws according to which people could be denaturalized who were a threat to the social

No paradox of contemporary politics is filled with a more poignant irony than the discrepancy between the efforts of well-meaning idealists who stubbornly insist on regarding as 'inalienable' those human rights, which are enjoyed only by citizens of the most prosperous and civilized countries, and the situation of the rightless themselves. Their situation has deteriorated just as stubbornly, until the internment camp – prior to the second World War the exception rather than the rule for the stateless – has become the routine solution for the problem of domicile of the 'displaced persons.'

Even the terminology applied to the stateless has deteriorated. The term 'stateless' at least acknowledged the fact that these persons had lost the protection of their government and required international agreements for safeguarding their legal status. The postwar term 'displaced persons' was invented during the war for the express purpose of liquidating statelessness once and for all by ignoring its existence. Nonrecognition of statelessness always means repatriation, *i.e.*, deportation to a country of origin, which either refuses to recognize the prospective repatriate as a citizen, or, on the contrary, urgently wants him back for punishment. Since nontotalitarian countries, in spite of their bad intentions inspired by the climate of war, generally have shied away from mass repatriations, the number of stateless people – twelve years after the end of the war – is larger than ever. The decision of the statesmen to solve the problem of statelessness by ignoring it is further revealed by the lack of any reliable statistics on the subject. This much is known, however: while there are one million 'recognized' stateless, there are more than ten million so-called '*de facto*' stateless; and whereas the relatively innocuous problem of the '*de jure*' stateless occasionally comes up at international conferences, the core of statelessness, which is identical with the refugee question, is simply not mentioned. Worse still, the number of potentially stateless people is continually on the increase. Prior to the last war, only totalitarian or

order. France threatened with denaturalization those of its new citizens who committed acts contrary to the interests of France (1927). Austria in 1933 could deprive of Austrian nationality any of her citizens who served or participated abroad in an action hostile to Austria. Germany, finally, in 1933 followed closely the various Russian nationality decrees since 1921 by stating that all persons 'residing abroad' could at will be deprived of German nationality.

half-totalitarian dictatorships resorted to the weapon of denaturalization with regard to those who were citizens by birth; now we have reached the point where even free democracies, as, for instance, the United States, were seriously considering depriving native Americans who are Communists of their citizenship. The sinister aspect of these measures is that they are being considered in all innocence. Yet, one need only remember the extreme care of the Nazis, who insisted that all Jews of non-German nationality 'should be deprived of their citizenship either prior to, or, at the latest, on the day of deportation' [25a] (for German Jews such a decree was not needed, because in the Third Reich there existed a law according to which all Jews who had left the territory – including, of course, those deported to a Polish camp – automatically lost their citizenship) in order to realize the true implications of statelessness.

The first great damage done to the nation-states as a result of the arrival of hundreds of thousands of stateless people was that the right of asylum, the only right that had ever figured as a symbol of the Rights of Man in the sphere of international relationships, was being abolished. Its long and sacred history dates back to the very beginnings of regulated political life. Since ancient times it has protected both the refugee and the land of refuge from situations in which people were forced to become outlaws through circumstances beyond their control. It was the only modern remnant of the medieval principle that *quidquid est in territorio est de territorio*, for in all other cases the modern state tended to protect its citizens beyond its own borders and to make sure, by means of reciprocal treaties, that they remained subject to the laws of their country. But though the right of asylum continued to function in a world organized into nation-states and, in individual instances, even survived both World Wars, it was felt to be an anachronism and in conflict with the international rights of the state. Therefore it cannot be found in written law, in no constitution

25a The quotation is taken from an order of Hauptsturmführer Dannecker, dated March 10, 1943, and referring to the 'deportation of 5,000 Jews from France, quota 1942.' The document (photostat in the Centre de Documentation Juive in Paris) is part of the Nuremberg Documents No. RF 1216. Identical arrangements were made for the Bulgarian Jews. Cf. *ibidem* the relevant memorandum by L. R. Wagner, dated April 3, 1943, Document NG 4180.

or international agreement, and the Covenant of the League of Nations never even so much as mentioned it.[26] It shares, in this respect, the fate of the Rights of Man, which also never became law but led a somewhat shadowy existence as an appeal in individual exceptional cases for which normal legal institutions did not suffice.[27]

The second great shock that the European world suffered through the arrival of the refugees[28] was the realization that it was impossible to get rid of them or transform them into nationals of the country of refuge. From the beginning everybody had agreed that there were only two ways to solve the problem: repatriation or naturalization.[29] When the example of the first Russian and Armenian waves proved

26 S. Lawford Childs (*op. cit.*) deplores the fact that the Covenant of the League contained 'no charter for political refugees, no solace for exiles.' The most recent attempt of the United Nations to obtain, at least for a small group of stateless – the so-called '*de jure* stateless' – an improvement of their legal status was no more than a mere gesture: namely, to gather the representatives of at least twenty states, but with the explicit assurance that participation in such a conference would entail no obligations whatsoever. Even under these circumstances it remained extremely doubtful whether the conference could be called. See the news item in the New York *Times*, October 17, 1954, p. 9.

27 The only guardians of the right of asylum were the few societies whose special aim was the protection of human rights. The most important of them, the French-sponsored Ligue des Droits de l'Homme with branches in all democratic European countries, behaved as though the question were still merely the saving of individuals persecuted for their political convictions and activities. This assumption, pointless already in the case of millions of Russian refugees, became simply absurd for Jews and Armenians. The Ligue was neither ideologically nor administratively equipped to handle the new problems. Since it did not want to face the new situation, it stumbled into functions which were much better fulfilled by any of the many charity agencies which the refugees had built up themselves with the help of their compatriots. When the Rights of Man became the object of an especially inefficient charity organization, the concept of human rights naturally was discredited a little more.

28 The many and varied efforts of the legal profession to simplify the problem by stating a difference between the stateless person and the refugee – such as maintaining 'that the status of a stateless person is characterized by the fact of his having no nationality, whereas that of a refugee is determined by his having lost diplomatic protection' (Simpson, *op. cit.*, p. 232) – were always defeated by the fact that 'all refugees are for practical purposes stateless' (Simpson, *op. cit.*, p. 4).

29 The most ironical formulation of this general expectation was made by R. Yewdall Jennings, 'Some International Aspects of the Refugee Question' in *British Yearbook of International Law*, 1939: 'The status of a refugee is not, of course, a permanent one. The aim is that he should rid himself of that status as soon as possible, either by repatriation or by naturalization in the country of refuge.'

that neither way gave any tangible results, the countries of refuge simply refused to recognize statelessness in all later arrivals, thereby making the situation of the refugees even more intolerable.[30] From the point of view of the governments concerned it was understandable enough that they should keep reminding the League of Nations 'that [its] Refugee work must be liquidated with the utmost rapidity';[31] they had many reasons to fear that those who had been ejected from the old trinity of state-people-territory, which still formed the basis of European organization and political civilization, formed only the beginning of an increasing movement, were only the first trickle from an ever-growing reservoir. It was obvious, and even the Evian Conference recognized it in 1938, that all German and Austrian Jews were potentially stateless; and it was only natural that the minority countries should be encouraged by Germany's example to try to use the same methods for getting rid of some of their minority populations.[32] Among the minorities the Jews and the Armenians ran the greatest risks and soon showed the highest proportion of statelessness; but they proved also that minority treaties did not necessarily offer protection

30 Only the Russians, in every respect the aristocracy of the stateless people, and the Armenians, who were assimilated to the Russian status, were ever officially recognized as 'stateless,' placed under the protection of the League of Nations' Nansen Office, and given traveling papers.

31 Childs, *op. cit.* The reason for this desperate attempt at promptness was the fear of all governments that even the smallest positive gesture 'might encourage countries to get rid of their unwanted people and that many might emigrate who would otherwise remain in their countries even under serious disabilities' (Louise W. Holborn, 'The Legal Status of Political Refugees, 1920–38,' in *American Journal of International Law*, 1938).

See also Georges Mauco (in *Esprit*, 7e année, No. 82, July, 1939, p. 590): 'An assimilation of the German refugees to the status of other refugees who were taken care of by the Nansen office would naturally have been the simplest and best solution for the German refugees themselves. But the governments did not want to extend the privileges already granted to a new category of refugees who, moreover, threatened to increase their number indefinitely.'

32 To the 600,000 Jews in Germany and Austria who were potentially stateless in 1938, must be added the Jews of Rumania (the president of the Rumanian Federal Commission for Minorities, Professor Dragomir, having just announced to the world the impending revision of the citizenship of all Rumanian Jews) and Poland (whose foreign minister Beck had officially declared that Poland had one million Jews too many). See Simpson, *op. cit.*, p. 235.

but could also serve as an instrument to single out certain groups for eventual expulsion.

Almost as frightening as these new dangers arising from the old trouble spots of Europe was the entirely new kind of behavior of all European nationals in 'ideological' struggles. Not only were people expelled from country and citizenship, but more and more persons of all countries, including the Western democracies, volunteered to fight in civil wars abroad (something which up to then only a few idealists or adventurers had done) even when this meant cutting themselves off from their national communities. This was the lesson of the Spanish Civil War and one of the reasons why the governments were so frightened by the International Brigade. Matters would not have been quite so bad if this had meant that people no longer clung so closely to their nationality and were ready eventually to be assimilated into another national community. But this was not at all the case. The stateless people had already shown a surprising stubbornness in retaining their nationality; in every sense the refugees represented separate foreign minorities who frequently did not care to be naturalized, and they never banded together, as the minorities had done temporarily, to defend common interests.[33] The International Brigade was organized

33 It is difficult to decide what came first, the nation-states' reluctance to naturalize refugees (the practice of naturalization became increasingly restricted and the practice of denaturalization increasingly common with the arrival of refugees) or the refugees' reluctance to accept another citizenship. In countries with minority populations like Poland, the refugees (Russians and Ukrainians) had a definite tendency to assimilate to the minorities without however demanding Polish citizenship. (See Simpson, *op. cit.*, p. 364.)

The behavior of Russian refugees is quite characteristic. The Nansen passport described its bearer as *'personne d'origine russe,'* because 'one would not have dared to tell the Russian émigré that he was without nationality or of doubtful nationality.' (See Marc Vichniac, 'Le Statut International des Apatrides,' in *Recueil des Cours de l'Académie de Droit International*, Vol. XXXIII, 1933.) An attempt to provide all stateless persons with uniform identity cards was bitterly contested by the holders of Nansen passports, who claimed that their passport was 'a sign of legal recognition of their peculiar status.' (See Jennings, *op. cit.*) Before the outbreak of the war even refugees from Germany were far from eager to be merged with the mass of the stateless, but preferred the description *'réfugié provenant d'Allemagne'* with its remnant of nationality.

More convincing than the complaints of European countries about the difficulties of assimilating refugees are statements from overseas which agree with the former that 'of all classes of European immigrants the least easy to assimilate are the South,

into national battalions in which the Germans felt they fought against Hitler and the Italians against Mussolini, just as a few years later, in the Resistance, the Spanish refugees felt they fought against Franco when they helped the French against Vichy. What the European governments were so afraid of in this process was that the new stateless people could no longer be said to be of dubious or doubtful nationality (*de nationalité indéterminée*). Even though they had renounced their citizenship, no longer had any connection with or loyalty to their country of origin, and did not identify their nationality with a visible, fully recognized government, they retained a strong attachment to their nationality. National splinter groups and minorities, without deep roots in their territory and with no loyalty or relationship to the state, had ceased to be characteristic only of the East. They had by now infiltrated, as refugees and stateless persons, the older nation-states of the West.

The real trouble started as soon as the two recognized remedies, repatriation and naturalization, were tried. Repatriation measures naturally failed when there was no country to which these people could be deported. They failed not because of consideration for the stateless person (as it may appear today when Soviet Russia claims its former citizens and the democratic countries must protect them from a repatriation they do not want); and not because of humanitarian sentiments on the part of the countries that were swamped with refugees; but because neither the country of origin nor any other agreed to accept the stateless person. It would seem that the very undeportability of the stateless person should have prevented a government's expelling him; but since the man without a state was 'an anomaly for whom there is no appropriate niche in the framework of the general law' [34] – an outlaw by definition – he was completely at the mercy of the police, which itself did not worry too much about committing a few illegal acts in order to diminish the country's burden of *indésirables*.[35]

---

Eastern, and Central Europeans.' (See 'Canada and the Doctrine of Peaceful Changes,' edited by H. F. Angus in *International Studies Conference: Demographic Questions: Peaceful Changes*, 1937, pp. 75–76.)

34 Jennings, *op. cit.*

35 A circular letter of the Dutch authorities (May 7, 1938) expressly considered each refugee as an 'undesirable alien,' and defined a refugee as an 'alien who left his country

In other words, the state, insisting on its sovereign right of expulsion, was forced by the illegal nature of statelessness into admittedly illegal acts.[36] It smuggled its expelled stateless into the neighboring countries, with the result that the latter retaliated in kind. The ideal solution of repatriation, to smuggle the refugee back into his country of origin, succeeded only in a few prominent instances, partly because a non-totalitarian police was still restrained by a few rudimentary ethical considerations, partly because the stateless person was as likely to be smuggled back from his home country as from any other, and last but not least because the whole traffic could go on only with neighboring countries. The consequences of this smuggling were petty wars between the police at the frontiers, which did not exactly contribute to good international relations, and an accumulation of jail sentences for the stateless who, with the help of the police of one country, had passed 'illegally' into the territory of another.

Every attempt by international conferences to establish some legal status for stateless people failed because no agreement could possibly replace the territory to which an alien, within the framework of existing law, must be deportable. All discussions about the refugee problems revolved around this one question: How can the refugee be made deportable again? The second World War and the DP camps were not necessary to show that the only practical substitute for a nonexistent homeland was an internment camp. Indeed, as early as

---

under the pressure of circumstances.' See 'L'Emigration, Problème Révolutionnaire,' in *Esprit*, 7e année, No. 82, July, 1939, p. 602.

36 Lawrence Preuss, *op. cit.*, describes the spread of illegality as follows: 'The initial illegal act of the denationalizing government ... puts the expelling country in the position of an offender of international law, because its authorities violate the law of the country to which the stateless person is expelled. The latter country, in turn, cannot get rid of him ... except by violating ... the law of a third country ... [The stateless person finds himself before the following alternative]: either he violates the law of the country where he resides ... or he violates the law of the country to which he is expelled.'

Sir John Fischer Williams ('Denationalisation,' in *British Year Book of International Law*, VII, 1927) concludes from this situation that denationalization is contrary to international law; yet at the Conférence pour la Codification du Droit International at the Hague in 1930, it was only the Finnish government which maintained that 'loss of nationality ... should never constitute a punishment ... nor be pronounced in order to get rid of an undesirable person through expulsion.'

the thirties this was the only 'country' the world had to offer the stateless.[37]

Naturalization, on the other hand, also proved to be a failure. The whole naturalization system of European countries fell apart when it was confronted with stateless people, and this for the same reasons that the right of asylum had been set aside. Essentially naturalization was an appendage to the nation-state's legislation that reckoned only with 'nationals,' people born in its territory and citizens by birth. Naturalization was needed in exceptional cases, for single individuals whom circumstances might have driven into a foreign territory. The whole process broke down when it became a question of handling mass applications for naturalization:[38] even from the purely administrative point of view, no European civil service could possibly have dealt with the problem. Instead of naturalizing at least a small portion of the new arrivals, the countries began to cancel earlier naturalizations, partly because of general panic and partly because the arrival of great masses of newcomers actually changed the always precarious position of naturalized citizens of the same origin.[39] Cancellation

37 Childs, *op. cit.*, after having come to the sad conclusion that 'the real difficulty about receiving a refugee is that if he turns out badly . . . there is no way of getting rid of him,' proposed 'transitional centers' to which the refugee could be returned even from abroad, which, in other words, should replace a homeland for deportation purposes.

38 Two instances of mass naturalization in the Near East were clearly exceptional: one involved Greek refugees from Turkey whom the Greek government naturalized en bloc in 1922 because it was actually a matter of repatriation of a Greek minority and not of foreign citizens; the other benefited Armenian refugees from Turkey in Syria, Lebanon, and other formerly Turkish countries, that is, a population with which the Near East had shared common citizenship only a few years ago.

39 Where a wave of refugees found members of their own nationality already settled in the country to which they immigrated – as was the case with the Armenians and Italians in France, for example, and with Jews everywhere – a certain retrogression set in in the assimilation of those who had been there longer. For their help and solidarity could be mobilized only by appealing to the original nationality they had in common with the newcomers. This point was of immediate interest to countries flooded by refugees but unable or unwilling to give them direct help or the right to work. In all these cases, national feelings of the older group proved to be 'one of the main factors in the successful establishment of the refugees' (Simpson, *op. cit.*, pp. 45–46), but by appealing to such national conscience and solidarity, the receiving countries naturally increased the number of unassimilated aliens. To take one particularly interesting instance, 10,000 Italian refugees were enough to postpone indefinitely the assimilation of almost one million Italian immigrants in France.

of naturalization or the introduction of new laws which obviously paved the way for mass denaturalization[40] shattered what little confidence the refugees might have retained in the possibility of adjusting themselves to a new normal life; if assimilation to the new country once looked a little shabby or disloyal, it was now simply ridiculous. The difference between a naturalized citizen and a stateless resident was not great enough to justify taking any trouble, the former being frequently deprived of important civil rights and threatened at any moment with the fate of the latter. Naturalized persons were largely assimilated to the status of ordinary aliens, and since the naturalized had already lost their previous citizenship, these measures simply threatened another considerable group with statelessness.

It was almost pathetic to see how helpless the European governments were, despite their consciousness of the danger of statelessness to their established legal and political institutions and despite all their efforts to stem the tide. Explosive events were no longer necessary. Once a number of stateless people were admitted to an otherwise normal country, statelessness spread like a contagious disease. Not only were naturalized citizens in danger of reverting to the status of statelessness, but living conditions for all aliens markedly deteriorated. In the thirties it became increasingly difficult to distinguish clearly between stateless refugees and normal resident aliens. Once the government tried to use its right and repatriate a resident alien against his will, he would do his utmost to find refuge in statelessness. During the first World War enemy aliens had already discovered the great advantages of statelessness. But what then had been the cunning of individuals who found a loophole in the law had now become the instinctive reaction of masses. France, Europe's greatest immigrant-reception area,[41] because she had regulated the chaotic labor market by calling in alien workers in times of need and deporting them in times

---

40 The French government, followed by other Western countries, introduced during the thirties an increasing number of restrictions for naturalized citizens: they were eliminated from certain professions for up to ten years after their naturalization, they had no political rights, etc.

41 Simpson, *op. cit.*, p. 289.

of unemployment and crisis, taught her aliens a lesson about the advantages of statelessness which they did not readily forget. After 1935, the year of mass repatriation by the Laval government from which only the stateless were saved, so-called 'economic immigrants' and other groups of earlier origin – Balkans, Italians, Poles, and Spaniards – mixed with the waves of refugees into a tangle that never again could be unraveled.

Much worse than what statelessness did to the time-honored and necessary distinctions between nationals and foreigners, and to the sovereign right of states in matters of nationality and expulsion, was the damage suffered by the very structure of legal national institutions when a growing number of residents had to live outside the jurisdiction of these laws and without being protected by any other. The stateless person, without right to residence and without the right to work, had of course constantly to transgress the law. He was liable to jail sentences without ever committing a crime. More than that, the entire hierarchy of values which pertain in civilized countries was reversed in his case. Since he was the anomaly for whom the general law did not provide, it was better for him to become an anomaly for which it did provide, that of the criminal.

The best criterion by which to decide whether someone has been forced outside the pale of the law is to ask if he would benefit by committing a crime. If a small burglary is likely to improve his legal position, at least temporarily, one may be sure he has been deprived of human rights. For then a criminal offense becomes the best opportunity to regain some kind of human equality, even if it be as a recognized exception to the norm. The one important fact is that this exception is provided for by law. As a criminal even a stateless person will not be treated worse than another criminal, that is, he will be treated like everybody else. Only as an offender against the law can he gain protection from it. As long as his trial and his sentence last, he will be safe from that arbitrary police rule against which there are no lawyers and no appeals. The same man who was in jail yesterday because of his mere presence in this world, who had no rights whatever and lived under threat of deportation, or who was dispatched without sentence and without trial to some kind of internment because he had tried to work and make a living, may become almost a full-fledged citizen because of a little theft. Even if he is penniless he can now get a lawyer, complain about his jailers, and he will be listened to respectfully. He is no longer the scum of the earth but important enough to be informed of all the details of the law under which he will be tried. He has become a respectable person.[42]

A much less reliable and much more difficult way to rise from an unrecognized anomaly to the status of recognized exception would be to become a genius. Just as the law knows only one difference between human beings, the difference between the normal noncriminal and the anomalous criminal, so a conformist society has recognized only one form of determined individualism, the genius. European bourgeois society wanted the genius to stay outside of human laws, to be a kind of monster whose chief social function was to create excitement, and it did not matter if he actually was an outlaw. Moreover, the loss of citizenship deprived people not only of protection, but also of all clearly established, officially recognized identity, a fact for which their eternal feverish efforts to obtain at least birth certificates from the country that denationalized them was a very exact symbol; one of their problems was solved when they achieved the degree of distinction that will rescue a man from the huge and nameless crowd. Only fame will eventually answer the repeated complaint of refugees of all social strata that 'nobody here knows who I am'; and it is true that the chances of the famous refugee are improved just as a dog with a name has a better chance to survive than a stray dog who is just a dog in general.[43]

The nation-state, incapable of providing a law for those who had

42 In practical terms, any sentence meted out to him will be of small consequence compared with an expulsion order, cancellation of a work permit, or a decree sending him into an internment camp. A West Coast Japanese-American who was in jail when the army ordered the internment of all Americans of Japanese ancestry would not have been forced to liquidate his property at too low a price; he would have remained right where he was, armed with a lawyer to look after his interests; and if he was so lucky as to receive a long sentence, he might have returned righteously and peacefully to his former business and profession, even that of a professional thief. His jail sentence guaranteed him the constitutional rights that nothing else – no protests of loyalty and no appeals – could have obtained for him once his citizenship had become doubtful.

43 The fact that the same principle of formation of an elite frequently worked in totalitarian concentration camps where the 'aristocracy' was composed of a majority of

lost the protection of a national government, transferred the whole matter to the police. This was the first time the police in Western Europe had received authority to act on its own, to rule directly over people; in one sphere of public life it was no longer an instrument to carry out and enforce the law, but had become a ruling authority independent of government and ministries.[44] Its strength and its emancipation from law and government grew in direct proportion to the influx of refugees. The greater the ratio of stateless and potentially stateless to the population at large – in prewar France it had reached 10 per cent of the total – the greater the danger of a gradual transformation into a police state.

It goes without saying that the totalitarian regimes, where the police had risen to the peak of power, were especially eager to consolidate this power through the domination over vast groups of people, who, regardless of any offenses committed by individuals, found themselves anyway beyond the pale of the law. In Nazi Germany, the Nuremberg Laws with their distinction between Reich citizens (full citizens) and nationals (second-class citizens without political rights) had paved the way for a development in which eventually all nationals of 'alien blood' could lose their nationality by official decree; only the outbreak of the war prevented a corresponding legislation, which had been prepared in detail.[44a] On the other hand, the increasing groups of

criminals and a few 'geniuses,' that is entertainers and artists, shows how closely related the social positions of these groups are.

44 In France, for instance, it was a matter of record that an order of expulsion emanating from the police was much more serious than one which was issued 'only' by the Ministry of Interior and that the Minister of Interior could only in rare cases cancel a police expulsion, while the opposite procedure was often merely a question of bribery. Constitutionally, the police is under the authority of the Ministry of Interior.

44a In February, 1938, the Reich and Prussian Ministry of Interior presented the 'draft of a law concerning the acquisition and loss of German nationality' which went far beyond the Nuremberg legislation. It provided that all children of 'Jews, Jews of mixed blood or persons of otherwise alien blood' (who could never become Reich citizens anyway) were also no longer entitled to the nationality, 'even if the father possesses German nationality by birth.' That these measures were no longer merely concerned with anti-Jewish legislation is evident from an opinion expressed July 19, 1939, by the Minister of Justice, who suggests that 'the words Jew and Jew of mixed blood should if possible be avoided in the law, to be replaced by "persons of alien blood," or "persons of non-German or non-Germanic [*nicht artverwandt*] blood." ' An interesting feature in

stateless in the nontotalitarian countries led to a form of lawlessness, organized by the police, which practically resulted in a co-ordination of the free world with the legislation of the totalitarian countries. That concentration camps were ultimately provided for the same groups in all countries, even though there were considerable differences in the treatment of their inmates, was all the more characteristic as the selection of the groups was left exclusively to the initiative of the totalitarian regimes: if the Nazis put a person in a concentration camp and if he made a successful escape, say, to Holland, the Dutch would put him in an internment camp. Thus, long before the outbreak of the war the police in a number of Western countries, under the pretext of 'national security,' had on their own initiative established close connections with the Gestapo and the GPU, so that one might say there existed an independent foreign policy of the police. This police-directed foreign policy functioned quite independently of the official governments; the relations between the Gestapo and the French police were never more cordial than at the time of Léon Blum's popular-front government, which was guided by a decidedly anti-German policy. Contrary to the governments, the various police organizations were never over-burdened with 'prejudices' against any totalitarian regime; the information and denunciations received from GPU agents were just as welcome to them as those from Fascist or Gestapo agents. They knew about the eminent role of the police apparatus in all totalitarian regimes, they knew about its elevated social status and political importance, and they never bothered to conceal their sympathies. That the Nazis eventually met with so disgracefully little resistance from the police in the countries they occupied, and that they were able to organize terror as much as they did with the assistance of these local

---

planning this extraordinary expansion of the stateless population in Nazi Germany concerns the foundlings, who are explicitly regarded as stateless, until 'an investigation of their racial characteristics can be made.' Here the principle that every individual is born with inalienable rights guaranteed by his nationality has been deliberately reversed: every individual is born rightless, namely stateless, unless subsequently other conclusions are reached.

The original dossier concerning the draft of this legislation, including the opinions of all Ministries and the *Wehrmacht* High Command, can be found in the archives of the Yiddish Scientific Institute in New York (G-75).

police forces, was due at least in part to the powerful position which the police had achieved over the years in their unrestricted and arbitrary domination of stateless and refugees.

Both in the history of the 'nation of minorities' and in the formation of a stateless people, Jews have played a significant role. They were at the head of the so-called minority movement because of their great need for protection (matched only by the need of the Armenians) and their excellent international connections, but above all because they formed a majority in no country and therefore could be regarded as the *minorité par excellence*, i.e., the only minority whose interests could be defended only by internationally guaranteed protection.[45]

The special needs of the Jewish people were the best possible pretext for denying that the Treaties were a compromise between the new nations' tendency forcefully to assimilate alien peoples *and* nationalities who for reasons of expediency could not be granted the right to national self-determination.

A similar incident made the Jews prominent in the discussion of the refugee and statelessness problem. The first *Heimatlose* or *apatrides*, as they were created by the Peace Treaties, were for the most part Jews who came from the succession states and were unable or unwilling to place themselves under the new minority protection of their homelands. Not until Germany forced German Jewry into emigration and statelessness did they form a very considerable portion of the stateless people. But in the years following Hitler's successful persecution of German Jews all the minority countries began to think in terms of expatriating their minorities, and it was only natural that they should start with the *minorité par excellence*, the only nationality that actually had no other protection than a minority system which by now had become a mockery.

The notion that statelessness is primarily a Jewish problem[46] was a

45 On the role of the Jews in formulating the Minority Treaties, see Macartney, *op. cit.*, pp. 4, 213, 281 and *passim*; David Erdstein, *Le Statut juridique des Minorités en Europe*, Paris, 1932, pp. 11 ff.; Oscar J. Janowsky, *op. cit.*

46 This was by no means only a notion of Nazi Germany, though only a Nazi author dared to express it: 'It is true that a refugee question will continue to exist even when there is no longer a Jewish question; but since Jews form such a high percentage of the

pretext used by all governments who tried to settle the problem by ignoring it. None of the statesmen was aware that Hitler's solution of the Jewish problem, first to reduce the German Jews to a nonrecognized minority in Germany, then to drive them as stateless people across the borders, and finally to gather them back from everywhere in order to ship them to extermination camps, was an eloquent demonstration to the rest of the world how really to 'liquidate' all problems concerning minorities and stateless. After the war it turned out that the Jewish question, which was considered the only insoluble one, was indeed solved – namely, by means of a colonized and then conquered territory – but this solved neither the problem of the minorities nor the stateless. On the contrary, like virtually all other events of our century, the solution of the Jewish question merely produced a new category of refugees, the Arabs, thereby increasing the number of the stateless and rightless by another 700,000 to 800,000 people. And what happened in Palestine within the smallest territory and in terms of hundreds of thousands was then repeated in India on a large scale involving many millions of people. Since the Peace Treaties of 1919 and 1920 the refugees and the stateless have attached themselves like a curse to all the newly established states on earth which were created in the image of the nation-state.

For these new states this curse bears the germs of a deadly sickness. For the nation-state cannot exist once its principle of equality before the law has broken down. Without this legal equality, which originally was destined to replace the older laws and orders of the feudal society, the nation dissolves into an anarchic mass of over- and underprivileged individuals. Laws that are not equal for all revert to rights and privileges, something contradictory to the very nature of nation-states. The clearer the proof of their inability to treat stateless people as legal persons and the greater the extension of arbitrary rule by police decree, the more difficult it is for states to resist the temptation to deprive all citizens of legal status and rule them with an omnipotent police.

---

refugees, the refugee question will be much simplified' (Kabermann, 'Das internationale Flüchtlingsproblem,' in *Zeitschrift für Politik*, Bd. 29, Heft 3, 1939).

## II: The Perplexities of the Rights of Man

The declaration of the Rights of Man at the end of the eighteenth century was a turning point in history. It meant nothing more nor less than that from then on Man, and not God's command or the customs of history, should be the source of Law. Independent of the privileges which history had bestowed upon certain strata of society or certain nations, the declaration indicated man's emancipation from all tutelage and announced that he had now come of age.

Beyond this, there was another implication of which the framers of the declaration were only half aware. The proclamation of human rights was also meant to be a much-needed protection in the new era where individuals were no longer secure in the estates to which they were born or sure of their equality before God as Christians. In other words, in the new secularized and emancipated society, men were no longer sure of these social and human rights which until then had been outside the political order and guaranteed not by government and constitution, but by social, spiritual, and religious forces. Therefore throughout the nineteenth century, the consensus of opinion was that human rights had to be invoked whenever individuals needed protection against the new sovereignty of the state and the new arbitrariness of society.

Since the Rights of Man were proclaimed to be 'inalienable,' irreducible to and undeducible from other rights or laws, no authority was invoked for their establishment; Man himself was their source as well as their ultimate goal. No special law, moreover, was deemed necessary to protect them because all laws were supposed to rest upon them. Man appeared as the only sovereign in matters of law as the people was proclaimed the only sovereign in matters of government. The people's sovereignty (different from that of the prince) was not proclaimed by the grace of God but in the name of Man, so that it seemed only natural that the 'inalienable' rights of man would find their guarantee and become an inalienable part of the right of the people to sovereign self-government.

In other words, man had hardly appeared as a completely emancipated, completely isolated being who carried his dignity within himself without reference to some larger encompassing order, when he disappeared again into a member of a people. From the beginning the paradox involved in the declaration of inalienable human rights was that it reckoned with an 'abstract' human being who seemed to exist nowhere, for even savages lived in some kind of a social order. If a tribal or other 'backward' community did not enjoy human rights, it was obviously because as a whole it had not yet reached that stage of civilization, the stage of popular and national sovereignty, but was oppressed by foreign or native despots. The whole question of human rights, therefore, was quickly and inextricably blended with the question of national emancipation; only the emancipated sovereignty of the people, of one's own people, seemed to be able to insure them. As mankind, since the French Revolution, was conceived in the image of a family of nations, it gradually became self-evident that the people, and not the individual, was the image of man.

The full implication of this identification of the rights of man with the rights of peoples in the European nation-state system came to light only when a growing number of people and peoples suddenly appeared whose elementary rights were as little safeguarded by the ordinary functioning of nation-states in the middle of Europe as they would have been in the heart of Africa. The Rights of Man, after all, had been defined as 'inalienable' because they were supposed to be independent of all governments; but it turned out that the moment human beings lacked their own government and had to fall back upon their minimum rights, no authority was left to protect them and no institution was willing to guarantee them. Or when, as in the case of the minorities, an international body arrogated to itself a nongovernmental authority, its failure was apparent even before its measures were fully realized; not only were the governments more or less openly opposed to this encroachment on their sovereignty, but the concerned nationalities themselves did not recognize a nonnational guarantee, mistrusted everything which was not clear-cut support of their 'national' (as opposed to their mere 'linguistic, religious, and ethnic') rights, and preferred either, like the Germans or Hungarians, to turn to the protection of the 'national' mother country, or, like the Jews, to some kind of interterritorial solidarity.[47]

The stateless people were as convinced as the minorities that loss of national rights was identical with loss of human rights, that the former inevitably entailed the latter. The more they were excluded from right in any form, the more they tended to look for a reintegration into a national, into their own national community. The Russian refugees were only the first to insist on their nationality and to defend themselves furiously against attempts to lump them together with other stateless people. Since them, not a single group of refugees or Displaced Persons has failed to develop a fierce, violent group consciousness and to clamor for rights as – and only as – Poles or Jews or Germans, etc.

Even worse was that all societies formed for the protection of the Rights of Man, all attempts to arrive at a new bill of human rights were sponsored by marginal figures – by a few international jurists without political experience or professional philanthropists supported by the uncertain sentiments of professional idealists. The groups they formed, the declarations they issued, showed an uncanny similarity in language and composition to that of societies for the prevention of cruelty to animals. No statesman, no political figure of any importance could possibly take them seriously; and none of the liberal or radical parties in Europe thought it necessary to incorporate into their program a new declaration of human rights. Neither before nor after the second World War have the victims themselves ever invoked these fundamental rights, which were so evidently denied them, in their many attempts to find a way out of the barbed-wire labyrinth into which events had driven them. On the contrary, the victims

47 Pathetic instances of this exclusive confidence in national rights were the consent, before the second World War, of nearly 75 per cent of the German minority in the Italian Tyrol to leave their homes and resettle in Germany, the voluntary repatriation of a German island in Slovenia which had been there since the fourteenth century or, immediately after the close of the war, the unanimous rejection by Jewish refugees in an Italian DP camp of an offer of mass naturalization by the Italian government. In the face of the experience of European peoples between the two wars, it would be a serious mistake to interpret this behavior simply as another example of fanatic nationalist sentiment; these people no longer felt sure of their elementary rights if these were not protected by a government to which they belonged by birth. See Eugene M. Kulisher, *op. cit.*

shared the disdain and indifference of the powers that be for any attempt of the marginal societies to enforce human rights in any elementary or general sense.

The failure of all responsible persons to meet the calamity of an ever-growing body of people forced to live outside the scope of all tangible law with the proclamation of a new bill of rights was certainly not due to ill will. Never before had the Rights of Man, solemnly proclaimed by the French and the American revolutions as the new fundament for civilized societies, been a practical political issue. During the nineteenth century, these rights had been invoked in a rather perfunctory way, to defend individuals against the increasing power of the state and to mitigate the new social insecurity caused by the industrial revolution. Then the meaning of human rights acquired a new connotation: they became the standard slogan of the protectors of the underprivileged, a kind of additional law, a right of exception necessary for those who had nothing better to fall back upon.

The reason why the concept of human rights was treated as a sort of stepchild by nineteenth-century political thought and why no liberal or radical party in the twentieth century, even when an urgent need for enforcement of human rights arose, saw fit to include them in its program seems obvious: civil rights – that is the varying rights of citizens in different countries – were supposed to embody and spell out in the form of tangible laws the eternal Rights of Man, which by themselves were supposed to be independent of citizenship and nationality. All human beings were citizens of some kind of political community; if the laws of their country did not live up to the demands of the Rights of Man, they were expected to change them, by legislation in democratic countries or through revolutionary action in despotisms.

The Rights of Man, supposedly inalienable, proved to be unenforceable – even in countries whose constitutions were based upon them – whenever people appeared who were no longer citizens of any sovereign state. To this fact, disturbing enough in itself, one must add the confusion created by the many recent attempts to frame a new bill of human rights, which have demonstrated that no one seems able to define with any assurance what these general human rights, as distinguished from the rights of citizens, really are. Although everyone seems to agree that the plight of these people consists precisely in their loss of the Rights of Man, no one seems to know which rights they lost when they lost these human rights.

The first loss which the rightless suffered was the loss of their homes, and this meant the loss of the entire social texture into which they were born and in which they established for themselves a distinct place in the world. This calamity is far from unprecedented; in the long memory of history, forced migrations of individuals or whole groups of people for political or economic reasons look like everyday occurrences. What is unprecedented is not the loss of a home but the impossibility of finding a new one. Suddenly, there was no place on earth where migrants could go without the severest restrictions, no country where they would be assimilated, no territory where they could found a new community of their own. This, moreover, had next to nothing to do with any material problem of overpopulation; it was a problem not of space but of political organization. Nobody had been aware that mankind, for so long a time considered under the image of a family of nations, had reached the stage where whoever was thrown out of one of these tightly organized closed communities found himself thrown out of the family of nations altogether.[48]

The second loss which the rightless suffered was the loss of government protection, and this did not imply just the loss of legal status in their own, but in all countries. Treaties of reciprocity and international agreements have woven a web around the earth that makes it possible for the citizen of every country to take his legal status with him no matter where he goes (so that, for instance, a German citizen under the Nazi regime might not be able to enter a mixed marriage abroad because of the Nuremberg laws). Yet, whoever is no longer caught in it finds himself out of legality altogether (thus during the last war stateless people were invariably in a worse position than enemy aliens who

48  The few chances for reintegration open to the new migrants were mostly based on their nationality: Spanish refugees, for instance, were welcomed to a certain extent in Mexico. The United States, in the early twenties, adopted a quota system according to which each nationality already represented in the country received, so to speak, the right to receive a number of former countrymen proportionate to its numerical part in the total population.

were still indirectly protected by their governments through international agreements).

By itself the loss of government protection is no more unprecedented than the loss of a home. Civilized countries did offer the right of asylum to those who, for political reasons, had been persecuted by their governments, and this practice, though never officially incorporated into any constitution, has functioned well enough throughout the nineteenth and even in our century. The trouble arose when it appeared that the new categories of persecuted were far too numerous to be handled by an unofficial practice destined for exceptional cases. Moreover, the majority could hardly qualify for the right of asylum, which implicitly presupposed political or religious convictions which were not outlawed in the country of refuge. The new refugees were persecuted not because of what they had done or thought, but because of what they unchangeably were – born into the wrong kind of race or the wrong kind of class or drafted by the wrong kind of government (as in the case of the Spanish Republican Army).[49]

The more the number of rightless people increased, the greater became the temptation to pay less attention to the deeds of the persecuting governments than to the status of the persecuted. And the first glaring fact was that these people, though persecuted under some political pretext, were no longer, as the persecuted had been throughout history, a liability and an image of shame for the persecutors; that they were not considered and hardly pretended to be active enemies (the few thousand Soviet citizens who voluntarily left Soviet Russia after the second World War and found asylum in democratic countries did more damage to the prestige of the Soviet Union than millions of refugees in the twenties who belonged to the wrong class), but that they were and appeared to be nothing but human beings whose very innocence – from every point of view, and especially that of the

49 How dangerous it can be to be innocent from the point of view of the persecuting government, became very clear when, during the last war, the American government offered asylum to all those German refugees who were threatened by the extradition paragraph in the German-French Armistice. The condition was, of course, that the applicant could prove that he had done something against the Nazi regime. The proportion of refugees from Germany who were able to fulfill this condition was very small, and they, strangely enough, were not the people who were most in danger.

persecuting government – was their greatest misfortune. Innocence, in the sense of complete lack of responsibility, was the mark of their rightlessness as it was the seal of their loss of political status.

Only in appearance therefore do the needs for a reinforcement of human rights touch upon the fate of the authentic political refugee. Political refugees, of necessity few in number, still enjoy the right to asylum in many countries, and this right acts, in an informal way, as a genuine substitute for national law.

One of the surprising aspects of our experience with stateless people who benefit legally from committing a crime has been the fact that it seems to be easier to deprive a completely innocent person of legality than someone who has committed an offense. Anatole France's famous quip, 'If I am accused of stealing the towers of Notre Dame, I can only flee the country,' has assumed a horrible reality. Jurists are so used to thinking of law in terms of punishment, which indeed always deprives us of certain rights, that they may find it even more difficult than the layman to recognize that the deprivation of legality, *i.e.*, of *all* rights, no longer has a connection with specific crimes.

This situation illustrates the many perplexities inherent in the concept of human rights. No matter how they have once been defined (life, liberty, and the pursuit of happiness, according to the American formula, or as equality before the law, liberty, protection of property, and national sovereignty, according to the French); no matter how one may attempt to improve an ambiguous formulation like the pursuit of happiness, or an antiquated one like unqualified right to property; the real situation of those whom the twentieth century has driven outside the pale of the law shows that these are rights of citizens whose loss does not entail absolute rightlessness. The soldier during the war is deprived of his right to life, the criminal of his right to freedom, all citizens during an emergency of their right to the pursuit of happiness, but nobody would ever claim that in any of these instances a loss of human rights has taken place. These rights, on the other hand, can be granted (though hardly enjoyed) even under conditions of fundamental rightlessness.

The calamity of the rightless is not that they are deprived of life, liberty, and the pursuit of happiness, or of equality before the law and freedom of opinion – formulas which were designed to solve problems *within* given communities – but that they no longer belong to any community whatsoever. Their plight is not that they are not equal before the law, but that no law exists for them; not that they are oppressed but that nobody wants even to oppress them. Only in the last stage of a rather lengthy process is their right to live threatened; only if they remain perfectly 'superfluous,' if nobody can be found to 'claim' them, may their lives be in danger. Even the Nazis started their extermination of Jews by first depriving them of all legal status (the status of second-class citizenship) and cutting them off from the world of the living by herding them into ghettos and concentration camps; and before they set the gas chambers into motion they had carefully tested the ground and found out to their satisfaction that no country would claim these people. The point is that a condition of complete rightlessness was created before the right to live was challenged.

The same is true even to an ironical extent with regard to the right of freedom which is sometimes considered to be the very essence of human rights. There is no question that those outside the pale of the law may have more freedom of movement than a lawfully imprisoned criminal or that they enjoy more freedom of opinion in the intern-ment camps of democratic countries than they would in any ordinary despotism, not to mention in a totalitarian country.[50] But neither phys-ical safety – being fed by some state or private welfare agency – nor freedom of opinion changes in the least their fundamental situation of rightlessness. The prolongation of their lives is due to charity and not to right, for no law exists which could force the nations to feed them; their freedom of movement, if they have it at all, gives them no right to residence which even the jailed criminal enjoys as a matter of course; and their freedom of opinion is a fool's freedom, for nothing they think matters anyhow

These last points are crucial. The fundamental deprivation of human rights is manifested first and above all in the deprivation of a

50 Even under the conditions of totalitarian terror, concentration camps sometimes have been the only place where certain remnants of freedom of thought and discussion still existed. See David Rousset, *Les Jours de Notre Mort*, Paris, 1947, *passim*, for freedom of discussion in Buchenwald, and Anton Ciliga, *The Russian Enigma*, London, 1940, p. 200, about 'isles of liberty,' 'the freedom of mind' that reigned in some of the Soviet places of detention.

place in the world which makes opinions significant and actions effective. Something much more fundamental than freedom and justice, which are rights of citizens, is at stake when belonging to the community into which one is born is no longer a matter of course and not belonging no longer a matter of choice, or when one is placed in a situation where, unless he commits a crime, his treatment by others does not depend on what he does or does not do. This extremity, and nothing else, is the situation of people deprived of human rights. They are deprived, not of the right to freedom, but of the right to action; not of the right to think whatever they please, but of the right to opinion. Privileges in some cases, injustices in most, blessings and doom are meted out to them according to accident and without any relation whatsoever to what they do, did, or may do.

We became aware of the existence of a right to have rights (and that means to live in a framework where one is judged by one's actions and opinions) and a right to belong to some kind of organized community, only when millions of people emerged who had lost and could not regain these rights because of the new global political situation. The trouble is that this calamity arose not from any lack of civilization, backwardness, or mere tyranny, but, on the contrary, that it could not be repaired, because there was no longer any 'uncivilized' spot on earth, because whether we like it or not we have really started to live in One World. Only with a completely organized humanity could the loss of home and political status become identical with expulsion from humanity altogether.

Before this, what we must call a 'human right' today would have been thought of as a general characteristic of the human condition which no tyrant could take away. Its loss entails the loss of the relevance of speech (and man, since Aristotle, has been defined as a being commanding the power of speech and thought), and the loss of all human relationship (and man, again since Aristotle, has been thought of as the 'political animal,' that is one who by definition lives in a community), the loss, in other words, of some of the most essential characteristics of human life. This was to a certain extent the plight of slaves, whom Aristotle therefore did not count among human beings. Slavery's fundamental offense against human rights was not that it took liberty away (which can happen in many other situations), but that it excluded a certain category of people even from the possibility of fighting for freedom – a fight possible under tyranny, and even under the desperate conditions of modern terror (but not under any conditions of concentration-camp life). Slavery's crime against humanity did not begin when one people defeated and enslaved its enemies (though of course this was bad enough), but when slavery became an institution in which some men were 'born' free and others slave, when it was forgotten that it was man who had deprived his fellow-men of freedom, and when the sanction for the crime was attributed to nature. Yet in the light of recent events it is possible to say that even slaves still belonged to some sort of human community; their labor was needed, used, and exploited, and this kept them within the pale of humanity. To be a slave was after all to have a distinctive character, a place in society – more than the abstract nakedness of being human and nothing but human. Not the loss of specific rights, then, but the loss of a community willing and able to guarantee any rights whatsoever, has been the calamity which has befallen ever-increasing numbers of people. Man, it turns out, can lose all so-called Rights of Man without losing his essential quality as man, his human dignity. Only the loss of a polity itself expels him from humanity.

The right that corresponds to this loss and that was never even mentioned among the human rights cannot be expressed in the categories of the eighteenth century because they presume that rights spring immediately from the 'nature' of man – whereby it makes relatively little difference whether this nature is visualized in terms of the natural law or in terms of a being created in the image of God, whether it concerns 'natural' rights or divine commands. The decisive factor is that these rights and the human dignity they bestow should remain valid and real even if only a single human being existed on earth; they are independent of human plurality and should remain valid even if a human being is expelled from the human community.

When the Rights of Man were proclaimed for the first time, they were regarded as being independent of history and the privileges which history had accorded certain strata of society. The new independence constituted the newly discovered dignity of man. From the beginning, this new dignity was of a rather ambiguous nature.

Historical rights were replaced by natural rights, 'nature' took the place of history, and it was tacitly assumed that nature was less alien than history to the essence of man. The very language of the Declaration of Independence as well as of the *Déclaration des Droits de l'Homme* – 'inalienable,' 'given with birth,' 'self-evident truths' – implies the belief in a kind of human 'nature' which would be subject to the same laws of growth as that of the individual and from which rights and laws could be deduced. Today we are perhaps better qualified to judge exactly what this human 'nature' amounts to; in any event it has shown us potentialities that were neither recognized nor even suspected by Western philosophy and religion, which for more than three thousand years have defined and redefined this 'nature.' But it is not only the, as it were, human aspect of nature that has become questionable to us. Ever since man learned to master it to such an extent that the destruction of all organic life on earth with man-made instruments has become conceivable and technically possible, he has been alienated from nature. Ever since a deeper knowledge of natural processes instilled serious doubts about the existence of natural laws at all, nature itself has assumed a sinister aspect. How should one be able to deduce laws and rights from a universe which apparently knows neither the one nor the other category?

Man of the twentieth century has become just as emancipated from nature as eighteenth-century man was from history. History and nature have become equally alien to us, namely, in the sense that the essence of man can no longer be comprehended in terms of either category. On the other hand, humanity, which for the eighteenth century, in Kantian terminology, was no more than a regulative idea, has today become an inescapable fact. This new situation, in which 'humanity' has in effect assumed the role formerly ascribed to nature or history, would mean in this context that the right to have rights, or the right of every individual to belong to humanity, should be guaranteed by humanity itself. It is by no means certain whether this is possible. For, contrary to the best-intentioned humanitarian attempts to obtain new declarations of human rights from international organizations, it should be understood that this idea transcends the present sphere of international law which still operates in terms of reciprocal agreements and treaties between sovereign states; and, for the time being, a sphere that is above the nations does not exist. Furthermore, this dilemma would by no means be eliminated by the establishment of a 'world government.' Such a world government is indeed within the realm of possibility, but one may suspect that in reality it might differ considerably from the version promoted by idealistic-minded organizations. The crimes against human rights, which have become a specialty of totalitarian regimes, can always be justified by the pretext that right is equivalent to being good or useful for the whole in distinction to its parts. (Hitler's motto that 'Right is what is good for the German people' is only the vulgarized form of a conception of law which can be found everywhere and which in practice will remain ineffectual only so long as older traditions that are still effective in the constitutions prevent this.) A conception of law which identifies what is right with the notion of what is good for – for the individual, or the family, or the people, or the largest number – becomes inevitable once the absolute and transcendent measurements of religion or the law of nature have lost their authority. And this predicament is by no means solved if the unit to which the 'good for' applies is as large as mankind itself. For it is quite conceivable, and even within the realm of practical political possibilities, that one fine day a highly organized and mechanized humanity will conclude quite democratically – namely by majority decision – that for humanity as a whole it would be better to liquidate certain parts thereof. Here, in the problems of factual reality, we are confronted with one of the oldest perplexities of political philosophy, which could remain undetected only so long as a stable Christian theology provided the framework for all political and philosophical problems, but which long ago caused Plato to say: 'Not man, but a god, must be the measure of all things.'

These facts and reflections offer what seems an ironical, bitter, and belated confirmation of the famous arguments with which Edmund Burke opposed the French Revolution's Declaration of the Rights of Man. They appear to buttress his assertion that human rights were an 'abstraction,' that it was much wiser to rely on an 'entailed inheritance' of rights which one transmits to one's children like life itself, and to claim one's rights to be the 'rights of an Englishman' rather than the inalienable rights of man.[51] According to Burke, the rights which we enjoy spring 'from within the nation,' so that neither natural law, nor divine command, nor any concept of mankind such as Robespierre's 'human race,' 'the sovereign of the earth,' are needed as a source of law.[52]

The pragmatic soundness of Burke's concept seems to be beyond doubt in the light of our manifold experiences. Not only did loss of national rights in all instances entail the loss of human rights; the restoration of human rights, as the recent example of the State of Israel proves, has been achieved so far only through the restoration or the establishment of national rights. The conception of human rights, based upon the assumed existence of a human being as such, broke down at the very moment when those who professed to believe in it were for the first time confronted with people who had indeed lost all other qualities and specific relationships – except that they were still human. The world found nothing sacred in the abstract nakedness of being human. And in view of objective political conditions, it is hard to say how the concepts of man upon which human rights are based – that he is created in the image of God (in the American formula), or that he is the representative of mankind, or that he harbors within himself the sacred demands of natural law (in the French formula) – could have helped to find a solution to the problem.

The survivors of the extermination camps, the inmates of concentration and internment camps, and even the comparatively happy stateless people could see without Burke's arguments that the abstract nakedness of being nothing but human was their greatest danger. Because of it they were regarded as savages and, afraid that they might end by being considered beasts, they insisted on their nationality, the last sign of their former citizenship, as their only remaining and recognized tie with humanity. Their distrust of natural, their preference for national, rights comes precisely from their realization that natural rights are granted even to savages. Burke had already feared that natural 'inalienable' rights would confirm only the 'right of the naked

51 Edmund Burke, *Reflections on the Revolution in France*, 1790, edited by E. J. Payne, Everyman's Library.
52 Robespierre, *Speeches*, 1927. Speech of April 24, 1793.

savage,'[53] and therefore reduce civilized nations to the status of savagery. Because only savages have nothing more to fall back upon than the minimum fact of their human origin, people cling to their nationality all the more desperately when they have lost the rights and protection that such nationality once gave them. Only their past with its 'entailed inheritance' seems to attest to the fact that they still belong to the civilized world.

If a human being loses his political status, he should, according to the implications of the inborn and inalienable rights of man, come under exactly the situation for which the declarations of such general rights provided. Actually the opposite is the case. It seems that a man who is nothing but a man has lost the very qualities which make it possible for other people to treat him as a fellow-man. This is one of the reasons why it is far more difficult to destroy the legal personality of a criminal, that is of a man who has taken upon himself the responsibility for an act whose consequences now determine his fate, than of a man who has been disallowed all common human responsibilities.

Burke's arguments therefore gain an added significance if we look only at the general human condition of those who have been forced out of all political communities. Regardless of treatment, independent of liberties or oppression, justice or injustice, they have lost all those parts of the world and all those aspects of human existence which are the result of our common labor, the outcome of the human artifice. If the tragedy of savage tribes is that they inhabit an unchanged nature which they cannot master, yet upon whose abundance or frugality they depend for their livelihood, that they live and die without leaving any trace, without having contributed anything to a common world, then these rightless people are indeed thrown back into a peculiar state of nature. Certainly they are not barbarians; some of them, indeed, belong to the most educated strata of their respective countries; nevertheless, in a world that has almost liquidated savagery, they appear as the first signs of a possible regression from civilization.

The more highly developed a civilization, the more accomplished the world it has produced, the more at home men feel within the

---

53 Introduction by Payne to Burke, *op. cit.*

human artifice – the more they will resent everything they have not produced, everything that is merely and mysteriously given them. The human being who has lost his place in a community, his political status in the struggle of his time, and the legal personality which makes his actions and part of his destiny a consistent whole, is left with those qualities which usually can become articulate only in the sphere of private life and must remain unqualified, mere existence in all matters of public concern. This mere existence, that is, all that which is mysteriously given us by birth and which includes the shape of our bodies and the talents of our minds, can be adequately dealt with only by the unpredictable hazards of friendship and sympathy, or by the great and incalculable grace of love, which says with Augustine, '*Volo ut sis* (I want you to be),' without being able to give any particular reason for such supreme and unsurpassable affirmation.

Since the Greeks, we have known that highly developed political life breeds a deep-rooted suspicion of this private sphere, a deep resentment against the disturbing miracle contained in the fact that each of us is made as he is – single, unique, unchangeable. This whole sphere of the merely given, relegated to private life in civilized society, is a permanent threat to the public sphere, because the public sphere is as consistently based on the law of equality as the private sphere is based on the law of universal difference and differentiation. Equality, in contrast to all that is involved in mere existence, is not given us, but is the result of human organization insofar as it is guided by the principle of justice. We are not born equal; we become equal as members of a group on the strength of our decision to guarantee ourselves mutually equal rights.

Our political life rests on the assumption that we can produce equality through organization, because man can act in and change and build a common world, together with his equals and only with his equals. The dark background of mere givenness, the background formed by our unchangeable and unique nature, breaks into the political scene as the alien which in its all too obvious difference reminds us of the limitations of human activity – which are identical with the limitations of human equality. The reason why highly developed political communities, such as the ancient city-states or modern nation-states, so often insist on ethnic homogeneity is that they hope to eliminate as far as possible those natural and always present differences and differentiations which by themselves arouse dumb hatred, mistrust, and discrimination because they indicate all too clearly those spheres where men cannot act and change at will, *i.e.*, the limitations of the human artifice. The 'alien' is a frightening symbol of the fact of difference as such, of individuality as such, and indicates those realms in which man cannot change and cannot act and in which, therefore, he has a distinct tendency to destroy. If a Negro in a white community is considered a Negro and nothing else, he loses along with his right to equality that freedom of action which is specifically human; all his deeds are now explained as 'necessary' consequences of some 'Negro' qualities; he has become some specimen of an animal species, called man. Much the same thing happens to those who have lost all distinctive political qualities and have become human beings and nothing else. No doubt, wherever public life and its law of equality are completely victorious, wherever a civilization succeeds in eliminating or reducing to a minimum the dark background of difference, it will end in complete petrifaction and be punished, so to speak, for having forgotten that man is only the master, not the creator of the world.

The great danger arising from the existence of people forced to live outside the common world is that they are thrown back, in the midst of civilization, on their natural givenness, on their mere differentiation. They lack that tremendous equalizing of differences which comes from being citizens of some commonwealth and yet, since they are no longer allowed to partake in the human artifice, they begin to belong to the human race in much the same way as animals belong to a specific animal species. The paradox involved in the loss of human rights is that such loss coincides with the instant when a person becomes a human being in general – without a profession, without a citizenship, without an opinion, without a deed by which to identify and specify himself – *and* different in general, representing nothing but his own absolutely unique individuality which, deprived of expression within and action upon a common world, loses all significance.

The danger in the existence of such people is twofold: first and more obviously, their ever-increasing numbers threaten our political life, our human artifice, the world which is the result of our common and co-ordinated effort in much the same, perhaps even more terrifying, way as the wild elements of nature once threatened the existence of man-made cities and countrysides. Deadly danger to any civilization is no longer likely to come from without. Nature has been mastered and no barbarians threaten to destroy what they cannot understand, as the Mongolians threatened Europe for centuries. Even the emergence of totalitarian governments is a phenomenon within, not outside, our civilization. The danger is that a global, universally interrelated civilization may produce barbarians from its own midst by forcing millions of people into conditions which, despite all appearances, are the conditions of savages.[54]

---

54 This modern expulsion from humanity has much more radical consequences than the ancient and medieval custom of outlawry. Outlawry, certainly the 'most fearful fate which primitive law could inflict,' placing the life of the outlawed person at the mercy of anyone he met, disappeared with the establishment of an effective system of law enforcement and was finally replaced by extradition treaties between the nations. It had been primarily a substitute for a police force, designed to compel criminals to surrender.

The early Middle Ages seem to have been quite conscious of the danger involved in 'civil death.' Excommunication in the late Roman Empire meant ecclesiastical death but left a person who had lost his membership in the church full freedom in all other respects. Ecclesiastical and civil death became identical only in the Merovingian era, and there excommunication 'in general practice [was] limited to temporary withdrawal or suspension of the rights of membership which might be regained.' See the articles 'Outlawry' and 'Excommunication' in the *Encyclopedia of Social Sciences*. Also the article 'Friedlosigkeit' in the *Schweizer Lexikon*.

# PART THREE

## Totalitarianism

*Normal men do not know that everything is possible.*

David Rousset

# CHAPTER TEN

# A Classless Society

## I: The Masses

Nothing is more characteristic of the totalitarian movements in general and of the quality of fame of their leaders in particular than the startling swiftness with which they are forgotten and the startling ease with which they can be replaced. What Stalin accomplished laboriously over many years through bitter factional struggles and vast concessions at least to the name of his predecessor – namely, to legitimate himself as Lenin's political heir – Stalin's successors attempted to do without concessions to the name of their predecessor, even though Stalin had thirty years' time and could manipulate a propaganda apparatus, unknown in Lenin's day, to immortalize his name. The same is true for Hitler, who during his lifetime exercised a fascination to which allegedly no one was immune,[1] and who after his defeat and

1 The 'magic spell' that Hitler cast over his listeners has been acknowledged many times, latterly by the publishers of *Hitlers Tischgespräche*, Bonn, 1951 (*Hitler's Table Talk*, American edition, New York, 1953; quotations from the original German edition). This fascination – 'the strange magnetism that radiated from Hitler in such a compelling manner' – rested indeed 'on the fanatical belief of this man in himself' (introduction by Gerhard Ritter, p. 14), on his pseudo-authoritative judgments about everything under the sun, and on the fact that his opinions – whether they dealt with the harmful effects of smoking or with Napoleon's policies – could always be fitted into an all-encompassing ideology.

Fascination is a social phenomenon, and the fascination Hitler exercised over his environment must be understood in terms of the particular company he kept. Society is always prone to accept a person offhand for what he pretends to be, so that a crackpot posing as a genius always has a certain chance to be believed. In modern society, with its characteristic lack of discerning judgment, this tendency is strengthened, so that someone who not only holds opinions but also presents them in a tone of unshakable conviction will not so easily forfeit his prestige, no matter how many

death is today so thoroughly forgotten that he scarcely plays any further role even among the neo-Fascist and neo-Nazi groups of postwar Germany. This impermanence no doubt has something to do with the proverbial fickleness of the masses and the fame that rests on them; more likely, it can be traced to the perpetual-motion mania of totalitarian movements which can remain in power only so long as they keep moving and set everything around them in motion. Therefore, in a certain sense this very impermanence is a rather flattering testimonial to the dead leaders insofar as they succeeded in contaminating their subjects with the specifically totalitarian virus; for if there is such a thing as a totalitarian personality or mentality, this extraordinary adaptability and absence of continuity are no doubt its outstanding characteristics. Hence it might be a mistake to assume that the inconstancy and forgetfulness of the masses signify that they are cured of the totalitarian delusion, which is occasionally identified with the Hitler or Stalin cult; the opposite might well be true.

It would be a still more serious mistake to forget, because of this impermanence, that the totalitarian regimes, so long as they are in power, and the totalitarian leaders, so long as they are alive, 'command and rest upon mass support' up to the end.[2] Hitler's rise to power

---

times he has been demonstrably wrong. Hitler, who knew the modern chaos of opinions from first-hand experience, discovered that the helpless seesawing between various opinions and 'the conviction . . . that everything is balderdash' (p. 281) could best be avoided by adhering to *one* of the many current opinions with 'unbending consistency.' The hair-raising arbitrariness of such fanaticism holds great fascination for society because for the duration of the social gathering it is freed from the chaos of opinions that it constantly generates. This 'gift' of fascination, however, has only social relevance; it is so prominent in the *Tischgespräche* because here Hitler played the game of society and was not speaking to his own kind but to the generals of the Wehrmacht, all of whom more or less belonged to 'society.' To believe that Hitler's successes were based on his 'powers of fascination' is altogether erroneous; with those qualities alone he would have never advanced beyond the role of a prominent figure in the salons.

2 See the illuminating remarks of Carlton J. H. Hayes on 'The Novelty of Totalitarianism in the History of Western Civilization,' in *Symposium on the Totalitarian State*, 1939. Proceedings of the American Philosophical Society, Philadelphia, 1940, Vol. LXXXII.

was legal in terms of majority rule[3] and neither he nor Stalin could have maintained the leadership of large populations, survived many interior and exterior crises, and braved the numerous dangers of relentless intra-party struggles if they had not had the confidence of the masses. Neither the Moscow trials nor the liquidation of the Röhm faction would have been possible if these masses had not supported Stalin and Hitler. The widespread belief that Hitler was simply an agent of German industrialists and that Stalin was victorious in the succession struggle after Lenin's death only through a sinister conspiracy are both legends which can be refuted by many facts but above all by the leaders' indisputable popularity.[4] Nor can their popularity be attributed to the victory of masterful and lying propaganda over ignorance and stupidity. For the propaganda of totalitarian movements which precede and accompany totalitarian regimes is invariably as frank as it is mendacious, and would-be totalitarian rulers usually start their careers by boasting of their past crimes and carefully outlining their future ones. The Nazis 'were convinced that evil-doing in our time has a morbid force of attraction,'[5] Bolshevik assurances inside and outside Russia that they do not recognize ordinary moral standards have become a mainstay of Communist propaganda, and experience has proved time and again that the propaganda value of evil deeds and general contempt for moral standards is independent

3 This was indeed 'the first large revolution in history that was carried out by applying the existing formal code of law at the moment of seizing power' (Hans Frank, *Recht und Verwaltung*, 1939, p. 8).

4 The best study of Hitler and his career is the new Hitler biography by Alan Bullock, *Hitler, A Study in Tyranny*, London, 1952. In the English tradition of political biographies it makes meticulous use of all available source material and gives a comprehensive picture of the contemporary political background. By this publication the excellent books of Konrad Heiden – primarily *Der Fuehrer: Hitler's Rise to Power*, Boston, 1944 – have been superseded in their details although they remain important for the general interpretation of events. For Stalin's career, Boris Souvarine, *Stalin: A Critical Survey of Bolshevism*, New York, 1939, is still a standard work. Isaac Deutscher, *Stalin: A Political Biography*, New York and London, 1949, is indispensable for its rich documentary material and great insight into the internal struggles of the Bolshevik party; it suffers from an interpretation which likens Stalin to – Cromwell, Napoleon, and Robespierre.

5 Franz Borkenau, *The Totalitarian Enemy*, London, 1940, p. 231.

of mere self-interest, supposedly the most powerful psychological factor in politics.

The attraction of evil and crime for the mob mentality is nothing new. It has always been true that the mob will greet 'deeds of violence with the admiring remark: it may be mean but it is very clever.'[6] The disturbing factor in the success of totalitarianism is rather the true selflessness of its adherents: it may be understandable that a Nazi or Bolshevik will not be shaken in his conviction by crimes against people who do not belong to the movement or are even hostile to it; but the amazing fact is that neither is he likely to waver when the monster begins to devour its own children and not even if he becomes a victim of persecution himself, if he is framed and condemned, if he is purged from the party and sent to a forced-labor or a concentration camp. On the contrary, to the wonder of the whole civilized world, he may even be willing to help in his own prosecution and frame his own death sentence if only his status as a member of the movement is not touched.[7] It would be naïve to consider this stubbornness of conviction which outlives all actual experiences and cancels all immediate self-interest a simple expression of fervent idealism. Idealism, foolish or heroic, always springs from some individual decision and conviction and is subject to experience and argument.[8] The fanaticism of

6 Quoted from the German edition of the 'Protocols of the Elders of Zion,' *Die Zionistischen Protokolle mit einem Vor- und Nachwort von Theodor Fritsch*, 1924, p. 29.

7 This, to be sure, is a specialty of the Russian brand of totalitarianism. It is interesting to note that in the early trial of foreign engineers in the Soviet Union, Communist sympathies were already used as an argument for self-accusation: 'All the time the authorities insisted on my admitting having committed acts of sabotage I had never done. I refused. I was told: "If you are in favour of the Soviet Government, as you pretend you are, prove it by your actions; the Government needs your confession."' Reported by Anton Ciliga, *The Russian Enigma*, London, 1940, p. 153.

A theoretical justification for this behavior was given by Trotsky: 'We can only be right with and by the Party, for history has provided no other way of being in the right. The English have a saying, "My country, right or wrong" ... We have much better historical justification in saying whether it is right or wrong in certain individual concrete cases, it is my party' (Souvarine, *op. cit.*, p. 361).

On the other hand, the Red Army officers who did not belong to the movement had to be tried behind closed doors.

8 The Nazi author Andreas Pfenning explicitly rejects the notion that the SA were fighting for an 'ideal' or were prompted by an 'idealistic experience.' Their 'basic experience came into existence in the course of the struggle.' 'Gemeinschaft und

totalitarian movements, contrary to all forms of idealism, breaks down the moment the movement leaves its fanaticized followers in the lurch, killing in them any remaining conviction that might have survived the collapse of the movement itself.[9] But within the organizational framework of the movement, so long as it holds together, the fanaticized members can be reached by neither experience nor argument; identification with the movement and total conformism seem to have destroyed the very capacity for experience, even if it be as extreme as torture or the fear of death.

The totalitarian movements aim at and succeed in organizing masses – not classes, like the old interest parties of the Continental nation-states; not citizens with opinions about, and interests in, the handling of public affairs, like the parties of Anglo-Saxon countries. While all political groups depend upon proportionate strength, the totalitarian movements depend on the sheer force of numbers to such an extent that totalitarian regimes seem impossible, even under otherwise favorable circumstances, in countries with relatively small populations.[10] After

---

Staatswissenschaft,' in *Zeitschrift für die gesamte Staatswissenschaft*, Band 96. Translation quoted from Ernst Fraenkel, *The Dual State*, New York and London, 1941, p. 192. From the extensive literature issued in pamphlet form by the main indoctrination center (*Hauptamt-Schulungsamt*) of the SS, it is quite evident that the word 'idealism' has been studiously avoided. Not idealism was demanded of SS members, but 'utter logical consistency in all questions of ideology and the ruthless pursuit of the political struggle' (Werner Best, *Die deutsche Polizei*, 1941, p. 99).

9 In this respect postwar Germany offers many illuminating examples. It was astonishing enough that American Negro troops were by no means received with hostility, in spite of the massive racial indoctrination undertaken by the Nazis. But equally startling was 'the fact that the Waffen-SS in the last days of German resistance against the Allies did not fight "to the last man"' and that this special Nazi combat unit 'after the enormous sacrifices of the preceding years, which far exceeded the proportionate losses of the Wehrmacht, in the last few weeks acted like any unit drawn from the ranks of civilians, and bowed to the hopelessness of the situation' (Karl O. Paetel, 'Die SS,' in *Vierteljahreshefte für Zeitgeschichte*, January, 1954).

10 The Moscow-dominated Eastern European governments rule for the sake of Moscow and act as agents of the Comintern; they are examples of the spread of the Moscow-directed totalitarian movement, not of native developments. The only exception seems to be Tito of Yugoslavia, who may have broken with Moscow because he realized that the Russian-inspired totalitarian methods would cost him a heavy percentage of Yugoslavia's population.

the first World War, a deeply antidemocratic, prodictatorial wave of semitotalitarian and totalitarian movements swept Europe; Fascist movements spread from Italy to nearly all Central and Eastern European countries (the Czech part of Czechoslovakia was one of the notable exceptions); yet even Mussolini, who was so fond of the term 'totalitarian state,' did not attempt to establish a full-fledged totalitarian regime[11] and contented himself with dictatorship and one-party rule. Similar nontotalitarian dictatorships sprang up in prewar Rumania, Poland, the Baltic states, Hungary, Portugal and Franco Spain. The Nazis, who had an unfailing instinct for such differences, used to comment contemptuously on the shortcomings of their Fascist allies while their genuine admiration for the Bolshevik regime in Russia (and the Communist Party in Germany) was matched and checked only by their contempt for Eastern European races.[12] The only man for

11 Proof of the nontotalitarian nature of the Fascist dictatorship is the surprisingly small number and the comparatively mild sentences meted out to political offenders. During the particularly active years from 1926 to 1932, the special tribunals for political offenders pronounced 7 death sentences, 257 sentences of 10 or more years imprisonment, 1,360 under 10 years, and sentenced many more to exile; 12,000, moreover, were arrested and found innocent, a procedure quite inconceivable under conditions of Nazi or Bolshevik terror. See E. Kohn-Bramstedt, *Dictatorship and Political Police: The Technique of Control by Fear*, London, 1945, pp. 51 ff.

12 Nazi political theorists have always emphatically stated that 'Mussolini's "ethical state" and Hitler's "ideological state" [*Weltanschauungsstaat*] cannot be mentioned in the same breath' (Gottfried Neesse, 'Die verfassungsrechtliche Gestaltung der Ein-Partei,' in *Zeitschrift für die gesamte Staatswissenschaft*, 1938, Band 98).

Goebbels on the difference between Fascism and National Socialism: '[Fascism] is . . . nothing like National Socialism. While the latter goes deep down to the roots, Fascism is only a superficial thing' (*The Goebbels Diaries 1942–1943*, ed. by Louis Lochner, New York, 1948, p. 71). '[The Duce] is not a revolutionary like the Führer or Stalin. He is so bound to his own Italian people that he lacks the broad qualities of a worldwide revolutionary and insurrectionist' (*ibid.*, p. 468).

Himmler expressed the same opinion in a speech delivered in 1943 at a Conference of Commanding Officers: 'Fascism and National Socialism are two fundamentally different things . . . there is absolutely no comparison between Fascism and National Socialism as spiritual, ideological movements.' See Kohn-Bramstedt, *op. cit.*, Appendix A.

Hitler recognized in the early twenties the affinity between the Nazi and the Communist movements: 'In our movement the two extremes come together: the Communists from the Left and the officers and the students from the Right. These two have always been the most active elements. . . . The Communists were the idealists of Socialism . . .' See Heiden, *op. cit.*, p. 147. Röhm, the chief of the SA, only repeated a current opinion when he wrote in the late twenties: 'Many things are between us and

whom Hitler had 'unqualified respect' was 'Stalin the genius,'[13] and while in the case of Stalin and the Russian regime we do not have (and presumably never will have) the rich documentary material that is available for Germany, we nevertheless know since Khrushchev's speech before the Twentieth Party Congress that Stalin trusted only one man and that was Hitler.[14]

The point is that in all these smaller European countries nontotalitarian dictatorships were preceded by totalitarian movements, so that it appeared that totalitarianism was too ambitious an aim, that although it had served well enough to organize the masses until the movement seized power, the absolute size of the country then forced the would-be totalitarian ruler of masses into the more familiar patterns of class or party dictatorship. The truth is that these countries simply did not control enough human material to allow for total

the Communists, but we respect the sincerity of their conviction and their willingness to bring sacrifices for their own cause, and this unites us with them' (Ernst Röhm, *Die Geschichte eines Hochverräters*, 1933, Volksausgabe, p. 273).

During the last war, the Nazis more readily recognized the Russians as their peers than any other nation. Hitler, speaking in May, 1943, at a conference of the Reichsleiter and Gauleiter, 'began with the fact that in this war bourgeoisie and revolutionary states are facing each other. It has been an easy thing for us to knock out the bourgeois states, for they were quite inferior to us in their upbringing and attitude. Countries with an ideology have an edge on bourgois states . . . [In the East] we met an opponent who also sponsors an ideology, even though a wrong one . . .' (*Goebbels Diaries*, p. 355). – This estimate was based on ideological, not on military considerations. Gottfried Neesse, *Partei und Staat*, 1936, gave the official version of the movement's struggle for power when he wrote: 'For us the united front of the *system* extends from the German National People's Party [*i.e.*, the extreme Right] to the Social Democrats. The Communist Party was an enemy outside of the *system*. During the first months of 1933, therefore, when the doom of the *system* was already sealed, we still had to fight a decisive battle against the Communist Party' (p. 76).

13 *Hitlers Tischgespräche*, p. 113. There we also find numerous examples showing that, contrary to certain postwar legends, Hitler never intended to defend 'the West' against Bolshevism but always remained ready to join 'the Reds' for the destruction of the West, even in the middle of the struggle against Soviet Russia. See especially pp. 95, 108, 113 ff., 158, 385.

14 We now know that Stalin was warned repeatedly of the imminent attack of Hitler on the Soviet Union. Even when the Soviet military attaché in Berlin informed him of the day of the Nazi attack, Stalin refused to believe that Hitler would violate the treaty. (See Khrushchev's 'Speech on Stalin,' text released by the State Department, New York *Times*, June 5, 1956.)

domination and its inherent great losses in population.[15] Without much hope for the conquest of more heavily populated territories, the tyrants in these small countries were forced into a certain old-fashioned moderation lest they lose whatever people they had to rule. This is also why Nazism, up to the outbreak of the war and its expansion over Europe, lagged so far behind its Russian counterpart in consistency and ruthlessness; even the German people were not numerous enough to allow for the full development of this newest form of government. Only if Germany had won the war would she have known a fully developed totalitarian rulership, and the sacrifices this would have entailed not only for the 'inferior races' but for the Germans themselves can be gleaned and evaluated from the legacy of Hitler's plans.[16]

15 The following information reported by Souvarine, op. cit., p. 669, seems to be an outstanding illustration: 'According to W. Krivitsky, whose excellent confidential source of information is the GPU: "Instead of the 171 million inhabitants calculated for 1937, only 145 million were found; thus nearly 30 million people in the USSR are missing."' And this, it should be kept in mind, occurred after the dekulakization of the early thirties which had cost an estimated 8 million human lives. See Communism in Action, U.S. Government, Washington, 1946, p. 140.

16 A large part of these plans, based on the original documents, can be found in Léon Poliakov's Bréviaire de la Haine, Paris, 1951, chapter 8 (American edition under the title Harvest of Hate, Syracuse, 1954; we quote from the original French edition), but only insofar as they referred to the extermination of non-Germanic peoples, above all those of Slavic origin. That the Nazi engine of destruction would not have stopped even before the German people is evident from a Reich health bill drafted by Hitler himself. Here he proposes to 'isolate' from the rest of the population all families with cases of heart or lung ailments among them, their physical liquidation being of course the next step in this program. This as well as several other interesting projects for a victorious postwar Germany are contained in a circular letter to the district leaders (Kreisleiter) of Hesse-Nassau in the form of a report on a discussion at the Fuehrer's headquarters concerning 'measures that before . . . and after victorious termination of the war' should be adopted. See the collection of documents in Nazi Conspiracy and Aggression, Washington, 1946, et seq., Vol. VII, p. 175. In the same context belongs the planned enactment of an 'over-all alien legislation,' by means of which the 'institutional authority' of the police – namely, to ship persons innocent of any offenses to concentration camps – was to be legalized and expanded. (See Paul Werner, SS-Standartenführer, in Deutsches Jugendrecht, Heft 4, 1944.)

In connection with this 'negative population policy,' which in its aim at extermination decidedly matches the Bolshevist party purges, it is important to remember that 'in this process of selection there can never be a standstill' (Himmler, 'Die Schutzstaffel,' in Grundlagen, Aufbau und Wirtschaftsordnung des nationalsozialistischen

In any event it was only during the war, after the conquests in the East furnished large masses of people and made the extermination camps possible, that Germany was able to establish a truly totalitarian rule. (Conversely, the chances for totalitarian rule are frighteningly good in the lands of traditional Oriental despotism, in India and China, where there is almost inexhaustible material to feed the power-accumulating and man-destroying machinery of total domination, and where, moreover, the mass man's typical feeling of superfluousness – an entirely new phenomenon in Europe, the concomitant of mass unemployment and the population growth of the last 150 years – has been prevalent for centuries in the contempt for the value of human life.) Moderation or less murderous methods of rule were hardly attributable to the governments' fear of popular rebellion; depopulation in their own country was a much more serious threat. Only where great masses are superfluous or can be spared without disastrous results of depopulation is totalitarian rule, as distinguished from a totalitarian movement, at all possible.

Totalitarian movements are possible wherever there are masses who for one reason or another have acquired the appetite for political organization. Masses are not held together by a consciousness of common interest and they lack that specific class articulateness which is expressed in determined, limited, and obtainable goals. The term masses applies only where we deal with people who either because of sheer numbers, or indifference, or a combination of both, cannot be integrated into any organization based on common interest, into political parties or municipal governments or professional organizations or trade unions. Potentially, they exist in every country and form the majority of those large numbers of neutral, politically indifferent people who never join a party and hardly ever go to the polls.

It was characteristic of the rise of the Nazi movement in Germany

---

Staates, No. 7b). 'The struggle of the Fuehrer and his party was a hitherto unattained selection . . . This selection and this struggle were ostensibly accomplished on January 30, 1933 . . . The Fuehrer and his old guard knew that the real struggle had just begun' (Robert Ley, *Der Weg zur Ordensburg*, o.D. Verlag der Deutschen Arbeitsfront. 'Not available for sale').

and of the Communist movements in Europe after 1930[17] that they recruited their members from this mass of apparently indifferent people whom all other parties had given up as too apathetic or too stupid for their attention. The result was that the majority of their membership consisted of people who never before had appeared on the political scene. This permitted the introduction of entirely new methods into political propaganda, and indifference to the arguments of political opponents; these movements not only placed themselves outside and against the party system as a whole, they found a membership that had never been reached, never been 'spoiled' by the party system. Therefore they did not need to refute opposing arguments and consistently preferred methods which ended in death rather than persuasion, which spelled terror rather than conviction. They presented disagreements as invariably originating in deep natural, social, or psychological sources beyond the control of the individual and therefore beyond the power of reason. This would have been a shortcoming only if they had sincerely entered into competition with other parties; it was not if they were sure of dealing with people who had reason to be equally hostile to all parties.

The success of totalitarian movements among the masses meant the end of two illusions of democratically ruled countries in general and of European nation-states and their party system in particular. The first was that the people in its majority had taken an active part in government and that each individual was in sympathy with one's own or somebody else's party. On the contrary, the movements showed that the politically neutral and indifferent masses could easily be the majority in a democratically ruled country, that therefore a democracy could function according to rules which are actively recognized by only a minority. The second democratic illusion exploded by the totalitarian movements was that these politically indifferent masses did not matter, that they were truly neutral and constituted no more than the inarticulate backward setting for the political life of the

17 F. Borkenau describes the situation correctly: 'The Communists had only very modest successes when they tried to win influence among the masses of the working class; their mass basis, therefore, if they had it at all, moved more and more away from the proletariat' ('Die neue Komintern,' in *Der Monat*, Berlin, 1949, Heft 4).

nation. Now they made apparent what no other organ of public opinion had ever been able to show, namely, that democratic government had rested as much on the silent approbation and tolerance of the indifferent and inarticulate sections of the people as on the articulate and visible institutions and organizations of the country. Thus when the totalitarian movements invaded Parliament with their contempt for parliamentary government, they merely appeared inconsistent: actually, they succeeded in convincing the people at large that parliamentary majorities were spurious and did not necessarily correspond to the realities of the country, thereby undermining the self-respect and the confidence of governments which also believed in majority rule rather than in their constitutions.

It has frequently been pointed out that totalitarian movements use and abuse democratic freedoms in order to abolish them. This is not just devilish cleverness on the part of the leaders or childish stupidity on the part of the masses. Democratic freedoms may be based on the equality of all citizens before the law; yet they acquire their meaning and function organically only where the citizens belong to and are represented by groups or form a social and political hierarchy. The breakdown of the class system, the only social and political stratification of the European nation-states, certainly was 'one of the most dramatic events in recent German history' [18] and as favorable to the rise of Nazism as the absence of social stratification in Russia's immense rural population (this 'great flaccid body destitute of political education, almost inaccessible to ideas capable of ennobling action' [19]) was to the Bolshevik overthrow of the democratic Kerensky government. Conditions in pre-Hitler Germany are indicative of the dangers implicit in the development of the Western part of the world since, with the end of the second World War, the same dramatic event of a breakdown of the class system repeated itself in almost all European countries, while events in Russia clearly indicate the direction which the inevitable revolutionary changes in Asia may take. Practically speaking, it will make little difference whether totalitarian movements adopt the pattern of Nazism or Bolshevism, organize the

18  William Ebenstein, *The Nazi State*, New York, 1943, p. 247.
19  As Maxim Gorky had described them. See Souvarine, *op. cit.*, p. 290.

masses in the name of race or class, pretend to follow the laws of life and nature or of dialectics and economics.

Indifference to public affairs, neutrality on political issues, are in themselves no sufficient cause for the rise of totalitarian movements. The competitive and acquisitive society of the bourgeoisie had produced apathy and even hostility toward public life not only, and not even primarily, in the social strata which were exploited and excluded from active participation in the rule of the country, but first of all in its own class. The long period of false modesty, when the bourgeoisie was content with being the dominating class in society without aspiring to political rule, which it gladly left to the aristocracy, was followed by the imperialist era, during which the bourgeoisie grew increasingly hostile to existing national institutions and began to claim and to organize itself for the exercise of political power. Both the early apathy and the later demand for monopolistic dictatorial direction of the nation's foreign affairs had their roots in a way and philosophy of life so insistently and exclusively centered on the individual's success or failure in ruthless competition that a citizen's duties and responsibilities could only be felt to be a needless drain on his limited time and energy. These bourgeois attitudes are very useful for those forms of dictatorship in which a 'strong man' takes upon himself the troublesome responsibility for the conduct of public affairs; they are a positive hindrance to totalitarian movements which can tolerate bourgeois individualism no more than any other kind of individualism. The apathetic sections of a bourgeois-dominated society, no matter how unwilling they may be to assume the responsibilities of citizens, keep their personalities intact if only because without them they could hardly expect to survive the competitive struggle for life.

The decisive differences between nineteenth-century mob organizations and twentieth-century mass movements are difficult to perceive because the modern totalitarian leaders do not differ much in psychology and mentality from the earlier mob leaders, whose moral standards and political devices so closely resembled those of the bourgeoisie. Yet, insofar as individualism characterized the bourgeoisie's as well as the mob's attitude to life, the totalitarian movements can rightly claim that they were the first truly antibourgeois parties; none of their nineteenth-century predecessors, neither the Society of the 10th of December which helped Louis Napoleon into power, the butcher brigades of the Dreyfus Affair, the Black Hundreds of the Russian pogroms, nor the pan-movements, ever involved their members to the point of complete loss of individual claims and ambition, or had ever realized that an organization could succeed in extinguishing individual identity permanently and not just for the moment of collective heroic action.

The relationship between the bourgeois-dominated class society and the masses which emerged from its breakdown is not the same as the relationship between the bourgeoisie and the mob which was a by-product of capitalist production. The masses share with the mob only one characteristic, namely, that both stand outside all social ramifications and normal political representation. The masses do not inherit, as the mob does – albeit in a perverted form – the standards and attitudes of the dominating class, but reflect and somehow pervert the standards and attitudes toward public affairs of all classes. The standards of the mass man were determined not only and not even primarily by the specific class to which he had once belonged, but rather by all-pervasive influences and convictions which were tacitly and inarticulately shared by all classes of society alike.

Membership in a class, although looser and never as inevitably determined by social origin as in the orders and estates of feudal society, was generally by birth, and only extraordinary gifts or luck could change it. Social status was decisive for the individual's participation in politics, and except in cases of national emergency when he was supposed to act only as a *national*, regardless of his class or party membership, he never was directly confronted with public affairs or felt directly responsible for their conduct. The rise of a class to greater importance in the community was always accompanied by the education and training of a certain number of its members for politics as a job, for paid (or, if they could afford it, unpaid) service in the government and representation of the class in Parliament. That the majority of people remained outside all party or other political organization was not important to anyone, and no truer for one particular class than another. In other words, membership in a class, its limited group obligations and traditional attitudes toward government, prevented the growth of a citizenry that felt individually and personally responsible for the rule of the country. This apolitical character of the nation-state's populations came to light only when the class system broke down and carried with it the whole fabric of visible and invisible threads which bound the people to the body politic.

The breakdown of the class system meant automatically the breakdown of the party system, chiefly because these parties, being interest parties, could no longer represent class interests. Their continuance was of some importance to the members of former classes who hoped against hope to regain their old social status and who stuck together not because they had common interests any longer but because they hoped to restore them. The parties, consequently, became more and more psychological and ideological in their propaganda, more and more apologetic and nostalgic in their political approach. They had lost, moreover, without being aware of it, those neutral supporters who had never been interested in politics because they felt that no parties existed to take care of their interests. So that the first signs of the breakdown of the Continental party system were not the desertion of old party members, but the failure to recruit members from the younger generation, and the loss of the silent consent and support of the unorganized masses who suddenly shed their apathy and went wherever they saw an opportunity to voice their new violent opposition.

The fall of protecting class walls transformed the slumbering majorities behind all parties into one great unorganized, structureless mass of furious individuals who had nothing in common except their vague apprehension that the hopes of party members were doomed, that, consequently, the most respected, articulate and representative members of the community were fools and that all the powers that be were not so much evil as they were equally stupid and fraudulent. It was of no great consequence for the birth of this new terrifying negative solidarity that the unemployed worker hated the status quo and the powers that be in the form of the Social Democratic Party, the expropriated small property owner in the form of a centrist or rightist party, and former members of the middle and upper classes in the form of the traditional extreme right. The number of this mass of generally dissatisfied and desperate men increased rapidly in

Germany and Austria after the first World War, when inflation and unemployment added to the disrupting consequences of military defeat; they existed in great proportion in all the succession states, and they have supported the extreme movements in France and Italy since the second World War.

In this atmosphere of the breakdown of class society the psychology of the European mass man developed. The fact that with monotonous but abstract uniformity the same fate had befallen a mass of individuals did not prevent their judging themselves in terms of individual failure or the world in terms of specific injustice. This self-centered bitterness, however, although repeated again and again in individual isolation, was not a common bond despite its tendency to extinguish individual differences, because it was based on no common interest, economic or social or political. Self-centeredness, therefore, went hand in hand with a decisive weakening of the instinct for self-preservation. Selflessness in the sense that oneself does not matter, the feeling of being expendable, was no longer the expression of individual idealism but a mass phenomenon. The old adage that the poor and oppressed have nothing to lose but their chains no longer applied to the mass men, for they lost much more than the chains of misery when they lost interest in their own well-being: the source of all the worries and cares which make human life troublesome and anguished was gone. Compared with their nonmaterialism, a Christian monk looks like a man absorbed in worldly affairs. Himmler, who knew so well the mentality of those whom he organized, described not only his SS-men, but the large strata from which he recruited them, when he said they were not interested in 'everyday problems' but only 'in ideological questions of importance for decades and centuries, so that the man . . . knows he is working for a great task which occurs but once in 2,000 years.' [20] The gigantic massing of individuals

20 Heinrich Himmler's speech on 'Organization and Obligation of the SS and the Police,' published in *National-politischer Lehrgang der Wehrmacht vom 15–23. Januar 1937.* Translation quoted from *Nazi Conspiracy and Aggression*, Office of the United States Chief of Counsel for the Prosecution of Axis Criminality, U.S. Government, Washington, 1946, IV, 616 ff.

produced a mentality which, like Cecil Rhodes some forty years before, thought in continents and felt in centuries.

Eminent European scholars and statesmen had predicted, from the early nineteenth century onward, the rise of the mass man and the coming of a mass age. A whole literature on mass behavior and mass psychology had demonstrated and popularized the wisdom, so familiar to the ancients, of the affinity between democracy and dictatorship, between mob rule and tyranny. They had prepared certain politically conscious and overconscious sections of the Western educated world for the emergence of demagogues, for gullibility, superstition, and brutality. Yet, while all these predictions in a sense came true, they lost much of their significance in view of such unexpected and unpredicted phenomena as the radical loss of self-interest,[21] the cynical or bored indifference in the face of death or other personal catastrophes, the passionate inclination toward the most abstract notions as guides for life, and the general contempt for even the most obvious rules of common sense.

The masses, contrary to prediction, did not result from growing equality of condition, from the spread of general education and its inevitable lowering of standards and popularization of content. (America, the classical land of equality of condition and of general education with all its shortcomings, knows less of the modern psychology of masses than perhaps any other country in the world.) It soon became apparent that highly cultured people were particularly attracted to mass movements and that, generally, highly differentiated individualism and sophistication did not prevent, indeed sometimes encouraged, the self-abandonment into the mass for which mass movements provided. Since the obvious fact that individualization and cultivation do not prevent the formation of mass attitudes was so unexpected, it has frequently been blamed upon the morbidity or nihilism of the modern intelligentsia, upon a supposedly typical intellectual self-hatred, upon the spirit's 'hostility to life' and antagonism to vitality. Yet, the much-slandered intellectuals were only the most illustrative example and the most articulate spokesmen for a much

---

21  Gustave Lebon, *La Psychologie des Foules*, 1895, mentions the peculiar selflessness of the masses. See chapter ii, paragraph 5.

more general phenomenon. Social atomization and extreme individualization preceded the mass movements which, much more easily and
earlier than they did the sociable, nonindividualistic members of the
traditional parties, attracted the completely unorganized, the typical
'nonjoiners' who for individualistic reasons always had refused to
recognize social links or obligations.

The truth is that the masses grew out of the fragments of a highly atomized society whose competitive structure and concomitant
loneliness of the individual had been held in check only through
membership in a class. The chief characteristic of the mass man is not
brutality and backwardness, but his isolation and lack of normal social
relationships. Coming from the class-ridden society of the nation-state,
whose cracks had been cemented with nationalistic sentiment, it is
only natural that these masses, in the first helplessness of their new
experience, have tended toward an especially violent nationalism, to
which mass leaders have yielded against their own instincts and purposes for purely demagogic reasons.[22]

Neither tribal nationalism nor rebellious nihilism is characteristic
of or ideologically appropriate to the masses as they were to the mob.
But the most gifted mass leaders of our time have still risen from the
mob rather than from the masses.[23] Hitler's biography reads like a textbook example in this respect, and the point about Stalin is that he
comes from the conspiratory apparatus of the Bolshevik party with
its specific mixture of outcasts and revolutionaries. Hitler's early
party, almost exclusively composed of misfits, failures, and adventurers, indeed represented the 'armed bohemians'[24] who were only the

22 The founders of the Nazi party referred to it occasionally even before Hitler took
over as a 'party of the Left.' An incident which occurred after the parliamentary elections of 1932 is also interesting: 'Gregor Strasser bitterly pointed out to his Leader that
before the elections the National Socialists in the Reichstag might have formed a
majority with the Center; now this possibility was ended, the two parties were less
than half of parliament . . . But with the Communists they still had a majority, Hitler
replied; no one can govern against us' (Heiden, op. cit., pp. 94 and 495, respectively).
23 Compare Carlton J. H. Hayes, op. cit., who does not differentiate between the mob
and the masses, thinks that totalitarian dictators 'have come from the masses rather
than from the classes.'
24 This is the central theory of K. Heiden, whose analyses of the Nazi movement are
still outstanding. 'From the wreckage of dead classes arises the new class of intellectuals, and at the head march the most ruthless, those with the least to lose, hence the

reverse side of bourgeois society and whom, consequently, the German bourgeoisie should have been able to use successfully for its own purposes. Actually, the bourgeoisie was as much taken in by the Nazis as was the Röhm–Schleicher faction in the Reichswehr, which also thought that Hitler, whom they had used as a stool-pigeon, or the SA, which they had used for militaristic propaganda and paramilitary training, would act as their agents and help in the establishment of a military dictatorship.[25] Both considered the Nazi movement in their own terms, in terms of the political philosophy of the mob,[26] and overlooked the independent, spontaneous support given the new mob leaders by masses as well as the mob leaders' genuine talents for creating new forms of organization. The mob as leader of these masses was no longer the agent of the bourgeoisie or of anyone else except the masses.

That totalitarian movements depended less on the structurelessness of a mass society than on the specific conditions of an atomized and individualized mass, can best be seen in a comparison of Nazism

strongest: the armed bohemians, to whom war is home and civil war fatherland' (*op. cit.*, p. 100).

25 The plot between Reichswehr General Schleicher and Röhm, the chief of the SA, consisted of a plan to bring all paramilitary formations under the military authority of the Reichswehr, which at once would have added millions to the German army. This, of course, would inevitably have led to a military dictatorship. In June, 1934, Hitler liquidated Röhm and Schleicher. The initial negotiations were started with the full knowledge of Hitler who used Röhm's connections with the Reichswehr to deceive German military circles about his real intentions. In April, 1932, Röhm testified in one of Hitler's lawsuits that the SA's military status had the full understanding of the Reichswehr. (For documentary evidence on the Röhm–Schleicher plan, see *Nazi Conspiracy*, V, 456 ff. See also Heiden, *op. cit.*, p. 450.) Röhm himself proudly reports his negotiations with Schleicher, which according to him were started in 1931. Schleicher had promised to put the SA under the command of Reichswehr officers in case of an emergency. (See *Die Memoiren des Stabschefs Röhm*, Saarbrücken, 1934, p. 170.) The militaristic character of the SA, shaped by Röhm and constantly fought by Hitler, continued to determine its vocabulary even after the liquidation of the Röhm faction. Contrary to the SS, the members of the SA always insisted on being the 'representatives of Germany's military will,' and for them the Third Reich was a 'military community [supported by] two pillars: Party and Wehrmacht' (see *Handbuch der SA*, Berlin, 1939, and Victor Lutze, 'Die Sturmabteilungen,' in *Grundlagen, Aufbau und Wirtschaftsordnung des nationalsozialistischen Staates*, No. 7a).

26 Röhm's autobiography especially is a veritable classic in this kind of literature.

and Bolshevism which began in their respective countries under very different circumstances. To change Lenin's revolutionary dictatorship into full totalitarian rule, Stalin had first to create artificially that atomized society which had been prepared for the Nazis in Germany by historical circumstances.

The October Revolution's amazingly easy victory occurred in a country where a despotic and centralized bureaucracy governed a structureless mass population which neither the remnants of the rural feudal orders nor the weak, nascent urban capitalist classes had organized. When Lenin said that nowhere in the world would it have been so easy to win power and so difficult to keep it, he was aware not only of the weakness of the Russian working class, but of anarchic social conditions in general, which favored sudden changes. Without the instincts of a mass leader – he was no orator and had a passion for public admission and analysis of his own errors, which is against the rules of even ordinary demagogy – Lenin seized at once upon all the possible differentiations, social, national, professional, that might bring some structure into the population, and he seemed convinced that in such stratification lay the salvation of the revolution. He legalized the anarchic expropriation of the landowners by the rural masses and established thereby for the first and probably last time in Russia that emancipated peasant class which, since the French Revolution, had been the firmest supporter of the Western nation-states. He tried to strengthen the working class by encouraging independent trade unions. He tolerated the timid appearance of a new middle class which resulted from the NEP policy after the end of the civil war. He introduced further distinguishing features by organizing, and sometimes inventing, as many nationalities as possible, furthering national consciousness and awareness of historical and cultural differences even among the most primitive tribes in the Soviet Union. It seems clear that in these purely practical political matters Lenin followed his great instincts for statesmanship rather than his Marxist convictions; his policy, at any rate, proves that he was more frightened by the absence of social and other structure than by the possible development of centrifugal tendencies in the newly emancipated nationalities or even by the growth of a new bourgeoisie out of the newly established middle and peasant classes. There is no doubt that Lenin suffered his greatest defeat when, with the outbreak of the civil war, the supreme power that he originally planned to concentrate in the Soviets definitely passed into the hands of the party bureaucracy; but even this development, tragic as it was for the course of the revolution, would not necessarily have led to totalitarianism. A one-party dictatorship added only one more class to the already developing social stratification of the country, *i.e.*, bureaucracy, which, according to socialist critics of the revolution, 'possessed the State as private property' (Marx).[27] At the moment of Lenin's death the roads were still open. The formation of workers, peasants, and middle classes need not necessarily have led to the class struggle which had been characteristic of European capitalism. Agriculture could still be developed on a collective, co-operative, or private basis, and the national economy was still free to follow a socialist, state-capitalist, or a free-enterprise pattern. None of these alternatives would have automatically destroyed the new structure of the country.

All these new classes and nationalities were in Stalin's way when he began to prepare the country for totalitarian government. In order to fabricate an atomized and structureless mass, he had first to liquidate the remnants of power in the Soviets which, as the chief organ of national representation, still played a certain role and prevented absolute rule by the party hierarchy. Therefore he first undermined the national Soviets through the introduction of Bolshevik cells from which alone the higher functionaries to the central committees were

27 It is well known that the anti-Stalinist splinter groups have based their criticism of the development of the Soviet Union on this Marxist formulation, and have actually never outgrown it. The repeated 'purges' of Soviet bureaucracy, which were tantamount to a liquidation of bureaucracy as a class, have never prevented them from seeing in it the dominating and ruling class of the Soviet Union. The following is the estimate of Rakovsky, writing in 1930 from his exile in Siberia: 'Under our eyes has formed and is being formed a great class of directors which has its internal subdivisions and which increases through calculated co-option and direct or indirect nominations ... The element which unites this original class is a form, also original, of private property, to wit, the State power' (quoted from Souvarine, *op. cit.*, p. 564). This analysis is indeed quite accurate for the development of the pre-Stalinist era. For the development of the relationship between party and Soviets, which is of decisive importance for the course of the October Revolution, see I. Deutscher, *The Prophet Armed: Trotsky 1879–1921*, 1954.

appointed.[28] By 1930, the last traces of former communal institutions had disappeared and had been replaced by a firmly centralized party bureaucracy whose tendencies toward Russification were not too different from those of the Czarist regime, except that the new bureaucrats were no longer afraid of literacy.

The Bolshevik government then proceeded to the liquidation of classes and started, for ideological and propaganda reasons, with the property-owning classes, the new middle class in the cities, and the peasants in the country. Because of the combination of numbers and property, the peasants up to then had been potentially the most powerful class in the Union; their liquidation, consequently, was more thorough and more cruel than that of any other group and was carried through by artificial famine and deportation under the pretext of expropriation of the kulaks and collectivization. The liquidation of the middle and peasant classes was completed in the early thirties; those who were not among the many millions of dead or the millions of deported slave laborers had learned 'who is master here,' had realized that their lives and the lives of their families depended not upon their fellow-citizens but exclusively on the whims of the government which they faced in complete loneliness without any help whatsoever from the group to which they happened to belong. The exact moment when collectivization produced a new peasantry bound by common interests, which owing to its numerical and economic key position in the country's economy again presented a potential danger to totalitarian rule, cannot be determined either from statistics or documentary sources. But for those who know how to read totalitarian 'source material' this moment had come two years before Stalin died, when he proposed to dissolve the collectives and transform them into larger units. He did not live to carry out this plan; this time the sacrifices

---

28 In 1927, 90 per cent of the village Soviets and 75 per cent of their chairmen were non-party members; the executive committees of the counties were made up of 50 per cent non-party members, while in the Central Committee 75 per cent of the delegates were party members. See the article on 'Bolshevism' by Maurice Dobb in the *Encyclopedia of Social Sciences*.

How the party members of the Soviets, by voting 'in conformity with the instructions they received from the permanent officials of the Party,' destroyed the Soviet system from within is described in detail in A. Rosenberg, *A History of Bolshevism*, London, 1934, chapter vi.

would have been still greater and the chaotic consequences for the total economy still more catastrophic than the liquidation of the first peasant class, but there is no reason to doubt that he might have succeeded; there is no class that cannot be wiped out if a sufficient number of its members are murdered.

The next class to be liquidated as a group were the workers. As a class they were much weaker and offered much less resistance than the peasants because their spontaneous expropriation of factory owners during the revolution, unlike the peasants' expropriation of landowners, had been frustrated at once by the government which confiscated the factories as state property under the pretext that the state belonged to the proletariat in any event. The Stakhanov system, adopted in the early thirties, broke up all solidarity and class consciousness among the workers, first by the ferocious competition and second by the temporary solidification of a Stakhanovite aristocracy whose social distance from the ordinary worker naturally was felt more acutely than the distance between the workers and the management. This process was completed in 1938 with the introduction of the labor book which transformed the whole Russian worker class officially into a gigantic forced-labor force.

On top of these measures came the liquidation of that bureaucracy which had helped to carry out the previous liquidation measures. It took Stalin about two years, from 1936 to 1938, to rid himself of the whole administrative and military aristocracy of the Soviet society; nearly all offices, factories, economic and cultural bodies, government, party, and military bureaus came into new hands, when 'nearly half the administrative personnel, party and nonparty, had been swept out,' and more than 50 per cent of all party members and 'at least eight million more' were liquidated.[29] Again the introduction of an interior

29 These figures are taken from Victor Kravchenko's book *I Chose Freedom: The Personal and Political Life of a Soviet Official*, New York, 1946, pp. 278 and 303. This is of course a highly questionable source. But since in the case of Soviet Russia we basically have nothing but questionable sources to resort to – meaning that we have to rely altogether on news stories, reports and evaluations of one kind or another – all we can do is use whatever information at least appears to have a high degree of probability. Some historians seem to think that the opposite method – namely, to use exclusively whatever material is furnished by the Russian government – is more reliable, but this is the not the case. It is precisely the official material that is nothing but propaganda.

passport, on which all departures from one city to another have to be registered and authorized, completed the destruction of the party bureaucracy as a class. As for its juridical status, the bureaucracy along with the party functionaries was now on the same level with the workers; it, too, had now become a part of the vast multitude of Russian forced laborers and its status as a privileged class in Soviet society was a thing of the past. And since this general purge ended with the liquidation of the highest police officials – the same who had organized the general purge in the first place – not even the cadres of the GPU which had carried out the terror could any longer delude themselves that as a group they represented anything at all, let alone power.

None of these immense sacrifices in human life was motivated by a *raison d'état* in the old sense of the term. None of the liquidated social strata was hostile to the regime or likely to become hostile in the fore-seeable future. Active organized opposition had ceased to exist by 1930 when Stalin, in his speech to the Sixteenth Party Congress, outlawed the rightist and leftist deviations inside the Party, and even these fee-ble oppositions had hardly been able to base themselves on any of the existing classes.[30] Dictatorial terror – distinguished from totalitarian terror insofar as it threatens only authentic opponents but not harm-less citizens without political opinions – had been grim enough to suffocate all political life, open or clandestine, even before Lenin's death. Intervention from abroad, which might ally itself with one of the dissatisfied sections in the population, was no longer a danger when, by 1930, the Soviet regime had been recognized by a majority of governments and concluded commercial and other international agreements with many countries. (Nor did Stalin's government elim-inate such a possibility as far as the people themselves were concerned: we know now that Hitler, if he had been an ordinary conqueror and not a rival totalitarian ruler, might have had an extraordinary chance to win for his cause at least the people of the Ukraine.)

30 Stalin's Report to the Sixteenth Congress denounced the devations as the 'reflec-tion' of the resistance of the peasant and petty bourgeois classes in the ranks of the Party. (See *Leninism*, 1933, Vol. II, chapter iii.) Against this attack the opposition was curiously defenseless because they too, and especially Trotsky, were 'always anxious to discover a struggle of classes behind the struggles of cliques' (Souvarine, *op. cit.*, p. 440).

If the liquidation of classes made no political sense, it was positively disastrous for the Soviet economy. The consequences of the artificial famine in 1933 were felt for years throughout the country; the introduction of the Stakhanov system in 1935, with its arbitrary speed-up of individual output and its complete disregard of the necessities for teamwork in industrial production, resulted in a 'chaotic imbalance' of the young industry.[31] The liquidation of the bureaucracy, that is, of the class of factory managers and engineers, finally deprived industrial enterprises of what little experience and know-how the new Russian technical intelligentsia had been able to acquire.

Equality of condition among their subjects has been one of the foremost concerns of despotisms and tyrannies since ancient times, yet such equalization is not sufficient for totalitarian rule because it leaves more or less intact certain nonpolitical communal bonds between the subjects, such as family ties and common cultural interests. If totalitarianism takes its own claim seriously, it must come to the point where it has 'to finish once and for all with the neutrality of chess,' that is, with the autonomous existence of any activity whatsoever. The lovers of 'chess for the sake of chess,' aptly compared by their liquidator with the lovers of 'art for art's sake,'[32] are not yet absolutely atomized elements in a mass society whose completely heterogeneous uniformity is one of the primary conditions for totalitarianism. From the point of view of totalitarian rulers, a society devoted to chess for the sake of chess is only in degree different and less dangerous than a class of farmers for the sake of farming. Himmler quite aptly defined the SS member as the new type of man who under no circumstances will ever do 'a thing for its own sake.'[33]

Mass atomization in Soviet society was achieved by the skillful use of repeated purges which invariably precede actual group liquidation. In order to destroy all social and family ties, the purges are conducted

31 Kravchenko, *op. cit.*, p. 187.
32 Souvarine, *op. cit.*, p. 575.
33 The watchword of the SS as formulated by Himmler himself begins with the words: 'There is no task that exists for its own sake.' See Gunter d'Alquen, 'Die SS,' in *Schriften der Hochschule für Politik*, 1939. The pamphlets issued by the SS solely for internal consumption emphasize time and again 'the absolute necessity for understanding the futility of everything that is an end in itself' (see *Der Reichsführer SS und Chef der deutschen Polizei*, undated, 'only for internal use within the police').

in such a way as to threaten with the same fate the defendant and all his ordinary relations, from mere acquaintances up to his closest friends and relatives. The consequence of the simple and ingenious device of 'guilt by association' is that as soon as a man is accused, his former friends are transformed immediately into his bitterest enemies; in order to save their own skins, they volunteer information and rush in with denunciations to corroborate the nonexistent evidence against him; this obviously is the only way to prove their own trustworthiness. Retrospectively, they will try to prove that their acquaintance or friendship with the accused was only a pretext for spying on him and revealing him as a saboteur, a Trotskyite, a foreign spy, or a Fascist. Merit being 'gauged by the number of your denunciations of close comrades,' [34] it is obvious that the most elementary caution demands that one avoid all intimate contacts, if possible – not in order to prevent discovery of one's secret thoughts, but rather to eliminate, in the almost certain case of future trouble, all persons who might have not only an ordinary cheap interest in your denunciation but an irresistible need to bring about your ruin simply because they are in danger of their own lives. In the last analysis, it has been through the development of this device to its farthest and most fantastic extremes that Bolshevik rulers have succeeded in creating an atomized and individualized society the like of which we have never seen before and which events or catastrophes alone would hardly have brought about.

Totalitarian movements are mass organizations of atomized, isolated individuals. Compared with all other parties and movements, their most conspicuous external characteristic is their demand for total, unrestricted, unconditional, and unalterable loyalty of the individual member. This demand is made by the leaders of totalitarian movements even before they seize power. It usually precedes the total organization of the country under their actual rule and it follows from the claim of their ideologies that their organization will encompass, in due course, the entire human race. Where, however,

---

34 The practice itself has been abundantly documented. W. Krivitsky, in his book *In Stalin's Secret Services* (New York, 1939), traces it directly to Stalin.

totalitarian rule has not been prepared by a totalitarian movement (and this, in contradistinction to Nazi Germany, was the case in Russia), the movement has to be organized afterward and the conditions for its growth have artificially to be created in order to make total loyalty – the psychological basis for total domination – at all possible. Such loyalty can be expected only from the completely isolated human being who, without any other social ties to family, friends, comrades, or even mere acquaintances, derives his sense of having a place in the world only from his belonging to a movement, his membership in the party.

Total loyalty is possible only when fidelity is emptied of all concrete content, from which changes of mind might naturally arise. The totalitarian movements, each in its own way, have done their utmost to get rid of the party programs which specified concrete content and which they inherited from earlier, nontotalitarian stages of development. No matter how radically they might have been phrased, every definite political goal which does not simply assert or circumscribe the claim to world rule, every political program which deals with issues more specific than 'ideological questions of importance for centuries' is an obstruction to totalitarianism. Hitler's greatest achievement in the organization of the Nazi movement, which he gradually built up from the obscure crackpot membership of a typically nationalistic little party, was that he unburdened the movement of the party's earlier program, not by changing or officially abolishing it, but simply by refusing to talk about it or discuss its points, whose relative moderateness of content and phraseology were very soon outdated.[35] Stalin's task in this as in other respects was much more formidable; the socialist program of the Bolshevik party was a much more troublesome burden[36] than the 25 points of an amateur economist and a crackpot

35  Hitler stated in *Mein Kampf* (2 vols., 1st German ed., 1925 and 1927 respectively. Unexpurgated translation, New York, 1939) that it was better to have an antiquated program than to allow a discussion of program (Book II, chapter v). Soon he was to proclaim publicly: 'Once we take over the government, the program will come of itself . . . The first thing must be an inconceivable wave of propaganda. That is a political action which would have little to do with the other problems of the moment.' See Heiden, *op. cit.*, p. 203.

36  Souvarine, in our opinion wrongly, suggests that Lenin had already abolished the role of a party program: 'Nothing could show more clearly the non-existence of

politician.[37] But Stalin achieved eventually, after having abolished the factions of the Russian party, the same result through the constant zigzag of the Communist Party lines, and the constant reinterpretation and application of Marxism which voided the doctrine of all its content because it was no longer possible to predict what course or action it would inspire. The fact that the most perfect education in Marxism and Leninism was no guide whatsoever for political behavior – that, on the contrary, one could follow the party line only if one repeated each morning what Stalin had announced the night before – naturally resulted in the same state of mind, the same concentrated obedience, undivided by any attempt to understand what one was doing, that Himmler's ingenious watchword for his SS-men expressed: 'My honor is my loyalty.'[38]

Lack of or ignoring of a party program is by itself not necessarily a sign of totalitarianism. The first to consider programs and platforms as needless scraps of paper and embarrassing promises, inconsistent with the style and impetus of a movement, was Mussolini with his Fascist philosophy of activism and inspiration through the historical moment itself.[39] Mere lust for power combined with contempt for 'talkative' articulation of what they intend to do with it is characteristic of all mob leaders, but does not come up to the standards of

---

Bolshevism as a doctrine except in Lenin's brain; every Bolshevik left to himself wandered from "the line" of his faction . . . for these men were bound together by their temperament and by the ascendancy of Lenin rather than by ideas' (*op. cit.*, p. 85).

37 Gottfried Feder's Program of the Nazi Party with its famous 25 points has played a greater role in the literature about the movement than in the movement itself.

38 The impact of the watchword, formulated by Himmler himself, is difficult to render. Its German equivalent: '*Meine Ehre heisst Treue*,' indicates an absolute devotion and obedience which transcends the meaning of mere discipline or personal faithfulness. *Nazi Conspiracy*, whose translations of German documents and Nazi literature are indispensable source material but, unfortunately, are very uneven, renders the SS watchword: 'My honor signifies faithfulness' (V, 346).

39 Mussolini was probably the first party leader who consciously rejected a formal program and replaced it with inspired leadership and action alone. Behind this act lay the notion that the actuality of the moment itself was the chief element of inspiration, which would only be hampered by a party program. The philosophy of Italian Fascism has been expressed by Gentile's 'actualism' rather than by Sorel's 'myths.' Compare also the article 'Fascism' in the *Encyclopedia of the Social Sciences*. The Program of 1921 was formulated when the movement had been in existence two years and contained, for the most part, its nationalist philosophy.

totalitarianism. The true goal of Fascism was only to seize power and establish the Fascist 'elite' as uncontested ruler over the country. Totalitarianism is never content to rule by external means, namely, through the state and a machinery of violence; thanks to its peculiar ideology and the role assigned to it in this apparatus of coercion, totalitarianism has discovered a means of dominating and terrorizing human beings from within. In this sense it eliminates the distance between the rulers and the ruled and achieves a condition in which power and the will to power, as we understand them, play no role, or at best, a secondary role. In substance, the totalitarian leader is nothing more nor less than the functionary of the masses he leads; he is not a power-hungry individual imposing a tyrannical and arbitrary will upon his subjects. Being a mere functionary, he can be replaced at any time, and he depends just as much on the 'will' of the masses he embodies as the masses depend on him. Without him they would lack external representation and remain an amorphous horde; without the masses the leader is a nonentity. Hitler, who was fully aware of this interdependence, expressed it once in a speech addressed to the SA: 'All that you are, you are through me; all that I am, I am through you alone.'[40] We are only too inclined to belittle such statements or to misunderstand them in the sense that acting is defined here in terms of giving and executing orders, as has happened too often in the political tradition and history of the West.[41] But this idea has always presupposed someone in command who thinks and wills, and then imposes his thought and will on a thought- and will-deprived group – be it by persuasion, authority, or violence. Hitler, however, was of the opinion that even 'thinking . . . [exists] only by virtue of giving or executing orders,'[42] and thereby eliminated even theoretically the distinction between thinking and acting on one hand, and between the rulers and the ruled on the other.

Neither National Socialism nor Bolshevism has ever proclaimed a new form of government or asserted that its goals were reached with the seizure of power and the control of the state machinery. Their idea

40 Ernst Bayer, *Die SA*, Berlin, 1938. Translation quoted from *Nazi Conspiracy*, IV, 783.
41 For the first time in Plato's *Statesman*, 305, where acting is interpreted in terms of *archein* and *prattein* – of ordering the start of an action and of executing this order
42 *Hitlers Tischgespräche*, p. 198.

of domination was something that no state and no mere apparatus of violence can ever achieve, but only a movement that is constantly kept in motion: namely, the permanent domination of each single individual in each and every sphere of life.[43] The seizure of power through the means of violence is never an end in itself but only the means to an end, and the seizure of power in any given country is only a welcome transitory stage but never the end of the movement. The practical goal of the movement is to organize as many people as possible within its framework and to set and keep them in motion; a political goal that would constitute the end of the movement simply does not exist.

## II: The Temporary Alliance Between the Mob and the Elite

What is more disturbing to our peace of mind than the unconditional loyalty of members of totalitarian movements, and the popular support of totalitarian regimes, is the unquestionable attraction these movements exert on the elite, and not only on the mob elements in society. It would be rash indeed to discount, because of artistic vagaries or scholarly naïveté, the terrifying roster of distinguished men whom totalitarianism can count among its sympathizers, fellow-travelers, and inscribed party members.

This attraction for the elite is as important a clue to the understanding of totalitarian movements (though hardly of totalitarian regimes) as their more obvious connection with the mob. It indicates the specific atmosphere, the general climate in which the rise of totalitarianism takes place. It should be remembered that the leaders of totalitarian movements and their sympathizers are, so to speak, older than the masses which they organize so that chronologically speaking the masses do not have to wait helplessly for the rise of their

43 *Mein Kampf*, Book I, chapter xi. See also, for example, Dieter Schwarz, *Angriffe auf die nationalsozialistische Weltanschauung*: Aus dem Schwarzen Korps, No. 2, 1936, who answers the obvious criticism that National Socialists after their rise to power continued to talk about 'a struggle': 'National Socialism as an ideology [*Weltanschauung*] will not abandon its struggle until . . . the way of life of each individual German has been shaped by its fundamental values and these are realized every day anew.'

own leaders in the midst of a decaying class society, of which they are the most outstanding product. Those who voluntarily left society before the wreckage of classes had come about, along with the mob, which was an earlier by-product of the rule of the bourgeoisie, stand ready to welcome them. The present totalitarian rulers and the leaders of totalitarian movements still bear the characteristic traits of the mob, whose psychology and political philosophy are fairly well known; what will happen once the authentic mass man takes over, we do not know yet, although it may be a fair guess that he will have more in common with the meticulous, calculated correctness of Himmler than with the hysterical fanaticism of Hitler, will more resemble the stubborn dullness of Molotov than the sensual vindictive cruelty of Stalin.

In this respect, the situation after the second World War in Europe does not differ essentially from that after the first; just as in the twenties the ideologies of Fascism, Bolshevism, and Nazism were formulated and the movements led by the so-called front generation, by those who had been brought up and still remembered distinctly the times before the war, so the present general political and intellectual climate of postwar totalitarianism is being determined by a generation which knew intimately the time and life which preceded the present. This is specifically true for France, where the breakdown of the class system came after the second instead of after the first War. Like the mob men and the adventurers of the imperialist era, the leaders of totalitarian movements have in common with their intellectual sympathizers the fact that both had been outside the class and national system of respectable European society even before this system broke down.

This breakdown, when the smugness of spurious respectability gave way to anarchic despair, seemed the first great opportunity for the elite as well as the mob. This is obvious for the new mass leaders whose careers reproduce the features of earlier mob leaders: failure in professional and social life, perversion and disaster in private life. The fact that their lives prior to their political careers had been failures, naïvely held against them by the more respectable leaders of the old parties, was the strongest factor in their mass appeal. It seemed to prove that individually they embodied the mass destiny of the time and that their desire to sacrifice everything for the movement, their assurance of devotion to those who had been struck by catastrophe, their determination never to be tempted back into the security of normal life, and their contempt for respectability were quite sincere and not just inspired by passing ambitions.

The postwar elite, on the other hand, was only slightly younger than the generation which had let itself be used and abused by imperialism for the sake of glorious careers outside of respectability, as gamblers and spies and adventurers, as knights in shining armor and dragon-killers. They shared with Lawrence of Arabia the yearning for 'losing their selves' and the violent disgust with all existing standards, with every power that be. If they still remembered the 'golden age of security,' they also remembered how they had hated it and how real their enthusiasm had been at the outbreak of the first World War. Not only Hitler and not only the failures thanked God on their knees when mobilization swept Europe in 1914.[44] They did not even have to reproach themselves with having been an easy prey for chauvinist propaganda or lying explanations about the purely defensive character of the war. The elite went to war with an exultant hope that everything they knew, the whole culture and texture of life, might go down in its 'storms of steel' (Ernst Jünger). In the carefully chosen words of Thomas Mann, war was 'chastisement' and 'purification'; 'war in itself, rather than victories, inspired the poet.' Or in the words of a student of the time, 'what counts is always the readiness to make a sacrifice, not the object for which the sacrifice is made'; or in the words of a young worker, 'it doesn't matter whether one lives a few years longer or not. One would like to have something to show for one's life.'[45] And long before one of Nazism's intellectual sympathizers announced, 'When I hear the word culture, I draw my revolver,' poets had proclaimed their disgust with 'rubbish culture' and called

44 See Hitler's description of his reaction to the outbreak of the first World War in *Mein Kampf*, Book I, chapter v.

45 See the collection of material on the 'inner chronicle of the first World War' by Hanna Hafkesbrink, *Unknown Germany*, New Haven, 1948, pp. 43, 45, 81, respectively. The great value of this collection for the imponderables of historical atmosphere makes the lack of similar studies for France, England, and Italy all the more deplorable.

poetically on 'ye Barbarians, Scythians, Negroes, Indians, to trample it down.'[46]

Simply to brand as outbursts of nihilism this violent dissatisfaction with the prewar age and subsequent attempts at restoring it (from Nietzsche and Sorel to Pareto, from Rimbaud and T. E. Lawrence to Jünger, Brecht, and Malraux, from Bakunin and Nechayev to Alexander Blok) is to overlook how justified disgust can be in a society wholly permeated with the ideological outlook and moral standards of the bourgeoisie. Yet it is also true that the 'front generation,' in marked contrast to their own chosen spiritual fathers, were completely absorbed by their desire to see the ruin of this whole world of fake security, fake culture, and fake life. This desire was so great that it outweighed in impact and articulateness all earlier attempts at a 'transformation of values,' such as Nietzsche had attempted, or a reorganization of political life as indicated in Sorel's writings, or a revival of human authenticity in Bakunin, or a passionate love of life in the purity of exotic adventures in Rimbaud. Destruction without mitigation, chaos and ruin as such assumed the dignity of supreme values.[47]

The genuineness of these feelings can be seen in the fact that very few of this generation were cured of their war enthusiasm by actual experience of its horrors. The survivors of the trenches did not become pacifists. They cherished an experience which, they thought, might serve to separate them definitely from the hated surroundings of respectability. They clung to their memories of four years of life in the trenches as though they constituted an objective criterion for the establishment of a new elite. Nor did they yield to the temptation to idealize this past; on the contrary, the worshipers of war were the first

---

46  *Ibid.*, pp. 20–21.

47  This started with a feeling of complete alienation from normal life. Wrote Rudolf Binding, for instance: 'More and more we are to be counted among the dead, among the estranged – because the greatness of the occurrence estranges and separates us – rather than among the banished whose return is possible' (*ibid.*, p. 160). A curious reminiscence of the front generation's elite claim can still be found in Himmler's account of how he finally hit upon his 'form of selection' for the reorganization of the SS: '. . . the most severe selection procedure is brought about by war, the struggle for life and death. In this procedure the value of blood is shown through achievement . . . War, however, is an exceptional circumstance, and a way had to be found to make selections in peace time' (*op. cit.*).

to concede that war in the era of machines could not possibly breed virtues like chivalry, courage, honor, and manliness,[48] that it imposed on men nothing but the experience of bare destruction together with the humiliation of being only small cogs in the majestic wheel of slaughter.

This generation remembered the war as the great prelude to the breakdown of classes and their transformation into masses. War, with its constant murderous arbitrariness, became the symbol for death, the 'great equalizer' [49] and therefore the true father of a new world order. The passion for equality and justice, the longing to transcend narrow and meaningless class lines, to abandon stupid privileges and prejudices, seemed to find in war a way out of the old condescending attitudes of pity for the oppressed and disinherited. In times of growing misery and individual helplessness, it seems as difficult to resist pity when it grows into an all-devouring passion as it is not to resent its very boundlessness, which seems to kill human dignity with a more deadly certainty than misery itself.

In the early years of his career, when a restoration of the European status quo was still the most serious threat to the ambitions of the mob,[50] Hitler appealed almost exclusively to these sentiments of the front generation. The peculiar selflessness of the mass man appeared here as yearning for anonymity, for being just a number and functioning only as a cog, for every transformation, in brief, which would wipe out the spurious identifications with specific types or predetermined functions within society. War had been experienced as that 'mightiest of all mass actions' which obliterated individual differences so that even suffering, which traditionally had marked off individuals through unique unexchangeable destinies, could now be interpreted as 'an instrument of historical progress.' [51] Nor did national distinctions limit

48 See, for instance, Ernst Jünger, *The Storm of Steel*, London, 1929.
49 Hafkesbrink, *op. cit.*, p. 156.
50 Heiden, *op. cit.*, shows how consistently Hitler sided with catastrophe in the early days of the movement, how he feared a possible recovery of Germany. 'Half a dozen times [*i.e.*, during the Ruhrputsch], in different terms, he declared to his storm troops that Germany was going under. "Our job is to insure the success of our movement"' (p. 167) – a success which at that moment depended upon the collapse of the fight in the Ruhr.
51 Hafkesbrink, *op. cit.*, pp. 156–157.

the masses into which the postwar elite wished to be immersed. The first World War, somewhat paradoxically, had almost extinguished genuine national feelings in Europe where, between the wars, it was far more important to have belonged to the generation of the trenches, no matter on which side, than to be a German or a Frenchman.[52] The Nazis based their whole propaganda on this indistinct comradeship, this 'community of fate,' and won over a great number of veteran organizations in all European countries, thereby proving how meaningless national slogans had become even in the ranks of the so-called Right, which used them for their connotation of violence rather than for their specific national content.

No single element in this general intellectual climate in postwar Europe was very new. Bakunin had already confessed, 'I do not want to be *I*, I want to be *We*,'[53] and Nechayev had preached the evangel of the 'doomed man' with 'no personal interests, no affairs, no sentiments, attachments, property, not even a name of his own.'[54] The antihumanist, antiliberal, anti-individualist, and anticultural instincts of the front generation, their brilliant and witty praise of violence, power, and cruelty, was preceded by the awkward and pompous 'scientific' proofs of the imperialist elite that a struggle of all against all is the law of the universe, that expansion is a psychological necessity before it is a political device, and that man has to behave by such universal laws.[55] What was new in the writings of the front generation was their high literary standard and great depth of

52 This feeling was already widespread during the war when Rudolf Binding wrote: '[This war] is not to be compared with a campaign. For there one leader pits his will against that of another. But in this War both adversaries lie on the ground, and only the War has its will' (*ibid.*, p. 67).

53 Bakunin in a letter written on February 7, 1870. See Max Nomad, *Apostles of Revolution*, Boston, 1939, p. 180.

54 The 'Catechism of the Revolutionist' was either written by Bakunin himself or by his disciple Nechayev. For the question of authorship and a translation of the complete text, see Nomad, *op. cit.*, pp. 227 ff. In any event, the 'system of complete disregard for any tenets of simple decency and fairness in [the revolutionist's] attitude towards other human beings ... went down in Russian revolutionary history under the name of "Nechayevshchina"' (*ibid.*, p. 224).

55 Outstanding among these political theorists of imperialism is Ernest Seillière, *Mysticisme et Domination: Essais de Critique Impérialiste*, 1913. See also Cargill Sprietsma, *We Imperialists: Notes on Ernest Seillière's Philosophy of Imperialism*, New York, 1931; G.

passion. The postwar writers no longer needed the scientific demonstrations of genetics, and they made little if any use of the collected works of Gobineau or Houston Stewart Chamberlain, which belonged already to the cultural household of the philistines. They read not Darwin but the Marquis de Sade.[56] If they believed at all in universal laws, they certainly did not particularly care to conform to them. To them, violence, power, cruelty, were the supreme capacities of men who had definitely lost their place in the universe and were much too proud to long for a power theory that would safely bring them back and reintegrate them into the world. They were satisfied with blind partisanship in anything that respectable society had banned, regardless of theory or content, and they elevated cruelty to a major virtue because it contradicted society's humanitarian and liberal hypocrisy.

If we compare this generation with the nineteenth-century ideologists, with whose theories they sometimes seem to have so much in common, their chief distinction is their greater authenticity and passion. They had been more deeply touched by misery, they were more concerned with the perplexities and more deadly hurt by hypocrisy than all the apostles of good will and brotherhood had been. And they could no longer escape into exotic lands, could no longer afford to be dragon-slayers among strange and exciting people. There was no escape from the daily routine of misery, meekness, frustration, and resentment embellished by a fake culture of educated talk; no conformity to the customs of fairy-tale lands could possibly save them from the rising nausea that this combination continuously inspired.

---

Monod in *La Revue Historique*, January, 1912; and Louis Estève, *Une nouvelle Psychologie de l'Impérialisme: Ernest Seillière*, 1913.

56 In France, since 1930, the Marquis de Sade has become one of the favored authors of the literary avant-garde. Jean Paulhan, in his Introduction to a new edition of Sade's *Les Infortunes de la Vertu*, Paris, 1946, remarks: 'When I see so many writers today consciously trying to deny artifice and the literary game for the sake of the inexpressible [*un évènement indicible*] . . . anxiously looking for the sublime in the infamous, for the great in the subversive . . . I ask myself . . . if our modern literature, in those parts which appear to us most vital – or at any rate most aggressive – has not turned entirely toward the past, and if it was not precisely Sade who determined it.' See also Georges Bataille, 'Le Secret de Sade,' in *La Critique*, Tome III, Nos. 15–16, 17, 1947.

This inability to escape into the wide world, this feeling of being caught again and again in the trappings of society – so different from the conditions which had formed the imperialist character – added a constant strain and the yearning for violence to the older passion for anonymity and losing oneself. Without the possibility of a radical change of role and character, such as the identification with the Arab national movement or the rites of an Indian village, the self-willed immersion in the suprahuman forces of destruction seemed to be a salvation from the automatic identification with pre-established functions in society and their utter banality, and at the same time to help destroy the functioning itself. These people felt attracted to the pronounced activism of totalitarian movements, to their curious and only seemingly contradictory insistence on both the primacy of sheer action and the overwhelming force of sheer necessity. This mixture corresponded precisely to the war experience of the 'front generation,' to the experience of constant activity within the framework of overwhelming fatality.

Activism, moreover, seemed to provide new answers to the old and troublesome question, 'Who am I?' which always appears with redoubled persistence in times of crisis. If society insisted, 'You are what you appear to be,' postwar activism replied: 'You are what you have done' – for instance, the man who for the first time had crossed the Atlantic in an airplane (as in Brecht's *Der Flug der Lindberghs*) – an answer which after the second World War was repeated and slightly varied by Sartre's 'You are your life' (in *Huis Clos*). The pertinence of these answers lies less in their validity as redefinitions of personal identity than in their usefulness for an eventual escape from social identification, from the multiplicity of interchangeable roles and functions which society had imposed. The point was to do something, heroic or criminal, which was unpredictable and undetermined by anybody else.

The pronounced activism of the totalitarian movements, their preference for terrorism over all other forms of political activity, attracted the intellectual elite and the mob alike, precisely because this terrorism was so utterly different from that of the earlier revolutionary societies. It was no longer a matter of calculated policy which saw in terrorist acts the only means to eliminate certain outstanding personalities who, because of their policies or position, had become the symbol of oppression. What proved so attractive was that terrorism had become a kind of philosophy through which to express frustration, resentment, and blind hatred, a kind of political expressionism which used bombs to express oneself, which watched delightedly the publicity given to resounding deeds and was absolutely willing to pay the price of life for having succeeded in forcing the recognition of one's existence on the normal strata of society. It was still the same spirit and the same game which made Goebbels, long before the eventual defeat of Nazi Germany, announce with obvious delight that the Nazis, in case of defeat, would know how to slam the door behind them and not to be forgotten for centuries.

Yet it is here if anywhere that a valid criterion may be found for distinguishing the elite from the mob in the pretotalitarian atmosphere. What the mob wanted, and what Goebbels expressed with great precision, was access to history even at the price of destruction. Goebbels' sincere conviction that 'the greatest happiness that a contemporary can experience today' is either to be a genius or to serve one,[57] was typical of the mob but neither of the masses nor the sympathizing elite. The latter, on the contrary, took anonymity seriously to the point of seriously denying the existence of genius; all the art theories of the twenties tried desperately to prove that the excellent is the product of skill, craftsmanship, logic, and the realization of the potentialities of the material.[58] The mob, and not the elite, was charmed by the 'radiant power of fame' (Stefan Zweig) and accepted enthusiastically the genius idolatry of the late bourgeois world. In this the mob of the twentieth century followed faithfully the pattern of earlier parvenus who also had discovered the fact that bourgeois society would rather open its doors to the fascinating 'abnormal,' the genius, the homosexual, or the Jew, than to simple merit. The elite's contempt for the genius and its yearning for anonymity was still witness of a spirit which neither the masses nor the mob were in a position to understand, and which, in the words of Robespierre, strove to assert the grandeur of man against the pettiness of the great.

57  Goebbels, *op. cit.*, p. 139.
58  The art theories of the Bauhaus were characteristic in this respect. See also Bertolt Brecht's remarks on the theater, *Gesammelte Werke*, London, 1938.

This difference between the elite and the mob notwithstanding, there is no doubt that the elite was pleased whenever the underworld frightened respectable society into accepting it on an equal footing. The members of the elite did not object at all to paying a price, the destruction of civilization, for the fun of seeing how those who had been excluded unjustly in the past forced their way into it. They were not particularly outraged at the monstrous forgeries in historiography of which all totalitarian regimes are guilty and which announce themselves clearly enough in totalitarian propaganda. They had convinced themselves that traditional historiography was a forgery in any case, since it had excluded the underprivileged and oppressed from the memory of mankind. Those who were rejected by their own time were usually forgotten by history, and insult added to injury had troubled all sensitive consciences ever since faith in a hereafter where the last would be the first had disappeared. Injustices in the past as well as the present became intolerable when there was no longer any hope that the scales of justice eventually would be set right. Marx's great attempt to rewrite world history in terms of class struggles fascinated even those who did not believe in the correctness of his thesis, because of his original intention to find a device by which to force the destinies of those excluded from official history into the memory of posterity.

The temporary alliance between the elite and the mob rested largely on this genuine delight with which the former watched the latter destroy respectability. This could be achieved when the German steel barons were forced to deal with and to receive socially Hitler the housepainter and self-admitted former derelict, as it could be with the crude and vulgar forgeries perpetrated by the totalitarian movements in all fields of intellectual life, insofar as they gathered all the subterranean, nonrespectable elements of European history into one consistent picture. From this viewpoint it was rather gratifying to see that Bolshevism and Nazism began even to eliminate those sources of their own ideologies which had already won some recognition in academic or other official quarters. Not Marx's dialectical materialism, but the conspiracy of 300 families; not the pompous scientificality of Gobineau and Chamberlain, but the 'Protocols of the Elders of Zion'; not the traceable influence of the Catholic Church and the role played by anticlericalism in Latin countries, but the backstairs literature about the Jesuits and the Freemasons became the inspiration for the rewriters of history. The object of the most varied and variable constructions was always to reveal official history as a joke, to demonstrate a sphere of secret influences of which the visible, traceable, and known historical reality was only the outward façade erected explicitly to fool the people.

To this aversion of the intellectual elite for official historiography, to its conviction that history, which was a forgery anyway, might as well be the playground of crackpots, must be added the terrible, demoralizing fascination in the possibility that gigantic lies and monstrous falsehoods can eventually be established as unquestioned facts, that man may be free to change his own past at will, and that the difference between truth and falsehood may cease to be objective and become a mere matter of power and cleverness, of pressure and infinite repetition. Not Stalin's and Hitler's skill in the art of lying but the fact that they were able to organize the masses into a collective unit to back up their lies with impressive magnificence, exerted the fascination. Simple forgeries from the viewpoint of scholarship appeared to receive the sanction of history itself when the whole marching reality of the movements stood behind them and pretended to draw from them the necessary inspiration for action.

The attraction which the totalitarian movements exert on the elite, so long as and wherever they have not seized power, has been perplexing because the patently vulgar and arbitrary, positive doctrines of totalitarianism are more conspicuous to the outsider and mere observer than the general mood which pervades the pretotalitarian atmosphere. These doctrines were so much at variance with generally accepted intellectual, cultural, and moral standards that one could conclude that only an inherent fundamental shortcoming of character in the intellectual, '*la trahison des clercs*' (J. Benda), or a perverse self-hatred of the spirit, accounted for the delight with which the elite accepted the 'ideas' of the mob. What the spokesmen of humanism and liberalism usually overlook, in their bitter disappointment and their unfamiliarity with the more general experiences of the time, is that an atmosphere in which all traditional values and propositions had evaporated (after the nineteenth-century ideologies had refuted each other and exhausted their vital appeal) in a sense made it easier to accept patently absurd propositions than the old truths which had become pious banalities, precisely because nobody could be expected to take the absurdities seriously. Vulgarity with its cynical dismissal of respected standards and accepted theories carried with it a frank admission of the worst and a disregard for all pretenses which were easily mistaken for courage and a new style of life. In the growing prevalence of mob attitudes and convictions – which were actually the attitudes and convictions of the bourgeoisie cleansed of hypocrisy – those who traditionally hated the bourgeoisie and had voluntarily left respectable society saw only the lack of hypocrisy and respectability, not the content itself.[59]

Since the bourgeoisie claimed to be the guardian of Western traditions and confounded all moral issues by parading publicly virtues which it not only did not possess in private and business life, but actually held in contempt, it seemed revolutionary to admit cruelty, disregard of human values, and general amorality, because this at least destroyed the duplicity upon which the existing society seemed to rest. What a temptation to flaunt extreme attitudes in the hypocritical twilight of double moral standards, to wear publicly the mask of cruelty if everybody was patently inconsiderate and pretended to be gentle, to parade wickedness in a world, not of wickedness, but of meanness! The intellectual elite of the twenties who knew little of the earlier connections between mob and bourgeoisie was certain that the old game of *épater le bourgeois* could be played to perfection if one started to shock society with an ironically exaggerated picture of its own behavior.

At that time, nobody anticipated that the true victims of this irony would be the elite rather than the bourgeoisie. The avant-garde did not know they were running their heads not against walls but against

59 The following passage by Röhm is typical of the feeling of almost the whole younger generation and not only of an elite: 'Hypocrisy and Pharisaism rule. They are the most conspicuous characteristics of society today . . . Nothing could be more lying than the so-called morals of society.' These boys 'don't find their way in the philistine world of bourgeois double morals and don't know any longer how to distinguish between truth and error' (*Die Geschichte eines Hochverräters*, pp. 267 and 269). The homosexuality of these circles was also at least partially an expression of their protest against society.

open doors, that a unanimous success would belie their claim to being a revolutionary minority, and would prove that they were about to express a new mass spirit or the spirit of the time. Particularly significant in this respect was the reception given Brecht's *Dreigroschenoper* in pre-Hitler Germany. The play presented gangsters as respectable businessmen and respectable businessmen as gangsters. The irony was somewhat lost when respectable businessmen in the audience considered this a deep insight into the ways of the world and when the mob welcomed it as an artistic sanction of gangsterism. The theme song in the play, 'Erst kommt das Fressen, dann kommt die Moral,' was greeted with frantic applause by exactly everybody, though for different reasons. The mob applauded because it took the statement literally; the bourgeoisie applauded because it had been fooled by its own hypocrisy for so long that it had grown tired of the tension and found deep wisdom in the expression of the banality by which it lived; the elite applauded because the unveiling of hypocrisy was such superior and wonderful fun. The effect of the work was exactly the opposite of what Brecht had sought by it. The bourgeoisie could no longer be shocked; it welcomed the exposure of its hidden philosophy, whose popularity proved they had been right all along, so that the only political result of Brecht's 'revolution' was to encourage everyone to discard the uncomfortable mask of hypocrisy and to accept openly the standards of the mob.

A reaction similar in its ambiguity was aroused some ten years later in France by Céline's *Bagatelles pour un Massacre*, in which he proposed to massacre all the Jews. André Gide was publicly delighted in the pages of the *Nouvelle Revue Française*, not of course because he wanted to kill the Jews of France, but because he rejoiced in the blunt admission of such a desire and in the fascinating contradiction between Céline's bluntness and the hypocritical politeness which surrounded the Jewish question in all respectable quarters. How irresistible the desire for the unmasking of hypocrisy was among the elite can be gauged by the fact that such delight could not even be spoiled by Hitler's very real persecution of the Jews, which at the time of Céline's writing was already in full swing. Yet aversion against the philosemitism of the liberals had much more to do with this reaction than hatred of Jews. A similar frame of mind explains the remarkable fact that

Hitler's and Stalin's widely publicized opinions about art and their persecution of modern artists have never been able to destroy the attraction which the totalitarian movements had for avant-garde artists; this shows the elite's lack of a sense of reality, together with its perverted selflessness, both of which resemble only too closely the fictitious world and the absence of self-interest among the masses. It was the great opportunity of the totalitarian movements, and the reason why a temporary alliance between the intellectual elite and the mob could come about, that in an elementary and undifferentiated way their problems had become the same and foreshadowed the problems and mentality of the masses.

Closely related to the attraction which the mob's lack of hypocrisy and the masses' lack of self-interest exerted on the elite was the equally irresistible appeal of the totalitarian movements' spurious claim to have abolished the separation between private and public life and to have restored a mysterious irrational wholeness in man. Since Balzac revealed the private lives of the public figures of French society and since Ibsen's dramatization of the 'Pillars of Society' had conquered the Continental theater, the issue of double morality was one of the main topics for tragedies, comedies, and novels. Double morality as practiced by the bourgeoisie became the outstanding sign of that *esprit de sérieux*, which is always pompous and never sincere. This division between private and public or social life had nothing to do with the justified separation between the personal and public spheres, but was rather the psychological reflection of the nineteenth-century struggle between *bourgeois* and *citoyen*, between the man who judged and used all public institutions by the yardstick of his private interests and the responsible citizen who was concerned with public affairs as the affairs of all. In this connection, the liberals' political philosophy, according to which the mere sum of individual interests adds up to the miracle of the common good, appeared to be only a rationalization of the recklessness with which private interests were pressed regardless of the common good.

Against the class spirit of the Continental parties, which had always admitted they represented certain interests, and against the 'opportunism' resulting from their conception of themselves as only parts of a total, the totalitarian movements asserted their 'superiority' in

that they carried a *Weltanschauung* by which they would take possession of man as a whole.[60] In this claim to totality the mob leaders of
the movements again formulated and only reversed the bourgeoisie's
own political philosophy. The bourgeois class, having made its way
through social pressure and, frequently, through an economic blackmail of political institutions, always believed that the public and visible
organs of power were directed by their own secret, non-public interests and influence. In this sense, the bourgeoisie's political philosophy
was always 'totalitarian'; it always assumed an identity of politics,
economics and society, in which political institutions served only as
the façade for private interests. The bourgeoisie's double standard,
its differentiation between public and private life, were a concession to
the nation-state which had desperately tried to keep the two spheres
apart.

What appealed to the elite was radicalism as such. Marx's hopeful
predictions that the state would wither away and a classless society
emerge were no longer radical, no longer Messianic enough. If Berdyaev is right in stating that 'Russian revolutionaries . . . had always been
totalitarian,' then the attraction which Soviet Russia exerted almost
equally on Nazi and Communist intellectual fellow-travelers lay precisely in the fact that in Russia 'the revolution was a religion and a
philosophy, not merely a conflict concerned with the social and political side of life.'[61] The truth was that the transformation of classes into
masses and the breakdown of the prestige and authority of political
institutions had brought to Western European countries conditions
which resembled those prevalent in Russia, so that it was no accident
that their revolutionaries also began to take on the typically Russian
revolutionary fanaticism which looked forward, not to change in
social or political conditions, but to the radical destruction of every
existing creed, value, and institution. The mob merely took advantage
of this new mood and brought about a short-lived alliance of

60 The role of the *Weltanschauung* in the formation of the Nazi movement has been
stressed many times by Hitler himself. In *Mein Kampf*, it is interesting to note that he
pretends to have understood the necessity of basing a party on a *Weltanschauung*
through the superiority of the Marxist parties. Book II, chapter i: '*Weltanschauung*
and Party.'

61 Nicolai Berdyaev, *The Origin of Russian Communism*, 1937, pp. 124–125.

revolutionaries and criminals, which also had been present in many revolutionary sects in Czarist Russia but conspicuously absent from the European scene.

The disturbing alliance between the mob and the elite, and the curious coincidence of their aspirations, had their origin in the fact that these strata had been the first to be eliminated from the structure of the nation-state and the framework of class society. They found each other so easily, if only temporarily, because they both sensed that they represented the fate of the time, that they were followed by unending masses, that sooner or later the majority of European peoples might be with them – as they thought, ready to make their revolution.

It turned out that they were both mistaken. The mob, the underworld of the bourgeois class, hoped that the helpless masses would help them into power, would support them when they attempted to forward their private interests, that they would be able simply to replace the older strata of bourgeois society and to instill into it the more enterprising spirit of the underworld. Yet totalitarianism in power learned quickly that enterprising spirit was not restricted to the mob strata of the population and that, in any event, such initiative could only be a threat to the total domination of man. Absence of scruple, on the other hand, was not restricted to the mob either and, in any event, could be taught in a relatively short time. For the ruthless machines of domination and extermination, the masses of co-ordinated philistines provided much better material and were capable of even greater crimes than so-called professional criminals, provided only that these crimes were well organized and assumed the appearance of routine jobs.

It is not fortuitous, then, that the few protests against the Nazis' mass atrocities against the Jews and Eastern European peoples were voiced not by the military men nor by any other part of the co-ordinated masses of respectable philistines, but precisely by those early comrades of Hitler who were typical representatives of the mob.[62] Nor

62 There is, for instance, the curious intervention of Wilhelm Kube, General Commissar in Minsk and one of the oldest members of the Party, who in 1941, *i.e.*, at the beginning of the mass murder, wrote to his chief: 'I certainly am tough and willing to co-operate in the solution of the Jewish question, but people who have been brought up

was Himmler, the most powerful man in Germany after 1936, one of those 'armed bohemians' (Heiden) whose features were distressingly similar to those of the intellectual elite. Himmler was himself 'more normal,' that is, more of a philistine, than any of the original leaders of the Nazi movement.[63] He was not a bohemian like Goebbels, or a sex criminal like Streicher, or a crackpot like Rosenberg, or a fanatic like Hitler, or an adventurer like Göring. He proved his supreme ability for organizing the masses into total domination by assuming that most people are neither bohemians, fanatics, adventurers, sex maniacs, crackpots, nor social failures, but first and foremost job holders and good family men.

The philistine's retirement into private life, his single-minded

---

in our own culture are, after all, different from the local bestial hordes. Are we to assign the task of slaughtering them to the Lithuanians and Letts who are discriminated against even by the indigenous population? I could not do it. I ask you to give me clear-cut instructions to take care of the matter in the most humane way for the sake of the prestige of our Reich and our Party.' This letter is published in Max Weinreich, *Hitler's Professors*, New York, 1946, pp. 153–154. Kube's intervention was quickly overruled, yet an almost identical attempt to save the lives of Danish Jews, made by W. Best, the Reich's plenipotentiary in Denmark, and a well-known Nazi, was more successful. See *Nazi Conspiracy*, V, 2.

Similarly Alfred Rosenberg, who had preached the inferiority of the Slav peoples, obviously never realized that his theories might one day mean their liquidation. Charged with the administration of the Ukraine, he wrote outraged reports about conditions there during the fall of 1942 after he had tried earlier to get direct intervention from Hitler himself. See *Nazi Conspiracy*, III, 83 ff., and IV, 62.

There are of course some exceptions to this rule. The man who saved Paris from destruction was General von Choltitz who, however, still 'feared that he would be deprived of his command as he had not executed his orders' even though he knew that the 'war had been lost for several years.' That he would have had the courage to resist the order 'to turn Paris into a mass of ruins' without the energetic support of a Nazi of old standing, Otto Abetz the Ambassador to France, appears dubious according to his own testimony during the trial of Abetz in Paris. See *New York Times*, July 21, 1949.

63 An Englishman, Stephen H. Roberts, *The House that Hitler Built*, London, 1939, describes Himmler as 'a man of exquisite courtesy and still interested in the simple things of life. He has none of the pose of those Nazis who act as demigods . . . No man looks less like his job than this police dictator of Germany, and I am convinced that nobody I met in Germany is more normal . . .' (pp. 89–90). – This reminds one in a curious way of the remark of Stalin's mother who according to Bolshevik propaganda said of him: 'An exemplary son. I wish everybody were like him' (Souvarine, *op. cit.*, p. 656).

devotion to matters of family and career was the last, and already degenerated, product of the bourgeoisie's belief in the primacy of private interest. The philistine is the bourgeois isolated from his own class, the atomized individual who is produced by the breakdown of the bourgeois class itself. The mass man whom Himmler organized for the greatest mass crimes ever committed in history bore the features of the philistine rather than of the mob man, and was the bourgeois who in the midst of the ruins of his world worried about nothing so much as his private security, was ready to sacrifice everything – belief, honor, dignity – on the slightest provocation. Nothing proved easier to destroy than the privacy and private morality of people who thought of nothing but safeguarding their private lives. After a few years of power and systematic co-ordination, the Nazis could rightly announce: 'The only person who is still a private individual in Germany is somebody who is asleep.'[64]

In all fairness to those among the elite, on the other hand, who at one time or another have let themselves be seduced by totalitarian movements, and who sometimes, because of their intellectual abilities, are even accused of having inspired totalitarianism, it must be stated that what these desperate men of the twentieth century did or did not do had no influence on totalitarianism whatsoever, although it did play some part in earlier, successful, attempts of the movements to force the outside world to take their doctrines seriously. Wherever totalitarian movements seized power, this whole group of sympathizers was shaken off even before the regimes proceeded toward their greatest crimes. Intellectual, spiritual, and artistic initiative is as dangerous to totalitarianism as the gangster initiative of the mob, and both are more dangerous than mere political opposition. The consistent persecution of every higher form of intellectual activity by the new mass leaders springs from more than their natural resentment against everything they cannot understand. Total domination does not allow for free initiative in any field of life, for any activity that is not entirely predictable. Totalitarianism in power invariably replaces all first-rate talents, regardless of their sympathies, with those

64  The remark was made by Robert Ley. See Kohn-Bramstedt, *op. cit.*, p. 178.

crackpots and fools whose lack of intelligence and creativity is still the best guarantee of their loyalty.[65]

65 Bolshevik policy, in this respect surprisingly consistent, is well known and hardly needs further comment. Picasso, to take the most famous instance, is not liked in Russia even though he has become a Communist. It is possible that André Gide's sudden reversal of attitude after seeing the Bolshevik reality in Soviet Russia (*Retour de l'URSS*) in 1936, definitely convinced Stalin of the uselessness of creative artists even as fellow-travelers. Nazi policy was distinguished from Bolshevik measures only insofar as it did not yet kill its first-rate talents.

It would be worthwhile to study in detail the careers of those comparatively few German scholars who went beyond mere co-operation and volunteered their services because they were convinced Nazis. (Weinreich, *op. cit.*, the only available study, and misleading because he does not distinguish between professors who adopted the Nazi creed and those who owed their careers exclusively to the regime, omits the earlier careers of the concerned scholars and thus indiscriminately puts well-known men of great achievement into the same category as crackpots.) Most interesting is the example of the jurist Carl Schmitt, whose very ingenious theories about the end of democracy and legal government still make arresting reading; as early as the middle thirties, he was replaced by the Nazis' own brand of political and legal theorists, such as Hans Frank, the later governor of Poland, Gottfried Neesse, and Reinhard Hoehn. The last to fall into disgrace was the historian Walter Frank, who had been a convinced antisemite and member of the Nazi party before it came to power, and who, in 1933, became director of the newly founded Reichsinstitut für Geschichte des Neuen Deutschlands with its famous Forschungsabteilung Judenfrage, and editor of the nine-volume *Forschungen zur Judenfrage* (1937–1944). In the early forties, Frank had to cede his position and influence to the notorious Alfred Rosenberg, whose *Der Mythos des 20. Jahrhunderts* certainly shows no aspiration whatsoever to 'scholarship.' Frank clearly was mistrusted for no other reason than that he was not a charlatan.

What neither the elite nor the mob that 'embraced' National Socialism with such fervor could understand was that 'one cannot embrace this Order . . . by accident. Above and beyond the willingness to serve stands the unrelenting necessity of selection that knows neither extenuating circumstances nor clemency' (*Der Weg der SS*, issued by the SS-Hauptamt-Schulungsamt, n.d., p. 4). In other words, concerning the selection of those who would belong to them the Nazis intended to make their own decisions, regardless of the 'accident' of any opinions. The same appears to be true for the selection of Bolshevists for the secret police. F. Beck and W. Godin report in *Russian Purge and the Extraction of Confession*, 1951, p. 160, that the members of the NKVD are claimed from the ranks of party members without having the slightest opportunity to volunteer for this 'career.'

# CHAPTER ELEVEN

# The Totalitarian Movement

## I: Totalitarian Propaganda

Only the mob and the elite can be attracted by the momentum of totalitarianism itself; the masses have to be won by propaganda. Under conditions of constitutional government and freedom of opinion, totalitarian movements struggling for power can use terror to a limited extent only and share with other parties the necessity of winning adherents and of appearing plausible to a public which is not yet rigorously isolated from all other sources of information.

It was recognized early and has frequently been asserted that in totalitarian countries propaganda and terror present two sides of the same coin.[1] This, however, is only partly true. Wherever totalitarianism possesses absolute control, it replaces propaganda with indoctrination and uses violence not so much to frighten people (this is done only in the initial stages when political opposition still exists) as to realize constantly its ideological doctrines and its practical lies. Totalitarianism will not be satisfied to assert, in the face of contrary

1 See, for instance, E. Kohn-Bramstedt, *Dictatorship and Political Police: The Technique of Control by Fear*, London, 1945, pp. 164 ff. The explanation is that 'terror without propaganda would lose most of its psychological effect, whereas propaganda without terror does not contain its full punch' (p. 175). What is overlooked in these and similar statements, which mostly go around in circles, is the fact that not only political propaganda but the whole of modern mass publicity contains an element of threat; that terror, on the other hand, can be fully effective without propaganda, so long as it is only a question of conventional political terror of tyranny. Only when terror is intended to coerce not merely from without but, as it were, from within, when the political regime wants more than power, is terror in need of propaganda. In this sense the Nazi theorist, Eugen Hadamovsky, could say in *Propaganda und nationale Macht*, 1933: 'Propaganda and violence are never contradictions. Use of violence can be part of the propaganda' (p. 22).

facts, that unemployment does not exist; it will abolish unemployment benefits as part of its propaganda.[2] Equally important is the fact that the refusal to acknowledge unemployment realized – albeit in a rather unexpected way – the old socialist doctrine: He who does not work shall not eat. Or when, to take another instance, Stalin decided to rewrite the history of the Russian Revolution, the propaganda of his new version consisted in destroying, together with the older books and documents, their authors and readers: the publication in 1938 of a new official history of the Communist Party was the signal that the superpurge which had decimated a whole generation of Soviet intellectuals had come to an end. Similarly, the Nazis in the Eastern occupied territories at first used chiefly antisemitic propaganda to win firmer control of the population. They neither needed nor used terror to support this propaganda. When they liquidated the greater part of the Polish intelligentsia, they did it not because of its opposition, but because according to their doctrine Poles had no intellect, and when they planned to kidnap blue-eyed and blond-haired children, they did not intend to frighten the population but to save 'Germanic blood.'[3]

2 'At that time, it was officially announced that unemployment was "liquidated" in Soviet Russia. The result of the announcement was that all unemployment benefits were equally "liquidated"' (Anton Ciliga, *The Russian Enigma*, London, 1940, p. 109).

3 The so-called 'Operation Hay' began with a decree dated February 16, 1942, by Himmler 'concerning [individuals] of German stock in Poland,' stipulating that their children should be sent to families 'that are willing [to accept them] without reservations, out of love for the good blood in them' (Nuremberg Document R 135, photostated by the Centre de Documentation Juive, Paris). It seems that in June, 1944, the Ninth Army actually kidnapped 40,000 to 50,000 children and subsequently transported them to Germany. A report on this matter, sent to the General Staff of the Wehrmacht in Berlin by a man called Brandenburg, mentions similar plans for the Ukraine (Document PS 031, published by Léon Poliakov in *Bréviaire de la Haine*, p. 317). Himmler himself made several references to this plan. (See *Nazi Conspiracy and Aggression*, Office of the United States Chief of Counsel for the Prosecution of Axis Criminality, U.S. Government, Washington, 1946, III, 640, which contains excerpts from Himmler's speech at Cracow in March, 1942; see also the comments on Himmler's speech at Bad Schachen in 1943 in Kohn-Bramstedt, *op. cit.*, p. 244.) How the selection of these children was arrived at can be gathered from medical certificates made out by Medical Section II at Minsk on August 10, 1942: 'The racial examination of Natalie Harpf, born August 14, 1922, showed a normally developed girl of predominantly East Baltic type with Nordic features.' – 'Examination of Arnold Cornies, born February 19, 1930, showed a normally developed boy, twelve years old, of predominantly Eastern type

Since totalitarian movements exist in a world which itself is non-totalitarian, they are forced to resort to what we commonly regard as propaganda. But such propaganda always makes its appeal to an external sphere – be it the nontotalitarian strata of the population at home or the nontotalitarian countries abroad. This external sphere to which totalitarian propaganda makes its appeal may vary greatly; even after the seizure of power totalitarian propaganda may address itself to those segments of its own population whose co-ordination was not followed by sufficient indoctrination. In this respect Hitler's speeches to his generals during the war are veritable models of propaganda, characterized mainly by the monstrous lies with which the Fuehrer entertained his guests in an attempt to win them over.[4] The external sphere can also be represented by groups of sympathizers who are not yet ready to accept the true aims of the movement; finally, it often happens that even party members are regarded by the Fuehrer's inner circle or the members of the elite formations as belonging to such an external sphere, and in this case they, too, are still in need of propaganda because they cannot yet be reliably dominated. In order not to overestimate the importance of the propaganda lies one should recall the much more numerous instances in which Hitler was completely sincere and brutally unequivocal in the definition of the movement's true aims, but they were simply not acknowledged by a public unprepared for such consistency.[5] But, basically speaking, totalitarian domination strives to

---

with Nordic features.' Signed: N. Wc. (Document in the archives of the Yiddish Scientific Institute, New York, No. Occ E 3a-17.)

For the extermination of the Polish intelligentsia, which, in Hitler's opinion, could be 'wiped out without qualms,' see Poliakov, *op. cit.*, p. 321, and Document NO 2472.

4 See *Hitlers Tischgespräche*. In the summer of 1942, he still talks about '[kicking] even the last Jew out of Europe' (p. 113) and resettling the Jews in Siberia or Africa (p. 311), or Madagascar, while in reality he had already decided on the 'final solution' prior to the Russian invasion, probably in 1940, and ordered the gas ovens to be set up in the fall of 1941 (see *Nazi Conspiracy and Aggression*, II, pp. 265 ff.; III, pp. 783 ff. Document PS 1104; V. pp. 322 ff. Document PS 2605). Himmler already knew in the spring of 1941 that 'the Jews [must be] exterminated to the last man by the end of the war. This is the unequivocal desire and command of the Fuehrer' (Dossier Kersten in the Centre de Documentation Juive).

5 In this connection there is a very interesting report, dated July 16, 1940, on a discussion at the Fuehrer's headquarters, in the presence of Rosenberg, Lammers and Keitel,

restrict propaganda methods solely to its foreign policy or to the branches of the movement abroad for the purpose of supplying them with suitable material. Whenever totalitarian indoctrination at home comes into conflict with the propaganda line for consumption abroad (which happened in Russia during the war, not when Stalin had concluded his alliance with Hitler, but when the war with Hitler brought him into the camp of the democracies), the propaganda is explained at home as a 'temporary tactical maneuver.'[6] As far as possible, this distinction between ideological doctrine for the initiated in the movement, who are no longer in need of propaganda, and unadulterated propaganda for the outside world is already established in the prepower existence of the movements. The relationship between propaganda and indoctrination usually depends upon the size of the movements on one hand, and upon outside pressure on the other. The smaller the movement, the more energy it will expend in mere propaganda; the greater the pressure on totalitarian regimes from the outside world – a pressure that even behind iron curtains cannot be ignored entirely – the more actively will the totalitarian dictators engage in propaganda. The essential point is that the necessities for propaganda are always dictated by the outside world and that the movements themselves do not actually propagate but indoctrinate. Conversely, indoctrination, inevitably coupled with terror, increases

---

which Hitler began by stating the following 'basic principles': 'It was now essential not to parade our ultimate goal before the entire world . . . Hence it must not be obvious that [the decrees for maintaining peace and order in the occupied territories] point to a final settlement. All necessary measures – executions, resettlements – can, and will be, carried out in spite of this.' This is followed by a discussion which makes no reference whatever to Hitler's words and in which Hitler no longer participates. He quite obviously had not been 'understood' (Document L 221 in the Centre de Documentation Juive).

6 For Stalin's confidence that Hitler would not attack Russia, see Isaac Deutscher, *Stalin: A Political Biography*, New York and London, 1949, pp. 454 ff., and especially the footnote on p. 458: 'It was only in 1948 that the Chief of the State Planning Commission, Vice-Premier N. Voznesensky, disclosed that the economic plans for the third quarter of 1941 had been based on the assumption of peace and that a new plan, suited for war, had been drafted only after the outbreak of hostilities.' Deutscher's estimate has now been solidly confirmed by Khrushchev's report on Stalin's reaction to the German attack on the Soviet Union. See his 'Speech on Stalin' at the Twentieth Congress as released by the State Department, New York *Times*, June 5, 1956.

with the strength of the movements or the totalitarian governments' isolation and security from outside interference.

Propaganda is indeed part and parcel of 'psychological warfare'; but terror is more. Terror continues to be used by totalitarian regimes even when its psychological aims are achieved: its real horror is that it reigns over a completely subdued population. Where the rule of terror is brought to perfection, as in concentration camps, propaganda disappears entirely; it was even expressly prohibited in Nazi Germany.[7] Propaganda, in other words, is one, and possibly the most important, instrument of totalitarianism for dealing with the nontotalitarian world; terror, on the contrary, is the very essence of its form of government. Its existence depends as little on psychological or other subjective factors as the existence of laws in a constitutionally governed country depends upon the number of people who transgress them.

Terror as the counterpart of propaganda played a greater role in Nazism than in Communism. The Nazis did not strike at prominent figures as had been done in the earlier wave of political crimes in Germany (the murder of Rathenau and Erzberger); instead, by killing small socialist functionaries or influential members of opposing parties, they attempted to prove to the population the dangers involved in mere membership. This kind of mass terror, which still operated on a comparatively small scale, increased steadily because neither the police nor the courts seriously prosecuted political offenders on the so-called Right. It was valuable as what a Nazi publicist has aptly called 'power propaganda':[8] it made clear to the population at large that the power of the Nazis was greater than that of the authorities and that it was safer to be a member of a Nazi paramilitary organization than a loyal Republican. This impression was greatly strengthened by the specific use the

7 'Education [in the concentration camps] consists of discipline, never of any kind of instruction on an ideological basis, for the prisoners have for the most part slave-like souls' (Heinrich Himmler, *Nazi Conspiracy*, IV, 616 ff.).

8 Eugen Hadamovsky, *op. cit.*, is outstanding in the literature on totalitarian propaganda. Without explicitly stating it, Hadamovsky offers an intelligent and revealing pro-Nazi interpretation of Hitler's own exposition on the subject in 'Propaganda and Organization,' in Book II, chapter xi of *Mein Kampf* (2 vols., 1st German edition, 1925 and 1927 respectively. Unexpurgated translation, New York, 1939). – See also F. A. Six, *Die politische Propaganda der NSDAP im Kampf um die Macht*, 1936, pp. 21 ff.

Nazis made of their political crimes. They always admitted them publicly, never apologized for 'excesses of the lower ranks' – such apologies were used only by Nazi sympathizers – and impressed the population as being very different from the 'idle talkers' of other parties.

The similarities between this kind of terror and plain gangsterism are too obvious to be pointed out. This does not mean that Nazism was gangsterism, as has sometimes been concluded, but only that the Nazis, without admitting it, learned as much from American gangster organizations as their propaganda, admittedly, learned from American business publicity.

More specific in totalitarian propaganda, however, than direct threats and crimes against individuals is the use of indirect, veiled, and menacing hints against all who will not heed its teachings and, later, mass murder perpetrated on 'guilty' and 'innocent' alike. People are threatened by Communist propaganda with missing the train of history, with remaining hopelessly behind their time, with spending their lives uselessly, just as they were threatened by the Nazis with living against the eternal laws of nature and life, with an irreparable and mysterious deterioration of their blood. The strong emphasis of totalitarian propaganda on the 'scientific' nature of its assertions has been compared to certain advertising techniques which also address themselves to masses. And it is true that the advertising columns of every newspaper show this 'scientificality,' by which a manufacturer proves with facts and figures and the help of a 'research' department that his is the 'best soap in the world.'[9] It is also true that there is a certain element of violence in the imaginative exaggerations of publicity men, that behind the assertion that girls who do not use this particular brand of soap may go through life with pimples and without a husband, lies the wild dream of monopoly, the dream that one day the manufacturer of the 'only soap that prevents pimples' may have the power to deprive of husbands all girls who do not use his soap. Science in the instances of both business publicity and totalitarian propaganda is obviously only a surrogate for power. The obsession of totalitarian

9 Hitler's analysis of 'War Propaganda' (*Mein Kampf*, Book I, chapter vi) stresses the business angle of propaganda and uses the example of publicity for soap. Its importance has been generally overestimated, while his later positive ideas on 'Propaganda and Organization' were neglected.

movements with 'scientific' proofs ceases once they are in power. The Nazis dismissed even those scholars who were willing to serve them, and the Bolsheviks use the reputation of their scientists for entirely unscientific purposes and force them into the role of charlatans.

But there is nothing more to the frequently overrated similarities between mass advertisement and mass propaganda. Businessmen usually do not pose as prophets and they do not constantly demonstrate the correctness of their predictions. The scientificality of totalitarian propaganda is characterized by its almost exclusive insistence on scientific prophecy as distinguished from the more old-fashioned appeal to the past. Nowhere does the ideological origin, of socialism in one instance and racism in the other, show more clearly than when their spokesmen pretend that they have discovered the hidden forces that will bring them good fortune in the chain of fatality. There is of course a great appeal to the masses in 'absolutist systems which represent all the events of history as depending upon the great first causes linked by the chain of fatality, and which, as it were, suppress men from the history of the human race' (in the words of Tocqueville). But it cannot be doubted either that the Nazi leadership actually believed in, and did not merely use as propaganda, such doctrines as the following: 'The more accurately we recognize and observe the laws of nature and life . . . so much the more do we conform to the will of the Almighty. The more insight we have into the will of the Almighty, the greater will be our successes.'[10] It is quite apparent that very few changes are needed to express Stalin's creed in two sentences which might run as follows: 'The more accurately we recognize and observe the laws of history and class struggle, so much the more do we conform to dialectic materialism. The more insight we have into dialectic materialism,

10 See Martin Bormann's important memorandum on the 'Relationship of National Socialism and Christianity' in *Nazi Conspiracy*, VI, 1036 ff. Similar formulations can be found time and again in the pamphlet literature issued by the SS for the 'ideological indoctrination' of its cadets. 'The laws of nature are subject to an unchangeable will that cannot be influenced. Hence it is necessary to recognize these laws' ('SS-Mann und Blutsfrage,' *Schriftenreihe für die weltanschauliche Schulung der Ordnungspolizei*, 1942). All these are nothing but variations of certain phrases taken from Hitler's *Mein Kampf*, of which the following is quoted as the motto for the pamphlet just mentioned: 'While man attempts to struggle against the iron logic of nature, he comes into conflict with the basic principles to which alone he owes his very existence as man.'

the greater will be our success.' Stalin's notion of 'correct leadership,'[11] at any rate, could hardly be better illustrated.

Totalitarian propaganda raised ideological scientificality and its technique of making statements in the form of predictions to a height of efficiency of method and absurdity of content because, demagogically speaking, there is hardly a better way to avoid discussion than by releasing an argument from the control of the present and by saying that only the future can reveal its merits. However, totalitarian ideologies did not invent this procedure, and were not the only ones to use it. Scientificality of mass propaganda has indeed been so universally employed in modern politics that it has been interpreted as a more general sign of that obsession with science which has characterized the Western world since the rise of mathematics and physics in the sixteenth century; thus totalitarianism appears to be only the last stage in a process during which 'science [has become] an idol that will magically cure the evils of existence and transform the nature of man.'[12] And there was, indeed, an early connection between scientificality and the rise of the masses. The 'collectivism' of masses was welcomed by those who hoped for the appearance of 'natural laws of historical development' which would eliminate the unpredictability of the individual's actions and behavior.[13] There has been cited the example of Enfantin who could already 'see the time approaching when the "art of moving the masses" will be so perfectly developed that the painter, the musician, and the poet will possess the power to please and to move with the same certainty as the mathematician solves a geometrical problem or the chemist analyses any substance,' and it has been concluded that modern propaganda was born then and there.[14]

Yet whatever the shortcomings of positivism, pragmatism, and behaviorism, and however great their influence on the formation of the nineteenth-century brand of common sense, it is not at all 'the

---

11 J. Stalin, *Leninism* (1933), Vol. II, chapter iii.

12 Eric Voegelin, 'The Origins of Scientism,' in *Social Research*, December, 1948.

13 See F. A. v. Hayek, 'The Counter-Revolution of Science,' in *Economica*, Vol. VIII (February, May, August, 1941), p. 13.

14 *Ibid.*, p. 137. The quotation is from the Saint-Simonist magazine *Producteur*, 1, 399.

cancerous growth of the utilitarian segment of existence'[15] which characterizes the masses to whom totalitarian propaganda and scientificality appeal. The positivists' conviction, as we know it from Comte, that the future is eventually scientifically predictable, rests on the evaluation of interest as an all-pervasive force in history and the assumption that objective laws of power can be discovered. Rohan's political theory that 'the kings command the peoples and the interest commands the king,' that objective interest is the rule 'that alone can never fail,' that 'rightly or wrongly understood, the interest makes governments live or die' is the traditional core of modern utilitarianism, positivist or socialist, but none of these theories assumes that it is possible 'to transform the nature of man' as totalitarianism indeed tries to do. On the contrary, they all implicitly or explicitly assume that human nature is always the same, that history is the story of changing objective circumstances and the human reactions to them, and that interest, rightly understood, may lead to a change of circumstances, but not to a change of human reactions as such. 'Scientism' in politics still presupposes that human welfare is its object, a concept which is utterly alien to totalitarianism.[16]

It is precisely because the utilitarian core of ideologies was taken for granted that the anti-utilitarian behavior of totalitarian governments, their complete indifference to mass interest, has been such a shock. This introduced into contemporary politics an element of unheard-of unpredictability. Totalitarian propaganda, however – although in the form of shifted emphasis – indicated even before totalitarianism could seize power how far the masses had drifted from mere concern with interest. Thus the suspicion of the Allies that the murder of the insane which Hitler ordered at the beginning of the war should be attributed to the desire to get rid of unnecessary mouths to feed was altogether unjustified.[17] Hitler was not forced by the war to

15 Voegelin, *op. cit.*
16 William Ebenstein, *The Nazi State*, New York, 1943, in discussing the 'Permanent War Economy' of the Nazi state is almost the only critic who has realized that 'the endless discussion . . . as to the socialist or capitalist nature of the German economy under the Nazi regime is largely artificial . . . [because it] tends to overlook the vital fact that capitalism and socialism are categories which relate to Western welfare economics' (p. 239).
17 The testimony of Karl Brandt, one of the physicians charged by Hitler with carrying out the program of euthanasia, is characteristic in this context (*Medical Trial. US against*

throw all ethical considerations overboard, but regarded the mass slaughter of war as an incomparable opportunity to start a murder program which, like all other points of his program, was calculated in terms of millennia.[18] Since virtually all of European history through many centuries had taught people to judge each political action by its *cui bono* and all political events by their particular underlying interests, they were suddenly confronted with an element of unprecedented unpredictability. Because of its demagogic qualities, totalitarian propaganda, which long before the seizure of power clearly indicated how little the masses were driven by the famous instinct of self-preservation, was not taken seriously. The success of totalitarian propaganda, however, does not rest so much on its demagoguery as on the knowledge that interest as a collective force can be felt only where stable social bodies provide the necessary transmission belts between the individual and the group; no effective propaganda based on mere interest can be carried on among masses whose chief characteristic is that they belong to no social or political body, and who therefore present a veritable chaos of individual interests. The fanaticism of members of totalitarian movements, so clearly different in quality from the greatest loyalty of members of ordinary parties, is produced by the lack of self-interest of masses who are quite prepared to sacrifice themselves. The Nazis have proved that one can lead a whole people into war with the slogan 'or else we shall go down' (something which the war propaganda of 1914 would have avoided carefully), and this is not in times of misery, unemployment, or frustrated national ambitions. The same spirit showed itself during the last months of a war

---

*Karl Brandt et al. Hearing of May 14, 1947*). Brandt vehemently protested against the suspicion that the project was initiated to eliminate superfluous food consumers; he emphasized that party members who brought up such arguments in the discussion had always been sharply rebuked. In his opinion, the measures were dictated solely by 'ethical considerations.' The same is, of course, true for the deportations. The files are filled with desperate memoranda written by the military complaining that the deportations of millions of Jews and Poles completely disregarded all 'military and economic necessities.' See Poliakov, *op. cit.*, p. 321, as well as the documentary material published there.

18 The decisive decree starting all subsequent mass murders was signed by Hitler on September 1, 1939 – the day the war broke out – and referred not merely to the insane (as is often erroneously assumed) but to all those who were 'incurably sick.' The insane were only the first to go.

that was obviously lost, when Nazi propaganda consoled an already badly frightened population with the promise that the Fuehrer 'in his wisdom had prepared an easy death for the German people by gassing them in case of defeat.'[19]

Totalitarian movements use socialism and racism by emptying them of their utilitarian content, the interests of a class or nation. The form of infallible prediction in which these concepts were presented has become more important than their content.[20] The chief qualification of a mass leader has become unending infallibility; he can never admit an error.[21] The assumption of infallibility, moreover, is based not so much on superior intelligence as on the correct interpretation of the essentially reliable forces in history or nature, forces which neither defeat nor ruin can prove wrong because they are bound to assert themselves in the long run.[22] Mass leaders in power have one concern which overrules all utilitarian considerations: to make their predictions come true. The Nazis did not hesitate to use, at the end of the war, the concentrated force of their still intact organization to bring about as complete a destruction of Germany as possible, in order to

19 See Friedrich Percyval Reck-Malleczewen, *Tagebuch eines Verzweifelten*, Stuttgart, 1947, p. 190.

20 Hitler based the superiority of ideological movements over political parties on the fact that ideologies (*Weltanschauungen*) always 'proclaim their infallibility' (*Mein Kampf*, Book II, chapter v, '*Weltanschauung* and Organization'). – The first pages of the official handbook for the Hitler Youth, *The Nazi Primer*, New York, 1938, consequently emphasize that all questions of *Weltanschauung*, formerly deemed 'unrealistic' and 'ununderstandable,' 'have become so clear, simple and *definite* [my italics] that every comrade can understand them and co-operate in their solution.'

21 The first among the 'pledges of the Party member,' as enumerated in the *Organisationsbuch der NSDAP*, reads: 'The Führer is always right.' Edition published in 1936, p. 8. But the *Dienstvorschrift für die P.O. der NSDAP*, 1932, p. 38, puts it this way: 'Hitler's decision is final!' Note the remarkable difference in phraseology.

'Their claim to be infallible, [that] neither of them has ever sincerely admitted an error' is in this respect the decisive difference between Stalin and Trotsky on one hand, and Lenin on the other. See Boris Souvarine, *Stalin: A Critical Survey of Bolshevism*, New York, 1939, p. 583.

22 That Hegelian dialectics should provide a wonderful instrument for always being right, because they permit the interpretation of all defeats as the beginning of victory, is obvious. One of the most beautiful examples of this kind of sophistry occurred after 1933 when the German Communists for nearly two years refused to recognize that Hitler's victory had been a defeat for the German Communist Party.

make true their prediction that the German people would be ruined in case of defeat.

The propaganda effect of infallibility, the striking success of posing as a mere interpreting agent of predictable forces, has encouraged in totalitarian dictators the habit of announcing their political intentions in the form of prophecy. The most famous example is Hitler's announcement to the German Reichstag in January, 1939: 'I want today once again to make a prophecy: In case the Jewish financiers . . . succeed once more in hurling the peoples into a world war, the result will be . . . the annihilation of the Jewish race in Europe.'[23] Translated into nontotalitarian language, this meant: I intend to make war and I intend to kill the Jews of Europe. Similarly Stalin, in the great speech before the Central Committee of the Communist Party in 1930 in which he prepared the physical liquidation of intraparty right and left deviationists, described them as representatives of 'dying classes.'[24] This definition not only gave the argument its specific sharpness but also announced, in totalitarian style, the physical destruction of those whose 'dying out' had just been prophesied. In both instances the same objective is accomplished: the liquidation is fitted into a historical process in which man only does or suffers what, according to immutable laws, is bound to happen anyway. As soon as the execution of the victims has been carried out, the 'prophecy' becomes a retrospective alibi: nothing happened but what had already been predicted.[25] It does not matter whether the 'laws of history' spell the 'doom' of the classes and their representatives, or whether the 'laws of nature . . . exterminate' all those elements – democracies, Jews, Eastern subhumans (*Untermenschen*), or the incurably sick – that are not 'fit to live'

23 Quoted from Goebbels: *The Goebbels Diaries (1942–1943)*, ed. by Louis Lochner, New York, 1948, p. 148.
24 Stalin, *op. cit., loc. cit.*
25 In a speech he made in September, 1942, when the extermination of the Jews was in full swing, Hitler explicitly referred to his speech of January 30, 1939 (published as a booklet titled *Der Führer vor dem ersten Reichstag Grossdeutschlands*, 1939), and to the Reichstag session of September 1, 1939, when he had announced that 'if Jewry should instigate an international world war to exterminate the Aryan peoples of Europe, not the Aryan peoples but Jewry will [rest of sentence drowned by applause]' (see *Der Führer zum Kriegswinterhilfswerk*, Schriften NSV, No. 14, p. 33).

anyway. Incidentally, Hitler too spoke of 'dying classes' that ought to be 'eliminated without much ado.'[26]

This method, like other totalitarian propaganda methods, is fool-proof only after the movements have seized power. Then all debate about the truth or falsity of a totalitarian dictator's prediction is as weird as arguing with a potential murderer about whether his future victim is dead or alive – since by killing the person in question the murderer can promptly provide proof of the correctness of his statement. The only valid argument under such conditions is promptly to rescue the person whose death is predicted. Before mass leaders seize the power to fit real-ity to their lies, their propaganda is marked by its extreme contempt for facts as such,[27] for in their opinion fact depends entirely on the power of man who can fabricate it. The assertion that the Moscow subway is the only one in the world is a lie only so long as the Bolsheviks have not the power to destroy all the others. In other words, the method of infallible prediction, more than any other totalitarian propaganda device, betrays its ultimate goal of world conquest, since only in a world completely under his control could the totalitarian ruler possibly realize all his lies and make true all his prophecies.

The language of prophetic scientificality corresponded to the needs of masses who had lost their home in the world and now were prepared to be reintegrated into eternal, all-dominating forces which by them-selves would bear man, the swimmer on the waves of adversity, to the shores of safety. 'We shape the life of our people and our legislation according to the verdicts of genetics,'[28] said the Nazis, just as the Bolshe-viks assure their followers that economic forces have the power of a verdict of history. They thereby promise a victory which is independent of 'temporary' defeats and failures in specific enterprises. For masses, in contrast to classes, want victory and success as such, in their most abstract form; they are not bound together by those special collective

---

26  In the speech of January 30, 1939, p. 19, as quoted above.

27  Konrad Heiden, *Der Fuehrer: Hitler's Rise to Power*, Boston, 1944, underlines Hitler's 'phenomenal untruthfulness,' 'the lack of demonstrable reality in nearly all his utter-ances,' his 'indifference to facts which he does not regard as vitally important' (pp. 368, 374). – In almost identical terms, Khrushchev describes 'Stalin's reluctance to consider life's realities' and his indifference to 'the real state of affairs,' *op. cit.* Stalin's opinion of the importance of facts is best expressed in his periodic revisions of Russian history.

28  *Nazi Primer*.

interests which they feel to be essential to their survival as a group and which they therefore may assert even in the face of overwhelming odds. More important to them than the cause that may be victorious, or the particular enterprise that may be a success, is the victory of no matter what cause, and success in no matter what enterprise.

Totalitarian propaganda perfects the techniques of mass propaganda, but it neither invents them nor originates their themes. These were prepared for them by fifty years of the rise of imperialism and disintegration of the nation-state, when the mob entered the scene of European politics. Like the earlier mob leaders, the spokesmen for totalitarian movements possessed an unerring instinct for anything that ordinary party propaganda or public opinion did not care or dare to touch. Everything hidden, everything passed over in silence, became of major significance, regardless of its own intrinsic importance. The mob really believed that truth was whatever respectable society had hypocritically passed over, or covered up with corruption.

Mysteriousness as such became the first criterion for the choice of topics. The origin of mystery did not matter; it could lie in a reasonable, politically comprehensible desire for secrecy, as in the case of the British Secret Services or the French Deuxième Bureau; or in the conspiratory need of revolutionary groups, as in the case of anarchist and other terrorist sects; or in the structure of societies whose original secret content had long since become well known and where only the formal ritual still retained the former mystery, as in the case of the Freemasons; or in age-old superstitions which had woven legends around certain groups, as in the case of the Jesuits and the Jews. The Nazis were undoubtedly superior in the selection of such topics for mass propaganda; but the Bolsheviks have gradually learned the trick, although they rely less on traditionally accepted mysteries and prefer their own inventions – since the middle thirties, one mysterious world conspiracy has followed another in Bolshevik propaganda, starting with the plot of the Trotskyites, followed by the rule of the 300 families, to the sinister imperialist (*i.e.*, global) machinations of the British or American Secret Services.[29]

29 It is interesting to note that the Bolsheviks during the Stalin era somehow accumulated conspiracies, that the discovery of a new one did not mean they would discard the former. The Trotskyite conspiracy started around 1930, the 300 families were added

The effectiveness of this kind of propaganda demonstrates one of the chief characteristics of modern masses. They do not believe in anything visible, in the reality of their own experience; they do not trust their eyes and ears but only their imaginations, which may be caught by anything that is at once universal and consistent in itself. What convinces masses are not facts, and not even invented facts, but only the consistency of the system of which they are presumably part. Repetition, somewhat overrated in importance because of the common belief in the masses' inferior capacity to grasp and remember, is important only because it convinces them of consistency in time.

What the masses refuse to recognize is the fortuitousness that pervades reality. They are predisposed to all ideologies because they explain facts as mere examples of laws and eliminate coincidences by inventing an all-embracing omnipotence which is supposed to be at the root of every accident. Totalitarian propaganda thrives on this escape from reality into fiction, from coincidence into consistency.

The chief disability of totalitarian propaganda is that it cannot fulfill this longing of the masses for a completely consistent, comprehensible, and predictable world without seriously conflicting with common sense. If, for instance, all the 'confessions' of political opponents in the Soviet Union are phrased in the same language and admit the same motives, the consistency-hungry masses will accept the fiction as supreme proof of their truthfulness; whereas common sense tells us that it is precisely their consistency which is out of this world and proves that they are a fabrication. Figuratively speaking, it is as though the masses demand a constant repetition of the miracle of the Septuagint, when, according to ancient legend, seventy isolated translators produced an identical Greek version of the Old Testament. Common sense can accept this tale only as a legend or a miracle; yet it could also be adduced as proof of the absolute faithfulness of every single word in the translated text.

In other words, while it is true that the masses are obsessed by a desire to escape from reality because in their essential homelessness

---

during the Popular Front period, from 1935 onward, British imperialism became an actual conspiracy during the Stalin–Hitler alliance, the 'American Secret Service' followed soon after the close of the war; the last, Jewish cosmopolitanism, had an obvious and disquieting resemblance to Nazi propaganda.

they can no longer bear its accidental, incomprehensible aspects, it is also true that their longing for fiction has some connection with those capacities of the human mind whose structural consistency is superior to mere occurrence. The masses' escape from reality is a verdict against the world in which they are forced to live and in which they cannot exist, since coincidence has become its supreme master and human beings need the constant transformation of chaotic and accidental conditions into a man-made pattern of relative consistency. The revolt of the masses against 'realism,' common sense, and all 'the plausibilities of the world' (Burke) was the result of their atomization, of their loss of social status along with which they lost the whole sector of communal relationships in whose framework common sense makes sense. In their situation of spiritual and social homelessness, a measured insight into the interdependence of the arbitrary and the planned, the accidental and the necessary, could no longer operate. Totalitarian propaganda can outrageously insult common sense only where common sense has lost its validity. Before the alternative of facing the anarchic growth and total arbitrariness of decay or bowing down before the most rigid, fantastically fictitious consistency of an ideology, the masses probably will always choose the latter and be ready to pay for it with individual sacrifices – and this not because they are stupid or wicked, but because in the general disaster this escape grants them a minimum of self-respect.

While it has been the specialty of Nazi propaganda to profit from the longing of the masses for consistency, Bolshevik methods have demonstrated, as though in a laboratory, its impact on the isolated mass man. The Soviet secret police, so eager to convince its victims of their guilt for crimes they never committed, and in many instances were in no position to commit, completely isolates and eliminates all real factors, so that the very logic, the very consistency of 'the story' contained in the prepared confession becomes overwhelming. In a situation where the dividing line between fiction and reality is blurred by the monstrosity and the inner consistency of the accusation, not only the strength of character to resist constant threats but great confidence in the existence of fellow human beings – relatives or friends or neighbors – who will never believe 'the story' are required to resist the temptation to yield to the mere abstract possibility of guilt.

To be sure, this extreme of an artificially fabricated insanity can be achieved only in a totalitarian world. Then, however, it is part of the propaganda apparatus of the totalitarian regimes to which confessions are not indispensable for punishment. 'Confessions' are as much a specialty of Bolshevik propaganda as the curious pedantry of legalizing crimes by retrospective and retroactive legislation was a specialty of Nazi propaganda. The aim in both cases is consistency.

Before they seize power and establish a world according to their doctrines, totalitarian movements conjure up a lying world of consistency which is more adequate to the needs of the human mind than reality itself; in which, through sheer imagination, uprooted masses can feel at home and are spared the never-ending shocks which real life and real experiences deal to human beings and their expectations. The force possessed by totalitarian propaganda – before the movements have the power to drop iron curtains to prevent anyone's disturbing, by the slightest reality, the gruesome quiet of an entirely imaginary world – lies in its ability to shut the masses off from the real world. The only signs which the real world still offers to the understanding of the unintegrated and disintegrating masses – whom every new stroke of ill luck makes more gullible – are, so to speak, its lacunae, the questions it does not care to discuss publicly, or the rumors it does not dare to contradict because they hit, although in an exaggerated and deformed way, some sore spot.

From these sore spots the lies of totalitarian propaganda derive the element of truthfulness and real experience they need to bridge the gulf between reality and fiction. Only terror could rely on mere fiction, and even the terror-sustained lying fictions of totalitarian regimes have not yet become entirely arbitrary, although they are usually cruder, more impudent, and, so to speak, more original than those of the movements. (It takes power, not propaganda skill, to circulate a revised history of the Russian Revolution in which no man by the name of Trotsky was ever commander-in-chief of the Red Army.) The lies of the movements, on the other hand, are much subtler. They attach themselves to every aspect of social and political life that is hidden from the public eye. They succeed best where the official authorities have surrounded themselves with an atmosphere of secrecy. In the eyes of the masses, they then acquire the reputation of superior 'realism' because they touch upon real conditions whose existence is being hidden. Revelations of scandals in high society, of corruption of politicians, everything that belongs to yellow journalism, becomes in their hands a weapon of more than sensational importance.

The most efficient fiction of Nazi propaganda was the story of a Jewish world conspiracy. Concentration on antisemitic propaganda had been a common device of demagogues ever since the end of the nineteenth century, and was widespread in the Germany and Austria of the twenties. The more consistently a discussion of the Jewish question was avoided by all parties and organs of public opinion, the more convinced the mob became that Jews were the true representatives of the powers that be, and that the Jewish issue was the symbol for the hypocrisy and dishonesty of the whole system.

The actual content of postwar antisemitic propaganda was neither a monopoly of the Nazis nor particularly new and original. Lies about a Jewish world conspiracy had been current since the Dreyfus Affair and based themselves on the existing international interrelationship and interdependence of a Jewish people dispersed all over the world. Exaggerated notions of Jewish world power are even older; they can be traced back to the end of the eighteenth century, when the intimate connection between Jewish business and the nation-states had become visible. The representation of *the* Jew as the incarnation of evil is usually blamed on remnants and superstitious memories from the Middle Ages, but is actually closely connected with the more recent ambiguous role which Jews played in European society since their emancipation. One thing was undeniable: in the postwar period Jews had become more prominent than ever before.

The point about the Jews themselves is that they grew prominent and conspicuous in inverse proportion to their real influence and position of power. Every decrease in the stability and force of the nation-states was a direct blow to Jewish positions. The partially successful conquest of the state by the nation made it impossible for the government machine to maintain its position above all classes and parties, and thereby nullified the value of alliances with the Jewish sector of the population, which was supposed also to stay outside the ranks of society and to be indifferent to party politics. The growing concern with foreign policy of the imperialist-minded bourgeoisie and its growing influence on the state machinery was accompanied by the steadfast refusal of the largest segment of Jewish wealth to engage itself in industrial enterprises and to leave the tradition of capital trading. All this taken together almost ended the economic usefulness to the state of the Jews as a group, and the advantages to themselves of social separation. After the first World War, Central European Jewries became as assimilated and nationalized as French Jewry had become during the first decades of the Third Republic.

How conscious the concerned states were of the changed situation came to light when, in 1917, the German government, following a long-established tradition, tried to use its Jews for tentative peace negotiations with the Allies. Instead of addressing itself to the established leaders of German Jewry, it went to the small and comparatively uninfluential Zionist minority which were still trusted in the old way precisely because they insisted on the existence of a Jewish people independent of citizenship, and could therefore be expected to render services which depended upon international connections and an international point of view. The step, however, turned out to have been a mistake for the German government. The Zionists did something that no Jewish banker had ever done before; they set their own conditions and told the government that they would only negotiate a peace without annexations and reparations.[30] The old Jewish indifference to political issues was gone; the majority could no longer be used, since it was no longer aloof from the nation, and the Zionist minority was useless because it had political ideas of its own.

The replacement of monarchical governments by republics in Central Europe completed the disintegration of Central European Jewries, just as the establishment of the Third Republic had done it in France some fifty years earlier. The Jews had already lost much of their influence when the new governments established themselves under conditions in which they lacked the power as well as the interest to protect their Jews. During the peace negotiations in Versailles, Jews were used chiefly as experts, and even antisemites admitted that the petty Jewish swindlers in the postwar era, mostly new arrivals (behind

---

30  See Chaim Weizmann's autobiography, *Trial and Error*, New York, 1949, p. 185.

whose fraudulent activities, which distinguished them sharply from their native coreligionists, lay an attitude which oddly resembled the old indifference to the standards of their environment), had no connections with the representatives of a supposed Jewish international.[31]

Among a host of competing antisemitic groups and in an atmosphere rife with antisemitism, Nazi propaganda developed a method of treating this subject which was different from and superior to all others. Still, not one Nazi slogan was new – not even Hitler's shrewd picture of a class struggle caused by the Jewish businessman who exploits his workers, while at the same time his brother in the factory courtyard incites them to strike.[32] The only new element was that the Nazi party demanded proof of non-Jewish descent for membership and that it remained, the Feder program notwithstanding, extremely vague about the actual measures to be taken against Jews once it came to power.[33] The Nazis placed the Jewish issue at the center of their propaganda in the sense that antisemitism was no longer a question of opinions about people different from the majority, or a concern of national politics,[34] but the intimate concern of every individual in his

31 See, for instance, Otto Bonhard, *Jüdische Geld- und Weltherrschaft?*, 1926, p. 57.

32 Hitler used this picture for the first time in 1922: 'Moses Kohn on the one side encourages his association to refuse the workers' demands, while his brother Isaac in the factory invites the masses . . .' to strike. (*Hitler's Speeches: 1922–1939*, ed. Baynes, London, 1942, p. 29.) It is noteworthy that no complete collection of Hitler's speeches was ever published in Nazi Germany, so that one is forced to resort to the English edition. That this was no accident can be seen from a bibliography compiled by Philipp Bouhler, *Die Reden des Führers nach der Machtübernahme*, 1940: only the public speeches were printed verbatim in the *Völkischer Beobachter*; as for speeches to the Fuehrerkorps and other party units, they were merely 'referred to' in that newspaper. They were not at any time meant for publication.

33 Feder's 25 points contain only standard measures demanded by all antisemitic groups: expulsion of naturalized Jews, and treatment of native Jews as aliens. Nazi antisemitic oratory was always much more radical than its program.

Waldemar Gurian, 'Antisemitism in Modern Germany,' in *Essays on Antisemitism*, ed. by Koppel S. Pinson, New York, 1946, p. 243, stresses the lack of originality in Nazi antisemitism: 'All these demands and views were not remarkable for their originality – they were self-evident in all nationalistic circles; what was remarkable was the demagogic and oratorical skill with which they were presented.'

34 A typical example of mere nationalistic antisemitism within the Nazi movement itself is Röhm who writes: 'And here again, my opinion differs from that of the national

personal existence; no one could be a member whose 'family tree' was not in order, and the higher the rank in the Nazi hierarchy, the farther back the family tree had to be traced.[35] By the same token, though less consistently, Bolshevism changed the Marxist doctrine of the inevitable final victory of the proletariat by organizing its members as 'born proletarians' and making other class origins shameful and scandalous.[36]

Nazi propaganda was ingenious enough to transform antisemitism into a principle of self-definition, and thus to eliminate it from the fluctuations of mere opinion. It used the persuasion of mass demagogy only as a preparatory step and never overestimated its lasting influence, whether in oratory or in print.[37] This gave the masses of atomized, undefinable, unstable and futile individuals a means of self-definition and identification which not only restored some of the self-respect they had formerly derived from their function in society, but also created a kind of spurious stability which made them better candidates for an organization. Through this kind of propaganda, the movement could set itself up as an artificial extension of the mass meeting and rationalize the essentially futile feelings of

---

philistine. Not: the Jew is to be blamed for everything! We are to be blamed for the fact that the Jew can rule today' (Ernst Röhm, *Die Geschichte eines Hochverräters*, 1933, Volksausgabe, p. 284).

35 SS applicants had to trace their ancestry back to 1750. Applicants for leading positions in the party were asked only three questions: 1. What have you done for the party? 2. Are you absolutely sound, physically, mentally, morally? 3. Is your family tree in order? See *Nazi Primer*.

It is characteristic for the affinity between the two systems that the elite and police formations of the Bolsheviks – the NKVD – also demanded proof of ancestry from their members. See F. Beck and W. Godin, *Russian Purge and the Extraction of Confession*, 1951.

36 Thus the totalitarian tendencies of McCarthyism in the United States showed most glaringly in the attempt not merely to persecute Communists, but to force every citizen to furnish proof of not being a Communist.

37 'One should not overestimate the influence of the press . . . it decreases in general while the influence of the organization increases' (Hadamovsky, *op. cit.*, p. 64). 'The newspapers are helpless when they are supposed to fight against the aggressive force of a living organization' (*ibid.*, p. 65). 'Power formations which have their origin in mere propaganda are fluctuating and can disappear quickly unless the violence of an organization supports the propaganda' (*ibid.*, p. 21).

self-importance and hysterical security that it offered to the isolated individuals of an atomized society.[38]

The same ingenious application of slogans, coined by others and tried out before, was apparent in the Nazis' treatment of other relevant issues. When public attention was equally focused on nationalism on one hand and socialism on the other, when the two were thought to be incompatible and actually constituted the ideological watershed between the Right and the Left, the 'National Socialist German Workers' Party' (Nazi) offered a synthesis supposed to lead to national unity, a semantic solution whose double trademark of 'German' and 'Worker' connected the nationalism of the Right with the internationalism of the Left. The very name of the Nazi movement stole the political contents of all other parties and pretended implicitly to incorporate them all. Combinations of supposedly antagonistic political doctrines (national-socialist, christian-social, etc.) had been tried, and successfully, before; but the Nazis realized their own combination in such a way that the whole struggle in Parliament between the socialists and the nationalists, between those who pretended to be workers first of all and those who were Germans first, appeared as a sham designed to hide ulterior sinister motives – for was not a member of the Nazi movement all these things at once?

It is interesting that even in their beginnings the Nazis were prudent enough never to use slogans which, like democracy, republic, dictatorship, or monarchy, indicated a specific form of government.[39] It is as though, in this one matter, they had always known that they would be entirely original. Every discussion about the actual form of their future government could be dismissed as empty talk about mere

38 'The mass-meeting is the strongest form of propaganda . . . [because] each individual feels more self-confident and more powerful in the unity of a mass' (*ibid*, p. 47). 'The enthusiasm of the moment becomes a principle and a spiritual attitude through organization and systematic training and discipline' (*ibid*., pp. 21–22).

39 In the isolated instances in which Hitler concerned himself with this question at all, he used to emphasize: 'Incidentally, I am not the head of a state in the sense of a dictator or monarch, but I am a leader of the German people' (see *Ausgewählte Reden des Führers*, 1939, p. 114). – Hans Frank expresses himself in the same spirit: 'The National Socialist Reich is not a dictatorial, let alone an arbitrary, regime. Rather, the National Socialist Reich rests on the mutual loyalty of the Führer and the people' (in *Recht und Verwaltung*, Munich, 1939, p. 15).

formalities – the state, according to Hitler, being only a 'means' for the conservation of the race, as the state, according to Bolshevik propaganda, is only an instrument in the struggle of classes.[40]

In another curious and roundabout way, however, the Nazis gave a propaganda answer to the question of what their future role would be, and that was in their use of the 'Protocols of the Elders of Zion' as a model for the future organization of the German masses for 'world empire.' The use of the Protocols was not restricted to the Nazis; hundreds of thousands of copies were sold in postwar Germany, and even their open adoption as a handbook of politics was not new.[41] Nevertheless, this forgery was mainly used for the purpose of denouncing the Jews and arousing the mob to the dangers of Jewish domination.[42] In

40 Hitler repeated many times: 'The state is only the means to an end. The end is: Conservation of race' (*Reden*, 1939, p. 125). He also stressed that his movement 'does not rest on the state idea, but is primarily based on the closed *Volksgemeinschaft*' (see *Reden*, 1933, p. 125, and the speech before the new generation of political leaders [*Führernachwuchs*], 1937, which is printed as an addendum in *Hitlers Tischgespräche*, p. 446). This, *mutatis mutandis*, is also the core of the complicated double talk which is Stalin's so-called 'state theory:' 'We are in favor of the State dying out, and at the same time we stand for the strengthening of the dictatorship of the proletariat which represents the most powerful and mighty authority of all forms of State which have existed up to the present day. The highest possible development of the power of the State with the object of preparing the conditions for the dying out of the State; that is the Marxist formula' (*op. cit., loc. cit.*).

41 Alexander Stein, *Adolf Hitler, Schüler der 'Weisen von Zion,'* Karlsbad, 1936, was the first to analyze by philological comparison the ideological identity of the teachings of the Nazis with that of the 'Elders of Zion.' See also R. M. Blank, *Adolf Hitler et les 'Protocoles des Sages de Sion,'* 1938.

The first to admit indebtedness to the teachings of the Protocols was Theodor Fritsch, the 'grand old man' of German postwar antisemitism. He writes in the epilogue to his edition of the *Protocols*, 1924: 'Our future statesmen and diplomats will have to learn from the oriental masters of villainy even the ABC of government, and for this purpose, the "Zionist Protocols" offer an excellent preparatory schooling.'

42 On the history of the Protocols, see John S. Curtiss, *An Appraisal of the Protocols of Zion*, 1942.

The fact that the Protocols were a forgery was irrelevant for propaganda purposes. The Russian publicist S. A. Nilus who published the second Russian edition in 1905 was already well aware of the doubtful character of this 'document' and added the obvious: 'But if it were possible to show its authenticity by documents or by the testimony of trustworthy witnesses, if it were possible to disclose the persons standing at the head of the world-wide plot . . . then . . . "the secret iniquity" could be broken . . .' Translation in Curtiss, *op. cit.*

terms of mere propaganda, the discovery of the Nazis was that the masses were not so frightened by Jewish world rule as they were interested in how it could be done, that the popularity of the Protocols was based on admiration and eagerness to learn rather than on hatred, and that it would be wise to stay as close as possible to certain of their outstanding formulas, as in the case of the famous slogan: 'Right is what is good for the German people,' which was copied from the Protocols' 'Everything that benefits the Jewish people is morally right and sacred.'[43]

The Protocols are a very curious and noteworthy document in many respects. Apart from their cheap Machiavellianism, their essential political characteristic is that in their crackpot manner they touch on every important political issue of the time. They are antinational in principle and picture the nation-state as a colossus with feet of clay. They discard national sovereignty and believe, as Hitler once put it, in a world empire on a national basis.[44] They are not satisfied with revolution in a particular country, but aim at the conquest and rule of the world. They promise the people that, regardless of superiority in numbers, territory, and state power, they will be able to achieve world conquest through organization alone. To be sure, part of their persuasive strength derives from very old elements of superstition. The notion of the uninterrupted existence of an international sect that has pursued the same revolutionary aims since antiquity is very old[45] and has played a role in political backstairs literature ever since the French Revolution, even though it did not occur to anyone writing

---

Hitler did not need Nilus to use the same trick: the best proof of their authenticity is that they have been proved to be a forgery. And he also adds the argument of their 'plausibility:' 'What many Jews may do unconsciously is here consciously made clear. And that is what counts' (*Mein Kampf*, Book I, chapter xi).

43 Fritsch, *op. cit.*, '[*Der Juden*] *oberster Grundsatz lautet: "Alles, was dem Volke Juda nützt, ist moralisch und ist heilig." '*

44 'World Empires spring from a national basis, but they expand soon far beyond it' (*Reden*).

45 Henri Rollin, *L'Apocalypse de Notre Temps*, Paris, 1939, who considers the popularity of the Protocols to be second only to the Bible (p. 40), shows the similarity between them and the *Monita Secreta*, first published in 1612 and still sold in 1939 on the streets of Paris, which claim to reveal a Jesuit conspiracy 'that justifies all villainies and all uses of violence . . . This is a real campaign against the established order' (p. 32).

at the end of the eighteenth century that the 'revolutionary sect,' this 'peculiar nation . . . in the midst of all civilized nations,' could be the Jews.[46]

It was the motif of a global conspiracy in the Protocols which appealed most to the masses, for it corresponded so well to the new power situation. (Hitler very early promised that the Nazi movement would 'transcend the narrow limits of modern nationalism,'[47] and during the war attempts were made within the SS to erase the word 'nation' from the National Socialist vocabulary altogether.) Only world powers seemed still to have a chance of independent survival and only global politics a chance of lasting results. That this situation should frighten the smaller nations which are not world powers is only too understandable. The Protocols seemed to show a way out that did not depend upon objective unalterable conditions, but only on the power of organization.

Nazi propaganda, in other words, discovered in 'the supranational

---

46 This whole literature is well represented by the Chevalier de Malet, *Recherches politiques et historiques qui prouvent l'existence d'une secte révolutionnaire*, 1817, who quotes extensively from earlier authors. The heroes of the French Revolution are to him '*mannequins*' of an '*agence secrète*,' the agents of the Freemasons. But Freemasonry is only the name which his contemporaries have given to a 'revolutionary sect' which has existed at all times and whose policy always has been to attack, 'remaining behind the scenes, manipulating the strings of the marionettes it thought convenient to put on the scene.' He starts by saying: 'Probably, it will be difficult to believe in a plan which was formed in antiquity and always followed with the same constancy . . . the authors of the Revolution are no more French than they are German, Italian, English, etc. They constitute a peculiar nation which was born and has grown in darkness, in the midst of all civilized nations, with the aim of subduing them all to its domination.'

For an extensive discussion of this literature, see E. Lesueur, *La Franc-Maçonnerie Artésienne au 18e siècle*, Bibliothèque d'Histoire Révolutionnaire, 1914. How persistent these conspiracy legends are in themselves, even under normal circumstances, can be seen by the enormous anti-Freemason crackpot literature in France, which is hardly less extensive than its antisemitic counterpart. A kind of compendium of all theories which saw in the French Revolution the product of secret conspiracy societies can be found in G. Bord, *La Franc-Maçonnerie en France des origines à 1815*, 1908.

47 *Reden*. – See the transcript of a session of the SS Committee on Labor Questions at SS headquarters in Berlin on January 12, 1943, where it was suggested that the word 'nation,' a concept being burdened with connotations of liberalism, should be eliminated as it was inadequate for the Germanic peoples (Document 705 – PS in *Nazi Conspiracy and Aggression*, V, 515).

because intensely national Jew' [48] the forerunner of the German master of the world and assured the masses that 'the nations that have been the first to see through the Jew and have been the first to fight him are going to take his place in the domination of the world.' [49] The delusion of an already existing Jewish world domination formed the basis for the illusion of future German world domination. This was what Himmler had in mind when he stated that 'we owe the art of government to the Jews,' namely, to the Protocols which 'the Führer [had] learned by heart.' [50] Thus the Protocols presented world conquest as a practical possibility, implied that the whole affair was only a question of inspired or shrewd know-how, and that nobody stood in the way of a German victory over the entire world but a patently small people, the Jews, who ruled it without possessing instruments of violence – an easy opponent, therefore, once their secret was discovered and their method emulated on a larger scale.

Nazi propaganda concentrated all these new and promising vistas in one concept which it labeled *Volksgemeinschaft*. This new community, tentatively realized in the Nazi movement in the pretotalitarian atmosphere, was based on the absolute equality of all Germans, an equality not of rights but of nature, and their absolute difference from all other people. [51] After the Nazis came to power, this concept gradually lost its importance and gave way to a general contempt for the German people (which the Nazis had always harbored but could not very well show publicly before) on one hand, [52] and a great eagerness,

48 *Hitler's Speeches*, ed. Baynes, p. 6.

49 Goebbels, *op. cit.*, p. 377. This promise, implied in all antisemitic propaganda of the Nazi type, was prepared by Hitler's 'The most extreme contrast to the Aryan is the Jew' (*Mein Kampf*, Book I, chapter xi).

50 Dossier Kersten, in the Centre de Documentation Juive.

51 Hitler's early promise (*Reden*), 'I shall never recognize that other nations have the same right as the German,' became official doctrine: 'The foundation of the national socialist outlook in life is the perception of the unlikeness of men' (*Nazi Primer*, p. 5).

52 For instance, Hitler in 1923: 'The German people consists for one third of heroes, for another third, of cowards, while the rest are traitors' (*Hitler's Speeches*, ed. Baynes, p. 76).

After the seizure of power this trend became more brutally outspoken. See, for instance, Goebbels in 1934: 'Who are the people to criticize? Party members? No. The rest of the German people? They should consider themselves lucky to be still alive. It would be too much of a good thing altogether, if those who live at our mercy should be

on the other, to enlarge their own ranks from 'Aryans' of other nations, an idea which had played only a small role in the prepower stage of Nazi propaganda.[53] The *Volksgemeinschaft* was merely the propagandistic preparation for an 'Aryan' racial society which in the end would have doomed all peoples, including the Germans.

To a certain extent, the *Volksgemeinschaft* was the Nazis' attempt to counter the Communist promise of a classless society. The propaganda appeal of the one over the other seems obvious if we disregard all ideological implications. While both promised to level all social and property differences, the classless society had the obvious connotation that everybody would be leveled to the status of a factory worker, while the *Volksgemeinschaft*, with its connotation of conspiracy for world conquest, held out a reasonable hope that every German could eventually become a factory owner. The even greater advantage of the *Volksgemeinschaft*, however, was that its establishment did not have to wait for some future time and did not depend upon objective conditions: it could be realized immediately in the fictitious world of the movement.

The true goal of totalitarian propaganda is not persuasion but organization – the 'accumulation of power without the possession of the means of violence.'[54] For this purpose, originality in ideological content can only be considered an unnecessary obstacle. It is no

---

allowed to criticize.' Quoted from Kohn-Bramstedt, *op. cit.*, pp. 178–179. – During the war Hitler declared: 'I am nothing but a magnet constantly moving across the German nation and extracting the steel from this people. And I have often stated that the time will come when all worth-while men in Germany are going to be in my camp. And those who will not be in my camp are worthless anyway.' Even then it was clear to Hitler's immediate environment what would happen to those who 'are worthless anyway' (see *Der grossdeutsche Freiheitskampf. Reden Hitlers vom 1. 9. 1939–10. 3. 1940*, p. 174). – Himmler meant the same when he said: 'The Führer does not think in German, but in Germanic terms' (Dossier Kersten, cf. above), except that we know from *Hitlers Tischgespräche* (pp. 315 ff.) that in those days he was already making fun even of the Germanic 'clamor' and thought in 'Aryan terms.'

53 Himmler in a speech to SS leaders at Kharkov in April, 1943 (*Nazi Conspiracy*, IV, 572 ff.): 'I very soon formed a Germanic SS in the various countries . . .' An early prepower indication of this non-national policy was given by Hitler (*Reden*): 'We shall certainly also receive into the new master class representatives of other nations, *i.e.*, those who deserve it because of their participation in our fight.'

54 Hadamovsky, *op. cit.*

accident that the two totalitarian movements of our time, so fright-fully 'new' in methods of rule and ingenious in forms of organization, have never preached a new doctrine, have never invented an ideology which was not already popular.[55] Not the passing successes of dema-gogy win the masses, but the visible reality and power of a 'living organization.' [56] Hitler's brilliant gifts as a mass orator did not win him his position in the movement but rather misled his opponents into underestimating him as a simple demagogue, and Stalin was able to defeat the greater orator of the Russian Revolution.[57] What distinguishes the totalitarian leaders and dictators is rather the simple-minded, single-minded purposefulness with which they choose those elements from existing ideologies which are best fitted to become the fundaments of another, entirely fictitious world. The fiction of the Pro-tocols was as adequate as the fiction of a Trotskyite conspiracy, for both contained an element of plausibility – the nonpublic influence of the Jews in the past; the struggle for power between Trotsky and Stalin – which not even the fictitious world of totalitarianism can safely do without. Their art consists in using, and at the same time transcending, the elements of reality, of verifiable experiences, in the chosen fiction, and in generalizing them into regions which then are definitely removed from all possible control by individual experience. With such generalizations, totalitarian propaganda establishes a world

55 Heiden, *op. cit.*, p. 139: Propaganda is not 'the art of instilling an opinion in the masses. Actually it is the art of receiving an opinion from the masses.'

56 Hadamovsky, *op. cit.*, *passim*. The term is taken from Hitler, *Mein Kampf* (Book II, chapter xi), where the 'living organization' of a movement is contrasted with the 'dead mechanism' of a bureaucratic party.

57 It would be a serious error to interpret totalitarian leaders in terms of Max Weber's category of the 'charismatic leadership.' See Hans Gerth, 'The Nazi Party,' in *American Journal of Sociology*, 1940, Vol. XLV. (A similar misunderstanding is also the shortcom-ing of Heiden's biography, *op. cit.*) Gerth describes Hitler as the charismatic leader of a bureaucratic party. This alone, in his opinion, can account for the fact that 'however flagrantly actions may have contradicted words, nothing could disrupt the firmly dis-ciplinary organization.' (This contradiction, by the way, is much more characteristic of Stalin who 'took care always to say the opposite of what he did, and to do the opposite of what he said.' Souvarine, *op. cit.*, p. 431.)

For the source of this misunderstanding see Alfred von Martin, 'Zur Soziologie der Gegenwart,' in *Zeitschrift für Kulturgeschichte*, Band 27, and Arnold Koettgen, 'Die Gesetzmässigkeit der Verwaltung im Führerstaat,' in *Reichsverwaltungsblatt*, 1936, both of whom characterize the Nazi state as a bureaucracy with charismatic leadership.

fit to compete with the real one, whose main handicap is that it is not logical, consistent, and organized. The consistency of the fiction and strictness of the organization make it possible for the generalization eventually to survive the explosion of more specific lies – the power of the Jews after their helpless slaughter, the sinister global conspiracy of Trotskyites after their liquidation in Soviet Russia and the murder of Trotsky.

The stubbornness with which totalitarian dictators have clung to their original lies in the face of absurdity is more than superstitious gratitude to what turned the trick, and, at least in the case of Stalin, cannot be explained by the psychology of the liar whose very success may make him his own last victim. Once these propaganda slogans are integrated into a 'living organization,' they cannot be safely eliminated without wrecking the whole structure. The assumption of a Jewish world conspiracy was transformed by totalitarian propaganda from an objective, arguable matter into the chief element of the Nazi reality; the point was that the Nazis *acted* as though the world were dominated by the Jews and needed a counterconspiracy to defend itself. Racism for them was no longer a debatable theory of dubious scientific value, but was being realized every day in the functioning hierarchy of a political organization in whose framework it would have been very 'unrealistic' to question it. Similarly, Bolshevism no longer needs to win an argument about class struggle, internationalism, and unconditional dependence of the welfare of the proletariat on the welfare of the Soviet Union; the functioning organization of the Comintern is more convincing than any argument or mere ideology can ever be.

The fundamental reason for the superiority of totalitarian propaganda over the propaganda of other parties and movements is that its content, for the members of the movement at any rate, is no longer an objective issue about which people may have opinions, but has become as real and untouchable an element in their lives as the rules of arithmetic. The organization of the entire texture of life according to an ideology can be fully carried out only under a totalitarian regime. In Nazi Germany, questioning the validity of racism and antisemitism when nothing mattered but race origin, when a career depended upon an 'Aryan' physiognomy (Himmler used to select the applicants for the SS from photographs) and the amount of food upon the number of one's Jewish grandparents, was like questioning the existence of the world.

The advantages of a propaganda that constantly 'adds the power of organization'[58] to the feeble and unreliable voice of argument, and thereby realizes, so to speak, on the spur of the moment, whatever it says, are obvious beyond demonstration. Foolproof against arguments based on a reality which the movements promised to change, against a counterpropaganda disqualified by the mere fact that it belongs to or defends a world which the shiftless masses cannot and will not accept, it can be disproved only by another, a stronger or better, reality.

It is in the moment of defeat that the inherent weakness of totalitarian propaganda becomes visible. Without the force of the movement, its members cease at once to believe in the dogma for which yesterday they still were ready to sacrifice their lives. The moment the movement, that is, the fictitious world which sheltered them, is destroyed, the masses revert to their old status of isolated individuals who either happily accept a new function in a changed world or sink back into their old desperate superfluousness. The members of totalitarian movements, utterly fanatical as long as the movement exists, will not follow the example of religious fanatics and die the death of martyrs (even though they were only too willing to die the death of robots).[59] Rather they will quietly give up the movement as a bad bet and look around for another promising fiction or wait until the former fiction regains enough strength to establish another mass movement.

The experience of the Allies who vainly tried to locate one self-confessed and convinced Nazi among the German people, 90 per cent of whom probably had been sincere sympathizers at one time or another, is not to be taken simply as a sign of human weakness or gross opportunism. Nazism as an ideology had been so fully 'realized'

58 Hadamovsky, *op. cit.*, p. 21. For totalitarian purposes it is a mistake to propagate their ideology through teaching or persuasion. In the words of Robert Ley, it can be neither 'taught' nor 'learned,' but only 'exercised' and 'practiced' (see *Der Weg zur Ordensburg*, undated).

59 R. Hoehn, one of the outstanding Nazi political theorists, interpreted this lack of a doctrine or even a common set of ideals and beliefs in the movement in his *Reichs-gemeinschaft und Volksgemeinschaft*, Hamburg, 1935: 'From the point of view of a folk community, every community of values is destructive' (p. 83).

that its content ceased to exist as an independent set of doctrines, lost its intellectual existence, so to speak; destruction of the reality therefore left almost nothing behind, least of all the fanaticism of believers.

## II: Totalitarian Organization

The forms of totalitarian organization, as distinguished from their ideological content and propaganda slogans, are completely new.[60] They are designed to translate the propaganda lies of the movement, woven around a central fiction – the conspiracy of the Jews, or the Trotskyites, or 300 families, etc. – into a functioning reality, to build up, even under nontotalitarian circumstances, a society whose members act and react according to the rules of a fictitious world. In contrast with seemingly similar parties and movements of Fascist or Socialist, nationalist or Communist orientation, all of which back up their propaganda with terrorism as soon as they have reached a certain stage of extremism (which mostly depends on the stage of desperation of their members), the totalitarian movement is really in earnest about its propaganda, and this earnestness is expressed much more frighteningly in the organization of its followers than in the physical liquidation of its opponents. Organization and propaganda (rather than terror and propaganda) are two sides of the same coin.[61]

The most strikingly new organizational device of the movements in their prepower stage is the creation of front organizations, the distinction drawn between party members and sympathizers. Compared to this invention, other typically totalitarian features, such as the appointment of functionaries from above and the eventual monopolization of appointments by one man are secondary in importance. The so-called 'leader principle' is in itself not totalitarian; it has borrowed

60 Hitler, discussing the relationship between *Weltanschauung* and organization, admits as a matter of course that the Nazis took over from other groups and parties the 'racial idea' (*die völkische Idee*) and acted as though they were its only representatives because they were the first to base a fighting organization on it and to formulate it for practical purposes. *Op. cit.*, Book II, chapter v.

61 See Hitler, 'Propaganda and Organization,' in *op. cit.*, Book II, chapter xi.

certain features from authoritarianism and military dictatorship which have greatly contributed toward obscuring and belittling the essentially totalitarian phenomenon. If the functionaries appointed from above possessed real authority and responsibility, we would have to do with a hierarchical structure in which authority and power are delegated and governed by laws. Much the same is true for the organization of an army and the military dictatorship established after its model; here, absolute power of command from the top down and absolute obedience from the bottom up correspond to the situation of extreme danger in combat, which is precisely why they are not totalitarian. A hierarchically organized chain of command means that the commander's power is dependent on the whole hierarchic system in which he operates. Every hierarchy, no matter how authoritarian in its direction, and every chain of command, no matter how arbitrary or dictatorial the content of orders, tends to stabilize and would have restricted the total power of the leader of a totalitarian movement.[62] In the language of the Nazis, the never-resting, dynamic 'will of the Fuehrer' – and not his orders, a phrase that might imply a fixed and circumscribed authority – becomes the 'supreme law' in a totalitarian state.[63] It is only from the position in which the totalitarian movement, thanks to its unique organization, places the leader – only from his functional importance for the movement – that the leader principle develops its totalitarian character. This is also borne out by the fact that both in Hitler's and Stalin's case the actual leader principle crystallized only rather slowly, and parallel with the progressive 'totalitarianization' of the movement.[64]

62 Himmler's vehemently urgent request 'not to issue any decree concerning the definition of the term "Jew" ' is a case in point; for 'with all these foolish commitments we will only be tying our hands' (Nuremberg Document No. 626, letter to Berger dated July 28, 1942, photostatic copy at the Centre de Documentation Juive).
63 The formulation 'The will of the Fuehrer is the supreme law' is found in all official rules and regulations governing the conduct of the Party and the SS. The best source on this subject is Otto Gauweiler, *Rechtseinrichtungen und Rechtsaufgaben der Bewegung*, 1939.
64 Heiden, *op. cit.*, p. 292, reports the following difference between the first and the following editions of *Mein Kampf*: The first edition proposes the election of party officials who only after their election are vested with 'unlimited power and authority'; all following editions establish appointment of party officials from above by the next higher leader. Naturally, for the stability of totalitarian regimes the appointment from above is a much more important principle than the 'unlimited authority' of the

An anonymity which contributes greatly to the weirdness of the whole phenomenon clouds the beginnings of this new organizational structure. We do not know who first decided to organize fellow-travelers into front organizations, who first saw in vaguely sympathizing masses – upon whom all parties used to count at election day but whom they considered to be too fluctuating for membership – not only a reservoir from which to draw party members, but a decisive force in itself. The early Communist-inspired organizations of sympathizers, such as the Friends of the Soviet Union or the Red Relief associations, developed into front organizations but were originally nothing more or less than what their names indicated: a gathering of sympathizers for financial or other (for instance, legal) help. Hitler was the first to say that each movement should divide the masses which have been won through propaganda into two categories, sympathizers and members. This in itself is interesting enough; even more significant is that he based this division upon a more general philosophy according to which most people are too lazy and cowardly for anything more than mere theoretical insight, and only a minority want to fight for their convictions.[65] Hitler, consequently, was the first to devise a conscious policy of constantly enlarging the ranks of sympathizers while at the same time keeping the number of

---

appointed official. In practice, the subleaders' authority was decisively limited through the Leader's absolute sovereignty. See below.

Stalin, coming from the conspiratory apparatus of the Bolshevik party, probably never thought this a problem. To him, appointments in the party machine were a question of accumulation of personal power. (Yet, it was only in the thirties, after he had studied Hitler's example, that he let himself be addressed as 'leader.') It must be admitted, however, that he could easily justify these methods by quoting Lenin's theory that 'the history of all countries shows that the working class, exclusively by its own effort, is able to develop only trade-union consciousness,' and that its leadership therefore necessarily comes from without. (See *What is to be done?*, first published in 1902, in *Collected Works*, Vol. IV, Book II.) The point is that Lenin considered the Communist Party as the 'most progressive' part of the working class and at the same time 'the lever of political organization' which 'directs the whole mass of the proletariat,' *i.e.*, an organization outside and above the class. (See W. H. Chamberlin, *The Russian Revolution, 1917–1921*, New York, 1935, II, 361.) Nevertheless, Lenin did not question the validity of inner-party democracy, though he was inclined to restrict democracy to the working class itself.

65 Hitler, *op. cit.*, Book II, chapter xi.

party members strictly limited.[66] This notion of a minority of party members surrounded by a majority of sympathizers comes very close to the later reality of front organizations – a term which indeed expresses most aptly their eventual function, and indicates the relationship between members and sympathizers within the movement itself. For the front organizations of sympathizers are no less essential to the functioning of the movement than its actual membership.

The front organizations surround the movements' membership with a protective wall which separates them from the outside, normal world; at the same time, they form a bridge back into normalcy, without which the members in the prepower stage would feel too sharply the differences between their beliefs and those of normal people, between the lying fictitiousness of their own and the reality of the normal world. The ingeniousness of this device during the movements' struggle for power is that the front organizations not only isolate the members but offer them a semblance of outside normalcy which wards off the impact of true reality more effectively than mere indoctrination. It is the difference between his own and the fellow-traveler's attitudes which confirms a Nazi or Bolshevik in his belief in the fictitious explanation of the world, for the fellow-traveler has the same convictions, after all, albeit in a more 'normal,' *i.e.*, less fanatic, more confused form; so that to the party member it appears that anyone whom the movement has not expressly singled out as an enemy (a Jew, a capitalist, etc.) is on his side, that the world is full of secret allies who merely cannot, as yet, summon up the necessary strength of mind and character to draw the logical conclusions from their own convictions.[67]

The world at large, on the other side, usually gets its first glimpse of a totalitarian movement through its front organizations. The

66 *Ibid.* This principle was strictly enforced as soon as the Nazis seized power. Of 7 million members of the Hitler Youth only 50,000 were accepted for party membership in 1937. See the preface by H. L. Childs to *The Nazi Primer*. – Compare also Gottfried Neesse, 'Die verfassungsrechtliche Gestaltung der Ein-Partei,' in *Zeitschift für die gesamte Staatswissenschaft*, 1938, Band 98, p. 678: 'Even the One-Party must never grow to the point where it would embrace the whole population. It is "total" because of its ideological influence on the nation.'

67 See Hitler's differentiation between the 'radical people' who alone were prepared to become members of the party and hundreds of thousands of sympathizers who were too 'cowardly' to make the necessary sacrifice. *Op. cit., loc. cit.*

sympathizers, who are to all appearances still innocuous fellow-citizens in a nontotalitarian society, can hardly be called single-minded fanatics; through them, the movements make their fantastic lies more generally acceptable, can spread their propaganda in milder, more respectable forms, until the whole atmosphere is poisoned with totalitarian elements which are hardly recognizable as such but appear to be normal political reactions or opinions. The fellow-traveler organizations surround the totalitarian movements with a mist of normality and respectability that fools the membership about the true character of the outside world as much as it does the outside world about the true character of the movement. The front organization functions both ways: as the façade of the totalitarian movement to the nontotalitarian world, and as the façade of this world, to the inner hierarchy of the movement.

Even more striking than this relationship is the fact that it is repeated on different levels within the movement itself. As party members are related to and separated from the fellow-travelers, so are the elite formations of the movement related to and separated from the ordinary members. If the fellow-traveler still appears to be a normal inhabitant of the outside world who has adopted the totalitarian creed as one may adopt the program of an ordinary party, the ordinary member of the Nazi or Bolshevik movement still belongs, in many respects, to the surrounding world: his professional and social relationships are not yet absolutely determined by his party membership, although he may realize – as distinguished from the mere sympathizer – that in case of conflict between his party allegiance and his private life, the former is supposed to be decisive. The member of a militant group, on the other hand, is wholly identified with the movement; he has no profession and no private life independent of it. Just as the sympathizers constitute a protective wall around the members of the movement and represent the outside world to them, so the ordinary membership surrounds the militant groups and represents the normal outside world to them.

A definite advantage of this structure is that it blunts the impact of one of the basic totalitarian tenets – that the world is divided into two gigantic hostile camps, one of which is the movement, and that the movement can and must fight the whole world – a claim which prepares the way for the indiscriminate aggressiveness of totalitarian regimes in power. Through a carefully graduated hierarchy of militancy in which each rank is the higher level's image of the nontotalitarian world because it is less militant and its members less totally organized, the shock of the terrifying and monstrous totalitarian dichotomy is vitiated and never fully realized; this type of organization prevents its members' ever being directly confronted with the outside world, whose hostility remains for them a mere ideological assumption. They are so well protected against the reality of the nontotalitarian world that they constantly underestimate the tremendous risks of totalitarian politics.

There is no doubt that the totalitarian movements attack the status quo more radically than did any of the earlier revolutionary parties. They can afford this radicalism, apparently so unsuited to mass organizations, because their organization offers a temporary substitute for ordinary, nonpolitical life, which totalitarianism actually seeks to abolish. The whole world of nonpolitical social relationships, from which the 'professional revolutionary' had to cut himself off or had to accept as they were, exists in the form of less militant groups in the movement; within this hierarchically organized world the fighters for world conquest and world revolution are never exposed to the shock inevitably generated by the discrepancy between 'revolutionary' beliefs and the 'normal' world. The reason why the movements in their prepower, revolutionary stage can attract so many ordinary philistines is that their members live in a fool's paradise of normalcy; the party members are surrounded by the normal world of sympathizers and the elite formations by the normal world of ordinary members.

Another advantage of the totalitarian pattern is that it can be repeated indefinitely and keeps the organization in a state of fluidity which permits it constantly to insert new layers and define new degrees of militancy. The whole history of the Nazi party can be told in terms of new formations within the Nazi movement. The SA, the stormtroopers (founded in 1922), were the first Nazi formation which was supposed to be more militant than the party itself;[68] in 1926, the SS was founded as the elite formation of the SA; after three years, the SS was separated from the SA and put under Himmler's command; it

68 See Hitler: chapter on the SA in *op. cit.*, Book II, chapter ix, second part.

took Himmler only a few more years to repeat the same game within the SS. One after the other, and each more militant than its predecessor, there now came into being, first, the Shock Troops,[69] then the Death Head units (the 'guard units for the concentration camps'), which later were merged to form the Armed SS (*Waffen-SS*), finally the Security Service (the 'ideological intelligence service of the Party,' and its executive arm for the 'negative population policy') and the Office for Questions of Race and Resettlement (*Rasse- und Siedlungswesen*), whose tasks were of a 'positive kind' – all of them developing out of the General SS, whose members, except for the higher Fuehrer Corps, remained in their civilian occupations. To all these new formations the member of the General SS now stood in the same relationship as the SA-man to the SS-man, or the party member to the SA-man, or the member of a front organization to a party member.[70] Now

69 In translating *Verfügungstruppe*, *i.e.*, the special units of the SS which originally were supposed to be at Hitler's special disposal, as shock troops, I follow O. C. Giles, *The Gestapo*, Oxford Pamphlets on World Affairs, No. 36, 1940.

70 The most important source for the organization and history of the SS is Himmler's 'Wesen und Aufgabe der SS und der Polizei,' in *Sammelheft ausgewählter Vorträge und Reden*, 1939. In the course of the war, when the ranks of the *Waffen-SS* had to be filled with enlistments owing to losses at the front, the *Waffen-SS* lost its elite character within the SS to such an extent that now the General SS, *i.e.*, the higher Fuehrer Corps, once again represented the real nuclear elite of the movement.

Very revealing documentary material for this last phase of the SS can be found in the archives of the Hoover Library, Himmler File, Folder 278. It shows that the SS went about its recruiting both among foreign workers and the native population by deliberately imitating the methods and rules of the French Foreign Legion. Enlistment among the Germans was based on an order by Hitler (never published) dated December, 1942, according to which 'the 1925 class [should] be drafted into the *Waffen-SS*' (Himmler in a letter to Bormann). Conscription and enlistment were handled ostensibly on a voluntary basis. Precisely what this amounted to can be seen from numerous reports of SS leaders entrusted with this assignment. A report dated July 21, 1943, describes how the police surround the hall in which French workers are to be enlisted, how the French first sing the *Marseillaise* and then try to jump out of the windows. Attempts among German youth were scarcely more encouraging. Although they were put under extraordinary pressure and told that 'they certainly would not want to join the "dirty gray hordes"' of the army, only 18 out of 220 members of the Hitler Youth reported for duty (according to a report of April 30, 1943, submitted by Häussler, head of Conscription Center Southwest of the *Waffen-SS*); all others preferred to join the Wehrmacht. It is possible that the greater losses of the SS, as compared with those of the Wehrmacht, entered into their decisions (see Karl O. Paetel, 'Die SS,' in *Vierteljahreshefte für Zeitgeschichte*, January, 1954). But that this factor alone could not have been decisive is proved

the General SS was charged not only with 'safeguarding the ... embodiments of the National Socialist idea,' but also with 'protecting the members of all special SS cadres from becoming detached from the movement itself.' [71]

This fluctuating hierarchy, with its constant addition of new layers and shifts in authority, is well known from secret control bodies, the secret police or espionage services, where new controls are always needed to control the controllers. In the prepower stage of the movements, total espionage is not yet possible; but the fluctuating hierarchy, similar to that of secret services, makes it possible, even without actual power, to degrade any rank or group that wavers or shows signs of decreasing radicalism by the mere insertion of a new more radical layer, hence driving the older group automatically in the direction of the front organization and away from the center of the movement. Thus, the Nazi elite formations were primarily inner-party organizations: the SA rose to the position of a superparty when the party appeared to lose in radicality and was then in turn and for similar reasons superseded by the SS.

The military value of the totalitarian elite formations, especially of the SA and the SS, is frequently overrated, while their purely inner-party significance has been somewhat neglected.[72] None of the Fascist Shirt-organizations was founded for specific defensive or aggressive purposes, though defense of the leaders or the ordinary party members usually was cited as a pretext.[73] The paramilitary form of Nazi and Fascist elite groups was the result of their being founded

by the following: As early as January, 1940, Hitler had ordered the drafting of SA-men into the *Waffen-SS*, and the results for Koenigsberg, based on a report that has been preserved, were listed as follows: 1807 SA-men were called up 'for police service'; of these, 1094 failed to report; 631 were found to be unfit; 82 were fit for service in the SS.

71 Werner Best, *op. cit.*, 1941, p. 99.

72 This, however, was not the fault of Hitler, who always insisted that the very name of the SA (*Sturmabteilung*) indicated that it was only 'a section of the movement' just like other party formations such as the propaganda department, the newspaper, the scientific institutes, etc. He also tried to dispel the illusions of the possible military value of a paramilitary formation and wanted training to be carried through according to the needs of the party and not according to the principles of an army. *Op. cit., loc. cit.*

73 The official reason for the foundation of the SA was protection of Nazi meetings, while the original task of the SS was protection of Nazi leaders.

as 'instruments of the ideological fight of the movement' [74] against the widespread pacifism in Europe after the first World War. For totalitarian purposes it was much more important to set up, as 'the expression of an aggressive attitude,' [75] a fake army which resembled as closely as possible the bogus army of the pacifists (unable to understand the constitutional place of an army within the political body, the pacifists had denounced all military institutions as bands of willful murderers), than to have a troop of well-trained soldiers. The SA and the SS were certainly model organizations for arbitrary violence and murder; they were hardly as well trained as the Black Reichswehr, and they were not equipped for a fight against regular troops. Militaristic propaganda was more popular in postwar Germany than military training, and uniforms did not enhance the military value of paramilitary troops, though they were useful as a clear indication of the abolition of civilian standards and morals; somehow these uniforms eased considerably the consciences of the murderers and also made them even more receptive to unquestioning obedience and unquestioned authority. Despite these militaristic trappings, the inner-party faction of the Nazis, which was primarily nationalistic and militaristic and therefore viewed the paramilitary troops not as mere party formations but as an illegal enlargement of the Reichswehr (which had been limited by the terms of the Versailles Peace Treaty), was the first to be liquidated. Röhm, the leader of the SA stormtroopers, had indeed dreamed of and negotiated for incorporation of his SA into the Reichswehr after the Nazis seized power. He was killed by Hitler because he tried to transform the new Nazi regime into a military dictatorship. [76] Hitler had

---

74 Hitler, *op. cit.*, *loc. cit.*

75 Ernst Bayer, *Die SA*, Berlin, 1938. Translation quoted from *Nazi Conspiracy*, IV.

76 Röhm's autobiography shows clearly how little his political convictions agreed with those of the Nazis. He always desired a *'Soldatenstaat'* and always insisted on the *'Primat des Soldaten vor dem Politiker' (op. cit.*, p. 349). Especially telling for his nontotalitarian attitude, or rather for his inability even to understand totalitarianism and its 'total' claim, is the following passage: 'I don't see why the following three things should not be compatible: my loyalty to the hereditary prince of the house of Wittelsbach and heir to Bavaria's crown; my admiration for the quartermaster-general of the World War [*i.e.*, Ludendorff], who today embodies the conscience of the German people; and my comradeship with the harbinger and bearer of the political struggle, Adolf Hitler' (p. 348). What ultimately cost Röhm his head was that after the seizure of power he envisioned a Fascist dictatorship patterned after the Italian regime, in which the

made it clear several years before that such a development was not desired by the Nazi movement when he dismissed Röhm – a real soldier whose experience in the war and in the organization of the Black Reichswehr would have made him indispensable to a serious military training program – from his position as chief of the SA and chose Himmler, a man without the slightest knowledge of military matters, as reorganizer of the SS.

Apart from the importance of the elite formations to the organizational structure of the movement, where they comprised the changing nuclei of militancy, their paramilitary character must be understood in connection with other professional party organizations, such as those for teachers, lawyers, physicians, students, university professors, technicians, and workers. All these were primarily duplicates of existing nontotalitarian professional societies, paraprofessional as the stormtroopers were paramilitary. It was characteristic that the more clearly the European Communist parties became branches of a Moscow-directed Bolshevik movement, the more they, too, used their front organizations to compete with existing purely professional groups. The difference between the Nazis and the Bolsheviks in this respect was only that the Nazis had a pronounced tendency to consider these paraprofessional formations as part of the party elite, while the Communists preferred to recruit from them the material for their front organizations. The important factor for the movements is that, even before they seize power, they give the impression that all elements of society are embodied in their ranks. (The ultimate goal of Nazi propaganda was to organize the whole German people as sympathizers.[77]) The Nazis went one step further in this game and set up a

---

Nazi party would 'break the chains of the party' and 'itself become the state,' which was exactly what Hitler meant to avoid under all circumstances. See Ernst Röhm, *Warum SA?*, speech before the diplomatic corps, December, 1933, Berlin, undated.

Within the Nazi party, the possibility of an SA–Reichswehr plot against the rule of the SS and the police apparently never was quite forgotten. Hans Frank, Governor General of Poland, in 1942, eight years after the murder of Röhm and General Schleicher, was suspected of wishing 'after the war . . . to inaugurate the greatest fight for justice [against the SS] with the assistance of the Armed Forces and the SA' (*Nazi Conspiracy*, VI, 747).

77 Hitler, *op. cit.*, Book II, chapter xi, states that propaganda attempts to force a doctrine on the whole people while the organization incorporates only a comparatively small proportion of its more militant members. – Compare also G. Neesse, *op. cit.*

series of fake departments which were modeled after the regular state administration, such as their own department of foreign affairs, education, culture, sport, etc. None of these institutions had more professional value than the imitation of the army represented by the stormtroopers, but together they created a perfect world of appearances in which every reality in the nontotalitarian world was slavishly duplicated in the form of humbug.

This technique of duplication, certainly useless for the direct overthrow of government, proved extremely fruitful in the work of undermining actively existing institutions and in the 'decomposition of the status quo'[78] which totalitarian organizations invariably prefer to an open show of force. If it is the task of movements 'to bore their way like polyps into all positions of power,'[79] then they must be ready for any specific social and political position. In accordance with their claim to total domination, every single organized group in the nontotalitarian society is felt to present a specific challenge to the movement to destroy it; every one needs, so to speak, a specific instrument of destruction. The practical value of the fake organizations came to light when the Nazis seized power and were ready at once to destroy the existing teachers' organizations with another teachers' organization, the existing lawyers' clubs with a Nazi-sponsored lawyers' club, etc. They could change overnight the whole structure of German society – and not just political life – precisely because they had prepared its exact counterpart within their own ranks. In this respect, the task of the paramilitary formations was finished when the regular military hierarchy could be placed, during the last stages of the war, under the authority of SS generals. The technique of this 'co-ordination' was as ingenious and irresistible as the deterioration of professional standards was swift and radical, although these results were more immediately felt in the highly technical and specialized field of warfare than anywhere else.

If the importance of paramilitary formations for totalitarian movements is not to be found in their doubtful military value, neither is it wholly in their fake imitation of the regular army. As elite formations

---

78  Hitler, *op. cit., loc. cit.*
79  Hadamovsky, *op. cit.*, p. 28.

they are more sharply separated from the outside world than any other group. The Nazis realized very early the intimate connection between total militancy and total separation from normality; the stormtroopers were never assigned to duty in their home communities, and the active cadres of the SA in the prepower stage, and of the SS under the Nazi regime, were so mobile and so frequently exchanged that they could not possibly get used to and take root in any other part of the ordinary world.[80] They were organized after the model of criminal gangs and used for organized murder.[81] These murders were publicly paraded and officially admitted by the upper Nazi hierarchy, so that open complicity made it well-nigh impossible for members to quit the movement even under the nontotalitarian government and even if they were not threatened, as they actually were, by their former comrades. In this respect, the function of the elite formations is the very opposite of that of the front organizations: while the latter lend the movement an air of respectability and inspire confidence, the former, by extending complicity, make every party member aware that he has left for good the normal world which outlaws murder and that he will be held accountable for all crimes committed by the elite.[82]

---

80 The Death Head units of the SS were placed under the following rules: 1. No brigade is called for duty in its native district. 2. Every unit is to change after three weeks' service. 3. Members are never to be sent into the streets alone or ever to display their Death Head insignia in public. See: *Secret Speech by Himmler to the German Army General Staff 1938* (the speech, however, was delivered in 1937, see *Nazi Conspiracy*, IV, 616, where only excerpts are published). Published by the American Committee for Anti-Nazi Literature.

81 Heinrich Himmler, *Die Schutzstaffel als antibolschewistische Kampforganisation*: Aus dem Schwarzen Korps, No. 3, 1936, said publicly: 'I know that there are people in Germany who get sick when they see this black coat. We understand that and don't expect to be loved by too many people.'

82 In his speeches to the SS Himmler always stressed committed crimes, underlining their gravity. About the liquidation of the Jews, for instance, he would say: 'I also want to talk to you quite frankly on a very grave matter. Among ourselves it should be mentioned quite frankly, and yet we will never speak of it publicly.' On the liquidation of the Polish intelligentsia: '. . . you should hear this but also forget it immediately . . .' (*Nazi Conspiracy*, IV, 558 and 553, respectively).

Goebbels, *op. cit.*, p. 266, notes in a similar vein: 'On the Jewish question, especially, we have taken a position from which there is no escape . . . Experience teaches that a movement and a people who have burned their bridges fight with much greater determination than those who are still able to retreat.'

This is achieved even in the prepower stage, when the leadership systematically claims responsibility for all crimes and leaves no doubt that they are committed for the ultimate good of the movement.

The artificial creation of civil-war conditions by which the Nazis blackmailed their way into power has more than the obvious advantage of stirring up trouble. For the movement, organized violence is the most efficient of the many protective walls which surround its fictitious world, whose 'reality' is proved when a member fears leaving the movement more than he fears the consequences of his complicity in illegal actions, and feels more secure as a member than as an opponent. This feeling of security, resulting from the organized violence with which the elite formations protect the party members from the outside world, is as important to the integrity of the fictitious world of the organization as the fear of its terror.

In the center of the movement, as the motor that swings it into motion, sits the Leader. He is separated from the elite formation by an inner circle of the initiated who spread around him an aura of impenetrable mystery which corresponds to his 'intangible preponderance.'[83] His position within this intimate circle depends upon his ability to spin intrigues among its members and upon his skill in constantly changing its personnel. He owes his rise to leadership to an extreme ability to handle inner-party struggles for power rather than to demagogic or bureaucratic-organizational qualities. He is distinguished from earlier types of dictators in that he hardly wins through simple violence. Hitler needed neither the SA nor the SS to secure his position as leader of the Nazi movement; on the contrary, Röhm, the chief of the SA and able to count upon its loyalty to his own person, was one of Hitler's inner-party enemies. Stalin won against Trotsky, who not only had a far greater mass appeal but, as chief of the Red Army, held

---

83 Souvarine, *op. cit.*, p. 648. – The way the totalitarian movements have kept the private lives of their leaders (Hitler and Stalin) absolutely secret contrasts with the publicity value which all democracies find in parading the private lives of Presidents, Kings, Prime Ministers, etc., in public. Totalitarian methods do not allow for an identification based on the conviction: Even the highest of us is only human.

Souvarine, *op. cit.*, p. xiii, quotes the most frequently used tags to describe Stalin: 'Stalin, the mysterious host of the Kremlin'; 'Stalin, impenetrable personality'; 'Stalin, the Communist Sphinx'; 'Stalin, the Enigma,' the 'insoluble mystery,' etc.

in his hands the greatest power potential in Soviet Russia at the time.[84] Not Stalin, but Trotsky, moreover, was the greatest organizational talent, the ablest bureaucrat of the Russian Revolution.[85] On the other hand, both Hitler and Stalin were masters of detail and devoted themselves in the early stages of their careers almost entirely to questions of personnel, so that after a few years hardly any man of importance remained who did not owe his position to them.[86]

Such personal abilities, however, though an absolute prerequisite for the first stages of such a career and even later far from insignificant, are no longer decisive when a totalitarian movement has been built up, has established the principle that 'the will of the Fuehrer is the Party's law,' and when its whole hierarchy has been efficiently trained for a single purpose – swiftly to communicate the will of the Leader to all ranks. When this has been achieved, the Leader is irreplaceable because the whole complicated structure of the movement would lose its *raison d'être* without his commands. Now, despite eternal cabals in the inner clique and unending shifts of personnel, with their tremendous accumulation of hatred, bitterness, and personal resentment, the Leader's position can remain secure against chaotic palace revolutions not because of his superior gifts, about which the men in his intimate surroundings frequently have no great illusions, but because of these men's sincere and sensible conviction that without him everything would be immediately lost.

The supreme task of the Leader is to impersonate the double function characteristic of each layer of the movement – to act as the magic defense of the movement against the outside world; and at the same time, to be the direct bridge by which the movement is connected

---

84 'If [Trotsky] had chosen to stage a military *coup d'état* he might perhaps have defeated the triumvirs. But he left office without the slightest attempt at rallying in his defence the army he had created and led for seven years' (Isaac Deutscher, *op. cit.*, p. 297).

85 The Commissariat for War under Trotsky 'was a model institution' and Trotsky was called in in all cases of disorder in other departments. Souvarine, *op. cit.*, p. 288.

86 The circumstances surrounding Stalin's death seem to contradict the infallibility of these methods. There is the possibility that Stalin, who, before he died, undoubtedly planned still another general purge, was killed by someone in his environment because no one felt safe any longer, but despite a great deal of circumstantial evidence this cannot be proved.

with it. The Leader represents the movement in a way totally different from all ordinary party leaders; he claims personal responsibility for every action, deed, or misdeed, committed by any member or functionary in his official capacity. This total responsibility is the most important organizational aspect of the so-called Leader principle, according to which every functionary is not only appointed by the Leader but is his walking embodiment, and every order is supposed to emanate from this one ever-present source. This thorough identification of the Leader with every appointed subleader and this monopoly of responsibility for everything which is being done are also the most conspicuous signs of the decisive difference between a totalitarian leader and an ordinary dictator or despot. A tyrant would never identify himself with his subordinates, let alone with every one of their acts;[87] he might use them as scapegoats and gladly have them criticized in order to save himself from the wrath of the people, but he would always maintain an absolute distance from all his subordinates and all his subjects. The Leader, on the contrary, cannot tolerate criticism of his subordinates, since they act always in his name; if he wants to correct his own errors, he must liquidate those who carried them out; if he wants to blame his mistakes on others, he must kill them.[88] For within this organizational framework a mistake can only be a fraud: the impersonation of the Leader by an impostor.

This total responsibility for everything done by the movement and this total identification with every one of its functionaries have the very practical consequence that nobody ever experiences a situation in which he has to be responsible for his own actions or can explain the reasons for them. Since the Leader has monopolized the right and

87 Thus Hitler personally cabled his responsibility for the Potempa murder to the SA assassins in 1932, although presumably he had nothing whatever to do with it. What mattered here was establishing a principle of identification, or, in the language of the Nazis, 'the mutual loyalty of the Leader and the people' on which 'the Reich rests' (Hans Frank, *op. cit.*).

88 'One of Stalin's distinctive characteristics . . . is systematically to throw his own misdeeds and crimes, as well as his political errors . . . on the shoulders of those whose discredit and ruin he is plotting' (Souvarine, *op. cit.*, p. 655). It is obvious that a totalitarian leader can choose freely whom he wants to impersonate his own errors since all acts committed by subleaders are supposed to be inspired by him, so that anybody can be forced into the role of an impostor.

possibility of explanation, he appears to the outside world as the only person who knows what he is doing, *i.e.*, the only representative of the movement with whom one may still talk in nontotalitarian terms and who, if reproached or opposed, cannot say: Don't ask me, ask the Leader. Being in the center of the movement, the Leader can act as though he were above it. It is therefore perfectly understandable (and perfectly futile) for outsiders to set their hopes time and again on a personal talk with the Leader himself when they have to deal with totalitarian movements or governments. The real mystery of the totalitarian Leader resides in an organization which makes it possible for him to assume the total responsibility for all crimes committed by the elite formations of the movement *and* to claim at the same time, the honest, innocent respectability of its most naïve fellow-traveler.[89]

The totalitarian movements have been called 'secret societies established in broad daylight.'[90] Indeed, little as we know of the socio-logical structure and the more recent history of secret societies, the

89 That it was Hitler himself – and not Himmler, or Bormann, or Goebbels – who always initiated the actually 'radical' measures; that they were always more radical than the proposals made by his immediate environment; that even Himmler was appalled when he was entrusted with the 'final solution' of the Jewish question – all this has now been proved by innumerable documents. And the fairy tale that Stalin was more moderate than the leftist factions of the Bolshevist Party is no longer believed, either. It is all the more important to remember that totalitarian leaders invariably try to appear more moderate to the outside world and that their real role – namely, to drive the movement forward at any price and if anything to step up its speed – remains carefully concealed. See, for instance, Admiral Erich Raeder's memo on 'My Relationship to Adolf Hitler and to the Party' in *Nazi Conspiracy*, VIII, 707 ff.: 'When information or rumours arose about radical measures of the Party and the Gestapo, one could come to the conclusion by the conduct of the Fuehrer that such measures were not ordered by the Fuehrer himself . . . In the course of future years, I gradually came to the conclusion that the Fuehrer himself always leaned toward the more radical solution without letting on outwardly.'

In the intraparty struggle which preceded his rise to absolute power, Stalin was care-ful always to pose as 'the man of the golden mean' (see Deutscher, *op. cit.*, pp. 295 ff.); though certainly no 'man of compromise,' he never abandoned this role altogether. When, for instance, in 1936 a foreign journalist questioned him about the movement's aim of world revolution, he replied: 'We have never had such plans and intentions . . . This is the product of a misunderstanding . . . a comic one, or rather a tragicomic one' (Deutscher, *op. cit.*, p. 422).

90 See Alexandre Koyré, 'The Political Function of the Modern Lie,' in *Contemporary Jewish Record*, June, 1945.

structure of the movements, unprecedented if compared with parties and factions, reminds one of nothing so much as of certain outstanding traits of secret societies.[91] Secret societies also form hierarchies according to degrees of 'initiation,' regulate the life of their members according to a secret and fictitious assumption which makes everything look as though it were something else, adopt a strategy of consistent lying to deceive the noninitiated external masses, demand unquestioning obedience from their members who are held together by allegiance to a frequently unknown and always mysterious leader, who himself is surrounded, or supposed to be surrounded, by a small group of initiated who in turn are surrounded by the half-initiated who form a 'buffer area' against the hostile profane world.[92] With secret societies, the totalitarian movements also share the dichotomous division of the world between 'sworn blood brothers' and an indistinct inarticulate mass of sworn enemies.[93] This distinction,

---

Hitler, *op. cit.*, Book II, chapter ix, discusses extensively the pros and cons of secret societies as models for totalitarian movements. His considerations actually led him to Koyré's conclusion, *i.e.*, to adopt the principles of secret societies without their secretiveness and to establish them in 'broad daylight.' There was, in the prepower stage of the movement, hardly anything which the Nazis consistently kept secret. It was only during the war, when the Nazi regime became fully totalitarianized and the party leadership found itself surrounded from all sides by the military hierarchy on which it depended for the conduct of the war, that the elite formations were instructed in no uncertain terms to keep everything connected with 'final solutions' – *i.e.*, deportations and mass exterminations – absolutely secret. This was also the time when Hitler began to act like the chief of a band of conspirators, but not without personally announcing and circulating this fact explicitly. During a discussion with the General Staff in May, 1939, Hitler laid down the following rules, which sound as if they had been copied from a primer for a secret society: '1. No one who need not know must be informed. 2. No one must know any more than he needs to. 3. No one must know any earlier than he has to' (quoted from Heinz Holldack, *Was wirklich geschah*, 1949, p. 378).

91 The following analysis follows closely Georg Simmel's 'Sociology of Secrecy and of Secret Societies,' in *The American Journal of Sociology*, Vol. XI, No. 4, January, 1906, which forms chapter v of his *Soziologie*, Leipzig, 1908, selections of which are translated by Kurt H. Wolff under the title *The Sociology of Georg Simmel*, 1950.

92 'Precisely because the lower grades of the society constitute a mediating transition to the actual center of the secret, they bring about the gradual compression of the sphere of repulsion around the same, which affords more secure protection than the abruptness of a radical standing wholly without or wholly within could secure' (*ibid.*, p. 489).

93 The terms 'sworn brothers,' 'sworn comrades,' 'sworn community,' etc., are repeated *ad nauseam* throughout Nazi literature, partly because of their appeal to

based on absolute hostility to the surrounding world, is very different from the ordinary parties' tendency to divide people into those who belong and those who don't. Parties and open societies in general will consider only those who expressly oppose them to be their enemies, while it has always been the principle of secret societies that 'whosoever is not expressly included is excluded.' [94] This esoteric principle seems to be entirely inappropriate for mass organizations; yet the Nazis gave their members at least the psychological equivalent for the initiation ritual of secret societies when, instead of simply excluding Jews from membership, they demanded proof of non-Jewish descent from their members and set up a complicated machine to shed light on the dark ancestry of some 80 million Germans. It was of course a comedy, and even an expensive one, when 80 million Germans set out to look for Jewish grandfathers; yet everybody came out of the examination with the feeling that he belonged to a group of included which stood against an imaginary multitude of ineligibles. The same principle is confirmed in the Bolshevik movement through repeated party purges which inspire in everybody who is not excluded a reaffirmation of his inclusion.

---

juvenile romanticism which was widespread in the German youth movement. It was mainly Himmler who used these terms in a more definite sense, introduced them into the 'central watchword' of the SS ('Thus we have fallen in line and march forward to a distant future following the unchangeable laws as a National Socialist order of Nordic men and as a sworn community of their tribes [*Sippen*],' see D'Alquen, *op. cit.*) and gave them their articulate meaning of 'absolute hostility' against all others (see Simmel, *op. cit.*, p. 489): 'Then when the mass of humanity of 1 to 1½ milliards [*sic!*] lines up against us, the Germanic people . . .' See Himmler's speech at the meeting of the SS Major Generals at Posen, October 4, 1943, *Nazi Conspiracy*, IV, 558.

94 Simmel, *op. cit.*, p. 490. – This, like so many other principles, was adopted by the Nazis after careful reflection on the implications of the 'Protocols of the Elders of Zion.' Hitler said as early as 1922: '[The gentlemen of the Right] have never yet understood that it is not necessary to be an enemy of the Jew to drag you one day . . . to the scaffold . . . it is quite enough . . . *not to be a Jew*: that will secure the scaffold for you' (*Hitler's Speeches*, p. 12). At that time, nobody could guess that this particular form of propaganda actually meant: One day, it will not be necessary to be an enemy of ours to be dragged to the scaffold; it will be quite enough to be a Jew, or, ultimately, a member of some other people, to be declared 'racially unfit' by some Health Commission. Himmler believed and preached that the whole SS was based on the principle that 'we must be honest, decent, loyal and comradely to members of our own blood and nobody else' (*op. cit., loc. cit.*).

Perhaps the most striking similarity between the secret societies and the totalitarian movements lies in the role of the ritual. The marches around the Red Square in Moscow are in this respect no less characteristic than the pompous formalities of the Nuremberg party days. In the center of the Nazi ritual was the so-called 'blood banner,' and in the center of the Bolshevik ritual stands the mummified corpse of Lenin, both of which introduce a strong element of idolatry into the ceremony. Such idolatry hardly is proof – as is sometimes asserted – of pseudoreligious or heretical tendencies. The 'idols' are mere organizational devices, familiar from the ritual of secret societies, which also used to frighten their members into secretiveness by means of frightful, awe-inspiring symbols. It is obvious that people are more securely held together through the common experience of a secret ritual than by the common sharing of the secret itself. That the secret of totalitarian movements is exposed in broad daylight does not necessarily change the nature of the experience.[95]

These similarities are not, of course, accidental; they cannot simply be explained by the fact that both Hitler and Stalin had been members of modern secret societies before they became totalitarian leaders – Hitler in the secret service of the Reichswehr and Stalin in the conspiracy section of the Bolshevik party. They are to some extent the natural outcome of the conspiracy fiction of totalitarianism whose organizations supposedly have been founded to counteract secret societies – the secret society of the Jews or the conspiratory society of the Trotskyites. What is remarkable in the totalitarian organizations is rather that they could adopt so many organizational devices of secret societies without ever trying to keep their own goal a secret. That the Nazis wanted to conquer the world, deport 'racially alien' peoples and exterminate those of 'inferior biological heritage,' that the Bolsheviks work for the world revolution, was never a secret; these aims, on the contrary, were always part of their propaganda. In other words, the totalitarian movements imitate all the paraphernalia of the secret societies but empty them of the only thing that could excuse, or was supposed to excuse, their methods – the necessity to safeguard a secret.

95 See Simmel, *op. cit.*, pp. 480–481.

In this, as in so many other respects, Nazism and Bolshevism arrived at the same organizational result from very different historical beginnings. The Nazis started with the fiction of a conspiracy and modeled themselves, more or less consciously, after the example of the secret society of the Elders of Zion, whereas the Bolsheviks came from a revolutionary party, whose aim was one-party dictatorship, passed through a stage in which the party was 'entirely apart and above everything' to the moment when the Politburo of the party was 'entirely apart from and above everything';[96] finally Stalin imposed upon this party structure the rigid totalitarian rules of its conspiratory sector and only then discovered the need for a central fiction to maintain the iron discipline of a secret society under the conditions of a mass organization. The Nazi development may be more logical, more consistent in itself, but the history of the Bolshevik party offers a better illustration of the essentially fictitious character of totalitarianism, precisely because the fictitious global conspiracies against and according to which the Bolshevik conspiracy is supposedly organized have not been ideologically fixed. They have changed – from the Trotskyites to the 300 families, then to various 'imperialisms' and recently to 'rootless cosmopolitanism' – and were adjusted to passing needs; yet at no moment and under none of the most various circumstances has it been possible for Bolshevism to do without some such fiction.

The means by which Stalin changed the Russian one-party dictatorship into a totalitarian regime and the revolutionary Communist parties all over the world into totalitarian movements was the liquidation of factions, the abolition of inner-party democracy and the transformation of national Communist parties into Moscow-directed branches of the Comintern. Secret societies in general, and the conspiratory apparatus of revolutionary parties in particular, have always been characterized by absence of factions, suppression of dissident opinions, and absolute centralization of command. All these measures have the obvious utilitarian purpose of protecting the members against persecution and the society against treason; the total obedience asked of each member and the absolute power in the hands of the chief were only inevitable by-products of practical necessities. The

96  Souvarine, *op. cit.*, p. 319, follows a formulation of Bukharin.

trouble, however, is that conspirators have an understandable tendency to think that the most efficient methods in politics in general are those of conspiratory societies and that if one can apply them in broad daylight and support them with a whole nation's instruments of violence, the possibilities for power accumulation become absolutely limitless.[97] The conspiratory sector of a revolutionary party can, as long as the party itself is still intact, be likened to the role of the army within an intact political body: although its own rules of conduct differ radically from those of the civilian body, it serves, remains subject to, and is controlled by it. Just as the danger of a military dictatorship arises when the army no longer serves but wants to dominate the body politic, so the danger of totalitarianism arises when the conspiratory sector of a revolutionary party emancipates itself from the control of the party and aspires to leadership. This is what happened to the Communist parties under the Stalin regime. Stalin's methods were always typical of a man who came from the conspiratory sector of the party: his devotion to detail, his emphasis on the personal side of politics, his ruthlessness in the use and liquidation of comrades and friends. His chief support in the succession struggle after Lenin's death came from the secret police[98] which at that time had already become one of the most important and powerful sections of the party.[99] It was only natural that the Cheka's sympathies should be with the representative of the conspiratory section, with the man who already looked upon it as a kind of secret society and therefore was likely to preserve and to expand its privileges.

The seizure of the Communist parties by their conspiratory sector,

97 Souvarine, *op. cit.*, p. 113, mentions that Stalin 'was always impressed by men who brought off "an affair." He looked on politics as an "affair" requiring dexterity.'

98 In the inner-party struggles during the twenties, 'the collaborators of the GPU were almost without exception fanatic adversaries of the Right and adherents of Stalin. The various services of the GPU were at that time the bulwarks of the Stalinist section' (Ciliga, *op. cit.*, p. 48). – Souvarine, *op. cit.*, p. 289, reports that Stalin even before had 'continued the police activity he had begun during the Civil War' and been the representative of the Politburo in the GPU.

99 Immediately after the civil war in Russia, *Pravda* stated 'that the formula "All power to the Soviets" had been replaced by "All power to the Chekas" . . . The end of the armed hostilities reduced military control . . . but left a ramified Cheka which perfected itself by simplification of its operation' (Souvarine, *op. cit.*, p. 251).

however, was only the first step in their transformation into totalitarian movements. It was not enough that the secret police in Russia and its agents in the Communist parties abroad played the same role in the movement as the elite formations which the Nazis had constituted in the form of paramilitary troops. The parties themselves had to be transformed, if the rule of the secret police was to remain stable. Liquidation of factions and inner-party democracy, consequently, was accompanied in Russia by the admission of large, politically uneducated and 'neutral' masses to membership, a policy which was quickly followed by the Communist parties abroad after the Popular Front policy had initiated it.

Nazi totalitarianism started with a mass organization which was only gradually dominated by elite formations, while the Bolsheviks started with elite formations and organized the masses accordingly. The result was the same in both cases. The Nazis, moreover, because of their militaristic tradition and prejudices, originally modeled their elite formations after the army, while the Bolsheviks from the beginning endowed the secret police with the exercise of supreme power. Yet after a few years this difference too disappeared: the chief of the SS became the chief of the secret police, and the SS formations were gradually incorporated into and replaced the former personnel of the Gestapo, even though this personnel already consisted of reliable Nazis.[100]

It is because of the essential affinity between the functioning of a secret society of conspirators and of the secret police organized to combat it that totalitarian regimes, based on a fiction of global conspiracy and aiming at global rule, eventually concentrate all power in the hands of the police. In the prepower stage, however, the 'secret societies in broad daylight' offer other organizational advantages. The obvious contradiction between a mass organization and an exclusive

---

100 The Gestapo was set up by Göring in 1933; Himmler was appointed chief of the Gestapo in 1934 and began at once to replace its personnel with his SS-men; at the end of the war, 75 per cent of all Gestapo agents were SS-men. It must also be considered that the SS units were particularly qualified for this job as Himmler had organized them, even in the prepower stage, for espionage duty among party members (Heiden, *op. cit.*, p. 308). For the history of the Gestapo, see Giles, *op. cit.*, and also *Nazi Conspiracy*, Vol. II, chapter xii.

society, which alone can be trusted to keep a secret, is of no importance compared with the fact that the very structure of secret and conspiratory societies could translate the totalitarian ideological dichotomy – the blind hostility of the masses against the existing world regardless of its divergences and differences – into an organizational principle. From the viewpoint of an organization which functions according to the principle that whoever is not included is excluded, whoever is not with me is against me, the world at large loses all the nuances, differentiations, and pluralistic aspects which had in any event become confusing and unbearable to the masses who had lost their place and their orientation in it.[101] What inspired them with the unwavering loyalty of members of secret societies was not so much the secret as the dichotomy between Us and all others. This could be kept intact by imitating the secret societies' organizational structure and emptying it of its rational purpose of safeguarding a secret. Nor did it matter if a conspiracy ideology was the origin of this development, as in the case of the Nazis, or a parasitic growth of the conspiratory sector of a revolutionary party, as in the case of the Bolsheviks. The claim inherent in totalitarian organization is that everything outside the movement is 'dying,' a claim which is drastically realized under the murderous conditions of totalitarian rule, but which even in the prepower stage appears plausible to the masses who escape from disintegration and disorientation into the fictitious home of the movement.

Totalitarian movements have proved time and again that they can command the same total loyalty in life and death which had been the prerogative of secret and conspiratory societies.[102] The complete absence of resistance in a thoroughly trained and armed troop like the SA in the face of the murder of a beloved leader (Röhm) and hundreds

101 It was probably one of the decisive ideological errors of Rosenberg, who fell from the Fuehrer's favor and lost his influence in the movement to men like Himmler, Bormann, and even Streicher, that his *Myth of the Twentieth Century* admits a racial pluralism from which only the Jews were excluded. He thereby violated the principle that whoever is not included ('the Germanic people') is excluded ('the mass of humanity'). Cf. note 87.

102 Simmel, *op. cit.*, p. 492, enumerates secret criminal societies in which the members voluntarily set up one commander whom they obey from then on without criticism and without limitation.

of close comrades was a curious spectacle. At that moment probably Röhm, and not Hitler, had the power of the Reichswehr behind him. But these incidents in the Nazi movement have by now been overshadowed by the ever-repeated spectacle of self-confessed 'criminals' in the Bolshevik parties. Trials based on absurd confessions have become part of an internally all-important and externally incomprehensible ritual. But, no matter how the victims are being prepared today, this ritual owes its existence to the probably unfabricated confessions of the old Bolshevik guard in 1936. Long before the time of the Moscow Trials men condemned to death would receive their sentences with great calm, an attitude 'particularly prevalent among members of the Cheka.'[103] So long as the movement exists, its peculiar form of organization makes sure that at least the elite formations can no longer conceive of a life outside the closely knit band of men who, even if they are condemned, still feel superior to the rest of the uninitiated world. And since this organization's exclusive aim has always been to deceive and fight and ultimately conquer the outside world, its members are satisfied to pay with their lives if only this helps again to fool the world.[104]

The chief value, however, of the secret or conspiratory societies' organizational structure and moral standards for purposes of mass organization does not even lie in the inherent guarantees of unconditional belonging and loyalty, and organizational manifestation of unquestioned hostility to the outside world, but in their unsurpassed capacity to establish and safeguard the fictitious world through consistent lying. The whole hierarchical structure of totalitarian movements, from naïve fellow-travelers to party members, elite formations, the intimate circle around the Leader, and the Leader himself, could be described in terms of a curiously varying mixture of gullibility and cynicism with which each member, depending upon

103 Ciliga, *op. cit.*, pp. 96–97. He also describes how in the twenties even ordinary prisoners in the GPU prison of Leningrad who had been condemned to death allowed themselves to be taken to execution 'without a word, without a cry of revolt against the Government that put them to death' (p. 183).

104 Ciliga reports how the condemned party members 'thought that if these executions saved the bureaucratic dictatorship as a whole, if they calmed the rebellious peasantry (or rather if they misled them into error), the sacrifice of their lives would not have been in vain' (*op. cit.*, pp. 96–97).

his rank and standing in the movement, is expected to react to the changing lying statements of the leaders and the central unchanging ideological fiction of the movement.

A mixture of gullibility and cynicism had been an outstanding characteristic of mob mentality before it became an everyday phenomenon of masses. In an ever-changing, incomprehensible world the masses had reached the point where they would, at the same time, believe everything and nothing, think that everything was possible and that nothing was true. The mixture in itself was remarkable enough, because it spelled the end of the illusion that gullibility was a weakness of unsuspecting primitive souls and cynicism the vice of superior and refined minds. Mass propaganda discovered that its audience was ready at all times to believe the worst, no matter how absurd, and did not particularly object to being deceived because it held every statement to be a lie anyhow. The totalitarian mass leaders based their propaganda on the correct psychological assumption that, under such conditions, one could make people believe the most fantastic statements one day, and trust that if the next day they were given irrefutable proof of their falsehood, they would take refuge in cynicism; instead of deserting the leaders who had lied to them, they would protest that they had known all along that the statement was a lie and would admire the leaders for their superior tactical cleverness.

What had been a demonstrable reaction of mass audiences became an important hierarchical principle for mass organizations. A mixture of gullibility and cynicism is prevalent in all ranks of totalitarian movements, and the higher the rank the more cynicism weighs down gullibility. The essential conviction shared by all ranks, from fellow-traveler to leader, is that politics is a game of cheating and that the 'first commandment' of the movement: 'The Fuehrer is always right,' is as necessary for the purposes of world politics, *i.e.*, worldwide cheating, as the rules of military discipline are for the purposes of war.[105]

The machine that generates, organizes, and spreads the monstrous

---

105 Goebbels' notion of the role of diplomacy in politics is characteristic: 'There is no doubt that one does best if one keeps the diplomats uninformed about the background of politics . . . Genuineness in playing an appeasement role is sometimes the most convincing argument for their political trustworthiness' (*op. cit.*, p. 87).

falsehoods of totalitarian movements depends again upon the position of the Leader. To the propaganda assertion that all happenings are scientifically predictable according to the laws of nature or economics, totalitarian organization adds the position of one man who has monopolized this knowledge and whose principal quality is that he 'was always right and will always be right.'[106] To a member of a totalitarian movement this knowledge has nothing to do with truth and this being right nothing to do with the objective truthfulness of the Leader's statements which cannot be disproved by facts, but only by future success or failure. The Leader is always right in his actions and since these are planned for centuries to come, the ultimate test of what he does has been removed beyond the experience of his contemporaries.[107]

The only group supposed to believe loyally and textually in the Leader's words are the sympathizers whose confidence surrounds the movement with an atmosphere of honesty and simple-mindedness, and helps the Leader to fulfill half his task, that is, to inspire confidence in the movement. The party members never believe public statements and are not supposed to, but are complimented by totalitarian propaganda on that superior intelligence which supposedly distinguishes them from the nontotalitarian outside world, which, in turn, they know only from the abnormal gullibility of sympathizers. Only Nazi sympathizers believed Hitler when he swore his famous legality oath before the supreme court of the Weimar Republic; members of the movement knew very well that he lied, and trusted him more than ever because he apparently was able to fool public opinion and the authorities. When in later years Hitler repeated the performance for the whole world, when he swore to his good intentions and at the same time most openly prepared his crimes, the admiration of the Nazi membership naturally was boundless. Similarly, only Bolshevik fellow-travelers believed in the dissolution of the Comintern, and only

---

106 Rudolf Hess in a broadcast in 1934. *Nazi Conspiracy*, I, 193.

107 Werner Best, *op. cit.*, explained: 'Whether the will of the government lays down the "right" rules ... is no longer a question of law, but a question of fate. For actual misuses ... will be punished more surely before history by fate itself with misfortune and overthrow and ruin, because of the violation of the "laws of life," than by a State Court of Justice.' Translation quoted from *Nazi Conspiracy*, IV, 490.

the nonorganized masses of the Russian people and the fellow-travelers abroad were meant to take at face value Stalin's prodemocratic statements during the war. Bolshevik party members were explicitly warned not to be fooled by tactical maneuvers and were asked to admire their Leader's shrewdness in betraying his allies.[108]

Without the organizational division of the movement into elite formations, membership, and sympathizers, the lies of the Leader would not work. The graduation of cynicism expressed in a hierarchy of contempt is at least as necessary in the face of constant refutation as plain gullibility. The point is that the sympathizers in front organizations despise their fellow-citizens' complete lack of initiation, the party members despise the fellow-travelers' gullibility and lack of radicalism, the elite formations despise for similar reasons the party membership, and within the elite formations a similar hierarchy of contempt accompanies every new foundation and development.[109] The result of this system is that the gullibility of sympathizers makes lies credible to the outside world, while at the same time the graduated cynicism of membership and elite formations eliminates the danger that the Leader will ever be forced by the weight of his own propaganda to make good his own statements and feigned respectability. It has been one of the chief handicaps of the outside world in dealing with totalitarian systems that it ignored this system and therefore trusted that, on one hand, the very enormity of totalitarian lies would be their undoing and that, on the other, it would be possible to take the Leader at his word and force him, regardless of his original intentions, to make it good. The totalitarian system, unfortunately, is foolproof against such normal consequences; its ingeniousness rests precisely on the elimination of that reality which either unmasks the liar or forces him to live up to his pretense.

While the membership does not believe statements made for public consumption, it believes all the more fervently the standard clichés of ideological explanation, the keys to past and future history which

108 See Kravchenko, *op. cit.*, p. 422: 'No properly indoctrinated Communist felt that the Party was "lying" in professing one set of policies in public and its very opposite in private.'
109 'The National Socialist despises his fellow German, the SA man the other National Socialists, the SS man the SA man' (Heiden, *op. cit.*, p. 308).

totalitarian movements took from nineteenth-century ideologies, and transformed, through organization, into a working reality. These ideological elements in which the masses had come to believe anyhow, albeit rather vaguely and abstractly, were turned into factual lies of an all-comprehensive nature (the domination of the world by the Jews instead of a general theory about races, the conspiracy of Wall Street instead of a general theory about classes) and integrated into a general scheme of action in which only the 'dying' – the dying classes of capitalist countries or the decadent nations – are supposed to stand in the way of the movement. In contrast to the movements' tactical lies which change literally from day to day, these ideological lies are supposed to be believed like sacred untouchable truths. They are surrounded by a carefully elaborated system of 'scientific' proofs which do not have to be convincing for the completely 'uninitiated,' but still appeal to some vulgarized thirst for knowledge by 'demonstrating' the inferiority of the Jews or the misery of people living under a capitalist system.

The elite formations are distinguished from the ordinary party membership in that they do not need such demonstrations and are not even supposed to believe in the literal truth of ideological clichés. These are fabricated to answer a quest for truth among the masses which in its insistence on explanation and demonstration still has much in common with the normal world. The elite is not composed of ideologists; its members' whole education is aimed at abolishing their capacity for distinguishing between truth and falsehood, between reality and fiction. Their superiority consists in their ability immediately to dissolve every statement of fact into a declaration of purpose. In distinction to the mass membership which, for instance, needs some demonstration of the inferiority of the Jewish race before it can safely be asked to kill Jews, the elite formations understand that the statement, all Jews are inferior, means, all Jews should be killed; they know that when they are told that only Moscow has a subway, the real meaning of the statement is that all subways should be destroyed, and are not unduly surprised when they discover the subway in Paris. The tremendous shock of disillusion which the Red Army suffered on its conquering trip to Europe could be cured only by concentration camps and forced exile for a large part of the occupation troops; but the police formations which accompanied the Army were prepared for the shock, not by different and more correct information – there is no secret training school in Soviet Russia which gives out authentic facts about life abroad – but simply by a general training in supreme contempt for all facts and all reality.

This mentality of the elite is no mere mass phenomenon, no mere consequence of social rootlessness, economic disaster, and political anarchy; it needs careful preparation and cultivation and forms a more important, though less easily recognizable, part of the curriculum of totalitarian leadership schools, the Nazi *Ordensburgen* for the SS troops, and the Bolshevik training centers for Comintern agents, than race indoctrination or the techniques of civil war. Without the elite and its artificially induced inability to understand facts as facts, to distinguish between truth and falsehood, the movement could never move in the direction of realizing its fiction. The outstanding negative quality of the totalitarian elite is that it never stops to think about the world as it really is and never compares the lies with reality. Its most cherished virtue, correspondingly, is loyalty to the Leader, who, like a talisman, assures the ultimate victory of lie and fiction over truth and reality.

The topmost layer in the organization of totalitarian movements is the intimate circle around the Leader, which can be a formal institution, like the Bolshevik Politburo, or a changing clique of men who do not necessarily hold office, like the entourage of Hitler. To them ideological clichés are mere devices to organize the masses, and they feel no compunction about changing them according to the needs of circumstances if only the organizing principle is kept intact. In this connection, the chief merit of Himmler's reorganization of the SS was that he found a very simple method for 'solving the problem of blood by action,' that is, for selecting the members of the elite according to 'good blood' and preparing them to 'carry on a racial struggle without mercy' against everyone who could not trace his 'Aryan' ancestry back to 1750, or was less than 5 feet 8 inches tall ('I know that people who have reached a certain height must possess the desired blood to some degree') or did not have blue eyes and blond hair.[110] The importance of

110 Himmler originally selected the candidates of the SS from photographs. Later a Race Commission, before which the applicant had to appear in person, approved or disapproved of his racial appearance. See Himmler on 'Organization and Obligation of the SS and the Police,' *Nazi Conspiracy*, IV, 616 ff.

this racism in action was that the organization became independent of almost all concrete teachings of no matter what racial 'science,' independent also of antisemitism insofar as it was a specific doctrine concerning the nature and role of the Jews, whose usefulness would have ended with their extermination.[111] Racism was safe and independent of the scientificality of propaganda once an elite had been selected by a 'race commission' and placed under the authority of special 'marriage laws,'[112] while at the opposite end and under the jurisdiction of this 'racial elite,' concentration camps existed for the sake of 'better demonstration of the laws of inheritance and race.'[113] On the strength of this 'living organization,' the Nazis could dispense with dogmatism and offer friendship to Semitic peoples, like the Arabs, or enter into alliances with the very representatives of the Yellow Peril, the Japanese. The reality of a race society, the formation of an elite selected from an allegedly racial viewpoint, would indeed have been a better safeguard for the doctrine of racism than the finest scientific or pseudo-scientific proof.

The policy-makers of Bolshevism show the same superiority to their own avowed dogmas. They are quite capable of interrupting every existing class struggle with a sudden alliance with capitalism

111 Himmler was well aware of the fact that it was one of his 'most important and lasting accomplishments' to have transformed the racial question from 'a negative concept based on matter-of-course antisemitism' into 'an organizational task for building up the SS' (*Der Reichsführer SS und Chef der deutschen Polizei*, 'exclusively for use within the police'; undated). Thus, 'for the first time, the racial question had been placed into, or, better still, had become the focal point, going far beyond the negative concept underlying the natural hatred of Jews. The revolutionary idea of the Fuehrer had been infused with warm lifeblood' (*Der Weg der SS. Der Reichsführer SS*. SS-Hauptamt-Schulungsamt. Dust jacket: 'Not for publication,' undated, p. 25).

112 As soon as he was appointed chief of the SS in 1929, Himmler introduced the principle of racial selection and marriage laws and added: 'The SS knows very well that this order is of great significance. Taunts, sneers or misunderstanding don't touch us; the future is ours.' Quoted from d'Alquen, *op. cit.* And again, fourteen years later, in his speech at Kharkov (*Nazi Conspiracy*, IV, 572 ff.), Himmler reminds his SS leaders that 'we were the first really to solve the problem of blood by action . . . and by problem of blood, we of course do not mean antisemitism. Antisemitism is exactly the same as delousing. Getting rid of lice is not a question of ideology. It is a matter of cleanliness . . . But for us the question of blood was a reminder of our own worth, a reminder of what is actually the basis holding this German people together.'

113 Himmler, *op. cit.*, *Nazi Conspiracy*, IV, 616 ff.

without undermining the reliability of their cadres or committing treason against their belief in class struggle. The dichotomous principle of class struggle having become an organizational device, having, as it were, petrified into uncompromising hostility against the whole world through the secret police cadres in Russia and the Comintern agents abroad, Bolshevik policy has become remarkably free of 'prejudices.'

It is this freedom from the content of their own ideologies which characterizes the highest rank of the totalitarian hierarchy. These men consider everything and everybody in terms of organization, and this includes the Leader who to them is neither an inspired talisman nor the one who is infallibly right, but the simple consequence of this type of organization; he is needed, not as a person, but as a function, and as such he is indispensable to the movement. In contrast, however, to other despotic forms of government, where frequently a clique rules and the despot plays only the representative role of a puppet ruler, totalitarian leaders are actually free to do whatever they please and can count on the loyalty of their entourage even if they choose to murder them.

The more technical reason for this suicidal loyalty is that succession to the supreme office is not regulated by any inheritance or other laws. A successful palace revolt would have as disastrous results for the movement as a whole as a military defeat. It is in the nature of the movement that once the Leader has assumed his office, the whole organization is so absolutely identified with him that any admission of a mistake or removal from office would break the spell of infallibility which surrounds the office of the Leader and spell doom to all those connected with the movement. It is not the truthfulness of the Leader's words but the infallibility of his actions which is the basis for the structure. Without it and in the heat of a discussion which presumes fallibility, the whole fictitious world of totalitarianism goes to pieces, overwhelmed at once by the factuality of the real world which only the movement steered in an infallibly right direction by the Leader was able to ward off.

However, the loyalty of those who believe neither in ideological clichés nor in the infallibility of the Leader also has deeper, nontechnical reasons. What binds these men together is a firm and sincere belief in human omnipotence. Their moral cynicism, their belief that every-thing is permitted, rests on the solid conviction that everything is possible. It is true that these men, few in number, are not easily caught in their own specific lies and that they do not necessarily believe in racism or economics, in the conspiracy of the Jews or of Wall Street. Yet they too are deceived, deceived by their impudent conceited idea that everything can be done and their contemptuous conviction that everything that exists is merely a temporary obstacle that superior organization will certainly destroy. Confident that power of organiza-tion can destroy power of substance, as the violence of a well-organized gang might rob a rich man of ill-guarded wealth, they constantly underestimate the substantial power of stable communities and over-estimate the driving force of a movement. Since, moreover, they do not actually believe in the factual existence of a world conspiracy against them, but use it only as an organizational device, they fail to understand that their own conspiracy may eventually provoke the whole world into uniting against them.

Yet no matter how the delusion of human omnipotence through organization is ultimately defeated, within the movement its practical consequence is that the entourage of the Leader, in case of disagree-ment with him, will never be very sure of their own opinions, since they believe sincerely that their disagreements do not really matter, that even the maddest device has a fair chance of success if properly organized. The point of their loyalty is not that they believe the Leader is infallible, but that they are convinced that everybody who com-mands the instruments of violence with the superior methods of totalitarian organization can become infallible. This delusion is greatly strengthened when totalitarian regimes hold the power to demonstrate the relativity of success and failure, and to show how a loss in substance can become a gain in organization. (The fantastic mismanagement of industrial enterprise in Soviet Russia led to the atomization of the working class, and the terrifying mistreatment of civilian prisoners in Eastern territories under Nazi occupation, though it caused a 'deplorable loss of labor,' 'thinking in terms of generations, [was] not to be regretted.'[114]) Moreover, the decision regarding success

114 Himmler in his speech at Posen, *Nazi Conspiracy*, IV, 558.

and failure under totalitarian circumstances is very largely a matter of organized and terrorized public opinion. In a totally fictitious world, failures need not be recorded, admitted, and remembered. Factuality itself depends for its continued existence upon the existence of the nontotalitarian world.

# CHAPTER TWELVE

# Totalitarianism in Power

When a movement, international in organization, all-comprehensive in its ideological scope, and global in its political aspiration, seizes power in one country, it obviously puts itself in a paradoxical situation. The socialist movement was spared this crisis, first, because the national question – and that meant the strategical problem involved in the revolution – had been curiously neglected by Marx and Engels, and, secondly, because it faced governmental problems only after the first World War had divested the Second International of its authority over the national members, which everywhere had accepted the primacy of national sentiments over international solidarity as an unalterable fact. In other words, when the time came for the socialist movements to seize power in their respective countries, they had already been transformed into national parties.

This transformation never occurred in the totalitarian, the Bolshevik and the Nazi movements. At the time it seized power the danger to the movement lay in the fact that, on one hand, it might become 'ossified' by taking over the state machine and frozen into a form of absolute government,[1] and that, on the other hand, its freedom of movement might be limited by the borders of the territory in which it came to power. To a totalitarian movement, both dangers are equally deadly: a development toward absolutism would put an end to the movement's interior drive, and a development toward nationalism would frustrate its exterior expansion, without which the movement

---

[1] The Nazis fully realized that the seizure of power might lead to the establishment of absolutism. 'National Socialism, however, has not spearheaded the struggle against liberalism in order to bog down in absolutism and start the game all over again' (Werner Best, *Die deutsche Polizei*, p. 20). The warning expressed here, as in countless other places, is directed against the state's claim to be absolute.

cannot survive. The form of government the two movements developed, or, rather, which almost automatically developed from their double claim to total domination and global rule, is best characterized by Trotsky's slogan of 'permanent revolution' although Trotsky's theory was no more than a socialist forecast of a series of revolutions, from the antifeudal bourgeois to the antibourgeois proletarian, which would spread from one country to the other.[2] Only the term itself suggests 'permanency,' with all its semi-anarchistic implications, and is, strictly speaking, a misnomer; yet even Lenin was more impressed by the term than by its theoretical content. In the Soviet Union, at any rate, revolutions, in the form of general purges, became a permanent institution of the Stalin regime after 1934.[3] Here, as in other instances, Stalin concentrated his attacks on Trotsky's half-forgotten slogan precisely because he had decided to use this technique.[4] In Nazi Germany,

2 Trotsky's theory, first pronounced in 1905, did of course not differ from the revolutionary strategy of all Leninists in whose eyes 'Russia herself was merely the first domain, the first rampart, of international revolution: her interests were to be subordinated to the supernational strategy of militant socialism. For the time being, however, the boundaries of both Russia and victorious socialism were the same' (Isaac Deutscher, *Stalin. A Political Biography*, New York and London, 1949, p. 243).

3 The year 1934 is significant because of the new Party statute, announced at the Seventeenth Party Congress, which provided that 'periodic . . . purges are to [be] carried out for the systematic cleansing of the Party.' (Quoted from A. Avtorkhanov, 'Social Differentiation and Contradictions in the Party,' *Bulletin of the Institute for the Study of the USSR*, Munich, February, 1956.) – The party purges during the early years of the Russian Revolution have nothing in common with their later totalitarian perversion into an instrument of permanent instability. The first purges were conducted by local control commissions before an open forum to which party and non-party members had free access. They were planned as a democratic control organ against bureaucratic corruption in the party and 'were to serve as a substitute for real elections' (Deutscher, *op. cit.*, pp. 233–34). – An excellent short survey of the development of the purges can be found in Avtorkhanov's recent article which also refutes the legend that the murder of Kirov gave rise to the new policy. The general purge had begun before Kirov's death which was no more than a 'convenient pretext to give it added drive.' In view of the many 'inexplicable and mysterious' circumstances surrounding Kirov's murder, one suspects that the 'convenient pretext' was carefully planned and executed by Stalin himself. See Khrushchev's 'Speech on Stalin,' New York *Times*, June 5, 1956.

4 Deutscher, *op. cit.*, p. 282, describes the first attack on Trotsky's 'permanent revolution' and Stalin's counterformulation of 'socialism in one country' as an accident of political maneuvering. In 1924, Stalin's 'immediate purpose was to discredit Trotsky . . . Searching in Trotsky's past, the triumvirs came across the theory of

a similar tendency toward permanent revolution was clearly discernible though the Nazis did not have time to realize it to the same extent. Characteristically enough, their 'permanent revolution' also started with the liquidation of the party faction which had dared to proclaim openly the 'next stage of the revolution' [5] – and precisely because 'the Fuehrer and his old guard knew that the real struggle had just begun.' [6] Here, instead of the Bolshevik concept of permanent revolution, we find the notion of a racial 'selection which can never stand still' thus requiring a constant radicalization of the standards by which the selection, *i.e.*, the extermination of the unfit, is carried out. [7] The point

---

"permanent revolution," which he had formulated in 1905 . . . It was in the course of that polemic that Stalin arrived at his formula of "socialism in one country." '

5  The liquidation of the Röhm faction in June, 1934, was preceded by a short interval of stabilization. At the beginning of the year, Rudolf Diels, the chief of the political police in Berlin, could report that there were no more illegal ('revolutionary') arrests by the SA and that older arrests of this kind were being investigated. (*Nazi Conspiracy*, U.S. Government, Washington, 1946, V, 205.) In April, 1934, Reichsminister of the Interior Wilhelm Frick, an old member of the Nazi Party, issued a decree to place restrictions upon the exercise of 'protective custody' (*ibid.*, III, 555) in consideration of the 'stabilization of the national situation.' (See *Das Archiv*, April, 1934, p. 31.) This decree, however, was never published (*Nazi Conspiracy*, VII, 1099; II, 259). The political police of Prussia had prepared a special report on the excesses of the SA for Hitler in the year 1933 and suggested the prosecution of the SA leaders named therein.

Hitler solved the situation by killing these SA leaders without legal proceedings *and* discharging all those police officers who had opposed the SA. (See the sworn affidavit of Rudolf Diels, *ibid.*, V, 224.) In this manner he had safeguarded himself completely against all legalization and stabilization. Among the numerous jurists who enthusiastically served the 'National Socialist idea' only very few comprehended what was really at stake. In this group belongs primarily Theodor Maunz, whose essay *Gestalt und Recht der Polizei* (Hamburg, 1943) is quoted with approval even by those authors, who, like Paul Werner, belonged to the higher Fuehrer Corps of the SS.

6  Robert Ley, *Der Weg zur Ordensburg* (undated, about 1936). 'Special edition . . . for the Fuehrer Corps of the Party . . . Not for free sale.'

7  Heinrich Himmler, 'Die Schutzstaffel,' in *Grundlagen, Aufbau und Wirtschaftsordnung des nationalsozialistischen Staates*, Nr. 7b. This constant radicalization of the principle of racial selection can be found in all phases of Nazi policy. Thus, the first to be exterminated were the full Jews, to be followed by those who were half-Jewish and one-quarter Jewish; or first the insane, to be followed by the incurably sick and, eventually, by all families in which there were any 'incurably sick.' The 'selection which can never stand still' did not stop before the SS itself, either. A Fuehrer decree dated May 19, 1943, ordered that all men who were bound to foreigners by family ties, marriage or friendship were to be eliminated from state, party, Wehrmacht and economy; this affected 1,200 SS leaders (see Hoover Library Archives, Himmler File, Folder 330).

is that both Hitler and Stalin held out promises of stability in order to hide their intention of creating a state of permanent instability.

There could have been no better solution for the perplexities inherent in the co-existence of a government and a movement, of both a totalitarian claim and limited power in a limited territory, of ostensible membership in a comity of nations in which each respects the other's sovereignty and claim to world rule, than this formula stripped of its original content. For the totalitarian ruler is confronted with a dual task which at first appears contradictory to the point of absurdity: he must establish the fictitious world of the movement as a tangible working reality of everyday life, and he must, on the other hand, prevent this new world from developing a new stability; for a stabilization of its laws and institutions would surely liquidate the movement itself and with it the hope for eventual world conquest. The totalitarian ruler must, at any price, prevent normalization from reaching the point where a new way of life could develop – one which might, after a time, lose its bastard qualities and take its place among the widely differing and profoundly contrasting ways of life of the nations of the earth. The moment the revolutionary institutions became a national way of life (that moment when Hitler's claim that Nazism is not an export commodity or Stalin's that socialism can be built in one country, would be more than an attempt to fool the nontotalitarian world), totalitarianism would lose its 'total' quality and become subject to the law of the nations, according to which each possesses a specific territory, people, and historical tradition which relates it to other nations – a plurality which *ipso facto* refutes every contention that any specific form of government is absolutely valid.

Practically speaking, the paradox of totalitarianism in power is that the possession of all instruments of governmental power and violence in one country is not an unmixed blessing for a totalitarian movement. Its disregard for facts, its strict adherence to the rules of a fictitious world, becomes steadily more difficult to maintain, yet remains as essential as it was before. Power means a direct confrontation with reality, and totalitarianism in power is constantly concerned with overcoming this challenge. Propaganda and organization no longer suffice to assert that the impossible is possible, that the incredible is true, that an insane consistency rules the world; the chief psychological support of totalitarian fiction – the active resentment of the status quo, which the masses refused to accept as the only possible world – is no longer there; every bit of factual information that leaks through the iron curtain, set up against the ever-threatening flood of reality from the other, nontotalitarian side, is a greater menace to totalitarian domination than counterpropaganda has been to totalitarian movements.

The struggle for total domination of the total population of the earth, the elimination of every competing nontotalitarian reality, is inherent in the totalitarian regimes themselves; if they do not pursue global rule as their ultimate goal, they are only too likely to lose whatever power they have already seized. Even a single individual can be absolutely and reliably dominated only under global totalitarian conditions. Ascendancy to power therefore means primarily the establishment of official and officially recognized headquarters (or branches in the case of satellite countries) for the movement and the acquisition of a kind of laboratory in which to carry out the experiment with or rather against reality, the experiment in organizing a people for ultimate purposes which disregard individuality as well as nationality, under conditions which are admittedly not perfect but are sufficient for important partial results. Totalitarianism in power uses the state administration for its long-range goal of world conquest and for the direction of the branches of the movement; it establishes the secret police as the executors and guardians of its domestic experiment in constantly transforming reality into fiction; and it finally erects concentration camps as special laboratories to carry through its experiment in total domination.

## I: The So-called Totalitarian State

History teaches that rise to power and responsibility affects deeply the nature of revolutionary parties. Experience and common sense were perfectly justified in expecting that totalitarianism in power would gradually lose its revolutionary momentum and utopian character, that the everyday business of government and the possession of real power would moderate the prepower claims of the movements and gradually destroy the fictitious world of their organizations. It seems, after all, to be in the very nature of things, personal or public, that extreme demands and goals are checked by objective conditions; and reality, taken as a whole, is only to a very small extent determined by the inclination toward fiction of a mass society of atomized individuals.

Many of the errors of the nontotalitarian world in its diplomatic dealings with totalitarian governments (the most conspicuous ones being confidence in the Munich pact with Hitler and the Yalta agreements with Stalin) can clearly be traced to an experience and a common sense which suddenly proved to have lost its grasp on reality. Contrary to all expectations, important concessions and greatly heightened international prestige did not help to reintegrate the totalitarian countries into the comity of nations or induce them to abandon their lying complaint that the whole world had solidly lined up against them. And far from preventing this, diplomatic victories clearly precipitated their recourse to the instruments of violence and resulted in all instances in increased hostility against the powers that had shown themselves willing to compromise.

These disappointments suffered by statesmen and diplomats find their parallel in the earlier disillusionment of benevolent observers and sympathizers with the new revolutionary governments. What they had looked forward to was the establishment of new institutions and the creation of a new code of law which, no matter how revolutionary in content, would lead to a stabilization of conditions and thus check the momentum of the totalitarian movements at least in the countries where they had seized power. What happened instead was that terror increased both in Soviet Russia and Nazi Germany in inverse ratio to the existence of internal political opposition, so that it looked as though political opposition had not been the pretext of terror (as liberal accusers of the regime were wont to assert) but the last impediment to its full fury.[8]

---

8 It is common knowledge that in Russia 'the repression of socialists and anarchists had grown in severity in the same ratio as the country became pacified' (Anton Ciliga, *The Russian Enigma*, London, 1940, p. 244). Deutscher, *op. cit.*, p. 218, thinks that the reason for the vanishing of the 'libertarian spirit of the revolution' at the moment of victory could be found in a changed attitude of the peasants: they turned against Bolshevism 'the more resolutely the more they became confident that the power of the

Even more disturbing was the handling of the constitutional question by the totalitarian regimes. In the early years of their power the Nazis let loose an avalanche of laws and decrees, but they never bothered to abolish officially the Weimar constitution; they even left the civil services more or less intact – a fact which induced many native and foreign observers to hope for restraint of the party and for rapid normalization of the new regime. But when with the issuance of the Nuremberg Laws this development had come to an end, it turned out that the Nazis themselves showed no concern whatsoever about their own legislation. Rather, there was 'only the constant going ahead on the road toward ever-new fields,' so that finally the 'purpose and scope of the secret state police' as well as of all other state or party institutions created by the Nazis could 'in no manner be covered by the laws and regulations issued for them.' [9] In practice, this permanent state of lawlessness found expression in the fact that 'a number of valid regulations [were] no longer made public.' [10] Theoretically, it corresponded to

---

landlords and the White generals had been broken.' This explanation seems rather weak in view of the dimensions which terror was to assume after 1930. It also fails to take into account that full terror did not break loose in the twenties but in the thirties, when the opposition of the peasant classes was no longer an active factor in the situation. – Khrushchev, too (*op. cit.*), notes that 'extreme repressive measures were not used' against the opposition during the fight against the Trotskyites and the Bukharinites, but that 'the repression against them began' much later after they had long been defeated.

Terror by the Nazi regime reached its peak during the war, when the German nation was actually 'united.' Its preparation goes back to 1936 when all organized interior resistance had vanished and Himmler proposed an expansion of the concentration camps. Characteristic of this spirit of oppression regardless of resistance is Himmler's speech at Kharkov before the SS leaders in 1943: 'We have only one task . . . to carry on the racial struggle without mercy . . . We will never let that excellent weapon, the dread and terrible reputation which preceded us in the battles for Kharkov, fade, but will constantly add new meaning to it' (*Nazi Conspiracy*, IV, 572 ff.).

9 See Theodor Maunz, *op. cit.*, pp. 5 and 49. – How little the Nazis thought of the laws and regulations they themselves had issued, and which were regularly published by W. Hoche under the title of *Die Gesetzgebung des Kabinetts Hitler* (Berlin, 1933 ff.), may be gathered from a random remark made by one of their constitutional jurists. He felt that in spite of the absence of a comprehensive new legal order there nevertheless had occurred a 'comprehensive reform' (see Ernst R. Huber, 'Die deutsche Polizei,' in *Zeitschrift für die gesamte Staatswissenschaft*, Band 101, 1940/1, pp. 273 ff.).

10 Maunz, *op. cit.*, p. 49. To my knowledge, Maunz is the only one among Nazi authors who has mentioned this circumstance and sufficiently emphasized it. Only by going

Hitler's dictum that 'the total state must not know any difference between law and ethics';[11] because if it assumed that the valid law is identical with the ethics common to all and springing from their consciences, then there is indeed no further necessity for public decrees. The Soviet Union, where the prerevolutionary civil services had been exterminated in the revolution and the regime had paid scant attention to constitutional questions during the period of revolutionary change, even went to the trouble of issuing an entirely new and very elaborate constitution in 1936 ('a veil of liberal phrases and premises over the guillotine in the background'[12]), an event which was hailed in Russia and abroad as the conclusion of the revolutionary period. Yet the publication of the constitution turned out to be the beginning of the gigantic superpurge which in nearly two years liquidated the existing administration and erased all traces of normal life and economic recovery which had developed in the four years after the liquidation of kulaks and enforced collectivization of the rural population.[13] From then on, the constitution of 1936 played exactly the same

through the five volumes of *Verfügungen, Anordnungen, Bekanntgaben*, which were collected and printed during the war by the party chancellery on instructions of Martin Bormann, is it possible to obtain an insight into this secret legislation by which Germany in fact was governed. According to the preface, the volumes were 'meant solely for internal party work and to be treated as confidential.' Four of these evidently very rare volumes, compared to which the Hoche collection of the legislation of Hitler's cabinet is merely a façade, are in the Hoover Library.

11 This was the Fuehrer's 'warning' to the jurists in 1933, quoted by Hans Frank, *Nationalsozialistische Leitsätze für ein neues deutsches Strafrecht*, Zweiter Teil, 1936, p. 8.

12 Deutscher, *op. cit.*, p. 381. – There were earlier attempts at establishing a constitution, in 1918 and 1924. The constitutional reform in 1944 under which some of the Soviet Republics were to have their own foreign representatives and their own armies, was a tactical maneuver designed to assure the Soviet Union of some additional votes in the United Nations.

13 See Deutscher, *op. cit.*, p. 375. – Upon close reading of Stalin's speech concerning the constitution (his report to the Extraordinary Eighth Soviet Congress of November 25, 1936) it becomes evident that it was never meant to be definitive. Stalin stated explicitly: 'This is the framework of our constitution at the given historical moment. Thus the draft of the new constitution represents the sum total of the road already traveled, the sum total of achievements already existing.' In other words, the constitution was already dated the moment it was announced, and was merely of historical interest. That this is not just an arbitrary interpretation is proved by Molotov, who in his speech about the constitution picks up Stalin's theme and underlines the provisional nature of the whole matter: 'We have realized only the first, the lower phase, of

role the Weimar constitution played under the Nazi regime: it was completely disregarded but never abolished; the only difference was that Stalin could afford one more absurdity – with the exception of Vishinsky, all those who had drafted the never-repudiated constitution were executed as traitors.

What strikes the observer of the totalitarian state is certainly not its monolithic structure. On the contrary, all serious students of the subject agree at least on the co-existence (or the conflict) of a dual authority, the party and the state. Many, moreover, have stressed the peculiar 'shapelessness' of the totalitarian government.[14] Thomas Masaryk saw early that 'the so-called Bolshevik system has never been anything but a complete absence of system';[15] and it is perfectly true that 'even an expert would be driven mad if he tried to unravel the relationships between Party and State' in the Third Reich.[16] It has also been frequently observed that the relationship between the two sources of authority, between state and party, is one of ostensible and real authority, so that the government machine is usually pictured as the powerless façade which hides and protects the real power of the party.[17]

---

Communism. Even this first phase of Communism, Socialism, is by no means completed; only its skeletal structure has been erected' (see *Die Verfassung des Sozialistischen Staates der Arbeiter und Bauern*, Editions Prométhée, Strasbourg, 1937, pp. 42 and 84).

14 'German constitutional life is thus characterized by its utter shapelessness, in contrast to Italy' (Franz Neumann, *Behemoth*, 1942, Appendix, p. 521).

15 Quoted from Boris Souvarine, *Stalin: A Critical Survey of Bolshevism*, New York, 1939, p. 695.

16 Stephen H. Roberts, *The House that Hitler Built*, London, 1939, p. 72.

17 Justice Robert H. Jackson, in his opening speech at the Nuremberg Trials, based his description of the political structure of Nazi Germany consistently on the co-existence of 'two governments in Germany – the real and the ostensible. The forms of the German Republic were maintained for a time and it was the outward and visible government. But the real authority in the State was outside of and above the law and rested in the Leadership Corps of the Nazi Party' (*Nazi Conspiracy*, I, 125). See also the distinction of Roberts, *op. cit.*, p. 101, between the party and a shadow state: 'Hitler obviously leans toward increasing the duplication of functions.'

Students of Nazi Germany seem agreed that the state had only ostensible authority. For the only exception, see Ernst Fraenkel, *The Dual State*, New York and London, 1941, who claims the co-existence of a 'normative and a prerogative state' living in constant friction as 'competitive and not complementary parts of the German Reich.' According to Fraenkel, the normative state was maintained by the Nazis for the protection of the

All levels of the administrative machine in the Third Reich were subject to a curious duplication of offices. With a fantastic thoroughness, the Nazis made sure that every function of the state administration would be duplicated by some party organ:[18] the Weimar division of Germany into states and provinces was duplicated by the Nazi division into *Gaue* whose borderlines, however, did not coincide, so that every given locality belonged, even geographically, to two altogether different administrative units.[19] Nor was the duplication of functions abandoned when, after 1933, outstanding Nazis occupied the official ministries of the state; when Frick, for instance, became Minister of the Interior or Guerthner Minister of Justice. These old and trusted party members, once they had embarked upon official nonparty careers, lost their power and became as uninfluential as other civil servants. Both came under the factual authority of Himmler, the rising chief of the police, who normally would have been subordinate to the Minister of the Interior.[20] Better known abroad has been the fate of

---

capitalist order and private property and had full authority in all economic matters, while the prerogative state of the party ruled supreme in all political matters.

18 'For those positions of state power which the National Socialists could not occupy with their own people, they created corresponding "shadow offices" in their own party organization, in this way setting up a second state beside the state . . .' (Konrad Heiden, *Der Fuehrer: Hitler's Rise to Power*, Boston, 1944, p. 616).

19 O. C. Giles, *The Gestapo*, Oxford Pamphlets on World Affairs, No. 36, 1940, describes the constant overlapping of party and state departments.

20 Characteristic is a memo of Minister of the Interior Frick, who resented the fact that Himmler, the leader of the SS, should have superior power. See *Nazi Conspiracy*, III, 547. – Noteworthy in this respect also are Rosenberg's notes about a discussion with Hitler in 1942: Rosenberg had never before the war held a state position but belonged to the intimate circle around Hitler. Now that he had become Reichsminister for the Eastern Occupied Territories, he was constantly confronted with 'direct actions' of other plenipotentiaries (chiefly SS-men) who overlooked him because he now belonged to the ostensible apparatus of the state. See *ibid.*, IV, 65 ff. The same happened to Hans Frank, Governor General of Poland. There were only two cases in which the attainment of ministerial rank did not entail any loss of power and prestige: that of Minister of Propaganda Goebbels, and of Minister of the Interior Himmler. As regards Himmler, we possess a memorandum, presumably from the year 1935, which illustrates the systematic singlemindedness of the Nazis in regulating the relations between party and state. This memorandum, which apparently originated in Hitler's immediate entourage and was found among the correspondence of the *Reichsadjudantur* of the Fuehrer and the Gestapo, contains a warning against making Himmler state secretary of the Ministry of the Interior because in that case he could 'no longer be a political leader'

the old German Foreign Affairs Office in the Wilhelmstrasse. The Nazis left its personnel nearly untouched and of course never abolished it; yet at the same time they maintained the prepower Foreign Affairs Bureau of the Party, headed by Rosenberg;[21] and since this office had specialized in maintaining contacts with Fascist organizations in Eastern Europe and the Balkans, they set up another organ to compete with the office in the Wilhelmstrasse, the so-called Ribbentrop Bureau, which handled foreign affairs in the West, and survived the departure of its chief as Ambassador to England, that is, his incorporation into the official apparatus of the Wilhelmstrasse. Finally, in addition to these party institutions, the Foreign Office received another duplication in the form of an SS Office, which was responsible 'for negotiations with all racially Germanic groups in Denmark, Norway, Belgium and the Netherlands.'[22] These examples prove that for the Nazis the duplication of offices was a matter of principle and not just an expedient for providing jobs for party members.

The same division between a real and an ostensible government developed from very different beginnings in Soviet Russia.[23] The ostensible government originally sprang from the All-Russian Soviet Congress, which during the civil war lost its influence and power to the Bolshevik party. This process started when the Red Army was made autonomous and the secret political police re-established as an organ of the party, and not of the Soviet Congress;[24] it was completed in 1923, during the first year

---

and 'would be alienated from the party.' Here, too, we find mention of the technical principle regulating the relations between party and state: 'A *Reichsleiter* [a high party functionary] must not be subordinated to a *Reichsminister* [a high state functionary].' (The undated, unsigned memorandum, entitled *Die geheime Staatspolizei*, can be found in the archives of the Hoover Library, File P. Wiedemann.)

21 See the 'Brief Report on Activities of Rosenberg's Foreign Affairs Bureau of the Party from 1933 to 1943,' *ibid.*, III, 27 ff.

22 Based on a Fuehrer decree of August 12, 1942. See *Verfügungen, Anordnungen, Bekanntgaben, op. cit.*, Nr. A 54/42.

23 'Behind the ostensible government was a real government,' which Victor Kravchenko (*I Chose Freedom: The Personal Life of a Soviet Official*, New York, 1946, p. 111) saw in the 'secret police system.'

24 See Arthur Rosenberg, *A History of Bolshevism*, London, 1934, chapter vi: 'There are in reality two political edifices in Russia that rise parallel to one another: the shadow government of the Soviets and the *de facto* government of the Bolshevik Party.'

of Stalin's General Secretaryship.[25] From then on, the Soviets became the shadow government in whose midst, through cells formed by Bolshevik party members, functioned the representatives of real power who were appointed and responsible to the Central Committee in Moscow. The crucial point in the later development was not the conquest of the Soviets by the party, but the fact that 'although it would have presented no difficulties, the Bolsheviks did not abolish the Soviets and used them as the decorative outward symbol of their authority.'[26]

The co-existence of an ostensible and a real government therefore was partly the outcome of the revolution itself and preceded Stalin's totalitarian dictatorship. Yet while the Nazis simply retained the existing administration and deprived it of all power, Stalin had to revive his shadow government, which in the early thirties had lost all its functions and was half forgotten in Russia; he introduced the Soviet constitution as the symbol of the existence as well as the powerlessness of the Soviets. (None of its paragraphs ever had the slightest practical significance for life and jurisdiction in Russia.) The ostensible Russian government, utterly lacking the glamour of tradition so necessary for a façade, apparently needed the sacred halo of written law. The totalitarian defiance of law and legality (which 'in spite of the greatest changes . . . still [remain] the expression of a permanently desired order')[27] found in the written Soviet constitution, as in the never-repudiated Weimar constitution, a permanent background for its own lawlessness, the permanent challenge to the nontotalitarian world and its standards whose helplessness and impotence could be demonstrated daily.[28]

25  Deutscher, *op. cit.*, pp. 255–256, sums up Stalin's report to the Twelfth Party Congress about the work of the personnel department during his first year in the General Secretariat: 'The year before only 27 per cent of the regional leaders of the trade unions were members of the party. At present 57 per cent of them were Communists. The percentage of Communists in the management of co-operatives had risen from 5 to 50 per cent; and in the commanding staffs of the armed forces from 16 to 24. The same happened in all other institutions which Stalin described as the "transmission belts" connecting the party with the people.'

26  Arthur Rosenberg, *op. cit., loc. cit.*

27  Maunz, *op. cit.*, p. 12.

28  The jurist and Obersturmbannfuehrer, Professor R. Hoehn, has expressed this in the following words: 'And there was still another thing which foreigners, but Germans, too, had to get used to: namely, that the task of the secret state police . . . was

Duplication of offices and division of authority, the co-existence of real and ostensible power, are sufficient to create confusion but not to explain the 'shapelessness' of the whole structure. One should not forget that only a building can have a structure, but that a movement – if the word is to be taken as seriously and as literally as the Nazis meant it – can have only a direction, and that any form of legal or governmental structure can be only a handicap to a movement which is being propelled with increasing speed in a certain direction. Even in the pre-power stage the totalitarian movements represented those masses that were no longer willing to live in any kind of structure, regardless of its nature; masses that had started to move in order to flood the legal and geographical borders securely determined by the government. Therefore, judged by our conceptions of government and state structure, these movements, so long as they find themselves physically still limited to a specific territory, necessarily must try to destroy all structure, and for this willful destruction a mere duplication of all offices into party and state institutions would not be sufficient. Since duplication involves a relationship between the façade of the state and the inner core of the party, it, too, would eventually result in some kind of structure, where the relationship between party and state would automatically end in a legal regulation which restricts and stabilizes their respective authority.[29]

---

taken over by a community of persons who originated within the movement, and continue to be rooted in it. That the term state police actually makes no allowance for this fact shall be mentioned here only in passing' (*Grundfragen der deutschen Polizei*, Report on the Constitutive Session of the Committee on Police Law of the Academy for German Law, October 11, 1936. Hamburg, 1937, with contributions by Frank, Himmler and Hoehn).

29 For example, such an attempt to circumscribe the separate responsibilities and to counter the 'anarchy of authority' was made by Hans Frank in *Recht und Verwaltung*, 1939, and again in an address titled *Technik des States*, in 1941. He expressed the opinion that 'legal guarantees' were not the 'prerogative of liberal systems of government' and that the administration should continue to be governed, as before, by the laws of the Reich, which now were inspired and guided by the program of the National Socialist party. It was precisely because he wanted to prevent such a new legal order at any price that Hitler never acknowledged the program of the Nazi party. Of party members who made such proposals he was wont to speak with contempt, describing them as 'eternally tied to the past,' as persons 'who are unable to leap across their own shadow' (Felix Kersten, *Totenkopf und Treue*, Hamburg).

As a matter of fact, duplication of offices, seemingly the result of the party–state problem in all one-party dictatorships, is only the most conspicuous sign of a more complicated phenomenon that is better defined as multiplication of offices than duplication. The Nazis were not content to establish *Gaue* in addition to the old provinces, but also introduced a great many other geographical divisions in accordance with the different party organizations: the territorial units of the SA were neither co-extensive with the *Gaue* nor with the provinces; they differed, moreover, from those of the SS and none of them corresponded to the zones dividing the Hitler Youth.[30] To this geographical confusion must be added the fact that the original relationship between real and ostensible power repeated itself throughout, albeit in an ever-changing way. The inhabitant of Hitler's Third Reich lived not only under the simultaneous and often conflicting authorities of competing powers, such as the civil services, the party, the SA, and the SS; he could never be sure and was never explicitly told whose authority he was supposed to place above all others. He had to develop a kind of sixth sense to know at a given moment whom to obey and whom to disregard.

Those, on the other hand, who had to execute the orders which the leadership, in the interest of the movement, regarded as genuinely necessary – in contradistinction to governmental measures, such orders were of course entrusted only to the party's elite formations – were not much better off. Mostly such orders were 'intentionally vague, and given in the expectation that their recipient would recognize the intent of the order giver, and act accordingly';[31] for the elite

30 'The 32 *Gaue* . . . do not coincide with the administrative or military regions, or even the 21 divisions of the SA, or the 10 regions of the SS, or the 23 zones of the Hitler Youth . . . Such discrepancies are the more remarkable because there is no reason for them' (Roberts, *op. cit.*, p. 98).

31 Nuremberg Documents, PS 3063 in the Centre de Documentation Juive in Paris. The document is a report of the supreme party court about 'events and party court proceedings connected with the antisemitic demonstrations of November 9, 1938.' On the basis of investigations by the police and the office of the Attorney General the supreme court came to the conclusion that 'the verbal instructions of the Reichspropagandaleiter must have been understood by all party leaders to mean that, to the outside, the party did not wish to appear as the instigator of the demonstration, but in reality was to organize and carry it through . . . The re-examination of the command echelons has shown . . . that the active National Socialist molded in the prepower

formations were by no means merely obligated to obey the orders of the Fuehrer (this was mandatory for all existing organizations anyway), but 'to execute the *will* of the leadership.'[32] And, as can be gathered from the lengthy proceedings concerning 'excesses' before the party courts, this was by no means one and the same thing. The only difference was that the elite formations, thanks to their special indoctrination for such purposes, had been trained to understand that certain 'hints meant more than their mere verbal contents.'[33]

Technically speaking, the movement within the apparatus of totalitarian domination derives its mobility from the fact that the leadership constantly shifts the actual center of power, often to other organizations, but without dissolving or even publicly exposing the groups that have thus been deprived of their power. In the early period of the Nazi regime, immediately after the Reichstag fire, the SA was the real authority and the party the ostensible one; power then shifted from the SA to the SS and finally from the SS to the Security Service.[34] The

---

struggle [*Kampfzeit*] takes it for granted that actions in which the party does not wish to appear in the role of organizer are not ordered with unequivocal clarity and down to the last detail. Hence he is accustomed to understand that an order may mean more than its verbal content, just as it has more or less become routine with the order giver, in the interests of the party . . . not to say everything and only to intimate what he wants to achieve by the order . . . Thus, the . . . orders – for instance, not the Jew Grünspan but all Jewry must be blamed for the death of Party Comrade vom Rath . . . pistols should be brought along . . . every SA-man now ought to know what he had to do – were understood by a number of subleaders to mean that Jewish blood would now have to be shed for the blood of Party Comrade vom Rath . . .' Particularly significant is the end of the report, in which the supreme party court quite openly takes exception to these methods: 'It is another question whether, in the interest of discipline, the order that is intentionally vague, and given in the expectation that its recipient will recognize the intent of the order giver and act accordingly, must not be relegated to the past.' Here, too, there were persons who, in Hitler's words, 'were unable to leap across their own shadow' and insisted upon legislative measures, because they did not understand that not the order but the *will* of the Fuehrer was the supreme law. Here, the difference between the mentality of the elite formations and the party agencies is particularly clear. 32 Best (*op. cit.*) puts it this way: 'So long as the police execute this will of the leadership, they are acting within the law; if the will of the leadership is transgressed, then not the police, but a member of the police, has committed a violation.'

33 See footnote 31.

34 In 1933, after the Reichstag fire, 'SA leaders were more powerful than Gauleiter. They also refused obedience to Göring.' See Rudolf Diels's sworn affidavit in *Nazi Conspiracy*, V, 224; Diels was chief of the political police under Göring.

point is that none of the organs of power was ever deprived of its right to pretend that it embodied the will of the Leader.[35] But not only was the will of the Leader so unstable that compared with it the whims of Oriental despots are a shining example of steadfastness; the consistent and ever-changing division between real secret authority and ostensible open representation made the actual seat of power a mystery by definition, and this to such an extent that the members of the ruling clique themselves could never be absolutely sure of their own position in the secret power hierarchy. Alfred Rosenberg, for instance, despite his long career in the party and his impressive accumulation of ostensible power and offices in the party hierarchy, still talked about the creation of a series of Eastern European States as a security wall against Moscow at a time when those invested with real power had already decided that no state structure would succeed the defeat of the Soviet Union and that the population of the Eastern occupied territories had become definitely stateless and could therefore be exterminated.[36] In other words, since knowledge of whom to obey and a comparatively permanent settlement of hierarchy would introduce an element of stability which is essentially absent from totalitarian rule, the Nazis constantly disavowed real authority whenever it had come into the open and created new instances of government compared with which the former became a shadow government – a game which obviously could go indefinitely. One of the most important technical differences between the Soviet and the National Socialist system is that Stalin, whenever he shifted the

---

35 The SA obviously resented its loss of rank and power in the Nazi hierarchy and tried desperately to keep up appearances. In their magazines – *Der SA-Mann*, *Das Archiv*, *etc.* – many indications, veiled and unveiled, of this impotent rivalry with the SS can be found. More interesting is that Hitler still in 1936, when the SA had already lost its power, would assure them in a speech: 'All that you are, you are through me; and all that I am, I am through you alone.' See Ernst Bayer, *Die SA*, Berlin, 1938. Translation quoted from *Nazi Conspiracy*, IV, 782.

36 Compare Rosenberg's speech of June, 1941: 'I believe that our political task will consist of . . . organizing these peoples in certain types of political bodies . . . and building them up against Moscow' with the 'Undated Memorandum for the Administration in the Occupied Eastern Territories': 'With the dissolution of the USSR after her defeat, no body politic is left in the Eastern territories and therefore . . . no citizenship for their population' (*Trial of the Major War Criminals*, Nuremberg, 1947, XXVI, p. 616 and 604, respectively).

power emphasis within his own movement from one apparatus to another, had the tendency to liquidate the apparatus together with its staff, while Hitler, in spite of his contemptuous comments on people who 'are unable to leap across their own shadows,' [37] was perfectly willing to continue using these shadows even though in another function.

The multiplication of offices was extremely useful for the constant shifting of power; the longer, moreover, a totalitarian regime stays in power, the greater becomes the number of offices and the possibility of jobs exclusively dependent upon the movement, since no office is abolished when its authority is liquidated. The Nazi regime started this multiplication with an initial co-ordination of all existing associations, societies, and institutions. The interesting thing in this nation-wide manipulation was that co-ordination did not signify incorporation into the already existing respective party organizations. The result was that up to the end of the regime, there were not one, but two National Socialist student organizations, two Nazi women's organizations, two Nazi organizations for university professors, lawyers, physicians, and so forth.[38] It was by no means sure, however, that in all cases the original party organization would be more powerful than its co-ordinated counterpart.[39] Nor could anybody predict with

---

37 *Hitlers Tischgespräche*, Bonn, 1951, p. 213. Usually, Hitler meant some high-ranking Nazi functionaries who had their reservations about murdering all those without compunctions, whom he described as 'human junk [*Gesox*]' (see pp. 248 ff. and *passim*).

38 For the variety of overlapping party organizations, see *Rang- und Organisationsliste der NSDAP*, Stuttgart, 1947, and *Nazi Conspiracy*, I, 178, which distinguishes four main categories: 1. *Gliederungen der NSDAP*, which had existed before its rise to power; 2. *Angeschlossene Verbände der NSDAP*, which comprise those societies which had been co-ordinated; 3. *Betreute Organisationen der NSDAP*; and 4. *Weitere nationalsozialistische Organisationen*. In nearly every category, one finds a different students', women's, teachers', and workers' organization.

39 The gigantic organization for public works, headed by Todt and later led by Albert Speer, was created by Hitler outside of all party hierarchies and affiliations. This organization might have been used against the authority of party or even police organizations. It is noteworthy that Speer could risk pointing out to Hitler (during a conference in 1942) the impossibility of organizing production under Himmler's regime, and even demand jurisdiction over slave labor and concentration camps. See *Nazi Conspiracy*, I, 916–917.

any assurance which party organ would rise in the ranks of the internal party hierarchy.[40]

A classical instance of this planned shapelessness occurred in the organization of scientific antisemitism. In 1933, an institute for study of the Jewish question (Institut zur Erforschung der Judenfrage) was founded in Munich which, since the Jewish question presumably had determined the whole of German history, quickly enlarged into a research institute for modern German history. Headed by the well-known historian Walter Frank, it transformed the traditional universities into seats of ostensible learning or façades. In 1940, another institute for the study of the Jewish question was founded in Frankfurt, headed by Alfred Rosenberg, whose standing as a party member was considerably higher. The Munich institute consequently was relegated to a shadowy existence; the Frankfurt, not the Munich institution was supposed to receive the treasures from looted European Jewish collections and become the seat of a comprehensive library on Judaism. Yet, when these collections actually arrived in Germany a few years later, their most precious parts went not to Frankfurt, but to Berlin, where they were received by Himmler's special Gestapo department for the liquidation (not merely the study) of the Jewish question, which was headed by Eichmann. None of the older institutions was ever abolished, so that in 1944 the situation was this: behind the façade of the universities' history departments stood threateningly the more real power of the Munich institute, behind which rose Rosenberg's institute in Frankfurt, and only behind these three façades, hidden and protected by them, lay the real center of authority, the *Reichssicherheitshauptamt*, a special division of the Gestapo.

The façade of the Soviet government, despite its written constitution, is even less impressive, erected even more exclusively for foreign observation than the state administration which the Nazis inherited and retained from the Weimar Republic. Lacking the Nazis' original

40 Such an innocuous and unimportant society, for instance, as the NSKK (the National Socialist corps of automobilists founded in 1930) was suddenly elevated, in 1933, to the status of an elite formation, sharing with the SA and the SS the privilege of an independent affiliated unit of the party. Nothing followed this rise in the ranks of the Nazi hierarchy; retrospectively, it looks like an idle threat to the SA and SS.

accumulation of offices in the period of co-ordination, the Soviet regime relies even more on constant creation of new offices to put the former centers of power in the shadow. The gigantic increase of the bureaucratic apparatus, inherent in this method, is checked by repeated liquidation through purges. Nevertheless, in Russia, too, we can distinguish at least three strictly separate organizations: the Soviet or state apparatus, the party apparatus, and the NKVD apparatus, each of which has its own independent department of economy, a political department, a ministry of education and culture, a military department, etc.[41]

In Russia, the ostensible power of the party bureaucracy as against the real power of the secret police corresponds to the original duplication of party and state as known in Nazi Germany, and the multiplication becomes evident only in the secret police itself, with its extremely complicated, widely ramified network of agents, in which one department is always assigned to supervising and spying on another. Every enterprise in the Soviet Union has its special department of the secret police, which spies on party members and ordinary personnel alike. Co-existent with this department is another police division of the party itself, which again watches everybody, including the agents of the NKVD, and whose members are not known to the rival body. Added to these two espionage organizations must be the unions in the factories, which must see to it that the workers fulfill their prescribed quotas. Far more important than these apparatuses, however, is 'the special department' of the NKVD which represents 'an NKVD within the NKVD,' *i.e.*, a secret police within the secret police.[42] All reports of these competing police agencies ultimately end up in the Moscow Central Committee and the Politburo. Here it is decided which of the reports is decisive and which of the police divisions shall be entitled to carry out the respective police measures.

41  F. Beck and W. Godin, *Russian Purge and the Extraction of Confession*, 1951, p. 153.
42  *Ibid.*, pp. 159 ff. – According to other reports, there are different examples of the staggering multiplication of the Soviet police apparatus, primarily the local and regional associations of the NKVD, which work independently of one another and which have their counterparts in the local and regional networks of party agents. It is in the nature of things that we know considerably less about Russian conditions than we do about those in Nazi Germany, especially as far as organizational details are concerned.

Neither the average inhabitant of the country nor any one of the police departments knows, of course, what decision will be made; today it may be the special division of the NKVD, tomorrow the party's network of agents; the day after, it may be the local committees or one of the regional bodies. Among all these departments there exists no legally rooted hierarchy of power or authority; the only certainty is that eventually one of them will be chosen to embody 'the will of the leadership.'

The only rule of which everybody in a totalitarian state may be sure is that the more visible government agencies are, the less power they carry, and the less is known of the existence of an institution, the more powerful it will ultimately turn out to be. According to this rule, the Soviets, recognized by a written constitution as the highest authority of the state, have less power than the Bolshevik party; the Bolshevik party, which recruits its members openly and is recognized as the ruling class, has less power than the secret police. Real power begins where secrecy begins. In this respect the Nazi and the Bolshevik states were very much alike; their difference lay chiefly in the monopolization and centralization of secret police services in Himmler on one hand, and the maze of apparently unrelated and unconnected police activities in Russia on the other.

If we consider the totalitarian state solely as an instrument of power and leave aside questions of administrative efficiency, industrial capacity, and economic productivity, then its shapelessness turns out to be an ideally suited instrument for the realization of the so-called Leader principle. A continuous competition between offices, whose functions not only overlap but which are charged with identical tasks,[43] gives opposition or sabotage almost no chance to become effective; a swift change of emphasis which relegates one office to the shadow and elevates another to authority can solve all problems without anybody's becoming aware of the change or of the fact that opposition had existed, the additional advantage of the system being that the opposing office is likely never to learn of its defeat, since it is either not abolished at all (as in the case of the Nazi regime) or it is

---

43 According to the testimony of one of his former employees (*Nazi Conspiracy*, VI, 461), it was 'a specialty of Himmler to give one task to two different people.'

liquidated much later and without any apparent connection with the specific matter. This can be done all the more easily since nobody, except those few initiated, knows the exact relationship between the authorities. Only once in a while does the nontotalitarian world catch a glimpse of these conditions, as when a high official abroad confesses that an obscure clerk in the Embassy had been his immediate superior. In retrospect it is often possible to determine why such a sudden loss of power occurred, or, rather, that it occurred at all. For instance, it is not hard to understand today why at the outbreak of war people like Alfred Rosenberg or Hans Frank were removed to state positions and thus eliminated from the real center of power, namely, the Fuehrer's inner circle.[44] The important thing is that they not only did not know the reasons for these moves, but presumably did not even suspect that such apparently exalted positions as Governor General of Poland or Reichsminister for all Eastern territories did not signify the climax but the end of their National Socialist careers.

The Leader principle does not establish a hierarchy in the totalitarian state any more than it does in the totalitarian movement; authority is not filtered down from the top through all intervening layers to the bottom of the body politic as is the case in authoritarian regimes. The factual reason is that there is no hierarchy without authority and that, in spite of the numerous misunderstandings concerning the so-called 'authoritarian personality,' the principle of authority is in all important respects diametrically opposed to that of totalitarian domination. Quite apart from its origin in Roman history, authority, no matter in what form, always is meant to restrict or limit freedom, but never to abolish it. Totalitarian domination, however, aims at abolishing freedom, even at eliminating human spontaneity in general, and by no means at a restriction of freedom no matter how tyrannical. Technically, this absence of any authority or hierarchy in the totalitarian

44 In the aforementioned address (see footnote 29) Hans Frank showed that at some point he wanted to stabilize the movement, and his numerous complaints as Governor General of Poland testify to a total lack of understanding of the deliberately anti-utilitarian tendencies of Nazi policy. He cannot understand why the subjected peoples are not exploited but exterminated. Rosenberg, in the eyes of Hitler, was racially unreliable because he meant to establish satellite states in the conquered Eastern territories and did not understand that Hitler's population policy aimed at depopulating these territories.

system is shown by the fact that between the supreme power (the Fuehrer) and the ruled there are no reliable intervening levels, each of which would receive its due share of authority and obedience. The will of the Fuehrer can be embodied everywhere and at all times, and he himself is not tied to any hierarchy, not even the one he might have established himself. Therefore, it is not accurate to say that the movement, after its seizure of power, founds a multiplicity of principalities in whose realm each little leader is free to do as he pleases and to imitate the big leader at the top.[45] The Nazi claim that 'the party is the order of fuehrers'[46] was an ordinary lie. Just as the infinite multiplication of offices and confusion of authority leads to a state of affairs in which every citizen feels himself directly confronted with the will of the Leader, who arbitrarily chooses the executing organ of his decisions, so the one and a half million 'fuehrers' throughout the Third Reich[47] knew very well that their authority derived directly from Hitler without the intervening levels of a functioning hierarchy.[48] The direct dependence was real and the intervening hierarchy, certainly of social importance, was an ostensible, spurious imitation of an authoritarian state.

The Leader's absolute monopoly of power and authority is most conspicuous in the relationship between him and his chief of police, who in a totalitarian country occupies the most powerful public position. Yet despite the enormous material and organizational power at his disposal as the head of a veritable police army and of the elite formations, the chief of police apparently is in no position ever to seize power and himself become the ruler of the country. Thus prior to

---

45 The notion of a division into 'little principalities' which formed 'a pyramid of power outside the law with the Fuehrer at its apex' is Robert H. Jackson's. See chapter xii of *Nazi Conspiracy*, II, 1 ff. In order to avoid the establishment of such an authoritarian state, Hitler, as early as 1934, issued the following party decree: 'The form of address "Mein Fuehrer" is reserved for the Fuehrer alone. I herewith forbid all subleaders of the NSDAP to allow themselves to be addressed as "Mein Reichsleiter," etc., either in words or in writing. Rather, the form of address has to be Pg. [Party Comrade] . . . or Gauleiter, etc.' See *Verfügungen, Anordnungen, Bekanntgaben, op. cit.*, decree of August 20, 1934.

46 See the *Organisationsbuch der NSDAP*.

47 See Chart 14 in Vol. VIII of *Nazi Conspiracy*.

48 All oaths in the party as well as the elite formations were taken on the person of Adolf Hitler.

Hitler's fall, Himmler never dreamed of touching Hitler's claim to leadership[49] and was never proposed as Hitler's successor. Even more interesting in this context is Beria's ill-fated attempt at seizing power after Stalin's death. Although Stalin had never permitted any of his police chiefs to enjoy a position comparable to that of Himmler during the last years of Nazi rule, Beria, too, disposed of enough troops to challenge the rule of the party after Stalin's death simply by occupying the whole of Moscow and all accesses to the Kremlin; nobody except the Red Army might have disrupted his claim to power and this would have led to a bloody civil war whose outcome would by no means have been assured. The point is that Beria voluntarily abandoned all his positions only a few days later even though he must have known that he would forfeit his life because for a matter of days he had dared to play off the power of the police against the power of the party.[50]

This lack of absolute power of course does not prevent the chief of police from organizing his enormous apparatus in accordance with totalitarian power principles. Thus it is most remarkable to see how Himmler after his appointment began the reorganization of the German police by introducing into the hitherto centralized apparatus of the secret police the multiplication of offices – *i.e.*, he apparently did what all experts of power who preceded the totalitarian regimes would have feared as decentralization leading to a diminution of power. To the service of the Gestapo Himmler first added the Security Service, originally a division of the SS and founded as an inner-party police body. While the main offices of the Gestapo and the Security Service were eventually centralized in Berlin, the regional branches of these two huge secret services retained their separate identities and

49 The first step of Himmler in this direction occurred in the fall of 1944, when he ordered on his own initiative that the gas installations in the extermination camps be dismantled and the mass slaughter be stopped. This was his way of initiating peace negotiations with the Western powers. Interestingly enough, Hitler apparently was never informed of these preparations; it seems that no one dared tell him that one of his most important war aims had already been given up. See Léon Poliakov, *Brévaire de la Haine*, 1951, p. 232.
50 For the events following Stalin's death, see Harrison E. Salisbury, *American in Russia*, New York, 1955.

each reported directly to Himmler's own office in Berlin.[51] In the course of the war, Himmler added two more intelligence services: one consisted of so-called inspectors who were supposed to control and co-ordinate the Security Service with the police and who were subject to the jurisdiction of the SS; the second was a specifically military intelligence bureau which acted independently of the Reich's military forces and finally succeeded in absorbing the army's own military intelligence.[52]

The complete absence of successful or unsuccessful palace revolutions is one of the most remarkable characteristics of totalitarian dictatorships. (With one exception no dissatisfied Nazis took part in the military conspiracy against Hitler of July, 1944.) On the surface, the Leader principle seems to invite bloody changes of personal power without a change of regime. This is but one of many indications that the totalitarian form of government has very little to do with lust for power or even the desire for a power-generating machine, with the game of power for power's sake which has been characteristic of the last stages of imperialist rule. Technically speaking, however, it is one of the most important indications that totalitarian government, all appearances notwithstanding, is not rule by a clique or a gang.[53] The evidence of Hitler's as well as Stalin's dictatorship points clearly to the fact that isolation of atomized individuals provides not only the mass basis for totalitarian rule, but is carried through to the very top of the whole structure. Stalin has shot almost everybody who could claim to belong to the ruling clique and has moved the members of the Politburo back and forth whenever a clique was on the point of consolidating itself. Hitler destroyed cliques in Nazi Germany with less drastic

51 See the excellent analysis of the structure of the Nazi police in *Nazi Conspiracy*, II, 250 ff., esp. p. 256.

52 *Ibid.*, p. 252.

53 Franz Neumann, *op. cit.*, pp. 521 ff., is doubtful 'whether Germany can be called a State. It is far more a gang where the leaders are perpetually compelled to agree after disagreements.' Konrad Heiden's works on Nazi Germany are representative for the theory of government by a clique. – As regards the formation of cliques around Hitler, *The Bormann Letters*, published by Trevor-Roper, are quite enlightening. In the trial of the doctors (the United States *vs.* Karl Brandt *et al.*, hearing of May 13, 1947), Victor Brack testified that as early as 1933 Bormann, acting no doubt on Hitler's orders, had begun to organize a group of persons who stood above state and party.

means – the only bloody purge having been directed against the Röhm clique which indeed was firmly kept together through the homosexuality of its leading members; he prevented their formation by constant shifts in power and authority, and frequent changes of intimates in his immediate surroundings, so that all former solidarity between those who had come into power with him quickly evaporated. It seems obvious, moreover, that the monstrous unfaithfulness which is reported in almost identical terms as the outstanding trait in both Hitler's and Stalin's characters did not allow them to preside over anything so lasting and durable as a clique. However that may be, the point is that there exists no interrelationship between those holding office; they are not bound together by equal status in a political hierarchy or the relationship between superiors and inferiors, or even the uncertain loyalties of gangsters. In Soviet Russia, everybody knows that the top manager of a big industrial concern can as well as the Minister of Foreign Affairs be demoted any day to the lowest social and political status, and that a complete unknown may step into his place. The gangster complicity, on the other hand, which played some role in the early stages of the Nazi dictatorship, loses all cohesive force, for totalitarianism uses its power precisely to spread this complicity through the population until it has organized the guilt of the whole people under its domination.[54]

The absence of a ruling clique has made the question of a successor to the totalitarian dictator especially baffling and troublesome. It is true that this issue has plagued all usurpers, and it is quite characteristic that none of the totalitarian dictators ever tried the old method of establishing a dynasty and appointing their sons. Against Hitler's numerous and therefore self-defeating appointments stands Stalin's method, which made the succession one of the most dangerous honors in the Soviet Union. Under totalitarian conditions, knowledge of the labyrinth of transmission belts equals supreme power, and every appointed successor who actually comes to know what is going on is automatically removed after a certain time. A valid and comparatively permanent appointment would indeed presuppose the existence of a clique whose members would share the Leader's monopoly of

54 Compare the author's contribution to the discussion of the problem of German guilt: 'Organized Guilt,' in *Jewish Frontier*, January, 1945.

knowledge of what is going on, which the Leader must avoid by all means. Hitler once explained this in his own terms to the supreme commanders of the Wehrmacht, who in the midst of the turmoil of war were presumably racking their brains over this problem: 'As the ultimate factor I must, in all modesty, name my own person: irreplaceable ... The destiny of the Reich depends on me alone.' [55] There is no need to look for any irony in the word modesty; the totalitarian leader, in marked contrast to all former usurpers, despots and tyrants, seems to believe that the question of his succession is not overly important, that no special qualities or training are needed for the job, that the country will eventually obey anybody who happens to hold the appointment at the moment of his death, and that no power-thirsty rivals will dispute his legitimacy.[56]

As techniques of government, the totalitarian devices appear simple and ingeniously effective. They assure not only an absolute power monopoly, but unparalleled certainty that all commands will always be carried out; the multiplicity of the transmission belts, the confusion of the hierarchy, secure the dictator's complete independence of all his inferiors and make possible the swift and surprising changes in policy for which totalitarianism has become famous. The body politic of the country is shock-proof because of its shapelessness.

The reasons why such extraordinary efficiency was never tried before are as simple as the device itself. The multiplication of offices

---

55 In a speech of November 23, 1939, quoted from *Trial of Major War Criminals*, Vol. 26, p. 332. That this pronouncement was more than a hysterical aberration dictated by chance is apparent from Himmler's speech (the stenographic transcript can be found in the archives of the Hoover Library, Himmler File, Folder 332) at the conference of mayors at Posen in March, 1944. It says: 'What values can we place onto the scales of history? The value of our own people ... The second, I would almost say, even greater value is the unique person of our Fuehrer Adolf Hitler ... who for the first time after two thousand years ... was sent to the Germanic race as a great leader ...'

56 See Hitler's statements on this question in *Hitlers Tischgespräche*, pp. 253 f. and 222 f.: The new Fuehrer would have to be elected by a 'senate'; the guiding principle for the Fuehrer's election must be that any discussion among the personalities participating in the election should cease for the duration of the proceedings. Within three hours Wehrmacht, party and all civil servants will have to be newly sworn in. 'He had no illusions about the fact that in this election of the supreme head of the state there might not always be an outstanding Fuehrer personality at the helm of the Reich.' But this entailed no dangers, 'so long as the over-all machinery functions properly.'

destroys all sense of responsibility and competence; it is not merely a tremendously burdensome and unproductive increase of administration, but actually hinders productivity because conflicting orders constantly delay real work until the order of the Leader has decided the matter. The fanaticism of the elite cadres, absolutely essential for the functioning of the movement, abolishes systematically all genuine interest in specific jobs and produces a mentality which sees every conceivable action as an instrument for something entirely different.[57] And this mentality is not confined to the elite but gradually pervades the entire population, the most intimate details of whose life and death depend upon political decisions – that is, upon causes and ulterior motives which have nothing to do with performance. Constant removal, demotion, and promotion make reliable teamwork impossible and prevent the development of experience. Economically speaking, slave labor is a luxury which Russia should not be able to afford; in a time of acute shortage of technical skill, the camps were filled with 'highly qualified engineers [who] compete for the right to do plumbing jobs, repair clocks, electric lighting and telephone.'[58] But then, from a purely utilitarian point of view, Russia should not have been able to afford the purges in the thirties that interrupted a long-awaited economic recovery, or the physical destruction of the Red Army general staff, which led almost to a defeat in the Russian-Finnish war.

Conditions in Germany were different in degree. In the beginning, the Nazis showed a certain tendency to retain technical and administrative skill, to allow profits in business, and to dominate economically without too much interference. At the outbreak of the war Germany was not yet completely totalitarianized, and if one accepts preparation for war as a rational motive, it must be conceded that until roughly 1942 her economy was allowed to function more or less rationally. The

57 One of the guiding principles for the SS formulated by Himmler himself reads: 'No task exists for its own sake.' See Gunter d'Alquen, *Die SS. Geschichte, Aufgabe und Organisation der Schutzstaffeln der NSDAP*, 1939, in Schriften der Hochschule für Politik.

58 See David J. Dallin and Boris I. Nicolaevsky, *Forced Labor in Russia*, 1947, who also report that during the war when mobilization had created an acute problem of manpower, the death rate in the labor camps was about 40 per cent during one year. In general, they estimate that the output of a worker in the camps is below 50 per cent of that of a free laborer.

preparation for war in itself is not anti-utilitarian, despite its prohibitive costs,[59] for it may indeed be much 'cheaper to seize the wealth and resources of other nations by conquest than to buy them from foreign countries or produce them at home.' [60] Economic laws of investment and production, of stabilizing gains and profits, and of exhaustion do not apply if one intends in any event to replenish the depleted home economy with loot from other countries; it is quite true, and the sympathizing German people were perfectly aware of it, that the famous Nazi slogan of 'guns or butter' actually meant 'butter through guns.' [61] It was not until 1942 that the rules of totalitarian domination began to outweigh all other considerations.

The radicalization began immediately at the outbreak of war; one may even surmise that one of Hitler's reasons for provoking this war was that it enabled him to accelerate the development in a manner that would have been unthinkable in peacetime.[62] The remarkable thing about this process, however, is that it was by no means checked by such a shattering defeat as Stalingrad, and that the danger of losing the war altogether was only another incitement to throw overboard all utilitarian considerations and make an all-out attempt to realize through ruthless total organization the goals of totalitarian racial ideology, no matter for how short a time.[63] After Stalingrad, the elite

59 Thomas Reveille, *The Spoil of Europe*, 1941, estimates that Germany during the first year of war was able to cover her entire preparatory war expenses of the years 1933 to 1939.

60 William Ebenstein, *The Nazi State*, p. 257.

61 *Ibid.*, p. 270.

62 This is supported by the fact that the decree to murder all incurably sick was issued on the day the war broke out, but even more so by Hitler's statements during the war, quoted by Goebbels (*The Goebbels Diaries*, ed. Louis P. Lochner, 1948) to the effect that 'the war had made possible for us the solution of a whole series of problems that could never have been solved in normal times,' and that, no matter how the war turned out, 'the Jews will certainly be the losers' (p. 314).

63 The Wehrmacht of course tried time and again to explain to the various party organs the dangers of a war conduct in which commands were issued with utter disregard for all military, civilian and economic necessities (see, for instance, Poliakov, *op. cit.*, p. 321). But even many high Nazi functionaries had difficulty understanding this neglect of all objective economic and military factors in the situation. They had to be told time and again that 'economic considerations should fundamentally remain unconsidered in the settlement of the [Jewish] problem' (*Nazi Conspiracy*, VI, 402), but still would complain that the interruption of a big building program in Poland 'would

formations which had been strictly separated from the people were greatly expanded; the ban on party membership for those in the armed forces was lifted and the military command was subordinated to SS commanders. The jealously guarded crime monopoly of the SS was abandoned and soldiers were assigned at will to duties of mass murder.[64] Neither military, nor economic, nor political considerations were allowed to interfere with the costly and troublesome program of mass exterminations and deportations.

If one considers these last years of Nazi rule and their version of a 'five-year plan,' which they had no time to carry out but which aimed at the extermination of the Polish and Ukrainian people, of 170 million Russians (as mentioned in one plan), the intelligentsia of Western Europe such as the Dutch and the people of Alsace and Lorraine, as well as of all those Germans who would be disqualified under the prospective Reich health bill or the planned 'community alien law,' the analogy to the Bolshevik five-year plan of 1929, the first year of clear-cut totalitarian dictatorship in Russia, is almost inescapable. Vulgar eugenic slogans in one case, high-sounding economic phrases in the other, were the prelude to 'a piece of prodigious insanity, in which all rules of logic and principles of economics were turned upside down.'[65]

To be sure, totalitarian dictators do not consciously embark upon

---

not have happened if the many thousands of Jews working at it had not been deported. Now the order is given that the Jews will have to be removed from the armament projects. I hope that this . . . order will soon be cancelled, for then the situation will be still worse.' This hope of Hans Frank, Governor General of Poland, was as little fulfilled as his later expectations of a militarily more sensible policy toward Poles and Ukrainians. His complaints are interesting (see his Diary in *Nazi Conspiracy*, IV, 902 ff.) because he is frightened exclusively by the anti-utilitarian aspect of Nazi policies during the war. 'Once we have won the war, then for all I care, mince-meat can be made of the Poles and the Ukrainians and all the others who run around here . . .'

64 Originally, only special units of the SS – the Death Head formations – were employed in the concentration camps. Later replacements came from the Armed SS divisions. From 1944 on, units of the regular armed forces were also employed but usually incorporated in the Armed SS. (See the Affidavit of a former SS official of the concentration camp of Neuengamme in *Nazi Conspiracy*, VII, 211.) How the active presence of the Wehrmacht made itself felt in the concentration camps has been described in Odd Nansen's concentration camp diary *Day After Day*, London, 1949. Unfortunately, it shows that these regular army troops were at least as brutal as the SS.

65 Deutscher, *op. cit.*, p. 326. This quotation carries weight because it comes from the most benevolent of Stalin's non-Communist biographers.

the road to insanity. The point is rather that our bewilderment about the anti-utilitarian character of the totalitarian state structure springs from the mistaken notion that we are dealing with a normal state after all – a bureaucracy, a tyranny, a dictatorship – from our overlooking the emphatic assertions by totalitarian rulers that they consider the country where they happened to seize power only the temporary headquarters of the international movement on the road to world conquest, that they reckon victories and defeats in terms of centuries or millennia, and that the global interests always overrule the local interests of their own territory.[66] The famous 'Right is what is good for the German people' was meant only for mass propaganda; Nazis were told that 'Right is what is good for the movement,' [67] and these two interests did by no means always coincide. The Nazis did not think that the Germans were a master race, to whom the world belonged, but that they should be led by a master race, as should all other nations, and that this race was only on the point of being born.[68] Not the

66 The Nazis were especially fond of reckoning in terms of millennia. Himmler's pronouncements that SS-men were solely interested in 'ideological questions whose importance counted in terms of decades and centuries' and that they 'served a cause which in two thousand years occurred only once' are repeated, with slight variations, throughout the entire indoctrination material issued by the SS-Hauptamt-Schulungsamt (*Wesen und Aufgabe der SS und der Polizei*, p. 160). – As for the Bolshevik version, the best reference is the program of the Communist International as formulated by Stalin as early as 1928 at the Party Congress in Moscow. Particularly interesting is the evaluation of the Soviet Union as 'the basis for the world movement, the center of international revolution, the greatest factor in world history. In the USSR, the world proletariat for the first time acquires a country . . .' (quoted from W. H. Chamberlin, *Blueprint for World Conquest*, 1946, where the programs of the Third International are reprinted verbatim).

67 This change of the official motto can be found in the *Organisationsbuch der NSDAP*, p. 7.

68 See Heiden, *op. cit.*, p. 722. – Hitler stated in a speech of November 23, 1937, before the future political leaders at the Ordensburg Sonthofen: Not 'ridiculously small tribes, tiny countries, states or dynasties . . . but only races [can] function as world conquerors. A race, however – at least in the conscious sense – we still have to become' (see *Hitlers Tischgespräche*, p. 445). – In complete harmony with this by no means accidental phrasing is a decree of August 9, 1941, in which Hitler prohibited the further use of the term 'German race' because it would lead to the 'sacrifice of the racial idea as such in favor of a mere nationality principle, and to the destruction of important conceptual preconditions of our whole racial and folk policy' (*Verfügungen, Anordnungen, Bekanntgaben*). It is obvious that the concept of a German race would have constituted an impediment to

Germans were the dawn of the master race, but the SS.[69] The 'Germanic world empire,' as Himmler said, or the 'Aryan' world empire, as Hitler would have put it, was in any event still centuries off.[70] For the 'movement' it was more important to demonstrate that it was possible to fabricate a race by annihilating other 'races' than to win a war with limited aims. What strikes the outside observer as a 'piece of prodigious insanity' is nothing but the consequence of the absolute primacy of the movement not only over the state, but also over the nation, the people and the positions of power held by the rulers themselves. The reason why the ingenious devices of totalitarian rule, with their absolute and unsurpassed concentration of power in the hands of a single man, were never tried out before, is that no ordinary tyrant was ever mad enough to discard all limited and local interests – economic, national, human, military – in favor of a purely fictitious reality in some indefinite distant future.

Since totalitarianism in power remains faithful to the original tenets of the movement, the striking similarities between the organizational devices of the movement and the so-called totalitarian state are hardly surprising. The division between party members and fellow-travelers organized in front organizations, far from disappearing, leads to the 'co-ordination' of the whole population, who are now organized as sympathizers. The tremendous increase in sympathizers is checked by limiting party strength to a privileged 'class' of a few millions and creating a superparty of several hundred thousand, the elite formations. Multiplication of offices, duplication of functions, and adaptation of the party–sympathizer relationship to the new conditions mean simply that the peculiar onion-like structure of the

---

the progressive 'selection' and extermination of undesirable parts among the German population which in those very years was being planned for the future.

69 Himmler consequently 'very soon formed a Germanic SS in the various countries' whom he told: 'We do not expect you to become German out of opportunism. But we do expect you to subordinate your national ideal to the greater racial and historical ideal, to the Germanic Reich' (Heiden, *op. cit.*). Its future task would be to form through 'the most copious breeding' a 'racial superstratum' which in another twenty to thirty years would 'present the whole of Europe with its leading class' (Himmler's speech at the meeting of the SS Major Generals at Posen in 1943, in *Nazi Conspiracy*, IV, 558 ff.).

70 Himmler, *ibid.*, p. 572.

movement, in which every layer was the front of the next more militant formation, is retained. The state machine is transformed into a
front organization of sympathizing bureaucrats whose function in
domestic affairs is to spread confidence among the masses of merely
co-ordinated citizens and whose foreign affairs consist in fooling the
outside, nontotalitarian world. The Leader, in his dual capacity as
chief of the state and leader of the movement, again combines in his
person the acme of militant ruthlessness and confidence-inspiring
normality.

One of the important differences between a totalitarian movement
and a totalitarian state is that the totalitarian dictator can and must
practice the totalitarian art of lying more consistently and on a larger
scale than the leader of a movement. This is partly the automatic consequence of swelling the ranks of fellow-travelers, and is partly due to
the fact that unpleasant statements by a statesman are not as easily
revoked as those of a demagogic party leader. For this purpose, Hitler
chose to fall back, without any detours, on the old-fashioned nationalism which he had denounced many times before his ascent to power;
by posing as a violent nationalist, claiming that National Socialism
was not an 'export commodity,' he appeased Germans and non-
Germans alike and implied that Nazi ambitions would be satisfied
when the traditional demands of a nationalist German foreign policy –
return of territories ceded in the Versailles treaties, *Anschluss* of
Austria, annexation of the German-speaking parts of Bohemia – were
fulfilled. Stalin likewise reckoned with both Russian public opinion
and the non-Russian world when he invented his theory of 'socialism
in one country' and threw the onus of world revolution on Trotsky.[71]

Systematic lying to the whole world can be safely carried out only
under the conditions of totalitarian rule, where the fictitious quality
of everyday reality makes propaganda largely superfluous. In their
prepower stage the movements can never afford to hide their true
goals to the same degree – after all, they are meant to inspire mass

71 Deutscher, *op. cit.*, describes Stalin's remarkable 'sensibility to all those psychological undercurrents . . . of which he set himself up as a mouthpiece' (p. 292). 'The very
name of Trotsky's theory, "permanent revolution," sounded like an ominous warning
to a tired generation . . . Stalin appealed directly to the horror of risk and uncertainty
that had taken possession of many Bolsheviks' (p. 291).

organizations. But, given the possibility to exterminate Jews like bed-bugs, namely, by poison gas, it is no longer necessary to propagate that Jews are bedbugs;[72] given the power to teach a whole nation the history of the Russian Revolution without mentioning the name of Trotsky, there is no further need for propaganda against Trotsky. But the use of the methods for carrying out the ideological goals can be 'expected' only from those who are 'ideologically utterly firm' – whether they have acquired such firmness in the Comintern schools or the special Nazi indoctrination centers – even if these goals continue to be publicized. On such occasions it invariably turns out that the mere sympathizers never realize what is happening.[73] This leads to the paradox that 'the secret society in broad daylight' is never more conspiratory in character and methods than after it has been recognized as a full-fledged member of the comity of nations. It is only logical that Hitler, prior to his seizure of power, resisted all attempts to organize the party and even the elite formations on a conspiratory basis; yet after 1933 he was quite eager to help transform the SS into a kind of secret society.[74] Similarly, the Moscow-directed Communist

72 Thus Hitler could afford to use the favorite cliché 'decent Jew' once he had begun to exterminate them, namely, in December, 1941, in the *Tischgespräche*, p. 346.

73 Hitler, therefore, speaking to members of the General Staff (Blomberg, Fritsch, Raeder) and high-ranking civilians (Neurath, Göring) in November, 1937, could permit himself to state openly that he needed depopulated space and reject the idea of conquering alien peoples. That this would automatically result in a policy of exterminating such peoples was evidently not realized by any one of his listeners.

74 This began with an order in July, 1934, by which the SS was elevated to the rank of an independent organization within the NSDAP, and completed by a top secret decree of August, 1938, which declared that the SS special formations, the Death Head Units and the Shock Troops (*Verfügungstruppen*) were neither part of the army nor of the police; the Death Head Units had 'to clear up special tasks of police nature' and the Shock Troops were 'a standing armed unit exclusively at my disposal' (*Nazi Conspiracy*, III, 459). Two subsequent decrees of October, 1939, and April, 1940, established special jurisdiction in general matters for all SS members (*ibid.*, II, 184). From then on all pamphlets issued by the SS indoctrination office carry such notations as 'Solely for use of the police.' 'Not for publication,' 'Exclusively for leaders and those entrusted with ideological education.' It would be worth while to compile a bibliography of the voluminous secret literature, which includes a great many legislative measures, that was printed during the Nazi era. Interestingly enough, there is not a single SA booklet among this type of literature, and this is probably the most conclusive proof that after 1934 the SA ceased to be an elite formation.

parties, in marked contrast to their predecessors, show a curious tendency to prefer the conditions of conspiracy even where complete legality is possible.[75] The more conspicuous the power of totalitarianism the more secret become its true goals. To know the ultimate aims of Hitler's rule in Germany, it was much wiser to rely on his propaganda speeches and *Mein Kampf* than on the oratory of the Chancellor of the Third Reich; just as it would have been wiser to distrust Stalin's words about 'socialism in one country,' invented for the passing purpose of seizing power after Lenin's death, and to take more seriously his repeated hostility to democratic countries. The totalitarian dictators have proved that they knew only too well the danger inherent in their pose of normality; that is, the danger of a true nationalist policy or of actually building socialism in one country. This they try to overcome through a permanent and consistent discrepancy between reassuring words and the reality of rule, by consciously developing a method of always doing the opposite of what they say.[76] Stalin has carried this art of balance, which demands more skill than the ordinary routine of diplomacy, to the point where a moderation in foreign policy or the political line of the Comintern is almost invariably accompanied by radical purges in the Russian party. It was certainly more than coincidence that the Popular Front policy and the drafting of the comparatively liberal Soviet constitution were accompanied by the Moscow Trials.

Evidence that totalitarian governments aspire to conquer the globe and bring all countries on earth under their domination can be found repeatedly in Nazi and Bolshevik literature. Yet these ideological programs, inherited from pretotalitarian movements (from the supranationalist antisemitic parties and the Pan-German dreams of empire in the case of the Nazis, from the international concept of revolutionary socialism in the case of the Bolsheviks) are not decisive. What is decisive is that totalitarian regimes really conduct their

---

75 Compare Franz Borkenau, 'Die neue Komintern,' in *Der Monat*, Berlin, 1949, Heft 4.
76 Instances are too obvious and too numerous to be quoted. This tactic, however, should not be simply identified with the enormous lack of faithfulness and truthfulness which all biographers of Hitler and Stalin report as outstanding traits of their character.

foreign policy on the consistent assumption that they will eventually achieve this ultimate goal, and never lose sight of it no matter how distant it may appear or how seriously its 'ideal' demands may conflict with the necessities of the moment. They therefore consider no country as permanently foreign, but, on the contrary, every country as their potential territory. Rise to power, the fact that in one country the fictitious world of the movement has become a tangible reality, creates a relationship to other nations which is similar to the situation of the totalitarian party under nontotalitarian rule: the tangible reality of the fiction, backed by internationally recognized state power, can be exported the same way contempt for parliament could be imported into a nontotalitarian parliament. In this respect, the prewar 'solution' of the Jewish question was the outstanding export commodity of Nazi Germany: expulsion of Jews carried an important portion of Nazism into other countries; by forcing Jews to leave the Reich passportless and penniless, the legend of the Wandering Jew was realized, and by forcing the Jews into uncompromising hostility against them, the Nazis had created the pretext for taking a passionate interest in all nations' domestic policies.[77]

How seriously the Nazis took their conspiratorial fiction, according to which they were the future rulers of the world, came to light in 1940 when – despite necessity, and in the face of all their all-too-real chances of winning over the occupied peoples of Europe – they started their depopulation policies in the Eastern territories, regardless of loss of manpower and serious military consequences, and introduced legislation which with retroactive force exported part of the Third Reich's penal code into the Western occupied countries.[78] There was hardly a more effective way of publicizing the Nazi claim to world rule than punishing as high treason every utterance or action against the Third Reich, no matter when, where, or by whom it had been made. Nazi

77 See the Circular Letter from the Ministry of Foreign Affairs to all German authorities abroad of January, 1939, in *Nazi Conspiracy*, VI, 87 ff.
78 In 1940, the Nazi government decreed that offenses ranging from high treason against the Reich to 'malicious agitatorial utterances against leading persons of the State or the Nazi Party' should be punished with retroactive force in all German occupied territories, no matter whether they had been committed by Germans or by natives of these countries. See Giles, *op. cit.* – For the disastrous consequences of the Nazi *'Siedlungspolitik'* in Poland and the Ukraine, see *Trial, op. cit.*, Vols. XXVI and XXIX.

law treated the whole world as falling potentially under its jurisdiction, so that the occupying army was no longer an instrument
of conquest that carried with it the new law of the conqueror, but
an executive organ which enforced a law which already supposedly
existed for everyone.

The assumption that Nazi law was binding beyond the German
border and the punishment of non-Germans were more than mere
devices of oppression. Totalitarian regimes are not afraid of the logical
implications of world conquest even if they work the other way around
and are detrimental to their own peoples' interests. Logically, it is
indisputable that a plan for world conquest involves the abolition of
differences between the conquering mother country and the conquered territories, as well as the difference between foreign and
domestic politics, upon which all existing nontotalitarian institutions
and all international intercourse are based. If the totalitarian conqueror conducts himself everywhere as though he were at home, by
the same token he must treat his own population as though he were a
foreign conqueror.[79] And it is perfectly true that the totalitarian movement seizes power in much the same sense as a foreign conqueror may
occupy a country which he governs not for its own sake but for the
benefit of something or somebody else. The Nazis behaved like foreign conquerors in Germany when, against all national interests, they
tried and half succeeded in converting their defeat into a final catastrophe for the whole German people; similarly in case of victory, they
intended to extend their extermination politics into the ranks of
'racially unfit' Germans.[80]

---

79 The term is Kravchenko's, *op. cit.*, p. 303, who, describing conditions in Russia after
the superpurge of 1936–1938, remarks: 'Had a foreign conqueror taken over the machinery of Soviet life . . . the change could hardly have been more thorough or more cruel.'
80 Hitler contemplated during the war the introduction of a National Health Bill:
'After national X-ray examination, the Fuehrer is to be given a list of sick persons, particularly those with lung and heart diseases. On the basis of the new Reich Health
Law . . . these families will no longer be able to remain among the public and can no
longer be allowed to produce children. What will happen to these families will be the
subject of further orders of the Fuehrer.' It does not need much imagination to guess
what these further orders would have been. The number of people no longer allowed
'to remain among the public' would have formed a considerable portion of the German
population (*Nazi Conspiracy*, VI, 175).

A similar attitude seems to have inspired Soviet foreign policy after the war. The cost of its aggressiveness to the Russian people themselves is prohibitive: it has forgone the great postwar loan from the United States which would have enabled Russia to reconstruct devastated areas and industrialize the country in a rational, productive way. The extension of Comintern governments throughout the Balkans and the occupation of large Eastern territories brought no tangible benefits, but on the contrary strained Russian resources still further. But this policy certainly served the interests of the Bolshevik movement, which has spread over almost half of the inhabited world.

Like a foreign conqueror, the totalitarian dictator regards the natural and industrial riches of each country, including his own, as a source of loot and a means of preparing the next step of aggressive expansion. Since this economy of systematic spoliation is carried out for the sake of the movement and not of the nation, no people and no territory, as the potential beneficiary, can possibly set a saturation point to the process. The totalitarian dictator is like a foreign conqueror who comes from nowhere, and his looting is likely to benefit nobody. Distribution of the spoils is calculated not to strengthen the economy of the home country but only as a temporary tactical maneuver. For economic purposes, the totalitarian regimes are as much at home in their countries as the proverbial swarms of locusts. The fact that the totalitarian dictator rules his own country like a foreign conqueror makes matters worse because it adds to ruthlessness an efficiency which is conspicuously lacking in tyrannies in alien surroundings. Stalin's war against the Ukraine in the early thirties was twice as effective as the terribly bloody German invasion and occupation.[81] This is the reason why

---

81 The total number of Russian dead in four years of war is estimated at between 12 and 21 million. Stalin exterminated in a single year in the Ukraine alone about 8 million people (estimate). See *Communism in Action*, U.S. Government, Washington, 1946, House Document No. 754, pp. 140–141. – Unlike the Nazi regime which kept rather accurate accounts on the number of its victims, there are no reliable figures for the millions of people who were killed in the Russian system. Nevertheless the following estimate, quoted by Souvarine, *op. cit.*, p. 669, carries some weight insofar as it stems from Walter Krivitsky, who had direct access to the information contained in the GPU files. According to these figures the census of 1937 in the Soviet Union, which Soviet statisticians had expected to reach 171 million persons, showed that there were actually

totalitarianism prefers quisling governments to direct rule despite the obvious dangers of such regimes.

The trouble with totalitarian regimes is not that they play power politics in an especially ruthless way, but that behind their politics is hidden an entirely new and unprecedented concept of power, just as behind their *Realpolitik* lies an entirely new and unprecedented concept of reality. Supreme disregard for immediate consequences rather than ruthlessness; rootlessness and neglect of national interests rather than nationalism; contempt for utilitarian motives rather than unconsidered pursuit of self-interest; 'idealism,' *i.e.*, their unwavering faith in an ideological fictitious world, rather than lust for power – these have all introduced into international politics a new and more disturbing factor than mere aggressiveness would have been able to do.

Power, as conceived by totalitarianism, lies exclusively in the force produced through organization. Just as Stalin saw every institution, independent of its actual function, only as a 'transmission belt connecting the party with the people' [82] and honestly believed that the most precious treasures of the Soviet Union were not the riches of its soil or the productive capacity of its huge manpower, but the 'cadres' of the party[83] (*i.e.*, the police), so Hitler, as early as 1929, saw the 'great thing' of the movement in the fact that sixty thousand men 'have outwardly become almost a unit, that actually these members are uniform not only in ideas, but that even the facial expression is almost the same. Look at these laughing eyes, this fanatical enthusiasm and you will discover . . . how a hundred thousand men in a movement become a single type.' [84] Whatever connection power had in the minds

---

only 145 millions. This would point to a loss in population of 26 millions, a figure which does not include the losses quoted above.

82 Deutscher, *op. cit.*, p. 256.

83 B. Souvarine, *op. cit.*, p. 605, quotes Stalin as saying at the height of terror in 1937: 'You must reach the understanding that of all the precious assets existing in the world, the most precious and decisive are the cadres.' All reports show that in Soviet Russia the secret police must be regarded as the real elite formation of the party. Characteristic for this nature of the police is that since the early twenties NKVD agents were 'not recruited on a voluntary basis,' but drawn from the ranks of the party. Furthermore, 'the NKVD could not be chosen as a career' (see Beck and Godin, *op. cit.*, p. 160).

84 Quoted from Heiden, *op. cit.*, p. 311.

of Western man with earthly possessions, with wealth, treasures, and riches, has been dissolved into a kind of dematerialized mechanism whose every move generates power as friction or galvanic currents generate electricity. The totalitarian division of states into Have and Have-not countries is more than a demagogic device; those who make it are actually convinced that the power of material possessions is negligible and only stands in the way of the development of organizational power. To Stalin constant growth and development of police cadres were incomparably more important than the oil in Baku, the coal and ore in the Urals, the granaries in the Ukraine, or the potential treasures of Siberia – in short the development of Russia's full power arsenal. The same mentality led Hitler to sacrifice all Germany to the cadres of the SS; he did not consider the war lost when German cities lay in rubble and industrial capacity was destroyed, but only when he learned that the SS troops were no longer reliable.[85] To a man who believed in organizational omnipotence against all mere material factors, military or economic, and who, moreover, calculated the eventual victory of his enterprise in centuries, defeat was not military catastrophe or threatened starvation of the population, but only the destruction of the elite formations which were supposed to carry the conspiracy for world rule through a line of generations to its eventual end.

The structurelessness of the totalitarian state, its neglect of material interests, its emancipation from the profit motive, and its nonutilitarian attitudes in general have more than anything else contributed to making contemporary politics well-nigh unpredictable. The inability of the nontotalitarian world to grasp a mentality which functions independently of all calculable action in terms of men and material, and is completely indifferent to national interest and the well-being of its people, shows itself in a curious dilemma of judgment: those who rightly understand the terrible efficiency of totalitarian organization and police are likely to overestimate the material force of totalitarian countries, while those who understand the wasteful incompetence of totalitarian economics are likely to

---

85 According to reports of the last meeting, Hitler decided to commit suicide after he had learned that the SS troops could no longer be trusted. See H. R. Trevor-Roper, *The Last Days of Hitler*, 1947, pp. 116 ff.

underestimate the power potential which can be created in disregard of all material factors.


## II: The Secret Police

Up to now we know only two authentic forms of totalitarian domination: the dictatorship of National Socialism after 1938, and the dictatorship of Bolshevism since 1930. These forms of domination differ basically from other kinds of dictatorial, despotic or tyrannical rule; and even though they have developed, with a certain continuity, from party dictatorships, their essentially totalitarian features are new and cannot be derived from one-party systems. The goal of one-party systems is not only to seize the government administration but, by filling all offices with party members, to achieve a complete amalgamation of state and party, so that after the seizure of power the party becomes a kind of propaganda organization for the government. This system is 'total' only in a negative sense, namely, in that the ruling party will tolerate no other parties, no opposition and no freedom of political opinion. Once a party dictatorship has come to power, it leaves the original power relationship between state and party intact; the government and the army exercise the same power as before, and the 'revolution' consists only in the fact that all government positions are now occupied by party members. In all these cases the power of the party rests on a monopoly guaranteed by the state and the party no longer possesses its own power center.

The revolution initiated by the totalitarian movements after they have seized power is of a considerably more radical nature. From the start, they consciously strive to maintain the essential differences between state and movement and to prevent the 'revolutionary' institutions of the movement from being absorbed by the government.[86]

86 Hitler frequently commented on the relationship between state and party, and always emphasized that not the state, but the race, or the 'united folk community,' was of primary importance (cf. the afore-quoted speech, reprinted as annex to the *Tischgespräche*). In his speech at the Nuremberg Parteitag of 1935, he gave this theory its most succinct expression: 'It is not the state that commands us, but we who command the state.' It is self-evident that, in practice, such powers of command are possible only if the institutions of the party remain independent from those of the state.

The problem of seizing the state machine without amalgamating with it is solved by permitting only those party members whose importance for the movement is secondary to rise in the state hierarchy. All real power is vested in the institutions of the movement, and outside the state and military apparatuses. It is inside the movement, which remains the center of action of the country, that all decisions are made; the official civil services are often not even informed of what is going on, and party members with the ambition to rise to the rank of ministers have in all cases paid for such 'bourgeois' wishes with the loss of their influence on the movement and of the confidence of its leaders.

Totalitarianism in power uses the state as its outward façade, to represent the country in the nontotalitarian world. As such, the totalitarian state is the logical heir of the totalitarian movement from which it borrows its organizational structure. Totalitarian rulers deal with nontotalitarian governments in the same way they dealt with parliamentary parties or intra-party factions before their rise to power and, though on an enlarged international scene, are again faced with the double problem of shielding the fictitious world of the movement (or the totalitarian country) from the impact of factuality and of presenting a semblance of normality and common sense to the normal outside world.

Above the state and behind the façades of ostensible power, in a maze of multiplied offices, underlying all shifts of authority and in a chaos of inefficiency, lies the power nucleus of the country, the superefficient and supercompetent services of the secret police.[86a] The emphasis on the police as the sole organ of power, and the corresponding neglect of the seemingly greater power arsenal of the army, which is characteristic of all totalitarian regimes, can still be partially explained by the totalitarian aspiration to world rule and its conscious abolition of the distinction between a foreign country and a home country, between foreign and domestic affairs. The military forces, trained to fight a foreign aggressor, have always been a dubious instrument for civil-war purposes; even under totalitarian conditions they

86a Otto Gauweiler, *Rechtseinrichtungen und Rechtsaufgaben der Bewegung*, 1939, notes expressly that Himmler's special position as Reichsfuehrer-SS and head of the German police rested on the fact that the police administration had achieved 'a genuine unity of party and state' which was not even attempted anywhere else in the government.

find it difficult to regard their own people with the eyes of a foreign conqueror.[87] More important in this respect, however, is that their value becomes dubious even in time of war. Since the totalitarian ruler conducts his policies on the assumption of an eventual world government, he treats the victims of his aggression as though they were rebels, guilty of high treason, and consequently prefers to rule occupied territories with police, and not with military forces.

Even before the movement seizes power, it possesses a secret police and spy service with branches in various countries. Later its agents receive more money and authority than the regular military intelligence service and are frequently the secret chiefs of embassies and consulates abroad.[88] Its main tasks consist in forming fifth columns, directing the branches of the movement, influencing the domestic policies of the respective countries, and generally preparing for the time when the totalitarian ruler – after overthrow of the government or military victory – can openly feel at home. In other words, the international branches of the secret police are the transmission belts which constantly transform the ostensibly foreign policy of the totalitarian state into the potentially domestic business of the totalitarian movement.

These functions, however, which the secret police fulfill in order to prepare the totalitarian utopia of world rule, are secondary to those required for the present realization of the totalitarian fiction in one country. The dominant role of the secret police in the domestic politics of totalitarian countries has naturally contributed much to the common misconception of totalitarianism. All despotisms rely heavily on secret services and feel more threatened by their own than by any foreign people. However, this analogy between totalitarianism and despotism holds only for the first stages of totalitarian rule, when there is still a political opposition. In this as in other respects totalitarianism takes advantage of, and gives conscious support to,

87 During the peasant revolts of the twenties in Russia, Voroshilov allegedly refused the support of the Red Army; this led to the introduction of special divisions of the GPU for punitive expeditions. See Ciliga, *op. cit.*, p. 95.
88 In 1935, the Gestapo agents abroad received 20 million marks while the regular espionage service of the Reichswehr had to get along with a budget of 8 million. See Pierre Dehillotte, *Gestapo*, Paris, 1940, p. 11.

nontotalitarian misconceptions, no matter how uncomplimentary they may be. Himmler, in his famous speech to the Reichswehr staff in 1937, assumed the role of an ordinary tyrant when he explained the constant expansion of the police forces by assuming the existence of a 'fourth theater in case of war, internal Germany.'[89] Similarly, Stalin at almost the same moment half succeeded in convincing the old Bolshevik guard, whose 'confessions' he needed, of a war threat against the Soviet Union and, consequently, an emergency in which the country must remain united even behind a despot. The most striking aspect of these statements was that both were made after all political opposition had been extinguished, that the secret services were expanded when actually no opponents were left to be spied upon. When war came, Himmler neither needed nor used his SS troops in Germany itself, except for the running of concentration camps and policing of foreign slave labor; the bulk of the armed SS served at the Eastern front where they were used for 'special assignments' – usually mass murder – and the enforcement of policy which frequently ran counter to the military as well as the Nazi civilian hierarchy. Like the secret police of the Soviet Union, the SS formations usually arrived after the military forces had pacified the conquered territory and had dealt with outright political opposition.

In the first stages of a totalitarian regime, however, the secret police and the party's elite formations still play a role similar to that in other forms of dictatorship and the well-known terror regimes of the past; and the excessive cruelty of their methods is unparalleled only in the history of modern Western countries. The first stage of ferreting out secret enemies and hunting down former opponents is usually combined with drafting the entire population into front organizations and re-educating old party members for voluntary espionage services, so that the rather dubious sympathies of the drafted sympathizers need not worry the specially trained cadres of the police. It is during this stage that a neighbor gradually becomes a more dangerous enemy to one who happens to harbor 'dangerous thoughts' than are the officially appointed police agents. The end of the first stage comes with the liquidation of open and secret resistance in any organized form; it

89  See *Nazi Conspiracy*, IV, 616 ff.

can be set at about 1935 in Germany and approximately 1930 in Soviet Russia.

Only after the extermination of real enemies has been completed and the hunt for 'objective enemies' begun does terror become the actual content of totalitarian regimes. Under the pretext of building socialism in one country, or using a given territory as a laboratory for a revolutionary experiment, or realizing the *Volksgemeinschaft*, the second claim of totalitarianism, the claim to total domination, is carried out. And although theoretically total domination is possible only under the conditions of world rule, the totalitarian regimes have proved that this part of the totalitarian utopia can be realized almost to perfection, because it is temporarily independent of defeat or victory. Thus Hitler could rejoice even in the midst of military setbacks over the extermination of Jews and the establishment of death factories; no matter what the final outcome, without the war it would never have been possible 'to burn the bridges' and to realize some of the goals of the totalitarian movement.[90]

The elite formations of the Nazi movement and the 'cadres' of the Bolshevik movement serve the goal of total domination rather than the security of the regime in power. Just as the totalitarian claim to world rule is only in appearance the same as imperialist expansion, so the claim to total domination only *seems* familiar to the student of despotism. If the chief difference between totalitarian and imperialist expansion is that the former recognizes no difference between a home and a foreign country, then the chief difference between a despotic and a totalitarian secret police is that the latter does not hunt secret thoughts and does not use the old method of secret services, the method of provocation.[91]

Since the totalitarian secret police begins its career after the

90 See note 62.

91 Maurice Laporte, *Histoire de l'Okhrana*, Paris, 1935, rightly called the method of provocation 'the foundation stone' of the secret police (p. 19).

In Soviet Russia, provocation, far from being the secret weapon of the secret police, has been used as the widely propagandized public method of the regime to gauge the temper of public opinion. The reluctance of the population to avail itself of the periodically recurring invitations to criticize or react to 'liberal' interludes in the terror regime shows that such gestures are understood as provocation on a mass scale. Provocation has indeed become the totalitarian version of public opinion polls.

pacification of the country, it always appears entirely superfluous to all outside observers – or, on the contrary, misleads them into thinking that there is some secret resistance.[92] The superfluousness of secret services is nothing new; they have always been haunted by the need to prove their usefulness and keep their jobs after their original task had been completed. The methods used for this purpose have made the study of the history of revolutions a rather difficult enterprise. It appears, for example, that there was not a single anti-government action under the reign of Louis Napoleon which had not been inspired by the police itself.[93] Similarly, the role of secret agents in all revolutionary parties in Czarist Russia strongly suggests that without their 'inspiring' provocative actions the course of the Russian revolutionary movement would have been far less successful.[94] Provocation, in other words, helped as much to maintain the continuity of tradition as it did to disrupt time and again the organization of the revolution.

This dubious role of provocation might have been one reason why the totalitarian rulers discarded it. Provocation, moreover, is clearly necessary only on the assumption that suspicion is not sufficient for arrest and punishment. None of the totalitarian rulers, of course, ever dreamed of conditions in which he would have to resort to provocation in order to trap somebody he thought to be an enemy. More

92 Interesting in this respect are the attempts made by Nazi civil servants in Germany to reduce the competence and the personnel of the Gestapo on the ground that Nazification of the country had been achieved, so that Himmler, who on the contrary wanted to expand the secret services at this moment (around 1934), had to exaggerate the danger coming from the 'internal enemies.' See *Nazi Conspiracy*, II, 259; V, 205; III, 547.

93 See Gallier-Boissière, *Mysteries of the French Secret Police*, 1938, p. 234.

94 It seems, after all, no accident that the foundation of the Okhrana in 1880 ushered in a period of unsurpassed revolutionary activities in Russia. In order to prove its usefulness, it had occasionally to organize murders, and its agents 'served despite themselves the ideas of those whom they denounced . . . If a pamphlet was distributed by a police agent or if the execution of a minister was organized by an Azev – the result was the same' (M. Laporte, *op. cit.*, p. 25). The more important executions moreover seem to have been police jobs – Stolypin and von Plehve. Decisive for the revolutionary tradition was the fact that in times of calm the police agents had to 'stir up anew the energies and stimulate the zeal' of the revolutionaries (*ibid.*, p. 71).

See also Bertram D. Wolfe, *Three Who Made a Revolution: Lenin, Trotsky, Stalin*, 1948, who calls this phenomenon 'Police Socialism.'

important than these technical considerations is the fact that totalitarianism defined its enemies ideologically before it seized power, so that categories of the 'suspects' were not established through police information. Thus the Jews in Nazi Germany or the descendants of the former ruling classes in Soviet Russia were not really suspected of any hostile action; they had been declared 'objective' enemies of the regime in accordance with its ideology.

The chief difference between the despotic and the totalitarian secret police lies in the difference between the 'suspect' and the 'objective enemy.' The latter is defined by the policy of the government and not by his own desire to overthrow it.[95] He is never an individual whose dangerous thoughts must be provoked or whose past justifies suspicion, but a 'carrier of tendencies' like the carrier of a disease.[96] Practically speaking, the totalitarian ruler proceeds like a man who persistently insults another man until everybody knows that the latter is his enemy, so that he can, with some plausibility, go and kill him in self-defense. This certainly is a little crude, but it works – as everybody will know who ever watched how certain successful careerists eliminate competitors.

The introduction of the notion of 'objective enemy' is much more decisive for the functioning of totalitarian regimes than the ideological definition of the respective categories. If it were only a matter of hating Jews or bourgeois, the totalitarian regimes could,

95 Hans Frank, who later became Governor General of Poland, made a typical differentiation between a person 'dangerous to the State' and a person who is 'hostile to the State.' The former implies an objective quality which is independent of will and behavior; the political police of the Nazis is concerned not just with actions hostile to the state but with 'all attempts – no matter what their aim – which in their effects endanger the State.' See *Deutsches Verwaltungsrecht*, pp. 420–430. Translation quoted from *Nazi Conspiracy*, IV, 881 ff. – In the words of Maunz, *op. cit.*, p. 44: 'By eliminating dangerous persons, the security measure . . . means to ward off a state of danger to the national community, independently of any offense that may have been committed by these persons. [It is a question of] warding off an *objective* danger.'

96 R. Hoehn, a Nazi jurist and member of the SS, said in an obituary on Reinhard Heydrich, who prior to his rule of Czechoslovakia had been one of the closest collaborators with Himmler: He regarded his opponents 'not as individuals but as carriers of tendencies endangering the state and therefore beyond the pale of the national community.' In *Deutsche Allgemeine Zeitung* of June 6, 1942; quoted from E. Kohn-Bramstedt, *Dictatorship and Political Police*, London, 1945.

after the commission of one gigantic crime, return, as it were, to the rules of normal life and government. As we know, the opposite is the case. The category of objective enemies outlives the first ideologically determined foes of the movement; new objective enemies are discovered according to changing circumstances: the Nazis, foreseeing the completion of Jewish extermination, had already taken the necessary preliminary steps for the liquidation of the Polish people, while Hitler even planned the decimation of certain categories of Germans;[97] the Bolsheviks, having started with descendants of the former ruling classes, directed their full terror against the kulaks (in the early thirties), who in turn were followed by Russians of Polish origin (between 1936 and 1938), the Tartars and the Volga Germans during the war, former prisoners of war and units of the occupational forces of the Red Army after the war, and Russian Jewry after the establishment of a Jewish state. The choice of such categories is never entirely arbitrary; since they are publicized and used for propaganda purposes of the movement abroad, they must appear plausible as possible enemies; the choice of a particular category may even be due to certain propaganda needs of the movement at large – as for instance the sudden entirely unprecedented emergence of governmental antisemitism in the Soviet Union, which may be calculated to win sympathies for the Soviet Union in the European satellite countries. The show trials which require subjective confessions of guilt from 'objectively' identified enemies are meant for these purposes; they can best be staged with those who have received a totalitarian indoctrination that enables them 'subjectively' to understand their own 'objective' harmfulness and to confess 'for the sake of the cause.'[98] The concept of the

97 As early as 1941, during a staff meeting in Hitler's headquarters, it was proposed to impose upon the Polish population those regulations by which the Jews had been prepared for the extermination camps: change of names if these were of German origin; death sentences for sexual intercourse between Germans and Poles (*Rassenschande*); obligation to wear a P-sign in Germany similar to the Yellow Star for Jews. See *Nazi Conspiracy*, VIII, 237 ff., and Hans Frank's diary in *Trial, op. cit.*, XXIX, 683. Naturally, the Poles themselves soon began to worry about what would happen to them when the Nazis had finished the extermination of the Jews (*Nazi Conspiracy*, IV, 916). – For Hitler's plans regarding the German people, see note 80.

98 Beck and Godin, *op. cit.*, p. 87. speak of the 'objective characteristics' which invited arrest in the USSR; among them was membership in the NKVD (p. 153). Subjective

'objective opponent,' whose identity changes according to the prevailing circumstances – so that, as soon as one category is liquidated, war may be declared on another – corresponds exactly to the factual situation reiterated time and again by totalitarian rulers: namely, that their regime is not a government in any traditional sense, but a *movement*, whose advance constantly meets with new obstacles that have to be eliminated. So far as one may speak at all of any legal thinking within the totalitarian system, the 'objective opponent' is its central idea.

Closely connected with this transformation of the suspect into the objective enemy is the change of position of the secret police in the totalitarian state. The secret services have rightly been called a state within the state, and this not only in despotisms but also under constitutional or semiconstitutional governments. The mere possession of secret information has always given this branch a decisive superiority over all other branches of the civil services and constituted an open threat to members of the government.[99] The totalitarian police, on the contrary, is totally subject to the will of the Leader, who alone can decide who the next potential enemy will be and who, as Stalin did, can also single out cadres of the secret police for liquidation. Since the police are no longer permitted to use provocation, they have been deprived of the only available means of perpetuating themselves independently of the government and have become entirely dependent on the higher authorities for the safeguarding of their jobs. Like the army in a nontotalitarian state, the police in totalitarian countries merely execute political policy and

---

insight into the objective necessity of arrest and confession could most easily be achieved with former members of the secret police. In the words of an ex-NKVD agent: 'My superiors know me and my work well enough, and if the party and the NKVD now require me to confess to such things they must have good reasons for what they are doing. My duty as a loyal Soviet citizen is not to withhold the confession required of me' (*ibid.*, p. 231).

99 Well known is the situation in France where ministers lived in constant fear of the secret '*dossiers*' of the police. For the situation in Czarist Russia, see Laporte, *op. cit.*, pp. 22–23: 'Eventually the Okhrana will wield a power far superior to the power of the more regular authorities ... The Okhrana ... will inform the Czar only of what it chooses to.'

have lost all the prerogatives which they held under despotic bureaucracies.[100]

The task of the totalitarian police is not to discover crimes, but to be on hand when the government decides to arrest a certain category of the population. Their chief political distinction is that they alone are in the confidence of the highest authority and know which political line will be enforced. This does not apply only to matters of high policy, such as the liquidation of a whole class or ethnic group (only the cadres of the GPU knew the actual goal of the Soviet government in the early thirties and only the SS formations knew that the Jews were to be exterminated in the early forties); the point about everyday life under totalitarian conditions is that only the agents of the NKVD in an industrial enterprise are informed of what Moscow wants when it orders, for instance, a speed-up in the fabrication of pipes – whether it simply wants more pipes, or to ruin the director of the factory, or to liquidate the whole management, or to abolish this particular factory, or, finally, to have this order repeated all over the nation so that a new purge can begin.

One of the reasons for the duplication of secret services whose agents are unknown to each other is that total domination needs the most extreme flexibility: to use our example, Moscow may not yet know, when it gives its order for pipes, whether it wants pipes – which are always needed – or a purge. Multiplication of secret services makes last-minute changes possible, so that one branch may be preparing to bestow the Order of Lenin on the director of the factory while another makes arrangements for his arrest. The efficiency of the police consists in the fact that such contradictory assignments can be prepared simultaneously.

Under totalitarian, as under other regimes, the secret police has a monopoly on certain vital information. But the kind of knowledge that can be possessed only by the police has undergone an important change: the police are no longer concerned with knowing what is going on in the heads of future victims (most of the time they ignore who these victims will be), and the police have become the trustees of

100 'Unlike the Okhrana, which had been a state within a state, the GPU is a department of the Soviet government . . . and its activities are much less independent' (Roger N. Baldwin, 'Political Police,' in *Encyclopedia of Social Sciences*).

the greatest state secrets. This automatically means a great improvement in prestige and position, even though it is accompanied by a definite loss of real power. The secret services no longer know anything that the Leader does not know better; in terms of power, they have sunk to the level of the executioner.

From a legal point of view, even more interesting than the change from the suspect to the objective enemy is the totalitarian replacement of the suspected offense by the possible crime. The possible crime is no more subjective than the objective enemy. While the suspect is arrested because he is thought to be capable of committing a crime that more or less fits his personality (or his suspected personality),[101] the totalitarian version of the possible crime is based on the logical anticipation of objective developments. The Moscow Trials of the old Bolshevik guard and the chiefs of the Red Army were classic examples of punishment for possible crimes. Behind the fantastic, fabricated charges one can easily detect the following logical calculation: developments in the Soviet Union might lead to a crisis, a crisis might lead to the overthrow of Stalin's dictatorship, this might weaken the country's military force and possibly bring about a situation in which the new government would have to sign a truce or even conclude an alliance with Hitler. Whereupon Stalin proceeded to declare that a plot for the overthrow of the government and a conspiracy with Hitler existed.[102] Against these 'objective,' though entirely improbable, possibilities stood only 'subjective' factors, such as the trustworthiness of

101 Typical of the concept of the suspect is the following story related by C. Pobyedonostzev in *L'Autocratie Russe: Mémoires politiques, correspondance officielle et documents inédits . . . 1881–1894*, Paris, 1927: General Cherevin of the Okhrana is asked, because the opposing party has hired a Jewish lawyer, to intervene in favor of a lady who is about to lose a lawsuit. Says the General: 'The same night I ordered the arrest of this cursed Jew and held him as a so-called politically suspect person . . . After all, could I treat in the same manner friends and a dirty Jew who may be innocent today but who was guilty yesterday or will be guilty tomorrow?'

102 The charges in the Moscow Trials 'were based . . . on a grotesquely brutalized and distorting anticipation of possible developments. [Stalin's] reasoning probably developed along the following lines: they may want to overthrow me in a crisis – I shall charge them with having made the attempt . . . A change of government may weaken Russia's fighting capacity; and if they succeed, they may be compelled to sign a truce with Hitler, and perhaps even agree to a cession of territory . . . I shall accuse them of having entered already into a treacherous alliance with Germany and ceded Soviet

the accused, their fatigue, their inability to understand what was going on, their firm conviction that without Stalin everything would be lost, their sincere hatred of Fascism – that is, a number of factual details which naturally lacked the consistency of the fictitious, logical, possible crime. Totalitarianism's central assumption that everything is possible thus leads through consistent elimination of all factual restraints to the absurd and terrible consequence that every crime the rulers can conceive of must be punished, regardless of whether or not it has been committed. The possible crime, like the objective enemy, is of course beyond the competence of the police, who can neither discover, invent, nor provoke it. Here again the secret services depend entirely upon the political authorities. Their independence as a state within the state is gone.

Only in one respect does the totalitarian secret police still resemble closely the secret services of nontotalitarian countries. The secret police has traditionally, *i.e.*, since Fouché, profited from its victims and has augmented the official state-authorized budget from certain unorthodox sources simply by assuming a position of partnership in activities it was supposed to suppress, such as gambling and prostitution.[103] These illegal methods of financing itself, ranging from friendly acceptance of bribes to outright blackmail, were a prominent factor in freeing the secret services from the public authorities and strengthened their position as a state within the state. It is curious to see that the financing of police activities with income from its victims has survived all other changes. In Soviet Russia, the NKVD is almost entirely dependent upon the exploitation of slave labor which, indeed, seems to yield no other profit and to serve no other purpose but the financing

---

territory.' This is I. Deutscher's brilliant explanation of the Moscow Trials, *op. cit.*, p. 377.

A good example of the Nazi version of the possible crime can be found in Hans Frank, *op. cit.*: 'A complete catalogue of attempts "dangerous to the State" can never be drawn up because it can never be foreseen what may endanger the leadership and the people some time in the future.' (Translation quoted from *Nazi Conspiracy*, IV, 881.)

103 The criminal methods of the secret police are of course no monopoly of the French tradition. In Austria, for example, the feared political police under Maria Theresa was organized by Kaunitz from the cadres of the so-called 'chastity commissars' who used to live by blackmail. See Moritz Bermann, *Maria Theresia und Kaiser Joseph II*, Vienna–Leipzig, 1881. I owe this reference to Robert Pick

of the huge secret apparatus.[104] Himmler first financed his SS troops, who were the cadres of the Nazi secret police, through the confiscation of Jewish property; he then concluded an agreement with Darré, the Minister of Agriculture, by which Himmler received the several hundred million marks which Darré earned annually by buying agricultural commodities cheaply abroad and selling them at fixed prices in Germany.[105] This source of regular income disappeared of course during the war; Albert Speer, the successor of Todt and the greatest employer of manpower in Germany after 1942, proposed a similar deal to Himmler in 1942; if Himmler agreed to release from SS authority the imported slave laborers whose work had been remarkably inefficient, the Speer organization would give him a certain percentage of the profits for the SS.[106] To such more or less regular sources of income, Himmler added the old blackmail methods of secret services in times of financial crisis: in their communities SS units formed groups of 'Friends of the SS' who had to 'volunteer' the necessary funds for the needs of the local SS men.[107] (It is noteworthy that in its various financial operations the Nazi secret police did not exploit its prisoners. Except in the last years of the war, when the use of human material in the concentration camps was no longer determined by Himmler alone, work in the camps 'had no rational purpose except that of increasing the burden and torture of the unfortunate prisoners.' [108])

104 That the huge police organization is paid with profits from slave labor is certain; surprising is that the police budget seems not even entirely covered by it; Kravchenko, *op. cit.*, mentions special taxes, imposed by the NKVD on convicted citizens who continue to live and work in freedom.

105 See Fritz Thyssen, *I Paid Hitler*, London, 1941.

106 See *Nazi Conspiracy*, I, 916–917. – The economic activity of the SS was consolidated in a central office for economic and administrative affairs. To the Treasury and Internal Revenue, the SS declared its financial assets as 'party property earmarked for special purposes' (letter of May 5, 1943, quoted from M. Wolfson, *Uebersicht der Gliederung verbrecherischer Nazi-Organisationen. Omgus*, December, 1947).

107 See Kohn-Bramstedt, *op. cit.*, p. 112. – The blackmail motive is clearly revealed if we consider that this kind of fund-raising was always organized by local SS units in the localities where they were stationed. See *Der Weg der SS*, issued by the SS-Hauptamt-Schulungsamt (undated), p. 14.

108 *Ibid.*, p. 124. – Certain compromises in this respect were made for those requirements pertaining to the maintenance of the camps and the personal needs of the SS. See Wolfson, *op. cit.*, letter of September 19, 1941, from Oswald Pohl, head of the WVH (*Wirtschafts- und Verwaltungs-Hauptamt*) to the Reichskommissar for price control. It

However, these financial irregularities are the sole, and not very important, traces of the secret police tradition. They are possible because of the general contempt of totalitarian regimes for economic and financial matters, so that methods which under normal conditions would be illegal, and would distinguish the secret police from other more respectable departments of the administration, no longer indicate that we are dealing here with a department which enjoys independence, is not controlled by other authorities, lives in an atmosphere of irregularity, nonrespectability, and insecurity. The position of the totalitarian secret police, on the contrary, has been completely stabilized, and its services are wholly integrated in the administration. Not only is the organization *not* beyond the pale of the law, but, rather, it is the embodiment of the law, and its respectability is above suspicion. It no longer organizes murders on its own initiative, no longer provokes offenses against state and society, and it sternly proceeds against all forms of bribery, blackmail and irregular financial gains. The moral lecture, coupled with very tangible threats, that Himmler could permit himself to deliver to his men in the middle of the war – 'We had the moral right . . . to wipe out this [Jewish] people bent on wiping us out, but we do not have the right to enrich ourselves in any manner whatsoever, be it by a fur coat, a watch, a single mark, or a cigarette' [109] – strikes a note that one would look for in vain in the history of the secret police. If it still is concerned with 'dangerous thoughts,' they are hardly ones which the suspected persons know to be dangerous; the regimentation of all intellectual and artistic life demands a constant re-establishment and revision of standards which naturally is accompanied by repeated eliminations of intellectuals whose 'dangerous thoughts' usually consist in certain ideas that were still entirely orthodox the day before. While, therefore, its police function in the accepted meaning of the word has become superfluous, the economic function of the secret police, sometimes thought to have replaced the first, is even more dubious. It is undeniable, to be sure, that the NKVD periodically rounds up a percentage of the Soviet

---

seems that all these economic activities in the concentration camps developed only during the war and under the pressure of acute labor shortage.

109 Himmler's speech of October, 1943, at Posen, *International Military Trials*, Nuremberg, 1945–46, Vol. 29, p. 146.

population and sends them into camps which are known under the flattering misnomer of forced-labor camps;[110] yet although it is quite possible that this is the Soviet Union's way of solving its unemployment problem, it is also generally known that the output in those camps is infinitely lower than that of ordinary Soviet labor and hardly suffices to pay the expenses of the police apparatus.

Neither dubious nor superfluous is the political function of the secret police, the 'best organized and the most efficient' of all government departments,[111] in the power apparatus of the totalitarian regime. It constitutes the true executive branch of the government through which all orders are transmitted. Through the net of secret agents, the totalitarian ruler has created for himself a directly executive transmission belt which, in distinction to the onion-like structure of the ostensible hierarchy, is completely severed and isolated from all other institutions.[112] In this sense, the secret police agents are the only openly

110 'Bek Bulat (the pen name of a former Soviet professor) has been able to study documents of the North Caucasian NKVD. From these documents it was obvious that in June, 1937, when the great purge was at its apex, the government prescribed the local NKVDs to have a certain percentage of the population arrested . . . The percentage varied from one province to the other, reaching 5 per cent in the least loyal areas. The average for the whole of the Soviet Union was about 3 per cent.' Reported by David J. Dallin in *The New Leader,* January 8, 1949. – Beck and Godin, *op. cit.,* p. 239, arrive at a slightly divergent and quite plausible assumption, according to which 'arrests were planned as follows: The NKVD files covered practically the whole population, and everyone was classified in a category. Thus statistics were available in every town showing how many former Whites, members of opposing parties, etc., were living in them. All incriminating material collected . . . and gathered from prisoners' confessions was also entered in the files, and each person's card was marked to show how dangerous he was considered; this depending on the amount of suspicious or incriminating material appearing in his file. As the statistics were regularly reported to higher authorities, it was possible to arrange a purge at any moment, with full knowledge of the exact number of persons in each category.'

111 Baldwin, *op. cit.*

112 The Russian secret-police cadres were as much at the 'personal disposal' of Stalin as the SS Shock Troops (*Verfügungstruppen*) were at the personal disposal of Hitler. Both, even if they are called to serve with the military forces in time of war, live under their own special jurisdiction. The special 'marriage laws' which served to segregate the SS from the rest of the population, were the first and most fundamental regulations which Himmler introduced when he took over the reorganization of the SS. Even prior to Himmler's marriage laws, in 1927, the SS was instructed by official decree 'never [to participate] in discussions at membership meetings' (*Der Weg der SS*, *op. cit.*).

ruling class in totalitarian countries and their standards and scale of values permeate the entire texture of totalitarian society.

From this viewpoint, it may not be too surprising that certain peculiar qualities of the secret police are general qualities of totalitarian society rather than peculiarities of the totalitarian secret police. The category of the suspect thus embraces under totalitarian conditions the total population; every thought that deviates from the officially prescribed and permanently changing line is already suspect, no matter in which field of human activity it occurs. Simply because of their capacity to think, human beings are suspects by definition, and this suspicion cannot be diverted by exemplary behavior, for the human capacity to think is also a capacity to change one's mind. Since, moreover, it is impossible ever to know beyond doubt another man's heart – torture in this context is only the desperate and eternally futile attempt to achieve what cannot be achieved – suspicion can no longer be allayed if neither a community of values nor the predictabilities of self-interest exist as social (as distinguished from merely psychological) realities. Mutual suspicion, therefore, permeates all social relationships in totalitarian countries and creates an all-pervasive atmosphere even outside the special purview of the secret police.

In totalitarian regimes provocation, once only the specialty of the secret agent, becomes a method of dealing with his neighbor which everybody, willingly or unwillingly, is forced to follow. Everyone, in a way, is the *agent provocateur* of everyone else; for obviously everybody will call himself an *agent provocateur* if ever an ordinary friendly exchange of 'dangerous thoughts' (or what in the meantime have become dangerous thoughts) should come to the attention of the authorities. Collaboration of the population in denouncing political opponents and volunteer service as stool pigeons are certainly not unprecedented, but in totalitarian countries they are so well organized that the work of specialists is almost superfluous. In a system of ubiquitous spying, where everybody may be a police agent and each individual feels himself under constant surveillance; under circumstances, moreover, where careers are extremely insecure and where

---

The same conduct is reported about the members of the NKVD, who kept deliberately to themselves and above all did not associate with other sections of the party aristocracy (Beck and Godin, *op. cit.*, p. 163).

the most spectacular ascents and falls have become everyday occurrences, every word becomes equivocal and subject to retrospective 'interpretation.'

The most striking illustration of the permeation of totalitarian society with secret police methods and standards can be found in the matter of careers. The double agent in nontotalitarian regimes served the cause he was supposed to combat almost as much as, and sometimes more than, the authorities. Frequently he harbored a sort of double ambition: he wanted to rise in the ranks of the revolutionary parties as well as in the ranks of the services. In order to win promotion in both fields, he had only to adopt certain methods which in a normal society belong to the secret daydreams of the small employee who depends on seniority for advancement: through his connections with the police, he could certainly eliminate his rivals and superiors in the party, and through his connections with the revolutionaries he had at least a chance to get rid of his chief in the police.[113] If we consider the career conditions in present Russian society, the similarity to such methods is striking. Not only do almost all higher officials owe their positions to purges that removed their predecessors, but promotions in all walks of life are accelerated in this way. About every ten years, a nation-wide purge makes room for the new generation, freshly graduated and hungry for jobs. The government has itself established those conditions for advancement which the police agent formerly had to create.

This regular violent turnover of the whole gigantic administrative machine, while it prevents the development of competence, has many advantages: it assures the relative youth of officials and prevents a stabilization of conditions which, at least in time of peace, are fraught with danger for totalitarian rule; by eliminating seniority and merit, it prevents the development of the loyalties that usually tie younger staff members to their elders, upon whose opinion and good will their advancement depends; it eliminates once and for all the dangers of unemployment and assures everyone of a job compatible with his education. Thus, in 1939, after the gigantic purge in the Soviet Union had

113 Typical is the splendid career of police agent Malinovsky, who ended as deputy of the Bolsheviks in parliament. See Bertram D. Wolfe, *op. cit.*, chapter xxxi.

come to an end, Stalin could note with great satisfaction that 'the Party was able to promote to leading posts in State or Party affairs more than 500,000 young Bolsheviks.' [114] The humiliation implicit in owing a job to the unjust elimination of one's predecessor has the same demoralizing effect that the elimination of the Jews had upon the German professions: it makes every jobholder a conscious accomplice in the crimes of the government, their beneficiary whether he likes it or not, with the result that the more sensitive the humiliated individual happens to be, the more ardently he will defend the regime. In other words, this system is the logical outgrowth of the Leader principle in its full implications and the best possible guarantee for loyalty, in that it makes every new generation depend for its livelihood on the current political line of the Leader which started the job-creating purge. It also realizes the identity of public and private interests, of which defenders of the Soviet Union used to be so proud (or, in the Nazi version, the abolition of the private sphere of life), insofar as every individual of any consequence owes his whole existence to the political interest of the regime; and when this factual identity of interest is broken and the next purge has swept him out of office, the regime makes sure that he disappears from the world of the living. In a not very different way, the double agent was identified with the cause of the revolution (without which he would lose his job), and not only with the secret police; in that sphere, too, a spectacular rise could end only in an anonymous death, since it was rather unlikely that the double game could be played forever. The totalitarian government, when it set such conditions for promotion in all careers as had previously prevailed only among social outcasts, has effected one of the most far-reaching changes in social psychology. The psychology of the double agent, who was willing to pay the price of a short life for the exalted existence of a few years at the peak, has necessarily become the philosophy in personal matters of the whole post-revolutionary generation in Russia, and to a lesser but still very dangerous extent, in postwar Germany.

This is the society, permeated by standards and living by methods which once had been the monopoly of the secret police, in which the

114 Quoted from Avtorkhanov, *op. cit.*

totalitarian secret police functions. Only in the initial stages, when a struggle for power is still going on, are its victims those who can be suspected of opposition. It then embarks upon its totalitarian career with the persecution of the objective enemy, which may be the Jews or the Poles (as in the case of the Nazis) or so-called 'counter-revolutionaries' – an accusation which 'in Soviet Russia . . . is established . . . before any question as to [the] behavior [of the accused] has arisen at all' – who may be people who at any time owned a shop or a house or 'had parents or grandparents who owned such things,' [115] or who happened to belong to one of the Red Army occupational forces, or were Russians of Polish origin. Only in its last and fully totalitarian stage are the concepts of the objective enemy and the logically possible crime abandoned, the victims chosen completely at random and, even without being accused, declared unfit to live. This new category of 'undesirables' may consist, as in the case of the Nazis, of the mentally ill or persons with lung and heart disease, or in the Soviet Union, of people who happen to have been taken up in that percentage, varying from one province to another, which is ordered to be deported.

This consistent arbitrariness negates human freedom more efficiently than any tyranny ever could. One had at least to be an enemy of tyranny in order to be punished by it. Freedom of opinion was not abolished for those who were brave enough to risk their necks. Theoretically, the choice of opposition remains in totalitarian regimes too; but such freedom is almost invalidated if committing a voluntary act only assures a 'punishment' that everyone else may have to bear anyway. Freedom in this system has not only dwindled down to its last and apparently still indestructible guarantee, the possibility of suicide, but has lost its distinctive mark because the consequences of its exercise are shared with completely innocent people. If Hitler had had the time to realize his dream of a General German Health Bill, the man suffering from a lung disease would have been subject to the same fate as a Communist in the early and a Jew in the later years of the Nazi regime. Similarly, the opponent of the regime in Russia, suffering the same fate as millions of people who are chosen for concentration

115 *The Dark Side of the Moon*, New York, 1947.

camps to make up certain quotas, only relieves the police of the burden of arbitrary choice. The innocent and the guilty are equally undesirable.

The change in the concept of crime and criminals determines the new and terrible methods of the totalitarian secret police. Criminals are punished, undesirables disappear from the face of the earth; the only trace which they leave behind is the memory of those who knew and loved them, and one of the most difficult tasks of the secret police is to make sure that even such traces will disappear together with the condemned man.

The Okhrana, the Czarist predecessor of the GPU, is reported to have invented a filing system in which every suspect was noted on a large card in the center of which his name was surrounded by a red circle; his political friends were designated by smaller red circles and his nonpolitical acquaintances by green ones; brown circles indicated persons in contact with friends of the suspect but not known to him personally; cross-relationships between the suspect's friends, political and nonpolitical, and the friends of his friends were indicated by lines between the respective circles.[116] Obviously the limitations of this method are set only by the size of the filing cards, and, theoretically, a gigantic single sheet could show the relations and cross-relationships of the entire population. And this is the utopian goal of the totalitarian secret police. It has given up the traditional old police dream which the lie detector is still supposed to realize, and no longer tries to find out who is who, or who thinks what. (The lie detector is perhaps the most graphic example of the fascination that this dream apparently exerts over the mentality of all policemen; for obviously the complicated measuring equipment can hardly establish anything except the cold-blooded or nervous temperament of its victims. Actually, the feeble-minded reasoning underlying the use of this mechanism can only be explained by the irrational wish that some form of mind reading were possible after all.) This old dream was terrible enough and since time immemorial has invariably led to torture and the most abominable cruelties. There was only one thing in its favor: it asked for the impossible. The modern dream of the totalitarian police, with

116 See Laporte, *op. cit.*, p. 39.

its modern techniques, is incomparably more terrible. Now the police dreams that one look at the gigantic map on the office wall should suffice at any given moment to establish who is related to whom and in what degree of intimacy; and, theoretically, this dream is not unrealizable although its technical execution is bound to be somewhat difficult. If this map really did exist, not even memory would stand in the way of the totalitarian claim to domination; such a map might make it possible to obliterate people without any traces, as if they had never existed at all.

If the reports of arrested NKVD agents can be trusted, the Russian secret police has come uncomfortably close to this ideal of totalitarian rule. The police has secret dossiers about each inhabitant of the vast country, carefully listing the many relationships that exist between people, from chance acquaintances to genuine friendship to family relations; for it is only to discover these relationships that the defendants, whose 'crimes' have anyway been established 'objectively' prior to their arrest, are questioned so closely. Finally, as for the gift of memory so dangerous to totalitarian rule, foreign observers feel that 'if it is true that elephants never forget, Russians seem to us to be the very opposite of elephants ... Soviet Russian psychology seems to make forgetfulness really possible.'[117]

How important to the total-domination apparatus this complete disappearance of its victims is can be seen in those instances where, for one reason or another, the regime was confronted with the memory of survivors. During the war, one SS commandant made the terrible mistake of informing a French woman of her husband's death in a German concentration camp; this slip caused a small avalanche of orders and instructions to all camp commandants, warning them that under no circumstances was information ever to be given to the outside world.[118] The point is that, as far as the French widow was concerned, her husband had supposedly ceased to live at the moment of his arrest, or rather had ceased ever to have lived. Similarly, the Soviet police officers, accustomed to this system since their birth, could only stare in amazement at those people in occupied Poland

---

117 Beck and Godin, *op. cit.*, pp. 234 and 127.
118 See *Nazi Conspiracy*, VII, 84 ff.

who tried desperately to find out what had happened to their friends and relatives under arrest.[119]

In totalitarian countries all places of detention ruled by the police are made to be veritable holes of oblivion into which people stumble by accident and without leaving behind them such ordinary traces of former existence as a body and a grave. Compared with this newest invention for doing away with people, the old-fashioned method of murder, political or criminal, is inefficient indeed. The murderer leaves behind him a corpse, and although he tries to efface the traces of his own identity, he has no power to erase the identity of his victim from the memory of the surviving world. The operation of the secret police, on the contrary, miraculously sees to it that the victim never existed at all.

The connection between secret police and secret societies is obvious. The establishment of the former always needed and used the argument of dangers arising from the existence of the latter. The totalitarian secret police is the first in history which neither needs nor uses these old-fashioned pretexts of all tyrants. The anonymity of its victims, who cannot be called enemies of the regime and whose identity is unknown to the persecutors until the arbitrary decision of the government eliminates them from the world of the living and exterminates their memory from the world of the dead, is beyond all secrecy, beyond the strictest silence, beyond the greatest mastery of double life that the discipline of conspiratory societies used to impose upon their members.

The totalitarian movements which, during their rise to power, imitate certain organizational features of secret societies and yet establish themselves in broad daylight, create a true secret society only after their ascendancy to rule. The secret society of totalitarian regimes is the secret police; the only strictly guarded secret in a totalitarian country, the only esoteric knowledge that exists, concerns the operations of the police and the conditions in the concentration camps.[120] Of course the

---

119 *The Dark Side of the Moon.*
120 'There was little in the SS that was not secret. The greatest secret was the practices in the concentration camps. Not even members of the Gestapo were admitted . . . to the camps without a special permit' (Eugen Kogon, *Der SS-Staat*, Munich, 1946, p. 297).

population at large and the party members specifically know all the general facts – that concentration camps exist, that people disappear, that innocent persons are arrested; at the same time, every person in a totalitarian country knows also that it is the greatest crime ever to talk about these 'secrets.' Inasmuch as man depends for his knowledge upon the affirmation and comprehension of his fellow-men, this generally shared but individually guarded, this never-communicated information loses its quality of reality and assumes the nature of a mere nightmare. Only those who are in possession of the strictly esoteric knowledge concerning the eventual new categories of undesirables and the operational methods of the cadres are in a position to communicate with each other about what actually constitutes the reality for all. They alone are in a position to believe in what they know to be true. This is their secret, and in order to guard this secret they are established as a secret organization. They remain members even if this secret organization arrests them, forces them to make confessions, and finally liquidates them. So long as they guard the secret they belong to the elite, and as a rule they do not betray it even when they are in the prisons and concentration camps.[121]

We already have noted that one of the many paradoxes that offend the common sense of the nontotalitarian world is the seemingly irrational use which totalitarianism makes of conspiratory methods. The totalitarian movements, apparently persecuted by the police, very sparingly use methods of conspiracy for the overthrow of the government in their struggle for power, whereas totalitarianism in power, after it has been recognized by all governments and seemingly outgrown its revolutionary stage, develops a true secret police as the nucleus of its government and power. It seems that official recognition is felt to be a greater menace to the conspiracy content of the totalitarian movement, a menace of interior disintegration, than the half-hearted police measures of nontotalitarian regimes.

The truth of the matter is that totalitarian leaders, though they are convinced that they must follow consistently the fiction and the rules of the fictitious world which were laid down during their struggle for

121 Beck and Godin, *op. cit.*, p. 169, report how the arrested NKVD officials 'took the greatest care never to reveal any NKVD secrets.'

power, discover only gradually the full implications of this fictitious world and its rules. Their faith in human omnipotence, their conviction that everything can be done through organization, carries them into experiments which human imaginations may have outlined but human activity certainly never realized. Their hideous discoveries in the realm of the possible are inspired by an ideological scientificality which has proved to be less controlled by reason and less willing to recognize factuality than the wildest fantasies of prescientific and prephilosophical speculation. They establish the secret society which now no longer operates in broad daylight, the society of the secret police or the political soldier or the ideologically trained fighter, in order to be able to carry out the indecent experimental inquiry into what is possible.

The totalitarian conspiracy against the nontotalitarian world, on the other hand, its claim to world domination, remains as open and unguarded under conditions of totalitarian rule as in the totalitarian movements. It is practically impressed upon the co-ordinated population of 'sympathizers' in the form of a supposed conspiracy of the whole world against their own country. The totalitarian dichotomy is propagated by making it a duty for every national abroad to report home as though he were a secret agent, and by treating every foreigner as a spy for his home government.[122] It is for the practical realization of this dichotomy rather than because of specific secrets, military and other, that iron curtains separate the inhabitants of a totalitarian country from the rest of the world. Their real secret, the concentration camps, those laboratories in the experiment of total domination, is shielded by the totalitarian regimes from the eyes of their own people as well as from all others.

For a considerable length of time the normality of the normal world is the most efficient protection against disclosure of totalitarian mass crimes. 'Normal men don't know that everything is possible,'[123]

---

122 Typical is the following dialogue reported in *Dark Side of the Moon*: 'To an admission that one had ever been outside Poland the next question invariably was: "And for whom were you spying? . . . One man . . . asked: "But you too have foreign visitors. Do you suppose they are all spies?" The answer was: "What do you think? Do you imagine we are so naïve as not to be perfectly aware of it?"'

123 David Rousset, *The Other Kingdom*, New York, 1947

refuse to believe their eyes and ears in the face of the monstrous, just as the mass men did not trust theirs in the face of a normal reality in which no place was left for them.[124] The reason why the totalitarian regimes can get so far toward realizing a fictitious, topsy-turvy world is that the outside nontotalitarian world, which always comprises a great part of the population of the totalitarian country itself, indulges also in wishful thinking and shirks reality in the face of real insanity just as much as the masses do in the face of the normal world. This common-sense disinclination to believe the monstrous is constantly strengthened by the totalitarian ruler himself, who makes sure that no reliable statistics, no controllable facts and figures are ever published, so that there are only subjective, uncontrollable, and unreliable reports about the places of the living dead.

Because of this policy, the results of the totalitarian experiment are only partially known. Although we have enough reports from concentration camps to assess the possibilities of total domination and to catch a glimpse into the abyss of the 'possible,' we do not know the extent of character transformation under a totalitarian regime. We know even less how many of the normal people around us would be willing to accept the totalitarian way of life – that is, to pay the price of a considerably shorter life for the assured fulfillment of all their career dreams. It is easy to realize the extent to which totalitarian propaganda and even some totalitarian institutions answer the needs of the new homeless masses, but it is almost impossible to know how many of them, if they are further exposed to a constant threat of unemployment, will gladly acquiesce to a 'population policy' that consists of regular elimination of surplus people, and how many, once they have fully grasped their growing incapacity to bear the burdens of modern life, will gladly conform to a system that, together with spontaneity, eliminates responsibility.

In other words, while we know the operation and the specific

---

124 The Nazis were well aware of the protective wall of incredulity which surrounded their enterprise. A secret report to Rosenberg about the massacre of 5,000 Jews in 1943 states explicitly: 'Imagine only that these occurrences would become known to the other side and exploited by them. Most likely such propaganda would have no effect only because people who hear and read about it simply would not be ready to believe it' (*Nazi Conspiracy*, I, 1001).

function of the totalitarian secret police, we do not know how well or to what an extent the 'secret' of this secret society corresponds to the secret desires and the secret complicities of the masses in our time.

## III: Total Domination

The concentration and extermination camps of totalitarian regimes serve as the laboratories in which the fundamental belief of totalitarianism that everything is possible is being verified. Compared with this, all other experiments are secondary in importance – including those in the field of medicine whose horrors are recorded in detail in the trials against the physicians of the Third Reich – although it is characteristic that these laboratories were used for experiments of every kind.

Total domination, which strives to organize the infinite plurality and differentiation of human beings as if all of humanity were just one individual, is possible only if each and every person can be reduced to a never-changing identity of reactions, so that each of these bundles of reactions can be exchanged at random for any other. The problem is to fabricate something that does not exist, namely, a kind of human species resembling other animal species whose only 'freedom' would consist in 'preserving the species.' [125] Totalitarian domination attempts to achieve this goal both through ideological indoctrination of the elite formations and through absolute terror in the camps; and the atrocities for which the elite formations are ruthlessly used become, as it were, the practical application of the ideological indoctrination – the testing ground in which the latter must prove itself – while the appalling spectacle of the camps themselves is supposed to furnish the 'theoretical' verification of the ideology.

The camps are meant not only to exterminate people and degrade human beings, but also serve the ghastly experiment of eliminating, under scientifically controlled conditions, spontaneity itself as an

125 In the *Tischgespräche*, Hitler mentions several times that he '[strives] for a condition in which each individual knows that he lives and dies for the preservation of his species' (p. 349). See also p. 347: 'A fly lays millions of eggs, all of which perish. But the flies remain.'

expression of human behavior and of transforming the human personality into a mere thing, into something that even animals are not; for
Pavlov's dog, which, as we know, was trained to eat not when it was
hungry but when a bell rang, was a perverted animal.

Under normal circumstances this can never be accomplished,
because spontaneity can never be entirely eliminated insofar as it is
connected not only with human freedom but with life itself, in the
sense of simply keeping alive. It is only in the concentration camps
that such an experiment is at all possible, and therefore they are not
only '*la société la plus totalitaire encore réalisée*' (David Rousset) but the
guiding social ideal of total domination in general. Just as the stability
of the totalitarian regime depends on the isolation of the fictitious
world of the movement from the outside world, so the experiment of
total domination in the concentration camps depends on sealing off
the latter against the world of all others, the world of the living in general, even against the outside world of a country under totalitarian
rule. This isolation explains the peculiar unreality and lack of credibility that characterize all reports from the concentration camps and
constitute one of the main difficulties for the true understanding of
totalitarian domination, which stands or falls with the existence of
these concentration and extermination camps; for, unlikely as it may
sound, these camps are the true central institution of totalitarian
organizational power.

There are numerous reports by survivors.[126] The more authentic
they are, the less they attempt to communicate things that evade
human understanding and human experience – sufferings, that is, that
transform men into 'uncomplaining animals.'[127] None of these reports
inspires those passions of outrage and sympathy through which men
have always been mobilized for justice. On the contrary, anyone

---

126  The best reports on Nazi concentration camps are David Rousset, *Les Jours de Notre
Mort*, Paris, 1947; Eugen Kogon, *op. cit.*; Bruno Bettelheim, 'On Dachau and Buchenwald' (from May, 1938, to April, 1939), in *Nazi Conspiracy*, VII, 824 ff. For Soviet
concentration camps, see the excellent collection of reports by Polish survivors published under the title *The Dark Side of the Moon*; also David J. Dallin, *op. cit.*, though his
reports are sometimes less convincing because they come from 'prominent' personalities who are intent on drawing up manifestos and indictments.

127  *The Dark Side of the Moon*; the introduction also stresses this peculiar lack of communication: 'They record but do not communicate.'

speaking or writing about concentration camps is still regarded as suspect; and if the speaker has resolutely returned to the world of the living, he himself is often assailed by doubts with regard to his own truthfulness, as though he had mistaken a nightmare for reality.[128]

This doubt of people concerning themselves and the reality of their own experience only reveals what the Nazis have always known: that men determined to commit crimes will find it expedient to organize them on the vastest, most improbable scale. Not only because this renders all punishments provided by the legal system inadequate and absurd; but because the very immensity of the crimes guarantees that the murderers who proclaim their innocence with all manner of lies will be more readily believed than the victims who tell the truth. The Nazis did not even consider it necessary to keep this discovery to themselves. Hitler circulated millions of copies of his book in which he stated that to be successful, a lie must be enormous – which did not prevent people from believing him as, similarly, the Nazis' proclamations, repeated *ad nauseam*, that the Jews would be exterminated like bedbugs (*i.e.*, with poison gas), prevented anybody from *not* believing them.

There is a great temptation to explain away the intrinsically incredible by means of liberal rationalizations. In each one of us, there lurks such a liberal, wheedling us with the voice of common sense. The road to totalitarian domination leads through many intermediate stages for which we can find numerous analogies and precedents. The extraordinarily bloody terror during the initial stage of totalitarian

128  See especially Bruno Bettelheim, *op. cit.*: 'It seemed as if I had become convinced that these horrible and degrading experiences somehow did not happen to "me" as subject but to "me" as an object. This experience was corroborated by the statements of other prisoners . . . It was as if I watched things happening in which I only vaguely participated . . . "This cannot be true, such things just do not happen." . . . The prisoners had to convince themselves that this was real, was really happening and not just a nightmare. They were never wholly successful.'

See also Rousset, *op. cit.*, p. 213: '. . . Those who haven't seen it with their own eyes can't believe it. Did you yourself, before you came here, take the rumors about the gas chambers seriously?

'No, I said.

'. . . You see? Well, they're all like you. The lot of them in Paris, London, New York, even at Birkenau, right outside the crematoriums . . . still incredulous, five minutes before they were sent down into the cellar of the crematorium . . .'

rule serves indeed the exclusive purpose of defeating the opponent and rendering all further opposition impossible; but total terror is launched only after this initial stage has been overcome and the regime no longer has anything to fear from the opposition. In this context it has been frequently remarked that in such a case the means have become the end, but this is after all only an admission, in paradoxical disguise, that the category 'the end justifies the means' no longer applies, that terror has lost its 'purpose,' that it is no longer the means to frighten people. Nor does the explanation suffice that the revolution, as in the case of the French Revolution, was devouring its own children, for the terror continues even after everybody who might be described as a child of the revolution in one capacity or another – the Russian factions, the power centers of party, the army, the bureaucracy – has long since been devoured. Many things that nowadays have become the specialty of totalitarian government are only too well known from the study of history. There have almost always been wars of aggression; the massacre of hostile populations after a victory went unchecked until the Romans mitigated it by introducing the *parcere subjectis*; through centuries the extermination of native peoples went hand in hand with the colonization of the Americas, Australia and Africa; slavery is one of the oldest institutions of mankind and all empires of antiquity were based on the labor of state-owned slaves who erected their public buildings. Not even concentration camps are an invention of totalitarian movements. They emerge for the first time during the Boer War, at the beginning of the century, and continued to be used in South Africa as well as India for 'undesirable elements'; here, too, we first find the term 'protective custody' which was later adopted by the Third Reich. These camps correspond in many respects to the concentration camps at the beginning of totalitarian rule; they were used for 'suspects' whose offenses could not be proved and who could not be sentenced by ordinary process of law. All this clearly points to totalitarian methods of domination; all these are elements they utilize, develop and crystallize on the basis of the nihilistic principle that 'everything is permitted,' which they inherited and already take for granted. But wherever these new forms of domination assume their authentically totalitarian structure they transcend this principle, which is still tied to the utilitarian motives and self-interest of the rulers, and try their hand in a realm that up to now has been completely unknown to us: the realm where 'everything is possible.' And, characteristically enough, this is precisely the realm that cannot be limited by either utilitarian motives or self-interest, regardless of the latter's content.

What runs counter to common sense is not the nihilistic principle that 'everything is permitted,' which was already contained in the nineteenth-century utilitarian conception of common sense. What common sense and 'normal people' refuse to believe is that everything is possible.[129] We attempt to understand elements in present or recollected experience that simply surpass our powers of understanding. We attempt to classify as criminal a thing which, as we all feel, no such category was ever intended to cover. What meaning has the concept of murder when we are confronted with the mass production of corpses? We attempt to understand the behavior of concentration-camp inmates and SS-men psychologically, when the very thing that must be realized is that the psyche *can* be destroyed even without the destruction of the physical man; that, indeed, psyche, character, and individuality seem under certain circumstances to express themselves only through the rapidity or slowness with which they disintegrate.[130] The end result in any case is inanimate men, *i.e.*, men who can no longer be psychologically understood, whose return to the psychologically or otherwise intelligibly human world closely resembles the resurrection of Lazarus. All statements of common sense, whether of a psychological or sociological nature, serve only to encourage those who think it 'superficial' to 'dwell on horrors.'[131]

If it is true that the concentration camps are the most consequential institution of totalitarian rule, 'dwelling on horrors' would seem to be indispensable for the understanding of totalitarianism. But recollection can no more do this than can the uncommunicative eyewitness report. In both these genres there is an inherent tendency to run away from the experience; instinctively or rationally, both

129  The first to understand this was Rousset in his *Univers Concentrationnaire*, 1947.
130  Rousset, *op. cit.*, p. 587.
131  See Georges Bataille in *Critique*, January, 1948, p. 72.

types of writer are so much aware of the terrible abyss that separates the world of the living from that of the living dead, that they
cannot supply anything more than a series of remembered occurrences that must seem just as incredible to those who relate them as
to their audience. Only the fearful imagination of those who have
been aroused by such reports but have not actually been smitten
in their own flesh, of those who are consequently free from the bestial, desperate terror which, when confronted by real, present
horror, inexorably paralyzes everything that is not mere reaction,
can afford to keep thinking about horrors. Such thoughts are useful
only for the perception of political contexts and the mobilization of
political passions. A change of personality of any sort whatever can no
more be induced by thinking about horrors than by the real experience of horror. The reduction of a man to a bundle of reactions
separates him as radically as mental disease from everything within
him that is personality or character. When, like Lazarus, he rises from
the dead, he finds his personality or character unchanged, just as he
had left it.

Just as the horror, or the dwelling on it, cannot affect a change of
character in him, cannot make men better or worse, thus it cannot
become the basis of a political community or party in a narrower
sense. The attempts to build up a European elite with a program of
intra-European understanding based on the common European experience of the concentration camps have foundered in much the same
manner as the attempts following the first World War to draw political conclusions from the international experience of the front
generation. In both cases it turned out that the experiences themselves
can communicate no more than nihilistic banalities.[132] Political consequences such as postwar pacifism, for example, derived from the
general fear of war, not from the experiences in war. Instead of producing a pacifism devoid of reality, the insight into the structure of
modern wars, guided and mobilized by fear, might have led to the
realization that the only standard for a necessary war is the fight
against conditions under which people no longer wish to live – and

132 Rousset's book contains many such 'insights' into human 'nature,' based chiefly on
the observation that after a while the mentality of the inmates is scarcely distinguishable from that of the camp guards.

our experiences with the tormenting hell of the totalitarian camps have enlightened us only too well about the possibility of such conditions.[133] Thus the fear of concentration camps and the resulting insight into the nature of total domination might serve to invalidate all obsolete political differentiations from right to left and to introduce beside and above them the politically most important yardstick for judging events in our time, namely: whether they serve totalitarian domination or not.

In any event, the fearful imagination has the great advantage to dissolve the sophistic-dialectical interpretations of politics which are all based on the superstition that something good might result from evil. Such dialectical acrobatics had at least a semblance of justification so long as the worst that man could inflict upon man was murder. But, as we know today, murder is only a limited evil, The murderer who kills a man – a man who has to die anyway – still moves within the realm of life and death familiar to us; both have indeed a necessary connection on which the dialectic is founded, even if it is not always conscious of it. The murderer leaves a corpse behind and does not pretend that his victim has never existed; if he wipes out any traces, they are those of his own identity, and not the memory and grief of the persons who loved his victim; he destroys a life, but he does not destroy the fact of existence itself.

The Nazis, with the precision peculiar to them, used to register their operations in the concentration camps under the heading 'under cover of the night (*Nacht und Nebel*).' The radicalism of measures to treat people as if they had never existed and to make them disappear in the literal sense of the word is frequently not apparent at first glance, because both the German and the Russian system are not uniform but consist of a series of categories in which people are treated very differently. In the case of Germany, these different categories used to exist in the same camp, but without coming into contact with each other; frequently, the isolation between the categories was even stricter than the isolation from the outside world. Thus, out of racial considerations, Scandinavian nationals during the war were quite differently

---

133 In order to avoid misunderstandings it may be appropriate to add that with the invention of the hydrogen bomb the whole war question has undergone another decisive change. A discussion of this question is of course beyond the theme of this book.

treated by the Germans than the members of other peoples, although the former were outspoken enemies of the Nazis. The latter in turn were divided into those whose 'extermination' was immediately on the agenda, as in the case of the Jews, or could be expected in the predictable future, as in the case of the Poles, Russians and Ukrainians, and into those who were not yet covered by instructions about such an over-all 'final solution,' as in the case of the French and Belgians. In Russia, on the other hand, we must distinguish three more or less independent systems. First, there are the authentic forced-labor groups that live in relative freedom and are sentenced for limited periods. Secondly, there are the concentration camps in which the human material is ruthlessly exploited and the mortality rate is extremely high, but which are essentially organized for labor purposes. And, thirdly, there are the annihilation camps in which the inmates are systematically wiped out through starvation and neglect.

The real horror of the concentration and extermination camps lies in the fact that the inmates, even if they happen to keep alive, are more effectively cut off from the world of the living than if they had died, because terror enforces oblivion. Here, murder is as impersonal as the squashing of a gnat. Someone may die as the result of systematic torture or starvation, or because the camp is overcrowded and superfluous human material must be liquidated. Conversely, it may happen that due to a shortage of new human shipments the danger arises that the camps become depopulated and that the order is now given to reduce the death rate at any price.[134] David Rousset called his report on the period in a German concentration camp 'Les Jours de Notre Mort,' and it is indeed as if there were a possibility to give permanence to the

---

134 This happened in Germany toward the end of 1942, whereupon Himmler served notice to all camp commandants 'to reduce the death rate at all costs.' For it had turned out that of the 136,000 new arrivals, 70,000 were already dead on reaching the camp or died immediately thereafter. See *Nazi Conspiracy*, IV, Annex II. – Later reports from Soviet Russian camps unanimously confirm that after 1949 – that is, when Stalin was still alive – the death rate in the concentration camps, which previously had reached up to 60 per cent of the inmates, was systematically lowered, presumably due to a general and acute labor shortage in the Soviet Union. This improvement in living conditions should not be confused with the crisis of the regime after Stalin's death which, characteristically enough, first made itself felt in the concentration camps. Cf. Wilhelm Starlinger, *Grenzen der Sowjetmacht*, Wurzburg, 1955.

process of dying itself and to enforce a condition in which both death and life are obstructed equally effectively.

It is the appearance of some radical evil, previously unknown to us, that puts an end to the notion of developments and transformations of qualities. Here, there are neither political nor historical nor simply moral standards but, at the most, the realization that something seems to be involved in modern politics that actually should never be involved in politics as we used to understand it, namely all or nothing – all, and that is an undetermined infinity of forms of human living-together, or nothing, for a victory of the concentration-camp system would mean the same inexorable doom for human beings as the use of the hydrogen bomb would mean the doom of the human race.

There are no parallels to the life in the concentration camps. Its horror can never be fully embraced by the imagination for the very reason that it stands outside of life and death. It can never be fully reported for the very reason that the survivor returns to the world of the living, which makes it impossible for him to believe fully in his own past experiences. It is as though he had a story to tell of another planet, for the status of the inmates in the world of the living, where nobody is supposed to know if they are alive or dead, is such that it is as though they had never been born. Therefore all parallels create confusion and distract attention from what is essential. Forced labor in prisons and penal colonies, banishment, slavery, all seem for a moment to offer helpful comparisons, but on closer examination lead nowhere.

Forced labor as a punishment is limited as to time and intensity. The convict retains his rights over his body; he is not absolutely tortured and he is not absolutely dominated. Banishment banishes only from one part of the world to another part of the world, also inhabited by human beings; it does not exclude from the human world altogether. Throughout history slavery has been an institution within a social order; slaves were not, like concentration-camp inmates, withdrawn from the sight and hence the protection of their fellow-men; as instruments of labor they had a definite price and as property a definite value. The concentration-camp inmate has no price, because he can always be replaced; nobody knows to whom he belongs, because he is never seen. From the point of view of normal society he is absolutely superfluous, although in times of acute labor shortage, as in Russia and in Germany during the war, he is used for work.

The concentration camp as an institution was not established for the sake of any possible labor yield; the only permanent economic function of the camps has been the financing of their own supervisory apparatus; thus from the economic point of view the concentration camps exist mostly for their own sake. Any work that has been performed could have been done much better and more cheaply under different conditions.[135] Especially Russia, whose concentration camps are mostly described as forced-labor camps because Soviet bureaucracy has chosen to dignify them with this name, reveals most clearly that forced labor is not the primary issue; forced labor is the normal condition of all Russian workers, who have no freedom of movement and can be arbitrarily drafted for work to any place at any time. The incredibility of the horrors is closely bound up with their economic uselessness. The Nazis carried this uselessness to the point of open anti-utility when in the midst of the war, despite the shortage of building material and rolling stock, they set up enormous, costly extermination factories and transported millions of people back and forth.[136] In the eyes of a strictly utilitarian world the obvious

135 See Kogon, *op. cit.*, p. 58: 'A large part of the work exacted in the concentration camps was useless, either it was superfluous or it was so miserably planned that it had to be done over two or three times.' Also Bettelheim, *op. cit.*, pp. 831–32: 'New prisoners particularly were forced to perform nonsensical tasks . . . They felt debased . . . and preferred even harder work when it produced something useful . . .' Even Dallin, who has built his whole book on the thesis that the purpose of Russian camps is to provide cheap labor, is forced to admit the inefficiency of camp labor, *op. cit.*, p. 105. – The current theories about the Russian camp system as an economic measure for providing a cheap labor supply would stand clearly refuted if recent reports on mass amnesties and the abolition of concentration camps should prove to be true. For if the camps had served an important economic purpose, the regime certainly could not have afforded their rapid liquidation without grave consequences for the whole economic system.

136 Apart from the millions of people whom the Nazis transported to the extermination camps, they constantly attempted new colonization plans – transported Germans from Germany or the occupied territories to the East for colonization purposes. This was of course a serious handicap for military actions and economic exploitation. For the numerous discussions on these subjects and the constant conflict between the Nazi civilian hierarchy in the Eastern occupied territories and the SS hierarchy see especially Vol. XXIX of *Trial of the Major War Criminals*, Nuremberg, 1947.

contradiction between these acts and military expediency gave the whole enterprise an air of mad unreality.

This atmosphere of madness and unreality, created by an apparent lack of purpose, is the real iron curtain which hides all forms of concentration camps from the eyes of the world. Seen from outside, they and the things that happen in them can be described only in images drawn from a life after death, that is, a life removed from earthly purposes. Concentration camps can very aptly be divided into three types corresponding to three basic Western conceptions of a life after death: Hades, Purgatory, and Hell. To Hades correspond those relatively mild forms, once popular even in non-totalitarian countries, for getting undesirable elements of all sorts – refugees, stateless persons, the asocial and the unemployed – out of the way; as DP camps, which are nothing other than camps for persons who have become superfluous and bothersome, they have survived the war. Purgatory is represented by the Soviet Union's labor camps, where neglect is combined with chaotic forced labor. Hell in the most literal sense was embodied by those types of camp perfected by the Nazis, in which the whole of life was thoroughly and systematically organized with a view to the greatest possible torment.

All three types have one thing in common: the human masses sealed off in them are treated as if they no longer existed, as if what happened to them were no longer of any interest to anybody, as if they were already dead and some evil spirit gone mad were amusing himself by stopping them for a while between life and death before admitting them to eternal peace.

It is not so much the barbed wire as the skillfully manufactured unreality of those whom it fences in that provokes such enormous cruelties and ultimately makes extermination look like a perfectly normal measure. Everything that was done in the camps is known to us from the world of perverse, malignant fantasies. The difficult thing to understand is that, like such fantasies, these gruesome crimes took place in a phantom world, which, however, has materialized, as it were, into a world which is complete with all sensual data of reality but lacks that structure of consequence and responsibility without which reality remains for us a mass of incomprehensible data. The result is that a place has been established where men can be tortured and slaughtered, and yet neither the tormentors nor the tormented, and least of all the outsider, can be aware that what is happening is anything more than a cruel game or an absurd dream.[137]

The films which the Allies circulated in Germany and elsewhere after the war showed clearly that this atmosphere of insanity and unreality is not dispelled by pure reportage. To the unprejudiced observer these pictures are just about as convincing as snapshots of mysterious substances taken at spiritualist séances.[138] Common sense reacted to the horrors of Buchenwald and Auschwitz with the plausible argument: 'What crime must these people have committed that such things were done to them!'; or, in Germany and Austria, in the midst of starvation, overpopulation, and general hatred: 'Too bad that they've stopped gassing the Jews'; and everywhere with the skeptical shrug that greets ineffectual propaganda.

If the propaganda of truth fails to convince the average person because it is too monstrous, it is positively dangerous to those who know from their own imaginings what they themselves are capable of doing and who are therefore perfectly willing to believe in the reality of what they have seen. Suddenly it becomes evident that things which for thousands of years the human imagination had banished to a realm beyond human competence can be manufactured right here on earth, that Hell and Purgatory, and even a shadow of their perpetual duration, can be established by the most modern methods of destruction and therapy. To these people (and they are more numerous in any large city than we like to admit) the totalitarian hell proves only that the power of man is greater than they ever dared to think, and that

137 Bettelheim, *op. cit.*, notes that the guards in the camps embraced an attitude toward the atmosphere of unreality similar to that of the prisoners themselves.

138 It is of some importance to realize that all pictures of concentration camps are misleading insofar as they show the camps in their last stages, at the moment the Allied troops marched in. There were no death camps in Germany proper, and at that point all extermination equipment had already been dismantled. On the other hand, what provoked the outrage of the Allies most and what gives the films their special horror – namely, the sight of the human skeletons – was not at all typical for the German concentration camps; extermination was handled systematically by gas, not by starvation. The condition of the camps was a result of the war events during the final months: Himmler had ordered the evacuation of all extermination camps in the East, the German camps were consequently vastly overcrowded, and he was no longer in a position to assure the food supply in Germany.

man can realize hellish fantasies without making the sky fall or the earth open.

These analogies, repeated in many reports from the world of the dying,[139] seem to express more than a desperate attempt at saying what is outside the realm of human speech. Nothing perhaps distinguishes modern masses as radically from those of previous centuries as the loss of faith in a Last Judgment: the worst have lost their fear and the best have lost their hope. Unable as yet to live without fear and hope, these masses are attracted by every effort which seems to promise a man-made fabrication of the Paradise they had longed for and of the Hell they had feared. Just as the popularized features of Marx's classless society have a queer resemblance to the Messianic Age, so the reality of concentration camps resembles nothing so much as medieval pictures of Hell.

The one thing that cannot be reproduced is what made the traditional conceptions of Hell tolerable to man: the Last Judgment, the idea of an absolute standard of justice combined with the infinite possibility of grace. For in the human estimation there is no crime and no sin commensurable with the everlasting torments of Hell. Hence the discomfiture of common sense, which asks: What crime must these people have committed in order to suffer so inhumanly? Hence also the absolute innocence of the victims: no man ever deserved this. Hence finally the grotesque haphazardness with which concentration-camp victims were chosen in the perfected terror state: such 'punishment' can, with equal justice and injustice, be inflicted on anyone.

In comparison with the insane end-result – concentration-camp society – the process by which men are prepared for this end, and the methods by which individuals are adapted to these conditions, are transparent and logical. The insane mass manufacture of corpses is preceded by the historically and politically intelligible preparation of living corpses. The impetus and what is more important, the silent consent to such unprecedented conditions are the products of those events which in a period of political disintegration suddenly and

139  That life in a concentration camp was simply a dragged-out process of dying is stressed by Rousset, *op. cit., passim.*

unexpectedly made hundreds of thousands of human beings homeless, stateless, outlawed and unwanted, while millions of human beings were made economically superfluous and socially burdensome by unemployment. This in turn could only happen because the Rights of Man, which had never been philosophically established but merely formulated, which had never been politically secured but merely proclaimed, have, in their traditional form, lost all validity.

The first essential step on the road to total domination is to kill the juridical person in man. This was done, on the one hand, by putting certain categories of people outside the protection of the law and forcing at the same time, through the instrument of denationalization, the nontotalitarian world into recognition of lawlessness; it was done, on the other, by placing the concentration camp outside the normal penal system, and by selecting its inmates outside the normal judicial procedure in which a definite crime entails a predictable penalty. Thus criminals, who for other reasons are an essential element in concentration-camp society, are ordinarily sent to a camp only on completion of their prison sentence. Under all circumstances totalitarian domination sees to it that the categories gathered in the camps – Jews, carriers of diseases, representatives of dying classes – have already lost their capacity for both normal or criminal action. Propagandistically this means that the 'protective custody' is handled as a 'preventive police measure,' [140] that is, a measure that deprives people of the ability to act. Deviations from this rule in Russia must be attributed to the catastrophic shortage of prisons and to a desire, so far unrealized, to transform the whole penal system into a system of concentration camps.[141]

The inclusion of criminals is necessary in order to make plausible the propagandistic claim of the movement that the institution exists for asocial elements.[142] Criminals do not properly belong in the

---

140 Maunz, *op. cit.*, p. 50, insists that criminals should never be sent to the camps for the time of their regular sentences.

141 The shortage of prison space in Russia has been such that in the year 1925–26, only 36 per cent of all court sentences could be carried out. See Dallin, *op. cit.*, pp. 158 ff.

142 'Gestapo and SS have always attached great importance to mixing the categories of inmates in the camps. In no camp have the inmates belonged exclusively to one category' (Kogon, *op. cit.*, p. 19).

concentration camps, if only because it is harder to kill the juridical person in a man who is guilty of some crime than in a totally innocent person. If they constitute a permanent category among the inmates, it is a concession of the totalitarian state to the prejudices of society, which can in this way most readily be accustomed to the existence of the camps. In order, on the other hand, to keep the camp system itself intact, it is essential as long as there is a penal system in the country that criminals should be sent to the camps only on completion of their sentence, that is when they are actually entitled to their freedom. Under no circumstances must the concentration camp become a calculable punishment for definite offenses.

The amalgamation of criminals with all other categories has moreover the advantage of making it shockingly evident to all other arrivals that they have landed on the lowest level of society. It soon turns out, to be sure, that they have every reason to envy the lowest thief and murderer; but meanwhile the lowest level is a good beginning. Moreover it is an effective means of camouflage: this happens only to criminals and nothing worse is happening than what deservedly happens to criminals.

The criminals everywhere constitute the aristocracy of the camps. (In Germany, during the war, they were replaced in the leadership by the Communists, because not even a minimum of rational work could be performed under the chaotic conditions created by a criminal administration. This was merely a temporary transformation of concentration camps into forced-labor camps, a thoroughly atypical phenomenon of limited duration.)[143] What places the criminals in the leadership is not so much the affinity between supervisory personnel and criminal elements – in the Soviet Union apparently the

---

In Russia, it has also been customary from the beginning to mix political prisoners and criminals. During the first ten years of Soviet power, the Left political groups enjoyed certain privileges; only with the full development of the totalitarian character of the regime 'after the end of the twenties, the politicals were even officially treated as inferior to the common criminals' (Dallin, *op. cit.*, pp. 177 ff.).

143 Rousset's book suffers from his overestimation of the influence of the German Communists, who dominated the internal administration of Buchenwald during the war.

supervisors are not, like the SS, a special elite trained to commit crimes[144] – as the fact that only criminals have been sent to the camp in connection with some definite activity. They at least know why they are in a concentration camp and therefore have kept a remnant of their juridical person. For the politicals this is only subjectively true; their actions, insofar as they were actions and not mere opinions or someone else's vague suspicions, or accidental membership in a politically disapproved group, are as a rule not covered by the normal legal system of the country and not juridically defined.[145]

To the amalgam of politicals and criminals with which concentration camps in Russia and Germany started out, was added at an early date a third element which was soon to constitute the majority of all concentration-camp inmates. This largest group has consisted ever since of people who had done nothing whatsoever that, either in their own consciousness or the consciousness of their tormenters, had any rational connection with their arrest. In Germany, after 1938, this element was represented by masses of Jews, in Russia by any groups which, for any reason having nothing to do with their actions, had incurred the disfavor of the authorities. These groups, innocent in every sense, are the most suitable for thorough experimentation in disfranchisement and destruction of the juridical person, and therefore they are both qualitatively and quantitatively the most essential category of the camp population. This principle was most fully realized in the gas chambers which, if only because of their enormous capacity, could not be intended for individual cases but only for people in general. In this connection, the following dialogue sums up the situation of the individual: 'For what purpose, may I ask, do the gas chambers exist?' – 'For what purpose

144 See for instance the testimony of Mrs. Buber-Neumann (former wife of the German Communist Heinz Neumann), who survived Soviet and German concentration camps: 'The Russians never . . . evinced the sadistic streak of the Nazis . . . Our Russian guards were decent men and not sadists, but they faithfully fulfilled the requirements of the inhuman system' (*Under Two Dictators*).

145 Bruno Bettelheim, 'Behavior in Extreme Situations,' in *Journal of Abnormal and Social Psychology*, Vol. XXXVIII, No. 4, 1943, describes the self-esteem of the criminals and the political prisoners as compared with those who have not done anything. The latter 'were least able to withstand the initial shock,' the first to disintegrate. Bettelheim blames this on their middle-class origin.

were you born?' [146] It is this third group of the totally innocent who in every case fare the worst in the camps. Criminals and politicals are assimilated to this category; thus deprived of the protective distinction that comes of their having done something, they are utterly exposed to the arbitrary. The ultimate goal, partly achieved in the Soviet Union and clearly indicated in the last phases of Nazi terror, is to have the whole camp population composed of this category of innocent people.

Contrasting with the complete haphazardness with which the inmates are selected are the categories, meaningless in themselves but useful from the standpoint of organization, into which they are usually divided on their arrival. In the German camps there were criminals, politicals, asocial elements, religious offenders, and Jews, all distinguished by insignia. When the French set up concentration camps after the Spanish Civil War, they immediately introduced the typical totalitarian amalgam of politicals with criminals and the innocent (in this case the stateless), and despite their inexperience proved remarkably inventive in creating meaningless categories of inmates.[147] Originally devised in order to prevent any growth of solidarity among the inmates, this technique proved particularly valuable because no one could know whether his own category was better or worse than someone else's. In Germany this eternally shifting though pedantically organized edifice was given an appearance of solidity by the fact that under any and all circumstances the Jews were the lowest category. The gruesome and grotesque part of it was that the inmates identified themselves with these categories, as though they represented a last authentic remnant of their juridical person. Even if we disregard all other circumstances, it is no wonder that a Communist of 1933 should have come out of the camps more Communistic than he went in, a Jew more Jewish, and, in France, the wife of a Foreign Legionary more convinced of the value of the Foreign Legion; it would seem as though these categories promised some last shred of predictable treatment, as though they embodied some last and hence most fundamental juridical identity.

146 Rousset, *op. cit.*, p. 71.
147 For conditions in French concentration camps, see Arthur Koestler, *Scum of the Earth*, 1941.

While the classification of inmates by categories is only a tactical, organizational measure, the arbitrary selection of victims indicates the essential principle of the institution. If the concentration camps had been dependent on the existence of political adversaries, they would scarcely have survived the first years of the totalitarian regimes. One only has to take a look at the number of inmates at Buchenwald in the years after 1936 in order to understand how absolutely necessary the element of the innocent was for the continued existence of the camps. 'The camps would have died out if in making its arrests the Gestapo had considered only the principle of opposition,'[148] and toward the end of 1937 Buchenwald, with less than 1,000 inmates, was close to dying out until the November pogroms brought more than 20,000 new arrivals.[149] In Germany, this element of the innocent was furnished in vast numbers by the Jews after 1938; in Russia, it consisted of random groups of the population which for some reason entirely unconnected with their actions had fallen into disgrace.[150] But if in Germany the really totalitarian type of concentration camp with its enormous majority of completely 'innocent' inmates was not established until 1938, in Russia it goes back to the early thirties, since up to 1930 the majority of the concentration-camp population still consisted of criminals, counterrevolutionaries and 'politicals' (meaning, in this case, members of deviationist factions). Since then there have been so many innocent people in the camps that it is difficult to classify them – persons who had some sort of contact with a foreign country, Russians of Polish origin (particularly in the years 1936 to 1938), peasants whose villages for some economic reason were liquidated, deported nationalities, demobilized soldiers of the Red Army who happened to belong to regiments that stayed too long abroad as occupation forces or had become prisoners of war in Germany, etc. But the existence of a political opposition is for a concentration-camp system only a pretext, and the purpose of the system is not achieved even when, under the most monstrous terror, the population becomes more or less voluntarily co-

---

148  Kogon, *op. cit.*, p. 6.
149  See *Nazi Conspiracy*, IV, 800 ff.
150  Beck and Godin, *op. cit.*, state explicitly that 'opponents constituted only a relatively small proportion of the [Russian] prison population' (p. 87), and that there was no connection whatever between 'a man's imprisonment and any offense' (p. 95).

ordinated, *i.e.*, relinquishes its political rights. The aim of an arbitrary system is to destroy the civil rights of the whole population, who ultimately become just as outlawed in their own country as the stateless and homeless. The destruction of a man's rights, the killing of the juridical person in him, is a prerequisite for dominating him entirely. And this applies not only to special categories such as criminals, political opponents, Jews, homosexuals, on whom the early experiments were made, but to every inhabitant of a totalitarian state. Free consent is as much an obstacle to total domination as free opposition.[151] The arbitrary arrest which chooses among innocent people destroys the validity of free consent, just as torture – as distinguished from death – destroys the possibility of opposition.

Any, even the most tyrannical, restriction of this arbitrary persecution to certain opinions of a religious or political nature, to certain modes of intellectual or erotic social behavior, to certain freshly invented 'crimes,' would render the camps superfluous, because in the long run no attitude and no opinion can withstand the threat of so much horror; and above all it would make for a new system of justice, which, given any stability at all, could not fail to produce a new juridical person in man, that would elude the totalitarian domination. The so-called '*Volksnutzen*' of the Nazis, constantly fluctuating (because what is useful today can be injurious tomorrow) and the eternally shifting party line of the Soviet Union which, being retroactive, almost daily makes new groups of people available for the concentration camps, are the only guaranty for the continued existence of the concentration camps, and hence for the continued total disfranchisement of man.

The next decisive step in the preparation of living corpses is the murder of the moral person in man. This is done in the main by making martyrdom, for the first time in history, impossible: 'How many

151 Bruno Bettelheim, 'On Dachau and Buchenwald,' when discussing the fact that most prisoners 'made their peace with the values of the Gestapo,' emphasizes that 'this was not the result of propaganda . . . the Gestapo insisted that it would prevent them from expressing their feelings anyway' (pp. 834–35).

Himmler explicitly prohibited propaganda of any kind in the camps. 'Education consists of discipline, never of any kind of instruction on an ideological basis.' 'On Organization and Obligation of the SS and the Police,' in *National-politischer Lehrgang der Wehrmacht*, 1937. Quoted from *Nazi Conspiracy*, IV, 616 ff.

people here still believe that a protest has even historic importance? This skepticism is the real masterpiece of the SS. Their great accomplishment. They have corrupted all human solidarity. Here the night has fallen on the future. When no witnesses are left, there can be no testimony. To demonstrate when death can no longer be postponed is an attempt to give death a meaning, to act beyond one's own death. In order to be successful, a gesture must have social meaning. There are hundreds of thousands of us here, all living in absolute solitude. That is why we are subdued no matter what happens.' [152]

The camps and the murder of political adversaries are only part of organized oblivion that not only embraces carriers of public opinion such as the spoken and the written word, but extends even to the families and friends of the victim. Grief and remembrance are forbidden. In the Soviet Union a woman will sue for divorce immediately after her husband's arrest in order to save the lives of her children; if her husband chances to come back, she will indignantly turn him out of the house. [153] The Western world has hitherto, even in its darkest periods, granted the slain enemy the right to be remembered as a self-evident acknowledgment of the fact that we are all men (and *only* men). It is only because even Achilles set out for Hector's funeral, only because the most despotic governments honored the slain enemy, only because the Romans allowed the Christians to write their martyrologies, only because the Church kept its heretics alive in the memory of men that all was not lost and never could be lost. The concentration camps, by making death itself anonymous (making it impossible to find out whether a prisoner is dead or alive) robbed death of its meaning as the end of a fulfilled life. In a sense they took away the individual's own death, proving that henceforth nothing belonged to him and he belonged to no one. His death merely set a seal on the fact that he had never really existed.

This attack on the moral person might still have been opposed by man's conscience which tells him that it is better to die a victim than to live as a bureaucrat of murder. Totalitarian terror achieved its most terrible triumph when it succeeded in cutting the moral person off

152  Rousset, *op. cit.*, p. 464.
153  See the report of Sergei Malakhov in Dallin, *op. cit.*, pp. 20 ff.

from the individualist escape and in making the decisions of conscience absolutely questionable and equivocal. When a man is faced with the alternative of betraying and thus murdering his friends or of sending his wife and children, for whom he is in every sense responsible, to their death; when even suicide would mean the immediate murder of his own family – how is he to decide? The alternative is no longer between good and evil, but between murder and murder. Who could solve the moral dilemma of the Greek mother, who was allowed by the Nazis to choose which of her three children should be killed?[154]

Through the creation of conditions under which conscience ceases to be adequate and to do good becomes utterly impossible, the consciously organized complicity of all men in the crimes of totalitarian regimes is extended to the victims and thus made really total. The SS implicated concentration-camp inmates – criminals, politicals, Jews – in their crimes by making them responsible for a large part of the administration, thus confronting them with the hopeless dilemma whether to send their friends to their death, or to help murder other men who happened to be strangers, and forcing them, in any event, to behave like murderers.[155] The point is not only that hatred is diverted from those who are guilty (the *capos* were more hated than the SS), but that the distinguishing line between persecutor and persecuted, between the murderer and his victim, is constantly blurred.[156]

Once the moral person has been killed, the one thing that still prevents men from being made into living corpses is the differentiation of the individual, his unique identity. In a sterile form such individuality can be preserved through a persistent stoicism, and it is certain that many men under totalitarian rule have taken and are each day still taking refuge in this absolute isolation of a personality without rights or conscience. There is no doubt that this part of the human person,

154 See Albert Camus in *Twice a Year*, 1947.
155 Rousset's book, *op. cit.*, consists largely of discussions of this dilemma by prisoners.
156 Bettelheim, *op. cit.*, describes the process by which the guards as well as the prisoners became 'conditioned' to the life in the camp and were afraid of returning to the outer world.

precisely because it depends so essentially on nature and on forces that cannot be controlled by the will, is the hardest to destroy (and when destroyed is most easily repaired).[157]

The methods of dealing with this uniqueness of the human person are numerous and we shall not attempt to list them. They begin with the monstrous conditions in the transports to the camps, when hundreds of human beings are packed into a cattle-car stark naked, glued to each other, and shunted back and forth over the countryside for days on end; they continue upon arrival at the camp, the well-organized shock of the first hours, the shaving of the head, the grotesque camp clothing; and they end in the utterly unimaginable tortures so gauged as not to kill the body, at any event not quickly. The aim of all these methods, in any case, is to manipulate the human body – with its infinite possibilities of suffering – in such a way as to make it destroy the human person as inexorably as do certain mental diseases of organic origin.

It is here that the utter lunacy of the entire process becomes most apparent. Torture, to be sure, is an essential feature of the whole totalitarian police and judiciary apparatus; it is used every day to make people talk. This type of torture, since it pursues a definite, rational aim, has certain limitations: either the prisoner talks within a certain time, or he is killed. To this rationally conducted torture another, irrational, sadistic type was added in the first Nazi concentration camps and in the cellars of the Gestapo. Carried on for the most part by the SA, it pursued no aims and was not systematic, but depended on the initiative of largely abnormal elements. The mortality was so high that only a few concentration-camp inmates of 1933 survived these first years. This type of torture seemed to be not so much a calculated political institution as a concession of the regime to its criminal and abnormal elements, who were thus rewarded for services rendered. Behind the blind bestiality of the SA, there often lay a deep hatred and

157 Bettelheim, *op. cit.*, describes how 'the main concern of the new prisoners seemed to be to remain intact as a personality' while the problem of the old prisoners was 'how to live as well as possible within the camp.'

Rousset, therefore, is right when he insists that the truth is that 'victim and executioner are alike ignoble; the lesson of the camps is the brotherhood of abjection' (p. 588).

resentment against all those who were socially, intellectually, or physically better off than themselves, and who now, as if in fulfillment of their wildest dreams, were in their power. This resentment, which never died out entirely in the camps, strikes us as a last remnant of humanly understandable feeling.[158]

The real horror began, however, when the SS took over the administration of the camps. The old spontaneous bestiality gave way to an absolutely cold and systematic destruction of human bodies, calculated to destroy human dignity; death was avoided or postponed indefinitely. The camps were no longer amusement parks for beasts in human form, that is, for men who really belonged in mental institutions and prisons; the reverse became true: they were turned into 'drill grounds,' on which perfectly normal men were trained to be full-fledged members of the SS.[159]

158 Rousset, *op. cit.*, p. 390, reports an SS-man haranguing a professor as follows: 'You used to be a professor. Well, you're no professor now. You're no big shot any more. You're nothing but a little runt now. Just as little as you can be. I'm the big fellow now.'
159 Kogon, *op. cit.*, p. 6, speaks of the possibility that the camps will be maintained as training and experimental grounds for the SS. He also gives a good report on the difference between the early camps administered by the SA and the later ones under the SS. 'None of these first camps had more than a thousand inmates . . . Life in them beggared all description. The accounts of the few old prisoners who survived those years agree that there was scarcely any form of sadistic perversion that was not practiced by the SA men. But they were all acts of individual bestiality, there was still no fully organized cold system, embracing masses of men. This was the accomplishment of the SS' (p. 7).

This new mechanized system eased the feeling of responsibility as much as was humanly possible. When, for instance, the order came to kill every day several hundred Russian prisoners, the slaughter was performed by shooting through a hole without seeing the victim. (See Ernest Feder, 'Essai sur la Psychologie de la Terreur,' in *Synthèses*, Brussels, 1946.) On the other hand, perversion was artificially produced in otherwise normal men. Rousset reports the following from a SS guard: 'Usually I keep on hitting until I ejaculate. I have a wife and three children in Breslau. I used to be perfectly normal. That's what they've made of me. Now when they give me a pass out of here, I don't go home. I don't dare look my wife in the face' (p. 273). – The documents from the Hitler era contain numerous testimonials for the average normality of those entrusted with carrying out Hitler's program of extermination. A good collection is found in Léon Poliakov's 'The Weapon of Antisemitism,' published by UNESCO in *The Third Reich*, London, 1955. Most of the men in the units used for these purposes were not volunteers but had been drafted from the ordinary police for these special assignments. But even trained SS-men found this kind of duty worse than front-line fighting. In his report of a mass execution by the SS, an eyewitness gives high praise to

The killing of man's individuality, of the uniqueness shaped in equal parts by nature, will, and destiny, which has become so self-evident a premise for all human relations that even identical twins inspire a certain uneasiness, creates a horror that vastly overshadows the outrage of the juridical-political person and the despair of the moral person. It is this horror that gives rise to the nihilistic generalizations which maintain plausibly enough that essentially all men alike are beasts.[160] Actually the experience of the concentration camps does show that human beings can be transformed into specimens of the human animal, and that man's 'nature' is only 'human' insofar as it opens up to man the possibility of becoming something highly unnatural, that is, a man.

After murder of the moral person and annihilation of the juridical person, the destruction of the individuality is almost always successful. Conceivably some laws of mass psychology may be found to explain why millions of human beings allowed themselves to be marched unresistingly into the gas chambers, although these laws would explain nothing else but the destruction of individuality. It is more significant that those individually condemned to death very seldom attempted to take one of their executioners with them, that there were scarcely any serious revolts, and that even in the moment of liberation there were very few spontaneous massacres of SS men. For to destroy individuality is to destroy spontaneity, man's power to begin something new out of his own resources, something that cannot be explained on the basis of reactions to environment and events.[161]

---

this troop which had been so 'idealistic' that it was able to bear 'the entire extermination without the help of liquor.'

That one wanted to eliminate all personal motives and passions during the 'exterminations' and hence keep the cruelties to a minimum is revealed by the fact that a group of doctors and engineers entrusted with handling the gas installations were making constant improvements that were not only designed to raise the productive capacity of the corpse factories but also to accelerate and ease the agony of death.

160 This is very prominent in Rousset's work. 'The social conditions of life in the camps have transformed the great mass of inmates, both the Germans and the deportees, regardless of their previous social position and education . . . into a degenerate rabble, entirely submissive to the primitive reflexes of the animal instinct' (p. 183).

161 In this context also belongs the astonishing rarity of suicides in the camps. Suicide occurred far more often before arrest and deportation than in the camp itself, which is of course partly explained by the fact that every attempt was made to prevent suicides

Nothing then remains but ghastly marionettes with human faces, which all behave like the dog in Pavlov's experiments, which all react with perfect reliability even when going to their own death, and which do nothing but react. This is the real triumph of the system: 'The triumph of the SS demands that the tortured victim allow himself to be led to the noose without protesting, that he renounce and abandon himself to the point of ceasing to affirm his identity. And it is not for nothing. It is not gratuitously, out of sheer sadism, that the SS men desire his defeat. They know that the system which succeeds in destroying its victim before he mounts the scaffold . . . is incomparably the best for keeping a whole people in slavery. In submission. Nothing is more terrible than these processions of human beings going like dummies to their death. The man who sees this says to himself: "For them to be thus reduced, what power must be concealed in the hands of the masters," and he turns away, full of bitterness but defeated.'[162]

If we take totalitarian aspirations seriously and refuse to be misled by the common-sense assertion that they are utopian and unrealizable, it develops that the society of the dying established in the camps is the only form of society in which it is possible to dominate man entirely. Those who aspire to total domination must liquidate all spontaneity, such as the mere existence of individuality will always engender, and track it down in its most private forms, regardless of how unpolitical and harmless these may seem. Pavlov's dog, the human specimen reduced to the most elementary reactions, the bundle of reactions that can always be liquidated and replaced by other bundles of reactions that behave in exactly the same way, is the model 'citizen' of a totalitarian state; and such a citizen can be produced only imperfectly outside of the camps.

The uselessness of the camps, their cynically admitted anti-utility,

---

which are, after all, spontaneous acts. From the statistical material for Buchenwald (*Nazi Conspiracy*, IV, 800 ff.) it is evident that scarcely more than one-half per cent of the deaths could be traced to suicide, that frequently there were only two suicides per year, although in the same year the total number of deaths reached 3,516. The reports from Russian camps mention the same phenomenon. Cf., for instance, Starlinger, *op. cit.*, p. 57.

162 Rousset, *op. cit.*, p. 525.

is only apparent. In reality they are more essential to the preservation of the regime's power than any of its other institutions. Without concentration camps, without the undefined fear they inspire and the very well-defined training they offer in totalitarian domination, which can nowhere else be fully tested with all of its most radical possibilities, a totalitarian state can neither inspire its nuclear troops with fanaticism nor maintain a whole people in complete apathy. The dominating and the dominated would only too quickly sink back into the 'old bourgeois routine'; after early 'excesses,' they would succumb to everyday life with its human laws; in short, they would develop in the direction which all observers counseled by common sense were so prone to predict. The tragic fallacy of all these prophecies, originating in a world that was still safe, was to suppose that there was such a thing as one human nature established for all time, to identify this human nature with history, and thus to declare that the idea of total domination was not only inhuman but also unrealistic. Meanwhile we have learned that the power of man is so great that he really can be what he wishes to be.

It is in the very nature of totalitarian regimes to demand unlimited power. Such power can only be secured if literally all men, without a single exception, are reliably dominated in every aspect of their life. In the realm of foreign affairs new neutral territories must constantly be subjugated, while at home ever-new human groups must be mastered in expanding concentration camps, or, when circumstances require liquidated to make room for others. The question of opposition is unimportant both in foreign and domestic affairs. Any neutrality, indeed any spontaneously given friendship, is from the standpoint of totalitarian domination just as dangerous as open hostility, precisely because spontaneity as such, with its incalculability, is the greatest of all obstacles to total domination over man. The Communists of non-Communist countries, who fled or were called to Moscow, learned by bitter experience that they constituted a menace to the Soviet Union. Convinced Communists are in this sense, which alone has any reality today, just as ridiculous and just as menacing to the regime in Russia, as, for example, the convinced Nazis of the Röhm faction were to the Nazis.

What makes conviction and opinion of any sort so ridiculous and dangerous under totalitarian conditions is that totalitarian regimes take the greatest pride in having no need of them, or of any human help of any kind. Men insofar as they are more than animal reaction and fulfillment of functions are entirely superfluous to totalitarian regimes. Totalitarianism strives not toward despotic rule over men, but toward a system in which men are superfluous. Total power can be achieved and safeguarded only in a world of conditioned reflexes, of marionettes without the slightest trace of spontaneity. Precisely because man's resources are so great, he can be fully dominated only when he becomes a specimen of the animal-species man.

Therefore character is a threat and even the most unjust legal rules are an obstacle; but individuality, anything indeed that distinguishes one man from another, is intolerable. As long as all men have not been made equally superfluous – and this has been accomplished only in concentration camps – the ideal of totalitarian domination has not been achieved. Totalitarian states strive constantly, though never with complete success, to establish the superfluity of man – by the arbitrary selection of various groups for concentration camps, by constant purges of the ruling apparatus, by mass liquidations. Common sense protests desperately that the masses are submissive and that all this gigantic apparatus of terror is therefore superfluous; if they were capable of telling the truth, the totalitarian rulers would reply: The apparatus seems superfluous to you only because it serves to make men superfluous.

The totalitarian attempt to make men superfluous reflects the experience of modern masses of their superfluity on an overcrowded earth. The world of the dying, in which men are taught they are superfluous through a way of life in which punishment is meted out without connection with crime, in which exploitation is practiced without profit, and where work is performed without product, is a place where senselessness is daily produced anew. Yet, within the framework of the totalitarian ideology, nothing could be more sensible and logical; if the inmates are vermin, it is logical that they should be killed by poison gas; if they are degenerate, they should not be allowed to contaminate the population; if they have 'slave-like souls' (Himmler), no one should waste his time trying to re-educate them. Seen through the eyes of the ideology, the trouble with the camps is almost that they make too much sense, that the execution of the doctrine is too consistent.

While the totalitarian regimes are thus resolutely and cynically emptying the world of the only thing that makes sense to the utilitarian expectations of common sense, they impose upon it at the same time a kind of supersense which the ideologies actually always meant when they pretended to have found the key to history or the solution to the riddles of the universe. Over and above the senselessness of totalitarian society is enthroned the ridiculous supersense of its ideological superstition. Ideologies are harmless, uncritical, and arbitrary opinions only as long as they are not believed in seriously. Once their claim to total validity is taken literally they become the nuclei of logical systems in which, as in the systems of paranoiacs, everything follows comprehensibly and even compulsorily once the first premise is accepted. The insanity of such systems lies not only in their first premise but in the very logicality with which they are constructed. The curious logicality of all isms, their simple-minded trust in the salvation value of stubborn devotion without regard for specific, varying factors, already harbors the first germs of totalitarian contempt for reality and factuality.

Common sense trained in utilitarian thinking is helpless against this ideological supersense, since totalitarian regimes establish a functioning world of no-sense. The ideological contempt for factuality still contained the proud assumption of human mastery over the world; it is, after all, contempt for reality which makes possible changing the world, the erection of the human artifice. What destroys the element of pride in the totalitarian contempt for reality (and thereby distinguishes it radically from revolutionary theories and attitudes) is the supersense which gives the contempt for reality its cogency, logicality, and consistency. What makes a truly totalitarian device out of the Bolshevik claim that the present Russian system is superior to all others is the fact that the totalitarian ruler draws from this claim the logically impeccable conclusion that without this system people never could have built such a wonderful thing as, let us say, a subway; from this, he again draws the logical conclusion that anyone who knows of the existence of the Paris subway is a suspect because he may cause people to doubt that one can do things only in the Bolshevik way.

This leads to the final conclusion that in order to remain a loyal Bolshevik, you have to destroy the Paris subway. Nothing matters but consistency.

With these new structures, built on the strength of supersense and driven by the motor of logicality, we are indeed at the end of the bourgeois era of profits and power, as well as at the end of imperialism and expansion. The aggressiveness of totalitarianism springs not from lust for power, and if it feverishly seeks to expand, it does so neither for expansion's sake nor for profit, but only for ideological reasons: to make the world consistent, to prove that its respective supersense has been right.

It is chiefly for the sake of this supersense, for the sake of complete consistency, that it is necessary for totalitarianism to destroy every trace of what we commonly call human dignity. For respect for human dignity implies the recognition of my fellow-men or our fellow-nations as subjects, as builders of worlds or cobuilders of a common world. No ideology which aims at the explanation of all historical events of the past and at mapping out the course of all events of the future can bear the unpredictability which springs from the fact that men are creative, that they can bring forward something so new that nobody ever foresaw it.

What totalitarian ideologies therefore aim at is not the transformation of the outside world or the revolutionizing transmutation of society, but the transformation of human nature itself. The concentration camps are the laboratories where changes in human nature are tested, and their shamefulness therefore is not just the business of their inmates and those who run them according to strictly 'scientific' standards; it is the concern of all men. Suffering, of which there has been always too much on earth, is not the issue, nor is the number of victims. Human nature as such is at stake, and even though it seems that these experiments succeed not in changing man but only in destroying him, by creating a society in which the nihilistic banality of *homo homini lupus* is consistently realized, one should bear in mind the necessary limitations to an experiment which requires global control in order to show conclusive results.

Until now the totalitarian belief that everything is possible seems to have proved only that everything can be destroyed. Yet, in their effort to prove that everything is possible, totalitarian regimes have discovered without knowing it that there are crimes which men can neither punish nor forgive. When the impossible was made possible it became the unpunishable, unforgivable absolute evil which could no longer be understood and explained by the evil motives of self-interest, greed, covetousness, resentment, lust for power, and cowardice; and which therefore anger could not revenge, love could not endure, friendship could not forgive. Just as the victims in the death factories or the holes of oblivion are no longer 'human' in the eyes of their executioners, so this newest species of criminals is beyond the pale even of solidarity in human sinfulness.

It is inherent in our entire philosophical tradition that we cannot conceive of a 'radical evil,' and this is true both for Christian theology, which conceded even to the Devil himself a celestial origin, as well as for Kant, the only philosopher who, in the word he coined for it, at least must have suspected the existence of this evil even though he immediately rationalized it in the concept of a 'perverted ill will' that could be explained by comprehensible motives. Therefore, we actually have nothing to fall back on in order to understand a phenomenon that nevertheless confronts us with its overpowering reality and breaks down all standards we know. There is only one thing that seems to be discernible: we may say that radical evil has emerged in connection with a system in which all men have become equally superfluous. The manipulators of this system believe in their own superfluousness as much as in that of all others, and the totalitarian murderers are all the more dangerous because they do not care if they themselves are alive or dead, if they ever lived or never were born. The danger of the corpse factories and holes of oblivion is that today, with populations and homelessness everywhere on the increase, masses of people are continuously rendered superfluous if we continue to think of our world in utilitarian terms. Political, social, and economic events everywhere are in a silent conspiracy with totalitarian instruments devised for making men superfluous. The implied temptation is well understood by the utilitarian common sense of the masses, who in most countries are too desperate to retain much fear of death. The Nazis and the Bolsheviks can be sure that their factories of annihilation which demonstrate the swiftest solution to the problem of overpopulation, of economically superfluous and socially rootless human masses, are as much of an attraction as a warning. Totalitarian solutions may well survive the fall of totalitarian regimes in the form of strong temptations which will come up whenever it seems impossible to alleviate political, social, or economic misery in a manner worthy of man.

# CHAPTER THIRTEEN

# Ideology and Terror: A Novel Form of Government

In the preceding chapers we emphasized repeatedly that the means of total domination are not only more drastic but that totalitarianism differs essentially from other forms of political oppression known to us such as despotism, tyranny and dictatorship. Wherever it rose to power, it developed entirely new political institutions and destroyed all social, legal and political traditions of the country. No matter what the specifically national tradition or the particular spiritual source of its ideology, totalitarian government always transformed classes into masses, supplanted the party system, not by one-party dictatorships, but by a mass movement, shifted the center of power from the army to the police, and established a foreign policy openly directed toward world domination. Present totalitarian governments have developed from one-party systems; whenever these became truly totalitarian, they started to operate according to a system of values so radically different from all others, that none of our traditional legal, moral, or common sense utilitarian categories could any longer help us to come to terms with, or judge, or predict their course of action.

If it is true that the elements of totalitarianism can be found by retracing the history and analyzing the political implications of what we usually call the crisis of our century, then the conclusion is unavoidable that this crisis is no mere threat from the outside, no mere result of some aggressive foreign policy of either Germany or Russia, and that it will no more disappear with the death of Stalin than it disappeared with the fall of Nazi Germany. It may even be that the true predicaments of our time will assume their authentic form – though not necessarily the cruelest – only when totalitarianism has become a thing of the past.

It is in the line of such reflections to raise the question whether totalitarian government, born of this crisis and at the same time its clearest and only unequivocal symptom, is merely a makeshift arrangement, which borrows its methods of intimidation, its means of organization and its instruments of violence from the well-known political arsenal of tyranny, despotism and dictatorships, and owes its existence only to the deplorable, but perhaps accidental failure of the traditional political forces – liberal or conservative, national or social-ist, republican or monarchist, authoritarian or democratic. Or whether, on the contrary, there is such a thing as the *nature* of totali-tarian government, whether it has its own essence and can be compared with and defined like other forms of government such as Western thought has known and recognized since the times of ancient philosophy. If this is true, then the entirely new and unprecedented forms of totalitarian organization and course of action must rest on one of the few basic experiences which men can have whenever they live together, and are concerned with public affairs. If there is a basic experience which finds its political expression in totalitarian domina-tion, then, in view of the novelty of the totalitarian form of government, this must be an experience which, for whatever reason, has never before served as the foundation of a body politic and whose general mood – although it may be familiar in every other respect – never before has pervaded, and directed the handling of, public affairs.

If we consider this in terms of the history of ideas, it seems extremely unlikely. For the forms of government under which men live have been very few; they were discovered early, classified by the Greeks and have proved extraordinarily long-lived. If we apply these findings, whose fundamental idea, despite many variations, did not change in the two and a half thousand years that separate Plato from Kant, we are tempted at once to interpret totalitarianism as some modern form of tyranny, that is a lawless government where power is wielded by one man. Arbitrary power, unrestricted by law, wielded in the interest of the ruler and hostile to the interests of the governed, on one hand, fear as the principle of action, namely fear of the people by the ruler and fear of the ruler by the people, on the other – these have been the hallmarks of tyranny throughout our tradition.

Instead of saying that totalitarian government is unprecedented, we could also say that it has exploded the very alternative on which all definitions of the essence of governments have been based in political philosophy, that is the alternative between lawful and lawless government, between arbitrary and legitimate power. That lawful government and legitimate power, on one side, lawlessness and arbitrary power on the other, belonged together and were inseparable has never been questioned. Yet, totalitarian rule confronts us with a totally different kind of government. It defies, it is true, all positive laws, even to the extreme of defying those which it has itself established (as in the case of the Soviet Constitution of 1936, to quote only the most outstanding example) or which it did not care to abolish (as in the case of the Weimar Constitution which the Nazi government never revoked). But it operates neither without guidance of law nor is it arbitrary, for it claims to obey strictly and unequivocally those laws of Nature or of History from which all positive laws always have been supposed to spring.

It is the monstrous, yet seemingly unanswerable claim of totalitarian rule that, far from being 'lawless,' it goes to the sources of authority from which positive laws received their ultimate legitimation, that far from being arbitrary it is more obedient to these suprahuman forces than any government ever was before, and that far from wielding its power in the interest of one man, it is quite prepared to sacrifice everybody's vital immediate interests to the execution of what it assumes to be the law of History or the law of Nature. Its defiance of positive laws claims to be a higher form of legitimacy which, since it is inspired by the sources themselves, can do away with petty legality. Totalitarian lawfulness pretends to have found a way to establish the rule of justice on earth – something which the legality of positive law admittedly could never attain. The discrepancy between legality and justice could never be bridged because the standards of right and wrong into which positive law translates its own source of authority – 'natural law' governing the whole universe, or divine law revealed in human history, or customs and traditions expressing the law common to the sentiments of all men – are necessarily general and must be valid for a countless and unpredictable number of cases, so that each concrete individual case with its unrepeatable set of circumstances somehow escapes it.

Totalitarian lawfulness, defying legality and pretending to

establish the direct reign of justice on earth, executes the law of History or of Nature without translating it into standards of right and wrong for individual behavior. It applies the law directly to mankind without bothering with the behavior of men. The law of Nature or the law of History, if properly executed, is expected to produce mankind as its end product; and this expectation lies behind the claim to global rule of all totalitarian governments. Totalitarian policy claims to transform the human species into an active unfailing carrier of a law to which human beings otherwise would only passively and reluctantly be subjected. If it is true that the link between totalitarian countries and the civilized world was broken through the monstrous crimes of totalitarian regimes, it is also true that this criminality was not due to simple aggressiveness, ruthlessness, warfare and treachery, but to a conscious break of that *consensus iuris* which, according to Cicero, constitutes a 'people,' and which, as international law, in modern times has constituted the civilized world insofar as it remains the foundation-stone of international relations even under the conditions of war. Both moral judgment and legal punishment presuppose this basic consent; the criminal can be judged justly only because he takes part in the *consensus iuris*, and even the revealed law of God can function among men only when they listen and consent to it.

At this point the fundamental difference between the totalitarian and all other concepts of law comes to light. Totalitarian policy does not replace one set of laws with another, does not establish its own *consensus iuris*, does not create, by one revolution, a new form of legality. Its defiance of all, even its own positive laws implies that it believes it can do without any *consensus iuris* whatever, and still not resign itself to the tyrannical state of lawlessness, arbitrariness and fear. It can do without the *consensus iuris* because it promises to release the fulfillment of law from all action and will of man; and it promises justice on earth because it claims to make mankind itself the embodiment of the law.

This identification of man and law, which seems to cancel the discrepancy between legality and justice that has plagued legal thought since ancient times, has nothing in common with the *lumen naturale* or the voice of conscience, by which Nature or Divinity as the sources of authority for the *ius naturale* or the historically revealed commands of

God, are supposed to announce their authority in man himself. This never made man a walking embodiment of the law, but on the contrary remained distinct from him as the authority which demanded consent and obedience. Nature or Divinity as the source of authority for positive laws were thought of as permanent and eternal; positive laws were changing and changeable according to circumstances, but they possessed a relative permanence as compared with the much more rapidly changing actions of men; and they derived this permanence from the eternal presence of their source of authority. Positive laws, therefore, are primarily designed to function as stabilizing factors for the ever changing movements of men.

In the interpretation of totalitarianism, all laws have become laws of movement. When the Nazis talked about the law of nature or when the Bolsheviks talk about the law of history, neither nature nor history is any longer the stabilizing source of authority for the actions of mortal men; they are movements in themselves. Underlying the Nazis' belief in race laws as the expression of the law of nature in man, is Darwin's idea of man as the product of a natural development which does not necessarily stop with the present species of human beings, just as under the Bolsheviks' belief in class struggle as the expression of the law of history lies Marx's notion of society as the product of a gigantic historical movement which races according to its own law of motion to the end of historical times when it will abolish itself.

The difference between Marx's historical and Darwin's naturalistic approach has frequently been pointed out, usually and rightly in favor of Marx. This has led us to forget the great and positive interest Marx took in Darwin's theories; Engels could not think of a greater compliment to Marx's scholarly achievements than to call him the 'Darwin of history.'[1] If one considers, not the actual achievement, but the basic philosophies of both men, it turns out that ultimately the movement of history and the movement of nature are one and the same. Darwin's

---

1 In his funeral speech on Marx, Engels said: 'Just as Darwin discovered the law of development of organic life, so Marx discovered the law of development of human history.' A similar comment is found in Engels' introduction to the edition of the *Communist Manifesto* in 1890, and in his introduction to the *Ursprung der Familie*, he once more mentions 'Darwin's theory of evolution' and 'Marx's theory of surplus value' side by side.

introduction of the concept of development into nature, his insistence that, at least in the field of biology, natural movement is not circular but unilinear, moving in an infinitely progressing direction, means in fact that nature is, as it were, being swept into history, that natural life is considered to be historical. The 'natural' law of the survival of the fittest is just as much a historical law and could be used as such by racism as Marx's law of the survival of the most progressive class. Marx's class struggle, on the other hand, as the driving force of history is only the outward expression of the development of productive forces which in turn have their origin in the 'labor-power' of men. Labor, according to Marx, is not a historical but a natural-biological force – released through man's 'metabolism with nature' by which he conserves his individual life and reproduces the species.[2] Engels saw the affinity between the basic convictions of the two men very clearly because he understood the decisive role which the concept of development played in both theories. The tremendous intellectual change which took place in the middle of the last century consisted in the refusal to view or accept anything 'as it is' and in the consistent interpretation of everything as being only a stage of some further development. Whether the driving force of this development was called nature or history is relatively secondary. In these ideologies, the term 'law' itself changed its meaning: from expressing the framework of stability within which human actions and motions can take place, it became the expression of the motion itself.

Totalitarian politics which proceeded to follow the recipes of ideologies has unmasked the true nature of these movements insofar as it clearly showed that there could be no end to this process. If it is the law of nature to eliminate everything that is harmful and unfit to live, it would mean the end of nature itself if new categories of the harmful and unfit-to-live could not be found; if it is the law of history that in a class struggle certain classes 'wither away,' it would mean the end of human history itself if rudimentary new classes did not form, so that they in turn could 'wither away' under the hands of totalitarian rulers. In other words, the law of killing by which totalitarian movements

2 For Marx's labor concept as 'an eternal nature-imposed necessity, without which there can be no metabolism between man and nature, and therefore no life,' see *Capital*, Vol. I, Part I, chs. 1 and 5. The quoted passage is from ch. 1, section 2.

seize and exercise power would remain a law of the movement even if they ever succeeded in making all of humanity subject to their rule.

By lawful government we understand a body politic in which positive laws are needed to translate and realize the immutable *ius naturale* or the eternal commandments of God into standards of right and wrong. Only in these standards, in the body of positive laws of each country, do the *ius naturale* or the Commandments of God achieve their political reality. In the body politic of totalitarian government, this place of positive laws is taken by total terror, which is designed to translate into reality the law of movement of history or nature. Just as positive laws, though they define transgressions, are independent of them – the absence of crimes in any society does not render laws superfluous but, on the contrary, signifies their most perfect rule – so terror in totalitarian government has ceased to be a mere means for the suppression of opposition, though it is also used for such purposes. Terror becomes total when it becomes independent of all opposition; it rules supreme when nobody any longer stands in its way. If lawfulness is the essence of non-tyrannical government and lawlessness is the essence of tyranny, then terror is the essence of totalitarian domination.

Terror is the realization of the law of movement; its chief aim is to make it possible for the force of nature or of history to race freely through mankind, unhindered by any spontaneous human action. As such, terror seeks to 'stabilize' men in order to liberate the forces of nature or history. It is this movement which singles out the foes of mankind against whom terror is let loose, and no free action of either opposition or sympathy can be permitted to interfere with the elimination of the 'objective enemy' of History or Nature, of the class or the race. Guilt and innocence become senseless notions; 'guilty' is he who stands in the way of the natural or historical process which has passed judgment over 'inferior races,' over individuals 'unfit to live,' over 'dying classes and decadent peoples.' Terror executes these judgments, and before its court, all concerned are subjectively innocent: the murdered because they did nothing against the system, and the murderers because they do not really murder but execute a death sentence pronounced by some higher tribunal. The rulers themselves do not claim to be just or wise, but only to execute historical or natural laws; they do not apply laws, but execute a movement in accordance with its inherent law. Terror is lawfulness, if law is the law of the movement of some suprahuman force, Nature or History.

Terror as the execution of a law of movement whose ultimate goal is not the welfare of men or the interest of one man but the fabrication of mankind, eliminates individuals for the sake of the species, sacrifices the 'parts' for the sake of the 'whole.' The suprahuman force of Nature or History has its own beginning and its own end, so that it can be hindered only by the new beginning and the individual end which the life of each man actually is.

Positive laws in constitutional government are designed to erect boundaries and establish channels of communication between men whose community is continually endangered by the new men born into it. With each new birth, a new beginning is born into the world, a new world has potentially come into being. The stability of the laws corresponds to the constant motion of all human affairs, a motion which can never end as long as men are born and die. The laws hedge in each new beginning and at the same time assure its freedom of movement, the potentiality of something entirely new and unpredictable; the boundaries of positive laws are for the political existence of man what memory is for his historical existence: they guarantee the pre-existence of a common world, the reality of some continuity which transcends the individual life span of each generation, absorbs all new origins and is nourished by them.

Total terror is so easily mistaken for a symptom of tyrannical government because totalitarian government in its initial stages must behave like a tyranny and raze the boundaries of man-made law. But total terror leaves no arbitrary lawlessness behind it and does not rage for the sake of some arbitrary will or for the sake of despotic power of one man against all, least of all for the sake of a war of all against all. It substitutes for the boundaries and channels of communication between individual men a band of iron which holds them so tightly together that it is as though their plurality had disappeared into One Man of gigantic dimensions. To abolish the fences of laws between men – as tyranny does – means to take away man's liberties and destroy freedom as a living political reality; for the space between men as it is hedged in by laws, is the living space of freedom. Total terror uses this old instrument of tyranny but destroys at the same time also the lawless, fenceless wilderness of fear and suspicion which tyranny leaves behind. This desert, to be sure, is no longer a living space of freedom, but it still provides some room for the fear-guided movements and suspicion-ridden actions of its inhabitants.

By pressing men against each other, total terror destroys the space between them; compared to the condition within its iron band, even the desert of tyranny, insofar as it is still some kind of space, appears like a guarantee of freedom. Totalitarian government does not just curtail liberties or abolish essential freedoms; nor does it, at least to our limited knowledge, succeed in eradicating the love for freedom from the hearts of man. It destroys the one essential prerequisite of all freedom which is simply the capacity of motion which cannot exist without space.

Total terror, the essence of totalitarian government, exists neither for nor against men. It is supposed to provide the forces of nature or history with an incomparable instrument to accelerate their movement. This movement, proceeding according to its own law, cannot in the long run be hindered; eventually its force will always prove more powerful than the most powerful forces engendered by the actions and the will of men. But it can be slowed down and is slowed down almost inevitably by the freedom of man, which even totalitarian rulers cannot deny, for this freedom – irrelevant and arbitrary as they may deem it – is identical with the fact that men are being born and that therefore each of them *is* a new beginning, begins, in a sense, the world anew. From the totalitarian point of view, the fact that men are born and die can be only regarded as an annoying interference with higher forces. Terror, therefore, as the obedient servant of natural or historical movement has to eliminate from the process not only freedom in any specific sense, but the very source of freedom which is given with the fact of the birth of man and resides in his capacity to make a new beginning. In the iron band of terror, which destroys the plurality of men and makes out of many the One who unfailingly will act as though he himself were part of the course of history or nature, a device has been found not only to liberate the historical and natural forces, but to accelerate them to a speed they never would reach if left to themselves. Practically speaking, this means that terror executes on the spot the death sentences which Nature is supposed to have pronounced on races or individuals who are 'unfit to live,' or History on 'dying classes,' without waiting for the slower and less efficient processes of nature or history themselves.

In this concept, where the essence of government itself has become motion, a very old problem of political thought seems to have found a solution similar to the one already noted for the discrepancy between legality and justice. If the essence of government is defined as lawfulness, and if it is understood that laws are the stabilizing forces in the public affairs of men (as indeed it always has been since Plato invoked Zeus, the god of the boundaries, in his *Laws*), then the problem of movement of the body politic and the actions of its citizens arises. Lawfulness sets limitations to actions, but does not inspire them; the greatness, but also the perplexity of laws in free societies is that they only tell what one should not, but never what one should do. The necessary movement of a body politic can never be found in its essence if only because this essence – again since Plato – has always been defined with a view to its permanence. Duration seemed one of the surest yardsticks for the goodness of a government. It is still for Montesquieu the supreme proof for the badness of tyranny that only tyrannies are liable to be destroyed from within, to decline by themselves, whereas all other governments are destroyed through exterior circumstances. Therefore what the definition of governments always needed was what Montesquieu called a 'principle of action' which, different in each form of government, would inspire government and citizens alike in their public activity and serve as a criterion, beyond the merely negative yardstick of lawfulness, for judging all action in public affairs. Such guiding principles and criteria of action are, according to Montesquieu, honor in a monarchy, virtue in a republic and fear in a tyranny.

In a perfect totalitarian government, where all men have become One Man, where all action aims at the acceleration of the movement of nature or history, where every single act is the execution of a death sentence which Nature or History has already pronounced, that is, under conditions where terror can be completely relied upon to keep the movement in constant motion, no principle of action separate from its essence would be needed at all. Yet as long as totalitarian rule has not conquered the earth and with the iron band of terror made each single man a part of one mankind, terror in its double function as essence of government and principle, not of action, but of motion, cannot be fully realized. Just as lawfulness in constitutional government is insufficient to inspire and guide men's actions, so terror in totalitarian government is not sufficient to inspire and guide human behavior.

While under present conditions totalitarian domination still shares with other forms of government the need for a guide for the behavior of its citizens in public affairs, it does not need and could not even use a principle of action strictly speaking, since it will eliminate precisely the capacity of man to act. Under conditions of total terror not even fear can any longer serve as an advisor of how to behave, because terror chooses its victims without reference to individual actions or thoughts, exclusively in accordance with the objective necessity of the natural or historical process. Under totalitarian conditions, fear probably is more widespread than ever before; but fear has lost its practical usefulness when actions guided by it can no longer help to avoid the dangers man fears. The same is true for sympathy or support of the regime; for total terror not only selects its victims according to objective standards; it chooses its executioners with as complete a disregard as possible for the candidate's conviction and sympathies. The consistent elimination of conviction as a motive for action has become a matter of record since the great purges in Soviet Russia and the satellite countries. The aim of totalitarian education has never been to instill convictions but to destroy the capacity to form any. The introduction of purely objective criteria into the selective system of the SS troops was Himmler's great organizational invention; he selected the candidates from photographs according to purely racial criteria. Nature itself decided, not only who was to be eliminated, but also who was to be trained as an executioner.

No guiding principle of behavior, taken itself from the realm of human action, such as virtue, honor, fear, is necessary or can be useful to set into motion a body politic which no longer uses terror as a means of intimidation, but whose essence *is* terror. In its stead, it has introduced an entirely new principle into public affairs that dispenses with human will to action altogether and appeals to the craving need for some insight into the law of movement according to which the terror functions and upon which, therefore, all private destinies depend.

The inhabitants of a totalitarian country are thrown into and caught in the process of nature or history for the sake of accelerating its movement; as such, they can only be executioners or victims of its inherent law. The process may decide that those who today eliminate races and individuals or the members of dying classes and decadent peoples are tomorrow those who must be sacrificed. What totalitarian rule needs to guide the behavior of its subjects is a preparation to fit each of them equally well for the role of executioner and the role of victim. This two-sided preparation, the substitute for a principle of action, is the ideology.

Ideologies – isms which to the satisfaction of their adherents can explain everything and every occurence by deducing it from a single premise – are a very recent phenomenon and, for many decades, played a negligible role in political life. Only with the wisdom of hindsight can we discover in them certain elements which have made them so disturbingly useful for totalitarian rule. Not before Hitler and Stalin were the great political potentialities of the ideologies discovered.

Ideologies are known for their scientific character: they combine the scientific approach with results of philosophical relevance and pretend to be scientific philosophy. The word 'ideology' seems to imply that an idea can become the subject matter of a science just as animals are the subject matter of zoology, and that the suffix -*logy* in ideology, as in zoology, indicates nothing but the *logoi*, the scientific statements made on it. If this were true, an ideology would indeed be a pseudo-science and a pseudo-philosophy, transgressing at the same time the limitations of science and the limitations of philosophy. Deism, for example, would then be the ideology which treats the idea of God, with which philosophy is concerned, in the scientific manner of theology for which God is a revealed reality. (A theology which is not based on revelation as a given reality but treats God as an idea would be as mad as a zoology which is no longer sure of the physical, tangible existence of animals.) Yet we know that this is only part of the truth. Deism, though it denies divine revelation, does not simply make 'scientific' statements on a God which is only an 'idea,' but uses the idea of God in order to explain the course of the world. The 'ideas' of isms – race in racism, God in deism, etc. – never form the subject matter of the ideologies and the suffix -*logy* never indicates simply a body of 'scientific' statements.

An ideology is quite literally what its name indicates: it is the logic of an idea. Its subject matter is history, to which the 'idea' is applied; the result of this application is not a body of statements about something that *is*, but the unfolding of a process which is in constant change. The ideology treats the course of events as though it followed the same 'law' as the logical exposition of its 'idea.' Ideologies pretend to know the mysteries of the whole historical process – the secrets of the past, the intricacies of the present, the uncertainties of the future – because of the logic inherent in their respective ideas.

Ideologies are never interested in the miracle of being. They are historical, concerned with becoming and perishing, with the rise and fall of cultures, even if they try to explain history by some 'law of nature.' The word 'race' in racism does not signify any genuine curiosity about the human races as a field for scientific exploration, but is the 'idea' by which the movement of history is explained as one consistent process.

The 'idea' of an ideology is neither Plato's eternal essence grasped by the eyes of the mind nor Kant's regulative principle of reason but has become an instrument of explanation. To an ideology, history does not appear in the light of an idea (which would imply that history is seen *sub specie* of some ideal eternity which itself is beyond historical motion) but as something which can be calculated by it. What fits the 'idea' into this new role is its own 'logic,' that is a movement which is the consequence of the 'idea' itself and needs no outside factor to set it into motion. Racism is the belief that there is a motion inherent in the very idea of race, just as deism is the belief that a motion is inherent in the very notion of God.

The movement of history and the logical process of this notion are supposed to correspond to each other, so that whatever happens, happens according to the logic of one 'idea.' However, the only possible movement in the realm of logic is the process of deduction from a premise. Dialectical logic, with its process from thesis through antithesis to synthesis which in turn becomes the thesis of the next dialectical movement, is not different in principle, once an ideology gets hold of it; the first thesis becomes the premise and its advantage for ideological explanation is that this dialectical device can explain away factual contradictions as stages of one identical, consistent movement.

As soon as logic as a movement of thought – and not as a necessary control of thinking – is applied to an idea, this idea is transformed into a premise. Ideological world explanations performed this operation long before it became so eminently fruitful for totalitarian reasoning. The purely negative coercion of logic, the prohibition of contradictions, became 'productive' so that a whole line of thought could be initiated, and forced upon the mind, by drawing conclusions in the manner of mere argumentation. This argumentative process could be interrupted neither by a new idea (which would have been another premise with a different set of consequences) nor by a new experience. Ideologies always assume that one idea is sufficient to explain everything in the development from the premise, and that no experience can teach anything because everything is comprehended in this consistent process of logical deduction. The danger in exchanging the necessary insecurity of philosophical thought for the total explanation of an ideology and its *Weltanschauung,* is not even so much the risk of falling for some usually vulgar, always uncritical assumption as of exchanging the freedom inherent in man's capacity to think for the strait jacket of logic with which man can force himself almost as violently as he is forced by some outside power.

The *Weltanschauungen* and ideologies of the nineteenth century are not in themselves totalitarian, and although racism and communism have become the decisive ideologies of the twentieth century they were not, in principle, any 'more totalitarian' than the others; it happened because the elements of experience on which they were originally based – the struggle between the races for world domination, and the struggle between the classes for political power in the respective countries – turned out to be politically more important than those of other ideologies. In this sense the ideological victory of racism and communism over all other isms was decided before the totalitarian movements took hold of precisely these ideologies. On the other hand, all ideologies contain totalitarian elements, but these are fully developed only by totalitarian movements, and this creates the deceptive impression that only racism and communism are totalitarian in character. The truth is, rather, that the real nature of all ideologies was revealed only in the role that the ideology plays in the apparatus of totalitarian domination. Seen from this aspect, there appear three specifically totalitarian elements that are peculiar to all ideological thinking.

First, in their claim to total explanation, ideologies have the tendency to explain not what is, but what becomes, what is born and passes away. They are in all cases concerned solely with the element of motion, that is, with history in the customary sense of the word. Ideologies are always oriented toward history, even when, as in the case of racism, they seemingly proceed from the premise of nature; here, nature serves merely to explain historical matters and reduce them to matters of nature. The claim to total explanation promises to explain all historical happenings, the total explanation of the past, the total knowledge of the present, and the reliable prediction of the future. Secondly, in this capacity ideological thinking becomes independent of all experience from which it cannot learn anything new even if it is a question of something that has just come to pass. Hence ideological thinking becomes emancipated from the reality that we perceive with our five senses, and insists on a 'truer' reality concealed behind all perceptible things, dominating them from this place of concealment and requiring a sixth sense that enables us to become aware of it. The sixth sense is provided by precisely the ideology, that particular ideological indoctrination which is taught by the educational institutions, established exclusively for this purpose, to train the 'political soldiers' in the *Ordensburgen* of the Nazis or the schools of the Comintern and the Cominform. The propaganda of the totalitarian movement also serves to emancipate thought from experience and reality; it always strives to inject a secret meaning into every public, tangible event and to suspect a secret intent behind every public political act. Once the movements have come to power, they proceed to change reality in accordance with their ideological claims. The concept of enmity is replaced by that of conspiracy, and this produces a mentality in which reality – real enmity or real friendship – is no longer experienced and understood in its own terms but is automatically assumed to signify something else.

Thirdly, since the ideologies have no power to transform reality, they achieve this emancipation of thought from experience through certain methods of demonstration. Ideological thinking orders facts into an absolutely logical procedure which starts from an axiomatically accepted premise, deducing everything else from it; that is, it proceeds with a consistency that exists nowhere in the realm of reality. The deducing may proceed logically or dialectically; in either case it involves a consistent process of argumentation which, because it thinks in terms of a process, is supposed to be able to comprehend the movement of the suprahuman, natural or historical processes. Comprehension is achieved by the mind's imitating, either logically or dialectically, the laws of 'scientifically' established movements with which through the process of imitation it becomes integrated. Ideological argumentation, always a kind of logical deduction, corresponds to the two aforementioned elements of the ideologies – the element of movement and of emancipation from reality and experience – first, because its thought movement does not spring from experience but is self-generated, and, secondly, because it transforms the one and only point that is taken and accepted from experienced reality into an axiomatic premise, leaving from then on the subsequent argumentation process completely untouched from any further experience. Once it has established its premise, its point of departure, experiences no longer interfere with ideological thinking, nor can it be taught by reality.

The device both totalitarian rulers used to transform their respective ideologies into weapons with which each of their subjects could force himself into step with the terror movement was deceptively simple and inconspicuous: they took them dead seriously, took pride the one in his supreme gift for 'ice cold reasoning' (Hitler) and the other in the 'mercilessness of his dialectics,' and proceeded to drive ideological implications into extremes of logical consistency which, to the onlooker, looked preposterously 'primitive' and absurd: a 'dying class' consisted of people condemned to death; races that are 'unfit to live' were to be exterminated. Whoever agreed that there are such things as 'dying classes' and did not draw the consequence of killing their members, or that the right to live had something to do with race and did not draw the consequence of killing 'unfit races,' was plainly either stupid or a coward. This stringent logicality as a guide to action permeates the whole structure of totalitarian movements and governments. It is exclusively the work of Hitler and Stalin who, although they did not add a single new thought to the ideas and propaganda slogans of their movements, for this reason alone must be considered ideologists of the greatest importance.

What distinguished these new totalitarian ideologists from their predecessors was that it was no longer primarily the 'idea' of the ideology – the struggle of classes and the exploitation of the workers or the struggle of races and the care for Germanic peoples – which appealed to them, but the logical process which could be developed from it. According to Stalin, neither the idea nor the oratory but 'the irresistible force of logic thoroughly overpowered [Lenin's] audience.' The power, which Marx thought was born when the idea seized the masses, was discovered to reside, not in the idea itself, but in its logical process which 'like a mighty tentacle seizes you on all sides as in a vise and from whose grip you are powerless to tear yourself away; you must either surrender or make up your mind to utter defeat.'[3] Only when the realization of the ideological aims, the classless society or the master race, was at stake, could this force show itself. In the process of realization, the original substance upon which the ideologies based themselves as long as they had to appeal to the masses – the exploitation of the workers or the national aspirations of Germany – is gradually lost, devoured as it were by the process itself: in perfect accordance with 'ice cold reasoning' and the 'irresistible force of logic,' the workers lost under Bolshevik rule even those rights they had been granted under Tsarist oppression and the German people suffered a kind of warfare which did not pay the slightest regard to the minimum requirements for survival of the German nation. It is in the nature of ideological politics – and is not simply a betrayal committed for the sake of self-interest or lust for power – that the real content of the ideology (the working class or the Germanic peoples), which

3 Stalin's speech of January 28, 1924; quoted from Lenin, *Selected Works*, Vol. I, p. 33, Moscow, 1947. – It is interesting to note that Stalin's 'logic' is among the few qualities that Khrushchev praises in his devastating speech at the Twentieth Party Congress.

originally had brought about the 'idea' (the struggle of classes as the law of history or the struggle of races as the law of nature), is devoured by the logic with which the 'idea' is carried out.

The preparation of victims and executioners which totalitarianism requires in place of Montesquieu's principle of action is not the ideology itself – racism or dialectical materialism – but its inherent logicality. The most persuasive argument in this respect, an argument of which Hitler like Stalin was very fond, is: You can't say A without saying B and C and so on, down to the end of the murderous alphabet. Here, the coercive force of logicality seems to have its source; it springs from our fear of contradicting ourselves. To the extent that the Bolshevik purge succeeds in making its victims confess to crimes they never committed, it relies chiefly on this basic fear and argues as follows: We are all agreed on the premise that history is a struggle of classes and on the role of the Party in its conduct. You know therefore that, historically speaking, the Party is always right (in the words of Trotsky: 'We can only be right with and by the Party, for history has provided no other way of being in the right.'). At this historical moment, that is in accordance with the law of history, certain crimes are due to be committed which the Party, knowing the law of history, must punish. For these crimes, the Party needs criminals; it may be that the Party, though knowing the crimes, does not quite know the criminals; more important than to be sure about the criminals is to punish the crimes, because without such punishment, History will not be advanced but may even be hindered in its course. You, therefore, either have committed the crimes or have been called by the Party to play the role of the criminal – in either case, you have objectively become an enemy of the Party. If you don't confess, you cease to help History through the Party, and have become a real enemy. – The coercive force of the argument is: if you refuse, you contradict yourself and, through this contradiction, render your whole life meaningless; the A which you said dominates your whole life through the consequences of B and C which it logically engenders.

Totalitarian rulers rely on the compulsion with which we can compel ourselves, for the limited mobilization of people which even they still need; this inner compulsion is the tyranny of logicality against which nothing stands but the great capacity of men to start something new. The tyranny of logicality begins with the mind's submission to logic as a never-ending process, on which man relies in order to engender his thoughts. By this submission, he surrenders his inner freedom as he surrenders his freedom of movement when he bows down to an outward tyranny. Freedom as an inner capacity of man is identical with the capacity to begin, just as freedom as a political reality is identical with a space of movement between men. Over the beginning, no logic, no cogent deduction can have any power, because its chain presupposes, in the form of a premise, the beginning. As terror is needed lest with the birth of each new human being a new beginning arise and raise its voice in the world, so the self-coercive force of logicality is mobilized lest anybody ever start thinking – which as the freest and purest of all human activities is the very opposite of the compulsory process of deduction. Totalitarian government can be safe only to the extent that it can mobilize man's own will power in order to force him into that gigantic movement of History or Nature which supposedly uses mankind as its material and knows neither birth nor death.

The compulsion of total terror on one side, which, with its iron band, presses masses of isolated men together *and* supports them in a world which has become a wilderness for them, and the self-coercive force of logical deduction on the other, which prepares each individual in his lonely isolation against all others, correspond to each other and need each other in order to set the terror-ruled movement into motion and keep it moving. Just as terror, even in its pre-total, merely tyrannical form ruins all relationships between men, so the self-compulsion of ideological thinking ruins all relationships with reality. The preparation has succeeded when people have lost contact with their fellowmen as well as the reality around them; for together with these contacts, men lose the capacity of both experience and thought. The ideal subject of totalitarian rule is not the convinced Nazi or the convinced Communist, but people for whom the distinction between fact and fiction (*i.e.*, the reality of experience) and the distinction between true and false (*i.e.*, the standards of thought) no longer exist.

The question we raised at the start of these considerations and to which we now return is what kind of basic experience in the living-together of men permeates a form of government whose essence is terror and whose principle of action is the logicality of ideological thinking. That such a combination was never used before in the varied forms of political domination is obvious. Still, the basic experience on which it rests must be human and known to men, insofar as even this most 'original' of all political bodies has been devised by, and is somehow answering the needs of, men.

It has frequently been observed that terror can rule absolutely only over men who are isolated against each other and that, therefore, one of the primary concerns of all tyrannical government is to bring this isolation about. Isolation may be the beginning of terror; it certainly is its most fertile ground; it always is its result. This isolation is, as it were, pretotalitarian; its hallmark is impotence insofar as power always comes from men acting together, 'acting in concert' (Burke); isolated men are powerless by definition.

Isolation and impotence, that is the fundamental inability to act at all, have always been characteristic of tyrannies. Political contacts between men are severed in tyrannical government and the human capacities for action and power are frustrated. But not all contacts between men are broken and not all human capacities destroyed. The whole sphere of private life with the capacities for experience, fabrication and thought are left intact. We know that the iron band of total terror leaves no space for such private life and that the self-coercion of totalitarian logic destroys man's capacity for experience and thought just as certainly as his capacity for action.

What we call isolation in the political sphere, is called loneliness in the sphere of social intercourse. Isolation and loneliness are not the same. I can be isolated – that is in a situation in which I cannot act, because there is nobody who will act with me – without being lonely; and I can be lonely – that is in a situation in which I as a person feel myself deserted by all human companionship – without being isolated. Isolation is that impasse into which men are driven when the political sphere of their lives, where they act together in the pursuit of a common concern, is destroyed. Yet isolation, though destructive of power and the capacity for action, not only leaves intact but is required for all so-called productive activities of men. Man insofar as he is *homo faber* tends to isolate himself with his work, that is to leave temporarily the realm of politics. Fabrication (*poiesis*, the making of things), as distinguished from action (*praxis*) on one hand and sheer labor on the other, is always performed in a certain isolation from common concerns, no matter whether the result is a piece of craftsmanship or of art. In isolation, man remains in contact with the world as the human artifice; only when the most elementary form of human creativity, which is the capacity to add something of one's own to the common world, is destroyed, isolation becomes altogether unbearable. This can happen in a world whose chief values are dictated by labor, that is where all human activities have been transformed into laboring. Under such conditions, only the sheer effort of labor which is the effort to keep alive is left and the relationship with the world as a human artifice is broken. Isolated man who lost his place in the political realm of action is deserted by the world of things as well, if he is no longer recognized as *homo faber* but treated as an *animal laborans* whose necessary 'metabolism with nature' is of concern to no one. Isolation then becomes loneliness. Tyranny based on isolation generally leaves the productive capacities of man intact; a tyranny over 'laborers,' however, as for instance the rule over slaves in antiquity, would automatically be a rule over lonely, not only isolated, men and tend to be totalitarian.

While isolation concerns only the political realm of life, loneliness concerns human life as a whole. Totalitarian government, like all tyrannies, certainly could not exist without destroying the public realm of life, that is, without destroying, by isolating men, their political capacities. But totalitarian domination as a form of government is new in that it is not content with this isolation and destroys private life as well. It bases itself on loneliness, on the experience of not belonging to the world at all, which is among the most radical and desperate experiences of man.

Loneliness, the common ground for terror, the essence of totalitarian government, and for ideology or logicality, the preparation of its executioners and victims, is closely connected with uprootedness and superfluousness which have been the curse of modern masses since the beginning of the industrial revolution and have become acute with the rise of imperialism at the end of the last century and the breakdown of political institutions and social traditions in our own time. To be uprooted means to have no place in the world, recognized and guaranteed by others; to be superfluous means not to belong to the world at all. Uprootedness can be the preliminary condition for super-fluousness, just as isolation can (but must not) be the preliminary condition for loneliness. Taken in itself, without consideration of its recent historical causes and its new role in politics, loneliness is at the same time contrary to the basic requirements of the human condition *and* one of the fundamental experiences of every human life. Even the experience of the materially and sensually given world depends upon my being in contact with other men, upon our *common* sense which regulates and controls all other senses and without which each of us would be enclosed in his own particularity of sense data which in themselves are unreliable and treacherous. Only because we have common sense, that is only because not one man, but men in the plural inhabit the earth can we trust our immediate sensual experience. Yet, we have only to remind ourselves that one day we shall have to leave this common world which will go on as before and for whose continuity we are superfluous in order to realize loneliness, the experience of being abandoned by everything and everybody.

Loneliness is not solitude. Solitude requires being alone whereas loneliness shows itself most sharply in company with others. Apart from a few stray remarks – usually framed in a paradoxical mood like Cato's statement (reported by Cicero, *De Re Publica*, I, 17): *numquam minus solum esse quam cum solus esset*, 'never was he less alone than when he was alone,' or, rather, 'never was he less lonely than when he was in solitude' – it seems that Epictetus, the emancipated slave philosopher of Greek origin, was the first to distinguish between loneliness and solitude. His discovery, in a way, was accidental, his chief interest being neither solitude nor loneliness, but being alone (*monos*) in the sense of absolute independence. As Epictetus sees it (*Dissertationes*, Book 3, ch. 13) the lonely man (*eremos*) finds himself surrounded by others with whom he cannot establish contact or to whose hostility he is exposed. The solitary man, on the contrary, is alone and therefore 'can be together with himself' since men have the capacity of 'talking with themselves.' In solitude, in other words, I am 'by myself,' together with my self, and therefore two-in-one, whereas in loneliness I am actually one, deserted by all others. All thinking, strictly speaking, is done in solitude and is a dialogue between me and myself; but this dialogue of the two-in-one does not lose contact with the world of my fellow-men because they are represented in the self with whom I lead the dialogue of thought. The problem of solitude is that this two-in-one needs the others in order to become one again: one unchangeable individual whose identity can never be mistaken for that of any other. For the confirmation of my identity I depend entirely upon other people; and it is the great saving grace of companionship for solitary men that it makes them 'whole' again, saves them from the dialogue of thought in which one remains always equivocal, restores the identity which makes them speak with the single voice of one unexchangeable person.

Solitude can become loneliness; this happens when all by myself I am deserted by my own self. Solitary men have always been in danger of loneliness, when they can no longer find the redeeming grace of companionship to save them from duality and equivocality and doubt. Historically, it seems as though this danger became sufficiently great to be noticed by others and recorded by history only in the nineteenth century. It showed itself clearly when philosophers, for whom alone solitude is a way of life and a condition of work, were no longer content with the fact that 'philosophy is only for the few' and began to insist that nobody 'understands' them. Characteristic in this respect is the anecdote reported from Hegel's deathbed which hardly could have been told of any great philosopher before him: 'Nobody has understood me except one; and he also misunderstood.' Conversely, there is always the chance that a lonely man finds himself and starts the thinking dialogue of solitude. This seems to have happened to Nietzsche in Sils Maria when he conceived *Zarathustra*. In two poems ('Sils Maria' and 'Aus hohen Bergen') he tells of the empty expectation and the yearning waiting of the lonely until suddenly *'um Mittag war's, da wurde Eins zu Zwei . . . / Nun feiern wir, vereinten Siegs gewiss, / das Fest der Feste; / Freund Zarathustra kam, der Gast der Gäste!'* ('Noon was, when One became Two . . . Certain of united victory we celebrate the feast of feasts; friend Zarathustra came, the guest of guests.')

What makes loneliness so unbearable is the loss of one's own self which can be realized in solitude, but confirmed in its identity only by the trusting and trustworthy company of my equals. In this situation, man loses trust in himself as the partner of his thoughts and that elementary confidence in the world which is necessary to make experiences at all. Self and world, capacity for thought and experience are lost at the same time.

The only capacity of the human mind which needs neither the self nor the other nor the world in order to function safely and which is as independent of experience as it is of thinking is the ability of logical reasoning whose premise is the self-evident. The elementary rules of cogent evidence, the truism that two and two equals four cannot be perverted even under the conditions of absolute loneliness. It is the only reliable 'truth' human beings can fall back upon once they have lost the mutual guarantee, the common sense, men need in order to experience and live and know their way in a common world. But this 'truth' is empty or rather no truth at all, because it does not reveal anything. (To define consistency as truth as some modern logicians do means to deny the existence of truth.) Under the conditions of loneliness, therefore, the self-evident is no longer just a means of the intellect and begins to be productive, to develop its own lines of 'thought.' That thought processes characterized by strict self-evident logicality, from which apparently there is no escape, have some connection with loneliness was once noticed by Luther (whose experiences in the phenomena of solitude and loneliness probably were second to no one's and who once dared to say that 'there must be a God because man needs one being whom he can trust') in a little-known remark on the Bible text 'it is not good that man should be alone': A lonely man, says Luther, 'always deduces one thing from the other and thinks everything to the worst.' [4] The famous extremism of totalitarian movements, far from having anything to do with true radicalism, consists indeed in this 'thinking everything to the worst,' in this deducing process which always arrives at the worst possible conclusions.

What prepares men for totalitarian domination in the non-totalitarian world is the fact that loneliness, once a borderline experience usually suffered in certain marginal social conditions like old age, has become an everyday experience of the evergrowing masses of our century. The merciless process into which totalitarianism drives

---

4 'Ein solcher (sc. einsamer) Mensch folgert immer eins aus dem andern und denkt alles zum Ärgsten.' In *Erbauliche Schriften*, 'Warum die Einsamkeit zu fliehen?'

and organizes the masses looks like a suicidal escape from this reality. The 'ice-cold reasoning' and the 'mighty tentacle' of dialectics which 'seizes you as in a vise' appears like a last support in a world where nobody is reliable and nothing can be relied upon. It is the inner coercion whose only content is the strict avoidance of contradictions that seems to confirm a man's identity outside all relationships with others. It fits him into the iron band of terror even when he is alone, and totalitarian domination tries never to leave him alone except in the extreme situation of solitary confinement. By destroying all space between men and pressing men against each other, even the productive potentialities of isolation are annihilated; by teaching and glorifying the logical reasoning of loneliness where man knows that he will be utterly lost if ever he lets go of the first premise from which the whole process is being started, even the slim chances that loneliness may be transformed into solitude and logic into thought are obliterated. If this practice is compared with that of tyranny, it seems as if a way had been found to set the desert itself in motion, to let loose a sand storm that could cover all parts of the inhabited earth.

The conditions under which we exist today in the field of politics are indeed threatened by these devastating sand storms. Their danger is not that they might establish a permanent world. Totalitarian domination, like tyranny, bears the germs of its own destruction. Just as fear and the impotence from which fear springs are antipolitical principles and throw men into a situation contrary to political action, so loneliness and the logical-ideological deducing the worst that comes from it represent an antisocial situation and harbor a principle destructive for all human living-together. Nevertheless, organized loneliness is considerably more dangerous than the unorganized impotence of all those who are ruled by the tyrannical and arbitrary will of a single man. Its danger is that it threatens to ravage the world as we know it – a world which everywhere seems to have come to an end – before a new beginning rising from this end has had time to assert itself.

Apart from such considerations – which as predictions are of little avail and less consolation – there remains the fact that the crisis of our time and its central experience have brought forth an entirely new form of government which as a potentiality and an ever-present danger is only too likely to stay with us from now on, just as other forms of government which came about at different historical moments and rested on different fundamental experiences have stayed with mankind regardless of temporary defeats – monarchies, and republics, tyrannies, dictatorships and despotism.

But there remains also the truth that every end in history necessarily contains a new beginning; this beginning is the promise, the only 'message' which the end can ever produce. Beginning, before it becomes a historical event, is the supreme capacity of man; politically, it is identical with man's freedom. *Initium ut esset homo creatus est* – 'that a beginning be made man was created' said Augustine.[5] This beginning is guaranteed by each new birth; it is indeed every man.

5  *De Civitate Dei*, Book 12, chapter 20.

*Bibliography*

## Part One: Antisemitism

Alhaiza, Adolphe, *Vérité sociologique gouvernementale et religieuse. Succinct résumé du Sociétarisme de Fourier comparé au socialisme de Marx*, Paris, 1919.

Anchel, Robert, 'Un Baron Juif au 18e siècle,' *Souvenir et Science*, vol. 1.

Arendt, Hannah, 'Why the Crémieux Decree Was Abrogated,' *Contemporary Jewish Record*, April, 1943; 'The Jew as Pariah. A Hidden Tradition,' *Jewish Social Studies*, vol. 6, no. 2, 1944; 'Organized Guilt,' *Jewish Frontier*, January, 1945.

Arland, Marcel, 'Review of F. Céline's *Bagatelle pour un Massacre*,' *Nouvelle Revue Française*, February, 1938.

Aron, Robert, *The Vichy Regime 1940–1944*, New York, 1958.

Bainville, Jacques, *La troisième République*, 1935.

Baron, Salo W., *Die Judenfrage auf dem Wiener Kongress*, Vienna, 1920; *A Social and Religious History of the Jews*, New York, 1937; 'The Jewish Question in the 19th Century,' *Journal of Modern History*, vol. X, 1938; *Modern Nationalism and Religion*, 1947.

Barrès, Maurice, *Scènes et doctrines du nationalisme*, Paris, 1899.

Basnage, J., *Histoire des Juifs*, La Haye, 1716.

Batault, Georges, *Le Problème juif. La renaissance de l'antisémitisme*, Paris, 1921.

Bauer, Bruno, *Die Judenfrage*, 1843.

Beaurepaire, Guesnay de, *Le Panama et la République*, 1899.

Bécourt, Renault, *Conspiration universelle du Judaisme, entièrement dévoilée; dédiée à tous les souverains d'Europe, à leurs ministres, aux hommes d'Etat et généralement à toutes les classes de la société, menacée de ces perfides projets*, 1835.

Bédarrida, Jassuda, *Les Juifs en France, en Italie et en Espagne,* 1859.

Benjamin, René, *Clémenceau dans la retraite,* Paris, 1930.

Bernanos, Georges, *Las grande peur des bien-pensants,* Paris, 1931; *Les grands cimetières sous la lune,* Paris, 1938.

Berndorff, H. R., *Diplomatische Unterwelt,* 1930.

Bertholet, Alfred, *Die Stellung der Juden zu den Fremden,* 1896; *Kulturgeschichte Israels,* 1919.

Bismarck, Otto von, *Gedanken und Erinnerungen,* 1909–1921.

Bloom, R. I., *The Economic Activities of the Jews of Amsterdam in the 17th and 18th Centuries,* 1937.

Bloy, Léon, *Le Salut par les Juifs,* 1892.

Boehlich, Walter, ed., *Der Berliner Antisemitismusstreit,* Frankfurt/M., 1965.

Boehmer, Heinrich, *Les Jésuites. Ouvrage traduit de l'allemand avec une introduction et des notes par G. Monod,* Paris, 1910.

Boerne, Ludwig, *Über die Judenverfolgung,* 1819; *Für die Juden,* 1819; *Briefe aus Paris, 1830–1833.*

Boh, Felix, *Der Konservatismus und die Judenfrage,* 1892.

Bondy-Dworsky, *Geschichte der Juden in Boehmen, Maehren und Schlesien,* Prague, 1906.

Boom, W. ten, *Entstehung des modernen Rassen-Antisemitismus,* Leipzig, 1928.

Bord, Gustave, *La Franc-Maçonnerie en France des origines à 1815,* 1908.

Botzenhart, Erich, 'Der politische Aufstieg des Judentums von der Emanzipation bis zur Revolution 1848,' in *Forschungen zur Judenfrage,* vol. 3, 1938.

Bourgin, Georges, 'Le Problème de la fonction économique des Juifs,' *Souvenir et Science,* vol. 3, nos. 2–4, 1932.

Brentano, Clemens v., *Der Philister vor, in und nach der Geschichte,* 1811.

Brogan, D. W., *The Development of Modern France 1870–1939,* 1941; *The French Nation: From Napoleon to Pétain 1814–1940,* New York, 1958.

Bronner, Fritz, 'Georg, Ritter v. Schoenerer,' *Volk im Werden,* vol. 7, no. 3, 1939.

Brugerette, Joseph, *Le Comte de Montlosier,* 1931.

Buch, Willi, *Fünfzig Jahre antisemitische Bewegung,* Munich, 1937.

Buchholz, Friedrich, *Untersuchungen über den Geburtsadel,* Berlin, 1807.

Buelow, Bernhard von, *Denkwürdigkeiten,* Berlin, 1930–1931.

Buelow, Heinrich von, *Geschichte des Adels*, 1903.

Busch, Moritz, 'Israel und die Gojim,' *Die Grenzboten*, 1879–1881; *Bismarck: Some Secret Pages of his History*, London, 1898.

Byrnes, Robert, *Antisemitism in Modern France*, New Brunswick, 1950.

Capefigue, Jean, *Histoire des grandes opérations financières*, 1855–1858.

Capéran, Louis, *L'Anticléricalisme et l'Affaire Dreyfus*, Toulouse, 1948.

Caro, Georg, *Sozial- und Wirtschaftsgeschichte der Juden im Mittelalter und der Neuzeit*, 1908–1920.

Caro, Joseph, 'Benjamin Disraeli, Juden und Judentum,' *Monatsschrift für Geschichte und Wissenschaft des Judentums*, 1932.

'Il caso di Alfredo Dreyfus,' *Civiltà Cattolica*, February 5, 1898.

Cassel, Selig, 'Geschichte der Juden,' in *Ersch und Gruber, Allgemeine Enzyklopädie der Wissenschaften und Künste*, section 2, vol. 27, 1850.

Céline, Ferdinand, *Bagatelle pour un massacre*, 1938; *L'Ecole des cadavres*, 1940.

Chamberlain, Houston Stewart, *The Foundations of the Nineteenth Century*, 1966, translation of the German edition of 1899.

Charensol, Georges, *L'Affaire Dreyfus et la Troisième République*, Paris, 1930.

Chesterton, Gilbert K., *The Return of Don Quixote*, 1927.

Chevrillon, André, 'Huit Jours à Rennes,' *La Grande Revue*, February, 1900.

Clarke, Edwin, *Benjamin Disraeli*, London, 1926.

Clémenceau, Georges, *L'Iniquité*, 1899; *Vers la Réparation*, 1899; *Contre la Justice*, 1900; *Des Juges*, 1901.

Corti, Egon Cesar, Conte, *The Rise of the House of Rothschild*, New York, 1927.

Dairvaell, Mathieu, *Histoire édifiante et curieuse de Rothschild, Roi des Juifs, suivi du récit de la catastrophe du 18 Juillet par un témoin oculaire*, 1846; *Guerre aux fripons, chronique secrète de la Bourse et des chemins de fer par l'auteur de 'Rothschild I, Roi des Juifs,'* 1846, 3rd ed.

Daudet, Léon, *Souvenirs des milieux littéraires, politiques et médicaux*, Paris, 1920; *Panorama de la Troisième République*, Paris, 1936.

Davidsohn, Ludwig, *Beiträge zur Sozial- und Wirtschaftsgeschichte der Berliner Juden vor der Emanzipation*, 1920.

Delitzsch, Franz, *Sind die Juden wirklich das auserwählte Volk?*, Leipzig, 1890.

Delitzsch, Friedrich, *Die grosse Täuschung*, 1920–1921.

Demachy, Edouard, *Les Rothschilds, une famille de financiers juifs au 19e siècle*, 1896.

Desachy, Paul, *Répertoire de l'Affaire Dreyfus*, 1894; *Bibliographie de l'Affaire Dreyfus*, 1905.

Diderot, Denis, 'Juif,' in *Encyclopédie*, vol. 9, 1765.

Diest Daber, Otto von, *Bismarck und Bleichroeder*, Munich, 1897.

Dilthey, Wilhelm, *Das Leben Schleiermachers*, 1870.

Dimier, Louis, *Vingt Ans d'Action Française*, Paris, 1926.

Disraeli, Benjamin, *Alroy*, 1833; *Coningsby*, 1844; *Tancred*, 1847; *Lord George Bentinck. A Political Biography*, 1852; *Lothair*, 1870; *Endymion*, 1881.

Dohm, Christian Wilhelm, *Über die bürgerliche Verbesserung der Juden*, 1781–1783; *Denkwürdigkeiten meiner Zeit*, Lemgo, 1814–1819.

Drumont, Edouard, *La France Juive*, 1885; *La dernière Bataille*, 1890; *La Fin d'un monde. De l'or, de la boue, du sang. Du Panama à l'anarchie*, 1896; *Le Testament d'un antisémite*, Paris, 1891; *Les Tréteaux du succès: les héros et les pitres*, Paris, 1901.

Dubnow, S. M., *Weltgeschichte des jüdischen Volkes*, 10 vols., 1929; *History of the Jews in Russia and Poland*. Translated from the Russian by I. Friedlaender, Philadelphia, 1918.

Duehring, Eugen Karl, *Die Judenfrage als Frage der Rassenschädlichkeit für Existenz, Sitte und Cultur der Völker mit einer weltgeschichtlichen Antwort*, 1880.

Dutrait-Crozon, Henri (pseudonym), *Précis de l'Affaire Dreyfus*, 1909, 2nd ed., 1924.


Ehrenberg, Richard, *Grosse Vermögen, ihre Entstehung und ihre Bedeutung*, Jena, 1902.

Eisemenger, J. A., *Entdecktes Judentum*, 1703. New edition by Schieferl, 1893.

Elbogen, Ismar, *Geschichte der Juden in Deutschland*, Berlin, 1935; 'Die Messianische Idee in der alten jüdischen Geschichte,' *Judaica*, 1912, *Festschrift Hermann Cohen*.

Emden, Paul H., 'The Story of the Vienna Creditanstalt,' *Menorah Journal*, vol. 28, no. 1, 1940.

Ewald, Joh. Ludwig, *Ideen über die nötige Organisation der Israeliten in christlichen Staaten*, 1816.

Fernandez, Ramon, 'La Vie sociale dans l'oeuvre de Marcel Proust,' *Les Cahiers Marcel Proust*, no. 2, 1927.

Foucault, André, *Un nouvel Aspect de l'Affaire Dreyfus* (Les Oeuvres Libres), 1938.

Fourier, Charles, *Théorie des quatre mouvements*, 1808; *Nouveau Monde Industriel*, 1829.

Frank, Walter, *Demokratie und Nationalismus in Frankreich*, Hamburg, 1933; *Hofprediger Adolf Stoecker und die christlich-soziale Bewegung*, 1st ed., 1928, 2nd revised ed., 1935; 'Neue Akten zur Affäre Dreyfus,' *Preussische Jahrbücher*, 1933, vol. 233; 'Apostata. Maximilian Harden und das wilhelminische Deutschland,' in *Forschungen zur Judenfrage*, vol. 3, 1938; 'Walter Rathenau und die blonde Rasse,' *ibidem*, vol. 4, 1940; 'Die Erforschung der Judenfrage. Rückblick und Ausblick,' *ibidem*, vol. 5, 1941.

Frantz, Constantin, *Der Nationalliberalismus und die Judenherrschaft*, Munich, 1874.

*Freemasonry, the Highway to Hell*, London, 1761. – *Freimaurerei, Weg zur Hölle*, translated from the English, 1768. – *La Franche Maçonnerie n'est que le chemin de l'enfer*, translated from the German, Frankfurt, 1769.

Freund, Ismar, *Die Emanzipation der Juden in Preussen*, Berlin, 1912.

Fries, Jacob Friedrich, *Über die Gefährdung des Wohlstandes und Charakters der Deutschen durch die Juden*, Heidelberg, 1816.

Fritsch, Theodor E., *Antisemiten-Katechismus*, 1892; editor, *Die Zionistischen Protokolle*, mit einem Vor und Nachwort von Theodor Fritsch, 1924; *Handbuch der Judenfrage*, revised edition, 1935.

Froude, J. A., *Lord Beaconsfield*, London, 1890.

Gentz, Friedrich, *Briefwechsel mit Adam Müller*, Stuttgart, 1857.

Gide, André, 'Review of F. Céline's *Bagatelle pour un massacre*,' *Nouvelle Revue Française*, April, 1938.

Giraudoux, Jean, *Pleins Pouvoirs*, 1939.

Glagau, Otto, *Der Börsen- und Gründungsschwindel*, Leipzig, 1876; *Der Bankrott des Nationalliberalismus und die Reaktion*, 8th ed., Berlin, 1878.

Goethe, Joh. Wolfgang von, 'Isachar Falkensohn Behr, Gedichte eines polnischen Juden, 1772, Mietau und Leipzig,' *Frankfurter Gelehrte Anzeigen*; *Wilhelm Meister*.

Goldberg, Isidor, 'Finanz- und Bankwesen,' in *Encyclopedia Judaica*, 1930.

Goldstein, Moritz, 'Deutsch-Jüdischer Parnass,' *Kunstwart*, March, 1912.

Graser, I. B., *Das Judentum und seine Reformen als Vorbedingung der vollständigen Aufnahme der Nation in den Staatsverband*, 1828.

Grattenauer, C. W. F., *Über die physische und moralische Verfassung der heutigen Juden. Stimme eines Kosmopoliten*, 1791. Reviewed in *Allgemeine deutsche Bibliothek*, vol. 112, 1792; *Wider die Juden*, 1802.

Grau, Wilhelm, *Die Judenfrage als Aufgabe der neuen deutschen Geschichte*, 1935; *Wilhelm v. Humboldt und das Problem der Juden*, Hamburg, 1935; 'Geschichte der Judenfrage,' *Historische Zeitschrift*, vol. 153, 1936.

Greenstone, Julius H., *The Messiah Idea in Jewish History*, Philadelphia, 1906.

Gressmann, Hugo, *Der Messias*, Göttingen, 1929.

Gruen, Karl, *Die Judenfrage*, 1844.

Grunwald, Max, *Samuel Oppenheimer und sein Kreis*, Vienna, 1913; 'Contributions à l'histoire des impôts et des professions des Juifs de Bohème, Moravie et Silésie depuis le 16e siècle,' *Revue des Etudes Juives*, vol. 82.

Gueneau, Louis, 'La Première Voie Ferrée de Bourgogne,' *Annales de Bourgogne*, 1930, 1931.

Gumplowicz, Ludwig, *Der Rassenkampt*, Innsbruck, 1883.

Gurian, Waldemar, *Die politischen und sozialen Ideen des französischen Katholizismus*, Munich-Gladbach, 1929; *Der integrale Nationalismus in Frankreich: Charles Maurras und die Action Française*, Frankfurt, 1931; 'Antisemitism in Modern Germany,' *Essays on Antisemitism*, ed. by K. S. Pinson, 1946.


Haeckel, Ernst, *Lebenswunder*, 1904.

Halévy, Daniel, 'Apologie pour notre passé,' *Cahiers de la Quinzaine*, sér. 11, no. 10, 1910.

Halperin, Rose A., *The American Reaction to the Dreyfus Case*, Master's Essay, Columbia University, 1941.

Harden, Maximilian, 'Händler und Soldaten,' *Die Zukunft*, 1898; 'Zum Schutz der Republik,' *ibid.*, July, 1922; 'Tönt die Glocke Grabgesang?', *ibid.*, July–August, 1922; *Köpfe*, Berlin, 1910.

Hauser, Otto, *Die Rasse der Juden*, 1933.

Heckscher, Eli F., *Mercantilism*, London, 1935.

Herder, J. G., *Briefe zur Beförderung der Humanität*, 1793–1797; 'Über die politische Bekehrung der Juden,' in his *Adrastea und das 18. Jahrhundert*, 1801–1803.

Herzog, Wilhelm, *Der Kampf einer Republik*, Zürich, 1933; and Rehfisch, Hans José (pseudonym: René Kestner), *L'Affaire Dreyfus*, a play, 1931.

Hoberg, Clemens August, 'Die geistigen Grundlagen des Antisemitismus im modernen Frankreich,' in *Forschungen zur Judenfrage*, vol. 4, 1940.

Hohenlohe-Schillingsfürst, Chlodwig von, *Denkwürdigkeiten der Reichskanzlerzeit*, edited by Karl Alexander v. Müller (Deutsche Geschichtsquellen des 19. Jahrhunderts, vol. 28), Stuttgart, 1931.

Holst, Ludolf, *Das Judentum in allen dessen Teilen. Aus einem staatswissenschaftlichen Standpunkt betrachtet*, Mainz, 1821.

Humboldt, Wilhelm von, 'Gutachten,' 1809, in J. Freund, *Die Emanzipation der Juden in Preussen*, Berlin, 1912; *Tagebücher*, ed. Leitzmann, Berlin, 1916–1918; *Wilhelm und Caroline von Humboldt in ihren Briefen*, Berlin, 1910.

Hyamson, A. M., *A History of the Jews in England*, 1928.


Jahn, F. L., *Deutsches Volkstum*, 1810.

Jöhlinger, Otto, *Bismarck und die Juden*, Berlin, 1921.

Jost, J. M., *Neuere Geschichte der Israeliten, 1815–1845*, Berlin, 1846.


Karbach, Oscar, 'The Founder of Modern Political Antisemitism: Georg von Schoenerer,' *Jewish Social Studies*, vol. 7, no. 1, January, 1945.

Katz, Jacob, *Exclusiveness and Tolerance, Jewish-Gentile Relations in Medieval and Modern Times*, New York, 1961.

*Kleines Jahrbuch des Nützlichen und Angenehmen für Israeliten*, 1847.

Koch, Ludwig, S.J., 'Juden' in *Jesuitenlexikon*, Paderborn, 1934.

Koehler, Max, *Beiträge zur neueren jüdischen Wirtschaftsgeschichte. Die Juden in Halberstadt und Umgebung* (Studien zur Geschichte der Wirtschaft und Geisteskultur, vol. 3), 1927.

Kohler, Max J., 'Some New Light on the Dreyfus Case,' *Studies in Jewish Bibliography and Related Subjects in Memory of A. S. Freidus*, New York, 1929.

Krakauer, J., *Geschichte der Juden in Frankfurt/Main, 1150–1824*, 1925–1927.

Kraus, Karl, *Untergang de Welt durch schwarze Magie*, 1925.

Krueger, Hans K., *Berliner Romantik und Berliner Judentum*, Dissertation, 1939.

Krug, W. Traugott, 'Über das Verhältnis verschiedener Religionsparteien zum Staate und über die Emanzipation der Juden,' *Minerva*, vol. 148, 1828.

K.V.T., 'The Dreyfus Case: A Study of French Opinion,' *The Contemporary Review*, vol. 74, October, 1898.

Labori, Fernand, 'Le Mal politique et les partis,' *La Grande Revue*, October–December, 1901; 'Notes de Plaidoiries pour le procès de Rennes,' *ibid.*, February, 1900.

Lachapelle, Georges, *Les Finances de la Troisième République*, Paris, 1937.

La Serve, Fleury, 'Les Juifs à Lyon,' *Revue du Lyonnais*, vol. 7, 1838.

Lazare, Bernard, *L'Antisémitisme, son histoire et ses causes*, 1894; *Une Erreur judiciaire; la vérité sur l'affaire Dreyfus*, 1896; *Contre l'Antisémitisme; histoire d'une polémique*, Paris, 1896; *Job's Dungheap*, New York, 1948.

Lazaron, Morris S., *Seed of Abraham*, New York, 1930.

Lecanuet, Edouard, *Les Signes avant-coureurs de la séparation, 1894–1910*, Paris, 1930.

Lemoine, Albert, *Napoléon I et les Juifs*, Paris, 1900.

Lestschinsky, Jacob, 'Die Umwandlung und Umschichtung des jüdischen Volkes im Laufe des letzten Jahrhunderts,' *Weltwirtschaftliches Archiv*, vol. 30, Kiel, 1929.

Lesueur, E., *La Franc-Maçonnerie Artésienne au 18e siècle* (Bibliothèque Révolutionnaire), 1914.

Leuillot, Paul, 'L'Usure judaïque en Alsace sous l'Empire et la Restauration,' *Annales Historiques de la Révolution Française*, vol. 7, 1930.

Levaillant, I., 'La Genèse de l'antisémitisme sous la Troisième République,' *Revue des Etudes Juives*, vol. 53, 1907.

Levinas, E., 'L'Autre dans Proust,' *Deucalion*, no. 2, 1947.

Lewinsohn, Richard, *Jüdische Weltfinanz?*, 1925; *Wie sie gross und reich wurden*, Berlin, 1927.

Lombard de Langres, Vincent, *Sociétés secrètes en Allemagne . . . de l'assassinat Kotzebue*, Paris, 1819.

Lombroso, César, *L'Antisémitisme*, 2nd edition, 1899, Paris.

Lucien-Brun, Henry, *La Condition des Juifs en France depuis 1789*, Paris, 1900.

Luxemburg, Rosa, 'Die sozialistische Krise in Frankreich,' *Die Neue Zeit*, vol. I, 1901.

Maier, Hans, 'Die Antisemiten,' *Deutsches Parteiwesen*, no. 2, Munich, 1911.

Maistre, Comte J. M. de, *Les Soirées de St. Petersburg*, 1821.

Malet, Chevalier de, *Recherches politiques et historiques qui prouvent l'existence d'une secte révolutionnaire*, 1817.

Marburg, Fritz, *Der Antisemitismus in der deutschen Republik*, Vienna, 1931.

Marcus, Jacob R., *The Rise and Destiny of the German Jews*, 1934.

Marr, Wilhelm, *Sieg des Judentums über das Germanentum vom nicht konfessionellen Standpunkt aus betrachtet*, 2nd ed., Berlin, 1879.

Martin du Gard, Roger, *Jean Barois*, 1913.

Marwitz, Fr. August Ludwig von der, 'Letzte Vorstellung der Stände des Lebusischen Kreises an den König,' 1811, *Werke*, ed. Meusel, Berlin, 1908; 'Über eine Reform des Adels,' 1812, *ibid.*; 'Von den Ursachen des Verfalls der preussischen Staaten', *ibid.*

Marx, Karl, 'Zur Judenfrage,' *Deutsch-französische Jahrbücher*, 1843.

Maurras, Charles, *Au Signe de Flore; Souvenirs de la vie politique; L'Affaire Dreyfus et la fondation de l'Action Française*, Paris, 1931; *Oeuvres Capitales*, Paris, 1954.

Mayer, Sigmund, *Die Wiener Juden; Kommerz, Kultur, Politik, 1700–1900*, 1917.

McDermot, George, C.S.P., 'Mr. Chamberlain's Foreign Policy and the Dreyfus Case,' *Catholic World*, vol. 67, September, 1898.

Mehring, Franz, *Die Lessinglegende*, 1906.

Mendelssohn, Moses, 'Schreiben an Lavater,' 1769, *Gesammelte Schriften*, Berlin, 1930, vol. 7; 'Vorrede zur Uebersetzung von Menasseh ben Israel, *Rettung der Juden*,' 1782, *Gesammelte Schriften*, Leipzig, 1843–1845, vol. 3.

Meyer, Rudolf, *Politische Gründer und die Korruption in Deutschland*, 1877.

Mirabeau, H. G. R. de, *Sur Moses Mendelssohn*, London, 1788.

Mommsen, Theodor, *Reden und Aufsätze*, Berlin, 1905.

Monypenny, W. F., and Buckle, G. E., *The Life of Benjamin Disraeli, Earl of Beaconsfield*, New York, 1929.

Morley, John, *Life of Gladstone*, 1903.

Much, Willi, *50 Jahre antisemitischer Bewegung*, Munich, 1937.

Mulert, Hermann, 'Antisemitismus,' *Die Religion in Geschichte und Gegenwart*, Tübingen, 1909.

Müller, Adam, *Ausgewählte Abhandlungen*, ed. J. Baxa, Jena, 1921.

Neuschäfer, Fritz Albrecht, *Georg, Ritter von Schoenerer*, Hamburg, 1935.

Nipperdey, Thomas, *Die Organisation der deutschen Parteien vor 1918*, Düsseldorf, 1961.

Paalzow, C. L., *Über das Bürgerrecht der Juden, übersetzt von einem Juden*, Berlin, 1803.

Paléologue, Maurice, 'L'Antisémitisme, moyen du gouvernement sous Alexandre II et Alexandre III,' *Annales Politiques et littéraires*, vol. 112, July, 1938; *Tagebuch der Affäre Dreyfus*, Stuttgart, 1957.

Parkes, James W., *The Emergence of the Jewish Problem, 1878–1939*, 1946.

Paulus, Heinrich, E. G., *Beiträge von jüdischen und christlichen Gelehrten zur Verbesserung der Bekenner des jüdischen Glaubens*, Frankfurt, 1817; *Die jüdische Nationalabsonderung nach Ursprung, Folgen und Besserungsmitteln*, 1831.

Péguy, Charles, 'Notre Jeunesse,' *Cahiers de la Quinzaine*, 1910; 'A Portrait of Bernard Lazare,' in Bernard Lazare, *Job's Dungheap*, New York, 1948.

Philipp, Alfred, *Die Juden und das Wirtschaftsleben. Eine antikritisch-bibliographische Studie zu W. Sombart, Die Juden und das Wirtschaftsleben*, Strasbourg, 1929.

Philippsohn, Ludwig, 'Tagescontrolle,' *Allgemeine Zeitung des Judentums*, 1839.

Picciotto, James, *Sketches of Anglo-Jewish History*, London, 1875.

Pichl, Eduard (pseudonym Herwig), *Georg Schoenerer*, 1938.

Pinner, Felix, *Deutsche Wirtschaftsführer*, 1924.

Praag, J. E. van, 'Marcel Proust, Témoin du Judaisme déjudaisé,' *Revue Juive de Genève*, nos. 48, 49, 50, 1937.

*Précis historique sur l'Affaire du Panama*, 1893.

Pribram, Alfred François, *Urkunden und Akten zur Geschichte der Juden in Wien*, Vienna, 1918.

Priebatsch, Felix, 'Die Judenpolitik der fürstlichen Absolutismus im 17. und 18. Jahrhundert,' *Forschungen und Versuche zur Geschichte des Mittelalters und der Neuzeit*, 1915.

Proust, Marcel, *Remembrance of Things Past*, 1932–1934.


Quillard, P., *Le Monument Henry*, Paris, 1899.


Rachel, Hugo, *Das Berliner Wirtschaftsleben im Zeitalter des Frühkapitalismus*, Berlin, 1931; 'Die Juden im Berliner Wirtschaftsleben zur Zeit des Merkantilismus,' *Zeitschrift für die Geschichte der Juden in Deutschland*, vol. 2.

Rachfahl, Felix, 'Das Judentum und die Genesis des modernen Kapitalismus,' *Preussische Jahrbücher*, vol. 147, 1912.

Ramlow, Gerhard, *Ludwig von der Marwitz und die Anfänge konservativer Politik und Staatsauffassung in Preussen* (Historische Studien, no. 185).

Rathenau, Walter, *Staat und Judentum. Zur Kritik der Zeit*, Berlin, 1912; *Von kommenden Dingen*, 1917.

Raymond, E. T., *Disraeli. The Alien Patriot*, New York, 1925.

Reeves, John, *The Rothschilds. The Financial Rulers of Nations*, London, 1887.

Rehberg, August Wilhelm von, *Über den deutschen Adel*, Berlin, 1804.

Reinach, Joseph, *L'Affaire Dreyfus*, Paris, 1903–1911; 'Le rôle d'Henri,' *La Grande Revue*, 1900, vol. 1.

Reinach, Théodore, *Histoire sommaire de l'Affaire Dreyfus*, Paris, 1924.

Riesser, Gabriel, *Über die Stellung der Bekenner des mosaischen Glaubens, an die Deutschen aller Konfessionen*, 1831; *Betrachtungen über die Verhältnisse der jüdischen Untertanen in der Preussischen Monarchie*, 1834.

Robinson, John, *Proofs of a Conspiracy against the Religions and Governments of Europe*, London, 1797. American edition, 1798; German translation, 1800; French translation, 1798–1799.

Roth, Cecil, *The Magnificent Rothschild*, 1939.

Ruehs, Christian Friedrich, 'Über die Ansprüche der Juden auf das deutsche Bürgerrecht,' *Zeitschrift für die neueste Geschichte der Völker und Staatenkunde*, Berlin, 1815; *Die Rechte des Christentums und des deutschen Volkes verteidigt gegen die Ansprüche der Juden und ihrer Verfechter*, 1815.

Ruppin, Arthur, *Soziologie der Juden*, Berlin, 1930.


Samter, N., *Judentaufen im 19. Jahrhundert. Mit besonderer Berücksichtigung Preussens*, 1906.

Savigny, Friedrich Karl von, *Beitrag zur Rechtsgeschichte des Adels im neueren Europa*, 1836.

Sayou, André, 'Les Juifs,' *Revue Economique Internationale*, 1912.

Schaeffle, A. E. Fr., 'Der "grosse Börsenkrach" des Jahres 1873,' *Zeitschrift für die gesamte Staatswissenschaft*, vol. 30, 1874.

Scharf-Scharffenstein, Hermann von, *Das geheime Treiben, der Einfluss und die Macht des Judentums in Frankreich seit 100 Jahren (1771–1871)*, Stuttgart, 1872.

Schay, Rudolf, *Juden in der deutschen Politik*, 1929.

Scheffer, Egon, *Der Siegeszug des Leihkapitals*, 1924.

Scheidler, K. H., 'Judenemanzipation,' in *Ersch und Gruber, Allgemeine Enzyklopaedie der Wissenschaften und Künste*, 2nd section, vol. 27, 1850.

Schlegel, Friedrich, *Philosophische Vorlesungen aus den Jahren 1804–1806*, Bonn, 1836.

Schleiermacher, Friedrich, *Briefe bei Gelegenheit der politischen theologischen Aufgabe und des Sendschreibens jüdischer Hausväter*, 1799, *Werke*, section I, vol. 5, 1846.

Schnee, H., *Die Hoffinanz und der moderne Staat*, 3 vols., Berlin, 1953–1955.

Schneider, K. H., 'Judenemanzipation,' in *Ersch und Gruber, Allgemeine Enzyklopaedie der Wissenschaften und Künste*, section 2, vol. 27, 1850.

Schudt, Johann Jacob, *Jüdische Merkwürdigkeiten*, Frankfurt, 1715–1717.

Schwertfeger, Bernhard, *Die Wahrheit über Dreyfus*, 1930.

S.F.S., 'The Jesuits and the Dreyfus Case,' *The Month*, vol. 93, February, 1899.

Shohet, D. M., *The Jewish Court in the Middle Ages*, New York, 1931.

Silbergleit, Heinrich, *Die Bevölkerungs- und Berufsverhältnisse der Juden im Deutschen Reich*, Berlin, 1930.

Silberner, Edmund, 'Charles Fourier on the Jewish Question,' *Jewish Social Studies*, October, 1946.

Simon, Yves, *La grande Crise de la République Française; observations sur la vie politique française de 1918–1938*, Montreal, 1941.

Sombart, Werner, *Die deutsche Volkswirtschaft im 19. Jahrhundert*, 1903; *Die Juden und das Wirtschaftsleben*, 1911; *Die Zukunft der Juden*, 1912; *Der Bourgeois*, 1913; *Studien zur Entwicklungsgeschichte des modernen Kapitalismus*, 1913.

Sonnenberg-Liebermann, Max von, *Beiträge zur Geschichte der antisemitischen Bewegung vom Jahre 1880–1885*, Berlin, 1885.

Sorel, Georges, *Réflexions sur la violence*, Paris, 1908; *La Révolution dreyfusienne*, Paris, 1911.

Stahl, F. J., *Der christliche Staat und sein Verhältnis zu Deismus und Judentum*, 1847.

Steinberg, A. S., 'Die weltanschaulichen Voraussetzungen der jüdischen Geschichtsschreibung,' *Dubnov-Festschrift*, 1930.

Stern, Selma, 'Die Juden in der Handelspolitik Friedrich Wilhelms I. von Preussen,' *Zeitschrift für die Geschichte der Juden in Deutschland*, vol. 5; *Der preussische Staat und die Juden*, 2 vols., Tübingen, 1962; *Jud*

*Suess*, 1929; 'Die Judenfrage in der Ideologie der Aufklärung und Romantik,' *Der Morgen*, vol. 11, 1935; *The Court Jew*, Philadelphia, 1950.

Stoecker, Adolf, *Reden und Aufsätze*, Leipzig, 1913.

Strauss, Raphael, 'The Jews in the Economic Evolution of Central Europe,' *Jewish Social Studies*, vol. III, no. 1, 1941.

Suarez, Georges, *La Vie orgueilleuse de Clémenceau*, Paris, 1930.

Sundheimer, Paul, 'Die jüdische Hochfinanz und der bayrische Staat im 18. Jahrhundert,' *Finanzarchiv*, vol. 41, 1924.


Thalheimer, Siegfried, *Macht und Gerechtigkeit – Ein Beitrag zur Geschichte des Falles Dreyfus*, München, 1958.

Théo-Daedalus (pseudonym), *L'Angleterre juive: Israël chez John Bull*, Bruxelles, 1913.

Thibaudet, Albert, *Les idées de Charles Maurras*, Paris, 1920.

Toussenel, Alphonse, *Les Juifs, rois de l'époque. L'histoire de la féodalité financière*, 3rd ed., 1846.

Treitschke, Heinrich von, 'Unsere Aussichten,' *Preussische Jahrbücher*, vol. 44, no. 5, 1879; 'Herr Graetz und sein Judentum,' *ibid.*, no. 6; 'Erwidrung an Mommsen,' *ibid.*, vol. 46, no. 6, 1881.


Ucko, Siegfried, 'Geistesgeschichtliche Grundlagen der Wissenschaft des Judentums,' *Zeitschrift für die Geschichte der Juden in Deutschland*, vol. 5, no. 1.


Vacher de Lapouge, Georges, *L'Aryen, son rôle social*, Paris, 1896; *Les Selections sociales*, Paris, 1896.

Vallée, Oscar de, *Manieurs d'argent, 1720–1857*, 1857.

Varigny, C. de, 'Les grandes Fortunes en Angleterre,' *Revue des deux Mondes*, June, 1888.

Varnhagen, August, *Tagebücher*, Leipzig, 1861.

Vernunft, Walfried, 'Juden und Katholiken in Frankreich,' *National-sozialistische Monatshefte*, October, 1938; 'Die Hintergründe des französischen Antisemitismus,' *ibid.*, June, 1939.

Voltaire, F. M. Arouet de, *Dictionnaire philosophique (Oeuvres complètes*, vol. 9, 1878); *Philosophie génerale: métaphysique, morale et Théologie (Oeuvres complètes*, vol. 40, 1785); *Essai sur les moeurs et l'esprit des nations (Oeuvres complètes*, vol. 12, 1878).

Waetjen, Hermann, 'Das Judentum und die Anfänge der modernen Kolonisation,' *Vierteljahrsschrift für Sozial- und Wirtschaftsgeschichte*, vol. 11.

Wagener, Hermann, 'Das Judentum und der Staat,' in *Wagener Staatslexikon*, 1815–1889; 'Das Judentum in der Fremde,' *ibid.*

Wawrzinek, Kurt, *Die Entstehung der deutschen Antisemitenparteien 1873–1890*, Berlin, 1927.

Weber, Eugen, *Action française – Royalism and Reaction in Twentieth-Century France*, Stanford, 1962.

Weber, Max, 'Die Börse,' in his *Gesammelte Aufsätze zur Soziologie und Sozialpolitik; Wirtschaftsgeschichte*, 1923; *Parlament und Regierung*, 1918.

Weil, Bruno, *L'Affaire Dreyfus*, Paris, 1930.

Weill, Alexandre, *Rothschild und die europäischen Staaten*, 1844.

Weill, George, 'Les Juifs et le Saint-Simonisme,' *Revue des Etudes Juives*, vol. 31.

Weinryb, S. B., *Neueste Wirtschaftsgeschichte der Juden in Russland und Polen (Historische Untersuchungen*, vol. 12), Berlin, 1934.

Zaccone, Pierre, *Histoire des sociétés secrètes politiques et religieuses depuis les temps les plus reculés jusqu'à nos jours*, 1847–1849.

Zielenziger, Kurt, *Die Juden in der deutschen Wirtschaft*, 1930.

Zola, Emile, 'J'Accuse,' *L'Aurore*, January 13, 1898; *Correspondance: lettres à Maître Labori*, Paris, 1929.

Zweig, Stefan, *The World of Yesterday: An Autobiography*, 1943.

## Part Two: Imperialism

*American Friends Service Bulletin, General Relief Bulletin*, March, 1943.

Andler, Charles, *Les Origines du Pangermanisme*, 1915.

Angus, H. F., editor, 'Canada and the Doctrine of Peaceful Changes,' *International Studies Conference. Demographic Questions. Peaceful Changes*, 1937.

Arndt, Ernst Moritz, *Ein Blick aus der Zeit auf die Zeit*, 1814; *Phantasien zur Berichtigung der Urteile über künftige deutsche Verfassungen*, 1815; *Erinnerungen aus Schweden*, 1818.

Azcarate, Pablo de, 'Minorities. League of Nations,' in *Encyclopaedia Britannica*, 1929.

Bangert, Otto, *Gold oder Blut*, 1927.

Barker, Ernest, *Political Theory in England from Herbert Spencer to the Present Day*, 1915; *Ideas and Ideals of the British Empire*, Cambridge, 1941.

Barnes, Leonard, *Caliban in Africa. An Impression of Colour Madness*, Philadelphia, 1931.

Barrès, Maurice, *Scènes et doctrines du nationalisme*, Paris, 1899.

Barzun, Jacques, *Race. A Study in Modern Superstition*, New York, 1937.

Bassermann, Ernst, 'Nationalliberale,' in *Handbuch der Politik*, vol. 2, 1914.

Bauer, Otto, *Die Nationalitätenfrage und die österreichische Sozialdemokratie*, Vienna, 1907.

Beamish, Henry Hamilton, *South Africa's Kosher Press*, London, 1937.

Becker, Paul, *Carl Peters, die Wirkung der deutschen Kolonialpolitik*, 1934.

Bell, Sir Hesketh, *Foreign Colonial Administration in the Far East*, 1928.

Benedict, Ruth, *Race, Science and Politics*, 1940.

Benians, E. A., 'The European Colonies,' *Cambridge Modern History. The Latest Age*, vol. 12, 1934.

Benjamin, Walter, *Über den Begriff der Geschichte*, in *Werke*, Frankfurt, 1955.

Bentwich, Norman, 'South Africa. Dominion of Racial Problems,' *The Political Quarterly*, vol. 10, no. 3, 1939.

Bérard, Victor, *L'Empire russe et le tsarisme*, 1905.

Bergstraesser, Ludwig, *Geschichte der politischen Parteien*, 1921.

Bibl, Viktor, *Der Zerfall Oesterreichs*, 1924.

Bluntschli, Johann Caspar, *Charakter und Geist der Politischen Parteien*, 1869.

Bodelsen, C. A., *Studies in Mid-Victorian Imperialism*, 1924.

Bodin, Jean, *Six Livres de la République*, 1576.

Bonhard, Otto, *Geschichte des alldeutschen Verbandes*, 1920.

Boulainvilliers, Comte Henri de, *Histoire de l'Ancien Gouvernement de la France*, 1727.

Braun, Robert, 'Political Parties. Succession States,' in *Encyclopedia of Social Sciences*.

Brie, Friedrich, *Imperialistische Strömungen in der englischen Literatur*, Halle, 1928; *Der Einfluss der Lehren Darwins auf den britischen Imperialismus*, 1927.

Bronner, Fritz, 'Georg, Ritter v. Schoenerer,' *Volk im Werden*, vol. 7, no. 3, 1939.

Bruecher, Heinz, 'Ernst Haeckel. Ein Wegbereiter biologischen Staatsdenkens,' *Nationalsozialistische Monatshefte*, no. 69, 1935.

Bruun, Geoffrey, *Europe and the French Empire*, 1938.

Bryce, Viscount James, *Studies in History and Jurisprudence*, 1901.

Bubnoff, Nicolai, *Kultur und Geschichte im russischen Denken der Gegenwart* (Osteuropa: Quellen und Studien, no. 2), 1927.

Buffon, Georges-Louis Leclerc, Comte de, *Histoire Naturelle*, 1769–1789.

Burke, Edmund, *Reflections on the Revolution in France* (1790), Everyman's Library; *Upon Party*, 1850, 2nd ed.

Burns, Elinor, *British Imperialism in Ireland*, 1931.


Cambridge History of the British Empire, vol. 5, *The Indian Empire 1858-1918*, 1932; vol. 8, *South Africa*, 1936.

Carlyle, Thomas, 'Occasional Discourse on the Nigger Question,' in *Critical and Miscellaneous Essays*.

Carr-Saunders, A. M., *World Population*, Oxford, 1936.

Carthill, Al. (pseudonym), *The Lost Dominion*, 1924.

Chamberlin, W. H., *The Russian Revolution, 1917–1927*, New York, 1935.

Cherikover, E., 'New Materials on the Pogroms in Russia at the Beginning of the Eighties,' *Historishe Shriftn*, vol. 2, Vilna, 1937.

Chesterton, Cecil, and Belloc, Hilaire, *The Party System*, London, 1911.

Chesterton, Gilbert K., *The Crimes of England*, 1915.

Childs, Stephen Lawford, 'Refugees – a Permanent Problem in International Organization,' in *War is not Inevitable, Problems of Peace*, 13th series, published by the International Labor Office, London, 1938.

Clapham, J. H., *The Abbé Siéyès*, London, 1912.

Class, Heinrich (pseudonym Einhart), *Deutsche Geschichte*, Leipzig, 1910; *Zwanzig Jahre alldeutscher Arbeit und Kämpfe*, Leipzig, 1910; (pseudonym Daniel Fryman), *Wenn ich der Kaiser wär. Politische Wahrheiten und Notwendigkeiten*, 1912.

Cleinow, Georg, *Die Zukunft Polens*, Leipzig, 1914.

Comte, Auguste, *Discours sur l'Ensemble du Positivisme*, 1848.

Conditions of India (no author, preface by Bertrand Russell), London, 1934.

Conrad, Joseph, 'The Heart of Darkness,' in his *Youth and Other Tales*, 1902; *Victory*, 1915.

Cooke, George W., *The History of Party*, London, 1836.

Coquart, A., *Pisarev et l'idéologie du nihilisme russe*, Paris, 1946.

Cromer, Lord, Evelyn Baring, 'The Government of Subject Races,' *Edinburgh Review*, January, 1908; 'Disraeli,' *Spectator*, November, 1912.

Crozier, John B., *History of Intellectual Development on the Lines of Modern Evolution*, 1897–1901.

Crozier, W. P., 'France and her "Black Empire,"' *New Republic*, January 23, 1924.

Curzon, Lord George N., *Problems of the Far East*, 1894.

Dance, E. H., *The Victorian Illusion*, London, 1928.

Danilewski, Nikolai Yakovlevich, *Russia and Europe*, 1871.

Darcy, Jean, *France et Angleterre, Cent années de rivalité coloniale*, 1904.

(Davidson, John), *Testament of John Davidson*, 1908.

Deckert, Emil, *Panlatinismus, Panslawismus und Panteutonismus in ihrer Bedeutung für die Weltlage*, Frankfurt, 1914.

Delbrück, Hans, 'Die Alldeutschen,' *Preussische Jahrbücher*, vol. 154, December, 1913; *Ludendorffs Selbstportrait*, Berlin, 1922.

Delos, J.-T., *La Nation*, Montreal, 1944.

Detweiler, E. G., 'The rise of modern race antagonism,' *American Journal of Sociology*, 1932.

Dilke, Charles W., *Problems of Greater Britain*, 4th ed., London, 1890.

Dornath, J. v., 'Die Herrschaft des Panslawismus,' *Preussische Jahrbücher*, vol. 95, Berlin, 1898.

Dreyfus, Robert, 'La Vie et les prophéties du Comte de Gobineau,' *Cahiers de la Quinzaine*, ser. 6, cahier 16, 1905.

Dubuat-Nançay, Comte Louis Gabriel, *Les Origines; ou, l'Ancien Gouvernement de la France, de l'Allemagne et de l'Italie*, 1789.

Duesberg, Jacques, 'Le Comte de Gobineau,' *Revue Générale*, 1939.

Duverger, Maurice, *Political Parties. Their Organization and Activity in the Modern State*, New York, 1959.

Ehrenberg, Hans, and Bubnoff, Nicolai, editors, *Östliches Christentum. Dokumente*, 1925.

Emden, Paul H., *Jews of Britain. A Series of Biographies*, London, 1944.

Erdstein, David, *Le Statut juridique des minorités en Europe*, Paris, 1932.

Estève, Louis, *Une nouvelle Psychologie de l'Impérialisme. Ernest Seillière*, 1913.

Faure, Elie, 'Gobineau et le Problème des races,' *Europe*, 1923.

Fiala, Vaclav, 'Les Partis politiques polonais,' *Monde Slave*, February, 1935.

Fischel, A., *Der Panslawismus bis zum Weltkriege*, 1919.

*The French Colonial Empire* (Information Department Papers, no. 25), published by the Royal Institute of International Affairs, London, 1941.

'Friedlosikeit,' in *Schweizer Lexikon*, 1945.

Froude, J. A., *Short Studies on Great Subjects*, 1867–1882.

Gagarin, Ivan S., *La Russie sera-t-elle catholique?*, 1856.

Galton, Sir Francis, *Hereditary Genius*, 1869.

Gehrke, Achim, *Die Rasse im Schrifttum*, 1933.

Gelber, N. M., 'The Russian Pogroms in the Early Eighties in the Light of the Austrian Diplomatic Correspondence,' *Historishe Shriftn*, vol. 2, Vilna, 1937

George, David Lloyd, *Memoirs of the Peace Conference*, Yale, 1939.

Gobineau, Clément Serpeille de, 'Le Gobinisme et la Pensée moderne,' *Europe*, 1923.

Gobineau, Comte Joseph-Arthur de, *Essai sur l'inégalité des races humaines*, 1853; *The Inequality of Human Races*, English ed., translated by Adrian Collins, 1915; 'Ce qui est arrivé à la France en 1870,' *Europe*, 1923.

Goerres, Josef, *Politische Schriften*, Munich, 1854–1874.

Gohier, Urbain, *La Race a parlé*, 1916.

Grégoire, Abbé Henri, *De la Littérature des Nègres, ou recherches sur leurs qualités morales*, Paris, 1808; *De la Noblesse de la peau ou du préjugé des blancs contre la couleur des Africains*, Paris, 1826.

Gregory, Theodore, *Ernst Oppenheimer and the Economic Development of Southern Africa*, New York, 1962.

Grell, Hugo, *Der alldeutsche Verband, seine Geschichte, seine Bestrebungen, seine Erfolge* (Flugschriften des alldeutschen Verbandes, no. 8), Munich, 1898.

Gunenin, E., *L'Épopée coloniale de la France*, 1932.

Hadsel, Winifred N., 'Can Europe's refugees find new Homes?', *Foreign Policy Reports*, vol. 10, no. 10, 1943.

Halévy, Elie, *L'Ere des Tyrannies*, Paris, 1938.

Hallgarten, W., *Vorkriegsimperialismus*, 1935

Hancock, William K., *Survey of British Commonwealth Affairs*, London, 1937–1942; *Smuts: The Sanguine Years, 1870–1919*, New York, 1962.

Hanotaux, Gabriel, 'Le Général Mangin,' *Revue des Deux Mondes*, vol. 27, 1925.

Harlow, Vincent, *The Character of British Imperialism*, 1939.

Harvey, Charles H., *The Biology of British Politics*, 1904.

Hasse, Ernst, *Deutsche Weltpolitik* (Flugschriften des Alldeutschen Verbandes, no. 5), 1897; *Deutsche Politik*, 1905–1906.

Hazeltine, H. D., 'Excommunication,' in *Encyclopedia of Social Sciences*.

Heinberg, John Gilbert, *Comparative Major European Governments, an Introductory Study*, New York, 1937.

Herrmann, Louis, *History of the Jews in South Africa*, 1935.

Hilferding, Rudolf, *Das Finanzkapital*, Vienna, 1910.

Hobbes, Thomas, *Leviathan* (1651), Cambridge Edition, 1935.

Hobson, J. H., 'Capitalism and Imperialism in South Africa,' *Contemporary Review*, 1900; *Imperialism* (1905), unrevised edition, 1938.

Hoetzsch, Otto, *Russland; eine Einführung auf Grund seiner Geschichte von 1904–1912*, Berlin, 1913.

Hoffmann, Karl, *Ölpolitik und angelsächsisches Imperium*, 1927.

Holborn, Louise W., 'The Legal Status of Political Refugees, 1920–1938,' *American Journal of International Law*, 1938.

Holcombe, Arthur N., 'Political Parties,' in *Encyclopedia of Social Sciences*.

Hotman, François, *Franco-Gallia*, 1573.

Huebbe-Schleiden, *Deutsche Kolonisation*, 1881.

Huxley, Thomas, *The Struggle for Existence in Human Society*, 1888.


Ipseri, H. P., 'Vom Begriff der Partei,' *Zeitschrift für die gesamte Staatswissenschaft*, 1940.


James, Selwyn, *South of the Congo*, New York, 1943.

Janeff, Janko, 'Der Untergang des Panslawismus,' *Nationalsozialistische Monatshefte*, no. 91, 1937.

Janowsky, Oscar J., *The Jews and Minority Rights*, New York, 1933; *Nationalities and National Minorities*, New York, 1945.

Jennings, R. Yewdall, 'Some International Aspects of the Refugee Question,' *British Yearbook of International Law*, 1939.


Kabermann, Heinz, 'Das internationale Flüchtlingsproblem,' *Zeitschrift für Politik*, vol. 29, no. 3, 1939.

Kaehler, Siegfried, editor, *Deutscher Staat und deutsche Parteien*, Munich, 1922.

Karbach, Oscar, 'The Founder of Modern Political Antisemitism: Georg von Schoenerer,' *Jewish Social Studies*, vol. 7, no. 1, January, 1945.

Kat Angelino, A. D. A. de, *Colonial Policy*, Chicago, 1931.

Kehr, Eckart, *Schlachtflottenbau und Parteipolitik*, 1930.

Kidd, Benjamin, *Social Evolution*, 1894.

Kiewiet, C. W. de, *A History of South Africa. Social and Economic*, Oxford, 1941.

Kipling, Rudyard, 'The First Sailor,' in his *Humorous Tales*, 1891; 'The Tomb of His Ancestor,' in his *The Day's Work*, 1898; *Stalky and Company*, 1899; *Kim*, 1900.

Klemm, Gustav, *Allgemeine Kulturgeschichte der Menschheit*, 1843–1852.

Klyuchevsky, V. O., *A History of Russia*, London, 1911–1931.

Koebner, Richard, and Schmidt, Helmut Dan, *Imperialism: The Story and Significance of a Political Word, 1840–1860*, New York, 1964.

Koestler, Arthur, *Scum of the Earth*, 1941.

Kohn, Hans, *Nationalism*, 1938; *Panslavism: History and Ideology*, Notre Dame, 1953.

Koyré, Alexandre, *Etudes sur l'histoire de la pensée philosophique en Russie*, Paris, 1950.

Kruck, Alfred, *Geschichte des alldeutschen Verbandes 1890–1939*, Wiesbaden, 1954.

Kuhlenbeck, L., *Rasse und Volkstum* (Flugschriften des alldeutschen Verbandes, no. 23).

Kulischer, Eugene M., *The Displacement of Population in Europe* (International Labor Office), Montreal, 1943.

Kulischer, J., *Allgemeine Wirtschaftsgeschichte*, 1928–1929.

Landsberg, P. L., 'Rassenideologie,' *Zeitschrift für Sozialforschung*, 1933.

Langer, William, *The Diplomacy of Imperialism*, 1890–1902.

Larcher, M., *Traité Elémentaire de Législation Algérienne*, 1903.

Lawrence, T. E., 'France, Britain and the Arabs,' *The Observer*, 1920; *Seven Pillars of Wisdom*, 1926; *Letters*, edited by David Garnett, New York, 1939.

Lehr, *Zwecke und Ziele des alldeutschen Verbandes* (Flugschriften des alldeutschen Verbandes, no. 14).

Lemonon, Ernest, *L'Europe et la politique britannique, 1882–1911*, 1912.

Levine, Louis, *Pan-Slavism and European Politics*, New York, 1914.

Lewis, Sir George Cornewall, *An Essay on the Government of Dependencies*, Oxford, 1844.

Lippincott, Benjamin E., *Victorian Critics of Democracy*, University of Minnesota, 1938.

Lossky, N. O., *Three Chapters from the History of Polish Messianism* (International Philosophical Library, vol. 2, no. 9), Prague, 1936.

Lovell, Reginald Ivan, *The Struggle for South Africa, 1875–1899*, New York, 1934.

Low, Sidney, 'Personal Recollections of Cecil Rhodes,' *Nineteenth Century*, vol. 51, May, 1902.

Ludendorff, Erich, *Die überstaatlichen Mächte im letzten Jahre des Weltkrieges*, Leipzig, 1927; *Die Judenmacht, ihr Wesen und Ende*, Munich, 1938; *Feldherrnworte*, 1938.

Luxemburg, Rosa, *Die Akkumulation des Kapitals* (1913), Berlin, 1923.


Macartney, C. A., *The Social Revolution in Austria*, Cambridge, 1926; *National States and National Minorities*, London, 1934.

Mahan, Alfred T., *The Problem of Asia and its Effect upon International Policies*, Boston, 1900.

Maine, Sir Henry, *Popular Government*, 1886.

Mangin, Charles Marie Emmanuel, *La Force noire*, 1910; *Des Hommes et des Faits*, Paris, 1923.

Mangold, Ewald K. B., *Frankreich und der Rassegedanke; eine politische Kernfrage Europas*, 1937.

Mansergh, Nicholas, *Britain and Ireland* (Longman's Pamphlets on the British Commonwealth), London, 1942; *South Africa 1960–1961*, New York, 1962.

Marcks, Erich, editor, *Lebensfragen des britischen Weltreichs*, 1921.

Marx, Karl, *The Eighteenth Brumaire of Louis Bonaparte* (1852), 1898.

Masaryk, Th. G., *Zur russischen Geschichts- und Religionsphilosophie*, 1913.

Mauco, Georges, 'L'Emigration, problème révolutionnaire,' *Esprit*, 7th year, no. 82, July, 1939.

Maunier, René, *Sociologie coloniale*, 1932–1936.

Metzer, E., *Imperialismus und Romantik*, Berlin, 1908.

Michaelis, Alfred, editor, *Die Rechtsverhältnisse der Juden in Preussen seit dem Beginn des 19. Jahrhunderts*, Berlin, 1910.

Michel, P. Charles, 'A Biological View of Our Foreign Policy,' *Saturday Review*, London, February, 1896.

Michell, Lewis, *Rhodes*, London, 1910.

Michels, Robert, 'Prolegomena zur Analyse des nationalen Leitgedankens,' *Jahrbuch für Soziologie*, vol. 2, 1927; *Political Parties; a sociological study of the oligarchical tendencies of modern democracy*, Glencoe, 1949.

Millin, S. Gertrude, *Rhodes*, London, 1933.

Molisch, Paul, *Geschichte der deutschnationalen Bewegung in Österreich*, Jena, 1926.

Montesquieu, C. L. de Secondat de, *Esprit des Lois*, 1748.

Morrison, T., *Imperial Rule in India*, 1899.

Multatuli (pseudonym for Eduard Douwes Dekker), *Max Havelaar*, 1868.


Nadolny, R., *Germanisierung oder Slavisierung?*, 1928.

Naumann, Friedrich, *Central Europe*, London, 1916.

Neame, L. E., *The History of Apartheid*, London, 1962.

Nettlau, Max, *Der Anarchismus von Proudhon zu Kropotkin*, 1927.

Neumann, Sigmund, *Die Stufen des preussischen Konservativismus* (Historische Studien, no. 190), 1930; *Die deutschen Parteien*, 1932.

Neuschäfer, Fritz Albrecht, *Georg, Ritter von Schoenerer*, Hamburg, 1935.

Nicolson, Harold, *Curzon: The Last Phase 1919–1925*, Boston, New York, 1934.

Nippold, Gottfried, *Der deutsche Chauvinismus*, 1913.

Novalis (pseudonym for Friedrich Hardenberg), *Neue Fragmentensammlung*, 1798.


Oakesmith, John, *Race and Nationality, an Inquiry into the Origin and Growth of Patriotism*, 1919.

Oertzen, A. F. von, *Nationalsozialismus und Kolonialfrage*, Berlin, 1935.

Oesterley, W. O. E., *The Evolution of the Messianic Idea*, London, 1908.


*Le Panlatinism, Confédération Gallo-Latine et Kelto-Gauloise . . . ou projet d'union fédérative . . .* , Paris, 1860.

Pearson, Karl, *National Life*, 1901.

Peters, Carl, 'Das Deutschtum als Rasse,' *Deutsche Monatsschrift*, April, 1905; *Die Gründung von Deutsch-Ostafrika. Kolonialpolitische Erinnerungen*, 1906.

Pichl, Eduard (pseudonym Herwig), *George Schoenerer*, 1938.

Pinon, René, *France et Allemagne*, 1912.

Pirenne, Henri, *A History of Europe from the Invasions to XVI Century*, London, 1939.

Plucknett, Theodore F. T., 'Outlawry,' in *Encyclopedia of Social Sciences*.

Pobyedonostzev, Constantin, *L'Autocratie russe. Mémoires politiques, correspondance officielle et documents inédits . . . 1881–1894*, Paris, 1927; *Reflections of a Russian Statesman*, London, 1898.

Preuss, Lawrence, 'La Dénationalisation imposée pour des motifs politiques,' *Revue Internationale Française du Droit des Gens*, vol. 4, nos. 1, 2, 5, 1937.

Priestley, H. J., *France Overseas; a study of modern imperialism*, New York, 1938.

Propyläen Weltgeschichte, vol. 10, *Das Zeitalter des Imperialismus*, 1933.

Pundt, Alfred, *Arndt and the National Awakening in Germany*, New York, 1935.

Reimer, E., *Pangermanisches Deutschland*, 1905.

Reismann-Grone, Th., *Überseepolitik oder Festlandspolitik?* (Flugschriften des alldeutschen Verbandes, no. 22), 1905.

Renan, Ernest, *Histoire générale et système comparé des langues*, 1863; *Qu'est-ce qu'une nation?*, Paris, 1882. English translation in *The Poetry of the Celtic Races, and Other Studies*, translated by William G. Hutchison, London, 1896.

Renner, Karl, *Der Kampf der österreichischen Nationen unter dem Staat*, 1902; *Österreichs Erneuerung. Politisch-programmatische Aufsätze*, Vienna, 1916; *Das Selbstbestimmungsrecht der Nationen*, Leipzig, 1918.

Richard, Gaston, *Le Conflit de l'autonomie nationale et de l'impérialisme*, 1916.

Ritter, Paul, *Kolonien im deutschen Schrifttum*, 1936.

Robert, Cyprienne, *Les deux Panslavismes*, 1847; *Le Monde slave*, 1852.

Robespierre, Maximilien de, *Oeuvres*, 1840; *Speeches*, 1927.

Robinson, Jacob, 'Staatsbürgerliche und wirtschaftliche Gleichberechtigung,' *Süddeutsche Monatshefte*, July, 1929.

Roepke, Wilhelm, 'Kapitalismus und Imperialismus,' *Zeitschrift für Schweizerische Statistik und Volkswirtschaft*, vol. 70, 1934.

Rohan, Henri, Duc de, *De l'Intérêt des princes et Etats de la Chrétienté*, 1638

Rohden, Peter R., editor, *Demokratie und Partei*, Vienna. 1932.

Rohrbach, Paul, *Der deutsche Gedanke in der Welt*, 1912; *Die alldeutsche Gefahr*, 1918.

Roscher, Wilhelm, *Die Grundlagen der Nationalökonomie*, 1900.

Rosenkranz, Karl, *Über den Begriff der politischen Partei*, 1843.

Roucek, Joseph, *The Minority Principle as a Problem of Political Science*, Prague, 1928.

Rozanov, Vassilij, *Fallen Leaves*, 1929.

Rudlin, W. A., 'Political Parties. Great Britain,' in *Encyclopedia of the Social Sciences*.

Russell, Lord John, *On Party*, 1850.


Samuel, Horace B., *Modernities*, London, 1914.

Schnee, Heinrich, *Nationalismus und Imperialismus*, 1928.

Schultze, Ernest, 'Die Judenfrage in Südafrika,' *Der Weltkampf*, vol. 15, no. 178, 1938.

Schumpeter, Joseph, 'Zur Soziologie der Imperialismen,' *Archiv für Sozialwissenschaften und Sozialpolitik*, vol. 46, 1918–1919.

Schuyler, Robert L., *The Fall of the Old Colonial System. A Study in British Free Trade, 1770–1870*, New York, 1945.

Seeley, John Robert, *The Expansion of England*, 1883.

Seillière, Ernest, *La Philosophie de l'impérialisme*, 1903–1906; *Mysticisme et domination. Essais de critique impérialiste*, 1913.

Sieveking, H. J., 'Wirtschaftsgeschichte,' in *Enzyklopädie der Rechts- und Staatswissenschaften*, vol. 47, 1935.

Siéyès, Abbé E. J., *Qu'est-ce que le Tiers Etat?*, 1789.

Simar, Théophile, *Etude Critique sur la formation de la doctrine des races au 18e et son expansion au 19e siècle*, Bruxelles, 1922.

Simpson, John Hope, *The Refugee Problem* (Institute of International Affairs), Oxford, 1939.

*Sitzungsbericht des Kongresses der organisierten nationalen Gruppen in den Staaten Europas*, 1933.

Solovyov, Vladimir, *Judaism and the Christian Question*, 1884.

Sommerland, Theo, *Der deutsche Kolonialgedanke und sein Werden im 19. Jahrhundert*, Halle, 1918

Spiess, Camille, *Impérialismes. Gobinisme en France*, Paris, 1917.

Sprietsma, Cargill, *We Imperialists. Notes on Ernest Seillière's Philosophy of Imperialism*, New York, 1931.

Staehlin, Karl, *Geschichte Russlands von den Anfängen bis zur Gegenwart*, 1923–1939; 'Die Entstehung des Panslawismus,' *Germano-Slavica*, no. 4, 1936.

Stephen, Sir James F., *Liberty, Equality, Fraternity*, 1873; 'Foundations of the Government of India,' *Nineteenth Century*, vol. 80, 1883.

Stoddard, Th. L., *Rising Tide of Color*, 1920.

Strieder, Jakob, 'Staatliche Finanznot und Genesis des modernen Grossunternehmertums,' *Schmollers Jahrbücher*, vol. 49, 1920.

Strzygowski, Josef, *Altai, Iran und Völkerwanderung*, Leipzig, 1917.

Suarès, André, *La Nation contre la race*, Paris, 1916.

Sumner, B. H., *Russia and the Balkans*, Oxford, 1937; *A Short History of Russia*, New York, 1949.

Sydacoff, Bresnitz von, *Die panslawistische Agitation und die südslawiche Bewegung in Österreich-Ungarn*, Berlin, 1899.

Szpotański, Stanislaw, 'Les Messies au 19e siècle,' *Revue Mondiale*, 1920.


Talleyrand, C. M. de, 'Essai sur les avantages à retirer des colonies nouvelles dans les circonstances présentes' (1799), *Académie des Sciences Coloniales, Annales*, vol. 3, 1929.

Thierry, A., *Lettres sur l'histoire de la France*, 1840.

Thompson, L. M., 'Afrikaner Nationalist Historiography and the Policy of Apartheid,' *The Journal of African History*, vol., III, no. 1, 1962.

Thring, Lord Henry, *Suggestions for Colonial Reform*, 1865.

Tirpitz, Alfred von, *Erinnerungen*, 1919.

Tocqueville, Alexis de, 'Lettres de Alexis de Tocqueville et de Arthur Gobineau,' *Revue des Deux Mondes*, vol. 199, 1907; *L'Ancien Régime et la Révolution*, 1856.

Tonsill, Ch. C., 'Racial Theories from Herder to Hitler,' *Thought*, vol. 15, 1940.

Townsend, Mary E., *Origin of Modern German Colonialism, 1871–1885*, New York, 1921; *Rise and Fall of Germany's Colonial Empire*, New York, 1930; *European Colonial Experience since 1871*, New York, 1941.

Trampler, Kurt, 'Völkerbund und Völkerfreiheit,' *Süddeutsche Monatshefte*, July, 1929.

Tyler, J. E., *The Struggle for Imperial Unity*, London, Toronto, New York, 1938.

Unwin, George, *Studies in Economic History*, ed. by R. H. Tawney, 1927.

Vichniac, Marc, 'Le Statut international des apatrides,' *Recueil des Cours de l'Académie de Droit International*, vol. 33, 1933.

Voegelin, Erich, *Rasse und Staat*, 1933; *Die Rassenidee in der Geistesgeschichte*, Berlin, 1933; 'The Origins of Scientism,' *Social Research*, December, 1948.

Voelker, K., *Die religiöse Wurzel des englischen Imperialismus*, Tübingen, 1924.

Vrba, Rudolf, *Russland und der Panslawismus; statistische und sozialpolitische Studien*, 1913.

Wagner, Adolf, *Vom Territorialstaat zur Weltmacht*, 1900.

Weber, Ernst, *Volk und Rasse. Gibt es einen deutschen Nationalstaat?*, 1933.

Webster, Charles Kingsley, 'Minorities. History,' in *Encyclopaedia Britannica*, 1929.

Wenck, Martin, *Alldeutsche Taktik*, 1917.

Werner, Bartholomäus von, *Die deutsche Kolonialfrage*, 1897.

Werner, Lothar, *Der alldeutsche Verband, 1890–1918* (Historische Studien, no. 278), Berlin, 1935.

Wertheimer, Mildred S., *The Pan-German League, 1890–1914*, 1924.

Westarp, Graf Kuno F. V. von, *Konservative Politik im letzten Jahrzehnt des Kaiserreiches*, 1935.

White, John S., 'Taine on Race and Genius,' *Social Research*, February, 1943.

Whiteside, Andrew G., 'Nationaler Sozialismus in Österreich vor 1918,' *Vierteljahrshefte für Zeitgeschichte*, 9. Jg. (1961).

Williams, Basil, *Cecil Rhodes*, London, 1921.

Williams, Sir John Fischer, 'Denationalisation,' *British Year Book of International Law*, vol. 7, 1927.

Winkler, Wilhelm, *Statistisches Handbuch der europäischen Nationalitäten*, Vienna, 1931.

Wirth, Max, *Geschichte der Handelskrisen*, 1873.

Wolmar, Wolfram von, 'Vom Panslawismus zum tschechischsowjetischen Bündnis,' *Nationalsozialistische Monatshefte*, no. 104, 1938.

Zetland, Lawrence J., *Lord Cromer*, 1932.

Ziegler, H. O., *Die moderne Nation*, Tübingen, 1931.

Zimmermann, Alfred, *Geschichte der deutschen Kolonialpolitik*, 1914.

Zoepfl, G., 'Kolonien und Kolonialpolitik,' in *Handwörterbuch der Staatswissenschaften*, 3rd edition.

## Part Three: Totalitarianism

*For kind permission to peruse and quote archival material, I thank the Hoover Library in Stanford, California, the Centre de Documentation Juive Contemporaine in Paris, and the Yiddish Scientific Institute in New York. Documents used in the Nuremberg Trials are quoted with their Nuremberg File Number, other documents are referred to with indication of their present location and archival number.*

Abel, Theodore, *Why Hitler Came into Power; an Answer Based on the Original Life Stories of Six Hundred of His Followers*, 1938.

Adler, H. G., *Theresienstadt 1941–1945*, Tübingen, 1955.

Alquen, Gunter d,' *Die SS. Geschichte, Aufgabe und Organisation der Schutzstaffeln der NSDAP* (Schriften der Hochschule für Politik), 1939.

Anweiler, Oskar, *Die Räte-Bewegung in Russland 1905–1921*, Leiden 1958; 'Lenin und der friedliche Übergang zum Sozialismus,' in *Osteuropa*, 1956, vol. VI.

Armstrong, John A., *The Soviet Bureaucratic Elite: A Study of the Ukrainian Apparatus*, New York, 1959; *The Politics of Totalitarianism*, New York, 1961.

Avtorkhanov, A., 'Social Differentiation and Contradictions in the Party,' *Bulletin of the Institute for the Study of the USSR*, Munich, February, 1956; *Stalin and the Soviet Communist Party: A Study in the Technology of Power*, New York, 1959; (pseudonym Uvalov), *The Reign of Stalin*, London, 1953.

Bakunin, Michael, *Oeuvres*, Paris, 1907; *Gesammelte Werke*, 1921–24.

Balabanoff, Angelica, *Impressions of Lenin*, Ann Arbor, 1964.

Baldwin, Roger N., 'Political Police,' in *Encyclopedia of Social Sciences*.

Bataille, Georges, 'Le Secret de Sade,' *La Critique*, vol. 3, nos. 15, 16, 17, 1947; 'Review of D. Rousset, *Les Jours de notre mort*,' *La Critique*, January, 1948.

Bauer, R. A., Inkeles, A., and Kluckhohn, C., *How the Soviet System Works*, Cambridge, 1956.

Bayer, Ernest, *Die SA*, Berlin, 1938.

Bayle, François, *Psychologie et Ethique du National-Socialisme. Etude Anthropologique des Dirigeants SS*, Paris, 1953.

Beck, F., and Godin, W., *Russian Purge and the Extraction of Confession*, London and New York, 1951.

Beckerath, Erwin von, 'Fascism,' in *Encyclopedia of Social Sciences*; *Wesen und Werden des faschistischen Staates*, Berlin, 1927.

Benn, Gottfried, *Der neue Staat und die Intellektuellen*, 1933.

Bennecke, H., *Hitler und die SA*, München, 1962.

Berdyaev, Nicolas, *The Origin of Russian Communism*, 1937.

Best, Werner, *Die deutsche Polizei*, 1940.

Bettelheim, Bruno, 'On Dachau and Buchenwald,' in *Nazi Conspiracy, op. cit.*, vol. 7; 'Behavior in Extreme Situations,' *Journal of Abnormal and Social Psychology*, vol. 38, no. 4, 1943.

Black, C. E., editor, *Rewriting Russian History*, New York, 1956.

Blanc, R. M., *Adolf Hitler et les 'Protocoles des Sages de Sion*,' 1938.

Boberach, Heinz, editor, *Meldungen aus dem Reich*, Neuwied and Berlin, 1965.

Bonhard, Otto, *Jüdische Geld- und Weltherrschaft?*, Berlin, 1926.

Borkenau, Franz, *The Totalitarian Enemy*, London, 1940; *The Communist International*, London, 1938; 'Die neue Komintern,' *Der Monat*, no. 4, 1949.

Bormann, Martin, 'Relationship of National Socialism and Christianity,' in *Nazi Conspiracy, op. cit.*, vol. 6; *The Bormann Letters*, ed. by H. R. Trevor-Roper, London, 1954.

Boucart, Robert, *Les Dessous de l'Intelligence Service*, 1937.

Bracher, Karl Dietrich, *Die Auflösung der Weimarer Republik*, 1955; 3rd ed., Villingen, 1960.

—, Sauer, Wolfgang, and Schulz, Gerhard, *Die nationalsozialistische Machtergreifung*, Köln & Opladen, 1960.

Bramsted, Ernest K., *Goebbels and National Socialist Propaganda 1925–1945*, Michigan, 1965.

Brecht, Bertolt, *Stücke*, 10 vols., Frankfurt, 1953–1959; *Gedichte*, 7 vols., Frankfurt, 1960–1964.

Broszat, Martin, *Der Nationalsozialismus*, Stuttgart, 1960.

—, Jacobson, Hans-Adolf, and Krausnick, Helmut, *Konzentrationslager, Kommissarbefehl, Judenverfolgung*, Olten/Freiburg, 1965.

Brzezinski, Zbigniew, *Ideology and Power in Soviet Politics*, New York, 1962; *The Permanent Purge – Politics in Soviet Totalitarianism*, Cambridge, 1956.

Buber-Neumann, Margarete, *Under Two Dictators*, New York, 1951.

Buchheim, Hans, 'Die SS in der Verfassung des Dritten Reiches,' *Vierteljahreshefte für Zeitgeschichte*, April, 1955; *Das Dritte Reich*, München, 1958; *Die SS und totalitäre Herrschaft*, München, 1962; *Die SS – das Herrschaftsinstrument – Befehl und Gehorsam*, Olten/Freiburg, 1965.

Bullock, Alan, *Hitler, a Study in Tyranny*, rev. ed., New York, 1964.

Camus, Albert, 'The Human Crisis,' *Twice a Year*, 1946–1947.

Carocci, Giampiero, *Storia del fascismo*, Milan, 1959.

Carr, E. H., *History of Soviet Russia*, 7 vols., New York, 1951–1964; *Studies in Revolution*, New York, 1964.

Céline, Ferdinand, *Bagatelle pour un massacre*, 1938; *L'Ecole des cadavres*, 1940.

Chamberlin, W. H., *Blueprint for World Conquest*, 1946; *The Russian Revolution* (1935), 1965.

Childs, H. L., and Dodd, W. E., editors, *The Nazi Primer*, New York, 1938.

Ciliga, Anton, *The Russian Enigma*, London, 1940.

Clark, Evelyn A., 'Adolf Wagner. From National Economist to National Socialist,' *Political Science Quarterly*, 1940, vol. 55, no. 3.

Cobban, Alfred, *National Self-determination*, London, New York, 1945; *Dictatorship: Its History and Theory*, New York, 1939.

*Communism in Action* (United States Government House Documents, no. 754), Washington, 1946.

Crankshaw, Edward, *Gestapo, Instrument of Tyranny*, London, 1956.

Curtiss, J. S., *An Appraisal of the Protocols of Zion*, New York, 1942.

Dallin, David J., *From Purge to Coexistence*, Chicago, 1964; 'Report on Russia,' *The New Leader*, January 8, 1949.

—, and Nicolaevsky, Boris I., *Forced Labor in Russia*, 1947.

Daniels, Robert, *The Conscience of the Revolution: Communist Opposition in Soviet Russia*, Cambridge, 1960.

*The Dark Side of the Moon* (preface by T. S. Eliot), New York, 1947.

Deakin, F. W., *The Brutal Friendship*, New York, 1963.

De Begnac, Yvon, *Palazzo Venezia – Storia di un regime*, Rome, 1950.

Dehillotte, Pierre, *Gestapo*, Paris, 1940.

Delarue, Jacques, *Histoire de la Gestapo*, Paris, 1962.

Deutscher, Isaac, *Stalin: A Political Biography*, New York and London, 1949; *Prophet Armed: Trotsky, 1879–1921*, 1954; *Prophet Unarmed: Trotsky, 1921–1929*, 1959; *The Prophet Outcast: Trotsky, 1929–1940*, 1963.

'Die nationalsozialistische Revolution,' *Dokumente der deutschen Politik*, vol. I.

Dobb, Maurice, 'Bolshevism,' in *Encyclopedia of Social Sciences*.

*Dokumente der deutschen Politik und Geschichte*, vol. IV.

Domarus, Max, *Hitler-Reden und Proklamationen 1932–1945*, 2 vols., 1963.

Doob, Leonard W., 'Goebbels' Principles of Propaganda,' in Katz, Daniel *et al.*, *Public Opinion and Propaganda*, New York, 1954.

Drucker, Peter F., *The End of Economic Man*, New York, 1939.

Ebenstein, William, *The Nazi State*, New York, 1943.

Ehrenburg, Ilya, *Memoirs: 1921–1941*, Cleveland, 1964; *The War: 1941–1945*, Cleveland, 1965.

Engels, Friedrich, Introduction to the *Communist Manifesto*, 1890; introduction to the *Ursprung der Familie*; Funeral Speech on Marx.

Erickson, John, *The Soviet High Command 1918–1941*, New York, 1961.

Eyck, Erich, *A History of the Weimar Republic*, Cambridge, 1962.

Fainsod, Merle, *How Russia Is Ruled*, 1963; *Smolensk under Soviet Rule*, 1958.

*The Fascist Era*, published by the Fascist Confederation of Industrialists, Rome, 1939.

Feder, Ernest, 'Essai sur la Psychologie de la terreur,' *Synthèses*, Bruxelles, 1946.

Feder, Gottfried, *Das Programm der N.S.D.A.P. und seine weltanschaulichen Grundgedanken* (Nationalsozialistische Bibliothek, no. 1).

Fedotow, G. P., 'Russia and Freedom,' *The Review of Politics*, vol. 8, no. 1, January, 1946.

Fest, J. C., *Das Gesicht des Dritten Reiches*, München, 1963.

Finer, Herman, *Mussolini's Italy*, New York (1935), 1965.

Fischer, Louis, *The Soviets in World Affairs*, London, New York, 1930; *Life of Lenin*, New York, 1964.

Flammery, Harry W., 'The Catholic Church and Fascism,' *Free World*, September, 1943.

Florinsky, M. T., *Fascism and National Socialism. A Study of the Economic and Social Politics of the Totalitarian State*, New York, 1938.

Forsthoff, Ernst, *Der totale Staat*, Hamburg, 1933.

Fraenkel, Ernst, *The Dual State*, New York and London, 1941.

Frank, Hans, *Nationalsozialistische Leitsätze für ein neues deutsches Strafrecht*, Berlin, 1935–1936; *Die Technik des Staates*, München, 1940; (editor) *Grundfragen der deutschen Polizei* (Akademie für deutsches Recht), Hamburg, 1937; *Recht und Verwaltung*, 1939; *Die Technik des Staates*, München, 1942; *Im Angesicht des Galgens*, München, 1953; editor, *Nationalsozialistisches Handbuch für Recht und Gesetzgebung*, München, 1935.

Freyer, Hans, *Pallas Athene, Ethik des politischen Volkes*, 1935.

Friedrich, C. J., editor, *Totalitarianism*, New York, 1954.

—, and Brzezinski, Z. K., *Totalitarian Dictatorship and Autocracy*, Cambridge, 1956.

Gallier-Boissière, Jean, *Mysteries of the French Secret Police*, 1938.

Gauweiler, Otto, *Rechtseinrichtungen und Rechtsaufgaben der Bewegung*, 1939.

Geigenmüller, Otto, *Die politische Schutzhaft im nationalistischen Deutschland*, 2nd ed., Würzburg, 1937.

Gerth, Hans, 'The Nazi Party,' *American Journal of Sociology*, vol. 45, 1940.

Gide, André, *Retour de l'URSS*, Paris, 1936.

Giles, O. C., *The Gestapo* (Oxford Pamphlets on World Affairs, no. 36), 1940.

Globke, Hans, *Kommentare zur Deutschen Rassegesetzgebung*, Munich-Berlin, 1936.

Goebbels, Joseph, *Wege ins Dritte Reich*, München, 1927; 'Der Faschismus und seine praktischen Ergebnisse,' *Schriften der deutschen Hochschule für Politik*, vol. I, Berlin, 1935; *Vom Kaiserhof zur Reichskanzlei*, 19. ed., München, 1937; 'Rassenfrage und Weltprogramm,'

*Pädagogisches Magazin*, Heft 139, 1934; *The Goebbels Diaries 1942–1943*, Louis Lochner, editor, New York, 1948; *Wesen und Gestalt des National-sozialismus*, Berlin, 1935.

Goslar, Hans, *Jüdische Weltherrschaft. Phantasiegebilde oder Wirklichkeit*, Berlin, 1918.

Grauert, Wilhelm, 'Die Entwicklung des Polizeirechts in national-sozialistischen Staat,' in *Deutsche Juristenzeitung*, 39, 1934.

Griffith, William E., editor, *Communism in Europe, Continuity, Change and the Sino-Soviet Dispute*, Cambridge, 1964.

Gross, Walter, *Der deutsche Rassengedanke und die Welt* (Schriften der Hochschule für Politik, no. 42), 1939; 'Die Rassen- und Bevölker-ungspolitik im Kampf um die geschichtliche Selbstbehauptung der Völker,' *Nationalsozialistische Monatshefte*, no. 115, October, 1939.

Guenther, Hans, *Rassenkunde des jüdischen Volkes*, 1930; *Rassenkunde des deutschen Volkes*, 1st ed., München, 1922.

Gul, Roman, *Les Maîtres de la Tcheka*, Paris, 1938.

Gurian, Waldemar, *Bolshevism: Theory and Practice*, New York, 1932; *Bolshevism. An Introduction to Soviet Communism*, Notre Dame, 1952.

Hadamovsky, Eugen, *Propaganda und nationale Macht*, 1933.

Hafkesbrink, Hanna, *Unknown Germany*, New Haven, 1948.

Hallgarten, Georg Wolfgang F., *Hitler, Reichswehr und Industrie. Zur Geschichte der Jahre 1918–1933*, Frankfurt/M., 1955.

Hamel, Walter, 'Die Polizei im neuen Reich,' in *Deutsches Recht*, vol. 5, 1935.

Hammer, Hermann, 'Die deutschen Ausgaben von Hitlers "Mein Kampf,"' in *Vierteljahrshefte für Zeitgeschichte*, 4 (1956).

Hartshorne, Edward G., *The German Universities and National Social-ism*, Cambridge, 1937.

Hayek, F. A., 'The Counter-Revolution of Science,' *Economics*, vol. 8, 1941.

Hayes, Carlton J. H., *Essays on Nationalism*, New York, 1926; Remarks on 'The Novelty of Totalitarianism in the History of Western Civil-ization,' *Symposium on the Totalitarian State, 1939. Proceedings of the American Philosophical Society*, vol. 82, Philadelphia, 1940; *A Gener-ation of Materialism*, New York, 1941.

Heiden, Konrad, *Der Führer. Hitler's Rise to Power*, Boston, 1944; *A History of National Socialism*, New York, 1935; *Adolf Hitler. Das*

*Zeitalter der Verantwortungslosigkeit. Eine Biographie*, vol. 1, Zürich, 1936; *Geschichte des Nationalsozialismus. Die Karriere einer Idee*, Berlin, 1932; *Geburt des Dritten Reiches. Die Geschichte des Nationalsozialismus bis Herbst 1933*, 2nd ed., Zürich, 1934.

Hesse, Fritz, *Das Spiel um Deutschland*, Munich, 1953.

Heydrich, Reinhard, 'Die Bekämpfung der Staatsfeinde,' in *Deutsches Recht*, vol. 6, 1936.

Hilberg, Raul, *The Destruction of the European Jews*, Chicago, 1961.

Himmler, Heinrich, 'Männerbund auf rassischer Grundlage,' *Das Schwarze Corps*, 38. Folge; *Die Schutzstaffel als antibolschewistische Kampforganisation* (Aus dem Schwarzen Korps, no. 3), 1936; 'Organization and Obligation of the SS and the Police,' published in *Nationalpolitischer Lehrgang der Wehrmacht vom 15.–23. Januar 1937*. Excerpts translated in *Nazi Conspiracy, op. cit.*, vol. 4; English edition: *Secret Speech by Himmler to the German Army General Staff*, published by the American Committee for Anti-Nazi Literature, 1938; *Grundfragen der deutschen Polizei*, Hamburg, 1937; 'Denkschriften Himmlers über die Behandlung der Fremdvölkischen im Osten' (May 1940), *Vierteljahrshefte für Zeitgeschichte*, 5. Jg. (1957); 'Die Schutzstaffel,' *Grundlagen, Aufbau und Wirtschaftsordnung des nationalsozialistischen Staates*, Nr. 7b.

Hitler, Adolf, *Mein Kampf*, 1925–1927. Unexpurgated English edition, New York, 1939; *Reden*, ed. by Ernst Boepple, München, 1933; *Hitler's Speeches, 1922–1939*, ed. by N. H. Baynes, London 1942; *Ausgewählte Reden des Führers*, 1939; *Die Reden des Führers nach der Machtübernahme*, 1940; *Der grossdeutsche Freiheitskampf*, Reden Hitlers vom 1.9.1939–10.3.1940; *Hitler's Table Talk*, New York, 1953; *Hitler's Secret Book*, New York, 1962; *Der grossdeutsche Freiheitskampf – Reden Adolf Hitlers*, vols. I and II, 3rd ed., München, 1943.

Hocke, Werner, ed., *Die Gesetzgebung des Kabinetts Hitler*, vol. 1, Berlin, 1933.

Hoehn, Reinhard, *Rechtsgemeinschaft und Volksgemeinschaft*, Hamburg, 1935.

Hoettl, Wilhelm, *The Secret Front: The Story of Nazi Political Espionage*, New York, 1954.

Holldack, Heinz, *Was wirklich geschah*, 1949.

Horneffer, Reinhold, 'Das Problem der Rechtsgeltung und der Restbestand der Weimarer Verfassung,' in *Zeitschrift für die gesamte Staatswissenschaft*, 99, 1938.

Höss, Rudolf, *Commandant of Auschwitz*, New York, 1960.

Hossbach, Friedrich, *Zwischen Wehrmacht und Hitler 1934–1938*, Wolfenbüttel-Hannover, 1949.

Huber, Ernst R., 'Die deutsche Polizei,' *Zeitschrift für die gesamte Staatswissenschaft*, vol. 101, 1940/1.

Hudal, Bischof Alois, *Die Grundlagen des Nationalsozialismus*, 1937.

Inkeles, A., and Bauer, R. A., *The Soviet Citizen: Daily Life in a Totalitarian Society*, Cambridge, 1959.

Jetzinger, Franz, *Hitlers Jugend*, Wien, 1956.

Jünger, Ernst, *The Storm of Steel*, London, 1929.

Keiser, Guenther, 'Der jüngste Konzentrationsprozess,' *Die Wirtschaftskurve*, vol. 18, no. 148, 1938.

Kennan, George F., *Russia and the West under Lenin and Stalin*, Boston, 1961.

Khrushchev, N., 'The Crimes of the Stalin Era,' edited and annotated by Boris Nicolaevsky, New York, *The New Leader*, 1956.

Klein, Fritz, 'Zur Vorbereitung der faschistischen Diktatur durch die deutsche Grossbourgeoisie 1929–1932,' *Zeitschrift für Geschichtswissenschaft*, 1. Jg. 1953.

Kluke, Paul, 'Nationalsozialistische Europaideologie,' *Vierteljahrshefte für Zeitgeschichte*, 8. Jg. 1960.

Koch, Erich, 'Sind wir Faschisten?', in *Arbeitertum* 1, H. 9 (1. Juli 1931).

Koellenreuter, Otto, *Volk und Staat in der Weltanschauung des Nationalsozialismus*, 1935; *Der deutsche Führerstaat*, Tübingen, 1934.

Koettgen, Arnold, 'Die Gesetzmässigkeit der Verwaltung im Führerstaat,' *Reichsverwaltungsblatt*, 1936.

Kogon, Eugen, *The Theory and Practice of Hell*, 1956.

Kohn-Bramstedt, Ernst, *Dictatorship and Political Police; the Technique of Control by Fear*, London, 1945.

Koyré, Alexandre, 'The Political Function of the Modern Lie,' *Contemporary Jewish Record*, June, 1945.

Kravchenko, Victor, *I Chose Freedom. The Personal and Political Life of a Soviet Official*, New York, 1946.

Krivitsky, W., *In Stalin's Secret Services*, New York, 1939.

Kuhn, Karl G., 'Die Judenfrage als weltgeschichtliches Problem,' in *Forschungen zur Judenfrage*, 1939.

Laporte, Maurice, *Histoire de l'Okhrana*, Paris, 1935.

Latour, Contamine de, 'Le Maréchal Pétain,' *Revue de Paris*, vol. 1.

Lebon, Gustave, *La Psychologie des foules*, 1895.

Lederer, Zdenek, *Ghetto Theresienstadt*, London, 1953.

Lenin, V. I., *What Is to Be Done?*, 1902; *State and Revolution*, 1917; *Imperialism, the Last Stage of Capitalism*, 1917.

Leutwein, Paul, editor, *Kämpfe um Afrika; sechs Lebensbilder*, Luebeck, 1936.

Lewy, Guenter, *The Catholic Church and Nazi Germany*, New York and Toronto, 1964.

Ley, Robert, *Der Weg zur Ordensburg*, no date.

Lösener, Bernhard, *Die Nürnberger Gesetze*, Berlin, 1936.

Lowenthal, Richard, *World Communism. The Disintegration of a Secular Faith*, New York, 1964.

Luedecke, Winfred, *Behind the Scenes of Espionage. Tales of the Secret Service*, 1929.

Luxemburg, Rosa, *The Russian Revolution*, Ann Arbor, 1961.

Martin, Alfred von, 'Zur Soziologie der Gegenwart,' *Zeitschrift für Kulturgeschichte*, vol. 27.

Massing, Paul W., *Rehearsal for Destruction*, New York, 1949.

Mathias, Erich, and Morsey, Rudolph, editors, *Das Ende der Parteien 1933*, Düsseldorf, 1960.

Maunz, Theodor, *Gestalt und Recht der Polizei*, Hamburg, 1943.

McKenzie, Kermit E., *Comintern and World Revolution 1928–1934*, New York, 1964.

Micaud, Charles A., *The French Right and Nazi Germany, 1933–1939*, 1943.

Moeller van den Bruck, Arthur, *Das Dritte Reich*, 1923; English edition *Germany's Third Empire*, New York, 1934.

Moore, Barrington, *Terror and Progress USSR; Some Sources of Change and Stability in the Soviet Dictatorship*, Cambridge, 1954.

Morstein Marx, Fritz, 'Totalitarian Politics,' *Symposium on the Totalitarian State*, 1939. *Proceedings of the American Philosophical Society*, vol. 82, Philadelphia, 1940.

Mosse, George J., *The Crisis of German Ideology: Intellectual Origins of the Third Reich*, New York, 1964.

Muller, H. S., 'The Soviet Master Race Theory,' *The New Leader*, July 30, 1949.

Müller, Josef, *Die Entwicklung des Rassenantisemitismus in den letzten Jahrzehnten des 19. Jahrhundert (Historische Studien*, H. 372), Berlin, 1940.

Mussolini, Benito, 'Relativismo et Fascismo,' *Diuturna*, Milano, 1924; *Four Speeches on the Corporate State*, Rome, 1935; *Opera Omnia di Benito Mussolini*, vol. IV, Florence, 1951.


Nansen, Odd, *Day after Day*, London, 1949.

*Nazi Conspiracy and Aggression*, Office of the United States Chief of Counsel for the Prosecution of Axis Criminality, U.S. Government, Washington, 1946.

*Nazi-Soviet Relations, 1939–1941. Documents from the Archives of the German Foreign Office*, edited by Raymond James Sontag and James Stuart Beddie, Washington, 1948.

Neesse, Gottfried, *Partei und Staat*, 1936; 'Die verfassungsrechtliche Gestaltung der Ein-Partei,' *Zeitschrift für die gesamte Staatswissenschaft*, vol. 98, 1938.

Neumann, Franz, *Behemoth*, 1942.

Neusüss-Hunkel, Ermenhild, *Die SS*, Hannover-Frankfurt a.M., 1956.

Newman, Bernard, *Secret Servant*, New York, 1936.

Nicolaevsky, Boris I., *Bolsheviks and Bureaucrats*, New York, 1965; *Power and the Soviet Elite*, New York, 1965; (—), *Letter of an Old Bolshevik*, New York, 1937.

Nicolai, Helmut, *Die rassengesetzliche Rechtslehre. Grundzüge einer national-sozialistischen Rechtsphilosophie* (Nationalsozialistische Bibliothek, H. 39), 3rd ed., München, 1934.

Nomad, Max, *Apostles of Revolution*, Boston, 1939.


Olgin, Moissaye J., *The Soul of the Russian Revolution*, New York, 1917.

*Organisationsbuch der NSDAP*, many editions.

Orlov, A., *The Secret History of Stalin's Crimes*, New York, 1953.

Ortega y Gasset, José, *The Revolt of the Masses*, New York, 1932.

Paetel, Karl O., 'Die SS,' *Vierteljahreshefte für Zeitgeschichte*, January, 1954; 'Der schwarze Orden. Zur Literatur über die "SS,"' in *Neue Politische Literatur*, 3, 1958.

Parsons, Talcott, 'Some Sociological Aspects of the Fascist Movement,' *Essays in Sociological Theory*, Glencoe, 1954.

Pascal, Pierre, *Avvakum et les débuts du raskol* (Institut Français de Leningrad, Bibliothèque, vol. 18), Paris, 1938.

Paulhan, Jean, 'Introduction' to Marquis de Sade, *Les Infortunes de la Vertu*, Paris, 1946.

Payne, Stanley G., *A History of Spanish Fascism*, Stanford, 1961.

Pencherlo, Alberto, 'Antisemitism,' in *Encyclopedia Italiana*.

Petegroski, D. W., 'Antisemitism, the Strategy of Hatred,' *Antioch Review*, vol. 1, no. 3, 1941.

Pfenning, Andreas, 'Gemeinschaft und Staatswissenschaft,' *Zeitschrift für die gesamte Staatswissenschaft*, vol. 96.

Poliakov, Léon, *Bréviaire de la Haine*, Paris, 1951; 'The Weapon of Antisemitism,' *The Third Reich*, London, 1955, UNESCO.

—, and Wulf, Josef, *Das Dritte Reich und die Juden*, Berlin, 1955.

Poncins, Léon de, *Les Forces secrètes de la Révolution; F∴ M∴-Judaïsme*, revised ed., 1929 (translated into German, English, Spanish, Portuguese); *Les Juifs Maîtres du Monde*, 1932; *La Dictature des puissances occultes; La F∴ M∴*, 1932; *La mystérieuse Internationale juive*, 1936; *La Guerre occulte*, 1936.

Rauschning, Hermann, *Hitler Speaks*, 1939; *The Revolt of Nihilism*, 1939.

Reck-Malleczewen, Friedrich Percyval, *Tagebuch eines Verzweifelten*, Stuttgart, 1947.

Reitlinger, Gerald, *The Final Solution*, 1953; *The SS – Alibi of a Nation*, London, 1956.

Reveille, Thomas, *The Spoil of Europe*, 1941.

Reventlow, Graf Ernst zu, *Deutschlands auswärtige Politik, 1888–1914*, 1916; *Judas Kampf und Niederlage in Deutschland*, 1937.

Riesman, David, 'The Politics of Persecution,' *Public Opinion Quarterly*, vol. 6, 1942; 'Democracy and Defamation,' *Columbia Law Review*, 1942.

Riess, Curt, *Joseph Goebbels: A Biography*, New York, 1948.

Ripka, Hubert, *Munich: Before and After*, London, 1939.

Ritter, Gerhard, *Carl Goerdeler's Struggle against Tyranny*, New York, 1958.

Roberts, Stephen H., *The House that Hitler Built*, London, 1939.

Robinson, Jacob, and Friedman, Philip, *Guide to Jewish History under Nazi Impact*, a bibliography published jointly by YIVO Institute for Jewish Research and Yad Washem, New York and Jerusalem, 1960.

Rocco, Alfredo, *Scritti e discorsi politici*, 3 vols., Milan, 1938.

Roehm, Ernst, *Die Geschichte eines Hochverräters*, Volksausgabe, 1933; *Die Memoiren des Stabschefs Roehm*, Saarbrücken, 1934; *Warren SA?*, Berlin, 1933; 'SA und deutsche Revolution,' in *Nationalsozialistische Monatshefte*, Nr. 31, 1933.

Rollin, Henri, *L'Apocalypse de notre temps*, Paris, 1939.

Rosenberg, Alfred, *Die Protokolle der Weisen von Zion und die jüdische Weltpolitik*, München, 1923; *Der Mythos des zwanzigsten Jahrhunderts*, 1930.

Rosenberg, Arthur, *A History of Bolshevism*, London, 1934; *Geschichte der deutschen Republik*, 1936.

Rousset, David, *Les Jours de notre mort*, Paris, 1947; *The Other Kingdom*, 1947.

Rush, Myron, *Political Succession in the USSR*, New York, 1965; *The Rise of Khrushchev*, Washington, 1958.

*SA-Geist im Betrieb. Vom Ringen um die Durchsetzung des deutschen Sozialismus*, edited by Oberste SA-Führung, München, 1938.

Salisbury, Harrison E., *Moscow Journal: The End of Stalin*, Chicago, 1961; *American in Russia*, New York, 1955.

Salvemini, Gaetano, *La terreur fasciste 1922–1926*, Paris, 1938; *The Fascist Dictatorship in Italy* (1927), New York, 1966.

Schäfer, Wolfgang, *NSDAP, Entwicklung und Struktur der Staatspartei des Dritten Reiches*, Hannover-Frankfurt a.M., 1956.

Schapiro, L., *The Communist Party of the Soviet Union*, 1960; *The Government and Politics of the Soviet Union*, New York, 1965.

Schellenberg, Walter, *The Schellenberg Memoirs*, London, 1956.

Schemann, Ludwig, *Die Rasse in den Geisteswissenschaften. Studie zur Geschichte des Rassengedankens*, 3 vols., München, Berlin, 1928.

Scheuner, Ulrich, 'Die nationale Revolution. Eine staatsrechtliche Untersuchung,' in *Archiv des öffentlichen Rechts* (1933/34).

Schmitt, Carl, *Politische Romantik*, Munich, 1925; *Staat, Bewegung, Volk*, 1934; 'Totaler Feind, totaler Krieg, totaler Staat,' *Völkerbund und Völkerrecht*, vol. 4, 1937; *Verfassungsrechtliche Aufsätze aus den Jahren 1924–1954. Materialien zu einer Verfassungslehre*, Berlin, 1958.

Schnabel, Raimund, *Macht ohne Moral. Eine Dokumentation über die SS*, Frankfurt/M., 1957.

Schumann, Fr. L., *The Nazi Dictatorship*, 1939.

Schwartz, Dieter, *Angriffe auf die nationalsozialistische Weltanschauung* (Aus dem Schwarzen Korps, no. 2), 1936.

Schwartz-Bostunitsch, Gregor, *Jüdischer Imperialismus*, 5th edition, 1939.

Seraphim, Hans-Günther, *Das politische Tagebuch Alfred Rosenbergs aus den Jahren 1934/5 und 1939/40*, Göttingen-Berlin-Frankfurt/M., 1956; 'SS-Verfügungstruppe und Wehrmacht,' in *Wehrwissenschaftliche Rundschau*, 5, 1955.

Seraphim, P. H., *Das Judentum im osteuropäischen Raum*, Essen, 1938; 'Der Antisemitismus in Osteuropa,' *Osteuropa*, vol. 14, no. 5, February, 1939.

Seton-Watson, Hugh, *From Lenin to Khrushchev*, New York, 1960.

Simmel, Georg, 'Sociology of Secrecy and of Secret Societies,' *The American Journal of Sociology*, vol. 11, no. 4, 1906; *The Sociology of Georg Simmel*, translated by K. H. Wolff, 1950.

Six, F. A., *Die politische Propaganda der NSDAP im Kampf um die Macht*, 1936.

Smith, Bruce, 'Police,' in *Encyclopedia of Social Sciences*.

Souvarine, Boris, *Stalin. A Critical Survey of Bolshevism*, New York, 1939; translated from the French *Staline, Aperçu historique du Bolshévisme*, Paris, 1935.

Spengler, Oswald, *The Decline of the West*, 1928–1929.

SS-Hauptamt-Schulungsamt, *Wesen und Aufgabe der SS und der Polizei*; *Der Weg der SS*; *SS-Mann und Blutsfrage. Die biologischen Grundlagen und ihre sinngemässe Anwendung für die Erhaltung und Mehrung des nordischen Blutes*.

Stalin, J. V., *Leninism*, London, 1933; *Mastering Bolshevism*, New York, 1946; *History of the Communist Party of the Soviet Union (Bolsheviks): Short Course*, New York, 1939.

Starlinger, Wilhelm, *Grenzen der Sowjetmacht*, Würzburg, 1955.

Starr, Joshua, 'Italy's Antisemites,' *Jewish Social Studies*, 1939.

Stein, Alexander, *Adolf Hitler, Schüler der 'Weisen von Zion,'* Karlsbad, 1936.

Stein, George H., *The Waffen SS: Hitler's Elite Guard at War, 1939–45*, Ithaca, 1966.

Stuckart, Wilhelm, and Globke, Hans, *Reichsbürgergesetz, Blutschutzgesetz und Ehegesundheitsgesetz (Kommentare zur deutschen Rassengesetzgebung)*, vol. 1, München, Berlin, 1936.


Tasca, Angelo (pseudonym Angelo Rossi), *The Rise of Italian Fascism, 1918–1922* (1938), New York, 1966.

Thyssen, Fritz, *I Paid Hitler*, London, 1941.

Tobias, Fritz, *The Reichstag Fire*, New York, 1964.

Trevor-Roper, H. R., *The Last Days of Hitler*, 1947.

*The Trial of the Major War Criminals*, 42 vols., Nürnberg, 1947–1948.

*Trials of War Criminals before the Nuremberg Military Tribunals*, 15 vols., Washington, 1949–1953.

Trotsky, Leon, *The History of the Russian Revolution*, New York, 1932.

Tucker, Robert C., *The Soviet Political Mind*, New York, 1963.

—, and Cohen, Stephen F., editors, *The Great Purge Trial*, New York, 1965.


Ulam, Adam B., *The Bolsheviks: The Intellectual and Political History of the Triumph of Communism in Russia*, New York, 1965; *The New Face of Soviet Totalitarianism*, Cambridge, 1963.

Ullmann, A., *La Police, quatrième Pouvoir*, Paris, 1935.


Vardys, V. Stanley, 'How the Baltic Republics Fare in the Soviet Union,' *Foreign Affairs*, April, 1966.

Vassilyev, A. T., *The Ochrana*, 1930.

Venturi, Franco, *Roots of Revolution. A History of the Populist and Socialist Movements in Nineteenth Century Russia* (1952), New York, 1966.

*Verfassung, Die, des Sozialistischen Staates der Arbeiter und Bauern*, Strasbourg, 1937.

Volkmann, Erich, Elster, Alexander, and Küchenhoff, Günther, editors, *Die Rechtsentwicklung der Jahre 1933 bis 1935/6*, Handwörterbuch der Rechtswissenschaft, vol. VIII, Berlin, Leipzig, 1937.

Warmbrunn, Werner, *The Dutch under German Occupation, 1940–1945*, Stanford, 1963.

Weinreich, Max, *Hitler's Professors*, New York, 1946.

Weissberg, Alexander, *The Accused*, New York, 1951.

Weizmann, Chaim, *Trial and Error*, New York, 1949.

Wighton, Charles, *Heydrich: Hitler's Most Evil Henchman*, Philadelphia, 1962.

Wirsing, Giselher, *Zwischeneuropa und die deutsche Zukunft*, Jena, 1932.

Wolfe, Bertram D., *Three Men Who Made a Revolution: Lenin – Trotsky – Stalin*, New York, 1948.

Wolin, Simon, and Slusser, Robert M., editors, *The Soviet Secret Police*, New York, 1957.


Zielinski, T., 'L'Empereur Claude et l'idée de la domination mondiale des Juifs,' *Revue Universelle*, Bruxelles, 1926–1927

# Index

*Authors are listed only in case of special discussion or reference. Subjects of footnotes are listed. Chapter headings and subheadings and bibliographical references are not included.*